Practical Programming in Tcl/Tk

Brent B. Welch
Ken Jones

with Jeffrey Hobbs

PRENTICE
HALL
PTR

Prentice Hall PTR
Upper Saddle River, NJ 07458
www.phptr.com

Library of Congress Cataloging-in-Publication available

Editorial/production supervision: *Kathleen M. Caren*
Executive Editor: *Mark Taub*
Editorial Assistant: *Noreen Regina*
Marketing Manager: *Kate Hargett*
Manufacturing Manager: *Maura Zaldivar*
Cover Design Director: *Jerry Votta*

ISBN   0-13-038560-3

Text printed in the United States at Courier Stoughton in Stoughton, Massachusetts.

10th   Printing   July 2008

Pearson Education LTD.
Pearson Education Australia PTY, Limited
Pearson Education Singapore, Pte. Ltd.
Pearson Education North Asia Ltd.
Pearson Education Canada, Ltd.
Pearson Educación de Mexico, S.A. de C.V.
Pearson Education—Japan
Pearson Education Malaysia, Pte. Ltd.

to

Jody,
Christopher, Daniel, and Michael

— Brent

✳

Dean,
for his support and patience

— Ken

Contents

List of Examples xxxiii

List of Tables xliii

Preface xlix

Part I. Tcl Basics 1

1. Tcl Fundamentals 3
   Tcl Commands 3
   Hello, World! 4
   Variables 5
   Command Substitution 5
   Math Expressions 6
   Backslash Substitution 7
   Grouping with Braces and Double Quotes 8
       Square Brackets Do Not Group 9
       Grouping before Substitution 9
       Grouping Math Expressions with Braces 10
       More Substitution Examples 10
   Procedures 11
   A Factorial Example 12
   More about Variables 13
       Funny Variable Names 14
       The unset Command 15
       Using info to Find Out about Variables 15
   More about Math Expressions 15
   Comments 16
   Substitution and Grouping Summary 17
   Fine Points 18
   Reference 20
       Backslash Sequences 20
       Arithmetic Operators 20
       Built-in Math Functions 21
       Core Tcl Commands 22

2. Getting Started 25
   The source Command 26

UNIX Tcl Scripts 26

Windows Start Menu 27

Macintosh OS 8/9 and ResEdit 28

    Macintosh OS X 28

The `console` Command 29

Command-Line Arguments 29

    Command-Line Options to Wish 30

Predefined Variables 31

3.   The Guestbook CGI Application 33

A Quick Introduction to HTML 34

CGI for Dynamic Pages 35

The `guestbook.cgi` Script 36

    Using a Script Library File 37

    Beginning the HTML Page 38

    Sample Output of the CGI Script 40

    Using a Tcl Array for the Database 41

Defining Forms and Processing Form Data 42

    The `newguest.html` Form 43

    The `ncgi` and `cgi.tcl` Packages 44

    The `newguest.cgi` Script 44

    Using Tcl Scripts to Store Data 46

Handling Errors in CGI Scripts 46

Next Steps 48

4.   String Processing in Tcl 49

The `string` Command 49

    String Indices 51

    Strings and Expressions 52

    String Matching 53

    Character Classes 54

    Mapping Strings 55

The `append` Command 56

The `format` Command 56

The `scan` Command 58

The `binary` Command 59

    Format Templates 59

    Examples 61

    Binary Data and File I/O 62

Related Chapters 62

5.   Tcl Lists 63

Tcl Lists 63
Constructing Lists 65
   The `list` command 65
   The `lappend` Command 66
   The `lset` Command 66
   The `concat` Command 67
Getting List Elements: `llength`, `lindex`, and `lrange` 68
Modifying Lists: `linsert` and `lreplace` 68
Searching Lists: `lsearch` 69
Sorting Lists: `lsort` 70
The `split` Command 71
The `join` Command 72
Related Chapters 73

6.   Control Structure Commands 75

`If Then Else` 76
`Switch` 77
   Comments in `switch` Commands 78
`While` 79
`Foreach` 79
   Multiple Loop Variables 81
   Multiple Value Lists 82
`For` 82
`Break` and `Continue` 83
`Catch` 83
   Catching More Than Errors 84
`Error` 85
`Return` 86

7.   Procedures and Scope 87

The `proc` Command 87
Changing Command Names with `rename` 89
Scope 89
The `global` Command 90
Call by Name Using `upvar` 91
Variable Aliases with `upvar` 92
   Associating State with Data 92
   Namespaces and `upvar` 93
   Commands That Take Variable Names 93

8. Tcl Arrays 95

Array Syntax 95
Complex Indices 96
Array Variables 96
The `array` Command 97
Converting Between Arrays and Lists 98
Passing Arrays by Name 99
Building Data Structures with Arrays 99
Simple Records 99
A Stack 101
A List of Arrays 102
A Simple In-Memory Database 103
Alternatives to Using Arrays 104

9. Working with Files and Programs 105

Running Programs with `exec` 105
The `auto_noexec` Variable 107
Limitations of `exec` on Windows 107
`AppleScript` on Macintosh 107
The `file` Command 108
Cross-Platform File Naming 110
Building up Pathnames: `file join` 110
Chopping Pathnames: `split`, `dirname`, `tail` 111
Manipulating Files and Directories 112
Copying Files 112
Creating Directories 112
Symbolic and Hard Links 113
Deleting Files 113
Renaming Files and Directories 113
File Attributes 114
Input/Output Command Summary 116
Opening Files for I/O 116
Opening a Process Pipeline 118
Expect 119
Reading and Writing 119
The `puts` and `gets` Commands 119
The `read` Command 120
Platform-Specific End of Line Characters 120
Random Access I/O 121
Closing I/O Channels 121
The Current Directory — `cd` and `pwd` 122
Matching File Names with `glob` 122

Expanding Tilde in File Names 124
The **exit** and **pid** Commands 124
Environment Variables 124
The **registry** Command 125

Part II. Advanced Tcl.............................. 127

10. Quoting Issues and Eval 129

Constructing Code with the **list** Command 130
    The **eval** Command 130
    Commands That Concatenate Their Arguments 131
    Commands That Use Callbacks 132
    Command Prefix Callbacks 132
    Constructing Procedures Dynamically 133
Exploiting the **concat** inside **eval** 134
    Using **eval** in a Wrapper Procedure. 134
    Correct Quoting with **eval** 136
The **uplevel** Command 138
The **subst** Command 140
    String Processing with **subst** 141

11. Regular Expressions 143

When to Use Regular Expressions 144
    Avoiding a Common Problem 144
Regular Expression Syntax 145
    Matching Characters 145
    Character Sets 145
    Quantifiers 146
    Alternation 147
    Anchoring a Match 147
    Backslash Quoting 147
    Matching Precedence 148
    Capturing Subpatterns 148
Advanced Regular Expressions 149
    Compatibility with Patterns in Tcl 8.0 149
    Backslash Escape Sequences 149
    Character Classes 150
    Nongreedy Quantifiers 151
    Bound Quantifiers 151
    Back References 151
    Look-ahead 152
    Character Codes 152

Collating Elements 153
Equivalence Classes 153
Newline Sensitive Matching 153
Embedded Options 154
Expanded Syntax 154
Syntax Summary 154
The `regexp` Command 158
A Pattern to Match URLs 159
Bugs When Mixing Greedy
and Non-Greedy Quantifiers 161
Sample Regular Expressions 161
The `regsub` Command 162
Transforming Data to Program with `regsub` 163
URL Decoding 164
CGI Argument Parsing 165
Decoding HTML Entities 166
A Simple HTML Parser 168
Stripping HTML Comments 170
Other Commands That Use Regular Expressions 170

12. **Script Libraries and Packages** 171
Locating Packages: The `auto_path` Variable 172
Using Packages 173
Loading Packages Automatically 173
Packages Implemented in C Code 174
Summary of Package Loading 175
The `package` Command 176
Libraries Based on the `tclIndex` File 176
The `unknown` Command 178
How Auto Loading Works 178
Disabling the Library Facility: `auto_noload` 178
Interactive Conveniences 179
Auto Execute 179
History 179
Abbreviations 179
Tcl Shell Library Environment 179
Locating the Tcl Script Library 180
`tcl_findLibrary` 180
Coding Style 181
A Module Prefix for Procedure Names 181
A Global Array for State Variables 182
The Official Tcl Style Guide 182

13. Reflection and Debugging 183

The `clock` Command 183
The `info` Command 186
   Variables 187
   Procedures 188
   The Call Stack 190
   Command Evaluation 190
   Scripts and the Library 191
   Version Numbers 192
   Execution Environment 192
Cross-Platform Support 193
Tracing Variables and Commands 193
   Command Tracing 194
   Read-Only Variables 195
   Creating an Array with Traces 196
Interactive Command History 196
   History Syntax 197
   A Comparison to C Shell History Syntax 198
Debugging 199
Tcl Dev Kit 200
   Debugger with Coverage 200
   Checker 200
   Compiler 200
   TclApp 201
   Tcl Service Manager 201
   Inspector 201
Other Tools 201
   The tkcon Console 201
   Critcl 201
   The `bgerror` Command 202
   The `tkerror` Command 202
Performance Tuning 202
   Time stamps in a Log 202
   The Tcl Compiler 203

14. Namespaces 205

Using Namespaces 205
Namespace Variables 207
   Qualified Names 208
Command Lookup 208
Nested Namespaces 209
Importing and Exporting Procedures 210

Callbacks and Namespaces 211
Introspection 212
The `namespace` Command 213
Converting Existing Packages to use Namespaces 213
`[incr Tcl]` Object System 214
`xotcl` Object System 215
Notes 215
    Names for Widgets, Images, and Interpreters 215
    The `variable` command at the global scope 215
    Auto Loading and `auto_import` 215
    Namespaces and `uplevel` 216
    Naming Quirks 216
    Miscellaneous 216

15. Internationalization 217
    Character Sets and Encodings 218
    The System Encoding 218
    File Encodings and `fconfigure` 219
    Scripts in Different Encodings 220
    Unicode and UTF-8 220
    The Binary Encoding 221
    Conversions Between Encodings 221
    The `encoding` Command 222
    Message Catalogs 222
    Specifying a Locale 223
    Managing Message Catalog Files 223
    Message Catalogs and Namespaces 225
    The `msgcat` package 226

16. Event-Driven Programming 227
    The Tcl Event Loop 227
    The `after` Command 228
    The `fileevent` Command 229
    The `vwait` Command 230
    The `fconfigure` Command 231
    Nonblocking I/O 232
    The `fblocked` Command 233
    Buffering 233
    End of Line Translations 234
    End of File Character 234
    Serial Devices 234
    Character Set Encodings 235

      Configuring Read-Write Channels 235

17. Socket Programming 237

     Networking Extensions for Tcl 238
        Scotty 238
        Standard Tcl Library 238
        HTTP 238
     Client Sockets 239
        Client Socket Options 239
     Server Sockets 240
        Server Socket Options 241
     The Echo Service 241
     Fetching a URL with HTTP 243
        Proxy Servers 244
        The `HEAD` Request 245
        The `GET` and `POST` Requests 247
        The `fcopy` Command 250
     The `http` Package 251
        `http::config` 251
        `http::geturl` 251
        `http::formatQuery` 254
        `http::register` and `http::unregister` 255
        `http::reset` 255
        `http::cleanup` 255
     Basic Authentication 255

18. TclHttpd Web Server 257

     Integrating TclHttpd with Your Application 258
        TclHttpd Architecture 258
        Adding Code to TclHttpd 259
        Custom Main Programs 260
     Domain Handlers 260
        Connection State and Query Data 261
        The `html` and `ncgi` Packages 261
        Returning Results 262
     Application Direct URLs 262
        Using Query Data 263
        Returning Other Content Types 264
     Document Types 265
     HTML + Tcl Templates 266
        Where to Put Your Tcl Code 267
        Templates for Site Structure 268

Using Variables for Important Site Information 271
Form Handlers 272
Application Direct Handlers 272
Template Form Handlers 274
Self-Posting Forms 274
The html Package 276
Programming Reference 277
Standard Application Direct URLs 281
Status 281
Debugging 281
Sending Email 283
The TclHttpd Distribution 284
Quick Start 284
Inside the Distribution 284
Server Configuration 285
Command Line Arguments 286
Server Name and Port 286
User and Group ID 287
Webmaster Email 287
Document Root 287
Other Document Settings 288
Document Templates 288
Log Files 289
CGI Directories 289

19. Multiple Interpreters and
Safe-Tcl 291
The interp Command 292
Creating Interpreters 293
The Interpreter Hierarchy 293
The Interpreter Name as a Command 294
Use list with interp eval 294
Safe Interpreters 295
Command Aliases 296
Alias Introspection 296
Hidden Commands 297
Substitutions 298
I/O from Safe Interpreters 299
The Safe Base 300
Security Policies 301
Limited Socket Access 302
Limited Temporary Files 304

Safe **after** Command 307

20. Safe-Tk and
the Browser Plugin 311

Tk in Child Interpreters 312
  Embedding Tk Windows 312
  Safe-Tk Restrictions 313
The Browser Plugin 314
  The **embed_args** and **plugin** Variables 314
  Example Plugins 314
  Setting Up the plugin 315
Security Policies and Browser Plugin 315
  The Browser Package 317
Configuring Security Policies 318
  The **config/plugin.cfg** File 318
  Policy Configuration Files 319
  Security Policy Features 319
  Creating New Security Policies 320

21. Multi-Threaded Tcl Scripts 321

What are Threads? 321
Thread Support in Tcl 322
  Obtaining a Thread-Enabled Tcl Interpreter 323
  Using Extensions in Multi-Threaded Scripts 323
Getting Started with the Thread Extension 324
  Creating Threads 324
  Creating Joinable Threads 326
Sending Messages to Threads 328
  Synchronous Message Sending 328
  Asynchronous Message Sending 329
Preserving and Releasing Threads 330
Error Handling 331
Shared Resources 332
Managing I/O Channels 333
  Accessing Files from Multiple Threads 333
  Transferring Channels between Threads 334
Shared Variables 337
Mutexes and Condition Variables 339
  Mutexes 339
  Condition Variables 340
Thread Pools 342
The **Thread** Package Commands 343

The **thread** Namespace 343
The **tsv** Namespace 346
The **tpool** Namespace 347

22. Tclkit and Starkits 349

Getting Started with Tclkit 350
    Inside a Starkit 350
    Deploying Applications as Starkits 350
Virtual File Systems 351
    Accessing a Zip File Through a VFS 352
Using sdx to Bundle Applications 352
    Creating a Simple Starkit 352
    Examining a Starkit 353
    Standard Package Organization 353
    Creating a Starpack 354
Exploring the Virtual File System in a Starkit 354
Creating **tclhttpd.kit** 356
Creating a Shared Starkit 357
Metakit 359
    Metakit Data Model 359
    Examining a Metakit Database 360
    Creating a Metakit View 361
    Storing Application Data in a Starkit 362
    Wikit and the Tcler's Wiki 363
More Ideas 363
    Document Bundles 364
    Self-Updating Applications 364
    Simple Installers 364

Part III. Tk Basics 365

23. Tk Fundamentals 367

Hello, World! in Tk 369
Naming Tk Widgets 370
Configuring Tk Widgets 371
Tk Widget Attributes and the Resource Database 372
    The Tk Manual Pages 372
Summary of the Tk Commands 373
    Widget Commands 373
    Widget Manipulation Commands 374
    Support Procedures 375
Other Widget Sets 375

BLT 375
Tix 376
[incr Tk] and [incr Widgets] 376
BWidgets 376
TkTable 376

24. Tk by Example 377

ExecLog 377
Window Title 379
A Frame for Buttons 380
Command Buttons 380
A Label and an Entry 380
Key Bindings and Focus 380
A Resizable Text and Scrollbar 381
The Run Procedure 381
The Log Procedure 382
The Stop Procedure 383
Cross-Platform Issues 383
The Example Browser 384
More about Resizing Windows 387
Managing Global State 387
Searching through Files 387
Cascaded Menus 388
A Read-Only Text Widget 389
A Tcl Shell 389
Text Marks, Tags, and Bindings 392
Multiple Interpreters 392
Native Look and Feel 392

25. The Pack Geometry Manager 395

Packing toward a Side 396
Shrinking Frames and pack propagate 396
Horizontal and Vertical Stacking 397
The Cavity Model 398
Packing Space and Display Space 399
The -fill Option 400
Internal Padding with -ipadx and -ipady 401
External Padding with -padx and -pady 402
Resizing and -expand 403
Anchoring 404
Packing Order 406
Introspection 406

Pack the Scrollbar First 407
Choosing the Parent for Packing 407
Unpacking a Widget 408
Packer Summary 408
   The **pack** Command 409
Window Stacking Order 409

26. The Grid Geometry Manager 411

A Basic Grid 411
   The **-sticky** Setting 412
   External Padding with **-padx** and **-pady** 413
   Internal Padding with **-ipadx** and **-ipady** 414
   Multiple Widgets in a Cell 414
Spanning Rows and Columns 415
Row and Column Constraints 416
   Row and Column Padding 416
   Minimum Size 417
   Managing Resize Behavior 417
   Uniform Columns 418
The **grid** Command 419

27. The Place Geometry Manager 421

place Basics 421
The Pane Manager 423
   Parsing Arguments and Maintaining State 424
   Sticky Geometry Settings 425
   Event Bindings 425
   Managing the Layout 425
The **place** Command 427

28. The Panedwindow Widget 429

Using the Panedwindow 429
   Manipulating the Pane Contents 430
Programming Panedwindow Widgets 432
Panedwindow Attributes 433

29. Binding Commands to Events 435

The **bind** Command 435
The **bindtags** Command 437
   Focus and Key Events 438
   Using **break** and **continue** in Bindings 438
   Defining New Binding Tags 439

Event Syntax 439
    Keyboard Events 440
    Mouse Events 441
    Other Events 442
    Bindings on Top-level Windows 443
Modifiers 443
Event Sequences 445
Virtual Events 446
Generating Events 447
Event Summary 448
    Event Command Syntax 448
    Event Keywords 448

Part IV. Tk Widgets 451

30. Buttons and Menus 453

Button Commands and Scope Issues 454
Buttons Associated with Tcl Variables 458
Button Attributes 459
Button Operations 461
Menus and Menubuttons 462
    A Menu Bar 464
    System Menus 464
    Pop-Up Menus 465
    Option Menus 465
    Multicolumn Palette Menus 465
Menu Bindings and Events 465
    Keyboard Traversal 465
    Menu Virtual Events 466
Manipulating Menus and Menu Entries 466
Menu Attributes 468
A Menu by Name Package 470
    Menu Accelerators 473

31. The Resource Database 475

An Introduction to Resources 475
    Resource Patterns 476
Loading Option Database Files 477
Adding Individual Database Entries 478
Accessing the Database 479
User-Defined Buttons 479
User-Defined Menus 481

Application and User Resources 483
Expanding Variables 484

32. Simple Tk Widgets 485

Frames, Labelframes, and Toplevel Windows 485
Attributes for Frames, Labelframes, and Toplevels 486
Using Labelframe Widgets 487
Embedding Other Applications 489
Toplevel Window Styles 489
The Label Widget 490
Label Width and Wrap Length 491
Label Attributes 491
The Message Widget 493
Message Attributes 494
Arranging Labels and Messages 494
The Scale Widget 495
Scale Bindings 495
Scale Attributes 496
Programming Scales 497
The **bell** Command 497

33. Scrollbars 499

Using Scrollbars 499
The Scrollbar Protocol 501
The Scrollbar **set** Operation 501
The **xview** and **yview** Operations 502
The Scrollbar Widget 503
Scrollbar Bindings 503
Scrollbar Attributes 504
Programming Scrollbars 505

34. The Entry and Spinbox Widgets 507

Using Entry Widgets 507
Validating Entry Contents 508
Tips for Using Entry Widgets 510
Using Spinbox Widgets 511
Entry and Spinbox Bindings 513
Entry and Spinbox Attributes 515
Programming Entry and Spinbox Widgets 517

35. The Listbox Widget 519

Using Listboxes 519

Manipulating Listbox Contents 519
Programming Listboxes 520
The Listbox Widget 522
Listbox Bindings and Events 524
Browse Select Mode 525
Single Select Mode 525
Extended Select Mode 526
Multiple Select Mode 527
Scroll Bindings 527
Listbox Virtual Events 528
Listbox Attributes 528
Geometry Gridding 529

36. The Text Widget 531

Text Indices 531
Inserting and Deleting Text 532
Index Arithmetic 533
Comparing Indices 533
Text Marks 534
Mark Gravity 534
Text Tags 535
Tag Attributes 535
Mixing Attributes from Different Tags 537
Line Spacing and Justification 538
Tab Stops 540
The Selection 540
Tag Bindings 540
Searching Text 542
Embedded Widgets 542
Embedded Images 544
Looking inside the Text Widget 545
Looking at Tags 546
Looking at Marks 546
Dumping the Contents 547
The Undo Mechanism 548
Text Bindings and Events 549
Text Bindings 549
Text Virtual Events 551
Text Operations 551
Text Attributes 554

37. The Canvas Widget 557

Canvas Coordinates 557
Hello, World! 558
　　Canvas Tags 559
The Min Max Scale Example 561
Canvas Objects 565
　　Canvas Widget and Canvas Object State Options 566
　　Dashed Lines 566
　　Arc Items 567
　　Bitmap Items 568
　　Image Items 569
　　Line Items 570
　　Oval Items 572
　　Polygon Items 573
　　Rectangle Items 574
　　Text Items 575
　　Window Items 579
Canvas Operations 581
Generating Postscript 583
Canvas Attributes 586
Hints 587
　　Screen Coordinates vs. Canvas Coordinates 587
　　Large Coordinate Spaces 587
　　Scaling and Rotation 588
　　Resources 588
　　Objects with Many Points 588
　　Selecting Canvas Items 588

Part V. Tk Details 589

38. Selections and the Clipboard 591

The Selection Model 591
The **selection** Command 593
The **clipboard** Command 594
Selection Handlers 595
　　A Canvas Selection Handler 595

39. Focus, Grabs, and Dialogs 599

Standard Dialogs 599
　　Message Box 600
　　File and Directory Dialogs 600

Color Dialog 602
Custom Dialogs 602
Input Focus 603
The `focus` Command 603
Keyboard Focus Traversal 604
Grabbing the Focus 604
The `tkwait` Command 605
Destroying Widgets 605
The `focus`, `grab`, `tkwait` sequence 605
Prompter Dialog 607
Keyboard Shortcuts and Focus 608
Animation with the `update` Command 608

40. Tk Widget Attributes 611

Configuring Attributes 611
Size 612
Borders and Relief 614
The Focus Highlight 616
Padding and Anchors 616
Putting It All Together 617

41. Color, Images, and Cursors 619

Colors 620
Color Palettes 621
Color Values 621
Colormaps and Visuals 624
Bitmaps and Images 625
The image Command 626
Bitmap Images 626
The `bitmap` Attribute 627
Photo Images 628
The Text Insert Cursor 631
The Mouse Cursor 632

42. Fonts and Text Attributes 635

Naming a Font 636
Named Fonts 637
System Fonts 637
Unicode Fonts 637
X Font Names 638
Font Failures before Tk 8.0 639
Font Metrics 640

The `font` Command 640
Text Attributes 641
    Layout 641
    Selection Attributes 642
Gridding, Resizing, and Geometry 642
A Font Selection Application 643

43. Send 647

The `send` Command 648
    Send and X Authority 648
The Sender Script 649
Communicating Processes 651
Remote `eval` through Sockets 652

44. Window Managers and Window Information 657

The `wm` Command 657
    Toplevel Size, Placement, and Decoration 658
    Icons 660
    Application Session State 661
    Miscellaneous Window Manager Operations 662
The `winfo` Command 663
    Sending Commands between Applications 664
    Widget Family Relationships 664
    Widget Size 665
    Widget Location 666
    Virtual Root Window 667
    Atoms and IDs 667
    Colormaps and Visuals 668
The `tk` Command 669

45. Managing User Preferences 671

App-Defaults Files 671
Defining Preferences 673
The Preferences User Interface 675
Managing the Preferences File 678
Tracing Changes to Preference Variables 680
Improving the Package 680

46. A User Interface to Bindings 683

A Pair of Listboxes Working Together 685
The Editing Interface 687
Saving and Loading Bindings 688

Part VI. C Programming 691

47. C Programming and Tcl 693

Basic Concepts 694
    Getting Started 694
    C Command Procedures and Data Objects 694
    SWIG 695
    Tcl Initialization 695
    Calling Out to Tcl Scripts 696
    Using the Tcl C Library 696
Creating a Loadable Package 697
    The `load` Command 697
    The Package Initialization Procedure 698
    Using `Tcl_PkgProvide` 699
A C Command Procedure 699
    The String Command Interface 700
    Result Codes from Command Procedures 702
    Managing the String Result 702
    The `Tcl_Obj` Command Interface 703
    Managing `Tcl_Obj` Reference Counts 704
    Modifying `Tcl_Obj` Values 705
    Pitfalls of Shared `Tcl_Obj` Values 706
The `blob` Command Example 707
    Creating and Destroying Hash Tables 708
    `Tcl_Alloc`, `ckalloc`, and `malloc` 710
    Parsing Arguments and `Tcl_GetIndexFromObj` 710
    Creating and Removing Elements from a Hash Table . 713
    Building a List 714
    Keeping References to `Tcl_Obj` Values 714
    Using `Tcl_Preserve` and `Tcl_Release` to Guard Data . 715
`CONST` in the Tcl 8.4 APIs 716
Strings and Internationalization 717
    The `DString` Interface 717
    Character Set Conversions 718
`Tcl_Main` and `Tcl_AppInit` 719
    `Tk_Main` 721
The Event Loop 723
Invoking Scripts from C 724
    Variations on Tcl_Eval 724
    Bypassing `Tcl_Eval` 725

48. Compiling Tcl and Extensions 729

Standard Directory Structure 730
   The Source Distribution 730
   The Installation Directory Structure 731
Building Tcl from Source 731
   Configure and Autoconf 732
   Standard Configure Flags 733
   Installation 735
Using Stub Libraries 735
Using `autoconf` 736
   The `tcl.m4` File 736
   Makefile Templates 737
The Sample Extension 737
   `configure.in` 738
   `Makefile.in` 739
   Standard Header Files 740
   Using the Sample Extension 740

49. Writing a Tk Widget in C 743

Initializing the Extension 744
The Widget Data Structure 744
The Widget Class Command 745
The Widget Instance Command 749
Configuring and Reconfiguring Attributes 752
Specifying Widget Attributes 756
Displaying the Clock 761
The Window Event Procedure 764
Final Cleanup 765

50. C Library Overview 767

An Overview of the Tcl C Library 768
   Application Initialization 768
   Creating and Deleting Interpreters 768
   Creating and Deleting Commands 768
   Dynamic Loading and Packages 768
   Managing the Result String 769
   Memory Allocation 769
   Lists 769
   Command Parsing 770
   Command Pipelines 770
   Tracing the Actions of the Tcl Interpreter 770
   Evaluating Tcl Commands 770

Reporting Script Errors 771
Manipulating Tcl Variables 771
Evaluating Expressions 772
Converting Numbers 772
Tcl Objects 772
Primitive Object Types 772
String Object Types 772
ByteArrays for Binary Data 773
Dynamic Strings 773
Character Set Encodings 773
AssocData for per Interpreter Data Structures 774
Hash Tables 774
Option Processing 775
Regular Expressions and String Matching 775
Event Loop Implementation 775
File Handlers 775
Timer Events 776
Idle Callbacks 776
Input/Output 776
I/O Channel Drivers 776
Manipulating File Names 777
Examining the File System 777
Virtual File System Implementations 778
Thread Support 778
Working with Signals 778
Exit Handlers 779
Macintosh 779
Panic 779
Miscellaneous 779
An Overview of the Tk C Library 779
Main Programs and Command-Line Arguments 779
Creating Windows 780
Application Name for Send 780
Configuring Windows 780
Command Options 780
Window Coordinates 781
Window Stacking Order 781
Window Information 781
Configuring Widget Attributes 781
The Selection and Clipboard 781
Event Loop Interface 781
Handling Window Events 782

Event Bindings 782
Keyboard Grab 782
Handling Graphic Protocol Errors 782
Using the Resource Database 783
Managing Bitmaps 783
Creating New Image Types 783
Using an Image in a Widget 783
Photo Image Types 783
Canvas Object Support 784
Geometry Management 784
String Identifiers (UIDS) 784
Colors, Colormaps, and Visuals 784
3D Borders 785
Mouse Cursors 785
Fonts and Text Display 785
Graphics Contexts 785
Allocate a Pixmap 786
Screen Measurements 786
Relief Style 786
Text Anchor Positions 786
Line Cap Styles 786
Line Join Styles 786
Dashed Lines 786
Text Justification Styles 786
Atoms 787
X Resource ID Management 787
Windows Application Handles 787

Part VII. Changes................................... 789

51. Tcl 7.4/Tk 4.0 791
wish 791
Obsolete Features 791
The cget Operation 792
Input Focus Highlight 792
Bindings 792
Scrollbar Interface 793
pack info 793
Focus 793
The send Command 794
Internal Button Padding 794
Radiobutton Value 794

Entry Widget 794
Menus 795
Listboxes 795
No `geometry` Attribute 795
Text Widget 796
Color Attributes 796
Color Allocation and `tk colormodel` 797
Canvas `scrollincrement` 797
The Selection 797
The `bell` Command 797

52. Tcl 7.5/Tk 4.1 799

Cross-Platform Scripts 799
    File Name Manipulation 799
    Newline Translations 799
    The `tcl_platform` Variable 800
    The `console` Command 800
The `clock` Command 800
The `load` Command 800
The `package` Command 801
Multiple `foreach` loop variables 801
Event Loop Moves from Tk to Tcl 801
Network Sockets 801
    `info hostname` 802
    The `fconfigure` Command 802
Multiple Interpreters and Safe-Tcl 802
The `grid` Geometry Manager 802
The Text Widget 802
The Entry Widget 802

53. Tcl 7.6/Tk 4.2 803

More `file` Operations 803
Virtual Events 803
Standard Dialogs 804
New `grid` Geometry Manager 804
Macintosh `unsupported1` Command 804

54. Tcl/Tk 8.0 805

The Tcl Compiler 805
    Compile-Time Errors 806
    Binary String Support 806
Namespaces 806

Safe-Tcl 806
New `lsort` 807
`tcl_precision` Variable 807
Year 2000 Convention 807
Http Package 807
Serial Line I/O 808
Platform-Independent Fonts 808
The `tk scaling` Command 808
Application Embedding 808
Native Menus and Menubars 808
CDE Border Width 809
Native Buttons and Scrollbars 809
Images in Text Widgets 809
No Errors from `destroy` 809
`grid rowconfigure` 809
The Patch Releases 809
    `fconfigure -error` 810
    `tcl_platform(debug)` 810
    `tcl_findLibrary` 810
    `auto_mkindex_old` 811
    Windows Keysyms for Start and Menu Keys 811
    The `MouseWheel` Event 811
    Transparent Fill on Canvas Text 811
    `safe::loadTk` 811

55. Tcl/Tk 8.1 813

Unicode and Internationalization 813
    `fconfigure -encoding` 813
    The `encoding` Command 814
    The `msgcat` Package 814
    UTF-8 and Unicode C API 814
Thread Safety 814
    The `testthread` Command 814
Advanced Regular Expressions 815
New String Commands 815
The DDE Extension 816
Miscellaneous 816
    Serial Line I/O 816
    `tcl_platform(user)` 816

56. Tcl/Tk 8.2 817

The Trf Patch 817

Faster String Operations 817
Empty Array Names 818
Browser Plugin Compatibility 818
Finer Control of Windows Serial Port Monitoring 818
Regular Expression Expanded Syntax Option 818

57. Tcl/Tk 8.3 819
New File Manipulation Commands and Options 819
New glob Options 820
Regular Expression Command Enhancements 820
Direct Return of scan Matches 820
Removing Duplicate List Elements with lsort 820
Deleting Elements from an Array 820
Enhanced clock Features 820
Support for Delayed Package Loading in pkg_mkIndex 821
The Img Patch 821
The Dash Patch 821
    Canvas Improvements 821
    Hidden Text 822
    Pointer Warping 822
    Entry Widget Validation 822
Other New Tk Features 822
    Listbox Enhancements 822
    New Directory Chooser Dialog 823
    Window Manager Interactions with Toplevel Windows 823
    Support Added for Windows System Cursors 823
    Mousewheel Support for Listbox and Text Widgets 823
    New Quadruple Event Modifier 823
    X Input Methods (XIM) 823
The Patch Releases 823
    Detection of Entry Validation Type 824
    Macintosh File Selection Dialog Enhancement 824
    State Attributes for Label Widgets 824
    Support for Windows Icons 824
    New Reference Pages 824

58. Tcl/Tk 8.4 825
64-Bit Support 826
    64-Bit Arithmetic 826
    64-Bit Value Conversions 826
    64-Bit Filesystem Support 826
    Native Word Size Detection 826

Additional Filesystem Features and Commands 826
    Virtual Filesystems 826
    New **file** Subcommands and **glob** Options 827
New and Enhanced List Commands 827
Array Searching and Statistics 828
Enhanced Support for Serial Communications 828
New String Comparison Operators 828
Command Tracing 828
Additional Introspection Commands 828
Other Tcl Changes 829
    Unsetting Nonexistent Variables 829
    Direct Return of Substituted String with **regsub** 829
    Increased Time Resolution on Windows 829
    Bug Fixed in **fcopy** to Respect Channel Encodings 829
New Tk Widgets 829
Text Widget Undo Mechanism and Other Enhancements 830
New **pack** and **grid** Features 830
    Asymmetric Padding 830
    Uniform Rows and Columns in **grid** 830
Displaying Both Text and an Image in a Widget 830
New Button Relief Attributes 831
Controlling the State of Entries and Listboxes 831
More Window Manager Interaction 831
Other Tk Changes 832
    Mouse Button Repeat Control 832
    Better Support for Image Transparency 832
    Selecting Multiple Files with **tk_getOpenFile** 832
    Fixed-Width Button Support on Windows Systems 832
    Easier Access to Clipboard Contents 832
    Determining if an Image is Used 832
    New Events and Substitutions for Window Managers 833
    Caret Management for Improved XIM/IME Support ... 833
    New **bell** Option to Prevent Resetting Screen Savers . 833
    Generating Postscript for Embedded Widgets 833

59. About The CD-ROM 835
    Technical Support 836

List of Examples

1.1   The "Hello, World!" example. 4
1.2   Tcl variables. 5
1.3   Command substitution. 5
1.4   Simple arithmetic. 6
1.5   Nested commands. 6
1.6   Built-in math functions. 6
1.7   Grouping expressions with braces. 7
1.8   Quoting special characters with backslash. 7
1.9   Continuing long lines with backslashes. 8
1.10   Grouping with double quotes vs. braces. 8
1.11   Embedded command and variable substitution. 9
1.12   Defining a procedure. 11
1.13   A `while` loop to compute factorial. 12
1.14   A recursive definition of factorial. 13
1.15   Using `set` to return a variable value. 14
1.16   Embedded variable references. 14
1.17   Using `info` to determine if a variable exists. 15
1.18   Controlling precision with `tcl_precision`. 15

2.1   A standalone Tcl script on UNIX. 26
2.2   A standalone Tk script on UNIX. 26
2.3   Using `/bin/sh` to run a Tcl script. 27
2.4   The `EchoArgs` script. 29

3.1   A simple CGI script. 36
3.2   Output of Example 3–1. 36
3.3   The `guestbook.cgi` script, version 1. 37
3.4   The `Cgi_Header` procedure. 38
3.5   The `guestbook.cgi` script, version 2. 39
3.6   Initial output of `guestbook.cgi` with no data. 40
3.7   Output of `guestbook.cgi` with guestbook data. 41
3.8   The `newguest.html` form. 43
3.9   The `newguest.cgi` script. 45
3.10   The `newguest.cgi` script with error handling. 47

4.1   Comparing strings with `string compare`. 52
4.2   Comparing strings with `string equal`. 53
4.3   Comparing strings with `eq`. 53
4.4   Mapping Microsoft World special characters to ASCII. 55

5.1   Constructing a list with the `list` command. 65
5.2   Using `lappend` to add elements to a list. 66

5.3   Using `lset` to set an element of a list. 66
5.4   Using `concat` to splice lists together. 67
5.5   Double quotes compared to the `concat` and `list` commands. 67
5.6   Modifying lists with `lreplace`. 68
5.7   Deleting a list element by value. 69
5.8   Sorting a list using a comparison function. 71
5.9   Use `split` to turn input data into Tcl lists. 72
5.10   Implementing `join` in Tcl. 73

6.1   A conditional `if then else` command. 76
6.2   Chained conditional with `elseif`. 77
6.3   Using `switch` for an exact match. 78
6.4   Using `switch` with substitutions in the patterns. 78
6.5   A `switch` with "fall through" cases. 78
6.6   Comments in `switch` commands. 79
6.7   A `while` loop to read standard input. 79
6.8   Looping with `foreach`. 80
6.9   Parsing command-line arguments. 80
6.10   Using `list` with `foreach`. 81
6.11   Multiple loop variables with `foreach`. 81
6.12   Multiple value lists with `foreach`. 82
6.13   A `for` loop. 82
6.14   A standard `catch` phrase. 83
6.15   A longer `catch` phrase. 84
6.16   There are several possible return values from `catch`. 84
6.17   Raising an error. 85
6.18   Preserving `errorInfo` when calling `error`. 85
6.19   Raising an error with `return`. 86

7.1   Default parameter values. 88
7.2   Variable number of arguments. 88
7.3   Variable scope and Tcl procedures. 90
7.4   A random number generator. 91
7.5   Print variable by name. 92
7.6   Improved `incr` procedure. 92

8.1   Using arrays. 96
8.2   Referencing an array indirectly. 97
8.3   Referencing an array indirectly using `upvar`. 97
8.4   `ArrayInvert` inverts an array. 99
8.5   Using arrays for records, version 1. 100
8.6   Using arrays for records, version 2. 100
8.7   Using arrays for records, version 3. 100
8.8   Using a list to implement a stack. 101
8.9   Using an array to implement a stack. 101
8.10   A list of arrays. 102

8.11   A list of arrays. 103
8.12   A simple in-memory database. 103

9.1   Using `exec` on a process pipeline. 106
9.2   Comparing file modify times. 114
9.3   Determining whether pathnames reference the same file. 115
9.4   Opening a file for writing. 117
9.5   A more careful use of `open`. 118
9.6   Opening a process pipeline. 118
9.7   Prompting for input. 119
9.8   A read loop using `gets`. 120
9.9   A read loop using `read` and `split`. 120
9.10   Copy a file and translate to native format. 121
9.11   Finding a file by name. 123
9.12   Printing environment variable values. 124

10.1   Using `list` to construct commands. 131
10.2   Generating procedures dynamically with a template. 133
10.3   Using `eval` with `$args`. 136
10.4   `lassign`: list assignment with `foreach`. 139
10.5   The `File_Process` procedure iterates over lines in a file. 140

11.1   Expanded regular expressions allow comments. 154
11.2   Using regular expressions to parse a string. 158
11.3   A pattern to match URLs. 159
11.4   An advanced regular expression to match URLs. 160
11.5   The `Url_Decode` procedure. 164
11.6   The `Cgi_List` and `Cgi_Query` procedures. 165
11.7   `Cgi_Parse` and `Cgi_Value` store query data in the `cgi` array. 166
11.8   `Html_DecodeEntity`. 167
11.9   `Html_Parse`. 168

12.1   Maintaining a `tclIndex` file. 177
12.2   Loading a `tclIndex` file. 178

13.1   Calculating clicks per second. 185
13.2   Printing a procedure definition. 188
13.3   Mapping form data onto procedure arguments. 189
13.4   Finding built-in commands. 190
13.5   Getting a trace of the Tcl call stack. 190
13.6   A procedure to read and evaluate commands. 191
13.7   Using `info script` to find related files. 192
13.8   Tracing variables. 195
13.9   Creating array elements with array traces. 196
13.10 Interactive `history` usage. 197
13.11 Implementing special history syntax. 198
13.12 A `Debug` procedure. 199

13.13 Time Stamps in log records. 203

14.1   Random number generator using namespaces. 206
14.2   Random number generator using qualified names. 209
14.3   Nested namespaces. 209
14.4   The code procedure to wrap callbacks. 212
14.5   Listing commands defined by a namespace. 212

15.1   MIME character sets and file encodings. 219
15.2   Using scripts in nonstandard encodings. 220
15.3   Three sample message catalog files. 224
15.4   Using `msgcat::mcunknown` to share message catalogs. 225

16.1   A read event file handler. 229
16.2   Using `vwait` to activate the event loop. 230
16.3   A read event file handler for a nonblocking channel. 233

17.1   Opening a client socket with a timeout. 240
17.2   Opening a server socket. 240
17.3   The echo service. 241
17.4   A client of the echo service. 242
17.5   Opening a connection to an HTTP server. 243
17.6   Opening a connection through a HTTP proxy. 244
17.7   `Http_Head` validates a URL. 245
17.8   Using `Http_Head`. 247
17.9   `Http_Get` fetches the contents of a URL. 247
17.10 `HttpGetText` reads `text` URLs. 249
17.11 `HttpCopyDone` is used with `fcopy`. 249
17.12 Downloading files with `http::geturl`. 254
17.13 Basic Authentication using `http::geturl`. 256

18.1   The `hello.tcl` file implements `/hello/world`. 259
18.2   A simple URL domain. 261
18.3   Application Direct URLs. 262
18.4   Alternate types for Application Direct URLs. 265
18.5   A sample document type handler. 265
18.6   A one-level site structure. 268
18.7   A two-level site structure. 268
18.8   A HTML + Tcl template file. 269
18.9   `SitePage` template procedure, version 1. 269
18.10 `SiteMenu` and `SiteFooter` template procedures. 270
18.11 The `SiteLink` procedure. 271
18.12 Mail form results with `/mail/forminfo`. 272
18.13 Mail message sent by `/mail/forminfo`. 273
18.14 Processing mail sent by `/mail/forminfo`. 273
18.15 Processing mail sent by `/mail/forminfo`, Safe-Tcl version. 274
18.16 A self-checking form procedure. 275

18.17 A page with a self-checking form. 276
18.18 Generating a table with `html::foreach`. 277
18.19 The `/debug/source` Application Direct URL implementation. 282

19.1   Creating and deleting an interpreter. 293
19.2   Creating a hierarchy of interpreters. 293
19.3   A command alias for `exit`. 296
19.4   Querying aliases. 296
19.5   Dumping aliases as Tcl commands. 297
19.6   Substitutions and hidden commands. 298
19.7   Opening a file for an unsafe interpreter. 300
19.8   The `Safesock` security policy. 302
19.9   The `Tempfile` security policy. 304
19.10 Restricted `puts` using hidden commands. 306
19.11 A safe `after` command. 308

20.1   Using `EMBED` to insert a Tclet. 314

21.1   Creating a separate thread to perform a lengthy operation. 325
21.2   Initializing a thread before entering its event loop. 325
21.3   Creating several threads in an application. 326
21.4   Using joinable threads to detect thread termination. 327
21.5   Examples of synchronous message sending. 328
21.6   Using a return variable with synchronous message sending.... 329
21.7   Executing commands after `thread::wait` returns. 331
21.8   Creating a custom thread error handler. 332
21.9   A basic implementation of a logging thread. 333
21.10 Deferring socket transfer until after the connection callback... 335
21.11 Working around Tcl's socket transfer bug. 335
21.12 A multi-threaded echo server. 335
21.13 Using a mutex to protect a shared resource. 339
21.14 Standard condition variable use for a signalling thread. 341
21.15 Standard condition variable use for a waiting thread. 341

22.1   Accessing a Zip file through a VFS. 352
22.2   The output of `sdx lsk hello.kit`. 353
22.3   The main program of a Starkit. 353
22.4   The `pkgIndex.tcl` in a Starkit. 354
22.5   A Starkit that examines its Virtual File System. 355
22.6   Creating a simple Starkit. 355
22.7   The contents of the `tclhttpd.vfs` directory, version 1. 356
22.8   The main program for the TclHttpd Starkit, version 1. 356
22.9   Contents of the `tclhttpd.vfs` directory, version 2. 357
22.10 The main program for the TclHttpd Starkit, version 2. 357
22.11 The Standard Tcl Library Starkit `main.tcl` file. 358

22.12   The main program for TclHttpd Starkit, version 3. 359
22.13   Examining the views in a Metakit database. 360
22.14   Examining data in a Metakit view. 360
22.15   Selecting data with `mk::select`. 361
22.16   Creating a new view. 362
22.17   Adding data to a view. 362
22.18   Storing data in a Starkit. 363

23.1   "Hello, World!" Tk program. 369
23.2   Looking at all widget attributes. 371

24.1   Logging the output of a program run with `exec`. 378
24.2   A platform-specific cancel event. 383
24.3   A browser for the code examples in the book. 384
24.4   A Tcl shell in a text widget. 389
24.5   Macintosh look and feel. 393
24.6   Windows look and feel. 393
24.7   UNIX look and feel. 394

25.1   Two frames packed inside the main frame. 396
25.2   Turning off geometry propagation. 397
25.3   A horizontal stack inside a vertical stack. 397
25.4   Even more nesting of horizontal and vertical stacks. 398
25.5   Mixing bottom and right packing sides. 399
25.6   Filling the display into extra packing space. 400
25.7   Using horizontal fill in a menu bar. 400
25.8   The effects of internal padding (`-ipady`)..............................401
25.9   Button padding vs. packer padding. 402
25.10 The look of a default button. 402
25.11 Resizing without the `expand` option. 403
25.12 Resizing with `expand` turned on.......................................404
25.13 More than one expanding widget. 404
25.14 Setup for anchor experiments. 404
25.15 The effects of noncenter anchors. 405
25.16 Animating the packing anchors. 405
25.17 Controlling the packing order...406
25.18 Packing into other relatives. 407

26.1   A basic grid...412
26.2   A grid with `sticky` settings. 412
26.3   A grid with row and column specifications.............................413
26.4   A grid with external padding..413
26.5   A grid with internal padding. 414
26.6   All combinations of `-sticky` settings. 414
26.7   Explicit row and column span. 415
26.8   Grid syntax row and column span.......................................416
26.9   Row padding compared to cell padding. 416

26.10 Gridding a text widget and scrollbar. 417
26.11 Uniform column width.. 418

27.1 Centering a window with `place`... 421
27.2 Covering a window with `place`. 422
27.3 Combining relative and absolute sizes. 422
27.4 Positioning a window above a sibling with `place`. 422
27.5 `Pane_Create` sets up vertical or horizontal panes....................... 423
27.6 `PaneDrag` adjusts the percentage. 426
27.7 `PaneGeometry` updates the layout.. 426

28.1 A panedwindow with complex managed widgets..................... 430

29.1 Bindings on different binding tags. 438
29.2 Output from the UNIX *xmodmap* program.............................. 445
29.3 Emacs-like binding convention for `Meta` and `Escape`. 446
29.4 Virtual events for cut, copy, and paste.................................... 446

30.1 A troublesome button command... 454
30.2 Fixing the troublesome situation. 455
30.3 A button associated with a Tcl procedure............................... 456
30.4 Radiobuttons and checkbuttons. 458
30.5 A command on a radiobutton or checkbutton. 459
30.6 A menu sampler. 463
30.7 A menu bar in Tk 8.0. 464
30.8 Using the `<<MenuSelect>>` virtual event. 466
30.9 A simple menu by name package.. 470
30.10 Using the Tk 8.0 menu bar facility.. 471
30.11 `MenuGet` maps from name to menu.. 471
30.12 Adding menu entries. 472
30.13 A wrapper for cascade entries. 472
30.14 Using the menu by name package. 473
30.15 Keeping the accelerator display up to date. 473

31.1 Reading an option database file. 477
31.2 A file containing resource specifications................................. 478
31.3 Using resources to specify user-defined buttons. 479
31.4 `Resource_ButtonFrame` defines buttons based on resources. 480
31.5 Using `Resource_ButtonFrame`. 480
31.6 Specifying menu entries via resources. 481
31.7 Defining menus from resource specifications. 482
31.8 `Resource_GetFamily` merges user and application resources. 483

32.1 Labelframe example.. 488
32.2 Using the `labelAnchor` option to position a labelframe's anchor. 488
32.3 Associating an existing label widget with a labelframe............ 489
32.4 Macintosh window styles. 489

32.5   A label that displays different strings...................................490
32.6   The message widget formats long lines of text.......................493
32.7   Controlling the text layout in a message widget. 493
32.8   A scale widget. 495

33.1   A text widget and two scrollbars. 500
33.2   Scroll_Set manages optional scrollbars. 501
33.3   Listbox with optional scrollbars...502

34.1   Associating entry widgets with variables and commands. 508
34.2   Restricting entry text to integer values...................................509
34.3   Reestablishing validation using an idle task. 510
34.4   A simple spinbox with calculated values.................................511
34.5   Formatting numeric values in a spinbox...................................512
34.6   Enumerating spinbox values and wrapping. 512
34.7   Using the spinbox readonly state..513

35.1   Using -listvariable to link a listbox and variable.......................520
35.2   Choosing items from a listbox. 520
35.3   Using the <<ListboxSelect>> virtual event.................................528

36.1   Tag configurations for basic character styles. 537
36.2   Line spacing and justification in the text widget. 538
36.3   An active text button. 541
36.4   Delayed creation of embedded widgets.....................................543
36.5   Using embedded images for a bulleted list. 544
36.6   Finding the current range of a text tag. 546
36.7   Dumping the text widget. 547
36.8   Dumping the text widget with a command callback. 547

37.1   A large scrolling canvas...558
37.2   The canvas "Hello, World!" example..559
37.3   A min max scale canvas example...561
37.4   Moving the markers for the min max scale. 563
37.5   Canvas arc items. 568
37.6   Canvas bitmap items. 569
37.7   Canvas image items. 570
37.8   A canvas stroke drawing example..571
37.9   Canvas oval items..573
37.10   Canvas polygon items..573
37.11   Dragging out a box...574
37.12   Simple edit bindings for canvas text items...............................576
37.13   Using a canvas to scroll a set of widgets. 579
37.14   Generating Postscript from a canvas. 585

38.1   Paste the PRIMARY or CLIPBOARD selection. 592
38.2   Separate paste actions. 593

38.3   Bindings for canvas selection... 595
38.4   Selecting objects.. 596
38.5   A canvas selection handler. 596
38.6   The copy and cut operations.. 597
38.7   Pasting onto the canvas... 598

39.1   Procedures to help build dialogs. 606
39.2   A simple dialog.. 607
39.3   A feedback procedure. 609

40.1   Equal-sized labels. 614
40.2   3D relief sampler.. 614
40.3   Padding provided by labels and buttons................................. 617
40.4   Anchoring text in a label or button. 617
40.5   Borders and padding. 617

41.1   Resources for reverse video... 621
41.2   Computing a darker color... 624
41.3   Specifying an image for a widget. 625
41.4   Specifying a bitmap for a widget. 627
41.5   The built-in bitmaps.. 627
41.6   The Tk cursors. 633

42.1   The `FontWidget` procedure handles missing fonts..................... 639
42.2   Font metrics... 640
42.3   A gridded, resizable listbox. 642
42.4   Font selection dialog... 643

43.1   The sender application. 650
43.2   Hooking the browser to an `eval` server................................... 651
43.3   Making the shell into an `eval` server. 652
43.4   Remote `eval` using sockets. 653
43.5   Reading commands from a socket... 653
43.6   The client side of remote evaluation. 654

44.1   Gridded geometry for a canvas.. 658
44.2   Telling other applications what your name is. 664

45.1   Preferences initialization... 672
45.2   Adding preference items. 673
45.3   Setting preference variables.. 674
45.4   Using the preferences package... 674
45.5   A user interface to the preference items. 675
45.6   Interface objects for different preference types. 676
45.7   Displaying the help text for an item. 678
45.8   Saving preferences settings to a file. 678
45.9   Read settings from the preferences file.................................... 679

45.10 Tracing a Tcl variable in a preference item. 680

46.1 A user interface to widget bindings. 684
46.2 `Bind_Display` presents the bindings for a widget or class. 685
46.3 Related listboxes are configured to select items together. 686
46.4 Controlling a pair of listboxes with one scrollbar. 686
46.5 Drag-scrolling a pair of listboxes together. 687
46.6 An interface to define bindings. 687
46.7 Defining and saving bindings. 689

47.1 The initialization procedure for a loadable package. 698
47.2 The `RandomCmd` C command procedure. 700
47.3 The `RandomObjCmd` C command procedure. 703
47.4 The `Tcl_Obj` structure. 705
47.5 The `Plus1ObjCmd` procedure. 706
47.6 The `Blob` and `BlobState` data structures. 708
47.7 The `Blob_Init` and `BlobCleanup` procedures. 709
47.8 The `BlobCmd` command procedure. 711
47.9 `BlobCreate` and `BlobDelete`. 713
47.10 The `BlobNames` procedure. 714
47.11 The `BlobN` and `BlobData` procedures. 715
47.12 The `BlobCommand` and `BlobPoke` procedures. 716
47.13 A canonical Tcl `main` program and `Tcl_AppInit` 720
47.14 A canonical Tk `main` program and `Tk_AppInit` 721
47.15 Calling C command procedure directly with `Tcl_Invoke` 725

49.1 The `Clock_Init` procedure. 744
49.2 The `Clock` widget data structure. 745
49.3 The `ClockCmd` command procedure. 746
49.4 The `ClockObjCmd` command procedure. 747
49.5 The `ClockInstanceCmd` command procedure. 749
49.6 The `ClockInstanceObjCmd` command procedure. 751
49.7 `ClockConfigure` allocates resources for the widget. 753
49.8 `ClockObjConfigure` allocates resources for the widget. 754
49.9 The `Tk_ConfigSpec` typedef. 756
49.10 Configuration specs for the clock widget. 757
49.11 The `Tk_OptionSpec` typedef. 758
49.12 The `Tk_OptionSpec` structure for the clock widget. 758
49.13 `ComputeGeometry` computes the widget's size. 761
49.14 The `ClockDisplay` procedure. 762
49.15 The `ClockEventProc` handles window events. 764
49.16 The `ClockDestroy` cleanup procedure. 765
49.17 The `ClockObjDelete` command. 766

List of Tables

1-1   Backslash sequences. 20
1-2   Arithmetic operators from highest to lowest precedence. 20
1-3   Built-in math functions. 21
1-4   Built-in Tcl commands. 22

2-1   Wish command line options. 30
2-2   Variables defined by *tclsh* and *wish*. 31

3-1   HTML tags used in the examples. 34

4-1   The `string` command. 50
4-2   Matching characters used with `string match`. 53
4-3   Character class names. 54
4-4   Format conversions. 57
4-5   Format flags. 58
4-6   Binary conversion types. 60

5-1   List-related commands. 64
5-2   Options to the `lsearch` command. 70

8-1   The `array` command. 98

9-1   Summary of the `exec` syntax for I/O redirection. 106
9-2   The `file` command options. 108
9-3   Array elements defined by `file stat`. 114
9-4   Platform-specific file attributes. 115
9-5   Tcl commands used for file access. 116
9-6   Summary of the `open` access arguments. 117
9-7   Summary of `POSIX` flags for the access argument. 117
9-8   `glob` command options. 122
9-9   The `registry` command. 126
9-10   The `registry` data types. 126

11-1   Additional advanced regular expression syntax. 155
11-2   Backslash escapes in regular expressions. 156
11-3   Character classes. 156
11-4   Embedded option characters used with the (?x) syntax. 157
11-5   Options to the `regexp` command. 158
11-6   Sample regular expressions. 161

12-1   Options to the `pkg_mkIndex` command. 174
12-2   The `package` command. 176

13-1   `clock format` keywords. 184
13-2   The `clock` command. 184

13-3   The `info` command. 187
13-4   The `history` command. 196
13-5   Special `history` syntax. 197

14-1   The `namespace` command. 213

15-1   The `encoding` command. 222
15-2   The `msgcat` package 226

16-1   The `after` command. 228
16-2   The `fileevent` command. 230
16-3   I/O channel properties controlled by `fconfigure`. 231
16-4   Serial line properties controlled by `fconfigure`. 232
16-5   End of line translation modes. 234

17-1   Options to the `http::geturl` command. 252
17-2   The `http` support procedures. 253
17-3   Elements of the `http::geturl` state array 253

18-1   `Httpd` support procedures. 277
18-2   `Url` support procedures. 278
18-3   `Doc` procedures for configuration. 278
18-4   `Doc` procedures for generating responses. 279
18-5   `Doc` procedures that support template processing. 279
18-6   Elements of the `page` array. 279
18-7   Elements of the `env` array. 280
18-8   Status Application Direct URLs. 281
18-9   Debug Application Direct URLs. 282
18-10   Application Direct URLS that email form results. 283
18-11   Basic TclHttpd parameters. 286

19-1   The `interp` command. 292
19-2   Commands hidden from safe interpreters. 295
19-3   The safe base master interface. 301
19-4   The safe base slave aliases. 301

20-1   Tk commands omitted from safe interpreters. 313
20-2   Aliases defined by the `browser` package. 317
20-3   The `browser::getURL` callbacks. 317

21-1   The commands of the `thread` namespace. 344
21-2   Thread configuration options. 345
21-3   The commands of the `tsv` namespace. 346
21-4   The commands of the `tpool` namespace. 347
21-5   Thread pool configuration options. 348

22-1   Return values of the `starkit::startup` procedure 358

23-1   Tk widget-creation commands. 373

23-2   Tk widget-manipulation commands. 374
23-3   Tk support procedures. 375

25-1   The `pack` command. 409
25-2   Packing options. 409

26-1   The `grid` command. 419
26-2   Grid widget options. 419

27-1   The `place` command. 427
27-2   Placement options. 427

28-1   Panedwindow operations. 432
28-2   Panedwindow attributes. 433
28-3   Panedwindow managed widget options. 433

29-1   Event types. 439
29-2   Event modifiers. 444
29-3   The `event` command. 448
29-4   A summary of the `event` keywords. 449

30-1   Resource names of attributes for all button widgets. 460
30-2   Button operations. 462
30-3   Menu entry index keywords 467
30-4   Menu operations. 467
30-5   Menu attribute resource names. 468
30-6   Attributes for menu entries 469

32-1   Attributes for frame, labelframe, and toplevel widgets. 486
32-2   Label Attributes. 492
32-3   Message Attributes 494
32-4   Bindings for scale widgets. 495
32-5   Attributes for scale widgets. 496
32-6   Operations on the scale widget. 497

33-1   Attributes for the scrollbar widget. 504
33-2   Bindings for the scrollbar widget. 504
33-3   Operations on the scrollbar widget. 505

34-1   Entry and spinbox validation substitutions. 509
34-2   Entry and spinbox bindings. 513
34-3   Entry and spinbox attribute resource names. 515
34-4   Entry and spinbox indices. 517
34-5   Entry and spinbox operations. 517

35-1   Listbox indices. 522
35-2   Listbox operations. 522
35-3   Listbox item configuration options. 524
35-4   The values for the `selectMode` of a listbox. 524
35-5   Bindings for `browse` selection mode. 525

35-6   Bindings for `single` selection mode. 525
35-7   Bindings for `extended` selection mode. 526
35-8   Bindings for `multiple` selection mode. 527
35-9   Listbox scroll bindings. 527
35-10   Listbox attribute resource names. 528

36-1   Text indices. 532
36-2   Index modifiers for text widgets. 533
36-3   Attributes for text tags. 536
36-4   Options to the `search` operation. 542
36-5   Window and image alignment options. 543
36-6   Options to the `window create` operation. 544
36-7   Options to the `image create` operation. 545
36-8   Bindings for the text widget. 549
36-9   Operations for the text widget. 551
36-10   Text attribute resource names. 554

37-1   Common canvas item attributes. 565
37-2   Canvas dash pattern characters 567
37-3   Arc attributes. 568
37-4   Bitmap attributes. 569
37-5   Image attributes. 570
37-6   Line attributes. 572
37-7   Polygon attributes. 574
37-8   Indices for canvas `text` items. 575
37-9   Canvas operations that apply to `text` items. 575
37-10   Text attributes 579
37-11   Window attributes. 581
37-12   Operations on a `canvas` widget. 581
37-13   Canvas `postscript` options. 584
37-14   Canvas attribute resource names. 586

38-1   The `selection` command. 594
38-2   The `clipboard` command. 594

39-1   Options to `tk_messageBox`. 600
39-2   Options to the standard file and directory dialogs. 600
39-3   Options to `tk_chooseColor`. 602
39-4   The `focus` command. 603
39-5   The `grab` command. 604
39-6   The `tkwait` command. 605

40-1   Size attribute resource names. 613
40-2   Border and relief attribute resource names. 615
40-3   Highlight attribute resource names. 616
40-4   Layout attribute resource names. 616

41-1   Color attribute resource names. 620

41-2   Windows system colors... 622
41-3   Macintosh system colors. 623
41-4   Visual classes for displays. 624
41-5   Summary of the image command. 626
41-6   Bitmap image options... 627
41-7   Photo image attributes. 628
41-8   Photo image operations. 629
41-9   Copy options for photo images... 630
41-10   Read options for photo images... 630
41-11   Write options for photo images. 631
41-12   Cursor attribute resource names. 631

42-1   Font attributes. 636
42-2   X Font specification components. 638
42-3   Layout attribute resource names 641
42-4   The font command... 641
42-5   Selection attribute resource names................................. 642

43-1   Options to the send command.. 648

44-1   Size, placement and decoration window manager operations. . 659
44-2   Window manager commands for icons. 661
44-3   Session-related window manager operations........................ 662
44-4   Miscellaneous window manager operations......................... 663
44-5   send command information... 664
44-6   Window hierarchy information.. 665
44-7   Window location information. 666
44-8   Window size information... 666
44-9   Virtual root window information. 667
44-10   Atom and window ID information. 668
44-11   Colormap and visual class information. 669
44-12   The tk command operations. 670

47-1   Defines to control the meaning of CONST in the Tcl APIs........... 717

48-1   The Tcl source directory structure. 730
48-2   The installation directory structure................................. 731
48-3   Standard configure flags... 734
48-4   TEA standard Makefile targets... 740

49-1   Configuration flags and corresponding C types. 760

51-1   Changes in color attribute names. 796

55-1   The testthread command... 815
55-2   The dde command options. 816

Preface

Tcl stands for *Tool Command Language*. Tcl is really two things: a scripting language, and an interpreter for that language that is designed to be easy to embed into your application. Tcl and its associated graphical user-interface toolkit, Tk, were designed and crafted by Professor John Ousterhout of the University of California, Berkeley. You can find these packages on the Internet and use them freely in your application, even if it is commercial. The Tcl interpreter has been ported from UNIX to DOS, PalmOS, VMS, Windows, OS/2, NT, and Macintosh environments. The Tk toolkit has been ported from the X window system to Windows and Macintosh.

I first heard about Tcl in 1988 while I was Ousterhout's Ph.D. student at Berkeley. We were designing a network operating system, Sprite. While the students hacked on a new kernel, John wrote a new editor and terminal emulator. He used Tcl as the command language for both tools so that users could define menus and otherwise customize those programs. This was in the days of X10, and he had plans for an X toolkit based on Tcl that would help programs cooperate with each other by communicating with Tcl commands. To me, this cooperation among tools was the essence of Tcl.

This early vision imagined that applications would be large bodies of compiled code and a small amount of Tcl used for configuration and high-level commands. John's editor, *mx*, and the terminal emulator, *tx*, followed this model. While this model remains valid, it has also turned out to be possible to write entire applications in Tcl. This is because the Tcl/Tk shell, *wish*, provides access to other programs, the file system, network sockets, plus the ability to create a graphical user interface. For better or worse, it is now common to find applications that contain thousands of lines of Tcl script.

This book was written because, while I found it enjoyable and productive to use Tcl and Tk, there were times when I was frustrated. In addition, working at Xerox PARC, with many experts in languages and systems, I was compelled to understand both the strengths and weaknesses of Tcl and Tk. Although many of my colleagues adopted Tcl and Tk for their projects, they were also just as quick to point out its flaws. In response, I have built up a set of programming techniques that exploit the power of Tcl and Tk while avoiding troublesome areas. This book is meant as a practical guide to help you get the most out of Tcl and Tk and avoid some of the frustrations I experienced.

It has been about 14 years since I was introduced to Tcl, and about eight years since the first edition of this book. During several of those years I worked under John Ousterhout, first at Sun Microsystems and then at Scriptics Corporation. There I remained mostly a Tcl programmer while others in our group have delved into the C implementation of Tcl itself. I've built applications like HTML editors, email user interfaces, Web servers, and the customer database we ran our business on. This experience is reflected in this book. The bulk of the book is about Tcl scripting, and the aspects of C programming to create Tcl extensions is given a lighter treatment. I have been lucky to remain involved in the core Tcl development, and I hope I can pass along the insights I have gained by working with Tcl.

Why Tcl?

As a scripting language, Tcl is similar to other UNIX shell languages such as the Bourne Shell (sh), the C Shell (csh), the Korn Shell (ksh), and Perl. Shell programs let you execute other programs. They provide enough programmability (variables, control flow, and procedures) to let you build complex scripts that assemble existing programs into a new tool tailored for your needs. Shells are wonderful for automating routine chores.

It is the ability to easily add a Tcl interpreter to your application that sets it apart from other shells. Tcl fills the role of an extension language that is used to configure and customize applications. There is no need to invent a configuration file format or a command language for your new application, or struggle to provide some sort of user-programmability for your tool. Instead, by adding a Tcl interpreter, you structure your application as a set of primitive operations that can be composed by a script to best suit the needs of your users. It also allows other programs to have programmatic control over your application, leading to suites of applications that work well together.

The Tcl C library has clean interfaces and is simple to use. The library implements the basic interpreter and a set of core scripting commands that implement variables, flow control, and procedures (see page 22). There is also a broad set of APIs that access operating system services to run other programs, access the file system, and use network sockets. Tk adds commands to create graphical user interfaces. The Tcl and Tk C APIs provide a "virtual machine" that is portable across UNIX, Windows, and Macintosh environments.

The Tcl virtual machine is extensible because your application can define new Tcl commands. These commands are associated with a C or C++ procedure that your application provides. The result is applications that are split into a set of primitives written in a compiled language and exported as Tcl commands. A Tcl script is used to compose the primitives into the overall application. The script layer has access to shell-like capability to run other programs, has access to the file system, and can call directly into the compiled part of the application through the Tcl commands you define. In addition, from the C programming level, you can call Tcl scripts, set and query Tcl variables, and even trace the execution of the Tcl interpreter.

There are many Tcl extensions freely available on the Internet. Most extensions include a C library that provides some new functionality, and a Tcl interface to the library. Examples include database access, telephone control, MIDI controller access, and *expect*, which adds Tcl commands to control interactive programs.

The most notable extension is Tk, a toolkit for graphical user interfaces. Tk defines Tcl commands that let you create and manipulate user interface widgets. The script-based approach to user interface programming has three benefits:

- Development is fast because of the rapid turnaround; there is no waiting for long compilations.
- The Tcl commands provide a higher-level interface than most standard C library user-interface toolkits. Simple user interfaces require just a handful of commands to define them. At the same time, it is possible to refine the user interface in order to get every detail just so. The fast turnaround aids the refinement process.
- The user interface can be factored out from the rest of your application. The developer can concentrate on the implementation of the application core and then fairly painlessly work up a user interface. The core set of Tk widgets is often sufficient for all your user interface needs. However, it is also possible to write custom Tk widgets in C, and again there are many contributed Tk widgets available on the network.

There are other choices for extension languages that include Visual Basic, Scheme, Elisp, Perl, Python, Ruby and Javascript. Your choice between them is partly a matter of taste. Tcl has simple constructs and looks somewhat like C. It is easy to add new Tcl primitives by writing C procedures. Tcl is very easy to learn, and I have heard many great stories of users completing impressive projects in a short amount of time (e.g., a few weeks), even though they never used Tcl before.

Java has exploded onto the computer scene since this book was first published. Java is a great systems programming language that in the long run could displace C and C++. This is fine for Tcl, which is designed to glue together building blocks written in any system programming language. Tcl was designed to work with C, but has been adapted to work with the Java Virtual Machine. Where I say "C or C++", you can now say "C, C++, or Java," but the details are a bit different with Java. This book does not describe the Tcl/Java interface, but you can find *TclBlend* on the CD-ROM. TclBlend loads the Java Virtual Machine into your Tcl application and lets you invoke Java methods. It also lets you implement Tcl commands in Java instead of C or C++. *Jacl* is a Tcl interpreter written in Java. It has some limitations compared with the native C-based Tcl interpreter, but *Jacl* is great if you cannot use the native interpreter.

Javascript is a language from Netscape that is designed to script interactions with Web pages. Javascript is important because of its use in HTML user interfaces. However, Tcl provides a more general purpose scripting solution that can be used in a wide variety of applications. The Tcl/Tk Web browser plugin provides a way to run Tcl in your browser. It turns out to be more of a Java alternative than a JavaScript alternative. The plugin lets you run Tcl applications inside your browser, while JavaScript gives you fine grain control over the browser and HTML display. The plugin is described in Chapter 20.

Tcl and Tk Versions

Tcl and Tk continue to evolve. See `http://www.beedub.com/book/` for updates and news about the latest Tcl releases. Tcl and Tk have had separate version numbers for historical reasons, but they are released in pairs that work together. The original edition of this book was based on Tcl 7.4 and Tk 4.0, and there were a few references to features in Tk 3.6. This fourth edition has been updated to reflect new features added through Tcl/Tk 8.4:

- Tcl 7.5 and Tk 4.1 had their final release in May 1996. These releases feature the port of Tk to the Windows and Macintosh environments. The Safe-Tcl security mechanism was introduced to support safe execution of network applets. There is also network socket support and a new Input/Output (I/O) subsystem to support high-performance event-driven I/O.
- Tcl 7.6 and Tk 4.2 had their final release in October 1996. These releases include improvements in Safe-Tcl, and improvements to the `grid` geometry manager introduced in Tk 4.1. Cross-platform support includes virtual events (e.g., `<<Copy>>` as opposed to `<Control-c>`), standard dialogs, and more file manipulation commands.
- Tcl 7.7 and Tk 4.3 were internal releases used for the development of the Tcl/Tk plug-in for the Netscape Navigator and Microsoft Internet Explorer Web browsers. Their development actually proceeded in parallel to Tcl 7.6 and Tk 4.2. The plug-in has been released for a wide variety of platforms, including Solaris/SPARC, Solaris/INTEL, SunOS, Linux, Digital UNIX, IRIX, HP/UX, Windows 95, Windows NT, and the Macintosh. The browser plug-in supports Tcl applets in Web pages and uses the sophisticated security mechanism of Safe-Tcl to provide safety.
- Tcl 8.0 features an on-the-fly compiler for Tcl that provides many-times faster Tcl scripts. Tcl 8.0 supports strings with embedded null characters. The compiler is transparent to Tcl scripts, but extension writers need to learn some new C APIs to take advantage of its potential. The release history of 8.0 spread out over a couple of years as John Ousterhout moved from

Sun Microsystems to Scriptics Corporation. The widely used 8.0p2 release was made in the fall of 1997, but the final patch release, 8.0.5, was made in the spring of 1999.

- Tk changed its version to match Tcl at 8.0. Tk 8.0 includes a new platform-independent font mechanism, native menus and menu bars, and more native widgets for better native look and feel on Windows and Macintosh.
- Tcl/Tk 8.1 features full Unicode support, a new regular expression engine that provides all the features found in Perl 5, and thread safety so that you can embed Tcl into multi threaded applications. Tk does a heroic job of finding the correct font to display your Unicode characters, and it adds a message catalog facility so that you can write internationalized applications. The release history of Tcl/Tk 8.1 also straddled the Sun to Scriptics transition. The first alpha release was made in the fall of 1997, and the final patch release, 8.1.1, was made in May 1999.
- Tcl/Tk 8.2 is primarily a bug fix and stabilization release. There are a few minor additions to the Tcl C library APIs to support more extensions without requiring core patches. Tcl/Tk 8.2 went rapidly into final release in the summer of 1999.
- Tcl/Tk 8.3 adds a broad collection of enhancements to Tcl and Tk. Tk started to get some long deserved attention with adoption of the Dash and Image patches from Jan Nijtmans. The 8.3.0 release was in February, 2000, and the last patch release, 8.3.5, was made in October, 2002.
- Tcl/Tk 8.4 features a focus on performance, the addition of the Virtual File System Interface, and 3 new core Tk widgets: spinbox, labeledframe, and panedwindow. This release was a long time in development. The first beta release was in June, 2000, and the 8.4.2 release was made in March, 2003.

Extending Tcl and Tk

Tcl is designed so that interesting additions can be made as extensions that do not require changes to the Tcl core. Many extensions are available today: You can find them on the Web at:

```
http://www.tcl.tk/resource/
```

However, some changes require changes to Tcl/Tk itself. If you are interested in contributing to the continued improvement of Tcl/Tk, you can help. There is a Tcl Core Team (TCT) and a formal Tcl Improvement Process (TIP). You can browse the current TIPs or contribute your own at:

```
http://www.tcl.tk/cgi-bin/tct/tip/
```

The Tcl and Tk source code is maintained on a SourceForge project:

```
http://www.sourceforge.net/projects/tcl
http://www.sourceforge.net/projects/tktoolkit
```

All bug reports and patch submissions are logged in a database. Source code patches that are made according to the Tcl Engineering Manual guidelines have the most chance of adoption. These guidelines describe code appearance (e.g., indentation), test suite requirements, and documentation requirements.

Tcl on the World Wide Web

Start with these World Wide Web pages about Tcl:

```
http://www.tcl.tk/
http://tcl.activestate.com/
http://www.purl.org/NET/Tcl-FAQ/
```

The Tcler's Wiki is a very active site that is updated by its users (i.e., by *you*) with lots of great information about Tcl and its extensions:

```
http://wiki.tcl.tk/
```

The home page for this book contains errata for all editions. This is the only URL I control personally, and I plan to keep it up-to-date indefinitely:

```
http://www.beedub.com/book/
```

The Prentice Hall Web site is:

```
http://www.prenhall.com/
```

Ftp Archives

These are some of the FTP sites that maintain Tcl archives:

```
ftp://ftp.tcl.tk/pub/tcl
ftp://src.doc.ic.ac.uk/packages/tcl/
ftp://ftp.luth.se/pub/unix/tcl/
ftp://ftp.sunet.se/pub/lang/tcl
ftp://ftp.cs.columbia.edu/archives/tcl
ftp://ftp.funet.fi/pub/languages/tcl
```

You can use a World Wide Web browser like *Mozilla*, *Netscape*, *Internet Explorer*, or *Lynx* to access these sites.

Newsgroups

The `comp.lang.tcl` newsgroup is very active. It provides a forum for questions and answers about Tcl. Announcements about Tcl extensions and applications are posted to the `comp.lang.tcl.announce` newsgroup. The following web service provides a convenient way to read newsgroups. Enter `comp.lang.tcl` in the search field on this page:

```
http://groups.google.com
```

Who Should Read This Book

This book is meant to be useful to the beginner in Tcl as well as the expert. For the beginner and expert alike, I recommend careful study of Chapter 1, *Tcl Fundamentals*. The programming model of Tcl is designed to be simple, but it is different from many programming languages. The model is based on string substitutions, and it is important that you understand it properly to avoid trouble in complex cases. The remainder of the book consists of examples that demonstrate how to use Tcl and Tk productively. For your reference, each chapter has tables that summarize the Tcl commands and Tk widgets they describe.

This book assumes that you have some programming experience, although you should be able to get by even if you are a complete novice. Knowledge of UNIX shell programming will help, but it is not required. Where aspects of window systems are relevant, I provide some background information. Chapter 2 describes the details of using Tcl and Tk on UNIX, Windows, and Macintosh.

How to Read This Book

This book is best used in a hands-on manner, trying the examples at the computer. The book tries to fill the gap between the terse Tcl and Tk manual pages, which are complete but lack context and examples, and existing Tcl programs that may or may not be documented or well written.

I recommend the on-line manual pages for the Tcl and Tk commands. They provide a detailed reference guide to each command. This book summarizes much of the information from the manual pages, but it does not provide the complete details, which can vary from release to release. HTML versions of the on-line manual pages can be found on the CD-ROM that comes with this book.

On-line Examples

The book comes with a CD-ROM that has source code for all of the examples, plus a selection of Tcl freeware found on the Internet. The CD-ROM is readable on UNIX, Windows, and Macintosh. There, you will find the versions of Tcl and Tk that were available as the book went to press. You can also retrieve the sources shown in the book from my personal Web site:

```
http://www.beedub.com/book/
```

Typographic Conventions

The more important examples are set apart with a title and horizontal rules, while others appear in-line. The examples use courier for Tcl and C code. When interesting results are returned by a Tcl command, those are presented below in *oblique courier*. The => is not part of the return value in the following example.

```
expr 5 + 8
=> 13
```

The courier font is also used when naming Tcl commands and C procedures within sentences.

The usage of a Tcl command is presented in the following example. The command name and constant keywords appear in courier. Variable values appear in *courier oblique*. Optional arguments are surrounded with question marks.

```
set varname ?value?
```

The name of a program is in italics:

xterm

Hot Tips

The icon in the margin marks a "hot tip" as judged by the reviewers of the book. The visual markers help you locate the more useful sections in the book. These are also listed in the index under Hot Tip.

Book Organization

The chapters of the book are divided into seven parts. The first part describes basic Tcl features. The first chapter describes the fundamental mechanisms that characterize the Tcl language. This is an important chapter that provides the basic grounding you will need to use Tcl effectively. Even if you have programmed in Tcl already, you should review Chapter 1. Chapter 2 goes over the details of using Tcl and Tk on UNIX, Windows, and Macintosh. Chapter 3 presents a sample application, a CGI script, that illustrates typical Tcl programming. The rest of Part I covers the basic Tcl commands in more detail, including string handling, data types, control flow, procedures, and scoping issues. Part I finishes with a description of the facilities for file I/O and running other programs.

Part II describes advanced Tcl programming. It starts with `eval`, which lets you generate Tcl programs on the fly. Regular expressions provide powerful string processing. If your data-processing application runs slowly, you can probably boost its performance significantly with the regular expression facilities. Namespaces partition the global scope of procedures and variables. Unicode and message catalogs support internationalized applications. Libraries and packages provide a way to organize your code for sharing among projects. The introspection facilities of Tcl tell you about the internal state of Tcl. Event driven I/O helps server applications manage several clients simultaneously. Network sockets are used to implement the HTTP protocol used to fetch pages on the World Wide Web.

The last few chapters in Part II describe platforms and frameworks for application development. Safe-Tcl is used to provide a secure environment to execute Tcl applets in a Web browser. *TclHttpd* is an extensible web server built in Tcl. You can build applications on top of this server, or embed it into your existing applications to give them a web interface. Starkits are an exciting new way to package and deploy Tcl/Tk applications. They use the new Virtual File System (VFS) facilities to embed a private file system right in the Starkit.

Part III introduces Tk. It gives an overview of the toolkit facilities. A few complete examples are examined in detail to illustrate the features of Tk. Event bindings associate Tcl commands with events like keystrokes and button clicks. Part III ends with three chapters on the Tk geometry managers that provide powerful facilities for organizing your user interface.

Part IV describes the Tk widgets. These include buttons, menus, scrollbars, labels, text entries, multiline and multifont text areas, drawing canvases, list-boxes, and scales. The Tk widgets are highly configurable and very programmable, but their default behaviors make them easy to use as well. The resource database that can configure widgets provides an easy way to control the overall look of your application.

Part V describes the rest of the Tk facilities. These include selections, keyboard focus, and standard dialogs. Fonts, colors, images, and other attributes that are common to the Tk widgets are described in detail. This part ends with a few larger Tk examples.

Part VI is an introduction to C programming and Tcl. The goal of this part is to get you started in the right direction when you need to extend Tcl with new commands written in C or integrate Tcl into custom applications.

Part VII provides a chapter for each of the Tcl/Tk releases covered by the book. These chapters provide details about what features were changed and added. They also provide a quick reference if you need to update a program or start to use a new version.

What's New in the Fourth Edition

The fourth edition is up-to-date with Tcl/Tk 8.4, which adds many new features. Tcl has a new Virtual File System (VFS) feature that lets you transparently embed a file system in your application, or make remote resources such as FTP and Web sites visible through the regular file system interface. Chapter 22 is a new chapter on Tclkit and Starkits that use the Metakit embedded database to store scripts and other files. The VFS makes these files appear in a private file system. Starkits provide a new way to package and deploy Tcl/Tk applications. Chapter 21 is a new chapter on using the multi-threading support in Tcl. This is very useful when embedding Tcl in threaded server applications. There are a number of new Tk features, including three new widgets. The spinbox (i.e., combobox) is like an entry widget with a drop-down selection box. The labeled frame provides a new way to decorate frames. The panedwindow is a specialized geometry manager that provides a new way to organize your user interfaces.

Other Tcl Books

This book was the second Tcl book after the original book by John Ousterhout, the creator of Tcl. Since then, many other Tcl books have been published. The following are just some of the books currently available.

Tcl / Tk: A Developer's Guide, 2nd Ed. (Academic Press, 2003) by Clif Flynt is a good example-oriented book that has been recently updated.

Tcl and the Tk Toolkit (Addison-Wesley, 1994) by John Ousterhout provides a broad overview of all aspects of Tcl and Tk, even though it covers only Tcl 7.3 and Tk 3.6. The book provides a more detailed treatment of C programming for Tcl extensions.

Exploring Expect (O'Reilly & Associates, Inc., 1995) by Don Libes is a great book about an extremely useful Tcl extension. *Expect* lets you automate the use of interactive programs like *ftp* and *telnet* that expect to interact with a user. By combining *Expect* and Tk, you can create graphical user interfaces for old applications that you cannot modify directly.

Tcl / Tk in a Nutshell (O'Reilly, 1999) by Paul Raines and Jeff Tranter is a handy reference guide. It covers several popular extensions including Expect, [incr Tcl], Tix, TclX, BLT, SybTcl, OraTcl, and TclODBC. There is a tiny pocket-reference guide for Tcl/Tk that may eliminate the need to thumb through my large book to find the syntax of a particular Tcl or Tk command.

Web Tcl Complete (McGraw Hill, 1999) by Steve Ball describes programming with the Tcl Web Server. It also covers Tcl/Java integration using *TclBlend*.

[incr Tcl] From The Ground Up (Osborn-McGraw Hill, 1999) by Chad Smith describes the [incr Tcl] object-oriented extension to Tcl.

Tcl / Tk for Programmers (IEEE Computer Society, 1998) by Adrian Zimmer describes Unix and Windows programming with Tcl/Tk. This book also includes solved exercises at the end of each chapter.

Building Network Management Tools with Tcl / Tk (Prentice Hall, 1998) by Dave Zeltserman and Gerald Puoplo. This describes how to build SNMP tools.

Graphical Applications with Tcl & Tk (M&T Books, 1997) by Eric Johnson is oriented toward Windows users. The second edition covers Tcl/Tk 8.0.

Tcl / Tk Tools (O'Reilly & Associates, Inc., 1997) by Mark Harrison describes many useful Tcl extensions. These include Oracle and Sybase interfaces, object-oriented language enhancements, additional Tk widgets, and much more. The chapters were contributed by the authors of the extensions, so they provide authoritative information on some excellent additions to the Tcl toolbox.

Effective Tcl / Tk Programming (Addison Wesley, 1997) by Michael McLennan and Mark Harrison illustrate Tcl and Tk with examples and application design guidelines.

First Edition Thanks

I would like to thank my managers and colleagues at Xerox PARC for their patience with me as I worked on this book. The tips and tricks in this book came partly from my own work as I helped lab members use Tcl, and partly from them as they taught me. Dave Nichols' probing questions forced me to understand the basic mechanisms of the Tcl interpreter. Dan Swinehart and Lawrence Butcher kept me sharp with their own critiques. Ron Frederick and Berry Kerchival adopted Tk for their graphical interfaces and amazed me with their rapid results. Becky Burwell, Rich Gold, Carl Hauser, John Maxwell, Ken Pier, Marvin Theimer, and Mohan Vishwanath made use of my early drafts, and their questions pointed out large holes in the text. Karin Petersen, Bill Schilit, and Terri Watson kept life interesting by using Tcl in very nonstandard ways. I especially thank my managers, Mark Weiser and Doug Terry, for their understanding and support.

I thank John Ousterhout for Tcl and Tk, which are wonderful systems built with excellent craftsmanship. John was kind enough to provide me with an advance version of Tk 4.0 so that I could learn about its new features well before its first beta release.

Thanks to the Tcl programmers out on the Net, from whom I learned many tricks. John LoVerso and Stephen Uhler are the hottest Tcl programmers I know.

Many thanks to the patient reviewers of early drafts: Pierre David, Clif Flynt, Simon Kenyon, Eugene Lee, Don Libes, Lee Moore, Joe Moss, Hador Shemtov, Frank Stajano, Charles Thayer, and Jim Thornton.

Many folks contributed suggestions by email: Miguel Angel, Stephen Bensen, Jeff Blaine, Tom Charnock, Brian Cooper, Patrick D'Cruze, Benoit Desrosiers, Ted Dunning, Mark Eichin, Paul Friberg, Carl Gauthier, David Gerdes, Klaus Hackenberg, Torkle Hasle, Marti Hearst, Jean-Pierre Herbert, Jamie Honan, Norman Klein, Joe Konstan, Susan Larson, Håkan Liljegren, Lionel Mallet, Dejan Milojicic, Greg Minshall, Bernd Mohr, Will Morse, Heiko Nardmann, Gerd Neugebauer, TV Raman, Cary Renzema, Rob Riepel, Dan Schenk, Jean-Guy Schneider, Elizabeth Scholl, Karl Schwamb, Rony Shapiro, Peter Simanyi, Vince Skahan, Bill Stumbo, Glen Vanderburg, Larry Virden, Reed Wade, and Jim Wight. Unfortunately, I could not respond to every suggestion, even some that were excellent.

Thanks to the editors and staff at Prentice Hall. Mark Taub has been very helpful as I progressed through my first book. Lynn Schneider and Kerry Reardon were excellent copy and production editors, respectively.

Second Edition Thanks

I get to thank John Ousterhout again, this time for supporting me as I worked in the Tcl/Tk group at Sun Microsystems. The rest of the group deserve a lot of credit for turning Tcl and Tk into a dynamite cross-platform solution. Scott Stanton led the Tk port to the PC. Ray Johnson led the Tk port to the Macintosh. Jacob Levy implemented the event-driven I/O system, Safe-Tcl, and the browser plug-in. Brian Lewis built the Tcl compiler. Ken Corey worked on Java integration and helped with the *SpecTcl* user interface builder. Syd Polk generalized the menu system to work with native widgets on the Macintosh and Windows. Colin Stevens generalized the font mechanism and worked on internationalization for Tk.

Stephen Uhler deserves special thanks for inspiring many of the cool examples I use in this book. He was the lead on the *SpecTcl* user interface builder. He built the core HTML display library on which I based an editor. We worked closely together on the first versions of *TclHttpd*. He taught me how to write compact, efficient Tcl code and to use regular expression substitutions in amazing ways. I hope he has learned at least a little from me.

Thanks again to Mark Taub, Eileen Clark, and Martha Williams at Prentice Hall. George Williams helped me assemble the files for the CD-ROM.

Third Edition Thanks

John Ousterhout continues his wonderful role as Tcl benefactor, now as founder of Scriptics Corporation. I'd like to thank every one of the great folks that I work with at Scriptics, especially the pioneering crew of Sarah Daniels, Scott Stanton, Ray Johnson, Bryan Surles, Melissa Chawla, Lee Bernhard, Suresh Sastry, Emil Scaffon, Pat P., Scott Redman, and Berry Kercheval. The rest of the gang deserves a big thanks for making Scriptics such an enjoyable place to work. Jerry Peek, who is a notable author himself, provided valuable advice and wonderfully detailed comments! Ken Jones told me about a great indexing tool.

I'd like to thank all the readers that drop me the encouraging note or probing question via email. I am always interested in new and interesting uses of Tcl!

Thanks to the editors at Prentice Hall: Mark Taub, Joan McNamara, and Joan Eurell. Mark continues to encourage me to come out with new editions, and the Joans helped me complete this third edition on time.

Fourth Edition Thanks

I'd like to thank Jeff Hobbs and Ken Jones for making this project happen. Jeff has done a great service to the Tcl community as "The Tcl Guy". His leadership and hard work have been responsible for the steady pace of new Tcl/Tk releases. Ken is a great Tcl teacher and his experiences teaching are reflected in his additions to the book for this 4th edition. Again, without these two lending a hand, I just wouldn't have found the time for this edition.

I'd like to thank the Tcl Core Team and the supporting cast of contributors to the Tcl/Tk code base. The TCT provides a great framework to keep Tcl a high quality software product that continues to adopt new an interesting features.

I'd like to thank Jean-Claude Wippler and Steve Landers for Metakit, Tclkit, and Starkits. These provide a delightful way to package and deploy Tcl applications. I expect to see a lot more from these technologies in the future. Several readers provided great feedback on the Starkit material: Robert Techentin, Steve Blinkhorn, Frank Sergeant, Arjen Markus, Uwe Koloska, Larry Virden, Tom Krehbiel, and Donald Porter.

I'd like to thank Prentice Hall for their continued support. Mark Taub continues his role as godfather of this book. Kathleen Caren was the able production editor for this edition.

Finally, I thank my wonderful wife Jody for her love, kindness, patience, wit, and understanding as I worked long hours. Happily, many of those hours were spent working from home. I now have three sons, Christopher, Daniel, and Michael, who get the credit for keeping me from degenerating into a complete nerd.

Contact the Author

I am always open to comments about this book. My email address is welch@acm.org. It helps me sort through my mail if you put the word "book" or the title of the book into the email subject line. Visit my Web site for current news about the book and my other interests. I maintain an errata page for each edition, so please consult that and feel free to send bug reports!

http://www.beedub.com/

P A R T   I

Tcl Basics

Part I introduces the basics of Tcl. Everyone should read Chapter 1, which describes the fundamental properties of the language. Tcl is really quite simple, so beginners can pick it up quickly. The experienced programmer should review Chapter 1 to eliminate any misconceptions that come from using other languages.

Chapter 2 is a short introduction to running Tcl and Tk on UNIX, Windows, and Macintosh systems. You may want to look at this chapter first so you can try out the examples as you read Chapter 1.

Chapter 3 presents a sample application, a CGI script, that implements a guestbook for a Web site. The example uses several facilities that are described in detail in later chapters. The goal is to provide a working example that illustrates the power of Tcl.

The rest of Part I covers basic programming with Tcl. Simple string processing is covered in Chapter 4. Tcl lists, which share the syntax rules of Tcl commands, are explained in Chapter 5. Control structure like loops and if statements are described in Chapter 6. Chapter 7 describes Tcl procedures, which are new commands that you write in Tcl. Chapter 8 discusses Tcl arrays. Arrays are the most flexible and useful data structure in Tcl. Chapter 9 describes file I/O and running other programs. These facilities let you build Tcl scripts that glue together other programs and process data in files.

After reading Part I you will know enough Tcl to read and understand other Tcl programs, and to write simple programs yourself.

Tcl Fundamentals

This chapter describes the basic syntax rules for the Tcl scripting language. It describes the basic mechanisms used by the Tcl interpreter: substitution and grouping. It touches lightly on the following Tcl commands: `puts`, `format`, `set`, `expr`, `string`, `while`, `incr`, and `proc`.

Tcl is a string-based command language. The language has only a few fundamental constructs and relatively little syntax, which makes it easy to learn. The Tcl syntax is meant to be simple. Tcl is designed to be a glue that assembles software building blocks into applications. A simpler glue makes the job easier. In addition, Tcl is interpreted when the application runs. The interpreter makes it easy to build and refine your application in an interactive manner. A great way to learn Tcl is to try out commands interactively. If you are not sure how to run Tcl on your system, see Chapter 2 for instructions for starting Tcl on UNIX, Windows, and Macintosh systems.

This chapter takes you through the basics of the Tcl language syntax. Even if you are an expert programmer, it is worth taking the time to read these few pages to make sure you understand the fundamentals of Tcl. The basic mechanisms are all related to strings and string substitutions, so it is fairly easy to visualize what is going on in the interpreter. The model is a little different from some other programming languages with which you may already be familiar, so it is worth making sure you understand the basic concepts.

Tcl Commands

Tcl stands for Tool Command Language. A command does something for you, like output a string, compute a math expression, or display a widget on the screen. Tcl casts everything into the mold of a command, even programming constructs like variable assignment and procedure definition. Tcl adds a tiny amount of syntax needed to properly invoke commands, and then it leaves all the hard work up to the command implementation.

The basic syntax for a Tcl command is:

```
command arg1 arg2 arg3 ...
```

The `command` is either the name of a built-in command or a Tcl procedure. White space (i.e., spaces or tabs) is used to separate the command name and its arguments, and a newline (i.e., the end of line character) or semicolon is used to terminate a command. Tcl does not interpret the arguments to the commands except to perform *grouping*, which allows multiple words in one argument, and *substitution*, which is used with programming variables and nested command calls. The behavior of the Tcl command processor can be summarized in three basic steps:

- Argument grouping.
- Value substitution of nested commands, variables, and backslash escapes.
- Command invocation. It is up to the command to interpret its arguments.
  This model is described in detail in this Chapter.

Hello, World!

Example 1–1 The "Hello, World!" example.

```
puts stdout {Hello, World!}
=> Hello, World!
```

In this example, the command is `puts`, which takes two arguments: an I/O stream identifier and a string. `puts` writes the string to the I/O stream along with a trailing newline character. There are two points to emphasize:

- Arguments are interpreted by the command. In the example, `stdout` is used to identify the standard output stream. The use of `stdout` as a name is a convention employed by `puts` and the other I/O commands. Also, `stderr` is used to identify the standard error output, and `stdin` is used to identify the standard input. Chapter 9 describes how to open other files for I/O.
- Curly braces are used to group words together into a single argument. The `puts` command receives `Hello, World!` as its second argument.

The braces are not part of the value.

The braces are syntax for the interpreter, and they get stripped off before the value is passed to the command. Braces group all characters, including newlines and nested braces, until a matching brace is found. Tcl also uses double quotes for grouping. Grouping arguments will be described in more detail later.

Variables

The `set` command is used to assign a value to a variable. It takes two arguments: The first is the name of the variable, and the second is the value. Variable names can be any length, and case *is* significant. In fact, you can use any character in a variable name.

It is not necessary to declare Tcl variables before you use them.

The interpreter will create the variable when it is first assigned a value. The value of a variable is obtained later with the dollar-sign syntax, illustrated in Example 1–2:

Example 1–2 Tcl variables.

```
set var 5
=> 5
set b $var
=> 5
```

The second `set` command assigns to variable `b` the value of variable `var`. The use of the dollar sign is our first example of substitution. You can imagine that the second `set` command gets rewritten by substituting the value of `var` for `$var` to obtain a new command.

```
set b 5
```

The actual implementation of substitution is more efficient, which is important when the value is large.

Command Substitution

The second form of substitution is *command substitution*. A nested command is delimited by square brackets, `[ ]`. The Tcl interpreter takes everything between the brackets and evaluates it as a command. It rewrites the outer command by replacing the square brackets and everything between them with the result of the nested command. This is similar to the use of backquotes in other shells, except that it has the additional advantage of supporting arbitrary nesting of commands.

Example 1–3 Command substitution.

```
set len [string length foobar]
=> 6
```

In Example 1–3, the nested command is:

```
string length foobar
```

This command returns the length of the string `foobar`. The `string` command is described in detail starting on page 49. The nested command runs first.

Then, command substitution causes the outer command to be rewritten as if it were:

```
set len 6
```

If there are several cases of command substitution within a single command, the interpreter processes them from left to right. As each right bracket is encountered, the command it delimits is evaluated. This results in a sensible ordering in which nested commands are evaluated first so that their result can be used in arguments to the outer command.

Math Expressions

The Tcl interpreter itself does not evaluate math expressions. Tcl just does grouping, substitutions and command invocations. The expr command is used to parse and evaluate math expressions.

Example 1–4 Simple arithmetic.

```
expr 7.2 / 4
=> 1.8
```

The math syntax supported by expr is the same as the C expression syntax. The expr command deals with integer, floating point, and boolean values. Logical operations return either 0 (false) or 1 (true). Integer values are promoted to floating point values as needed. Octal values are indicated by a leading zero (e.g., 033 is 27 decimal). Hexadecimal values are indicated by a leading 0x. Scientific notation for floating point numbers is supported. A summary of the operator precedence is given on page 20.

You can include variable references and nested commands in math expressions. The following example uses expr to add the value of x to the length of the string foobar. As a result of the innermost command substitution, the expr command sees 6 + 7, and len gets the value 13:

Example 1–5 Nested commands.

```
set x 7
set len [expr [string length foobar] + $x]
=> 13
```

The expression evaluator supports a number of built-in math functions. (For a complete listing, see page 21.) Example 1–6 computes the value of *pi*:

Example 1–6 Built-in math functions.

```
set pi [expr 2*asin(1.0)]
=> 3.1415926535897931
```

The implementation of `expr` is careful to preserve accurate numeric values and avoid conversions between numbers and strings. However, you can make `expr` operate more efficiently by grouping the entire expression in curly braces. The explanation has to do with the byte code compiler that Tcl uses internally, and its effects are explained in more detail on page 15. For now, you should be aware that these expressions are all valid and run faster than the examples shown above:

Example 1–7 Grouping expressions with braces.

```
expr {7.2 / 4}
set len [expr {[string length foobar] + $x}]
set pi [expr {2*asin(1.0)}]
```

Backslash Substitution

The final type of substitution done by the Tcl interpreter is *backslash substitution*. This is used to quote characters that have special meaning to the interpreter. For example, you can specify a literal dollar sign, brace, or bracket by quoting it with a backslash. As a rule, however, if you find yourself using lots of backslashes, there is probably a simpler way to achieve the effect you are striving for. In particular, the `list` command described on page 65 will do quoting for you automatically. In Example 1–8 backslash is used to get a literal `$`:

Example 1–8 Quoting special characters with backslash.

```
set dollar \$foo
=> $foo
set x $dollar
=> $foo
```

Only a single round of interpretation is done.

The second `set` command in the example illustrates an important property of Tcl. The value of `dollar` does not affect the substitution performed in the assignment to `x`. In other words, the Tcl parser does not care about the value of a variable when it does the substitution. In the example, the value of `x` and `dollar` is the string `$foo`. In general, you do not have to worry about the value of variables until you use `eval`, which is described in Chapter 10.

You can also use backslash sequences to specify characters with their Unicode, hexadecimal, or octal value:

```
set escape \u001b
set escape \0x1b
set escape \033
```

The value of variable `escape` is the ASCII ESC character, which has character code `27`. Table 1–1 on page 20 summarizes backslash substitutions.

A common use of backslashes is to continue long commands on multiple lines. This is necessary because a newline terminates a command. The backslash in the next example is required; otherwise the expr command gets terminated by the newline after the plus sign.

Example 1–9 Continuing long lines with backslashes.

```
set totalLength [expr [string length $one] + \
        [string length $two]]
```

There are two fine points to escaping newlines. First, if you are grouping an argument as described in the next section, then you do not need to escape new-lines; the newlines are automatically part of the group and do not terminate the command. Second, a backslash as the last character in a line is converted into a space, and all the white space at the beginning of the next line is replaced by this substitution. In other words, the backslash-newline sequence also consumes all the leading white space on the next line.

Grouping with Braces and Double Quotes

Double quotes and curly braces are used to group words together into one argu-ment. The difference between double quotes and curly braces is that quotes allow substitutions to occur in the group, while curly braces prevent substitutions. This rule applies to command, variable, and backslash substitutions.

Example 1–10 Grouping with double quotes vs. braces.

```
set s Hello
=> Hello
puts stdout "The length of $s is [string length $s]."
=> The length of Hello is 5.
puts stdout {The length of $s is [string length $s].}
=> The length of $s is [string length $s].
```

In the second command of Example 1–10, the Tcl interpreter does variable and command substitution on the second argument to puts. In the third com-mand, substitutions are prevented, so the string is printed as is.

In practice, grouping with curly braces is used when substitutions on the argument must be delayed until a later time (or never done at all). Examples include loops, conditional statements, and procedure declarations. Double quotes are useful in simple cases like the puts command previously shown.

Another common use of quotes is with the format command. This is similar to the C printf function. The first argument to format is a format specifier that often includes special characters like newlines, tabs, and spaces. The easiest way to specify these characters is with backslash sequences (e.g., \n for newline and \t for tab). The backslashes must be substituted before the format command is called, so you need to use quotes to group the format specifier.

```
puts [format "Item: %s\t%5.3f" $name $value]
```

Here `format` is used to align a name and a value with a tab. The `%s` and `%5.3f` indicate how the remaining arguments to `format` are to be formatted. Note that the trailing `\n` usually found in a C `printf` call is not needed because `puts` provides one for us. For more information about the `format` command, see page 56.

Square Brackets Do Not Group

The square bracket syntax used for command substitution does not provide grouping. Instead, a nested command is considered part of the current group. In the command below, the double quotes group the last argument, and the nested command is just part of that group.

```
puts stdout "The length of $s is [string length $s]."
```

If an argument is made up of only a nested command, you do not need to group it with double-quotes because the Tcl parser treats the whole nested command as part of the group.

```
puts stdout [string length $s]
```

The following is a redundant use of double quotes:

```
puts stdout "[expr $x + $y]"
```

Grouping before Substitution

The Tcl parser makes a single pass through a command as it makes grouping decisions and performs string substitutions. Grouping decisions are made before substitutions are performed, which is an important property of Tcl. This means that the values being substituted do not affect grouping because the grouping decisions have already been made.

The following example demonstrates how nested command substitution affects grouping. A nested command is treated as an unbroken sequence of characters, regardless of its internal structure. It is included with the surrounding group of characters when collecting arguments for the main command.

Example 1–11 Embedded command and variable substitution.

```
set x 7; set y 9
puts stdout $x+$y=[expr $x + $y]
=> 7+9=16
```

In Example 1–11, the second argument to `puts` is:

```
$x+$y=[expr $x + $y]
```

The white space inside the nested command is ignored for the purposes of grouping the argument. By the time Tcl encounters the left bracket, it has already done some variable substitutions to obtain:

```
7+9=
```

When the left bracket is encountered, the interpreter calls itself recursively to evaluate the nested command. Again, the $x and $y are substituted before calling `expr`. Finally, the result of `expr` is substituted for everything from the left bracket to the right bracket. The `puts` command gets the following as its second argument:

```
7+9=16
```

Grouping before substitution.

The point of this example is that the grouping decision about `puts`'s second argument is made before the command substitution is done. Even if the result of the nested command contained spaces or other special characters, they would be ignored for the purposes of grouping the arguments to the outer command. Grouping and variable substitution interact the same as grouping and command substitution. Spaces or special characters in variable values do not affect grouping decisions because these decisions are made before the variable values are substituted.

If you want the output to look nicer in the example, with spaces around the + and =, then you must use double quotes to explicitly group the argument to `puts`:

```
puts stdout "$x + $y = [expr $x + $y]"
```

The double quotes are used for grouping in this case to allow the variable and command substitution on the argument to `puts`.

Grouping Math Expressions with Braces

It turns out that `expr` does its own substitutions inside curly braces. This is explained in more detail on page 15. This means you can write commands like the one below and the substitutions on the variables in the expression still occur:

```
puts stdout "$x + $y = [expr {$x + $y}]"
```

More Substitution Examples

If you have several substitutions with no white space between them, you can avoid grouping with quotes. The following command sets `concat` to the value of variables a, b, and c all concatenated together:

```
set concat $a$b$c
```

Again, if you want to add spaces, you'll need to use quotes:

```
set concat "$a $b $c"
```

In general, you can place a bracketed command or variable reference anywhere. The following computes a command name:

```
[findCommand $x] arg arg
```

When you use Tk, you often use widget names as command names:

```
$text insert end "Hello, World!"
```

Procedures

Tcl uses the `proc` command to define procedures. Once defined, a Tcl procedure is used just like any of the other built-in Tcl commands. The basic syntax to define a procedure is:

```
proc name arglist body
```

The first argument is the name of the procedure being defined. The second argument is a list of parameters to the procedure. The third argument is a *command body* that is one or more Tcl commands.

The procedure name is case sensitive, and in fact it can contain any characters. Procedure names and variable names do not conflict with each other. As a convention, this book begins procedure names with uppercase letters and it begins variable names with lowercase letters. Good programming style is important as your Tcl scripts get larger. Tcl coding style is discussed in Chapter 12.

Example 1–12 Defining a procedure.

```
proc Diag {a b} {
    set c [expr {sqrt($a * $a + $b * $b)}]
    return $c
}
puts "The diagonal of a 3, 4 right triangle is [Diag 3 4]"
=> The diagonal of a 3, 4 right triangle is 5.0
```

The `Diag` procedure defined in the example computes the length of the diagonal side of a right triangle given the lengths of the other two sides. The `sqrt` function is one of many math functions supported by the `expr` command. The variable `c` is local to the procedure; it is defined only during execution of `Diag`. Variable scope is discussed further in Chapter 7. It is not really necessary to use the variable `c` in this example. The procedure can also be written as:

```
proc Diag {a b} {
    return [expr {sqrt($a * $a + $b * $b)}]
}
```

The `return` command is used to return the result of the procedure. The `return command` is optional in this example because the Tcl interpreter returns the value of the last command in the body as the value of the procedure. So, the procedure could be reduced to:

```
proc Diag {a b} {
    expr {sqrt($a * $a + $b * $b)}
}
```

Note the stylized use of curly braces in the example. The curly brace at the end of the first line starts the third argument to `proc`, which is the command body. In this case, the Tcl interpreter sees the opening left brace, causing it to ignore newline characters and scan the text until a matching right brace is found. *Double quotes have the same property.* They group characters, including newlines, until another double quote is found. The result of the grouping is that the third argument to proc is a sequence of commands. When they are evaluated later, the embedded newlines will terminate each command.

The other crucial effect of the curly braces around the procedure body is to delay any substitutions in the body until the time the procedure is called. For example, the variables a, b, and c are not defined until the procedure is called, so we do not want to do variable substitution at the time Diag is defined.

The proc command supports additional features such as having variable numbers of arguments and default values for arguments. These are described in detail in Chapter 7.

A Factorial Example

To reinforce what we have learned so far, below is a longer example that uses a while loop to compute the factorial function:

Example 1–13 A while loop to compute factorial.

```
proc Factorial {x} {
    set i 1; set product 1
    while {$i <= $x} {
        set product [expr {$product * $i}]
        incr i
    }
    return $product
}
Factorial 10
=> 3628800
```

The semicolon is used on the first line to remind you that it is a command terminator just like the newline character. The while loop is used to multiply all the numbers from one up to the value of x. The first argument to while is a boolean expression, and its second argument is a command body to execute. The while command and other control structures are described in Chapter 6.

The same math expression evaluator used by the expr command is used by while to evaluate the boolean expression. There is no need to explicitly use the expr command in the first argument to while, even if you have a much more complex expression.

The loop body and the procedure body are grouped with curly braces in the same way. The opening curly brace must be on the same line as proc and while. If you like to put opening curly braces on the line after a while or if statement, you must escape the newline with a backslash:

```
    while {$i < $x} \
    {
        set product ...
    }
```

Always group expressions and command bodies with curly braces.

Curly braces around the boolean expression are crucial because they delay variable substitution until the `while` command implementation tests the expression. The following example is an infinite loop:

```
set i 1; while $i<=10 {incr i}
```

The loop will run indefinitely.[*] The reason is that the Tcl interpreter will substitute for `$i` *before* `while` is called, so `while` gets a constant expression `1<=10` that will always be true. You can avoid these kinds of errors by adopting a consistent coding style that groups expressions with curly braces:

```
set i 1; while {$i<=10} {incr i}
```

The `incr` command is used to increment the value of the loop variable `i`. This is a handy command that saves us from the longer command:

```
set i [expr {$i + 1}]
```

The `incr` command can take an additional argument, a positive or negative integer by which to change the value of the variable. Using this form, it is possible to eliminate the loop variable `i` and just modify the parameter `x`. The loop body can be written like this:

```
while {$x > 1} {
    set product [expr {$product * $x}]
    incr x -1
}
```

Example 1–14 shows factorial again, this time using a recursive definition. A recursive function is one that calls itself to complete its work. Each recursive call decrements `x` by one, and when `x` is one, then the recursion stops.

Example 1–14 A recursive definition of factorial.

```
proc Factorial {x} {
    if {$x <= 1} {
        return 1
    } else {
        return [expr {$x * [Factorial [expr {$x - 1}]]}]
    }
}
```

More about Variables

The `set` command will return the value of a variable if it is only passed a single argument. It treats that argument as a variable name and returns the current value of the variable. The dollar-sign syntax used to get the value of a variable is really just an easy way to use the `set` command. Example 1–15 shows a trick you can play by putting the name of one variable into another variable:

---

[*] Ironically, Tcl 8.0 introduced a byte-code compiler, and the first releases of Tcl 8.0 had a bug in the compiler that caused this loop to terminate! This bug is fixed in the 8.0.5 patch release.

Example 1–15 Using set to return a variable value.

```
set var {the value of var}
=> the value of var
set name var
=> var
set name
=> var
set $name
=> the value of var
```

This is a somewhat tricky example. In the last command, $name gets substituted with var. Then, the set command returns the value of var, which is the value of var. Nested set commands provide another way to achieve a level of indirection. The last set command above can be written as follows:

```
set [set name]
=> the value of var
```

Using a variable to store the name of another variable may seem overly complex. However, there are some times when it is very useful. There is even a special command, upvar, that makes this sort of trick easier. The upvar command is described in detail in Chapter 7.

Funny Variable Names

The Tcl interpreter makes some assumptions about variable names that make it easy to embed variable references into other strings. By default, it assumes that variable names contain only letters, digits, and the underscore. The construct $foo.o represents a concatenation of the value of foo and the literal ".o".

If the variable reference is not delimited by punctuation or white space, then you can use curly braces to explicitly delimit the variable name (e.g., ${x}). You can also use this to reference variables with funny characters in their name, although you probably do not want variables named like that. If you find yourself using funny variable names, or computing the names of variables, then you may want to use the upvar command.

Example 1–16 Embedded variable references.

```
set foo filename
set object $foo.o
=> filename.o
set a AAA
set b abc${a}def
=> abcAAAdef
set .o yuk!
set x ${.o}y
=> yuk!y
```

The `unset` Command

You can delete a variable with the `unset` command:

```
unset ?-nocomplain? ?--? varName varName2 ...
```

Any number of variable names can be passed to the `unset` command. However, `unset` will raise an error if a variable is not already defined, unless the `-nocomplain` is given. Use `--` to `unset` a variable named `-nocomplain`.

Using `info` to Find Out about Variables

The existence of a variable can be tested with the `info exists` command. For example, because `incr` requires that a variable exist, you might have to test for the existence of the variable first.

Example 1–17 Using `info` to determine if a variable exists.

```
if {![info exists foobar]} {
    set foobar 0
} else {
    incr foobar
}
```

Example 7–6 on page 92 implements a version of `incr` which handles this case.

More about Math Expressions

This section describes a few fine points about math in Tcl scripts. In Tcl 7.6 and earlier versions math is not that efficient because of conversions between strings and numbers. The `expr` command must convert its arguments from strings to numbers. It then does all its computations with double precision floating point values. The result is formatted into a string that has, by default, 12 significant digits. This number can be changed by setting the `tcl_precision` variable to the number of significant digits desired. Seventeen digits of precision are enough to ensure that no information is lost when converting back and forth between a string and an IEEE double precision number:

Example 1–18 Controlling precision with `tcl_precision`.

```
expr 1 / 3
=> 0
expr 1 / 3.0
=> 0.333333333333
set tcl_precision 17
=> 17
expr 1 / 3.0
# The trailing 1 is the IEEE rounding digit
=> 0.33333333333333331
```

In Tcl 8.0 and later versions, the overhead of conversions is eliminated in most cases by the built-in compiler. Even so, Tcl was not designed to support math-intensive applications. You may want to implement math-intensive code in a compiled language and register the function as a Tcl command as described in Chapter 47.

There is support for string comparisons by `expr`, so you can test string values in `if` statements. You must use quotes so that `expr` knows to do string comparisons:

```
if {$answer == "yes"} { ... }
```

However, the `string compare` and `string equal` commands described in Chapter 4 are more reliable because `expr` may do conversions on strings that look like numbers. The issues with string operations and `expr` are discussed on page 52. Tcl 8.4 introduced `eq` and `ne` `expr` operators to allow strict string based comparison.

Expressions can include variable and command substitutions and still be grouped with curly braces. This is because an argument to `expr` is subject to two rounds of substitution: one by the Tcl interpreter, and a second by `expr` itself. Ordinarily this is not a problem because math values do not contain the characters that are special to the Tcl interpreter. The second round of substitutions is needed to support commands like `while` and `if` that use the expression evaluator internally.

Grouping expressions can make them run more efficiently.

You should always group expressions in curly braces and let `expr` do command and variable substitutions. Otherwise, your values may suffer extra conversions from numbers to strings and back to numbers. Not only is this process slow, but the conversions can lose precision in certain circumstances. For example, suppose x is computed from a math function:

```
set x [expr {sqrt(2.0)}]
```

At this point the value of x is a double-precision floating point value, just as you would expect. If you do this:

```
set two [expr $x * $x]
```

then you may or may not get 2.0 as the result! This is because Tcl will substitute $x and `expr` will concatenate all its arguments into one string, and then parse the expression again. In contrast, if you do this:

```
set two [expr {$x * $x}]
```

then `expr` will do the substitutions, and it will be careful to preserve the floating point value of x. The expression will be more accurate and run more efficiently because no string conversions will be done. The story behind Tcl values is described in more detail in Chapter 47 on C programming and Tcl.

Comments

Tcl uses the pound character, #, for comments. Unlike in many other languages, the # must occur at the beginning of a command. A # that occurs elsewhere is not treated specially. An easy trick to append a comment to the end of a command is to precede the # with a semicolon to terminate the previous command:

```
# Here are some parameters
set rate 7.0      ;# The interest rate
set months 60     ;# The loan term
```

One subtle effect to watch for is that a backslash effectively continues a comment line onto the next line of the script. In addition, a semicolon inside a comment is not significant. Only a newline terminates comments:

```
# Here is the start of a Tcl comment \
and some more of it; still in the comment
```

The behavior of a backslash in comments is pretty obscure, but it can be exploited as shown in Example 2–3 on page 27.

A surprising property of Tcl comments is that curly braces inside comments are still counted for the purposes of finding matching brackets. The motivation for this odd feature was to keep the original Tcl parser simpler. However, it means that the following will not work as expected to comment out an alternate version of an if expression:

```
# if {boolean expression1} {
if {boolean expression2} {
    some commands
}
```

The previous sequence results in an extra left curly brace, and probably a complaint about a missing close brace at the end of your script! A technique I use to comment out large chunks of code is to put the code inside an if block that will never execute:

```
if {0} {
unused code here
}
```

Substitution and Grouping Summary

The following rules summarize the fundamental mechanisms of grouping and substitution that are performed by the Tcl interpreter before it invokes a command:

- Command arguments are separated by white space, unless arguments are grouped with curly braces or double quotes as described below.
- Grouping with curly braces, { }, prevents substitutions. Braces nest. The interpreter includes all characters between the matching left and right brace in the group, including newlines, semicolons, and nested braces. The enclosing (i.e., outermost) braces are not included in the group's value.

- Grouping with double quotes, " ", allows substitutions. The interpreter groups everything until another double quote is found, including newlines and semicolons. The enclosing quotes are not included in the group of characters. A double-quote character can be included in the group by quoting it with a backslash, (e.g., \").
- Grouping decisions are made before substitutions are performed, which means that the values of variables or command results do not affect grouping.
- A dollar sign, $, causes variable substitution. Variable names can be any length, and case is significant. If variable references are embedded into other strings, or if they include characters other than letters, digits, and the underscore, they can be distinguished with the ${varname} syntax.
- Square brackets, [ ], cause command substitution. Everything between the brackets is treated as a command, and everything including the brackets is replaced with the result of the command. Nesting is allowed.
- The backslash character, \, is used to quote special characters. You can think of this as another form of substitution in which the backslash and the next character or group of characters are replaced with a new character.
- Substitutions can occur anywhere unless prevented by curly brace grouping. Part of a group can be a constant string, and other parts of it can be the result of substitutions. Even the command name can be affected by substitutions.
- A single round of substitutions is performed before command invocation. The result of a substitution is not interpreted a second time. This rule is important if you have a variable value or a command result that contains special characters such as spaces, dollar signs, square brackets, or braces. Because only a single round of substitution is done, you do not have to worry about special characters in values causing extra substitutions.

Fine Points

- A common error is to forget a space between arguments when grouping with braces or quotes. This is because white space is used as the separator, while the braces or quotes only provide grouping. If you forget the space, you will get syntax errors about unexpected characters after the closing brace or quote. The following is an error because of the missing space between } and {:

```
if {$x > 1}{puts "x = $x"}
```

- A double quote is only used for grouping when it comes after white space. This means you can include a double quote in the middle of a group without quoting it with a backslash. This requires that curly braces or white space delimit the group. I do not recommend using this obscure feature, but this is what it looks like:

```
set silly a"b
```

- When double quotes are used for grouping, the special effect of curly braces is turned off. Substitutions occur everywhere inside a group formed with double quotes. In the next command, the variables are still substituted:

```
set x xvalue
set y "foo {$x} bar"
=> foo {xvalue} bar
```

- When double quotes are used for grouping and a nested command is encountered, the nested command can use double quotes for grouping, too.

```
puts "results [format "%f %f" $x $y]"
```

- Spaces are *not* required around the square brackets used for command substitution. For the purposes of grouping, the interpreter considers everything between the square brackets as part of the current group. The following sets x to the concatenation of two command results because there is no space between] and [.

```
set x [cmd1][cmd2]
```

- Newlines and semicolons are ignored when grouping with braces or double quotes. They get included in the group of characters just like all the others. The following sets x to a string that contains newlines:

```
set x "This is line one.
This is line two.
This is line three."
```

- During command substitution, newlines and semicolons *are* significant as command terminators. If you have a long command that is nested in square brackets, put a backslash before the newline if you want to continue the command on another line. This was illustrated in Example 1–9 on page 8.
- A dollar sign followed by something other than a letter, digit, underscore, or left parenthesis is treated as a literal dollar sign. The following sets x to the single character $.

```
set x $
```

Reference

Backslash Sequences

Table 1–1 Backslash sequences.

\a	Bell. ($0x7$)
\b	Backspace. ($0x8$)
\f	Form feed. ($0xc$)
\n	Newline. ($0xa$)
\r	Carriage return. ($0xd$)
\t	Tab. ($0x9$)
\v	Vertical tab. ($0xb$)
\<newline>	Replace the newline and the leading white space on the next line with a space.
\\	Backslash. ('\')
ooo	Octal specification of character code. 1, 2, or 3 octal digits (0-7).
\x*hh*	Hexadecimal specification of character code. 1 or 2 hex digits. Be careful when using this in a string of characters, because all hexadecimal characters following the \x will be consumed, but only the last 2 will specify the value.
\u*hhhh*	Hexadecimal specification of a 16-bit Unicode character value. 4 hex digits.
c	Replaced with literal *c* if *c* is not one of the cases listed above. In particular, \\$, \\", \\{, \\}, \\], and \\[are used to obtain these characters.

Arithmetic Operators

Table 1–2 Arithmetic operators from highest to lowest precedence.

- ~ !	Unary minus, bitwise NOT, logical NOT.
* / %	Multiply, divide, remainder.
+ -	Add, subtract.
<< >>	Left shift, right shift.
< > <= >=	Comparison: less, greater, less or equal, greater or equal.
== != eq ne	Equal, not equal, string equal (Tcl 8.4), string not equal (Tcl 8.4).
&	Bitwise AND.
^	Bitwise XOR.
|	Bitwise OR.
&&	Logical AND.
||	Logical OR.
x?*y*:*z*	If *x* then *y* else *z*.

Built-in Math Functions

Table 1–3 Built-in math functions.

acos(*x*)	Arccosine of *x*.
asin(*x*)	Arcsine of *x*.
atan(*x*)	Arctangent of *x*.
atan2(*y*,*x*)	Rectangular (*x*,*y*) to polar (*r*,*th*). atan2 gives *th*.
ceil(*x*)	Least integral value greater than or equal to *x*.
cos(*x*)	Cosine of *x*.
cosh(*x*)	Hyperbolic cosine of *x*.
exp(*x*)	Exponential, e^x.
floor(*x*)	Greatest integral value less than or equal to *x*.
fmod(*x*,*y*)	Floating point remainder of *x*/*y*.
hypot(*x*,*y*)	Returns sqrt(*x**x + *y**y). *r* part of polar coordinates.
log(*x*)	Natural log of *x*.
log10(*x*)	Log base 10 of *x*.
pow(*x*,*y*)	*x* to the *y* power, x^y.
sin(*x*)	Sine of *x*.
sinh(*x*)	Hyperbolic sine of *x*.
sqrt(*x*)	Square root of *x*.
tan(*x*)	Tangent of *x*.
tanh(*x*)	Hyperbolic tangent of *x*.
abs(*x*)	Absolute value of *x*.
double(*x*)	Promote *x* to floating point.
int(*x*)	Truncate *x* to an integer.
round(*x*)	Round *x* to an integer.
rand()	Return a random floating point value between 0.0 and 1.0.
srand(*x*)	Set the seed for the random number generator to the integer *x*.
wide(*x*)	Promote *x* to a wide (64-bit) integer. (Tcl 8.4)

Core Tcl Commands

The pages listed in Table 1–4 give the primary references for the command.

Table 1–4 Built-in Tcl commands.

Command	Pg.	Description
after	228	Schedule a Tcl command for later execution.
append	56	Append arguments to a variable's value. No spaces added.
array	97	Query array state and search through elements.
binary	59	Convert between strings and binary data.
break	83	Exit loop prematurely.
catch	83	Trap errors.
cd	122	Change working directory.
clock	183	Get the time and format date strings.
close	121	Close an open I/O stream.
concat	65	Concatenate arguments with spaces between. Splices lists.
console	29	Control the console used to enter commands interactively.
continue	83	Continue with next loop iteration.
error	85	Raise an error.
eof	116	Check for end of file.
eval	130	Concatenate arguments and evaluate them as a command.
exec	105	Fork and execute a UNIX program.
exit	124	Terminate the process.
expr	6	Evaluate a math expression.
fblocked	233	Poll an I/O channel to see if data is ready.
fconfigure	231	Set and query I/O channel properties.
fcopy	250	Copy from one I/O channel to another.
file	108	Query the file system.
fileevent	229	Register callback for event-driven I/O.
flush	116	Flush output from an I/O stream's internal buffers.
for	82	Loop construct similar to C `for` statement.
foreach	79	Loop construct over a list, or lists, of values.
format	56	Format a string similar to C `sprintf`.
gets	119	Read a line of input from an I/O stream.

Table 1–4 Built-in Tcl commands. (Continued)

glob	122	Expand a pattern to matching file names.
global	90	Declare global variables.
history	196	Use command-line history.
if	76	Test a condition. Allows else and elseif clauses.
incr	12	Increment a variable by an integer amount.
info	186	Query the state of the Tcl interpreter.
interp	292	Create additional Tcl interpreters.
join	72	Concatenate list elements with a given separator string.
lappend	66	Add elements to the end of a list.
lindex	68	Fetch an element of a list.
linsert	68	Insert elements into a list.
list	65	Create a list out of the arguments.
llength	68	Return the number of elements in a list.
load	697	Load shared libraries that define Tcl commands.
lrange	68	Return a range of list elements.
lreplace	68	Replace elements of a list.
lsearch	69	Search for an element of a list that matches a pattern.
lset	62	Set an element in a list. (Tcl 8.4)
lsort	70	Sort a list.
namespace	213	Create and manipulate namespaces.
open	116	Open a file or process pipeline for I/O.
package	175	Provide or require code packages.
pid	124	Return the process ID.
proc	87	Define a Tcl procedure.
puts	119	Output a string to an I/O stream.
pwd	122	Return the current working directory.
read	120	Read blocks of characters from an I/O stream.
regexp	158	Match regular expressions.
regsub	162	Substitute based on regular expressions.
rename	88	Change the name of a Tcl command.
return	86	Return a value from a procedure.

Table 1–4 Built-in Tcl commands. (Continued)

scan	58	Parse a string according to a format specification.
seek	121	Set the seek offset of an I/O stream.
set	5	Assign a value to a variable.
socket	239	Open a TCP/IP network connection.
source	26	Evaluate the Tcl commands in a file.
split	71	Chop a string up into list elements.
string	49	Operate on strings.
subst	140	Substitute embedded commands and variable references.
switch	77	Test several conditions.
tell	121	Return the current seek offset of an I/O stream.
time	202	Measure the execution time of a command.
trace	193	Monitor variable assignments.
unknown	178	Handle unknown commands.
unset	13	Delete variables.
uplevel	138	Execute a command in a different scope.
upvar	91	Reference a variable in a different scope.
variable	207	Declare namespace variables.
vwait	230	Wait for a variable to be modified.
while	79	Loop until a boolean expression is false.

C H A P T E R   **2**

Getting Started

This chapter explains how to run Tcl and Tk on different operating system platforms: UNIX, Windows, and Macintosh. Tcl commands discussed are: `source`, `console` and `info`.

*T*his chapter explains how to run Tcl scripts on different computer systems. While you can write Tcl scripts that are portable among UNIX, Windows, and Macintosh, the details about getting started are different for each system. If you are looking for a current version of Tcl/Tk, use the CD-ROM or check the URLs listed in the Preface on page *liv*.

The main Tcl/Tk program is *wish*. *Wish* stands for windowing shell, and with it you can create graphical applications that run on all these platforms. The name of the program is a little different on each of the UNIX, Windows, and Macintosh systems. On UNIX it is just *wish*. On Windows you will find *wish.exe*, and on the Macintosh the application name is *Wish*. A version number may also be part of the name, such as *wish8.0*, *wish83.exe*, or *Wish 8.4*. The differences among versions are introduced on page *lii*, and described in more detail in Part VII of the book. This book will use *wish* to refer to all of these possibilities.

Tk adds Tcl commands that are used to create graphical user interfaces, and Tk is described in Part III. You can run Tcl without Tk if you do not need a graphical interface, such as with the CGI script discussed in Chapter 3. In this case the program is *tclsh*, *tclsh.exe* or *Tclsh*.

When you run *wish,* it displays an empty window and prompts for a Tcl command with a % prompt. You can enter Tcl commands interactively and experiment with the examples in this book. On Windows and Macintosh, a console window is used to prompt for Tcl commands. On UNIX, your terminal window is used. As described later, you can also set up standalone Tcl/Tk scripts that are self-contained applications.

The source Command

It is a good idea to try out the examples in this book as you read along. The high-lighted examples from the book are on the CD-ROM in the exsource folder. You can edit these scripts in your favorite editor. Save your examples to a file and then execute them with the Tcl source command:

```
source filename
```

The source command reads Tcl commands from a file and evaluates them just as if you had typed them interactively.

Chapter 3 develops a sample application. To get started, just open an editor on a file named cgi1.tcl. Each time you update this file you can save it, reload it into Tcl with the source command, and test it again. Development goes quickly because you do not wait for things to compile!

UNIX Tcl Scripts

On UNIX you can create a standalone Tcl or Tcl/Tk script much like an sh or csh script. The trick is in the first line of the file that contains your script. If the first line of a file begins with #!pathname, then UNIX uses pathname as the inter-preter for the rest of the script. The "Hello, World!" program from Chapter 1 is repeated in Example 2–1 with the special starting line:

Example 2–1 A standalone Tcl script on UNIX.

```
#!/usr/local/bin/tclsh
puts stdout {Hello, World!}
```

The Tk hello world program from Chapter 23 is shown in Example 2–2:

Example 2–2 A standalone Tk script on UNIX.

```
#!/usr/local/bin/wish
button .hello -text Hello -command {puts "Hello, World!"}
pack .hello -padx 10 -pady 10
```

The actual pathnames for *tclsh* and *wish* may be different on your system. If you type the pathname for the interpreter wrong, you receive a confusing "command not found" error. You can find out the complete pathname of the Tcl interpreter with the info nameofexecutable command. This is what appears on my system:

```
info nameofexecutable
=> /home/welch/install/linux-ix86/bin/tclsh8.4
```

Watch out for long pathnames.

On most UNIX systems, this special first line is limited to 32 characters, including the #!. If the pathname is too long, you may end up with /bin/sh trying to interpret your script, giving you syntax errors. You might try using a symbolic link from a short name to the true, long name of the interpreter. However, watch out for systems like older versions of Solaris in which the script interpreter cannot be a symbolic link. Fortunately, Solaris doesn't impose a 32-character limit on the pathname, so you can just use a long pathname.

The next example shows a trick that works around the pathname length limitation in all cases. The trick comes from a posting to `comp.lang.tcl` by Kevin Kenny. It takes advantage of a difference between comments in Tcl and the Bourne shell. Tcl comments are described on page 16. In the example, the `exec` Bourne shell command that runs the Tcl interpreter is hidden in a comment as far as Tcl is concerned, but it is visible to `/bin/sh`. The `exec` command (in `/bin/sh`) replaces the current program, so that is all that the Bourne shell processes; Tcl interprets the rest of the script.

Example 2–3 Using `/bin/sh` to run a Tcl script.

```
#!/bin/sh
# The backslash makes the next line a comment in Tcl \
exec /some/very/long/path/to/wish "$0" ${1+"$@"}
#  ... Tcl script goes here ...
```

You do not even have to know the complete pathname of *tclsh* or *wish* to use this trick. You can just do the following:

```
#!/bin/sh
# Run wish from the users PATH \
exec wish -f "$0" ${1+"$@"}
```

The drawback of an incomplete pathname is that many sites have different versions of *wish* and *tclsh* that correspond to different versions of Tcl and Tk. In addition, some users may not have these programs in their PATH.

You can hide more than one Bourne shell command in a script with this trick. For example, you might need to set environment variables:

```
#!/bin/sh
# \
export LD_LIBRARY_PATH=/usr/local/lib
# \
exec /usr/local/bin/tclsh "$0" ${1+"$@"}
```

Windows Start Menu

You can add your Tcl/Tk programs to the Windows start menu. The command is the complete name of the *wish.exe* program and the name of the script. The trick is that the name of *wish.exe* has a space in it in the default configuration, so you must use quotes. Your start command will look something like this:

```
"c:\Program Files\Tcl84\wish84.exe" "c:\My Files\script.tcl"
```
This starts `c:\My Files\script.tcl` as a standalone Tcl/Tk program.

Macintosh OS 8/9 and *ResEdit*

If you want to create a self-contained Tcl/Tk application on Macintosh OS 8 or 9, you must copy the *Wish* program and add a Macintosh resource named `tclshrc` that has the start-up Tcl code. The Tcl code can be a single `source` command that reads your script file. Here are step-by-step instructions to create the resource using *ResEdit*:

- First, make a copy of *Wish* and open the copy in *ResEdit*.
- Pull down the `Resource` menu and select `Create New Resource` operation to make a new `TEXT` resource.
- *ResEdit* opens a window and you can type in text. Type in a `source` command that names your script:
  ```
  source "Hard Disk:Tcl/Tk 8.3:Applications:MyScript.tcl"
  ```
- Set the name of the resource to be `tclshrc`. You do this through the `Get Resource Info` dialog under the `Resources` menu in *ResEdit*.

This sequence of commands is captured in an application called *Drag n Drop Tclets*, which comes with the Macintosh Tcl distribution. If you drag a Tcl script onto this icon, it will create a copy of *Wish* and create the `tclshrc` text resource that has a `source` command that will load that script.

If you have a Macintosh development environment, you can build a version of *Wish* that has additional resources built right in. You add the resources to the `applicationInit.r` file. If a resource contains Tcl code, you use it like this:
```
source -rcrc resource
```

If you don't want to edit resources, you can just use the *Wish* `Source` menu to select a script to run.

Macintosh OS X

Mac OS X can run the same Tcl/Tk as Macintosh system 8 or 9. However, the preferred version for Mac OS X is *Tcl/Tk Aqua*, which uses the native windowing system known as Aqua. There are some differences in the application structure due to the new application framework used when building this variant. *Wish* checks the `Resources/Scripts` directory in its application bundle for a file called `AppMain.tcl`, if found it is used as the startup script and the `Scripts` folder is added to the `auto_path`. This is similar in spirit to the `tclshrc` resource described above. Daniel Steffen deserves a great deal of credit for the *Tcl/Tk Aqua* port and his continued support of the Macintosh platform. He has put together a great distribution that includes many popular extensions, which you can find on the CD-ROM. You can find out more about Tcl/Tk on Macintosh through these URLs:

```
http://wiki.tcl.tk/macos/
http://www.maths.mq.edu.au/~steffen/tcltk/
```

The console Command

The Windows and Macintosh platforms have a built-in console that is used to enter Tcl commands interactively. You can control this console with the console command. The console is visible by default. Hide the console like this:

```
console hide
```

Display the console like this:

```
console show
```

The console is implemented by a second Tcl interpreter. You can evaluate Tcl commands in that interpreter with:

```
console eval command
```

There is an alternate version of this console called *TkCon*. It is included on the CD-ROM, and you can find current versions on the Internet. *TkCon* was created by Jeff Hobbs and has lots of nice features. You can use *TkCon* on Unix systems, too. Some of its features were added to console in 8.4.

Command-Line Arguments

If you run a script from the command line, for example from a UNIX shell, you can pass the script command-line arguments. You can also specify these arguments in the shortcut command in Windows. For example, under UNIX you can type this at a shell:

```
% myscript.tcl arg1 arg2 arg3
```

In Windows, you can have a shortcut that runs *wish* on your script and also passes additional arguments:

```
"c:\Program Files\Tcl84\wish.exe" c:\your\script.tcl arg1
```

The Tcl shells pass the command-line arguments to the script as the value of the argv variable. The number of command-line arguments is given by the argc variable. The name of the program, or script, is not part of argv nor is it counted by argc. Instead, it is put into the argv0 variable. Table 2–2 lists all the predefined variables in the Tcl shells. argv is a list, so you can use the lindex command, which is described on page 63, to extract items from it:

```
set arg1 [lindex $argv 0]
```

The following script prints its arguments (foreach is described on page 79):

Example 2–4 The EchoArgs script.

```
# Tcl script to echo command line arguments
puts "Program: $argv0"
puts "Number of arguments: $argc"
set i 0
foreach arg $argv {
    puts "Arg $i: $arg"
    incr i
}
```

Command-Line Options to *Wish*

Some command-line options are interpreted by *wish*, and they do not appear in the `argv` variable. The general form of the *wish* command line is:

```
wish ?options? ?script? ?arg1 arg2?
```

If no script is specified, then *wish* just enters an interactive command loop. Table 2–1 lists the options that *wish* supports:

Table 2–1 Wish command line options.

`-colormap new`	Use a new private colormap. See page 624.
`-display` *display*	Use the specified X *display*. UNIX only.
`-geometry` *geometry*	The size and position of the window. See page 658.
`-name` *name*	Specify the Tk application name. See page 648.
`-sync`	Run X synchronously. UNIX only.
`-use` *id*	Use the window specified by *id* for the main window. See page 667.
`-visual` *visual*	Specify the visual for the main window. See page 624.
`--`	Terminate options to *wish*.

Predefined Variables

Table 2–2 Variables defined by *tclsh* and *wish*.

argc	The number of command-line arguments.
argv	A list of the command-line arguments.
argv0	The name of the script being executed. If being used interactively, argv0 is the name of the shell program.
embed_args	The list of arguments in the <EMBED> tag. Tcl applets only. See page 314.
env	An array of the environment variables. See page 124.
tcl_interactive	True (one) if the *tclsh* is prompting for commands.
tcl_library	The script library directory.
tcl_patchLevel	Modified version number, e.g., 8.0b1.
tcl_platform	Array containing operating system information. See page 192.
tcl_prompt1	If defined, this is a command that outputs the prompt.
tcl_prompt2	If defined, this is a command that outputs the prompt if the current command is not yet complete.
tcl_version	Version number.
auto_path	The search path for script library directories. See page 172.
auto_index	A map from command name to a Tcl command that defines it.
auto_noload	If set, the library facility is disabled.
auto_noexec	If set, the auto execute facility is disabled.
geometry	(*wish* only). The value of the -geometry argument.

The Guestbook CGI Application

This chapter presents a simple Tcl program that computes a Web page. The chapter provides a brief background to HTML and the CGI interface to Web servers. The chapter uses the `ncgi` package from the standard Tcl library.

This chapter presents a complete, but simple, guestbook program that computes an HTML document, or Web page, based on the contents of a simple database. The basic idea is that a user with a Web browser visits a page that is computed by the program. The details of how the page gets from your program to the user with the Web browser vary from system to system. The Tcl Web Server described in Chapter 18 comes with this guestbook example already set up. You can also use these scripts on your own Web server, but you will need help from your Webmaster to set things up.

The chapter provides a very brief introduction to HTML and CGI programming. HTML is a way to specify text formatting, including hypertext links to other pages on the World Wide Web. CGI is a standard for communication between a Web server that delivers documents and a program that computes documents for the server. There are many books on these subjects alone.

A guestbook is a place for visitors to sign their name and perhaps provide other information. We will build a guestbook that takes advantage of the World Wide Web. Our guests can leave their address as a Universal Resource Location (URL). The guestbook will be presented as a page that has hypertext links to all these URLs so that other guests can visit them. The program works by keeping a simple database of the guests, and it generates the guestbook page from the database.

The Tcl scripts described in this chapter use commands and techniques that are described in more detail in later chapters. The goal of the examples is to demonstrate the power of Tcl without explaining every detail. If the examples in this chapter raise questions, you can follow the references to examples in other chapters that do go into more depth.

A Quick Introduction to HTML

Web pages are written in a text markup language called HTML (HyperText Markup Language). The idea of HTML is that you annotate, or mark up, regular text with special tags that indicate structure and formatting. For example, the title of a Web page is defined like this:

```
<TITLE>My Home Page</TITLE>
```

The tags provide general formatting guidelines, but the browsers that display HTML pages have freedom in how they display things. This keeps the markup simple. The general syntax for HTML tags is:

```
<tag parameters>normal text</tag>
```

As shown here, the tags usually come in pairs. The open tag may have some parameters, and the close tag name begins with a slash. The case of a tag is not considered, so `<title>`, `<Title>`, and `<TITLE>` are all valid and mean the same thing. The corresponding close tag could be `</title>`, `</Title>`, `</TITLE>`, or even `</TiTlE>`.

The `<A>` tag defines hypertext links that reference other pages on the Web. The hypertext links connect pages into a Web so that you can move from page to page to page and find related information. It is the flexibility of the links that makes the Web so interesting. The `<A>` tag takes an `HREF` parameter that defines the destination of the link. If you wanted to link to my home page, you would put this in your page:

```
<A HREF="http://www.beedub.com/">Brent Welch</A>
```

When this construct appears in a Web page, your browser typically displays "Brent Welch" in blue underlined text. When you click on that text, your browser switches to the page at the address "http://www.beedub.com/". There is a lot more to HTML, of course, but this should give you a basic idea of what is going on in the examples. Table 3–1 summarizes the HTML tags that will be used in the examples:

Table 3–1   HTML tags used in the examples.

HTML	Main tag that surrounds the whole document.
HEAD	Delimits head section of the HTML document.
TITLE	Defines the title of the page.
BODY	Delimits the body section. Lets you specify page colors.

Table 3–1 HTML tags used in the examples. (Continued)

H1 – H6	HTML defines 6 heading levels: H1, H2, H3, H4, H5, H6.
P	Start a new paragraph.
BR	One blank line.
B	Bold text.
I	Italic text.
A	Used for hypertext links.
IMG	Specify an image.
DL	Definition list.
DT	Term clause in a definition list.
DD	Definition clause in a definition list.
UL	An unordered list.
LI	A bulleted item within a list.
TABLE	Create a table.
TR	A table row.
TD	A cell within a table row.
FORM	Defines a data entry form.
INPUT	A one-line entry field, checkbox, radio button, or submit button.
TEXTAREA	A multiline text field.

CGI for Dynamic Pages

There are two classes of pages on the Web: static and dynamic. A static page is written and stored on a Web server, and the same thing is returned each time a user views the page. This is the easy way to think about Web pages. You have some information to share, so you compose a page and tinker with the HTML tags to get the information to look good. If you have a home page, it is probably in this class.

In contrast, a dynamic page is computed each time it is viewed. This is how pages that give up-to-the-minute stock prices work, for example. A dynamic page does not mean it includes animations; it just means that a program computes the page contents when a user visits the page. The advantage of this approach is that a user might see something different each time he or she visits the page. As we shall see, it is also easier to maintain information in a database of some sort and generate the HTML formatting for the data with a program.

A CGI (Common Gateway Interface) program is used to compute Web pages. The CGI standard defines how inputs are passed to the program as well as a way to identify different types of results, such as images, plain text, or HTML markup. A CGI program simply writes the contents of the document to its standard output, and the Web server takes care of delivering the document to the user's Web browser. Example 3–1 is a very simple CGI script:

Example 3–1 A simple CGI script.

```
puts "Content-Type: text/html"
puts ""
puts "<TITLE>The Current Time</TITLE>"
puts "The time is <B>[clock format [clock seconds]]</B>"
```

The program computes a simple HTML page that has the current time. Each time a user visits the page, she will see the current time on the server. The server that has the CGI program and the user viewing the page might be on different sides of the planet. The output of the program is divided into two sections: the protocol header and the page contents. In this simple example, the protocol header just has a `Content-Type` line that tells your Web browser what kind of data comes next. A blank line separates the protocol header from the page, which starts with a <TITLE> tag, in this case.

The `clock` command is used twice: once to get the current time in seconds, and a second time to format the time into a nice-looking string. The `clock` command is described in detail on page 183. Fortunately, there is no conflict between the markup syntax used by HTML and the Tcl syntax for embedded commands, so we can mix the two in the argument to the `puts` command. Double quotes are used to group the argument to `puts` so that the `clock` command will be executed. Example 3–2 shows what the output of the program will look like:

Example 3–2 Output of Example 3–1.

```
Content-Type: text/html

<TITLE>The Current Time</TITLE>
The time is <B>Wed Jul 10 14:29:36 2002</B>
```

This example is a bit sloppy in its use of HTML, but it should display properly in most Web browsers. Example 3–3 includes all the required tags for a proper HTML document.

The guestbook.cgi Script

The `guestbook.cgi` script computes a page that lists all the registered guests. Example 3–3 is shown first, and then each part of it is discussed in more detail later. One thing to note right away is that the HTML tags are generated by procedures that hide the details of the HTML syntax. The first lines of the script use the UNIX trick to have *tclsh* interpret the script. This is described on page 26:

Example 3–3 The guestbook.cgi script, version 1.

```
#!/bin/sh
# guestbook.cgi
# Implement a simple guestbook page.
# The set of visitors is kept in a simple database.
# The newguest.cgi script will update the database.
# \
exec tclsh "$0" ${1+"$@"}

# The guestbook.data file has the database
# The datafile is in the same directory as the script

set dir [file dirname [info script]]
set datafile [file join $dir guestbook.data]

puts "text/html"
puts ""
set title "Brent's Guestbook"
puts "<HTML><HEAD><TITLE>$title</TITLE></HEAD>"
puts "<BODY BGCOLOR=white TEXT=black>"
puts "<H1>$title</H1>"

if {![file exists $datafile]} {
    puts "No registered guests, yet.
        <P>
        Be the first
        <A href='newguest.html'>registered guest!</A>"
} else {
    puts "The following folks have registered in my GuestBook.
        <P>
        <A href='newguest.html'>Register</A>
        <H2>Guests</H2>"
    catch {source $datafile}
    foreach name [lsort [array names Guestbook]] {
        set item $Guestbook($name)
        set homepage [lindex $item 0]
        set markup [lindex $item 1]
        puts "<H3><A href=$homepage>$name</A></H3>"
        puts $markup
    }
}
puts "</BODY></HTML>"
```

Using a Script Library File

If you write one CGI script, you are likely to write several. You could start making copies and modifying your first script, but that quickly becomes hard to maintain. If you learn something new after writing your third script, will you remember to update the first two scripts you wrote? Probably not. The best way to approach this problem is to create a collection of Tcl procedures in a file that you share among all your CGI scripts.

The Standard Tcl Library, *tcllib*, provides several packages of procedures that you can use. Later in this chapter, we will look at the `ncgi` package that helps handle form data. Before we do that, let's start a simple collection of our own procedures and learn how to share them among several different CGI scripts. Suppose you have a file `cgihacks.tcl` that contains your Tcl procedures. The `source` command loads that file into your script. The naive approach shown here probably won't work:

```
source cgihacks.tcl
```

Loading a file from the same directory as your script

The problem is that the current directory of the CGI process may not be the same as the directory that contains the CGI script or the `cgihacks.tcl` file. You can use the `info script` command to find out where the CGI script is, and from that load the supporting file. The `file dirname` and `file join` commands manipulate file names in a platform-independent way. They are described on page 108. I use the following trick to avoid putting absolute file names into my scripts, which would have to be changed if the program moves later:

```
set dir [file dirname [info script]]
source [file join $dir cgihacks.tcl]
```

You can also create script libraries as described in Chapter 12. That chapter describes tools to create an index of procedures so an application can quickly load the procedures it needs, and how to create packages of procedures so you can keep your code organized. However you set them up, it is always a good idea to have a library of procedures you share with other applications.

Beginning the HTML Page

The way you start your HTML page is a great candidate for capturing in a Tcl procedure. For example, I like to have the page title appear in the TITLE tag in the head, and repeated in an H1 tag at the beginning of the body. You may also have a favorite set of colors or fonts that you want to specify in the BODY tag. By putting all this into a Tcl procedure, you can make it easy to share this among all your scripts. If your tastes change tomorrow, then you can change the Tcl procedure in one spot and affect all CGI scripts that share the procedure. Example 3–4 shows `Cgi_Header` that generates a simple standard page header:

Example 3–4 The `Cgi_Header` procedure.

```
proc Cgi_Header {title {body {bgcolor=white text=black}}} {
    puts stdout "Content-Type: text/html

<HTML>
<HEAD>
<TITLE>$title</TITLE>
</HEAD>
<BODY $body>
<H1>$title</H1>"
}
```

The `Cgi_Header` procedure takes as arguments the title for the page and some optional parameters for the HTML BODY tag. The procedure definition uses the syntax for an optional parameter, so you do not have to pass `bodyparams` to `Cgi_Header`. The default specifies black text on a white background to avoid the standard gray background of most browsers. Default values for procedure parameters are described on page 87.

Example 3–5 The `guestbook.cgi` script, version 2.

```
#!/bin/sh
# guestbook.cgi
# Implement a simple guestbook page.
# The set of visitors is kept in a simple database.
# The newguest.cgi script will update the database.
# \
exec tclsh "$0" ${1+"$@"}

# The guestbook.data file has the database
# The datafile is in the same directory as the script

set dir [file dirname [info script]]
set datafile [file join $dir guestbook.data]

# Load our supporting Tcl procedures to define Cgi_Header

source [file join $dir cgihacks.tcl]
Cgi_Header "Brent's Guestbook"

if {![file exists $datafile]} {
    puts "No registered guests, yet.
        <P>
        Be the first
        <A href='newguest.html'>registered guest!</A>"
} else {
    puts "The following folks have registered in my GuestBook.
        <P>
        <A href='newguest.html'>Register</A>
        <h2>Guests</h2>"
    catch {source $datafile}
    foreach name [lsort [array names Guestbook]] {
        set item $Guestbook($name)
        set homepage [lindex $item 0]
        set markup [lindex $item 1]
        puts "<H3><A href=$homepage>$name</A></H3>"
        puts $markup
    }
}
puts "</BODY></HTML>"
```

Example 3–5 is a new version of the original CGI script that loads the `cgi-hacks.tcl` file and uses `Cgi_Header`. The `Cgi_Header` procedure just contains a single `puts` command that generates the standard boilerplate that appears at the beginning of the output. Note that several lines are grouped together with double quotes. Double quotes are used so that the variable references mixed into the HTML are substituted properly. The output of the `Cgi_Header` procedure matches what we wrote by hand in Example 3–3.

Sample Output of the CGI Script

The program tests to see whether there are any registered guests or not. The `file` command, which is described in detail on page 108, is used to see whether there is any data. The exclamation point means "not" in a boolean expression:

```
if {![file exists $datafile]} {
```

If the database file does not exist, a different page is displayed to encourage a registration. The page includes a hypertext link to a registration page, `newguest.html`, which is described on page 43. The output of the program would be as below in Example 3–6 if there were no data file:

Example 3–6 Initial output of `guestbook.cgi` with no data.

```
Content-Type: text/html

<HTML>
<HEAD>
<TITLE>Brent's Guestbook</TITLE>
</HEAD>
<BODY BGCOLOR=white TEXT=black>
<H1>Brent's Guestbook</H1>
<P>
No registered guests.
    <P>
    Be the first
    <A HREF="newguest.html">registered guest!</A>
</BODY></HTML>
```

Note the inconsistent indentation of the HTML that comes from the indentation in the `puts` command used for that part of the page. The browser doesn't care about white space in the HTML. You have a choice between lining up the Tcl commands in your CGI script, or lining up the HTML output. Here we have two different examples. The `Cgi_Header` procedure produces output that is lined up, but the procedure definition looks a bit odd. The main script, in contrast, keeps its Tcl commands neatly indented, but that shows up in the output. If you generate most of your HTML from code, you may choose to keep your code tidy.

Example 3–7 shows the output of the `guestbook.cgi` script when there is some data in the data file:

Example 3–7 Output of `guestbook.cgi` with guestbook data.

```
Content-Type: text/html

<HTML>
<HEAD>
<TITLE>Brent's Guestbook</TITLE>
</HEAD>
<BODY BGCOLOR=white TEXT=black>
<H1>Brent's Guestbook</H1>
<P>
The following folks have registered in my guestbook.
    <P>
    <A HREF='newguest.html'>Register</A>
    <H2>Guests</H2>
<H3><A HREF="http://www.beedub.com/">Brent Welch</A></H3>
<IMG SRC="http://www.beedub.com/welch.gif">
</BODY></HTML>
```

Using a Tcl Array for the Database

The data file contains Tcl commands that define an array that holds the guestbook data. If this file is kept in the same directory as the `guestbook.cgi` script, then you can compute its name:

```
set dir [file dirname [info script]]
set datafile [file join $dir guestbook.data]
```

By using Tcl commands to represent the data, we can load the data with the `source` command. The `catch` command is used to protect the script from a bad data file, which will show up as an error from the `source` command. Catching errors is described in detail on page 85:

```
catch {source $datafile}
```

The `Guestbook` variable is the array defined in `guestbook.data`. Array variables are the topic of Chapter 8. Each element of the array is defined with a Tcl command that looks like this:

```
set Guestbook(key) {url markup}
```

The person's name is the array index, or key. The value of the array element is a Tcl list with two elements: their URL and some additional HTML markup that they can include in the guestbook. Tcl lists are the topic of Chapter 5. The following example shows what the command looks like with real data:

```
set {Guestbook(Brent Welch)} {
    http://www.beedub.com/
    {<img src=http://www.beedub.com/welch.gif>}
}
```

The spaces in the name result in additional braces to group the whole variable name and each list element. This syntax is explained on page 96. Do not worry about it now. We will see on page 46 that all the braces in the previous statement are generated automatically. The main point is that the person's name is the key, and the value is a list with two elements.

The `array names` command returns all the indices, or keys, in the array, and the `lsort` command sorts these alphabetically. The `foreach` command loops over the sorted list, setting the loop variable `x` to each key in turn:

```
foreach name [lsort [array names Guestbook]] {
```

The `lsort` command will sort the names based on the person's first name. You can have `lsort` sort things in a variety of ways. One trick we can use here is to have `lsort` treat each key as a list and sort on the last item in the list (i.e., the last name):

```
foreach name [lsort -index end [array names Guestbook]] {
```

The `lsort` command is described in more detail on page 70. The `foreach` command assigns `name` to each key of the `Guestbook` array. We get the value like this:

```
set item $Guestbook($name)
```

The two list elements are extracted with `lindex`, which is described on page 68.

```
set homepage [lindex $item 0]
set markup [lindex $item 1]
```

We generate the HTML for the guestbook entry as a level-three header that contains a hypertext link to the guest's home page. We follow the link with any HTML markup text that the guest has supplied to embellish his or her entry:

```
puts "<H3><a href=$homepage>$name</a></H3>"
puts $markup
```

The `homepage` and `markup` variables are not strictly necessary, and the code could be written more compactly without them. However, the variables make the code more understandable. Here is what it looks like without the temporary variables:

```
puts "<H3><a href=[lindex $item 0]>$name</a></H3>"
puts [lindex $item 1]
```

Defining Forms and Processing Form Data

The `guestbook.cgi` script only generates output. The other half of CGI deals with input from the user. Input is more complex for two reasons. First, we have to define another HTML page that has a form for the user to fill out. Second, the data from the form is organized and encoded in a standard form that must be decoded by the script. Example 3–8 on page 43 defines a very simple form, and the procedure that decodes the form data is shown in Example 11–6 on page 165.

The guestbook page contains a link to `newguest.html`. This page contains a form that lets a user register his or her name, home page URL, and some additional HTML markup. The form has a submit button. When a user clicks that button in her browser, the information from the form is passed to the `newguest.cgi` script. This script updates the database and computes another page for the user that acknowledges the user's contribution.

The `newguest.html` Form

An HTML form contains tags that define data entry fields, buttons, checkboxes, and other elements that let the user specify values. For example, a one-line entry field that is used to enter the home page URL is defined like this:

```
<INPUT TYPE=text NAME=url>
```

The `INPUT` tag is used to define several kinds of input elements, and its `type` parameter indicates what kind. In this case, `TYPE=text` creates a one-line text entry field. The submit button is defined with an `INPUT` tag that has `TYPE=submit`, and the `VALUE` parameter becomes the text that appears on the submit button:

```
<INPUT TYPE=submit NAME=submit VALUE=Register>
```

A general type-in window is defined with the `TEXTAREA` tag. This creates a multiline, scrolling text field that is useful for specifying lots of information, such as a free-form comment. In our case, we will let guests type in HTML that will appear with their guestbook entry. The text between the open and close `TEXTAREA` tags is inserted into the type-in window when the page is first displayed.

```
<TEXTAREA NAME=markup ROWS=10 COLS=50>Hello.</TEXTAREA>
```

A common parameter to the form tags is `NAME=`*something*. This name identifies the data that will come back from the form. The tags also have parameters that affect their display, such as the label on the submit button and the size of the text area. Those details are not important for our example. The complete form is shown in Example 3–8:

Example 3–8 The `newguest.html` form.

```
<HTML>
<HEAD>
<TITLE>Register in my Guestbook</TITLE>
</HEAD>
<BODY BGCOLOR=white TEXT=black>

<FORM ACTION="newguest.cgi" METHOD="POST">

<H1>Register in my Guestbook</H1>
<UL>
<LI>Name <INPUT TYPE="text" NAME="name" SIZE="40">
<LI>URL  <INPUT TYPE="text" NAME="url" SIZE="40">
<P>
If you don't have a home page, you can use an email URL like
"mailto:welch@acm.org"
<LI>Additional HTML to include after your link:
<BR>

<TEXTAREA NAME="html" COLS="60" ROWS="15">
</TEXTAREA>
<LI><INPUT TYPE="submit" NAME="new" VALUE="Add me to your
guestbook">
<LI><INPUT TYPE="submit" NAME="update" VALUE="Update my
guestbook entry">
```

```
</UL>
</FORM>

</BODY>
</HTML>
```

The ncgi and cgi.tcl Packages

The `newguest.cgi` script uses the `ncgi` package to process form data. This is one of many packages available in the Standard Tcl Library, commonly known as "tcllib". If you don't have tcllib installed, you can find it on the CD-ROM, on SourceForge at `www.sf.net/projects/tcllib`, or via the main `www.tcl.tk` Web site. If your Tcl installation includes tcllib, then you use the `package` command to load the package.

```
package require ncgi
```

The procedures in the `ncgi` package are in the `ncgi` namespace. Tcl namespaces are described in detail in Chapter 14. Procedures in a namespace are qualified with the name of the namespace and :: syntax. For example, the standard setup procedure for a CGI script is `ncgi::parse`.

The "n" in ncgi is for "new". Don Libes wrote the original package for CGI scripts known as `cgi.tcl`. There is also the `cgilib.tcl` package that contains Cgi_Header and some other procedures described in earlier editions of this book. The `ncgi` and `html` packages of tcllib provide most of the features in both `cgi.tcl` and `cgilib.tcl`, but follow the standard namespace conventions use by the packages in tcllib. You can still find `cgi.tcl` on the Web at

```
http://expect.nist.gov/cgi.tcl/
```

The newguest.cgi Script

When the user clicks the Submit button in her browser, the data from the form is passed to the program identified by the `ACTION` parameter of the form tag. That program takes the data, does something useful with it, and then returns a new page for the browser to display. In our case, the `FORM` tag names `newguest.cgi` as the program to handle the data:

```
<FORM ACTION=newguest.cgi METHOD=POST>
```

The CGI specification defines how the data from the form is passed to the program. The data is encoded and organized so that the program can figure out the values the user specified for each form element. The encoding is handled rather nicely with some regular expression tricks that are done in `ncgi::parse`. `ncgi::parse` saves the form data, and `ncgi::value` gets a form value in the script. These procedures are described in Example 11–6 on page 165. Example 3–9 starts out by calling `ncgi::parse`:

Example 3–9 The `newguest.cgi` script.

```
#!/bin/sh
# \
exec tclsh "$0" ${1+"$@"}

# Use the ncgi package from tcllib to process form data

package require ncgi
ncgi::parse

# Load our data file and supporting procedures

set dir [file dirname [info script]]
set datafile [file join $dir guestbook.data]
source [file join $dir cgihacks.tcl]

# Open the datafile in append mode

if {[catch {open $datafile a} out]} {
    Cgi_Header "Guestbook Registration Error" \
        {BGCOLOR=black TEXT=red}
    puts "<P>Cannot open the data file<P>"
    puts $out;# the error message
    exit 0
}

# Append a Tcl set command that defines the guest's entry

puts $out ""
puts $out [list set Guestbook([ncgi::value name]) \
    [list [ncgi::value url] [ncgi::value html]]]
close $out

# Return a page to the browser

Cgi_Header "Guestbook Registration Confirmed" \
    {BGCOLOR=white TEXT=black}

puts "
<TABLE BORDER=1>
<TR><TD>Name</TD>
<TD>[ncgi::value name]</TD></TR>
<TR><TD>URL</TD>
<TD><A HREF='[ncgi::value url]'>[ncgi::value url]</A></TD></TR>
<TR><TD>Extra HTML</TD>
<TD>[ncgi::value html]</TD></TR>
</TABLE>
"

puts </BODY></HTML>
```

Using Tcl Scripts to Store Data

The main idea of the `newguest.cgi` script is that it saves the data to a file as a Tcl command that defines an element of the `Guestbook` array. This lets the `guestbook.cgi` script simply load the data by using the Tcl `source` command. This trick of storing data as a Tcl script saves us from the chore of defining a new file format and writing code to parse it. Instead, we can rely on the well-tuned Tcl implementation to do the hard work for us efficiently.

The script opens the datafile in append mode so that it can add a new record to the end. Opening files is described in detail on page 116. The script uses a `catch` command to guard against errors. If an error occurs, a page explaining the error is returned to the user. Working with files is one of the most common sources of errors (permission denied, disk full, file-not-found, and so on), so I always open the file inside a `catch` statement:

```
if {[catch {open $datafile a} out]} {
    # an error occurred
} else {
    # open was ok

}
```

In this command, the variable `out` gets the result of the `open` command, which is either a file descriptor or an error message. This style of using `catch` is described in detail in Example 6–14 on page 83.

Use list to generate Tcl commands.

The script writes the data as a Tcl `set` command. The `list` command is used to format the data properly:

```
puts $out [list set Guestbook([ncgi::value name]) \
    [list [ncgi::value url] [ncgi::value html]]]
```

There are two lists. First, the `url` and `html` values are formatted into one list. This list will be the value of the array element. Then the whole Tcl command is formed as a list. In simplified form, the command is generated from this:

```
list set variable value
```

Using the `list` command ensures that the result will always be a valid Tcl command that sets the variable to the given value. This is a very important technique. If you want to generate Tcl commands, the best way to do it is to generate lists using list manipulation commands. The `list` command is described in more detail on page 65.

Handling Errors in CGI Scripts

One of the more frustrating aspects of CGI programming is that errors in your script result in blank browser pages, and it may be difficult or impossible to find any trace of the error message. The other main problem is that your Web server may not be configured properly to find your CGI script. I use two simple tricks to track down the source of these errors. The first trick simply verifies that my script has run at all by creating an empty file somewhere on the Web server. On a UNIX system, you can put this line at the beginning of your script:

```
close [open /tmp/my_cgi_script_ran w]
```

When you aim the browser at your CGI script, it should at least create the file. If not, then the Web server cannot find your script, or it cannot find the Tclsh required by your script. Double-check your setup and the #! line in your script. On Windows, your best bet may be to use the TclHttpd Web server, which has a built-in ability to run Tcl CGI scripts. TclHttpd has other even cooler ways to generate pages, too.

If your script suddenly stops working after you've modified it, then you have introduced a programming bug. I generally put all of the script into a catch statement and print out any errors that occur. That way the errors will be displayed by the browser instead of filed into the void by your Web server. Example 3–10 shows the newguest.cgi script rewritten so the catch statement surrounds all the statements. At the end, the value of the errorInfo variable is printed out if an error has occurred:

Example 3–10 The newguest.cgi script with error handling.

```
#!/bin/sh
# \
exec tclsh "$0" ${1+"$@"}

# Trap all errors

if {[catch {

# Use the ncgi package from tcllib to process form data

package require ncgi
ncgi::parse

# Load our data file and supporting procedures

set dir [file dirname [info script]]
set datafile [file join $dir guestbook.data]
source [file join $dir cgihacks.tcl]

# Open the datafile in append mode

set out [open $datafile a]

# Append a Tcl set command that defines the guest's entry

puts $out ""
puts $out [list set Guestbook([ncgi::value name]) \
    [list [ncgi::value url] [ncgi::value html]]]
close $out

# Return a page to the browser
```

```
Cgi_Header "Guestbook Registration Confirmed" \
    {BGCOLOR=white TEXT=black}

puts "
<TABLE BORDER=1>
<TR><TD>Name</TD>
<TD>[ncgi::value name]</TD></TR>
<TR><TD>URL</TD>
<TD><A HREF='[ncgi::value url]'>[ncgi::value url]</A></TD></TR>
<TR><TD>Extra HTML</TD>
<TD>[ncgi::value html]</TD></TR>
</TABLE>
</BODY></HTML>
"

# End of main script

} err]} {

    # Error occurred - display in the Web page

    puts "Content-Type: text/plain"
    puts ""
    puts "CGI error occurred in [info script]"
    puts $errorInfo

}
```

Next Steps

There are a number of details that can be added to this example. Users may want to update their entry, for example. They could do that now, but they would have to retype everything. They might also like a chance to check the results of their registration and make changes before committing them. This requires another page that displays their guest entry as it would appear on a page, and also has the fields that let them update the data.

The details of how a CGI script is hooked up with a Web server vary from server to server. You should ask your local Webmaster for help if you want to try this out on your local Web site. The Tcl Web Server comes with this guestbook example already set up, plus it has a number of other very interesting ways to generate pages. My own taste in Web page generation has shifted from CGI to a template-based approach supported by the Tcl Web Server. This is the topic of Chapter 18.

The next few chapters describe basic Tcl commands and data structures. We return to the CGI example in Chapter 11 on regular expressions.

CHAPTER 4

String Processing in Tcl

This chapter describes string manipulation and simple pattern matching. Tcl commands described are: `string`, `append`, `format`, `scan`, and `binary`. The `string` command is a collection of several useful string manipulation operations.

Strings are the basic data item in Tcl, so it should not be surprising that there are a large number of commands to manipulate strings. A closely related topic is pattern matching, in which string comparisons are made more powerful by matching a string against a pattern. This chapter describes a simple pattern matching mechanism that is similar to that used in many other shell languages. Chapter 11 describes a more complex and powerful regular expression pattern matching mechanism.

The string Command

The `string` command is really a collection of operations you can perform on strings. The following example calculates the length of the value of a variable.

```
set name "Brent Welch"
string length $name
=> 11
```

The first argument to `string` determines the operation. You can ask `string` for valid operations by giving it a bad one:

```
string junk
=> bad option "junk": should be bytelength, compare,
equal, first, index, is, last, length, map, match, range,
repeat, replace, tolower, totitle, toupper, trim, trim-
left, trimright, wordend, or wordstart
```

This trick of feeding a Tcl command bad arguments to find out its usage is common across many commands. Table 4–1 summarizes the `string` command.

Table 4–1 The `string` command.

`string bytelength str`	Returns the number of bytes used to store a string, which may be different from the character length returned by `string length` because of UTF-8 encoding. See page 220 of Chapter 15 about Unicode and UTF-8.
`string compare ?-nocase? ?-length len? str1 str2`	Compares strings lexicographically. Use `-nocase` for case insensitive comparison. Use `-length` to limit the comparison to the first `len` characters. Returns 0 if equal, -1 if `str1` sorts before `str2`, else 1.
`string equal ?-nocase? str1 str2`	Compares strings and returns 1 if they are the same. Use `-nocase` for case insensitive comparison.
`string first subString string ?startIndex?`	Returns the index in `string` of the first occurrence of `subString`, or -1 if `string` is not found. `startIndex` may be specified to start in the middle of `string`.
`string index string index`	Returns the character at the specified `index`. An index counts from zero. Use `end` for the last character.
`string is class ?-strict? ?-failindex varname? string`	Returns 1 if `string` belongs to `class`. If `-strict`, then empty strings never match, otherwise they always match. If `-failindex` is specified, then `varname` is assigned the index of the character in `string` that prevented it from being a member of `class`. See Table 4–3 on page 54 for character class names.
`string last subString string ?startIndex?`	Returns the index in `string` of the last occurrence of `subString`, or -1 if `subString` is not found. `startIndex` may be specified to start in the middle of `string`.
`string length string`	Returns the number of characters in `string`.
`string map ?-nocase? charMap string`	Returns a new string created by mapping characters in `string` according to the input, output list in `charMap`. See page 55.
`string match ?-nocase? pattern str`	Returns 1 if `str` matches the `pattern`, else 0. Glob-style matching is used. See page 53.
`string range str i j`	Returns the range of characters in `str` from `i` to `j`.
`string repeat str count`	Returns `str` repeated `count` times.
`string replace str first last ?newstr?`	Returns a new string created by replacing characters `first` through `last` with `newstr`, or nothing.
`string tolower string ?first? ?last?`	Returns `string` in lower case. `first` and `last` determine the range of `string` on which to operate.

Table 4–1 The `string` command. (Continued)

`string totitle string` `?first? ?last?`	Capitalizes `string` by replacing its first character with the Unicode title case, or upper case, and the rest with lower case. `first` and `last` determine the range of `string` on which to operate.
`string toupper string` `?first? ?last?`	Returns `string` in upper case. `first` and `last` determine the range of `string` on which to operate.
`string trim string` `?chars?`	Trims the characters in `chars` from both ends of `string`. `chars` defaults to whitespace.
`string trimleft string` `?chars?`	Trims the characters in `chars` from the beginning of `string`. `chars` defaults to whitespace.
`string trimright string` `?chars?`	Trims the characters in `chars` from the end of `string`. `chars` defaults to whitespace.
`string wordend str ix`	Returns the index in `str` of the character after the word containing the character at index `ix`.
`string wordstart str ix`	Returns the index in `str` of the first character in the word containing the character at index `ix`.

These are the string operations I use most:

- The `equal` operation, which is shown in Example 4–2 on page 53.
- String `match`. This pattern matching operation is described on page 53.
- The `tolower`, `totitle`, and `toupper` operations convert case.
- The `trim`, `trimright`, and `trimleft` operations are handy for cleaning up strings.

These new operations were added in Tcl 8.1 (actually, they first appeared in the 8.1.1 patch release):

- The `equal` operation, which is simpler than using `string compare`.
- The `is` operation that test for kinds of strings. String classes are listed in Table 4–3 on page 54.
- The `map` operation that translates characters (e.g., like the Unix *tr* command.)
- The `repeat` and `replace` operations.
- The `totitle` operation, which is handy for capitalizing words.

String Indices

Several of the string operations involve string indices that are positions within a string. Tcl counts characters in strings starting with zero. The special index `end` is used to specify the last character in a string:

```
string range abcd 2 end
=> cd
```

Tcl 8.1 added syntax for specifying an index relative to the end. Specify end-N to get the Nth character before the end. For example, the following command returns a new string that drops the first and last characters from the original:

```
string range $string 1 end-1
```

There are several operations that pick apart strings: first, last, wordstart, wordend, index, and range. If you find yourself using combinations of these operations to pick apart data, it may be faster if you can do it with the regular expression pattern matcher described in Chapter 11.

Strings and Expressions

Strings can be compared with expr, if, and while using the comparison operators eq, ne, ==, !=, < and >. However, there are a number of subtle issues that can cause problems. First, you must quote the string value so that the expression parser can identify it as a string type. Then, you must group the expression with curly braces to prevent the double quotes from being stripped off by the main interpreter:

```
if {$x == "foo"} command
```

expr *is only reliable for string comparison when using* eq *or* ne.

Despite the quotes, the expression operators that work on numbers and strings first convert try converting items to numbers if possible, and then converts them back if it detects a case of string comparison. The conversion back is always done as a decimal number. This can lead to unexpected conversions between strings that look like hexadecimal or octal numbers. The following boolean expression is true!

```
if {"0xa" == "10"} { puts stdout ack! }
=> ack!
```

A safe way to compare strings is to use the string compare and string equal operations. The eq and ne expr operators were introduced in 8.4 to allow more compact strict string comparison. These operations also work faster because the unnecessary conversions are eliminated. Like the C library strcmp function, string compare returns 0 if the strings are equal, minus 1 if the first string is lexicographically less than the second, or 1 if the first string is greater than the second:

Example 4–1 Comparing strings with string compare.

```
if {[string compare $s1 $s2] == 0} {
    # strings are equal
}
```

The string equal command added in Tcl 8.1 makes this simpler:

Example 4–2 Comparing strings with `string equal`.

```
if {[string equal $s1 $s2]} {
    # strings are equal
}
```

The `eq` operator added in Tcl 8.4 is semantically equal, but more compact. It also avoids any internal format conversions. There is also a `ne` operator to efficiently test for inequality.

Example 4–3 Comparing strings with `eq`.

```
if {$s1 eq $s2} {
    # strings are equal
}
```

String Matching

The `string match` command implements *glob*-style pattern matching that is modeled after the file name pattern matching done by various UNIX shells. The heritage of the word "glob" is rooted in UNIX, and Tcl preserves this historical oddity in the `glob` command that does pattern matching on file names. The `glob` command is described on page 122. Table 4–2 shows the three constructs used in `string match` patterns:

Table 4–2 Matching characters used with `string match`.

`*`	Match any number of any characters.
`?`	Match exactly one character.
`[chars]`	Match any character in `chars`.

Any other characters in a pattern are taken as literals that must match the input exactly. The following example matches all strings that begin with a:

```
string match a* alpha
=> 1
```

To match all two-letter strings:

```
string match ?? XY
=> 1
```

To match all strings that begin with either a or b:

```
string match {[ab]*} cello
=> 0
```

Be careful! Square brackets are also special to the Tcl interpreter, so you will need to wrap the pattern up in curly braces to prevent it from being interpreted as a nested command. Another approach is to put the pattern into a variable:

```
set pat {[ab]*x}
string match $pat box
=> 1
```

You can specify a range of characters with the syntax `[x-y]`. For example, `[a-z]` represents the set of all lower-case letters, and `[0-9]` represents all the digits. You can include more than one range in a set. Any letter, digit, or the underscore is matched with:

```
string match {[a-zA-Z0-9_]} $char
```

The set matches only a single character. To match more complicated patterns, like one or more characters from a set, then you need to use regular expression matching, which is described on page 158.

If you need to include a literal `*`, `?`, or bracket in your pattern, preface it with a backslash:

```
string match {*\?} what?
=> 1
```

In this case the pattern is quoted with curly braces because the Tcl interpreter is also doing backslash substitutions. Without the braces, you would have to use two backslashes. They are replaced with a single backslash by Tcl before `string match` is called.

```
string match *\\? what?
```

Character Classes

The `string is` command tests a string to see whether it belongs to a particular *class*. This is useful for input validation. For example, to make sure something is a number, you do:

```
if {![string is integer -strict $input]} {
    error "Invalid input. Please enter a number."
}
```

Classes are defined in terms of the Unicode character set, which means they are more general than specifying character sets with ranges over the ASCII encoding. For example, `alpha` includes many characters outside the range of `[A-Za-z]` because of different characters in other alphabets. The classes are listed in Table 4–3.

Table 4–3 Character class names.

`alnum`	Any alphabet or digit character.
`alpha`	Any alphabet character.
`ascii`	Any character with a 7-bit character code (i.e., less than 128.)
`boolean`	A valid Tcl boolean value, such as 0, 1, `true`, `false` (in any case).
`control`	Character code less than 32, and not NULL.

Table 4–3 Character class names. (Continued)

`digit`	Any digit character.
`double`	A valid floating point number.
`false`	A valid Tcl boolean false value, such as 0 or `false` (in any case).
`graph`	Any printing characters, not including space characters.
`integer`	A valid integer.
`lower`	A string in all lower case.
`print`	A synonym for `alnum`.
`punct`	Any punctuation character.
`space`	Space, tab, newline, carriage return, vertical tab, backspace.
`true`	A valid Tcl boolean true value, such as 1 or `true` (in any case).
`upper`	A string all in upper case.
`wordchar`	Alphabet, digit, and the underscore.
`xdigit`	Valid hexadecimal digits.

Mapping Strings

The `string map` command translates a string based on a character map. The map is in the form of a input, output list. Wherever a string contains an input sequence, that is replaced with the corresponding output. For example:

```
string map {f p d l} food
=> pool
```

The inputs and outputs can be more than one character and they do not have to be the same length:

```
string map {f p d ll oo u} food
=> pull
```

Example 4–4 is more practical. It uses `string map` to replace fancy quotes and hyphens produced by Microsoft Word into ASCII equivalents. It uses the `open`, `read`, and `close` file operations that are described in Chapter 9, and the `fconfigure` command described on page 234 to ensure that the file format is UNIX friendly.

Example 4–4 Mapping Microsoft World special characters to ASCII.

```
proc Dos2Unix {filename} {
    set input [open $filename]
    set output [open $filename.new]
    fconfigure $output -translation lf
    puts $output [string map {
        \223    "
        \224    "
```

```
        \222    '
        \226    -
    } [read $input]]
    close $input
    close $output
}
```

The append Command

The append command takes a variable name as its first argument and concatenates its remaining arguments onto the current value of the named variable.
The variable is created if it does not already exist:

```
set foo z
append foo a b c
set foo
=> zabc
```

The append *command is efficient with large strings.*

The append command provides an efficient way to add items to the end of a
string. It modifies a variable directly, so it can exploit the memory allocation
scheme used internally by Tcl. Using the append command like this:

```
append x " some new stuff"
```

is always faster than this:

```
set x "$x some new stuff"
```

The lappend command described on page 65 has similar performance benefits when working with Tcl lists.

The format Command

The format command is similar to the C printf function. It formats a string
according to a format specification:

```
format spec value1 value2 ...
```

The spec argument includes literals and keywords. The literals are placed
in the result as is, while each keyword indicates how to format the corresponding
argument. The keywords are introduced with a percent sign, %, followed by zero
or more modifiers, and terminate with a conversion specifier. The most general
keyword specification for each argument contains up to six parts:

- position specifier
- flags
- field width
- precision
- word length
- conversion character

Example keywords include `%f` for floating point, `%d` for integer, and `%s` for string format. Use `%%` to obtain a single percent character. The following examples use double quotes around the `format` specification. This is because often the format contains white space, so grouping is required, as well as backslash substitutions like `\t` or `\n`, and the quotes allow substitution of these special characters. Table 4–4 lists the conversion characters:

Table 4–4 Format conversions.

d	Signed integer.
u	Unsigned integer.
i	Signed integer. The argument may be in hex (0x) or octal (0) format.
o	Unsigned octal.
x or X	Unsigned hexadecimal. 'x' gives lowercase results.
c	Map from an integer to the ASCII character it represents.
s	A string.
f	Floating point number in the format `a.b`.
e or E	Floating point number in scientific notation, `a.bE+-c`.
g or G	Floating point number in either `%f` or `%e` format, whichever is shorter.

A position specifier is *i*`$`, which means take the value from argument *i* as opposed to the normally corresponding argument. The position counts from 1. If a position is specified for one format keyword, the position must be used for all of them. If you group the format specification with double quotes, you need to quote the `$` with a backslash:

```
set lang 2
format "%${lang}\$s" one un uno
=> un
```

The position specifier is useful for picking a string from a set, such as this simple language-specific example. The message catalog facility described in Chapter 15 is a much more sophisticated way to solve this problem. The position is also useful if the same value is repeated in the formatted string.

The flags in a format are used to specify padding and justification. In the following examples, the `#` causes a leading `0x` to be printed in the hexadecimal value. The zero in `08` causes the field to be padded with zeros. Table 4–5 summarizes the format flag characters.

```
format "%#x" 20
=> 0x14
format "%#08x" 10
=> 0x0000000a
```

After the flags you can specify a minimum field width value. The value is

Table 4–5 Format flags.

–	Left justify the field.
+	Always include a sign, either + or -.
space	Precede a number with a space, unless the number has a leading sign. Useful for packing numbers close together.
0	Pad with zeros.
#	Leading 0 for octal. Leading 0x for hex. Always include a decimal point in floating point. Do not remove trailing zeros (%g).

padded to this width with spaces, or with zeros if the 0 flag is used:

```
format "%-20s %3d" Label 2
=> Label                  2
```

You can compute a field width and pass it to `format` as one of the arguments by using `*` as the field width specifier. In this case the next argument is used as the field width instead of the value, and the argument after that is the value that gets formatted.

```
set maxl 8
format "%-*s = %s" $maxl Key Value
=> Key      = Value
```

The precision comes next, and it is specified with a period and a number. For `%f` and `%e` it indicates how many digits come after the decimal point. For `%g` it indicates the total number of significant digits used. For `%d` and `%x` it indicates how many digits will be printed, padding with zeros if necessary.

```
format "%6.2f %6.2d" 1 1
=>   1.00     01
```

The storage length part comes last but it only became useful in Tcl 8.4 where wide integer support was added. Otherwise Tcl maintains all floating point values in double-precision, and all integers as long words. Wide integers are a minimum of 64-bits wide. By adding the `l` (long) word length specifier, we can see the difference between regular and wide integers.

```
format %u -1
=> 4294967295
format %lu -1
=> 18446744073709551615
```

The scan Command

The `scan` command parses a string according to a format specification and assigns values to variables. It returns the number of successful conversions it made, unless no capture variables are given, in which case it returns the scan matches in a list. The general form of the command is:

```
scan string format ?var? ?var? ?var? ...
```

The format for `scan` is nearly the same as in the `format` command. The `%c` scan format converts one character to its decimal value.

The `scan` format includes a set notation. Use square brackets to delimit a set of characters. The set matches one or more characters that are copied into the variable. A dash is used to specify a range. The following scans a field of all lowercase letters.

```
scan abcABC {%[a-z]} result
=> 1
set result
=> abc
```

If the first character in the set is a right square bracket, then it is considered part of the set. If the first character in the set is ^, then characters *not* in the set match. Again, put a right square bracket immediately after the ^ to include it in the set. Nothing special is required to include a left square bracket in the set. As in the previous example, you will want to protect the format with braces, or use backslashes, because square brackets are special to the Tcl parser.

The `binary` Command

Tcl 8.0 added support for binary strings. Previous versions of Tcl used null-terminated strings internally, which foils the manipulation of some types of data. Tcl now uses counted strings, so it can tolerate a null byte in a string value without truncating it.

This section describes the `binary` command that provides conversions between strings and packed binary data representations. The `binary format` command takes values and packs them according to a template. For example, this can be used to format a floating point vector in memory suitable for passing to Fortran. The resulting binary value is returned:

```
binary format template value ?value ...?
```

The `binary scan` command extracts values from a binary string according to a similar template. For example, this is useful for extracting data stored in binary data file. It assigns values to a set of Tcl variables:

```
binary scan value template variable ?variable ...?
```

Format Templates

The format template consists of type keys and counts. The count is interpreted differently depending on the type. For types like integer (`i`) and double (`d`), the count is a repetition count (e.g., `i3` means three integers). For strings, the count is a length (e.g., `a3` means a three-character string). If no count is specified, it defaults to 1. If count is `*`, then `binary scan` uses all the remaining bytes in the value.

Several type keys can be specified in a template. Each key-count combination moves an imaginary cursor through the binary data. There are special type keys to move the cursor. The x key generates null bytes in `binary format`, and it skips over bytes in `binary scan`. The @ key uses its *count* as an absolute byte offset to which to set the cursor. As a special case, @* skips to the end of the data. The x key backs up *count* bytes. The types are summarized in Table 4–6. In the table, *count* is the optional count following the type letter.

Table 4–6 Binary conversion types.

a	A character string of length *count*. Padded with nulls in `binary format`.
A	A character string of length *count*. Padded with spaces in `binary format`. Trailing nulls and blanks are discarded in `binary scan`.
b	A binary string of length *count*. Low-to-high order.
B	A binary string of length *count*. High-to-low order.
h	A hexadecimal string of length *count*. Low-to-high order.
H	A hexadecimal string of length *count*. High-to-low order. (More commonly used than h.)
c	An 8-bit character code. The *count* is for repetition.
s	A 16-bit integer in little-endian byte order. The *count* is for repetition.
S	A 16-bit integer in big-endian byte order. The *count* is for repetition.
i	A 32-bit integer in little-endian byte order. The *count* is for repetition.
I	A 32-bit integer in big-endian byte order. The *count* is for repetition.
f	Single-precision floating point value in native format. The *count* is for repetition.
d	Double-precision floating point value in native format. The *count* is for repetition.
w	A 64-bit integer in little-endian byte order. The *count* is for repetition. (Tcl 8.4)
W	A 64-bit integer in big-endian byte order. The *count* is for repetition. (Tcl 8.4)
x	Pack *count* null bytes with `binary format`. Skip *count* bytes with `binary scan`.
X	Backup *count* bytes.
@	Skip to absolute position specified by *count*. If *count* is *, skip to the end.

Numeric types have a particular byte order that determines how their value is laid out in memory. The type keys are lowercase for little-endian byte order (e.g., Intel) and uppercase for big-endian byte order (e.g., SPARC and Motorola). Different integer sizes are 16-bit (s or S), 32-bit (i or I), and, with Tcl 8.4 or greater, 64-bit (w or W). Note that the official byte order for data transmitted over a network is big-endian. Floating point values are always machine-specific, so it only makes sense to format and scan these values on the same machine.

There are three string types: character (a or A), binary (b or B), and hexadec-imal (h or H). With these types the *count* is the length of the string. The a type pads its value to the specified length with null bytes in `binary format` and the A type pads its value with spaces. If the value is too long, it is truncated. In `binary scan`, the A type strips trailing blanks and nulls.

A binary string consists of zeros and ones. The b type specifies bits from low-to-high order, and the B type specifies bits from high-to-low order. A hexa-decimal string specifies 4 bits (i.e., nybbles) with each character. The h type spec-ifies nybbles from low-to-high order, and the H type specifies nybbles from high-to-low order. The B and H formats match the way you normally write out num-bers.

Examples

When you experiment with `binary format` and `binary scan`, remember that Tcl treats things as strings by default. A "6", for example, is the character 6 with character code 54 or 0x36. The c type returns these character codes:

```
set input 6
binary scan $input "c" 6val
set 6val
=> 54
```

You can scan several character codes at a time:

```
binary scan abc "c3" list
=> 1
set list
=> 97 98 99
```

The previous example uses a single type key, so `binary scan` sets one corre-sponding Tcl variable. If you want each character code in a separate variable, use separate type keys:

```
binary scan abc "ccc" x y z
=> 3
set z
=> 99
```

Use the H format to get hexadecimal values:

```
binary scan 6 "H2" 6val
set 6val
=> 36
```

Use the a and A formats to extract fixed width fields. Here the * count is used to get all the rest of the string. Note that A trims trailing spaces:

```
binary scan "hello world " a3x2A* first second
puts "\"$first\" \"$second\""
=> "hel" " world"
```

Use the @ key to seek to a particular offset in a value. The following com-mand gets the second double-precision number from a vector. Assume the vector is read from a binary data file:

```
binary scan $vector "@8d" double
```

With `binary format`, the `a` and `A` types create fixed width fields. `A` pads its field with spaces, if necessary. The value is truncated if the string is too long:

```
binary format "A9A3" hello world
=> hello    wor
```

An array of floating point values can be created with this command:

```
binary format "f*" 1.2 3.45 7.43 -45.67 1.03e4
```

Remember that floating point values are always in native format, so you have to read them on the same type of machine that they were created. With integer data you specify either big-endian or little-endian formats. The `tcl_platform` variable described on page 193 can tell you the byte order of the current platform.

Binary Data and File I/O

When working with binary data in files, you need to turn off the newline translations and character set encoding that Tcl performs automatically. These are described in more detail on pages 120 and 219. For example, if you are generating binary data, the following command puts your standard output in binary mode:

```
fconfigure stdout -translation binary -encoding binary
puts [binary format "B8" 11001010]
```

Related Chapters

- To learn more about manipulating data in Tcl, read about lists in Chapter 5 and arrays in Chapter 8.
- For more about pattern matching, read about regular expressions in Chapter 11.
- For more about file I/O, see Chapter 9.
- For information on Unicode and other Internationalization issues, see Chapter 15.

Tcl Lists

This chapter describes Tcl lists. Tcl commands described are: `list`, `lindex`, `llength`, `lrange`, `lappend`, `linsert`, `lreplace`, `lsearch`, `lset`, `lsort`, `concat`, `join`, **and** `split`.

Lists in Tcl have the same structure as Tcl commands. All the rules you learned about grouping arguments in Chapter 1 apply to creating valid Tcl lists. However, when you work with Tcl lists, it is best to think of lists in terms of operations instead of syntax. Tcl commands provide operations to put values into a list, get elements from lists, count the elements of lists, replace elements of lists, and so on. It is a good habit to use commands like `list` and `lappend` to construct lists, instead of creating them by hand. Lists are used with commands such as `foreach` that take lists as arguments. In addition, lists are important when you are building up a command to be evaluated later. Delayed command evaluation with `eval` is described in Chapter 10, and similar issues with Tk callback commands are described in Chapter 30.

However, Tcl lists are not often the right way to build complicated data structures in scripts. You may find Tcl arrays more useful, and they are the topic of Chapter 8. List operations are also not right for handling unstructured data such as user input. Use regular expressions instead, which are described in Chapter 11.

Tcl Lists

A Tcl list is a sequence of values. When you write out a list, it has the same syntax as a Tcl command. A list has its elements separated by white space. Braces or quotes can be used to group words with white space into a single list element. Because of the relationship between lists and commands, the list-related commands described in this chapter are used often when constructing Tcl commands.

Since Tcl 8.0, lists are really 1-dimensional object arrays.

Early versions of Tcl represented all values as strings. Lists were just strings with special syntax to group their elements. The string representation was parsed on each list access, so you could have performance problems with large lists. The performance of lists was improved by the Tcl compiler added in Tcl 8.0. The Tcl runtime now stores lists using an C array of pointers to each element. (The `Tcl_Obj` type is described on page 694.) Tcl can access any element in the list with the same cost. Appending new elements to a list is made efficient by over allocating the array so there is room to grow. The internal format also records the number of list elements, so getting the length of a list is cheap. However, you can still get into performance trouble if you use a big Tcl list like a string, e.g., for output. Tcl will convert the list into a string representation if you print it to a file, or manipulate it with string commands. Table 5–1 describes Tcl commands for lists.

Table 5–1 List-related commands.

`list arg1 arg2 ...`	Creates a list out of all its arguments.
`lindex list ?i ...?`	Returns the *i*th element from `list`. Specifying multiple index elements allows you to descend into nested lists easily.
`llength list`	Returns the number of elements in `list`.
`lrange list i j`	Returns the *i*th through *j*th elements from `list`.
`lappend listVar arg ...`	Appends elements to the value of `listVar`.
`linsert list index arg arg ...`	Inserts elements into `list` before the element at position `index`. Returns a new list.
`lreplace list i j arg arg ...`	Replaces elements *i* through *j* of `list` with the `args`. Returns a new list.
`lsearch ?options? list value`	Returns the index of the element in `list` that matches the `value` according to the `options`. Glob matching is the default. Returns -1 if not found.
`lset listVar ?i ...? newValue`	Set the *i*th element in variable `listVar` to `newValue`. (Tcl 8.4)
`lsort ?switches? list`	Sorts elements of the list according to the switches: `-ascii`, `-dictionary`, `-integer`, `-real`, `-increasing`, `-decreasing`, `-index ix`, `-unique`, `-command command`. Returns a new list.
`concat list list ...`	Joins multiple lists together into one list.
`join list joinString`	Merges the elements of a list together by separating them with `joinString`.
`split string splitChars`	Splits a string up into list elements, using the characters in `splitChars` as boundaries between list elements.

Constructing Lists

Constructing a list can be tricky if you try to write the proper list syntax by hand. The manual approach works for simple cases. In more complex cases, however, you should use Tcl commands that build lists. Using list commands eliminates the struggle to get the grouping and quoting right, and the list is maintained in an efficient internal format. If you create lists by hand with quoting, there is additional overhead to parse the string representation the first time you use the list.

The `list` command

The `list` command constructs a list out of its arguments so that there is one list element for each argument. The simple beauty of `list` is that any special characters in the list elements do not matter. Spaces inside an element do not cause it to become more than one list element. The `list` command is efficient, too. It doesn't matter if `list` is making a list of three single-character values, or three 10 kilobyte values. The cost to make that three element list is the same in either case. The most compelling uses of list involve making lists out of variables that could have arbitrary values, as shown in Example 5–1.

Example 5–1 Constructing a list with the `list` command.

```
set x {1 2}
=> 1 2
set y \$foo
=> $foo
set l1 [list $x "a b" $y]
=> {1 2} {a b} {$foo}
set l2 [list $l1 $x]
=> {{1 2} {a b} {$foo}} {1 2}
```

The `list` command does automatic quoting.
The first list, `l1`, has three elements. The values of the elements do not affect the list structure. The second list, `l2`, has two elements, the value of `l1` and the value of `x`. Internally Tcl shares values instead of making copies, so constructing lists out of other values is quite efficient.

When you first experiment with Tcl lists, the treatment of curly braces can be confusing. In the assignment to `x`, for example, the curly braces disappear. However, they seem to come back again when `$x` is put into a bigger list. Also, the double quotes around `a b` get changed into curly braces. What's going on? There are three steps in the process. In the first step, the Tcl parser groups arguments to the `list` command. In the grouping process, the braces and quotes are syntax that define groups. These syntax characters get stripped off. The braces and quotes are not part of the values being grouped. In the second step, the `list` command creates an internal list structure. This is an array of references to each value. In the third step the value is printed out. This step requires conversion of the list into a string representation. The string representation of the list uses curly braces to group values back into list elements.

The `lappend` Command

The `lappend` command is used to append elements to the end of a list. The first argument to `lappend` is the name of a Tcl variable, and the rest of the arguments are added to the variable's value as new list elements. Like `list`, `lappend` operates efficiently on the internal representation of the list value. It is always more efficient to use `lappend` than to try and append elements by hand.

Example 5–2 Using `lappend` to add elements to a list.

```
lappend new 1 2
=> 1 2
lappend new 3 "4 5"
=> 1 2 3 {4 5}
set new
=> 1 2 3 {4 5}
```

The `lappend` command is unique among the list-related commands because its first argument is the name of a list-valued variable, while all the other commands take list values as arguments. You can call `lappend` with the name of an undefined variable and the variable will be created.

The `lset` Command

The `lset` command was introduced in Tcl 8.4 to make it easier, and more efficient, to set one element of a list or nested list. Like `lappend`, the first argument to `lset` is the name of a list variable. The last argument is the value to set. The middle arguments, if any, specify which element to set. If no index is specified, the whole variable is set to the new value. If the index is a single integer, or end-*integer*, then that element of the list is set. If you have a nested list, then you can specify several indices, and each one navigates into the nested list structure. This is illustrated in Example 5–3. If you specify several indices they can be separate arguments, or grouped into a list. Range checking in `lset` is strict and an error will be thrown for indices given outside of the list or sublist range. The new value of the list in the variable is returned, although you rarely need this because `lset` modifies the list variable directly.

Example 5–3 Using `lset` to set an element of a list.

```
lset new "a b c"
=> a b c
lset new 1 "d e"
=> a {d e} c
lset new 1 0 "g h"
=> a {{g h} e} c
```

The concat Command

The `concat` command is useful for splicing lists together. It works by concatenating its arguments, separating them with spaces. This joins multiple lists into one list where the top-level list elements in each input list become top-level list elements in the resulting list:

Example 5–4 Using `concat` to splice lists together.

```
set x {4 5 6}
set y {2 3}
set z 1
concat $z $y $x
=> 1 2 3 4 5 6
```

Double quotes behave much like the `concat` command. In simple cases, double quotes behave exactly like `concat`. However, the `concat` command trims extra white space from the end of its arguments before joining them together with a single separating space character. Example 5–5 compares the use of `list`, `concat`, and double quotes:

Example 5–5 Double quotes compared to the `concat` and `list` commands.

```
set x {1 2}
=> 1 2
set y "$x 3"
=> 1 2 3
set y [concat $x 3]
=> 1 2 3
set s { 2 }
=>  2
set y "1 $s 3"
=> 1  2  3
set y [concat 1 $s 3]
=> 1 2 3
set z [list $x $s 3]
=> {1 2} { 2 } 3
```

The distinction between `list` and `concat` becomes important when Tcl commands are built dynamically. The basic rule is that `list` and `lappend` preserve list structure, while `concat` (or double quotes) eliminates one level of list structure. The distinction can be subtle because there are examples where `list` and `concat` return the same results. Unfortunately, this can lead to data-dependent bugs. Throughout the examples of this book, you will see the `list` command used to safely construct lists. This issue is discussed more in Chapter 10.

Getting List Elements: `llength`, `lindex`, and `lrange`

The `llength` command returns the number of elements in a list.

```
llength {a b {c d} "e f g" h}
=> 5
llength {}
=> 0
```

The `lindex` command returns a particular element of a list. It takes an index; list indices count from zero.

```
set x {1 2 3}
lindex $x 1
=> 2
```

You can use the keyword `end` to specify the last element of a list, or the syntax `end-N` to count back from the end of the list. The following commands are equivalent ways to get the element just before the last element in a list.

```
lindex $list [expr {[llength $list] - 2}]
lindex $list end-1
```

The `lrange` command returns a range of list elements. It takes a list and two indices as arguments. Again, `end` or `end-N` can be used as an index:

```
lrange {1 2 3 {4 5}} 2 end
=> 3 {4 5}
```

Modifying Lists: `linsert` and `lreplace`

The `linsert` command inserts elements into a list value at a specified index. If the index is zero or less, then the elements are added to the front. If the index is equal to or greater than the length of the list, then the elements are appended to the end. Otherwise, the elements are inserted before the element that is currently at the specified index. The following command adds to the front of a list:

```
linsert {1 2} 0 new stuff
=> new stuff 1 2
```

`lreplace` replaces a range of list elements with new elements. If you don't specify any new elements, you effectively delete elements from a list.

Note: `linsert` and `lreplace` do not modify an existing list like the `lappend` and `lset` commands. Instead, they return a new list value. In the Example 5–6, the `lreplace` command does not change the value of x:

Example 5–6 Modifying lists with `lreplace`.

```
set x [list a {b c} e d]
=> a {b c} e d
lreplace $x 1 2 B C
=> a B C d
lreplace $x 0 0
=> {b c} e d
```

Searching Lists: `lsearch`

`lsearch` returns the index of a value in the list, or -1 if it is not present. `lsearch` supports pattern matching in its search. Simple pattern matching is the default, and this can be disabled with the `-exact` option. The glob pattern matching `lsearch` uses is described in more detail on page 53. The `-regexp` option lets you specify the list value with a regular expression. Regular expressions are described in Chapter 11.

In the following example, the glob pattern `l*` matches the value `list`, and `lsearch` returns the index of that element in the input list:

```
lsearch {here is a list} l*
=> 3
```

Example 5–7 shows `ldelete` as a combination of `lreplace` and `lsearch`:

Example 5–7 Deleting a list element by value.

```
proc ldelete { list value } {
    set ix [lsearch -exact $list $value]
    if {$ix >= 0} {
        return [lreplace $list $ix $ix]
    } else {
        return $list
    }
}
```

Tcl 8.4 added several features to `lsearch`, including typed searching, optimized searches for sorted lists, and the ability to find all matching elements of a list. The `lsearch` typed searches use the internal object representation for efficiency and speed. For example, if you have a list of numbers, the `-integer` option tells `lsearch` to leave the values in their native integer format. Otherwise it would convert them to strings as it did the search. If your list has been sorted, the `-sorted` option tells `lsearch` to perform an efficient binary search. Sorting lists is described on page 70.

The `-inline` option returns the list value instead of the index. This is most useful when you are matching a pattern, and it works well with the `-all` option that returns all matching indices, or values:

```
set foo {the quick brown fox jumped over a lazy dog}
lsearch -inline -all $foo *o*
=> brown fox over dog
```

The `lsearch` options are described in Table 5-2:

Table 5–2 Options to the `lsearch` command.

`-all`	Search for all items that match and return a list of matching indices.
`-ascii`	The list elements are to be compared as ascii strings. Only meaningful when used with `-exact` or `-sorted`.
`-decreasing`	Assume list elements are in decreasing order. Only meaningful when used with `-sorted`.
`-dictionary`	The list elements are to be compared using dictionary-style comparison. Only meaningful when used with `-exact` or `-sorted`.
`-exact`	Do exact string matching. Mutually exclusive with `-glob` and `-regexp`.
`-glob`	Do glob-style pattern matching (default). Mutually exclusive with `-exact` and `-regexp`.
`-increasing`	Assume list elements are in increasing order. Only meaning when used with `-sorted`.
`-inline`	Return the actual matching element(s) instead of the index to the element. An empty string is returned if no elements match.
`-integer`	The list elements are to be compared as integers. Only meaning when used with `-exact` or `-sorted`.
`-not`	Negate the sense of the match.
`-real`	Examine all elements as real (floating-point) values. Only meaning when used with `-exact` or `-sorted`.
`-regexp`	Do regular expression pattern matching. Mutually exclusive with `-exact` and `-glob`. Regular expressions are described in Chapter 11.
`-sorted`	Specifies that the list is presorted, so Tcl can do a faster binary search to find the pattern.
`-start ix`	Specify the start index in the list to begin searching.

Sorting Lists: `lsort`

You can sort a list in a variety of ways with `lsort`. The list is not sorted in place. Instead, a new list value is returned. The basic types of sorts are specified with the `-ascii`, `-dictionary`, `-integer`, or `-real` options. The `-increasing` or `-decreasing` option indicate the sorting order. The default option set is `-ascii -increasing`. An ASCII sort uses character codes, and a dictionary sort folds together case and treats digits like numbers. For example:

```
lsort -ascii {a Z n2 n100}
=> Z a n100 n2
lsort -dictionary {a Z n2 n100}
=> a n2 n100 Z
```

You can provide your own sorting function for special-purpose sorting. For example, suppose you have a list of names, where each element is itself a list containing the person's first name, middle name (if any), and last name. The default sorts by everyone's first name. If you want to sort by their last name, you need to supply a sorting command.

Example 5–8 Sorting a list using a comparison function.

```
proc NameCompare {a b} {
    set alast [lindex $a end]
    set blast [lindex $b end]
    set res [string compare $alast $blast]
    if {$res != 0} {
        return $res
    } else {
        return [string compare $a $b]
    }
}
set list {{Brent B. Welch} {John Ousterhout} {Miles Davis}}
=> {Brent B. Welch} {John Ousterhout} {Miles Davis}
lsort -command NameCompare $list
=> {Miles Davis} {John Ousterhout} {Brent B. Welch}
```

The `NameCompare` procedure extracts the last element from each of its arguments and compares those. If they are equal, then it just compares the whole of each argument.

Tcl 8.0 added a `-index` option to `lsort` that can be used to sort lists on an index. Instead of using `NameCompare`, you could do this:

```
lsort -index end $list
```

Tcl 8.3 added a `-unique` option that removes duplicates during sort:

```
lsort -unique {a b a z c b}
=> a b c z
```

The `split` Command

The `split` command takes a string and turns it into a list by breaking it at specified characters and ensuring that the result has the proper list syntax. The `split` command provides a robust way to turn input lines into proper Tcl lists:

```
set line {welch:*:28405:100:Brent Welch:/usr/welch:/bin/csh}
split $line :
=> welch * 28405 100 {Brent Welch} /usr/welch /bin/csh
lindex [split $line :] 4
=> Brent Welch
```

Do not use list operations on arbitrary data.

Even if your data has space-separated words, you should be careful when using list operators on arbitrary input data. Otherwise, stray double quotes or curly braces in the input can result in invalid list structure and errors in your script. Your code will work with simple test cases, but when invalid list syntax appears in the input, your script will raise an error. The next example shows what happens when input is not a valid list. The syntax error, an unmatched quote, occurs in the middle of the list. However, you cannot access any of the list because the lindex command tries to convert the value to a list before returning any part of it.

Example 5–9 Use split to turn input data into Tcl lists.

```
set line {this is "not a tcl list}
lindex $line 1
=> unmatched open quote in list
lindex [split $line] 2
=> "not
```

The default separator character for split is white space, which contains spaces, tabs, and newlines. If there are multiple separator characters in a row, these result in empty list elements; the separators are not collapsed. The following command splits on commas, periods, spaces, and tabs. The backslash–space sequence is used to include a space in the set of characters. You could also group the argument to split with double quotes:

```
set line "\tHello, world."
split $line \ ,.\t
=> {} Hello {} world {}
```

A trick that splits each character into a list element is to specify an empty string as the split character. This lets you get at individual characters with list operations:

```
split abc {}
=> a b c
```

However, if you write scripts that process data one character at a time, they may run slowly. Read Chapter 11 about regular expressions for hints on really efficient string processing and using regexp for a multi-character split routine.

The join Command

The join command is the inverse of split. It takes a list value and reformats it with specified characters separating the list elements. In doing so, it removes any curly braces from the string representation of the list that are used to group the top-level elements. For example:

```
join {1 {2 3} {4 5 6}} :
=> 1:2 3:4 5 6
```

If the treatment of braces is puzzling, remember that the first value is parsed into a list. The braces around element values disappear in the process. Example 5–10 shows a way to implement join in a Tcl procedure, which may help to understand the process:

Example 5–10 Implementing `join` in Tcl.

```
proc join {list sep} {
    set s {}  ;# s is the current separator
    set result {}
    foreach x $list {
        append result $s $x
        set s $sep
    }
    return $result
}
```

Related Chapters

- Arrays are the other main data structure in Tcl. They are described in Chapter 8.
- List operations are used when generating Tcl code dynamically. Chapter 10 describes these techniques when using the `eval` command.
- The `foreach` command loops over the values in a list. It is described on page 79 in Chapter 6.

Control Structure Commands

This chapter describes the Tcl commands that implement control structures: if, switch, foreach, while, for, break, continue, catch, error, and return.

*C*ontrol structure in Tcl is achieved with commands, just like everything else. There are looping commands: while, foreach, and for. There are conditional commands: if and switch. There is an error handling command: catch. Finally, there are some commands to fine-tune control structures: break, continue, return, and error.

A control structure command often has a command body that is executed later, either conditionally or in a loop. In this case, it is important to group the command body with curly braces to avoid substitutions at the time the control structure command is invoked. Group with braces, and let the control structure command trigger evaluation at the proper time. A control structure command returns the value of the last command it chose to execute.

Another pleasant property of curly braces is that they group things together while including newlines. The examples use braces in a way that is both readable and convenient for extending the control structure commands across multiple lines.

Commands like if, for, and while involve boolean expressions. They use the expr command internally, so there is no need for you to invoke expr explicitly to evaluate their boolean test expressions.

If Then Else

The `if` command is the basic conditional command. If an expression is true, then execute one command body; otherwise, execute another command body. The second command body (the `else` clause) is optional. The syntax of the command is:

        if *expression* ?then? *body1* ?else? ?*body2*?

The `then` and `else` keywords are optional. In practice, I omit `then` but use `else` as illustrated in the next example. I always use braces around the command bodies, even in the simplest cases:

Example 6–1 A conditional `if then else` command.

```
if {$x == 0} {
    puts stderr "Divide by zero!"
} else {
    set slope [expr $y/$x]
}
```

Curly brace positioning is important.

The style of this example takes advantage of the way the Tcl interpreter parses commands. Recall that newlines are command terminators, except when the interpreter is in the middle of a group defined by braces or double quotes. The stylized placement of the opening curly brace at the end of the first and third lines exploits this property to extend the `if` command over multiple lines.

The first argument to `if` is a boolean expression. As a matter of style this expression is grouped with curly braces. The expression evaluator performs variable and command substitution on the expression. Using curly braces ensures that these substitutions are performed at the proper time. It is possible to be lax in this regard, with constructs such as:

        if $x break continue

This is a sloppy, albeit legitimate, `if` command that will either break out of a loop or continue with the next iteration depending on the value of variable x. This style is fragile and error prone. Instead, always use braces around the command bodies to avoid trouble later when you modify the command. The following is much better (use `then` if it suits your taste):

```
if {$x} {
    break
} else {
    continue
}
```

When you are testing the result of a command, you can get away without using curly braces around the command, like this:

        if [*command*] *body1*

However, it turns out that you can execute the `if` statement more efficiently if you always group the expression with braces, like this:

        if {[*command*]} *body1*

You can create chained conditionals by using the `elseif` keyword. Again, note the careful placement of curly braces that create a single `if` command:

Example 6–2 Chained conditional with `elseif`.

```
if {$key < 0} {
    incr range 1
} elseif {$key == 0} {
    return $range
} else {
    incr range -1
}
```

Any number of conditionals can be chained in this manner. However, the `switch` command provides a more powerful way to test multiple conditions.

Switch

The `switch` command is used to branch to one of many command bodies depending on the value of an expression. The choice can be made on the basis of pattern matching as well as simple comparisons. Pattern matching is discussed in more detail in Chapter 4 and Chapter 11. The general form of the command is:

```
switch flags value pat1 body1 pat2 body2 ...
```

Any number of pattern-body pairs can be specified. If multiple patterns match, only the body of the first matching pattern is evaluated. You can also group all the pattern-body pairs into one argument:

```
switch flags value { pat1 body1 pat2 body2 ... }
```

The first form allows substitutions on the patterns but will require backslashes to continue the command onto multiple lines. This is shown in Example 6–4 on page 78. The second form groups all the patterns and bodies into one argument. This makes it easy to group the whole command without worrying about newlines, but it suppresses any substitutions on the patterns. This is shown in Example 6–3. In either case, you should always group the command bodies with curly braces so that substitution occurs only on the body with the pattern that matches the value.

There are four possible flags that determine how *value* is matched.

`-exact`	Matches the *value* exactly to one of the patterns. This is the default.
`-glob`	Uses glob-style pattern matching. See page 53.
`-regexp`	Uses regular expression pattern matching. See page 144.
`--`	No flag (or end of flags). Necessary when *value* can begin with -.

The `switch` command raises an error if any other flag is specified or if the *value* begins with -. In practice I always use the `--` flag before *value* so that I don't have to worry about that problem.

If the pattern associated with the last body is `default`, then this command body is executed if no other patterns match. The `default` keyword works only on the last pattern-body pair. If you use the `default` pattern on an earlier body, it will be treated as a pattern to match the literal string `default`:

Example 6–3 Using `switch` for an exact match.

```
switch -exact -- $value {
    foo { doFoo; incr count(foo) }
    bar { doBar; return $count(foo)}
    default { incr count(other) }
}
```

If you have variable references or backslash sequences in the patterns, then you cannot use braces around all the pattern-body pairs. You must use backslashes to escape the newlines in the command:

Example 6–4 Using `switch` with substitutions in the patterns.

```
switch -regexp -- $value \
    ^$key { body1 }\
    \t### { body2 }\
    {[0-9]*} { body3 }
```

In this example, the first and second patterns have substitutions performed to replace `$key` with its value and `\t` with a tab character. The third pattern is quoted with curly braces to prevent command substitution; square brackets are part of the regular expression syntax, too. (See page Chapter 11.)

If the body associated with a pattern is just a dash, -, then the `switch` command "falls through" to the body associated with the next pattern. You can tie together any number of patterns in this manner.

Example 6–5 A `switch` with "fall through" cases.

```
switch -glob -- $value {
    X* -
    Y* { takeXorYaction $value }
}
```

Comments in `switch` Commands

A comment can occur only where the Tcl parser expects a command to begin. This restricts the location of comments in a `switch` command. You must put them inside the command body associated with a pattern, as shown in Example 6–6. If you put a comment at the same level as the patterns, the `switch` command will try to interpret the comment as one or more pattern-body pairs.

Example 6–6 Comments in `switch` commands.

```
switch -- $value {
    # this comment confuses switch
    pattern { # this comment is ok }
}
```

While

The `while` command takes two arguments, a test and a command body:

    while booleanExpr body

The `while` command repeatedly tests the boolean expression and then executes the body if the expression is true (nonzero). Because the test expression is evaluated again before each iteration of the loop, it is crucial to protect the expression from any substitutions before the `while` command is invoked. The following is an infinite loop (see also Example 1–13 on page 12):

    set i 0 ; while $i<10 {incr i}

The following behaves as expected:

    set i 0 ; while {$i<10} {incr i}

It is also possible to put nested commands in the boolean expression. The following example uses `gets` to read standard input. The `gets` command returns the number of characters read, returning -1 upon end of file. Each time through the loop, the variable `line` contains the next line in the file:

Example 6–7 A `while` loop to read standard input.

```
set numLines 0 ; set numChars 0
while {[gets stdin line] >= 0} {
    incr numLines
    incr numChars [string length $line]
}
```

Foreach

The `foreach` command loops over a command body assigning one or more loop variables to each of the values in one or more lists. Multiple loop variables, which were introduced in Tcl 7.5, are a very useful feature. The syntax for the simple case of a single variable and a single list is:

    foreach loopVar valueList commandBody

The first argument is the name of a variable, and the command body is executed once for each element in the list with the loop variable taking on successive values in the list. The list can be entered explicitly, as in the next example:

Example 6–8 Looping with `foreach`.

```
set i 1
foreach value {1 3 5 7 11 13 17 19 23} {
    set i [expr $i*$value]
}
set i
=> 111546435
```

It is also common to use a list-valued variable or command result instead of a static list value. The next example loops through command-line arguments. The variable `argv` is set by the Tcl interpreter to be a list of the command-line arguments given when the interpreter was started:

Example 6–9 Parsing command-line arguments.

```
# argv is set by the Tcl shells
# possible flags are:
# -max integer
# -force
# -verbose
set state flag
set force 0
set verbose 0
set max 10
foreach arg $argv {
    switch -- $state {
        flag {
            switch -glob -- $arg {
                -f*    {set force 1}
                -v*    {set verbose 1}
                -max   {set state max}
                default {error "unknown flag $arg"}
            }
        }
        max {
            set max $arg
            set state flag
        }
    }
}
```

The loop uses the `state` variable to keep track of what is expected next, which in this example is either a flag or the integer value for `-max`. The `--` flag to `switch` is *required* in this example because the `switch` command complains about a bad flag if the pattern begins with a `-` character. The `-glob` option lets the user abbreviate the `-force` and `-verbose` options.

 If the list of values is to contain variable values or command results, then the `list` command should be used to form the list. Avoid double quotes because if any values or command results contain spaces or braces, the list structure will be reparsed, which can lead to errors or unexpected results.

Example 6–10 Using `list` with `foreach`.

```
foreach x [list $a $b [foo]] {
    puts stdout "x = $x"
}
```

The loop variable x will take on the value of a, the value of b, and the result of the `foo` command, regardless of any special characters or whitespace in those values.

Multiple Loop Variables

You can have more than one loop variable with `foreach`. Suppose you have two loop variables x and y. In the first iteration of the loop, x gets the first value from the value list and y gets the second value. In the second iteration, x gets the third value and y gets the fourth value. This continues until there are no more values. If there are not enough values to assign to all the loop variables, the extra variables get the empty string as their value.

Example 6–11 Multiple loop variables with `foreach`.

```
foreach {key value} {orange 55 blue 72 red 24 green} {
    puts "$key: $value"
}
orange: 55
blue: 72
red: 24
green:
```

If you have a command that returns a short list of values, then you can abuse the `foreach` command to assign the results of the commands to several variables all at once. For example, suppose the command `MinMax` returns two values as a list: the minimum and maximum values. Here is one way to get the values:

```
set result [MinMax $list]
set min [lindex $result 0]
set max [lindex $result 1]
```

The `foreach` command lets us do this much more compactly:

```
foreach {min max} [MinMax $list] {break}
```

The `break` in the body of the `foreach` loop guards against the case where the command returns more values than we expected. This trick is encapsulated into the `lassign` procedure in Example 10–4 on page 139.

Multiple Value Lists

The `foreach` command has the ability to loop over multiple value lists in parallel. In this case, each value list can also have one or more variables. The `foreach` command keeps iterating until all values are used from all value lists. If a value list runs out of values before the last iteration of the loop, its corresponding loop variables just get the empty string for their value.

Example 6–12 Multiple value lists with `foreach`.

```
foreach {k1 k2} {orange blue red green black} value {55 72 24} {
    puts "$k1 $k2: $value"
}
orange blue: 55
red green: 72
black : 24
```

For

The `for` command is similar to the C `for` statement. It takes four arguments:

```
for initial test final body
```

The first argument is a command to initialize the loop. The second argument is a boolean expression that determines whether the loop body will execute. The third argument is a command to execute after the loop body:

Example 6–13 A `for` loop.

```
for {set i 0} {$i < 10} {incr i 3} {
    lappend aList $i
}
set aList
=> 0 3 6 9
```

You could use `for` to iterate over a list, but you should really use `foreach` instead. Code like the following is slow and cluttered:

```
for {set i 0} {$i < [llength $list]} {incr i} {
    set value [lindex $list $i]
}
```

This is the same as:

```
foreach value $list {
}
```

Break and Continue

You can control loop execution with the break and continue commands. The break command causes immediate exit from a loop, while the continue command causes the loop to continue with the next iteration. There is no goto command in Tcl.

Catch

Until now we have ignored the possibility of errors. In practice, however, a command will raise an error if it is called with the wrong number of arguments, or if it detects some error condition particular to its implementation. An uncaught error aborts execution of a script.[*] The catch command is used to trap such errors. It takes two arguments:

```
catch command ?resultVar?
```

The first argument to catch is a command body. The second argument is the name of a variable that will contain the result of the command, or an error message if the command raises an error. catch returns zero if there was no error caught, or a nonzero error code if it did catch an error.

You should use curly braces to group the command instead of double quotes because catch invokes the full Tcl interpreter on the command. If double quotes are used, an extra round of substitutions occurs before catch is even called. The simplest use of catch looks like the following:

```
catch { command }
```

A more careful catch phrase saves the result and prints an error message:

Example 6–14 A standard catch phrase.

```
if {[catch { command arg1 arg2 ... } result]} {
    puts stderr $result
} else {
    # command was ok, result contains the return value
}
```

A more general catch phrase is shown in the next example. Multiple commands are grouped into a command body. The errorInfo variable is set by the Tcl interpreter after an error to reflect the stack trace from the point of the error:

---

[*] More precisely, the Tcl script unwinds and the current Tcl_Eval procedure in the C runtime library returns TCL_ERROR. There are three cases. In interactive use, the Tcl shell prints the error message. In Tk, errors that arise during event handling trigger a call to bgerror, a Tcl procedure you can implement in your application. In your own C code, you should check the result of Tcl_Eval and take appropriate action in the case of an error.

Example 6–15 A longer `catch` phrase.

```
if {[catch {
    command1
    command2
    command3
} result]} {
    global errorInfo
    puts stderr $result
    puts stderr "*** Tcl TRACE ***"
    puts stderr $errorInfo
} else {
    # command body ok, result of last command is in result
}
```

These examples have not grouped the call to `catch` with curly braces. This is acceptable because `catch` always returns an integer, so the `if` command will parse correctly. However, if we had used `while` instead of `if`, then curly braces would be necessary to ensure that the `catch` phrase was evaluated repeatedly.

Catching More Than Errors

The `catch` command catches more than just errors. If the command body contains `return`, `break`, or `continue` commands, these terminate the command body and are reflected by `catch` as nonzero return codes. You need to be aware of this if you try to isolate troublesome code with a `catch` phrase. An innocent looking `return` command will cause the `catch` to signal an apparent error. The next example uses `switch` to find out exactly what `catch` returns. Nonerror cases are passed up to the surrounding code by invoking `return`, `break`, or `continue`:

Example 6–16 There are several possible return values from `catch`.

```
switch [catch {
    command1
    command2
    ...
} result] {
    0 {                          # Normal completion }
    1 {                          # Error case }
    2 { return $result    ;# return from procedure}
    3 { break             ;# break out of the loop}
    4 { continue          ;# continue loop}
    default {                    # User-defined error codes }
}
```

Error

The error command raises an error condition that terminates a script unless it is trapped with the catch command. The command takes up to three arguments:

        error *message ?info? ?code?*

The *message* becomes the error message stored in the result variable of the catch command.

If the *info* argument is provided, then the Tcl interpreter uses this to initialize the errorInfo global variable. That variable is used to collect a stack trace from the point of the error. If the *info* argument is not provided, then the error command itself is used to initialize the errorInfo trace.

Example 6–17 Raising an error.

```
proc foo {} {
    error bogus
}
foo
=> bogus
set errorInfo
=> bogus
    while executing
"error bogus"
    (procedure "foo" line 2)
    invoked from within
"foo"
```

In the previous example, the error command itself appears in the trace. One common use of the info argument is to preserve the errorInfo that is available after a catch. In the next example, the information from the original error is preserved:

Example 6–18 Preserving errorInfo when calling error.

```
if {[catch {foo} result]} {
    global errorInfo
    set savedInfo $errorInfo
    # Attempt to handle the error here, but cannot...
    error $result $savedInfo
}
```

The *code* argument specifies a concise, machine-readable description of the error. It is stored into the global errorCode variable. It defaults to NONE. Many of the file system commands return an errorCode that has three elements: POSIX, the error name (e.g., ENOENT), and the associated error message:

        POSIX ENOENT {No such file or directory}

In addition, your application can define error codes of its own. Catch phrases can examine the code in the global errorCode variable and decide how to respond to the error.

Return

The `return` command is used to return from a procedure. It is needed if return is to occur before the end of the procedure body, or if a constant value needs to be returned. As a matter of style, I also use `return` at the end of a procedure, even though a procedure returns the value of the last command executed in the body.

Exceptional return conditions can be specified with some optional arguments to `return`. The complete syntax is:

```
return ?-code c? ?-errorinfo i? ?-errorcode ec? string
```

The `-code` option value is one of `ok`, `error`, `return`, `break`, `continue`, or an integer. `ok` is the default if `-code` is not specified.

The `-code error` option makes `return` behave much like the `error` command. The `-errorcode` option sets the global `errorCode` variable, and the `-errorinfo` option initializes the `errorInfo` global variable. When you use `return -code error`, there is no `error` command in the stack trace. Compare Example 6–17 with Example 6–19:

Example 6–19 Raising an error with `return`.

```
proc bar {} {
    return -code error bogus
}
catch {bar} result
=> 1
set result
=> bogus
set errorInfo
=> bogus
    while executing
"bar"
```

The `return`, `break`, and `continue` code options take effect in the caller of the procedure doing the exceptional return. If `-code return` is specified, then the calling procedure returns. If `-code break` is specified, then the calling procedure breaks out of a loop, and if `-code continue` is specified, then the calling procedure continues to the next iteration of the loop. These `-code` options to `return` enable the construction of new control structures entirely in Tcl. The following example implements the `break` command with a Tcl procedure:

```
proc break {} {
    return -code break
}
```

You can return integer-valued codes of your own with `return -code`, and trap them with `catch` in order to create your own control structures. There are also a number of exception packages available on the net that provide Java-like `try-catch-except` structures for Tcl, although the Tcl exception mechanism strikes a nice balance between simplicity and power.

Procedures and Scope

Procedures encapsulate a set of commands, and they introduce a local scope
for variables. Commands described are: proc, global, and upvar.

*P*rocedures parameterize a commonly used sequence of commands. In addition, each procedure has a new local scope for variables. The scope of a variable is the range of commands over which it is defined. Originally, Tcl had one global scope for shared variables, local scopes within procedures, and one global scope for procedures. Tcl 8.0 added *namespaces* that provide new scopes for procedures and global variables. For simple applications you can ignore namespaces and just use the global scope. Namespaces are described in Chapter 14.

The proc Command

A Tcl procedure is defined with the proc command. It takes three arguments:

```
proc name params body
```
The first argument is the procedure name, which is added to the set of commands understood by the Tcl interpreter. The name is case sensitive and can contain any characters. Procedure names do not conflict with variable names. The second argument is a list of parameter names. The last argument is the body of the procedure.

Once defined, a Tcl procedure is used just like any other Tcl command. When it is called, each argument is assigned to the corresponding parameter and the body is evaluated. The result of the procedure is the result returned by the last command in the body. The return command can be used to return a specific value.

Procedures can have default parameters so that the caller can leave out some of the command arguments. A default parameter is specified with its name and default value, as shown in the next example:

Example 7–1 Default parameter values.

```
proc P2 {a {b 7} {c -2} } {
    expr $a / $b + $c
}
P2 6 3
=> 0
```

Here the procedure P2 can be called with one, two, or three arguments. If it is called with only one argument, then the parameters b and c take on the values specified in the proc command. If two arguments are provided, then only c gets the default value, and the arguments are assigned to a and b. At least one argument and no more than three arguments can be passed to P2.

A procedure can take a variable number of arguments by specifying the args keyword as the last parameter. When the procedure is called, the args parameter is a list that contains all the remaining values:

Example 7–2 Variable number of arguments.

```
proc ArgTest {a {b foo} args} {
    foreach param {a b args} {
        puts stdout "\t$param = [set $param]"
    }
}
set x one
set y {two things}
set z \[special\$
ArgTest $x
=> a = one
   b = foo
   args =
ArgTest $y $z
=> a = two things
   b = [special$
   args =
ArgTest $x $y $z
=> a = one
   b = two things
   args = {[special$}
ArgTest $z $y $z $x
=> a = [special$
   b = two things
   args = {[special$} one
```

The effect of the list structure in args is illustrated by the treatment of variable z in Example 7–2. The value of z has special characters in it. When $z is passed as the value of parameter `b`, its value comes through to the procedure unchanged. When `$z` is part of the optional parameters, quoting is automatically added to create a valid Tcl list as the value of `args`. Example 10–3 on page 136 illustrates a technique that uses `eval` to undo the effect of the added list structure.

Changing Command Names with `rename`

The `rename` command changes the name of a command. There are two main uses for `rename`. The first is to augment an existing procedure. Before you redefine it with `proc`, rename the existing command:

```
rename foo foo.orig
```

From within the new implementation of `foo` you can invoke the original command as `foo.orig`. Existing users of `foo` will transparently use the new version.

The other thing you can do with `rename` is completely remove a command by renaming it to the empty string. For example, you might not want users to execute `UNIX` programs, so you could disable `exec` with the following command:

```
rename exec {}
```

Command renaming and deletion can be traced with the `trace` command described in Chapter 13.

Scope

By default there is a single, global scope for procedure names. This means that you can use a procedure anywhere in your script. Variables defined outside any procedure are global variables. However, as described below, global variables are not automatically visible inside procedures. There is a different namespace for variables and procedures, so you could have a procedure and a global variable with the same name without conflict. You can use the namespace facility described in Chapter 7 to manage procedures and global variables.

Each procedure has a local scope for variables. That is, variables introduced in the procedure live only for the duration of the procedure call. After the procedure returns, those variables are undefined. Variables defined outside the procedure are not visible to a procedure unless the `upvar` or `global` scope commands are used. You can also use qualified names to name variables in a namespace scope. The `global` and `upvar` commands are described later in this chapter. Qualified names are described on page 208. If the same variable name exists in an outer scope, it is unaffected by the use of that variable name inside a procedure.

In Example 7–3, the variable `a` in the global scope is different from the parameter `a` to `P1`. Similarly, the global variable `b` is different from the variable `b` inside `P1`:

Example 7–3 Variable scope and Tcl procedures.

```
set a 5
set b -8
proc P1 {a} {
    set b 42
    if {$a < 0} {
        return $b
    } else {
        return $a
    }
}
P1 $b
=> 42
P1 [expr {$a*2}]
=> 10
```

The global Command

Global scope is the toplevel scope. This scope is outside of any procedure. Variables defined at the global scope must be made accessible to the commands inside a procedure by using the global command. The syntax for global is:

> global *varName1 varName2 ...*

The global command goes inside a procedure.

The global command adds a global variable to the current scope. A common mistake is to have a single global command and expect that to apply to all procedures. However, a global command in the global scope has no effect. Instead, you must put a global command in all procedures that access the global variable. The variable can be undefined at the time the global command is used. When the variable is defined, it becomes visible in the global scope.

Example 7–4 shows a random number generator. Before we look at the example, let me point out that the best way to get random numbers in Tcl is to use the rand() math function:

> expr rand()
>
> => .137287362934

The point of the example is to show a state variable, the seed, that has to persist between calls to random, so it is kept in a global variable. The choice of randomSeed as the name of the global variable associates it with the random number generator. It is important to pick names of global variables carefully to avoid conflict with other parts of your program. For comparison, Example 14–1 on page 206 uses namespaces to hide the state variable:

Example 7–4 A random number generator.[*]

```
proc RandomInit { seed } {
    global randomSeed
    set randomSeed $seed
}
proc Random {} {
    global randomSeed
    set randomSeed [expr ($randomSeed*9301 + 49297) % 233280]
    return [expr $randomSeed/double(233280)]
}
proc RandomRange { range } {
    expr int([Random]*$range)
}
RandomInit [pid]
=> 5049
Random
=> 0.517686899863
Random
=> 0.217176783265
RandomRange 100
=> 17
```

Call by Name Using upvar

Use the upvar command when you need to pass the name of a variable, as opposed to its value, into a procedure. The upvar command associates a local variable with a variable in a scope up the Tcl call stack. The syntax of the upvar command is:

```
upvar ?level? varName localvar
```

The *level* argument is optional, and it defaults to 1, which means one level up the Tcl call stack. You can specify some other number of frames to go up, or you can specify an absolute frame number with a *#number* syntax. Level #0 is the global scope, so the global foo command is equivalent to:

```
upvar #0 foo foo
```

The variable in the uplevel stack frame can be either a scalar variable, an array element, or an array name. In the first two cases, the local variable is treated like a scalar variable. In the case of an array name, then the local variable is treated like an array. The use of upvar and arrays is discussed further in Chapter 8 on page 99. The following procedure uses upvar to print the value of a variable given its name.

---

[*] Adapted from *Exploring Expect* by Don Libes, O'Reilly & Associates, Inc., 1995, and from *Numerical Recipes in C* by Press et al., Cambridge University Press, 1988.

Example 7–5 Print variable by name.

```
proc PrintByName { varName } {
    upvar 1 $varName var
    puts stdout "$varName = $var"
}
```

You can use `upvar` to fix the `incr` command. One drawback of the built-in `incr` is that it raises an error if the variable does not exist. We can define a new version of `incr` that initializes the variable if it does not already exist:

Example 7–6 Improved `incr` procedure.

```
proc incr { varName {amount 1}} {
    upvar 1 $varName var
    if {[info exists var]} {
        set var [expr $var + $amount]
    } else {
        set var $amount
    }
    return $var
}
```

Variable Aliases with `upvar`

The `upvar` command is useful in any situation where you have the name of a variable stored in another variable. In Example 7–2 on page 88, the loop variable `param` holds the names of other variables. Their value is obtained with this construct:

```
        puts stdout "\t$param = [set $param]"
```

Another way to do this is to use `upvar`. It eliminates the need to use awkward constructs like `[set $param]`. If the variable is in the same scope, use zero as the scope number with `upvar`. The following is equivalent:

```
        upvar 0 $param x
        puts stdout "\t$param = $x"
```

Associating State with Data

Suppose you have a program that maintains state about a set of objects like files, URLs, or people. You can use the name of these objects as the name of a variable that keeps state about the object. The `upvar` command makes this more convenient:

```
        upvar #0 $name state
```

Using the name directly like this is somewhat risky. If there were an object named x, then this trick might conflict with an unrelated variable named x elsewhere in your program. You can modify the name to make this trick more robust:

```
upvar #0 state$name state
```

Your code can pass *name* around as a handle on an object, then use `upvar` to get access to the data associated with the object. Your code is just written to use the `state` variable, which is an alias to the state variable for the current object. This technique is illustrated in Example 17–7 on page 245.

Namespaces and `upvar`

You can use `upvar` to create aliases for namespace variables, too. Namespaces are described in Chapter 14. For example, as an alternative to reserving all global variables beginning with `state`, you can use a namespace to hide these variables:

```
upvar #0 state::$name state
```

Now `state` is an alias to the namespace variable. This `upvar` trick works from inside any namespace.

Commands That Take Variable Names

Several Tcl commands involve variable names. For example, the Tk widgets can be associated with a global Tcl variable. The `vwait` and `tkwait` commands also take variable names as arguments.

Upvar aliases do not work with Tk widget text variables.

The aliases created with `upvar` do not work with these commands, nor do they work if you use `trace`, which is described on page 193. Instead, you must use the actual name of the global variable. To continue the above example where `state` is an alias, you cannot:

```
vwait state(foo)
button .b -textvariable state(foo)
```

Instead, you must

```
vwait state$name\(foo)
button .b -textvariable state$name\(foo)
```

The backslash turns off the array reference so Tcl does not try to access `name` as an array. You do not need to worry about special characters in `$name`, except parentheses. Once the name has been passed into the Tk widget it will be used directly as a variable name. Text variables for labels are explained on page 490, and text variables for entry widgets are illustrated in Example 34–1 on page 508.

Tcl Arrays

This chapter describes Tcl arrays, which provide a flexible mechanism to build many other data structures in Tcl. Tcl command described is: `array`.

An array is a Tcl variable with a string-valued index. You can think of the index as a key, and the array as a collection of related data items identified by different keys. The index, or key, can be any string value. Internally, an array is implemented with a hash table, so the cost of accessing each array element is about the same. Before Tcl 8.0, arrays had a performance advantage over lists that took time to access proportional to the size of the list.

The flexibility of arrays makes them an important tool for the Tcl programmer. A common use of arrays is to manage a collection of variables, much as you use a C struct or Pascal record. This chapter shows how to create several simple data structures using Tcl arrays.

Array Syntax

The index of an array is delimited by parentheses. The index can have any string value, and it can be the result of variable or command substitution. Array elements are defined with `set`:

```
set arr(index) value
```

The value of an array element is obtained with `$` substitution:

```
set foo $arr(index)
```

Example 8–1 uses the loop variable value `$i` as an array index. It sets `arr(x)` to the product of $1 * 2 * \ldots * x$:

Example 8–1 Using arrays.

```
set arr(0) 1
for {set i 1} {$i <= 10} {incr i} {
    set arr($i) [expr {$i * $arr([expr {$i-1}])}]
}
```

Complex Indices

An array index can be any string, like `orange`, `5`, `3.1415`, or `foo,bar`. The examples in this chapter, and in this book, often use indices that are pretty complex strings to create flexible data structures. As a rule of thumb, you can use any string for an index, but avoid using a string that contains spaces.

Parentheses are not a grouping mechanism.

The main Tcl parser does not know about array syntax. All the rules about grouping and substitution described in Chapter 1 are still the same in spite of the array syntax described here. Parentheses do not group like curly braces or quotes, which is why a space causes problems. If you have complex indices, use a comma to separate different parts of the index. If you use a space in an index instead, then you have a quoting problem. The space in the index needs to be quoted with a backslash, or the whole variable reference needs to be grouped:

```
set {arr(I'm asking for trouble)} {I told you so.}
set arr(I'm\ asking\ for\ trouble) {I told you so.}
```

If the array index is stored in a variable, then there is no problem with spaces in the variable's value. The following works well:

```
set index {I'm asking for trouble}
set arr($index) {I told you so.}
```

Array Variables

You can use an array element as you would a simple variable. For example, you can test for its existence with `info exists`, increment its value with `incr`, and append elements to it with `lappend`:

```
if {[info exists stats($event)]} {incr stats($event)}
```

You can delete an entire array, or just a single array element with `unset`. Using `unset` on an array is a convenient way to clear out a big data structure.

It is an error to use a variable as both an array and a normal variable. The following is an error:

```
set arr(0) 1
set arr 3
=> can't set "arr": variable is array
```

The name of the array can be the result of a substitution. This is a tricky situation, as shown in Example 8–2:

Example 8–2 Referencing an array indirectly.

```
set name TheArray
=> TheArray
set ${name}(xyz) {some value}
=> some value
set x $TheArray(xyz)
=> some value
set x ${name}(xyz)
=> TheArray(xyz)
set x [set ${name}(xyz)]
=> some value
```

A better way to deal with this situation is to use the `upvar` command, which is introduced on page 91. The previous example is much cleaner when `upvar` is used:

Example 8–3 Referencing an array indirectly using `upvar`.

```
set name TheArray
=> TheArray
upvar 0 $name a
set a(xyz) {some value}
=> some value
set x $TheArray(xyz)
=> some value
```

The `array` Command

The `array` command returns information about array variables. The `array names` command returns the index names that are defined in the array. If the array variable is not defined, then `array names` just returns an empty list. It allows easy iteration through an array with a `foreach` loop:

```
foreach index [array names arr pattern] {
    # use arr($index)
}
```

The order of the names returned by `array names` is arbitrary. It is essentially determined by the hash table implementation of the array. You can limit what names are returned by specifying a *pattern* that matches indices. The pattern is the kind supported by the `string match` command, which is described on page 53.

It is also possible to iterate through the elements of an array one at a time using the search-related commands listed in Table 8–1. The ordering is also random, and I find the `foreach` over the results of `array names` much more convenient. If your array has an extremely large number of elements, or if you need to manage an iteration over a long period of time, then the array search operations might be more appropriate. Frankly, I never use them. Table 8–1 summarizes the `array` command:

Table 8–1 The `array` command.

`array exists arr`	Returns 1 if `arr` is an array variable.
`array get arr ?pattern?`	Returns a list that alternates between an index and the corresponding array value. `pattern` selects matching indices. If not specified, all indices and values are returned.
`array names arr ?mode? ?pattern?`	Returns the list of all indices defined for `arr`, or those that match `pattern`. `mode` specifies the pattern type and may be `-exact`, `-glob` (default) or `-regexp`.
`array set arr list`	Initializes the array `arr` from `list`, which has the same form as the list returned by `array get`.
`array size arr`	Returns the number of indices defined for `arr`.
`array unset arr ?pattern?`	Unset elements in `arr` matching the specified glob-style `pattern`. If not specified, unset `arr`. (Tcl 8.3)
`array startsearch arr`	Returns a search token for a search through `arr`.
`array nextelement arr id`	Returns the value of the next element in `arr` in the search identified by the token `id`. Returns an empty string if no more elements remain in the search.
`array anymore arr id`	Returns 1 if more elements remain in the search.
`array donesearch arr id`	Ends the search identified by `id`.
`array statistics arr`	Returns statistics about the array hash table. (Tcl 8.4)

Converting Between Arrays and Lists

The `array get` and `array set` operations are used to convert between an array and a list. The list returned by `array get` has an even number of elements. The first element is an index, and the next is the corresponding array value. The list elements continue to alternate between index and value. The list argument to `array set` must have the same structure.

```
array set fruit {
    best    kiwi
    worst   peach
    ok      banana
}
array get fruit
=> ok banana best kiwi worst peach
```

Another way to loop through the contents of an array is to use `array get` and the two-variable form of the `foreach` command.

```
foreach {key value} [array get fruit] {
    # key is ok, best, or worst
    # value is some fruit
}
```

Passing Arrays by Name

The `upvar` command works on arrays. You can pass an array name to a procedure and use the `upvar` command to get an indirect reference to the array variable in the caller's scope. This is illustrated in Example 8–4, which inverts an array. As with `array names`, you can specify a pattern to `array get` to limit what part of the array is returned. This example uses `upvar` because the array names are passed into the `ArrayInvert` procedure. The inverse array does not need to exist before you call `ArrayInvert`.

Example 8–4 `ArrayInvert` inverts an array.

```
proc ArrayInvert {arrName inverseName {pattern *}} {
    upvar $arrName array $inverseName inverse
    foreach {index value} [array get array $pattern] {
        set inverse($value) $index
    }
}
```

Building Data Structures with Arrays

This section describes several data structures you can build with Tcl arrays. These examples are presented as procedures that implement access functions to the data structure. Wrapping up your data structures in procedures is good practice. It shields the user of your data structure from the details of its implementation.

Use arrays to collect related variables.

A good use for arrays is to collect together a set of related variables for a module, much as one would use a record in other languages. By collecting these together in an array that has the same name as the module, name conflicts between different modules are avoided. Also, in each of the module's procedures, a single `global` statement will suffice to make all the state variables visible. You can also use `upvar` to manage a collection of arrays, as shown in Example 8–9 on page 101.

Simple Records

Suppose we have a database of information about people. The following examples show three different ways to store the employee name, ID, manager, and phone number. Each example implements `Emp_AddRecord` that stores the values, and one example accessor function that returns information about the employee (e.g., `Emp_Manager`.) By using simple procedures to return fields of the record, the implementation is hidden so that you can change it more easily. Example 8–5 uses on array for each field. The name of the person is the index into each array:

Example 8–5 Using arrays for records, version 1.

```
proc Emp_AddRecord {id name manager phone} {
    global employeeID employeeManager \
        employeePhone employeeName
    set employeeID($name) $id
    set employeeManager($name) $manager
    set employeePhone($name) $phone
    set employeeName($id) $name
}
proc Emp_Manager {name} {
    global employeeManager
    return $employeeManager($name)
}
```

The employeeName array provides a secondary key. It maps from the employee ID to the name so that the other information can be obtained if you have an ID instead of a name. Example 8–6 implements the same little database using a single array with more complex indices:

Example 8–6 Using arrays for records, version 2.

```
proc Emp_AddRecord {id name manager phone} {
    global employee
    set employee(id,$name) $id
    set employee(manager,$name) $manager
    set employee(phone,$name) $phone
    set employee(name,$id) $name
}
proc Emp_Manager {name} {
    global employee
    return $employee(manager,$name)
}
```

Example 8–7 shows the last approach. Each array element is a list of fields, and the accessor functions hide the lindex command used to pick out the right field. Here the cross referencing by ID is implement differently. If we can assume that names and IDs are distinct, we can keep the cross reference in the same array:

Example 8–7 Using arrays for records, version 3.

```
proc Emp_AddRecord {id name manager phone} {
    global employee
    set employee($name) [list $name $id $manager $phone]
    set employee($id) $name
}
proc Emp_Manager {name} {
    global employee
    return [lindex $employee($name) 2]
}
```

The difference between these three approaches is partly a matter of taste. Using a single array can be more convenient because there are fewer variables to manage. Using the lists for the fields is probably the most space efficient because there are fewer elements in the array, but maintaining the `lindex` offsets is tedious. In any case, you should hide the implementation in a small set of procedures.

A Stack

A stack can be implemented with either a list or an array. If you use a list, then the push and pop operations have a runtime cost that is proportional to the size of the stack. If the stack has a few elements this is fine. If there are a lot of items in a stack, you may wish to use arrays instead.

Example 8–8 Using a list to implement a stack.

```
proc Push { stack value } {
    upvar $stack list
    lappend list $value
}
proc Pop { stack } {
    upvar $stack list
    set value [lindex $list end]
    set list [lrange $list 0 [expr [llength $list]-2]]
    return $value
}
```

In these examples, the name of the stack is a parameter, and `upvar` is used to convert that into the data used for the stack. The variable is a list in Example 8–8 and an array in Example 8–9. The user of the stack module does not have to know.

The array implementation of a stack uses one array element to record the number of items in the stack. The other elements of the array have the stack values. The `Push` and `Pop` procedures both guard against a nonexistent array with the `info exists` command. When the first assignment to `S(top)` is done by `Push`, the array variable is created in the caller's scope. The example uses array indices in two ways. The `top` index records the depth of the stack. The other indices are numbers, so the construct `$S($S(top))` is used to reference the top of the stack.

Example 8–9 Using an array to implement a stack.

```
proc Push { stack value } {
    upvar $stack S
    if {![info exists S(top)]} {
        set S(top) 0
    }
    set S($S(top)) $value
    incr S(top)
}
```

```
proc Pop { stack } {
    upvar $stack S
    if {![info exists S(top)]} {
        return {}
    }
    if {$S(top) == 0} {
        return {}
    } else {
        incr S(top) -1
        set x $S($S(top))
        unset S($S(top))
        return $x
    }
}
```

A List of Arrays

Suppose you have many arrays, each of which stores some data, and you want to maintain an overall ordering among the data sets. One approach is to keep a Tcl list with the name of each array in order. Example 8–10 defines `RecordInsert` to add an array to the list, and an iterator function, `RecordIterate`, that applies a script to each array in order. The iterator uses `upvar` to make `data` an alias for the current array. The script is executed with `eval`, which is described in detail in Chapter 10. The Tcl commands in `script` can reference the arrays with the name `data`:

Example 8–10 A list of arrays.

```
proc RecordAppend {listName arrayName} {
    upvar $listName list
    lappend list $arrayName
}
proc RecordIterate {listName script} {
    upvar $listName list
    foreach arrayName $list {
        upvar #0 $arrayName data
        eval $script
    }
}
```

Another way to implement this list-of-records structure is to keep references to the arrays that come before and after each record. Example 8–11 shows the insert function and the iterator function when using this approach. Once again, `upvar` is used to set up `data` as an alias for the current array in the iterator. In this case, the loop is terminated by testing for the existence of the next array. It is perfectly all right to make an alias with `upvar` to a nonexistent variable. It is also all right to change the target of the `upvar` alias. One detail that is missing from the example is the initialization of the very first record so that its `next` element is the empty string:

Example 8–11 A list of arrays.

```
proc RecordInsert {recName afterThis} {
    upvar $recName record $afterThis after
    set record(next) $after(next)
    set after(next) $recName
}
proc RecordIterate {firstRecord body} {
    upvar #0 $firstRecord data
    while {[info exists data]} {
        eval $body
        upvar #0 $data(next) data
    }
}
```

A Simple In-Memory Database

Suppose you have to manage a lot of records, each of which contain a large chunk of data and one or more key values you use to look up those values. The procedure to add a record is called like this:

```
Db_Insert keylist datablob
```

The `datablob` might be a name, value list suitable for passing to `array set`, or simply a large chunk of text or binary data. One implementation of `Db_Insert` might just be:

```
foreach key $keylist {
    lappend Db($key) $datablob
}
```

The problem with this approach is that it duplicates the data chunks under each key. A better approach is to use two arrays. One stores all the data chunks under a simple ID that is generated automatically. The other array stores the association between the keys and the data chunks. Example 8–12, which uses the namespace syntax described in Chapter 14, illustrates this approach. The example also shows how you can easily dump data structures by writing `array set` commands to a file, and then load them later with a `source` command:

Example 8–12 A simple in-memory database.

```
namespace eval db {
    variable data        ;# Array of data blobs
    variable uid 0       ;# Index into data
    variable index       ;# Cross references into data
}
proc db::insert {keylist datablob} {
    variable data
    variable uid
    variable index
    set data([incr uid]) $datablob
    foreach key $keylist {
        lappend index($key) $uid
```

```
        }
    }
    proc db::get {key} {
        variable data
        variable index
        set result {}
        if {![info exist index($key)]} {
            return {}
        }
        foreach uid $index($key) {
            lappend result $data($uid)
        }
        return $result
    }
    proc db::save {filename} {
        variable uid
        set out [open $filename w]
        puts $out [list namespace eval db \
            [list variable uid $uid]]
        puts $out [list array set db::data [array get db::data]]
        puts $out [list array set db::index [array get db::index]]
        close $out
    }
    proc db::load {filename} {
        source $filename
    }
```

Alternatives to Using Arrays

While Tcl arrays are flexible and general purpose, they are not always the best solution to your data structure problems. If you find yourself building elaborate data structures, you should consider implementing a C library to encapsulate the data structure and expose it to the scripting level with Tcl commands. For example, Chapter 47 implements a `blob` data structure in C. You can also use the SWIG code generator can quickly generate a Tcl command interface for a C API. Find out about SWIG at *http://www.swig.org*.

The Metakit embedded database provides an efficient, easy, scriptable database for Tcl. It is more powerful than the simple "flat file" databases implemented in this Chapter, but it is not a full SQL database. It is part of Tclkit, or you can use it with the `mk4tcl` extension. Tclkit and Metakit are described in Chapter 22.

Working with Files and Programs

This chapter describes how to run programs, examine the file system, and access environment variables through the env array. Tcl commands described are: exec, file, open, close, read, write, puts, gets, flush, seek, tell, glob, pwd, cd, exit, pid, and registry.

*T*his chapter describes how to run programs and access the file system from Tcl. These commands were designed for UNIX. In Tcl 7.5 they were implemented in the Tcl ports to Windows and Macintosh. There are facilities for naming files and manipulating file names in a platform-independent way, so you can write scripts that are portable across systems. These capabilities enable your Tcl script to be a general-purpose glue that assembles other programs into a tool that is customized for your needs. Tcl 8.4 added support for 64-bit file systems, where available.

Running Programs with exec

The exec command runs programs from your Tcl script.[*] For example:

```
set d [exec date]
```

The standard output of the program is returned as the value of the exec command. However, if the program writes to its standard error channel or exits with a nonzero status code, then exec raises an error. If you do not care about the exit status, or you use a program that insists on writing to standard error, then you can use catch to mask the errors:

```
catch {exec program arg arg} result
```

---

[*] Unlike other UNIX shell exec commands, the Tcl exec does not replace the current process with the new one. Instead, the Tcl library forks first and executes the program as a child process.

The `exec` command supports a full set of *I/O redirection* and *pipeline* syntax. Each process normally has three I/O channels associated with it: standard input, standard output, and standard error. With I/O redirection, you can divert these I/O channels to files or to I/O channels you have opened with the Tcl `open` command. A pipeline is a chain of processes that have the standard output of one command hooked up to the standard input of the next command in the pipeline. Any number of programs can be linked together into a pipeline.

Example 9–1 Using `exec` on a process pipeline.

```
set n [exec sort < /etc/passwd | uniq | wc -1 2> /dev/null]
```

Example 9–1 uses `exec` to run three programs in a pipeline. The first program is `sort`, which takes its input from the file `/etc/passwd`. The output of `sort` is piped into `uniq`, which suppresses duplicate lines. The output of `uniq` is piped into `wc`, which counts the lines. The error output of the command is diverted to the null device to suppress any error messages. Table 9–1 provides a summary of the syntax understood by the `exec` command.

Table 9–1 Summary of the `exec` syntax for I/O redirection.

`-keepnewline`	(First argument.) Do not discard trailing newline from the result.
`|`	Pipes standard output from one process into another.
`|&`	Pipes both standard output and standard error output.
`< fileName`	Takes input from the named file.
`<@ fileId`	Takes input from the I/O channel identified by `fileId`.
`<< value`	Takes input from the given `value`.
`> fileName`	Overwrites `fileName` with standard output.
`2> fileName`	Overwrites `fileName` with standard error output.
`>& fileName`	Overwrites `fileName` with both standard error and standard out.
`>> fileName`	Appends standard output to the named file.
`2>> fileName`	Appends standard error to the named file.
`>>& fileName`	Appends both standard error and standard output to the named file.
`>@ fileId`	Directs standard output to the I/O channel identified by `fileId`.
`2>@ fileId`	Directs standard error to the I/O channel identified by `fileId`.
`>&@ fileId`	Directs both standard error and standard output to the I/O channel.
`&`	As the last argument, indicates pipeline should run in background.

A trailing `&` causes the program to run in the background. In this case, the process identifier is returned by the `exec` command. Otherwise, the `exec` command blocks during execution of the program, and the standard output of the program is the return value of `exec`. The trailing newline in the output is trimmed off, unless you specify `-keepnewline` as the first argument to `exec`.

If you look closely at the I/O redirection syntax, you'll see that it is built up from a few basic building blocks. The basic idea is that `|` stands for pipeline, `>` for output, and `<` for input. The standard error is joined to the standard output by `&`. Standard error is diverted separately by using `2>`. You can use your own I/O channels by using `@`.

The `auto_noexec` Variable

The Tcl shell programs are set up during interactive use to attempt to execute unknown Tcl commands as programs. For example, you can get a directory listing by typing:

```
ls
```

instead of:

```
exec ls
```

This is handy if you are using the Tcl interpreter as a general shell. It can also cause unexpected behavior when you are just playing around. To turn this off, define the `auto_noexec` variable:

```
set auto_noexec anything
```

Limitations of `exec` on Windows

Windows 3.1 has an unfortunate combination of special cases that stem from console-mode programs, 16-bit programs, and 32-bit programs. In addition, pipes are really just simulated by writing output from one process to a temporary file and then having the next process read from that file. If `exec` or a process pipeline fails, it is because of a fundamental limitation of Windows. The good news is that Windows 98 and Windows NT cleaned up most of the problems with `exec`. Windows NT, Window 2000, and Windows XP are pretty robust.

Tcl 8.0p2 was the last release to officially support Windows 3.1. That release includes `Tcl1680.dll`, which is necessary to work with the win32s subsystem. If you copy that file into the same directory as the other Tcl DLLs, you may be able to use some later releases of Tcl on Windows 3.1. However, Tcl 8.3 completely removed support for win32s while adding support for Windows XP-64.

AppleScript on Macintosh

The `exec` command is not provided on the Macintosh. Tcl ships with an `AppleScript` extension that lets you control other Macintosh applications. You can find documentation in the `AppleScript.html` that goes with the distribution.

You must use `package require` to load the `AppleScript` command:

```
package require Tclapplescript
AppleScript junk
=> bad option "junk": must be compile, decompile, delete,
execute, info, load, run, or store.
```

The `file` Command

The `file` command provides several ways to check the status of files in the file system. For example, you can find out if a file exists, what type of file it is, and other file attributes. There are facilities for manipulating files in a platform-independent manner. Table 9–2 provides a summary of the various forms of the `file` command. They are described in more detail later. Note that several operations have been added since the introduction of the `file` command; the table indicates the version of Tcl in which they were added.

Table 9–2 The `file` command options.

`file atime name ?time?`	Returns access time as a decimal string. If *time* is specified, the access time of the file is set.
`file attributes name ?option? ?value? ...`	Queries or sets file attributes. (Tcl 8.0)
`file channels ?pattern?`	Returns the open channels in this interpreter, optionally filtered by the glob-style *pattern*. (Tcl 8.3)
`file copy ?-force? source destination`	Copies file *source* to file *destination*. The *source* and *destination* can be directories. (Tcl 7.6)
`file delete ?-force? name`	Deletes the named file. (Tcl 7.6)
`file dirname name`	Returns parent directory of file *name*.
`file executable name`	Returns 1 if *name* has execute permission, else 0.
`file exists name`	Returns 1 if *name* exists, else 0.
`file extension name`	Returns the part of *name* from the last dot (i.e., .) to the end. The dot is included in the return value.
`file isdirectory name`	Returns 1 if *name* is a directory, else 0.
`file isfile name`	Returns 1 if *name* is not a directory, symbolic link, or device, else 0.
`file join path path...`	Joins pathname components into a new pathname. (Tcl 7.5)

Table 9–2 The `file` command options. (Continued)

`file link ?-type?` `   name ?target?`	Returns the link pointed to by *name*, or creates a link to *target* if it is specified. *type* can be `-hard` or `-symbolic`. (Tcl 8.4)
`file lstat name var`	Places attributes of the link *name* into *var*.
`file mkdir name`	Creates directory *name*. (Tcl 7.6)
`file mtime name` `   ?time?`	Returns modify time of *name* as a decimal string. If *time* is specified, the modify time of the file is set.
`file nativename name`	Returns the platform-native version of *name*. (Tk 8.0).
`file normalize name`	Returns a unique, absolute, path for *name* while eliminating extra `/`, `/ .`, and `/ . .` components. (Tcl 8.4)
`file owned name`	Returns 1 if current user owns the file *name*, else 0.
`file pathtype name`	`relative`, `absolute`, or `volumerelative`. (Tcl 7.5)
`file readable name`	Returns 1 if *name* has read permission, else 0.
`file readlink name`	Returns the contents of the symbolic link *name*.
`file rename ?-force?` `   old new`	Changes the name of *old* to *new*. (Tcl 7.6)
`file rootname name`	Returns all but the extension of *name* (i.e., up to but not including the last `.` in *name*).
`file separator` `   ?name?`	Returns the default file separator character on this file system, or the separator character for *name* if it is specified. (Tcl 8.4)
`file size name`	Returns the number of bytes in *name*.
`file split name`	Splits *name* into its pathname components. (Tcl 7.5)
`file stat name var`	Places attributes of *name* into array *var*. The elements defined for *var* are listed in Table 9–3.
`file system name`	Returns a tuple of the filesystem for *name* (e.g. `native` or `vfs`) and the platform-specific type for *name* (e.g `NTFS` or `FAT32`). (Tcl 8.4)
`file tail name`	Returns the last pathname component of *name*.
`file type name`	Returns type identifier, which is one of: `file`, `directory`, `characterSpecial`, `blockSpecial`, `fifo`, `link`, or `socket`.
`file volumes name`	Returns the available file volumes on this computer. On Unix, this always returns `/`. On Windows, this would be a list like `{a:/ c:/}`. (Tcl 8.3)
`file writable name`	Returns 1 if *name* has write permission, else 0.

Cross-Platform File Naming

Files are named differently on UNIX, Windows, and Macintosh. UNIX separates file name components with a forward slash (/), Macintosh separates components with a colon (:), and Windows separates components with a backslash (\). In addition, the way that absolute and relative names are distinguished is different. For example, these are absolute pathnames for the Tcl script library (i.e., $tcl_library) on Macintosh, Windows, and UNIX, respectively:

```
Disk:System Folder:Extensions:Tool Command Language:tcl7.6
c:\Program Files\Tcl\lib\Tcl7.6
/usr/local/tcl/lib/tcl7.6
```

The good news is that Tcl provides operations that let you deal with file pathnames in a platform-independent manner. The file operations described in this chapter allow either native format or the UNIX naming convention. The backslash used in Windows pathnames is especially awkward because the back-slash is special to Tcl. Happily, you can use forward slashes instead:

```
c:/Program Files/Tcl/lib/Tcl7.6
```

There are some ambiguous cases that can be specified only with native pathnames. On my Macintosh, Tcl and Tk are installed in a directory that has a slash in it. You can name it only with the native Macintosh name:

```
Disk:Applications:Tcl/Tk 4.2
```

Another construct to watch out for is a leading // in a file name. This is the Windows syntax for network names that reference files on other computers. You can avoid accidentally constructing a network name by using the `file join` command described next. Of course, you can use network names to access remote files.

If you must communicate with external programs, you may need to construct a file name in the native syntax for the current platform. You can construct these names with `file join` described later. You can also convert a UNIX-like name to a native name with `file nativename`.

Several of the `file` operations operate on pathnames as opposed to returning information about the file itself. You can use the `dirname`, `extension`, `join`, `normalize`, `pathtype`, `rootname`, `split`, and `tail` operations on any string; there is no requirement that the pathnames refer to an existing file.

Building up Pathnames: `file join`

You can get into trouble if you try to construct file names by simply joining components with a slash. If part of the name is in native format, joining things with slashes will result in incorrect pathnames on Macintosh and Windows. The same problem arises when you accept user input. The user is likely to provide file names in native format. For example, this construct will not create a valid pathname on the Macintosh because $tcl_library is in native format:

```
set file $tcl_library/init.tcl
```

Use `file join` to construct file names.

The platform-independent way to construct file names is with `file join`. The following command returns the name of the `init.tcl` file in native format:

```
set file [file join $tcl_library init.tcl]
```

The `file join` operation can join any number of pathname components. In addition, it has the feature that an absolute pathname overrides any previous components. For example (on UNIX), `/b/c` is an absolute pathname, so it overrides any paths that come before it in the arguments to `file join`:

```
file join a b/c d
=> a/b/c/d
file join a /b/c d
=> /b/c/d
```

On Macintosh, a relative pathname starts with a colon, and an absolute pathname does not. To specify an absolute path, you put a trailing colon on the first component so that it is interpreted as a volume specifier. These relative components are joined into a relative pathname:

```
file join a :b:c d
=> :a:b:c:d
```

In the next case, `b:c` is an absolute pathname with `b:` as the volume specifier. The absolute name overrides the previous relative name:

```
file join a b:c d
=> b:c:d
```

The file join operation converts UNIX-style pathnames to native format. For example, on Macintosh you get this:

```
file join /usr/local/lib
=> usr:local:lib
```

Chopping Pathnames: `split`, `dirname`, `tail`

The `file split` command divides a pathname into components. It is the inverse of `file join`. The `split` operation detects automatically if the input is in native or UNIX format. The results of `file split` may contain some syntax to help resolve ambiguous cases when the results are passed back to `file join`. For example, on Macintosh a UNIX-style pathname is split on slash separators. The Macintosh syntax for a volume specifier (`Disk:`) is returned on the leading component:

```
file split "/Disk/System Folder/Extensions"
=> Disk: {System Folder} Extensions
```

A common reason to split up pathnames is to divide a pathname into the directory part and the file part. This task is handled directly by the `dirname` and `tail` operations. The `dirname` operation returns the parent directory of a pathname, while `tail` returns the trailing component of the pathname:

```
file dirname /a/b/c
=> /a/b
```

```
file tail /a/b/c
=> c
```

For a pathname with a single component, the `dirname` option returns ".", on UNIX and Windows, or ":" on Macintosh. This is the name of the current directory.

The `extension` and `root` options are also complementary. The `extension` option returns everything from the last period in the name to the end (i.e., the file suffix including the period.) The `root` option returns everything up to, but not including, the last period in the pathname:

```
file root /a/b.c
=> /a/b
file extension /a/b.c
=> .c
```

Manipulating Files and Directories

Tcl 7.6 added file operations to copy files, delete files, rename files, and create directories. In earlier versions it was necessary to `exec` other programs to do these things, except on Macintosh, where `cp`, `rm`, `mv`, `mkdir`, and `rmdir` were built in. These commands are no longer supported on the Macintosh. Your scripts should use the `file` command operations described below to manipulate files in a platform-independent way.

File name patterns are not directly supported by the `file` operations. Instead, you can use the `glob` command described on page 122 to get a list of file names that match a pattern.

Copying Files

The `file copy` operation copies files and directories. The following example copies *file1* to *file2*. If *file2* already exists, the operation raises an error unless the `-force` option is specified:

```
file copy ?-force? file1 file2
```

Several files can be copied into a destination directory. The names of the source files are preserved. The `-force` option indicates that files under *directory* can be replaced:

```
file copy ?-force? file1 file2 ... directory
```

Directories can be recursively copied. The `-force` option indicates that files under *dir2* can be replaced:

```
file copy ?-force? dir1 dir2
```

Creating Directories

The `file mkdir` operation creates one or more directories:

```
file mkdir dir dir ...
```

It is *not* an error if the directory already exists. Furthermore, intermediate directories are created if needed. This means that you can always make sure a directory exists with a single `mkdir` operation. Suppose `/tmp` has no subdirectories at all. The following command creates `/tmp/sub1` and `/tmp/sub1/sub2`:

```
file mkdir /tmp/sub1/sub2
```

The `-force` option is not understood by `file mkdir`, so the following command accidentally creates a folder named `-force`, as well as one named `oops`.

```
file mkdir -force oops
```

Symbolic and Hard Links

The `file link` operation allows the user to manipulate links. Hard links are directory entries that directly reference an existing file or directory. Symbolic (i.e., soft) links are files that contain the name of another file or directory. Generally, opening a link opens the file referenced by the link. Operating system support for links varies. Unix supports both types of links. Classic Macintosh only supports symbolic links (i.e., aliases). Windows 95/98/ME do not support links at all, while Windows NT/2000/XP support symbolic links to directories and hard links to files.

With only a single argument, `file link` returns the value of a symbolic link, or raises an error if the file is not a symbolic link. With two pathname arguments, the first is the name of the link, and the second is the name of the file referenced by the link. If you leave out the `-hard` or `-symbolic`, the appropriate link type is created for the current platform:

```
file link the_link the_existing_file
```

Deleting Files

The `file delete` operation deletes files and directories. It is *not* an error if the files do not exist. A non-empty directory is not deleted unless the `-force` option is specified, in which case it is recursively deleted:

```
file delete ?-force? name name ...
```

To delete a file or directory named `-force`, you must specify a nonexistent file before the `-force` to prevent it from being interpreted as a flag (`-force -force` won't work):

```
file delete xyzzy -force
```

Renaming Files and Directories

The `file rename` operation changes a file's name from *old* to *new*. The `-force` option causes *new* to be replaced if it already exists.

```
file rename ?-force? old new
```

Using `file rename` is the best way to update an existing file. First, generate the new version of the file in a temporary file. Then, use `file rename` to replace the old version with the new version. This ensures that any other programs that access the file will not see the new version until it is complete.

File Attributes

There are several file operations that return specific file attributes: `atime`, `executable`, `exists`, `isdirectory`, `isfile`, `mtime`, `owned`, `readable`, `readlink`, `size` and `type`. Refer to Table 9–2 on page 108 for their function. The following command uses `file mtime` to compare the modify times of two files. If you have ever resorted to piping the results of *ls -l* into *awk* in order to derive this information in other shell scripts, you will appreciate this example:

Example 9–2 Comparing file modify times.

```
proc newer { file1 file2 } {
    if {![file exists $file2]} {
        return 1
    } else {
        # Assume file1 exists
        expr {[file mtime $file1] > [file mtime $file2]}
    }
}
```

You can use the optional *time* argument to mtime and atime to set the file's time attributes, like the Unix `touch` command. The `stat` and `lstat` operations return a collection of file attributes. They take a third argument that is the name of an array variable, and they initialize that array with elements that contain the file attributes. If the file is a symbolic link, then the `lstat` operation returns information about the link itself and the `stat` operation returns information about the target of the link.

Table 9–3 Array elements defined by `file stat`.

`atime`	The last access time, in seconds.
`ctime`	The last change time (not the create time), in seconds.
`dev`	The device identifier, an integer.
`gid`	The group owner, an integer.
`ino`	The file number (i.e., inode number), an integer.
`mode`	The permission bits.
`mtime`	The last modify time, in seconds.
`nlink`	The number of links, or directory references, to the file.
`size`	The number of bytes in the file.
`type`	`file`, `directory`, `characterSpecial`, `blockSpecial`, `fifo`, `link`, or `socket`.
`uid`	The owner's user ID, an integer.

The array elements are listed in Table 9–3. All the element values are decimal strings, except for `type`, which can have the values returned by the `type` option. The element names are based on the UNIX `stat` system call. Use the `file attributes` command described later to get other platform-specific attributes.

Example 9–3 uses the device (`dev`) and inode (`ino`) attributes of a file to determine whether two pathnames reference the same file. These attributes are UNIX specific; they are not well defined on Windows and Macintosh.

Example 9–3 Determining whether pathnames reference the same file.

```
proc fileeq { path1 path2 } {
    file stat $path1 stat1
    file stat $path2 stat2
    expr {$stat1(ino) == $stat2(ino) && \
          $stat1(dev) == $stat2(dev)}
}
```

The `file attributes` operation was added in Tcl 8.0 to provide access to platform-specific attributes. The `attributes` operation lets you set and query attributes. The interface uses option-value pairs. With no options, all the current values are returned.

```
file attributes book.doc
=> -creator FRAM -hidden 0 -readonly 0 -type MAKR
```

These Macintosh attributes are explained in Table 9–4. The four-character type codes used on Macintosh are illustrated on page 600. With a single option, only that value is returned:

```
file attributes book.doc -readonly
=> 0
```

The attributes are modified by specifying one or more option–value pairs. Setting attributes can raise an error if you do not have the right permissions:

```
file attributes book.doc -readonly 1 -hidden 0
```

Table 9–4 Platform-specific file attributes.

`-permissions` *mode*	File permission bits. *mode* is an octal number or symbolic representation (e.g. a+x) with bits defined by the chmod system call, or a simplified ls-style string of the form rwxrwxrwx (must be 9 characters). (UNIX)
`-group` *ID*	The group owner of the file. (UNIX)
`-owner` *ID*	The owner of the file. (UNIX)
`-archive` *bool*	The archive bit, which is set by backup programs. (Windows)
`-system` *bool*	If set, then you cannot remove the file. (Windows)
`-longname`	The long (expanded) version of the pathname. Read-only. (Windows)
`-shortname`	The short (8.3) version of the pathname. Read-only. (Windows)

Table 9–4 Platform-specific file attributes. (Continued)

-hidden *bool*	If set, then the file does not appear in listings. (Windows, Macintosh)
-readonly *bool*	If set, then you cannot write the file. (Windows, Macintosh)
-creator *type*	*type* is 4-character code of creating application. (Macintosh)
-type *type*	*type* is 4-character type code. (Macintosh)

Input/Output Command Summary

The following sections describe how to open, read, and write files. The basic model is that you open a file, read or write it, then close the file. Network sockets also use the commands described here. Socket programming is discussed in Chapter 17, and more advanced *event-driven* I/O is described in Chapter 16. Table 9–5 lists the basic commands associated with file I/O:

Table 9–5 Tcl commands used for file access.

open *what* ?*access*? ?*permissions*?	Returns channel ID for a file or pipeline.
puts ?-nonewline? ?*channel*? *string*	Writes a string.
gets *channel* ?*varname*?	Reads a line.
read *channel* ?*numBytes*?	Reads *numBytes* bytes, or all data.
read -nonewline *channel*	Reads all bytes and discard the last \n.
tell *channel*	Returns the seek offset.
seek *channel offset* ?*origin*?	Sets the seek offset. *origin* is one of start, current, or end.
eof *channel*	Queries end-of-file status.
flush *channel*	Writes buffers of a channel.
close *channel*	Closes an I/O channel.

Opening Files for I/O

The open command sets up an I/O channel to either a file or a pipeline of processes. The return value of open is an identifier for the I/O channel. Store the result of open in a variable and use the variable as you used the stdout, stdin, and stderr identifiers in the examples so far. The basic syntax is:

open *what* ?*access*? ?*permissions*?

The *what* argument is either a file name or a pipeline specification similar to that used by the exec command. The *access* argument can take two forms, either a short character sequence that is compatible with the fopen library routine, or a list of POSIX access flags. Table 9–6 summarizes the first form, while Table 9–7 summarizes the POSIX flags. If *access* is not specified, it defaults to read.

Example 9–4 Opening a file for writing.

```
set fileId [open /tmp/foo w 0600]
puts $fileId "Hello, foo!"
close $fileId
```

The *permissions* argument is a value used for the permission bits on a newly created file. UNIX uses three bits each for the owner, group, and everyone else. The bits specify read, write, and execute permission. These bits are usually specified with an octal number, which has a leading zero, so that there is one octal digit for each set of bits. The default permission bits are 0666, which grant read/write access to everybody. Example 9–4 specifies 0600 so that the file is readable and writable only by the owner. 0775 would grant read, write, and execute permissions to the owner and group, and read and execute permissions to everyone else. You can set other special properties with additional high-order bits. Consult the UNIX manual page on *chmod* command for more details.

Table 9–6 Summary of the open access arguments.

r	Opens for reading. The file must exist.
r+	Opens for reading and writing. The file must exist.
w	Opens for writing. Truncate if it exists. Create if it does not exist.
w+	Opens for reading and writing. Truncate or create.
a	Opens for writing. Data is appended to the file.
a+	Opens for reading and writing. Data is appended.

Table 9–7 Summary of POSIX flags for the access argument.

RDONLY	Opens for reading.
WRONLY	Opens for writing.
RDWR	Opens for reading and writing.
APPEND	Opens for append.
CREAT	Creates the file if it does not exist.
EXCL	If CREAT is also specified, then the file cannot already exist.
NOCTTY	Prevents terminal devices from becoming the controlling terminal.
NONBLOCK	Does not block during the open.
TRUNC	Truncates the file if it exists.

The following example illustrates how to use a list of POSIX access flags to open a file for reading and writing, creating it if needed, and not truncating it. This is something you cannot do with the simpler form of the access argument:

```
set fileId [open /tmp/bar {RDWR CREAT}]
```

Catch errors from open.

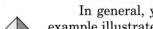

In general, you should check for errors when opening files. The following example illustrates a catch phrase used to open files. Recall that catch returns 1 if it catches an error; otherwise, it returns zero. It treats its second argument as the name of a variable. In the error case, it puts the error message into the variable. In the normal case, it puts the result of the command into the variable:

Example 9–5 A more careful use of open.

```
if [catch {open /tmp/data r} fileId] {
    puts stderr "Cannot open /tmp/data: $fileId"
} else {
    # Read and process the file, then...
    close $fileId
}
```

Opening a Process Pipeline

You can open a process pipeline by specifying the pipe character, |, as the first character of the first argument. The remainder of the pipeline specification is interpreted just as with the exec command, including input and output redirection. The second argument determines which end of the pipeline open returns. The following example runs the UNIX *sort* program on the password file, and it uses the split command to separate the output lines into list elements:

Example 9–6 Opening a process pipeline.

```
set input [open "|sort /etc/passwd" r]
set contents [split [read $input] \n]
close $input
```

You can open a pipeline for both read and write by specifying the r+ access mode. In this case, you need to worry about buffering. After a puts, the data may still be in a buffer in the Tcl library. Use the flush command to force the data out to the spawned processes before you try to read any output from the pipeline. You can also use the fconfigure command described on page 233 to force line buffering. Remember that read-write pipes will not work at all with Windows 3.1 because pipes are simulated with files. Event-driven I/O is also very useful with pipes. It means you can do other processing while the pipeline executes, and simply respond when the pipe generates data. This is described in Chapter 16.

Expect

If you are trying to do sophisticated things with an external application, you will find that the *Expect* extension provides a much more powerful interface than a process pipeline. *Expect* adds Tcl commands that are used to control interactive applications. It is extremely useful for automating a variety of applications such as ssh, Telnet, and programs under test. Tcl is able to handle simple FTP sessions, telnet and many command line controllable applications, but *Expect* has extra control at the tty level that is essential for certain applications. It comes on some systems as a specially built Tcl shell named *expect*, and it is also available as an extension that you can dynamically load into Tcl shells with:

```
package require Expect
```

Expect was created by Don Libes at the National Institute of Standards and Technology (NIST). *Expect* is described in *Exploring Expect* (Libes, O'Reilly & Associates, Inc., 1995). You can find the software on the CD and on the web at:

```
http://expect.nist.gov/
```

Reading and Writing

The standard I/O channels are already open for you. There is a standard input channel, a standard output channel, and a standard error output channel. These channels are identified by stdin, stdout, and stderr, respectively. Other I/O channels are returned by the open command, and by the socket command described on page 239.

There may be cases when the standard I/O channels are not available. The *wish* shells on Windows and Macintosh have no standard I/O channels. Some UNIX window managers close the standard I/O channels when you start programs from window manager menus. You can also close the standard I/O channels with close.

The puts and gets Commands

The puts command writes a string and a newline to the output channel. There are a couple of details about the puts command that we have not yet used. It takes a -nonewline argument that prevents the newline character that is normally appended to the output channel. This is used in the prompt example below. The second feature is that the channel identifier is optional, defaulting to stdout if not specified. Note that you must use flush to force output of a partial line. This is illustrated in Example 9–7.

Example 9–7 Prompting for input.

```
puts -nonewline "Enter value: "
flush stdout ;# Necessary to get partial line output
set answer [gets stdin]
```

The gets command reads a line of input, and it has two forms. In the previous example, with just a single argument, gets returns the line read from the specified I/O channel. It discards the trailing newline from the return value. If end of file is reached, an empty string is returned. You must use the eof command to tell the difference between a blank line and end-of-file. eof returns 1 if there is end of file. Given a second *varName* argument, gets stores the line into a named variable and returns the number of bytes read. It discards the trailing newline, which is not counted. A -1 is returned if the channel has reached the end of file.

Example 9–8 A read loop using gets.

```
while {[gets $channel line] >= 0} {
    # Process line
}
close $channel
```

The read Command

The read command reads blocks of data, and this capability is often more efficient. There are two forms for read: You can specify the -nonewline argument or the *numBytes* argument, but not both. Without *numBytes*, the whole file (or what is left in the I/O channel) is read and returned. The -nonewline argument causes the trailing newline to be discarded. Given a byte count argument, read returns that amount, or less if there is not enough data in the channel. The trailing newline is not discarded in this case.

Example 9–9 A read loop using read and split.

```
foreach line [split [read $channel] \n] {
    # Process line
}
close $channel
```

For moderate-sized files, it is about 10 percent faster to loop over the lines in a file using the read loop in the second example. In this case, read returns the whole file, and split chops the file into list elements, one for each line. For small files (less than 1K) it doesn't really matter. For large files (megabytes) you might induce paging with this approach.

Platform-Specific End of Line Characters

Tcl automatically detects different end of line conventions. On UNIX, text lines are ended with a newline character (\n). On Macintosh, they are terminated with a carriage return (\r). On Windows, they are terminated with a carriage return, newline sequence (\r\n). Tcl accepts any of these, and the line terminator can even change within a file. All these different conventions are converted to the UNIX style so that once read, text lines are always terminated with a newline character (\n). Both the `read` and `gets` commands do this conversion.

During output, text lines are generated in the platform-native format. The automatic handling of line formats means that it is easy to convert a file to native format. You just need to read it in and write it out:

```
puts -nonewline $out [read $in]
```

To suppress conversions, use the `fconfigure` command, which is described in more detail on page 234.

Example 9–10 demonstrates a `File_Copy` procedure that translates files to native format. It is complicated because it handles directories.

Example 9–10 Copy a file and translate to native format.

```
proc File_Copy {src dest} {
    if {[file isdirectory $src]} {
        file mkdir $dest
        foreach f [glob -nocomplain [file join $src *]] {
            File_Copy $f [file join $dest [file tail $f]]
        }
        return
    }
    if {[file isdirectory $dest]} {
        set dest [file join $dest [file tail $src]]
    }
    set in [open $src]
    set out [open $dest w]
    puts -nonewline $out [read $in]
    close $out ; close $in
}
```

Random Access I/O

The `seek` and `tell` commands provide random access to I/O channels. Each channel has a current position called the *seek offset*. Each read or write operation updates the seek offset by the number of bytes transferred. The current value of the offset is returned by the `tell` command. The `seek` command sets the seek offset by an amount, which can be positive or negative, from an origin which is either `start`, `current`, or `end`. If you are dealing with files greater than 2GB in size, you will need Tcl 8.4 for its 64-bit file system support.

Closing I/O Channels

The `close` command is just as important as the others because it frees operating system resources associated with the I/O channel. If you forget to close a channel, it will be closed when your process exits. However, if you have a long-running program, like a Tk script, you might exhaust some operating system resources if you forget to close your I/O channels.

The `close` command can raise an error.

If the channel was a process pipeline and any of the processes wrote to their standard error channel, then Tcl believes this is an error. The error is raised when the channel to the pipeline is finally closed. Similarly, if any of the processes in the pipeline exit with a nonzero status, `close` raises an error.

The Current Directory — cd and pwd

Every process has a current directory that is used as the starting point when resolving a relative pathname. The `pwd` command returns the current directory, and the `cd` command changes the current directory. Example 9–11 uses these commands.

Matching File Names with glob

The `glob` command expands a pattern into the set of matching file names. The general form of the `glob` command is:

```
glob ?options? pattern ?pattern? ...
```

The pattern syntax is similar to the `string match` patterns:

- `*` matches zero or more characters.
- `?` matches a single character.
- `[abc]` matches a set of characters.
- `{a,b,c}` matches any of `a`, `b`, or `c`.
- All other characters must match themselves.

Table 9–8 lists the options for the `glob` command.

Table 9–8 `glob` command options.

`-directory dir`	Search for files in the directory `dir`. (Tcl 8.3)
`-join`	The remaining `pattern` arguments are treated as a single pattern obtained by joining them with directory separators. (Tcl 8.3)
`-nocomplain`	Causes `glob` to return an empty list if no files match. Otherwise an error is raised.
`-path path`	Search for files in the given path prefix `path`. Allows you to search in areas that may contain glob-sensitive characters. (Tcl 8.3)
`-tails`	Only return the part of each file found that follows the last directory named in the `-directory` or `-path` argument. (Tcl 8.4)
`-types types`	Only return files matching the types specified.
`--`	Signifies the end of flags. Must be used if `pattern` begins with a `-`.

Unlike the glob matching in *csh*, the Tcl `glob` command matches only the names of existing files. In *csh*, the `{a,b}` construct can match nonexistent names. In addition, the results of `glob` are not sorted. Use the `lsort` command to sort its result if you find it important.

Example 9–11 shows the `FindFile` procedure, which traverses the file system hierarchy using recursion. At each iteration it saves its current directory and then attempts to change to the next subdirectory. A `catch` guards against bogus names. The `glob` command matches file names:

Example 9–11 Finding a file by name.

```
proc FindFile { startDir namePat } {
    set pwd [pwd]
    if {[catch {cd $startDir} err]} {
        puts stderr $err
        return
    }
    foreach match [glob -nocomplain -- $namePat] {
        puts stdout [file join $startDir $match]
    }
    foreach file {[glob -nocomplain *]} {
        if [file isdirectory $file] {
            FindFile [file join $startDir $file] $namePat
        }
    }
    cd $pwd
}
```

The `-types` option allows for special filtered matching similar to the UNIX `find` command. The first form is like the -type option of find: b (block special file), c (character special file), d (directory), f (plain file), l (symbolic link), p (named pipe), or s (socket), where multiple types may be specified in the list. Glob will return all files which match at least one of the types given.

The second form specifies types where all the types given must match. These are r (readable), w (writable) and x (executable) as file permissions, and `readonly` and `hidden` as special cases. On the Macintosh, MacOS types and creators are also supported, where any item which is four characters long is assumed to be a MacOS type (e.g. TEXT). Items which are of the form {macintosh type XXXX} or {macintosh creator XXXX} will match types or creators respectively. Unrecognized types, or specifications of multiple MacOS types/creators will signal an error.

The two forms may be mixed, so `-types {d f r w}` will find all regular files OR directories that have both read AND write permissions.

I. Tcl Basics

Expanding Tilde in File Names

The `glob` command also expands a leading tilde (~) in filenames. There are two cases:

- ~/ expands to the current user's home directory.
- ~*user* expands to the home directory of *user*.

If you have a file that starts with a literal tilde, you can avoid the tilde expansion by adding a leading ./ (e.g., ./~foobar).

The `exit` and `pid` Commands

The `exit` command terminates your script. Note that `exit` causes termination of the whole process that was running the script. If you supply an integer-valued argument to `exit`, then that becomes the exit status of the process.

The `pid` command returns the process ID of the current process. This can be useful as the seed for a random number generator because it changes each time you run your script. It is also common to embed the process ID in the name of temporary files.

You can also find out the process IDs associated with a process pipeline with `pid`:

```
set pipe [open "|command"]
set pids [pid $pipe]
```

There is no built-in mechanism to control processes in the Tcl core. On UNIX systems you can `exec` the *kill* program to terminate a process:

```
exec kill $pid
```

Environment Variables

Environment variables are a collection of string-valued variables associated with each process. The process's environment variables are available through the global array `env`. The name of the environment variable is the index, (e.g., `env(PATH)`), and the array element contains the current value of the environment variable. If assignments are made to `env`, they result in changes to the corresponding environment variable. Environment variables are inherited by child processes, so programs run with the `exec` command inherit the environment of the Tcl script. The following example prints the values of environment variables.

Example 9–12 Printing environment variable values.

```
proc printenv { args } {
    global env
    set maxl 0
    if {[llength $args] == 0} {
        set args [lsort [array names env]]
```

```
        }
        foreach x $args {
            if {[string length $x] > $maxl} {
                set maxl [string length $x]
            }
        }
        incr maxl 2
        foreach x $args {
            puts stdout [format "%*s = %s" $maxl $x $env($x)]
        }
    }
    printenv USER SHELL TERM
    =>
    USER    = welch
    SHELL   = /bin/csh
    TERM    = tx
```

Note: Environment variables can be initialized for Macintosh applications by editing a resource of type STR# whose name is Tcl Environment Variables. This resource is part of the *tclsh* and *wish* applications. Follow the directions on page 28 for using *ResEdit*. The format of the resource values is *NAME=VALUE*.

The `registry` Command

Windows uses the *registry* to store various system configuration information. The Windows tool to browse and edit the registry is called *regedit*. Tcl provides a registry command. It is a loadable package that you must load by using:

```
package require registry
```

The registry structure has keys, value names, and typed data. The value names are stored under a key, and each value name has data associated with it. The keys are organized into a hierarchical naming system, so another way to think of the value names is as an extra level in the hierarchy. The main point is that you need to specify both a key name and a value name in order to get something out of the registry. The key names have one of the following formats:

```
\\hostname\rootname\keypath
rootname\keypath
rootname
```

The *rootname* is one of HKEY_LOCAL_MACHINE, HKEY_PERFORMANCE_DATA, HKEY_USERS, HKEY_CLASSES_ROOT, HKEY_CURRENT_USER, HKEY_CURRENT_CONFIG, or HKEY_DYN_DATA. Tables 9–9 and 9–10 summarize the registry command and data types:

Table 9–9 The `registry` command.

`registry delete key ?valueName?`	Deletes the `key` and the named value, or it deletes all values under the key if `valueName` is not specified.
`registry get key valueName`	Returns the value associated with `valueName` under `key`.
`registry keys key ?pat?`	Returns the list of keys or value names under `key` that match `pat`, which is a `string match` pattern.
`registry set key`	Creates `key`.
`registry set key valueName data ?type?`	Creates `valueName` under `key` with value `data` of the given `type`. Types are listed in Table 9–10.
`registry type key valueName`	Returns the type of `valueName` under `key`.
`registry values key ?pat?`	Returns the names of the values stored under `key` that match `pat`, which is a `string match` pattern.

Table 9–10 The `registry` data types.

`binary`	Arbitrary binary data.
`none`	Arbitrary binary data.
`expand_sz`	A string that contains references to environment variables with the %VARNAME% syntax.
`dword`	A 32-bit integer.
`dword_big_endian`	A 32-bit integer in the other byte order. It is represented in Tcl as a decimal string.
`link`	A symbolic link.
`multi_sz`	An array of strings, which are represented as a Tcl list.
`resource_list`	A device driver resource list.

Advanced Tcl

Part II describes advanced programming techniques that support sophisticated applications. The Tcl interfaces remain simple, so you can quickly construct powerful applications.

Chapter 10 describes `eval`, which lets you create Tcl programs on the fly. There are tricks with using `eval` correctly, and a few rules of thumb to make your life easier.

Chapter 11 describes regular expressions. This is the most powerful string processing facility in Tcl. This chapter includes a cookbook of useful regular expressions.

Chapter 12 describes the library and package facility used to organize your code into reusable modules.

Chapter 13 describes introspection and debugging. Introspection provides information about the state of the Tcl interpreter.

Chapter 14 describes namespaces that partition the global scope for variables and procedures. Namespaces help you structure large Tcl applications.

Chapter 15 describes the features that support Internationalization, including Unicode, other character set encodings, and message catalogs.

Chapter 16 describes event-driven I/O programming. This lets you run process pipelines in the background. It is also very useful with network socket programming, which is the topic of Chapter 17.

Chapter 18 describes TclHttpd, a Web server built entirely in Tcl. You can build applications on top of TclHttpd, or integrate the server into existing applications to give them a web interface. TclHttpd also supports regular Web sites.

Chapter 19 describes Safe-Tcl and using multiple Tcl interpreters. If an interpreter is safe, then you can grant it restricted functionality. This is ideal for supporting network applets that are downloaded from untrusted sites, which is described in Chapter 20.

Chapter 21 describes how to use the `Thread` extension to create multi-threaded Tcl scripts. The extension provides threads, synchronization with mutexes and condition variables, shared variables, and thread pools.

Chapter 22 describes how to package and deploy Tcl applications as Starkits. A Virtual File System facility is used to create a private file system inside the Starkit to hold the scripts, graphics, and documentation that make up your application.

Quoting Issues and Eval

II. Advanced Tcl

This chapter describes explicit calls to the interpreter with the `eval` command. An extra round of substitutions is performed that results in some useful effects. The chapter describes the quoting problems with `eval` and the ways to avoid them. The `uplevel` command evaluates commands in a different scope. The `subst` command does substitutions but no command invocation.

*D*ynamic evaluation makes Tcl flexible and powerful, but it can be tricky to use properly. The basic idea is that you create a string and then use the `eval` command to interpret that string as a command or a series of commands. Creating program code on the fly is easy with an interpreted language like Tcl, and very hard, if not impossible, with a statically compiled language like C++ or Java. There are several ways that dynamic code evaluation is used in Tcl:

- In some cases, a simple procedure isn't quite good enough, and you need to glue together a command from a few different pieces and then execute the result using `eval`. This often occurs with *wrappers*, which provide a thin layer of functionality over existing commands.
- *Callbacks* are script fragments that are saved and evaluated later in response to some event. Examples include the commands associated with Tk buttons, `fileevent` I/O handlers, and `after` timer handlers. Callbacks are a flexible way to link different parts of an application together.
- You can add new control structures to Tcl using the `uplevel` command. For example, you can write a function that applies a command to each line in a file or each node in a tree.
- You can have a mixture of code and data, and just process the code part with the `subst` command. For example, this is useful in HTML templates described in Chapter 18. There are also some powerful combinations of `subst` and `regsub` described in Chapter 11.

Constructing Code with the `list` Command

It can be tricky to assemble a command so that it is evaluated properly by `eval`. The same difficulties apply to commands like `after`, `uplevel`, and the Tk `send` command, all of which have similar properties to `eval`, except that the command evaluation occurs later or in a different context. Constructing commands dynamically is a source of many problems. The worst part is that you can write code that works sometimes but not others, which can be very confusing.

Use `list` when constructing commands.

The root of the quoting problems is the internal use of `concat` by `eval` and similar commands to concatenate their arguments into one command string. The `concat` can lose some important list structure so that arguments are not passed through as you expect. The general strategy to avoid these problems is to use `list` and `lappend` to explicitly form the command callback as a single, well-structured list.

The `eval` Command

The `eval` command results in another call to the Tcl interpreter. If you construct a command dynamically, you must use `eval` to interpret it. For example, suppose we want to construct the following command now but execute it later:

```
puts stdout "Hello, World!"
```

In this case, it is sufficient to do the following:

```
set cmd {puts stdout "Hello, World!"}
=> puts stdout "Hello, World!"
# sometime later...
eval $cmd
=> Hello, World!
```

In this case, the value of `cmd` is passed to Tcl. All the standard grouping and substitution are done again on the value, which is a `puts` command.

However, suppose that part of the command is stored in a variable, but that variable will not be defined at the time `eval` is used. We can artificially create this situation like this:

```
set string "Hello, World!"
set cmd {puts stdout $string}
=> puts stdout $string
unset string
eval $cmd
=> can't read "string": no such variable
```

In this case, the command contains `$string`. When this is processed by `eval`, the interpreter looks for the current value of `string`, which is undefined. This example is contrived, but the same problem occurs if `string` is a local variable, and `cmd` will be evaluated later in the global scope.

A common mistake is to use double quotes to group the command. That will
let $string be substituted now. However, this works only if string has a simple
value, but it fails if the value of string contains spaces or other Tcl special characters:

```
set cmd "puts stdout $string"
=> puts stdout Hello, World!
eval $cmd
=> bad argument "World!": should be "nonewline"
```

The problem is that we have lost some important structure. The identity of
$string as a single argument gets lost in the second round of parsing by eval.
The solution to this problem is to construct the command using list, as shown
in the following example:

Example 10–1 Using `list` to construct commands.

```
set string "Hello, World!"
set cmd [list puts stdout $string]
=> puts stdout {Hello, World!}
unset string
eval $cmd
=> Hello, World!
```

The trick is that list has formed a list containing three elements: puts,
stdout, and the value of string. The substitution of $string occurs before list
is called, and list takes care of grouping that value for us. In contrast, using
double quotes is equivalent to:

```
set cmd [concat puts stdout $string]
```

Double quotes lose list structure.

The problem here is that concat does not preserve list structure. The main
lesson is that you should use list to construct commands if they contain variable values or command results that must be substituted now. If you use double
quotes, the values are substituted but you lose proper command structure. If you
use curly braces, then values are not substituted until later, which may not be in
the right context.

Commands That Concatenate Their Arguments

The uplevel, after and send commands concatenate their arguments into
a command and execute it later in a different context. The uplevel command is
described on page 138, after is described on page 228, and send is described on
page 648. Whenever I discover such a command, I put it on my danger list and
make sure I explicitly form a single command argument with list instead of letting the command concat items for me. Get in the habit now:

```
after 100 [list doCmd $param1 $param2]
send $interp [list doCmd $param1 $param2] ;# Safe!
```

The danger here is that `concat` and `list` can result in the same thing, so you can be led down the rosy garden path only to get errors later when values change. The two previous examples always work. The next two work only if `param1` and `param2` have values that are single list elements:

```
after 100 doCmd $param1 $param2
send $interp doCmd $param1 $param2;# Unsafe!
```

If you use other Tcl extensions that provide `eval`-like functionality, carefully check their documentation to see whether they contain commands that `concat` their arguments into a command. For example, Tcl-DP, which provides a network version of `send`, `dp_send`, also uses `concat`.

Commands That Use Callbacks

The general strategy of passing out a command or script to call later is a flexible way to assemble different parts of an application, and it is widely used by Tcl commands. Examples include commands that are called when users click on Tk buttons, commands that are called when I/O channels have data ready, or commands that are called when clients connect to network servers. It is also easy to write your own procedures or C extensions that accept scripts and call them later in response to some event.

These other callback situations may not appear to have the "`concat` problem" because they take a single script argument. However, as soon as you use double quotes to group that argument, you have created the `concat` problem all over again. So, all the caveats about using `list` to construct these commands still apply.

Command Prefix Callbacks

There is a variation on command callbacks called a *command prefix*. In this case, the command is given additional arguments when it is invoked. In other words, you provide only part of the command, the command prefix, and the module that invokes the callback adds additional arguments before using `eval` to invoke the command.

For example, when you create a network server, you supply a procedure that is called when a client makes a connection. That procedure is called with three additional arguments that indicate the client's socket, IP address, and port number. This is described in more detail on page 240. The tricky thing is that you can define your callback procedure to take four (or more) arguments. In this case you specify some of the parameters when you define the callback, and then the socket subsystem specifies the remaining arguments when it makes the callback. The following command creates the server side of a socket:

```
set virtualhost www.beedub.com
socket -server [list Accept $virtualhost] 8080
```

However, you define the `Accept` procedure like this:

```
proc Accept {myname sock ipaddr port} { ... }
```

The `myname` parameter is set when you construct the command prefix. The remaining parameters are set when the callback is invoked. The use of `list` in this example is not strictly necessary because "we know" that `virtualhost` will always be a single list element. However, using `list` is just a good habit when forming callbacks, so I always write the code this way.

There are many other examples of callback arguments that are really command prefixes. Some of these include the scrolling callbacks between Tk scrollbars and their widgets, the command aliases used with Safe Tcl, the sorting functions in `lsort`, and the completion callback used with `fcopy`. Example 13–6 on page 191 shows how to use `eval` to make callbacks from Tcl procedures.

Constructing Procedures Dynamically

The previous examples have all focused on creating single commands by using list operations. Suppose you want to create a whole procedure dynamically. Unfortunately, this can be particularly awkward because a procedure body is not a simple list. Instead, it is a sequence of commands that are each lists, but they are separated by newlines or semicolons. In turn, some of those commands may be loops and `if` commands that have their own command bodies. To further compound the problem, you typically have two kinds of variables in the procedure body: some that are to be used as values when constructing the body, and some that are to be used later when executing the procedure. The result can be very messy.

The main trick to this problem is to use either `format` or `regsub` to process a template for your dynamically generated procedure. If you use format, then you can put `%s` into your templates where you want to insert values. You may find the positional notation of the format string (e.g., `%1$s` and `%2$s`) useful if you need to repeat a value in several places within your procedure body. The following example is a procedure that generates a new version of other procedures. The new version includes code that counts the number of times the procedure was called and measures the time it takes to run:

Example 10–2 Generating procedures dynamically with a template.

```
proc TraceGen {procName} {
    rename s$procName $procName-orig
    set arglist {}
    foreach arg [info args $procName-orig] {
        append arglist "\$$arg "
    }
    proc $procName [info args $procName-orig] [format {
        global _trace_count _trace_msec
        incr _trace_count(%1$s)
        incr _trace_msec(%1$s) [lindex [time {
            set result [%1$s-orig %2$s]
        } 1] 0]
        return $result
    } $procName $arglist]
}
```

Suppose that we have a trivial procedure `foo`:

```
proc foo {x y} {
    return [expr $x * $y]
}
```

If you run `TraceGen` on it and look at the results, you see this:

```
TraceGen foo
info body foo
=>
    global _trace_count _trace_msec
    incr _trace_count(foo)
    incr _trace_msec(foo) [lindex [time {
        set result [foo-orig $x $y]
    } 1] 0]
    return $result
```

The tracing provided by `TraceGen` is similar to what you can achieve with the features of the Tcl 8.4 `trace` command. With command tracing, which is described on page 194, you can track the calls and results of procedures.

Exploiting the `concat` inside `eval`

The previous section warns about the danger of concatenation when forming commands. However, there are times when concatenation is done for good reason. This section illustrates cases where the `concat` done by `eval` is useful in assembling a command by concatenating multiple lists into one list. A `concat` is done internally by `eval` when it gets more than one argument:

```
    eval list1 list2 list3 ...
```

The effect of `concat` is to join all the lists into one list; a new level of list structure is *not* added. This is useful if the lists are fragments of a command. It is common to use this form of `eval` with the `args` construct in procedures. Use the `args` parameter to pass optional arguments through to another command. Invoke the other command with `eval`, and the values in `$args` get concatenated onto the command properly. The special `args` parameter is illustrated in Example 7–2 on page 88.

Using `eval` in a Wrapper Procedure.

Here, we illustrate the use of `eval` and `$args` with a simple Tk example. In Tk, the `button` command creates a button in the user interface. The `button` command can take many arguments, and commonly you simply specify the text of the button and the Tcl command that is executed when the user clicks on the button:

```
    button .foo -text Foo -command foo
```

After a button is created, it is made visible by packing it into the display. The `pack` command can also take many arguments to control screen placement. Here, we just specify a side and let the packer take care of the rest of the details:

```
pack .foo -side left
```

Even though there are only two Tcl commands to create a user interface button, we will write a procedure that replaces the two commands with one. Our first version might be:

```
proc PackedButton {name txt cmd} {
    button $name -text $txt -command $cmd
    pack $name -side left
}
```

This is not a very flexible procedure. The main problem is that it hides the full power of the Tk `button` command, which can really take more than 30 widget configuration options, such as `-background`, `-cursor`, `-relief`, and more. They are listed on page 459. For example, you can easily make a red button like this:

```
button .foo -text Foo -command foo -background red
```

A better version of `PackedButton` uses `args` to pass through extra configuration options to the `button` command. The `args` parameter is a list of all the extra arguments passed to the Tcl procedure. My first attempt to use `$args` looked like this, but it was not correct:

```
proc PackedButton {name txt cmd args} {
    button $name -text $txt -command $cmd $args
    pack $name -side left
}
PackedButton .foo "Hello, World!" {exit} -background red
=> unknown option "-background red"
```

The problem is that `$args` is a list value, and `button` gets the whole list as a single argument. Instead, `button` needs to get the elements of `$args` as individual arguments.

Use `eval` with `$args`

In this case, you can use `eval` because it concatenates its arguments to form a single list before evaluation. The single list is, by definition, the same as a single Tcl command, so the `button` command parses correctly. Here we give `eval` two lists, which it joins into one command:

```
eval {button $name -text $txt -command $cmd} $args
```

The use of the braces in this command is discussed in more detail below. We also generalize our procedure to take some options to the `pack` command. This argument, `pack`, must be a list of packing options. The final version of `Packed-Button` is shown in Example 10–3:

Example 10–3 Using `eval` with `$args`.

```
# PackedButton creates and packs a button.
proc PackedButton {path txt cmd {pack {-side right}} args} {
    eval {button $path -text $txt -command $cmd} $args
    eval {pack $path} $pack
}
```

In `PackedButton`, both `pack` and `args` are list-valued parameters that are used as parts of a command. The internal `concat` done by `eval` is perfect for this situation. The simplest call to `PackedButton` is:

```
PackedButton .new "New" { New }
```

The quotes and curly braces are redundant in this case but are retained to convey some type information. The quotes imply a string label, and the braces imply a command. The `pack` argument takes on its default value, and the `args` variable is an empty list. The two commands executed by `PackedButton` are:

```
button .new -text New -command New
pack .new -side right
```

`PackedButton` creates a horizontal stack of buttons by default. The packing can be controlled with a packing specification:

```
PackedButton .save "Save" { Save $file } {-side left}
```

The two commands executed by `PackedButton` are:

```
button .new -text Save -command { Save $file }
pack .new -side left
```

The remaining arguments, if any, are passed through to the button command. This lets the caller fine-tune some of the button attributes:

```
PackedButton .quit Quit { Exit } {-side left -padx 5} \
    -background red
```

The two commands executed by `PackedButton` are:

```
button .quit -text Quit -command { Exit } -background red
pack .quit -side left -padx 5
```

You can see a difference between the `pack` and `args` argument in the call to `PackedButton`. You need to group the packing options explicitly into a single argument. The `args` parameter is automatically made into a list of all remaining arguments. In fact, if you group the extra button parameters, it will be a mistake:

```
PackedButton .quit Quit { Exit } {-side left -padx 5} \
    {-background red}
=> unknown option "-background red"
```

Correct Quoting with `eval`

What about the peculiar placement of braces in `PackedButton`?

```
eval {button $path -text $txt -command $cmd} $args
```

By using braces, we control the number of times different parts of the command are seen by the Tcl evaluator. Without any braces, everything goes through two rounds of substitution. The braces prevent one of those rounds. In the above command, only `$args` is substituted twice. Before `eval` is called, the `$args` is replaced with its list value. Then, `eval` is invoked, and it concatenates its two list arguments into one list, which is now a properly formed command. The second round of substitutions done by `eval` replaces the `txt` and `cmd` values.

Do not use double quotes with `eval`.

You may be tempted to use double quotes instead of curly braces in your uses of `eval`. *Don't give in!* Using double quotes is, mostly likely, wrong. Suppose the first `eval` command is written like this:

```
eval "button $path -text $txt -command $cmd $args"
```

Incidentally, the previous is equivalent to:

```
eval button $path -text $txt -command $cmd $args
```

These versions happen to work with the following call because `txt` and `cmd` have one-word values with no special characters in them:

```
PackedButton .quit Quit { Exit }
```

The button command that is ultimately evaluated is:

```
button .quit -text Quit -command { Exit }
```

In the next call, an error is raised:

```
PackedButton .save "Save As" [list Save $file]
=> unknown option "As"
```

This is because the button command is this:

```
button .save -text Save As -command Save /a/b/c
```

But it should look like this instead:

```
button .save -text {Save As} -command {Save /a/b/c}
```

The problem is that the structure of the `button` command is now wrong. The value of `txt` and `cmd` are substituted first, before `eval` is even called, and then the whole command is parsed again. The worst part is that sometimes using double quotes works, and sometimes it fails. The success of using double quotes depends on the value of the parameters. When those values contain spaces or special characters, the command gets parsed incorrectly.

Braces: the one true way to group arguments to `eval`.

To repeat, the safe construct is:

```
eval {button $path -text $txt -command $cmd} $args
```

The following variations are also correct. The first uses `list` to do quoting automatically, and the others use backslashes or braces to prevent the extra round of substitutions:

```
eval [list button $path -text $txt -command $cmd] $args
eval button \$path -text \$txt -command \$cmd $args
eval button {$path} -text {$txt} -command {$cmd} $args
```

Finally, here is one more *incorrect* approach that tries to quote by hand:

```
eval "button {$path} -text {$txt} -command {$cmd} $args"
```

The problem is that double quotes disable the quoting you normally expect with curly braces. Consider this little example that uses double quotes. The curly braces around $blob have no special effect, and the interpreter sees unbalanced braces:

```
set blob "foo\{bar space"
=> foo{bar space
eval "puts {$blob}"
=> missing close brace
```

If we group instead with curly braces, then the variable substitution occurs once, after the arguments to puts have been grouped, and there is no error.

```
eval puts {$blob}
=> foo{bar space
```

You can also be successful using list:

```
eval puts [list $blob]
```

Of course, these simple examples are contrived, but they illustrate the need to be careful with your list construction when using eval!

The uplevel Command

The uplevel command is similar to eval, except that it evaluates a command in a different scope than the current procedure. It is useful for defining new control structures entirely in Tcl. The syntax for uplevel is:

```
uplevel ?level? command ?list1 list2 ...?
```

As with upvar, the level parameter is optional, but recommended for good style, and defaults to 1, which means to execute the command in the scope of the calling procedure. The other common use of level is #0, which means to evaluate the command in the global scope. You can count up farther than one (e.g., 2 or 3), or count down from the global level (e.g., #1 or #2), but these cases rarely make sense.

When you specify the command argument, you must be aware of any substitutions that might be performed by the Tcl interpreter before uplevel is called. If you are entering the command directly, protect it with curly braces so that substitutions occur in the other scope. The following affects the variable x in the caller's scope:

```
uplevel {set x [expr $x + 1]}
```

However, the following will use the value of x in the current scope to define the value of x in the calling scope, which is probably not what was intended:

```
uplevel "set x [expr $x + 1]"
```

If you are constructing the command dynamically, again use list. This fragment is used later in Example 10–4:

```
uplevel [list foreach $args $valueList {break}]
```

It is common to have the command in a variable. This is the case when the command has been passed into your new control flow procedure as an argument.

In this case, you should evaluate the command one level up. Put the level in explicitly to avoid cases where `$cmd` looks like a number!

```
uplevel 1 $cmd
```

Another common scenario is reading commands from users as part of an application. In this case, you should evaluate the command at the global scope. Example 16–2 on page 230 illustrates this use of `uplevel`:

```
uplevel #0 $cmd
```

If you are assembling a command from a few different lists, such as the `args` parameter, then you can use `concat` to form the command:

```
uplevel [concat $cmd $args]
```

The lists in `$cmd` and `$args` are concatenated into a single list, which is a valid Tcl command. Like `eval`, `uplevel` uses `concat` internally if it is given extra arguments, so you can leave out the explicit use of `concat`. The following commands are equivalent:

```
uplevel [concat $cmd $args]
uplevel "$cmd $args"
uplevel $cmd $args
```

Example 10–4 shows list assignment using the `foreach` trick described on Page 81. List assignment is useful if a command returns several values in a list. The `lassign` procedure assigns the list elements to several variables. The `lassign` procedure hides the `foreach` trick, but it must use the `uplevel` command so that the loop variables get assigned in the correct scope. The `list` command is used to construct the `foreach` command that is executed in the caller's scope. This is necessary so that `$variables` and `$values` get substituted before the command is evaluated in the other scope.

Example 10–4 `lassign`: list assignment with `foreach`.

```
# Assign a set of variables from a list of values.
# If there are more values than variables, they are returned.
# If there are fewer values than variables,
# the variables get the empty string.

proc lassign {valueList args} {
    if {[llength $args] == 0} {
        error "wrong # args: lassign list varname ?varname..?"
    }
    if {[llength $valueList] == 0} {
        # Ensure one trip through the foreach loop
        set valueList [list {}]
    }
    uplevel 1 [list foreach $args $valueList {break}]
    return [lrange $valueList [llength $args] end]
}
```

Example 10–5 illustrates a new control structure with the `File_Process` procedure that applies a callback to each line in a file. The call to `uplevel` allows the `callback` to be concatenated with the `line` to form the command. The `list` command is used to quote any special characters in `line`, so it appears as a single argument to the command.

Example 10–5 The `File_Process` procedure iterates over lines in a file.

```
proc File_Process {file callback} {
    set in [open $file]
    while {[gets $in line] >= 0} {
        uplevel 1 $callback [list $line]
    }
    close $in
}
```

What is the difference between these two commands?

```
uplevel 1 [list $callback $line]
uplevel 1 $callback [list $line]
```

The first form limits `callback` to be the name of the command, while the second form allows `callback` to be a command prefix. Once again, what is the bug with this version?

```
uplevel 1 $callback $line
```

The arbitrary value of `$line` is concatenated to the `callback` command, and it is likely to be a malformed command when executed.

The `subst` Command

The `subst` command is useful when you have a mixture of Tcl commands, Tcl variable references, and plain old data. The `subst` command looks through the data for square brackets, dollar signs, and backslashes, and it does substitutions on those. It leaves the rest of the data alone:

```
set a "foo bar"
subst {a=$a date=[exec date]}
=> a=foo bar date=Thu Dec 15 10:13:48 PST 1994
```

The `subst` command does not honor the quoting effect of curly braces. It does substitutions regardless of braces:

```
subst {a=$a date={[exec date]}}
=> a=foo bar date={Thu Dec 15 10:15:31 PST 1994}
```

You can use backslashes to prevent variable and command substitution.

```
subst {a=\$a date=\[exec date]}
=> a=$a date=[exec date]
```

You can use other backslash substitutions like \uXXXX to get Unicode characters, \n to get newlines, or \-newline to hide newlines.

The subst command takes flags that limit the substitutions it will perform. The flags are -nobackslashes, -nocommands, or -novariables. You can specify one or more of these flags before the string that needs to be substituted:

```
subst -novariables {a=$a date=[exec date]}
=> a=$a date=Thu Dec 15 10:15:31 PST 1994
```

String Processing with subst

The subst command can be used with the regsub command to do efficient, two-step string processing. In the first step, regsub is used to rewrite an input string into data with embedded Tcl commands. In the second step, subst or eval replaces the Tcl commands with their result. By artfully mapping the data into Tcl commands, you can dynamically construct a Tcl script that processes the data. The processing is efficient because the Tcl parser and the regular expression processor have been highly tuned. Chapter 11 has several examples that use this technique.

II. Advanced Tcl

Regular Expressions

This chapter describes regular expression pattern matching and string processing based on regular expression substitutions. These features provide the most powerful string processing facilities in Tcl. Tcl commands described are: `regexp` and `regsub`.

*R*egular expressions are a formal way to describe string patterns. They provide a powerful and compact way to specify patterns in your data. Even better, there is a very efficient implementation of the regular expression mechanism due to Henry Spencer. If your script does much string processing, it is worth the effort to learn about the `regexp` command. Your Tcl scripts will be compact and efficient. This chapter uses many examples to show you the features of regular expressions.

Regular expression substitution is a mechanism that lets you rewrite a string based on regular expression matching. The `regsub` command is another powerful tool, and this chapter includes several examples that do a lot of work in just a few Tcl commands. Stephen Uhler has shown me several ways to transform input data into a Tcl script with `regsub` and then use `subst` or `eval` to process the data. The idea takes a moment to get used to, but it provides a very efficient way to process strings.

Tcl 8.1 added a new regular expression implementation that supports Unicode and *advanced regular expressions* (ARE). This implementation adds more syntax and escapes that makes it easier to write patterns, once you learn the new features! If you know Perl, then you are already familiar with these features. The Tcl advanced regular expressions are almost identical to the Perl 5 regular expressions. The new features include a few very minor incompatibilities with the regular expressions implemented in earlier versions of Tcl 8.0, but these rarely occur in practice. The new regular expression package supports Unicode, of course, so you can write patterns to match Japanese or Hindi documents!

When to Use Regular Expressions

Regular expressions can seem overly complex at first. They introduce their own syntax and their own rules, and you may be tempted to use simpler commands like `string first`, `string range`, or `string match` to process your strings. However, often a single regular expression command can replace a sequence of several `string` commands. Not only do you have to write less code, but you often get a performance improvement because the regular expression matcher is implemented in optimized C code, so pattern matching is fast.

The regular expression matcher does more than test for a match. It also tells you what part of your input string matches the pattern. This is useful for picking data out of a large input string. In fact, you can capture several pieces of data in just one match by using subexpressions. The `regexp` Tcl command makes this easy by assigning the matching data to Tcl variables. If you find yourself using `string first` and `string range` to pick out data, remember that `regexp` can do it in one step instead.

The regular expression matcher is structured so that patterns are first compiled into an form that is efficient to match. If you use the same pattern frequently, then the expensive compilation phase is done only once, and all your matching uses the efficient form. These details are completely hidden by the Tcl interface. If you use a pattern twice, Tcl will nearly always be able to retrieve the compiled form of the pattern. As you can see, the regular expression matcher is optimized for lots of heavy-duty string processing.

Avoiding a Common Problem

Group your patterns with curly braces.

One of the stumbling blocks with regular expressions is that they use some of the same special characters as Tcl. Any pattern that contains brackets, dollar signs, or spaces must be quoted when used in a Tcl command. In many cases you can group the regular expression with curly braces, so Tcl pays no attention to it. However, when using Tcl 8.0 (or earlier) you may need Tcl to do backslash substitutions on part of the pattern, and then you need to worry about quoting the special characters in the regular expression.

Advanced regular expressions eliminate this problem because backslash substitution is now done by the regular expression engine. Previously, to get `\n` to mean the newline character (or `\t` for tab) you had to let Tcl do the substitution. With Tcl 8.1, `\n` and `\t` inside a regular expression mean newline and tab. In fact, there are now about 20 backslash escapes you can use in patterns. Now more than ever, remember to group your patterns with curly braces to avoid conflicts between Tcl and the regular expression engine.

The patterns in the first sections of this chapter ignore this problem. The sample expressions in Table 11–7 on page 161 are quoted for use within Tcl scripts. Most are quoted simply by putting the whole pattern in braces, but some are shown without braces for comparison.

Regular Expression Syntax

This section describes the basics of regular expression patterns, which are found in all versions of Tcl. There are occasional references to features added by advanced regular expressions, but they are covered in more detail starting on page 149. There is enough syntax in regular expressions that there are five tables that summarize all the options. These tables appear together starting at page 154.

A regular expression is a sequence of the following items:

- A literal character.
- A matching character, character set, or character class.
- A repetition quantifier.
- An alternation clause.
- A subpattern grouped with parentheses.

Matching Characters

Most characters simply match themselves. The following pattern matches an `a` followed by a `b`:

```
ab
```

The general wild-card character is the period, ".". It matches any single character. The following pattern matches an `a` followed by any character:

```
a.
```

Remember that matches can occur anywhere within a string; a pattern does not have to match the whole string. You can change that by using anchors, which are described on page 147.

Character Sets

The matching character can be restricted to a set of characters with the `[xyz]` syntax. Any of the characters between the two brackets is allowed to match. For example, the following matches either `Hello` or `hello`:

```
[Hh]ello
```

The matching set can be specified as a range over the character set with the `[x-y]` syntax. The following matches any digit:

```
[0-9]
```

There is also the ability to specify the complement of a set. That is, the matching character can be anything except what is in the set. This is achieved with the `[^xyz]` syntax. Ranges and complements can be combined. The following matches anything except the uppercase and lowercase letters:

```
[^a-zA-Z]
```

Using special characters in character sets.

If you want a] in your character set, put it immediately after the initial opening bracket. You do not need to do anything special to include [in your character set. The following matches any square brackets or curly braces:

    []{[{}]

Most regular expression syntax characters are no longer special inside character sets. This means you do not need to backslash anything inside a bracketed character set except for backslash itself. The following pattern matches several of the syntax characters used in regular expressions:

    [][+*?()|\\]

Advanced regular expressions add names and backslash escapes as shorthand for common sets of characters like white space, alpha, alphanumeric, and more. These are described on page 149 and listed in Table 11–3 on page 156.

Quantifiers

Repetition is specified with *, for zero or more, +, for one or more, and ?, for zero or one. These *quantifiers* apply to the previous item, which is either a matching character, a character set, or a subpattern grouped with parentheses. The following matches a string that contains b followed by zero or more a's:

    ba*

You can group part of the pattern with parentheses and then apply a quantifier to that part of the pattern. The following matches a string that has one or more sequences of ab:

    (ab)+

The pattern that matches anything, even the empty string, is:

    .*

These quantifiers have a *greedy* matching behavior: They match as many characters as possible. Advanced regular expressions add nongreedy matching, which is described on page 151. For example, a pattern to match a single line might look like this:

    .*\n

However, as a greedy match, this will match all the lines in the input, ending with the last newline in the input string. The following pattern matches up through the first newline.

    [^\n]*\n

We will shorten this pattern even further on page 151 by using nongreedy quantifiers. There are also special newline sensitive modes you can turn on with some options described on page 153.

Alternation

Alternation lets you test more than one pattern at the same time. The matching engine is designed to be able to test multiple patterns in parallel, so alternation is efficient. Alternation is specified with |, the pipe symbol. Another way to match either `Hello` or `hello` is:

```
hello|Hello
```

You can also write this pattern as:

```
(h|H)ello
```

or as:

```
[hH]ello
```

Anchoring a Match

By default a pattern does not have to match the whole string. There can be unmatched characters before and after the match. You can anchor the match to the beginning of the string by starting the pattern with ^, or to the end of the string by ending the pattern with $. You can force the pattern to match the whole string by using both. All strings that begin with spaces or tabs are matched with:

```
^[ \t]+
```

If you have many text lines in your input, you may be tempted to think of ^ as meaning "beginning of line" instead of "beginning of string." By default, the ^ and $ anchors are relative to the whole input, and embedded newlines are ignored. Advanced regular expressions support options that make the ^ and $ anchors line-oriented. They also add the \A and \Z anchors that always match the beginning and end of the string, respectively.

Backslash Quoting

Use the backslash character to turn off these special characters :

```
.  *  ?  +  [  ]  (  )  ^  $  |  \
```

For example, to match the plus character, you will need:

```
\+
```

Remember that this quoting is not necessary inside a bracketed expression (i.e., a character set definition.) For example, to match either plus or question mark, either of these patterns will work:

```
(\+|\?)
[+?]
```

To match a single backslash, you need two. You must do this everywhere, even inside a bracketed expression. Or you can use \B, which was added as part of advanced regular expressions. Both of these match a single backslash:

```
\\
\B
```

Unknown backslash sequences are an error.

Versions of Tcl before 8.1 ignored unknown backslash sequences in regular expressions. For example, `\=` was just =, and `\w` was just w. Even `\n` was just n, which was probably frustrating to many beginners trying to get a newline into their pattern. Advanced regular expressions add backslash sequences for tab, newline, character classes, and more. This is a convenient improvement, but in rare cases it may change the semantics of a pattern. Usually these cases are where an unneeded backslash suddenly takes on meaning, or causes an error because it is unknown.

Matching Precedence

If a pattern can match several parts of a string, the matcher takes the match that occurs earliest in the input string. Then, if there is more than one match from that same point because of alternation in the pattern, the matcher takes the longest possible match. The rule of thumb is: *first, then longest*. This rule gets changed by nongreedy quantifiers that prefer a shorter match.

Watch out for *, which means zero or more, because zero of anything is pretty easy to match. Suppose your pattern is:

```
[a-z]*
```

This pattern will match against 123abc, but not how you expect. Instead of matching on the letters in the string, the pattern will match on the zero-length substring at the very beginning of the input string! This behavior can be seen by using the `-indices` option of the `regexp` command described on page 158. This option tells you the location of the matching string instead of the value of the matching string.

Capturing Subpatterns

Use parentheses to capture a subpattern. The string that matches the pattern within parentheses is remembered in a matching variable, which is a Tcl variable that gets assigned the string that matches the pattern. Using parentheses to capture subpatterns is very useful. Suppose we want to get everything between the `<td>` and `</td>` tags in some HTML. You can use this pattern:

```
<td>([^<]*)</td>
```

The matching variable gets assigned the part of the input string that matches the pattern inside the parentheses. You can capture many subpatterns in one match, which makes it a very efficient way to pick apart your data. Matching variables are explained in more detail on page 158 in the context of the `regexp` command.

Sometimes you need to introduce parentheses but you do not care about the match that occurs inside them. The pattern is slightly more efficient if the matcher does not need to remember the match. Advanced regular expressions add noncapturing parentheses with this syntax:

```
(?:pattern)
```

Advanced Regular Expressions

The syntax added by advanced regular expressions is mostly just shorthand notation for constructs you can make with the basic syntax already described. There are also some new features that add additional power: nongreedy quantifiers, back references, look-ahead patterns, and named character classes. If you are just starting out with regular expressions, you can ignore most of this section, except for the one about backslash sequences. Once you master the basics, of if you are already familiar with regular expressions in Tcl (or the UNIX *vi* editor or *grep* utility), then you may be interested in the new features of advanced regular expressions.

Compatibility with Patterns in Tcl 8.0

Advanced regular expressions add syntax in an upward compatible way. Old patterns continue to work with the new matcher, but advanced regular expressions will raise errors if given to old versions of Tcl. For example, the question mark is used in many of the new constructs, and it is artfully placed in locations that would not be legal in older versions of regular expressions. The added syntax is summarized in Table 11–2 on page 155.

If you have unbraced patterns from older code, they are very likely to be correct in Tcl 8.1 and later versions. For example, the following pattern picks out everything up to the next newline. The pattern is unbraced, so Tcl substitutes the newline character for each occurrence of \n. The square brackets are quoted so that Tcl does not think they delimit a nested command:

```
regexp "(\[^\n\]+)\n" $input
```

The above command behaves identically when using advanced regular expressions, although you can now also write it like this:

```
regexp {([^\n]+)\n} $input
```

The curly braces hide the brackets from the Tcl parser, so they do not need to be escaped with backslash. This saves us two characters and looks a bit cleaner.

Backslash Escape Sequences

The most significant change in advanced regular expression syntax is backslash substitutions. In Tcl 8.0 and earlier, a backslash is only used to turn off special characters such as: . + * ? [ ] . Otherwise it was ignored. For example, \n was simply n to the Tcl 8.0 regular expression engine. This was a source of confusion, and it meant you could not always quote patterns in braces to hide their special characters from Tcl's parser. In advanced regular expressions, \n now means the newline character to the regular expression engine, so you should never need to let Tcl do backslash processing.

Again, *always group your pattern with curly braces* to avoid confusion.

Advanced regular expressions add a lot of new backslash sequences. They are listed in Table 11–4 on page 156. Some of the more useful ones include \s,

II. Advanced Tcl

which matches space-like characters, \w, which matches letters, digit, and the underscore, \y, which matches the beginning or end of a word, and \B, which matches a backslash.

Character Classes

Character classes are names for sets of characters. The named character class syntax is valid only inside a bracketed character set. The syntax is:

```
[:identifier:]
```

For example, alpha is the name for the set of uppercase and lowercase letters. The following two patterns are *almost* the same:

```
[A-Za-z]
[[:alpha:]]
```

The difference is that the alpha character class also includes accented characters like è. If you match data that contains nonASCII characters, the named character classes are more general than trying to name the characters explicitly.

There are also backslash sequences that are shorthand for some of the named character classes. The following patterns to match digits are equivalent:

```
[0-9]
[[:digit:]]
\d
```

The following patterns match space-like characters including backspace, form feed, newline, carriage return, tag, and vertical tab:

```
[ \b\f\n\r\t\v]
[[:space:]]
\s
```

The named character classes and the associated backslash sequence are listed in Table 11–3 on page 156.

You can use character classes in combination with other characters or character classes inside a character set definition. The following patterns match letters, digits, and underscore:

```
[[:digit:][:alpha:]_]
[\d[:alpha:]_]
[[:alnum:]_]
\w
```

Note that \d, \s and \w can be used either inside or outside character sets. When used outside a bracketed expression, they form their own character set. There are also \D, \S, and \W, which are the complement of \d, \s, and \w. These escapes (i.e., \D for not-a-digit) cannot be used inside a bracketed character set.

There are two special character classes, [[:<:]] and [[:>:]], that match the beginning and end of a word, respectively. A word is defined as one or more characters that match \w.

Nongreedy Quantifiers

The *, +, and ? characters are *quantifiers* that specify repetition. By default these match as many characters as possible, which is called *greedy* matching. A *nongreedy* match will match as few characters as possible. You can specify non-greedy matching by putting a question mark after these quantifiers. Consider the pattern to match "one or more of not-a-newline followed by a newline." The not-a-newline must be explicit with the greedy quantifier, as in:

```
[^\n]+\n
```

Otherwise, if the pattern were just

```
.+\n
```

then the "." could well match newlines, so the pattern would greedily consume everything until the very last newline in the input. A nongreedy match would be satisfied with the very first newline instead:

```
.+?\n
```

By using the nongreedy quantifier we've cut the pattern from eight characters to five. Another example that is shorter with a nongreedy quantifier is the HTML example from page 148. The following pattern also matches everything between `<td>` and `</td>`:

```
<td>(.*?)</td>
```

Even ? can be made nongreedy, ??, which means it prefers to match zero instead of one. This only makes sense inside the context of a larger pattern. Send me email if you have a compelling example for it!

Bound Quantifiers

The {m,n} syntax is a quantifier that means match at least m and at most n of the previous matching item. There are two variations on this syntax. A simple {m} means match exactly m of the previous matching item. A {m, } means match m or more of the previous matching item. All of these can be made nongreedy by adding a ? after them.

Back References

A back reference is a feature you cannot easily get with basic regular expressions. A back reference matches the value of a subpattern captured with parentheses. If you have several sets of parentheses you can refer back to different captured expressions with \1, \2, and so on. You count by left parentheses to determine the reference.

For example, suppose you want to match a quoted string, where you can use either single or double quotes. You need to use an alternation of two patterns to match strings that are enclosed in double quotes or in single quotes:

```
("[^"]*"|'[^']*')
```

With a back reference, \1, the pattern becomes simpler:

```
('|").*?\1
```

The first set of parenthesis matches the leading quote, and then the \1 refers back to that particular quote character. The nongreedy quantifier ensures that the pattern matches up to the first occurrence of the matching quote.

Look-ahead

Look-ahead patterns are subexpressions that are matched but do not consume any of the input. They act like constraints on the rest of the pattern, and they typically occur at the end of your pattern. A positive look-ahead causes the pattern to match if it also matches. A negative look-ahead causes the pattern to match if it would not match. These constraints make more sense in the context of matching variables and in regular expression substitutions done with the `regsub` command. For example, the following pattern matches a filename that begins with A and ends with `.txt`

```
^A.*\.txt$
```

The next version of the pattern adds parentheses to group the file name suffix.

```
^A.*(\.txt$)
```

The parentheses are not strictly necessary, but they are introduced so that we can compare the pattern to one that uses look-ahead. A version of the pattern that uses look-ahead looks like this:

```
^A.*(?=\.txt$)
```

The pattern with the look-ahead constraint matches only the part of the filename before the `.txt`, but only if the `.txt` is present. In other words, the `.txt` is not consumed by the match. This is visible in the value of the matching variables used with the `regexp` command. It would also affect the substitutions done in the `regsub` command.

There is negative look-ahead too. The following pattern matches a filename that begins with A and does not end with `.txt`.

```
^A.*(?!\.txt$)
```

Writing this pattern without negative look-ahead is awkward.

Character Codes

The `\nn` and `\mmm` syntax, where *n* and *m* are digits, can also mean an 8-bit character code corresponding to the octal value *nn* or *mmm*. This has priority over a back reference. However, I just wouldn't use this notation for character codes. Instead, use the Unicode escape sequence, `\unnnn`, which specifies a 16-bit value. The `\xnn` sequence also specifies an 8-bit character code. Unfortunately, the `\x` escape consumes all hex digits after it (not just two!) and then truncates the hexadecimal value down to 8 bits. This misfeature of `\x` is not considered a bug and will probably not change even in future versions of Tcl.

The `\Uyyyyyyyy` syntax is reserved for 32-bit Unicode, but I don't expect to see that implemented anytime soon.

Collating Elements

Collating elements are characters or long names for characters that you can use inside character sets. Currently, Tcl only has some long names for various ASCII punctuation characters. Potentially, it could support names for every Unicode character, but it doesn't because the mapping tables would be huge. This section will briefly mention the syntax so that you can understand it if you see it. But its usefulness is still limited.

Within a bracketed expression, the following syntax is used to specify a collating element:

```
[.identifier.]
```

The identifier can be a character or a long name. The supported long names can be found in the `generic/regc_locale.c` file in the Tcl source code distribution. A few examples are shown below:

```
[.c.]
[.#.]
[.number-sign.]
```

Equivalence Classes

An equivalence class is all characters that sort to the same position. This is another feature that has limited usefulness in the current version of Tcl. In Tcl, characters sort by their Unicode character value, so there are no equivalence classes that contain more than one character! However, you could imagine a character class for 'o', 'ò', and other accented versions of the letter o. The syntax for equivalence classes within bracketed expressions is:

```
[=char=]
```

where `char` is any one of the characters in the character class. This syntax is valid only inside a character class definition.

Newline Sensitive Matching

By default, the newline character is just an ordinary character to the matching engine. You can make the newline character special with two options: `lineanchor` and `linestop`. You can set these options with flags to the `regexp` and `regsub` Tcl commands, or you can use the embedded options described later in Table 11–5 on page 157.

The `lineanchor` option makes the ^ and $ anchors work relative to newlines. The ^ matches immediately after a newline, and $ matches immediately before a newline. These anchors continue to match the very beginning and end of the input, too. With or without the `lineanchor` option, you can use \A and \Z to match the beginning and end of the string.

The `linestop` option prevents . (i.e., period) and character sets that begin with ^ from matching a newline character. In other words, unless you explicitly include \n in your pattern, it will not match across newlines.

II. Advanced Tcl

Embedded Options

You can start a pattern with embedded options to turn on or off case sensitivity, newline sensitivity, and expanded syntax, which is explained in the next section. You can also switch from advanced regular expressions to a literal string, or to older forms of regular expressions. The syntax is a leading:

    (?chars)

where `chars` is any number of option characters. The option characters are listed in Table 11–5 on page 157.

Expanded Syntax

Expanded syntax lets you include comments and extra white space in your patterns. This can greatly improve the readability of complex patterns. Expanded syntax is turned on with a `regexp` command option or an embedded option.

Comments start with a # and run until the end of line. Extra white space and comments can occur anywhere except inside bracketed expressions (i.e., character sets) or within multicharacter syntax elements like `(?=`. When you are in expanded mode, you can turn off the comment character or include an explicit space by preceding them with a backslash. Example 11–1 shows a pattern to match URLs. The leading `(?x)` turns on expanded syntax. The whole pattern is grouped in curly braces to hide it from Tcl. This example is considered again in more detail in Example 11–3 on page 159:

Example 11–1 Expanded regular expressions allow comments.

```
regexp {(?x)          # A pattern to match URLS
       ([^:]+):       # The protocol before the initial colon
       //([^:/]+)     # The server name
       (:([0-9]+))?   # The optional port number
       (/.*)          # The trailing pathname
} $input
```

Syntax Summary

Table 11–1 summarizes the syntax of regular expressions available in all versions of Tcl:

Table 11–1 Basic regular expression syntax.

.	Matches any character.
*	Matches zero or more instances of the previous pattern item.
+	Matches one or more instances of the previous pattern item.

Table 11–1 Basic regular expression syntax. (Continued)

?	Matches zero or one instances of the previous pattern item.
( )	Groups a subpattern. The repetition and alternation operators apply to the preceding subpattern.
|	Alternation.
[ ]	Delimit a set of characters. Ranges are specified as [x-y]. If the first character in the set is ^, then there is a match if the remaining characters in the set are *not* present.
^	Anchor the pattern to the beginning of the string. Only when first.
$	Anchor the pattern to the end of the string. Only when last.

Advanced regular expressions, which were introduced in Tcl 8.1, add more syntax that is summarized in Table 11–2:

Table 11–2 Additional advanced regular expression syntax.

{m}	Matches m instances of the previous pattern item.
{m}?	Matches m instances of the previous pattern item. Nongreedy.
{m, }	Matches m or more instances of the previous pattern item.
{m, }?	Matches m or more instances of the previous pattern item. Nongreedy.
{m,n}	Matches m through n instances of the previous pattern item.
{m,n}?	Matches m through n instances of the previous pattern item. Nongreedy.
*?	Matches zero or more instances of the previous pattern item. Nongreedy.
+?	Matches one or more instances of the previous pattern item. Nongreedy.
??	Matches zero or one instances of the previous pattern item. Nongreedy.
(?:re)	Groups a subpattern, re, but does not capture the result.
(?=re)	Positive look-ahead. Matches the point where re begins.
(?!re)	Negative look-ahead. Matches the point where re does not begin.
(?abc)	Embedded options, where abc is any number of option letters listed in Table 11–5.
\c	One of many backslash escapes listed in Table 11–4.
[: :]	Delimits a character class within a bracketed expression. See Table 11–3.
[. .]	Delimits a collating element within a bracketed expression.
[= =]	Delimits an equivalence class within a bracketed expression.

Table 11–3 lists the named character classes defined in advanced regular expressions and their associated backslash sequences, if any. Character class names are valid inside bracketed character sets with the [:class:] syntax.

Table 11–3 Character classes.

alnum	Upper and lower case letters and digits.
alpha	Upper and lower case letters.
blank	Space and tab.
cntrl	Control characters: \u0001 through \u001F.
digit	The digits zero through nine. Also \d.
graph	Printing characters that are not in cntrl or space.
lower	Lowercase letters.
print	The same as alnum.
punct	Punctuation characters.
space	Space, newline, carriage return, tab, vertical tab, form feed. Also \s.
upper	Uppercase letters.
xdigit	Hexadecimal digits: zero through nine, a-f, A-F.

Table 11–4 lists backslash sequences supported in Tcl 8.1.

Table 11–4 Backslash escapes in regular expressions.

\a	Alert, or "bell", character.
\A	Matches only at the beginning of the string.
\b	Backspace character, \u0008.
\B	Synonym for backslash.
\cX	Control-X.
\d	Digits. Same as [[:digit:]]
\D	Not a digit. Same as [^[:digit:]]
\e	Escape character, \u001B.
\f	Form feed, \u000C.
\m	Matches the beginning of a word.
\M	Matches the end of a word.
\n	Newline, \u000A.
\r	Carriage return, \u000D.
\s	Space. Same as [[:space:]]
\S	Not a space. Same as [^[:space:]]
\t	Horizontal tab, \u0009.

Table 11-4 Backslash escapes in regular expressions. (Continued)

\u*XXXX*	A 16-bit Unicode character code.
\v	Vertical tab, \u000B.
\w	Letters, digit, and underscore. Same as [[:alnum:]_]
\W	Not a letter, digit, or underscore. Same as [^[:alnum:]_]
\x*hh*	An 8-bit hexadecimal character code. Consumes all hex digits after \x.
\y	Matches the beginning or end of a word.
\Y	Matches a point that is not the beginning or end of a word.
\Z	Matches the end of the string.
\0	NULL, \u0000
x	Where *x* is a digit, this is a back-reference.
xy	Where *x* and *y* are digits, either a decimal back-reference, or an 8-bit octal character code.
xyz	Where *x*, *y* and *z* are digits, either a decimal back-reference or an 8-bit octal character code.

Table 11-5 lists the embedded option characters used with the (?*abc*) syntax.

Table 11-5 Embedded option characters used with the (?*x*) syntax.

b	The rest of the pattern is a basic regular expression (a la *vi* or *grep*).
c	Case sensitive matching. This is the default.
e	The rest of the pattern is an extended regular expression (*a la* Tcl 8.0).
i	Case insensitive matching.
m	Synonym for the n option.
n	Newline sensitive matching . Both lineanchor and linestop mode.
p	Partial newline sensitive matching. Only linestop mode.
q	The rest of the pattern is a literal string.
s	No newline sensitivity. This is the default.
t	Tight syntax; no embedded comments. This is the default.
w	Inverse partial newline-sensitive matching. Only lineanchor mode.
x	Expanded syntax with embedded white space and comments.

II. Advanced Tcl

The `regexp` Command

The `regexp` command provides direct access to the regular expression matcher. Not only does it tell you whether a string matches a pattern, it can also extract one or more matching substrings. The return value is 1 if some part of the string matches the pattern; it is 0 otherwise. Its syntax is:

```
regexp ?flags? pattern string ?match sub1 sub2...?
```

The *flags* are described in Table 11–6:

Table 11–6 Options to the `regexp` command.

`-nocase`	Lowercase characters in *pattern* can match either lowercase or uppercase letters in *string*.
`-indices`	The match variables each contain a pair of numbers that are in indices delimiting the match within *string*. Otherwise, the matching string itself is copied into the match variables.
`-expanded`	The pattern uses the expanded syntax discussed on page 154.
`-line`	The same as specifying both `-lineanchor` and `-linestop`.
`-lineanchor`	Change the behavior of ^ and $ so they are line-oriented as discussed on page 153.
`-linestop`	Change matching so that . and character classes do not match newlines as discussed on page 153.
`-about`	Useful for debugging. It returns information about the pattern instead of trying to match it against the input.
`--`	Signals the end of the options. You must use this if your pattern begins with –.

The *pattern* argument is a regular expression as described earlier. If *string* matches *pattern*, then `regexp` stores the results of the match in the variables provided. These match variables are optional. If present, *match* is set to the part of the string that matched the pattern. The remaining variables are set to the substrings of *string* that matched the corresponding subpatterns in *pattern*. The correspondence is based on the order of left parentheses in the pattern to avoid ambiguities that can arise from nested subpatterns.

Example 11–2 uses `regexp` to pick the hostname out of the DISPLAY environment variable, which has the form:

```
hostname:display.screen
```

Example 11–2 Using regular expressions to parse a string.

```
set env(DISPLAY) sage:0.1
regexp {([^:]*):} $env(DISPLAY) match host
=> 1
set match
=> sage:
set host
=> sage
```

The pattern involves a complementary set, `[^:]`, to match anything except a colon. It uses repetition, `*`, to repeat that zero or more times. It groups that part into a subexpression with parentheses. The literal colon ensures that the DISPLAY value matches the format we expect. The part of the string that matches the complete pattern is stored into the `match` variable. The part that matches the subpattern is stored into `host`. The whole pattern has been grouped with braces to quote the square brackets. Without braces it would be:

```
regexp (\[^:\]*): $env(DISPLAY) match host
```

With advanced regular expressions the nongreedy quantifier `*?` can replace the complementary set:

```
regexp (.*?): $env(DISPLAY) match host
```

This is quite a powerful statement, and it is efficient. If we had only had the `string` command to work with, we would have needed to resort to the following, which takes roughly twice as long to interpret:

```
set i [string first : $env(DISPLAY)]
if {$i >= 0} {
    set host [string range $env(DISPLAY) 0 [expr $i-1]]
}
```

A Pattern to Match URLs

Example 11–3 demonstrates a pattern with several subpatterns that extract the different parts of a URL. There are lots of subpatterns, and you can determine which match variable is associated with which subpattern by counting the left parenthesis. The pattern will be discussed in more detail after the example:

Example 11–3 A pattern to match URLs.

```
set url http://www.beedub.com:80/index.html
regexp {([^:]+)://([^:/]+)(:([0-9]+))?(/.*)} $url \
    match protocol server x port path
=> 1
set match
=> http://www.beedub.com:80/index.html
set protocol
=> http
set server
=> www.beedub.com
set x
=> :80
set port
=> 80
set path
=> /index.html
```

Let's look at the pattern one piece at a time. The first part looks for the protocol, which is separated by a colon from the rest of the URL. The first part of the pattern is one or more characters that are not a colon, followed by a colon. This matches the `http:` part of the URL:

```
[^:]+:
```

Using nongreedy `+?` quantifier, you could also write that as:

```
.+?:
```

The next part of the pattern looks for the server name, which comes after two slashes. The server name is followed either by a colon and a port number, or by a slash. The pattern uses a complementary set that specifies one or more characters that are *not* a colon or a slash. This matches the `//www.beedub.com` part of the URL:

```
//[^:/]+
```

The port number is optional, so a subpattern is delimited with parentheses and followed by a question mark. An additional set of parentheses are added to capture the port number without the leading colon. This matches the `:80` part of the URL:

```
(:([0-9]+))?
```

The last part of the pattern is everything else, starting with a slash. This matches the `/index.html` part of the URL:

```
/.*
```

Use subpatterns to parse strings.

To make this pattern really useful, we delimit several subpatterns with parentheses:

```
([^:]+)://([^:/]+)(:([0-9]+))?(/.*)
```

These parentheses do not change the way the pattern matches. Only the optional port number really needs the parentheses in this example. However, the `regexp` command gives us access to the strings that match these subpatterns. In one step `regexp` can test for a valid URL and divide it into the protocol part, the server, the port, and the trailing path.

The parentheses around the port number include the : before the digits. We've used a dummy variable that gets the : and the port number, and another match variable that just gets the port number. By using noncapturing parentheses in advanced regular expressions, we can eliminate the unused match variable. We can also replace both complementary character sets with a nongreedy `.+?` match. Example 11–4 shows this variation:

Example 11–4 An advanced regular expression to match URLs.

```
set url http://www.beedub.com:80/book/
regexp {(.+?)://(.+?)(?::([0-9]+))?(/.*)$} $url \
    match protocol server port path
=> 1
set match
=> http://www.beedub.com:80/book/
```

```
set protocol
=> http
set server
=> www.beedub.com
set port
=> 80
set path
=> /book/
```

Bugs When Mixing Greedy and Non-Greedy Quantifiers

If you have a regular expression pattern that uses both greedy and non-greedy quantifiers, then you can quickly run into trouble. The problem is that in complex cases there can be ambiguous ways to resolve the quantifiers. Unfortunately, what happens in practice is that Tcl tends to make all the quantifiers either greedy, or all of them non-greedy. Example 11–4 has a $ at the end to force the last greedy term to go to the end of the string. In theory, the greediness of the last subpattern should match all the characters out to the end of the string. In practice, Tcl makes all the quantifiers non-greedy, so the anchor is necessary to force the pattern to match to the end of the string.

Sample Regular Expressions

The table in this section lists regular expressions as you would use them in Tcl commands. Most are quoted with curly braces to turn off the special meaning of square brackets and dollar signs. Other patterns are grouped with double quotes and use backslash quoting because the patterns include backslash sequences like \n and \t. In Tcl 8.0 and earlier, these must be substituted by Tcl before the `regexp` command is called. In these cases, the equivalent advanced regular expression is also shown.

Table 11–7 Sample regular expressions.

`{^[yY]}`	Begins with y or Y, as in a Yes answer.
`{^(yes|YES|Yes)$}`	Exactly "yes", "Yes", or "YES".
`{^[^ \t:\]+:}`	Begins with colon-delimited field that has no spaces or tabs.
`{^\S+?:}`	Same as above, using \S for "not space".
`"^\[ \t]*$"`	A string of all spaces or tabs.
`{(?n)^\s*$}`	A blank line using newline sensitive mode.
`"(\n|^)\[^\n\]*(\n|$)"`	A blank line, the hard way.
`{^[A-Za-z]+$}`	Only letters.
`{^[[:alpha:]]+$}`	Only letters, the Unicode way.

Table 11-7 Sample regular expressions. (Continued)

`{[A-Za-z0-9_]+}`	Letters, digits, and the underscore.
`{\w+}`	Letters, digits, and the underscore using `\w`.
`{[][${}\\]}`	The set of Tcl special characters:] [$ { } \
`"\[^\n\]*\n"`	Everything up to a newline.
`{.*?\n}`	Everything up to a newline using nongreedy `*?`
`{\.}`	A period.
`{[][$^?+*()|\\]}`	The set of regular expression special characters:][$ ^ ? + * ( ) | \
`<H1>(.*?)</H1>`	An `H1` HTML tag. The subpattern matches the string between the tags.
`<!--.*?-->`	HTML comments.
`{[0-9a-hA-H][0-9a-hA-H]}`	2 hex digits.
`{[[:xdigit:]]{2}}`	2 hex digits, using advanced regular expressions.
`{\d{1,3}}`	1 to 3 digits, using advanced regular expressions.

The `regsub` Command

The `regsub` command does string substitution based on pattern matching. It is very useful for processing your data. It can perform simple tasks like replacing sequences of spaces and tabs with a single space. It can perform complex data transforms, too, as described in the next section. Its syntax is:

        regsub ?*switches*? *pattern string subspec varname*

The `regsub` command returns the number of matches and replacements, or 0 if there was no match. `regsub` copies *string* to *varname*, replacing occurrences of *pattern* with the substitution specified by *subspec*. If the pattern does not match, then *string* is copied to *varname* without modification. The optional switches include:

- `-all`, which means to replace all occurrences of the pattern. Otherwise, only the first occurrence is replaced.
- The `-nocase`, `-expanded`, `-line`, `-linestop`, and `-lineanchor` switches are the same as in the `regexp` command. They are described on page 158.
- The `--` switch separates the pattern from the switches, which is necessary if your pattern begins with a `-`.

The replacement pattern, *subspec*, can contain literal characters as well as the following special sequences:

- `&` is replaced with the string that matched the pattern.
- `\x` , where *x* is a number, is replaced with the string that matched the corresponding subpattern in *pattern*. The correspondence is based on the order of left parentheses in the pattern specification.

The following replaces a user's home directory with a ~:

```
regsub ^$env(HOME)/ $pathname ~/ newpath
```

The following constructs a C compile command line given a filename:

```
set file tclIO.c
regsub {(([^\.]*)\.c$} $file {cc -c & -o \1.o} ccCmd
```

The matching pattern captures everything before the trailing `.c` in the file name. The `&` is replaced with the complete match, `tclIO.c`, and `\1` is replaced with `tclIO`, which matches the pattern between the parentheses. The value assigned to `ccCmd` is:

```
cc -c tclIO.c -o tclIO.o
```

We could execute that with:

```
eval exec $ccCmd
```

The following replaces sequences of multiple space characters with a single space:

```
regsub -all {\s+} $string " " string
```

It is perfectly safe to specify the same variable as the input value and the result. Even if there is no match on the pattern, the input string is copied into the output variable.

The `regsub` command can count things for us. The following command counts the newlines in some text. In this case the substitution is not important:

```
set numLines [regsub -all \n $text {} ignore]
```

Transforming Data to Program with `regsub`

One of the most powerful combinations of Tcl commands is `regsub` and `subst`. This section describes a few examples that use `regsub` to transform data into Tcl commands, and then use `subst` to replace those commands with a new version of the data. This technique is very efficient because it relies on two subsystems that are written in highly optimized C code: the regular expression engine and the Tcl parser. These examples are primarily written by Stephen Uhler.

URL Decoding

When a URL is transmitted over the network, it is encoded by replacing special characters with a %*xx* sequence, where *xx* is the hexadecimal code for the character. In addition, spaces are replaced with a plus (+). It would be tedious and very inefficient to scan a URL one character at a time with Tcl statements to undo this encoding. It would be more efficient to do this with a custom C program, but still very tedious. Instead, a combination of regsub and subst can efficiently decode the URL in just a few Tcl commands.

Replacing the + with spaces requires quoting the + because it is the one-or-more special character in regular expressions:

```
regsub -all {\+} $url { } url
```

The %*xx* are replaced with a format command that will generate the right character:

```
regsub -all {%([0-9a-hA-H][0-9a-hA-H])} $url \
    {[format %c 0x\1]} url
```

The %c directive to format tells it to generate the character from a character code number. We force a hexadecimal interpretation with a leading 0x. Advanced regular expressions let us write the "2 hex digits" pattern a bit more cleanly:

```
regsub -all {%([[:xdigit:]]{2})} $url \
    {[format %c 0x\1]} url
```

The resulting string is passed to subst to get the format commands substituted:

```
set url [subst $url]
```

For example, if the input is %7ewelch, the result of the regsub is:

```
[format %c 0x7e]welch
```

And then subst generates:

```
~welch
```

Example 11–5 encapsulates this trick in the Url_Decode procedure.

Example 11–5 The Url_Decode procedure.

```
proc Url_Decode {url} {
    regsub -all {\+} $url { } url
    regsub -all {%([[:xdigit:]]{2})} $url \
        {[format %c 0x\1]} url
    return [subst $url]
}
```

CGI Argument Parsing

Example 11–6 builds upon `Url_Decode` to decode the inputs to a CGI program that processes data from an HTML form. Each form element is identified by a name, and the value is URL encoded. All the names and encoded values are passed to the CGI program in the following format:

```
name1=value1&name2=value2&name3=value3
```

Example 11–6 shows `Cgi_List` and `Cgi_Query`. `Cgi_Query` receives the form data from the standard input or the `QUERY_STRING` environment variable, depending on whether the form data is transmitted with a `POST` or `GET` request. These `HTTP` operations are described in detail in Chapter 17. `Cgi_List` uses `split` to get back a list of names and values, and then it decodes them with `Url_Decode`. It returns a Tcl-friendly name, value list that you can either iterate through with a `foreach` command, or assign to an array with `array set`:

Example 11–6 The `Cgi_List` and `Cgi_Query` procedures.

```
proc Cgi_List {} {
    set query [Cgi_Query]
    regsub -all {\+} $query { } query
    set result {}
    foreach {x} [split $query &=] {
        lappend result [Url_Decode $x]
    }
    return $result
}
proc Cgi_Query {} {
    global env
    if {![info exists env(QUERY_STRING)] ||
            [string length $env(QUERY_STRING)] == 0} {
        if {[info exists env(CONTENT_LENGTH)] &&
                [string length $env(CONTENT_LENGTH)] != 0} {
            set query [read stdin $env(CONTENT_LENGTH)]
        } else {
            gets stdin query
        }
        set env(QUERY_STRING) $query
        set env(CONTENT_LENGTH) 0
    }
    return $env(QUERY_STRING)
}
```

An HTML form can have several form elements with the same name, and this can result in more than one value for each name. If you blindly use `array set` to map the results of `Cgi_List` into an array, you will lose the repeated values. Example 11–7 shows `Cgi_Parse` and `Cgi_Value` that store the query data in a global `cgi` array. `Cgi_Parse` adds list structure whenever it finds a repeated form value. The global `cgilist` array keeps a record of how many times a form value is repeated. The `Cgi_Value` procedure returns elements of the global `cgi` array, or the empty string if the requested value is not present.

Example 11–7 Cgi_Parse and Cgi_Value store query data in the cgi array.

```
proc Cgi_Parse {} {
    global cgi cgilist
    catch {unset cgi cgilist}
    set query [Cgi_Query]
    regsub -all {\+} $query { } query
    foreach {name value} [split $query &=] {
        set name [CgiDecode $name]
        if {[info exists cgilist($name)] &&
                ($cgilist($name) == 1)} {
            # Add second value and create list structure
            set cgi($name) [list $cgi($name) \
                [Url_Decode $value]]
        } elseif {[info exists cgi($name)]} {
            # Add additional list elements
            lappend cgi($name) [CgiDecode $value]
        } else {
            # Add first value without list structure
            set cgi($name) [CgiDecode $value]
            set cgilist($name) 0    ;# May need to listify
        }
        incr cgilist($name)
    }
    return [array names cgi]
}
proc Cgi_Value {key} {
    global cgi
    if {[info exists cgi($key)]} {
        return $cgi($key)
    } else {
        return {}
    }
}
proc Cgi_Length {key} {
    global cgilist
    if {[info exist cgilist($key)]} {
        return $cgilist($key)
    } else {
        return 0
    }
}
```

Decoding HTML Entities

The next example is a decoder for HTML *entities*. In HTML, special characters are encoded as entities. If you want a literal < or > in your document, you
encode them as the entities < and >, respectively, to avoid conflict with the
<*tag*> syntax used in HTML. HTML syntax is briefly described in Chapter 3 on
page 34. Characters with codes above 127 such as copyright © and egrave è are
also encoded. There are named entities, such as < for < and è for è.
You can also use decimal-valued entities such as © for ©. Finally, the trailing semicolon is optional, so &lt or < can both be used to encode <.

The entity decoder is similar to `Url_Decode`. In this case, however, we need to be more careful with `subst`. The text passed to the decoder could contain special characters like a square bracket or dollar sign. With `Url_Decode` we can rely on those special characters being encoded as, for example, `%24`. Entity encoding is different (do not ask me why URLs and HTML have different encoding standards), and dollar signs and square brackets are not necessarily encoded. This requires an additional pass to quote these characters. This `regsub` puts a backslash in front of all the brackets, dollar signs, and backslashes.

```
regsub -all {[][$\\]} $text {\\&} new
```

The decimal encoding (e.g., `&#169;`) is also more awkward than the hexadecimal encoding used in URLs. We cannot force a decimal interpretation of a number in Tcl. In particular, if the entity has a leading zero (e.g., `&#010;`) then Tcl interprets the value (e.g., `010`) as octal. The `scan` command is used to do a decimal interpretation. It scans into a temporary variable, and `set` is used to get that value:

```
regsub -all {&#([0-9][0-9]?[0-9]?);?}  $new \
    {[format %c [scan \1 %d tmp; set tmp]]} new
```

With advanced regular expressions, this could be written as follows using bound quantifiers to specify one to three digits:

```
regsub -all {&#(\d{1,3});?}  $new \
    {[format %c [scan \1 %d tmp;set tmp]]} new
```

The named entities are converted with an array that maps from the entity names to the special character. The only detail is that unknown entity names (e.g., `&foobar;`) are not converted. This mapping is done inside `HtmlMapEntity`, which guards against invalid entities.

```
regsub -all {&([a-zA-Z]+)(;?)} $new \
    {[HtmlMapEntity \1 \\\2 ]} new
```

If the input text contained:

```
[x &lt; y]
```

then the `regsub` would transform this into:

```
\[x [HtmlMapEntity lt \; ] y\]
```

Finally, `subst` will result in:

```
[x < y]
```

Example 11–8 `Html_DecodeEntity`.

```
proc Html_DecodeEntity {text} {
    if {![regexp & $text]} {return $text}
    regsub -all {[][$\\]} $text {\\&} new
    regsub -all {&#([0-9][0-9]?[0-9]?);?}  $new {\
        [format %c [scan \1 %d tmp;set tmp]]} new
    regsub -all {&([a-zA-Z]+)(;?)} $new \
        {[HtmlMapEntity \1 \\\2 ]} new
    return [subst $new]
}
```

```
proc HtmlMapEntity {text {semi {}}} {
    global htmlEntityMap
    if {[info exist htmlEntityMap($text)]} {
        return $htmlEntityMap($text)
    } else {
        return $text$semi
    }
}
# Some of the htmlEntityMap
array set htmlEntityMap {
    lt <   gt >   amp &
    aring \xe5   atilde \xe3
    copy  \xa9   ecirc \xea   egrave \xe8
}
```

A Simple HTML Parser

The following example is the brainchild of Stephen Uhler. It uses `regsub` to transform HTML into a Tcl script. When it is evaluated the script calls a procedure to handle each tag in an HTML document. This provides a general framework for processing HTML. Different callback procedures can be applied to the tags to achieve different effects. For example, the `html_library-0.3` package on the CD-ROM uses `Html_Parse` to display HTML in a Tk text widget.

Example 11–9 `Html_Parse`.

```
proc Html_Parse {html cmd {start {}}} {

    # Map braces and backslashes into HTML entities
    regsub -all \{ $html {\&ob;} html
    regsub -all \} $html {\&cb;} html
    regsub -all {\\} $html {\&bsl;} html

    # This pattern matches the parts of an HTML tag
    set s" \t\r\n"    ;# white space
    set exp <(/?)(\[^$s>]+)\[$s]*(\[^>]*)>

    # This generates a call to cmd with HTML tag parts
    # \1 is the leading /, if any
    # \2 is the HTML tag name
    # \3 is the parameters to the tag, if any
    # The curly braces at either end group of all the text
    # after the HTML tag, which becomes the last arg to $cmd.
    set sub "\}\n$cmd {\\2} {\\1} {\\3} \{"
    regsub -all $exp $html $sub html

    # This balances the curly braces,
    # and calls $cmd with $start as a pseudo-tag
    # at the beginning and end of the script.
    eval "$cmd {$start} {} {} {$html}"
    eval "$cmd {$start} / {} {}"
}
```

The main `regsub` pattern can be written more simply with advanced regular expressions:

```
set exp {<(/?)(\S+?)\s*(.*?)>}
```

An example will help visualize the transformation. Given this HTML:

```
<Title>My Home Page</Title>
<Body bgcolor=white text=black>
<H1>My Home</H1>
This is my <b>home</b> page.
```

and a call to `Html_Parse` that looks like this:

```
Html_Parse $html {Render .text} hmstart
```

then the generated program is this:

```
Render .text {hmstart} {} {} {}
Render .text {Title} {} {} {My Home Page}
Render .text {Title} {/} {} {
}
Render .text {Body} {} {bgcolor=white text=black} {
}
Render .text {H1} {} {} {My Home}
Render .text {H1} {/} {} {
This is my }
Render .text {b} {} {} {home}
Render .text {b} {/} {} { page.
}
Render .text {hmstart} / {} {}
```

One overall point to make about this example is the difference between using `eval` and `subst` with the generated script. The decoders shown in Examples 11–5 and 11–8 use `subst` to selectively replace encoded characters while ignoring the rest of the text. In `Html_Parse` we must process all the text. The main trick is to replace the matching text (e.g., the HTML tag) with some Tcl code that ends in an open curly brace and starts with a close curly brace. This effectively groups all the unmatched text.

When `eval` is used this way you must do something with any braces and backslashes in the unmatched text. Otherwise, the resulting script does not parse correctly. In this case, these special characters are encoded as HTML entities. We can afford to do this because the `cmd` that is called must deal with encoded entities already. It is not possible to quote these special characters with backslashes because all this text is inside curly braces, so no backslash substitution is performed. If you try that the backslashes will be seen by the `cmd` callback.

Finally, I must admit that I am always surprised that this works:

```
eval "$cmd {$start} {} {} {$html}"
```

I always forget that `$start` and `$html` are substituted in spite of the braces. This is because double quotes are being used to group the argument, so the quoting effect of braces is turned off.

Stripping HTML Comments

The `Html_Parse` procedure does not correctly handle HTML comments. The problem is that the syntax for HTML commands allows tags inside comments, so there can be > characters inside the comment. HTML comments are also used to hide Javascript inside pages, which can also contain >. We can fix this with a pass that eliminates the comments.

The comment syntax is this:

```
<!-- HTML comment, could contain <markup> -->
```

Using nongreedy quantifiers, we can strip comments with a single `regsub`:

```
regsub -all <!--.*?--> $html {} html
```

Using only greedy quantifiers, it is awkward to match the closing --> without getting stuck on embedded > characters, or without matching too much and going all the way to the end of the last comment. Time for another trick:

```
regsub -all --> $html \x81 html
```

This replaces all the end comment sequences with a single character that is not allowed in HTML. Now you can delete the comments like this:

```
regsub -all "<!--\[^\x81\]*\x81" $html {} html
```

Other Commands That Use Regular Expressions

Several Tcl commands use regular expressions.

- `lsearch` takes a `-regexp` flag so that you can search for list items that match a regular expression. The `lsearch` command is described on page 69.
- `switch` takes a `-regexp` flag, so you can branch based on a regular expression match instead of an exact match or a `string match` style match. The `switch` command is described on page 77.
- The Tk text widget can search its contents based on a regular expression match. Searching in the text widget is described on page 542.
- The *Expect* Tcl extension can match the output of a program with regular expressions. *Expect* is the subject of its own book, *Exploring Expect* (O'Reilly, 1995) by Don Libes.

Script Libraries and Packages

Collections of Tcl commands are kept in libraries and organized into packages.
Tcl automatically loads libraries as an application uses their commands.
Tcl commands discussed are: `package`, `pkg_mkIndex`,
`auto_mkindex`, `unknown`, and `tcl_findLibrary`.

*L*ibraries group useful sets of Tcl proce-
dures so that they can be used by multiple applications. For example, you could
use any of the code examples that come with this book by creating a script
library and then directing your application to check in that library for missing
procedures. One way to structure a large application is to have a short main
script and a library of support scripts. The advantage of this approach is that not
all the Tcl code needs to be loaded to start the application. Applications start up
quickly, and as new features are accessed, the code that implements them is
loaded automatically.

The Tcl package facility supports version numbers and has a *provide/
require* model of use. Typically, each file in a library provides one package with a
particular version number. Packages also work with shared object libraries that
implement Tcl commands in compiled code, which are described in Chapter 47. A
package can be provided by a combination of script files and object files. Applications specify which packages they require and the libraries are loaded automatically. The package facility is an alternative to the auto loading scheme used in
earlier versions of Tcl. You can use either mechanism, and this chapter describes
them both.

If you create a package you may wish to use the namespace facility to avoid
conflicts between procedures and global variables used in different packages.
Namespaces are the topic of Chapter 14. Before Tcl 8.0 you had to use your own
conventions to avoid conflicts. This chapter explains a simple coding convention
for large Tcl programs. I use this convention in exmh, a mail user interface that

has grown from about 2,000 to over 35,000 lines of Tcl code. A majority of the code has been contributed by the exmh user community. Such growth might not have been possible without coding conventions.

Locating Packages: The `auto_path` Variable

The package facility assumes that Tcl libraries are kept in well-known directories. The list of well-known directories is kept in the `auto_path` Tcl variable. This is initialized by `tclsh` and `wish` to include the Tcl script library directory, the Tk script library directory (for `wish`), and the parent directory of the Tcl script library directory. For example, on my Macintosh `auto_path` is a list of these three directories:

```
Disk:System Folder:Extensions:Tool Command Language:tcl8.4
Disk:System Folder:Extensions:Tool Command Language
Disk:System Folder:Extensions:Tool Command Language:tk8.4
```

On my Windows 95 machine the `auto_path` lists these directories:

```
c:\Program Files\Tcl\lib\Tcl8.4
c:\Program Files\Tcl\lib
c:\Program Files\Tcl\lib\Tk8.4
```

On my UNIX workstation the `auto_path` lists these directories:

```
/usr/local/tcl/lib/tcl8.4
/usr/local/tcl/lib
/usr/local/tcl/lib/tk8.4
```

The package facility searches these directories and their subdirectories for packages. The easiest way to manage your own packages is to create a directory at the same level as the Tcl library:

```
/usr/local/tcl/lib/welchbook
```

Packages in this location, for example, will be found automatically because the `auto_path` list includes `/usr/local/tcl/lib`. You can also add directories to the `auto_path` explicitly:

```
lappend auto_path directory
```

One trick I often use is to put the directory containing the main script into the `auto_path`. The following command sets this up:

```
lappend auto_path [file dirname [info script]]
```

If your code is split into `bin` and `lib` directories, then scripts in the `bin` directory can add the adjacent `lib` directory to their `auto_path` with this command:

```
lappend auto_path \
    [file join [file dirname [info script]] ../lib]
```

Using Packages

Each script file in a library declares what package it implements with the `package provide` command:

```
package provide name version
```

The *name* identifies the package, and the *version* has a *major.minor* format. The convention is that the minor version number can change and the package implementation will still be compatible. If the package changes in an incompatible way, then the major version number should change. For example, Chapter 17 defines several procedures that use the HTTP network protocol. These include `http::geturl`, `http::wait`, and `http::cleanup`. The file that contains the procedures starts with this command:

```
package provide http 2.4
```

Case is significant in package names. In particular, the package that comes with Tcl is named `http` — all lowercase.

More than one file can contribute to the same package simply by specifying the same *name* and *version*. In addition, different versions of the same package can be kept in the same directory but in different files.

An application specifies the packages it needs with the `package require` command:

```
package require name ?version? ?-exact?
```

If the *version* is left off, then the highest available version is loaded. Otherwise the highest version with the same major number is loaded. For example, if the client requires version 1.1, version 1.2 could be loaded if it exists, but versions 1.0 and 2.0 would not be loaded. You can restrict the package to a specific version with the `-exact` flag. If no matching version can be found, then the `package require` command raises an error.

Loading Packages Automatically

The `package require` command depends on an index to record which files implement which packages. The index must be maintained by you, your project librarian, or your system administrator when packages change. The index is created by the `pkg_mkIndex` command, which puts the index into a `pkgIndex.tcl` file in each library directory. The `pkg_mkIndex` command takes the name of a directory and one or more *glob* patterns that specify files within that directory. File name patterns are described on page 122. The syntax is:

```
pkg_mkIndex ?options? directory pattern ?pattern ...?
```

For example:

```
pkg_mkIndex /usr/local/lib/welchbook *.tcl
pkg_mkIndex -lazy /usr/local/lib/Sybtcl *.so
```

The `pkg_mkIndex` command sources or loads all the files matched by the pattern, detects what packages they provide, and computes the index. You should be aware of this behavior because it works well only for libraries. If the `pkg_mkIndex` command hangs or starts random applications, it is because it sourced an application file instead of a library file.

The package index, `pkgIndex.tcl`, is sourced in response to a `package require` command. The index instructs the package loading mechanism how to define the package. By default, `source` or `load` commands are specified so that packages are defined immediately as a side effect of `package require`. This is called *direct loading*. However, the original package index system used a *deferred loading* scheme layered on the `auto_load` mechanism and the `unknown` command hook, which is described on page 178. If you want deferred loading, use the `-lazy` option to `pkg_mkIndex`. The default behavior of `pkg_mkIndex` switched from `-lazy` to `-direct` in Tcl 8.3. The `pkg_mkIndex` options are summarized in Table 12–1.

Table 12–1 Options to the `pkg_mkIndex` command.

`-direct`	Generates an index with `source` and `load` commands in it. This results in packages being loaded directly as a result of `package require`. This is the default starting with Tcl 8.3.
`-lazy`	Generates an index that populates the `auto_index` array for deferred loading of commands. This behavior was the default prior to Tcl 8.3.
`-load` *pattern*	Dynamically loads packages that match *pattern* into the slave interpreter used to compute the index. A common reason to need this is with the `tcb-load` package needed to load `.tbc` files compiled with *TclPro Compiler*.
`-verbose`	Displays the name of each file processed and any errors that occur.

Packages Implemented in C Code

The files in a library can be either script files that define Tcl procedures or binary files in shared library format that define Tcl commands in compiled code (i.e., a Dynamic Link Library (DLL)). Chapter 47 describes how to implement Tcl commands in C. There is a C API to the package facility that you use to declare the package name for your commands. This is shown in Example 47–1 on page 698. Chapter 37 also describes the Tcl `load` command that is used instead of `source` to link in shared libraries. The `pkg_mkIndex` command also handles shared libraries:

```
pkg_mkIndex directory *.tcl *.so *.shlib *.dll
```

In this example, `.so`, `.shlib`, and `.dll` are file suffixes for shared libraries on UNIX, Macintosh, and Windows systems, respectively. You can have packages that have some of their commands implemented in C, and some implemented as Tcl procedures. The script files and the shared library must simply declare that they implement the same package. The `pkg_mkIndex` procedure will detect this and set up the `auto_index,` so some commands are defined by sourcing scripts, and some are defined by loading shared libraries.

If your file servers support more than one machine architecture, such as Solaris and Linux systems, you probably keep the shared library files in machine-specific directories. In this case the `auto_path` should also list the machine-specific directory so that the shared libraries there can be loaded automatically. If your system administrator configured the Tcl installation properly, this should already be set up. If not, or you have your shared libraries in a nonstandard place, you must append the location to the `auto_path` variable.

Summary of Package Loading

The basic structure of package loading works like this:

- An application does a `package require` command. If the package is already loaded, the command just returns the version number of the already loaded package. If is not loaded, the following steps occur.
- The package facility checks to see if it knows about the package. If it does, then it runs the Tcl scripts registered with the `package ifneeded` command. These commands either load the package or set it up to be loaded automatically when its commands are first used.
- If the package is unknown, the `tclPkgUnknown` procedure is called to find it. Actually, you can specify what procedure to call to do the lookup with the `package unknown` command, but the standard one is `tclPkgUnknown`.
- The `tclPkgUnknown` procedure looks through the `auto_path` directories and their subdirectories for `pkgIndex.tcl` files. It sources those to build an internal database of packages and version information. The `pkgIndex.tcl` files contain calls to `package ifneeded` that specify what to do to define the package. You can use the `pkg_mkIndex` command to create your `pkgIndex.tcl` files, or you can create them by hand.
- In the case of deferred package loading, the `tclPkgSetup` procedure defines the `auto_index` array to contain the correct `source` or `load` commands to define each command in the package. Automatic loading and the `auto_index` array are described in more detail later.

As you can see, there are several levels of processing involved in finding packages. The system is flexible enough that you can change the way packages are located and how packages are loaded. The `-lazy` scenario is complicated because it uses the delayed loading of source code that is described in the next section. Using the `-direct` flag to `pkg_mkIndex` simplifies the situation. In any case, it all boils down to three key steps:

- Use `pkg_mkIndex` to maintain your index files. Decide at this time whether or not to use direct or lazy package loading.
- Put the appropriate `package require` and `package provide` commands in your code.
- Ensure that your library directories, or their parent directories, are listed in the `auto_path` variable.

II. Advanced Tcl

The package Command

The `package` command has several operations that are used primarily by the `pkg_mkIndex` procedure and the automatic loading facility. These operations are summarized in Table 12–2.

Table 12–2 The `package` command.

`package forget` *package*	Deletes registration information for package.
`package ifneeded` *package* ?*command*?	Queries or sets the command used to set up automatic loading of a package.
`package names`	Returns the set of registered packages.
`package provide` *package version*	Declares that a script file defines commands for *package* with the given *version*.
`package present` *package* ?*version*? ?-exact?	Equivalent to `package require`, except that no attempt to load the package is made if it is not loaded.
`package require` *package* ?*version*? ?-exact?	Declares that a script uses *package*. The –exact flag specifies that the exact `version` must be loaded. Otherwise, the highest matching version is loaded.
`package unknown` ?*command*?	Queries or sets the *command* used to locate packages.
`package vcompare` *v1 v2*	Compares version *v1* and *v2*. Returns 0 if they are equal, -1 if *v1* is less than *v2*, or 1 if *v1* is greater than *v2*.
`package versions` *package*	Returns which versions of the package are registered.
`package vsatisfies` *v1 v2*	Returns 1 if *v1* is greater or equal to *v2* and still has the same major version number. Otherwise returns 0.

Libraries Based on the `tclIndex` File

You can create libraries without using the `package` command. The basic idea is that a directory has a library of script files, and an index of the Tcl commands defined in the library is kept in a `tclIndex` file. The drawback is that versions are not supported and you may need to adjust the `auto_path` to list your library directory. The main advantage of this approach is that this mechanism has been part of Tcl since the earliest versions. If you currently maintain a library using `tclIndex` files, it will still work.

You must generate the index that records what procedures are defined in the library. The `auto_mkindex` procedure creates the index, which is stored in a file named `tclIndex` that is kept in the script library directory. (Watch out for the difference in capitalization between `auto_mkindex` and `pkg_mkIndex`!) Suppose all the examples from this book are in the directory `/usr/local/tcl/welchbook`. You can make the examples into a script library by creating the `tclIndex` file:

```
auto_mkindex /usr/local/tcl/welchbook *.tcl
```

You will need to update the `tclIndex` file if you add procedures or change any of their names. A conservative approach to this is shown in the next example. It is conservative because it re-creates the index if anything in the library has changed since the `tclIndex` file was last generated, whether or not the change added or removed a Tcl procedure.

Example 12–1 Maintaining a `tclIndex` file.

```
proc Library_UpdateIndex { libdir } {
    set index [file join $libdir tclIndex]
    if {![file exists $index]} {
        set doit 1
    } else {
        set age [file mtime $index]
        set doit 0
        # Changes to directory may mean files were deleted
        if {[file mtime $libdir] > $age} {
            set doit 1
        } else {
            # Check each file for modification
            foreach file [glob [file join $libdir *.tcl]] {
                if {[file mtime $file] > $age} {
                    set doit 1
                    break
                }
            }
        }
    }
    if { $doit } {
        auto_mkindex $libdir *.tcl
    }
}
```

The `auto_path` variable contains a list of directories to search for unknown commands. To continue our example, you can make the procedures in the book examples available by putting this command at the beginning of your scripts:

```
lappend auto_path /usr/local/tcl/welchbook
```

This has no effect if you have not created the `tclIndex` file. If you want to be extra careful, you can call `Library_UpdateIndex`. This will update the index if you add new things to the library.

```
lappend auto_path /usr/local/tcl/welchbook
Library_UpdateIndex /usr/local/tcl/welchbook
```

This will not work if there is no `tclIndex` file at all because Tcl won't be able to find the implementation of `Library_UpdateIndex`. Once the `tclIndex` has been created for the first time, then this will ensure that any new procedures added to the library will be installed into `tclIndex`. In practice, if you want this sort of automatic update, it is wise to include something like the `Library_UpdateIndex` procedure directly into your application as opposed to loading it from the library it is supposed to be maintaining.

The unknown Command

The unknown command implements automatic loading of Tcl commands. Whenever the Tcl interpreter encounters a command that it does not know about, it calls the unknown command with the name of the missing command. The unknown command is implemented in Tcl, so you are free to provide your own mechanism to handle unknown commands. This chapter describes the behavior of the default implementation of unknown, which can be found in the init.tcl file in the Tcl library. The info library command returns the location of the library.

How Auto Loading Works

The unknown command uses an array named auto_index. One element of the array is defined for each procedure that can be automatically loaded. The auto_index array is initialized by the package mechanism or by tclIndex files. The value of an auto_index element is a command that defines the procedure. Typical commands are:

```
source [file join $dir bind_ui.tcl]
load [file join $dir mime.so] Mime
```

The $dir gets substituted with the name of the directory that contains the library file, so the result is a source or load command that defines the missing Tcl command. The substitution is done with eval, so you could initialize auto_index with any commands at all. Example 12–2 is a simplified version of the code that reads the tclIndex file.

Example 12–2 Loading a tclIndex file.

```
# This is a simplified part of the auto_load_index procedure.
# Go through auto_path from back to front.
set i [expr [llength $auto_path]-1]
for {} {$i >= 0} {incr i -1} {
    set dir [lindex $auto_path $i]
    if [catch {open [file join $dir tclIndex]} f] {
        # No index
        continue
    }
    # eval the file as a script. Because eval is
    # used instead of source, an extra round of
    # substitutions is performed and $dir gets expanded
    # The real code checks for errors here.
    eval [read $f]
    close $f
}
```

Disabling the Library Facility: auto_noload

If you do not want the unknown procedure to try and load procedures, you can set the auto_noload variable to disable the mechanism:

```
set auto_noload anything
```

Auto loading is quite fast. I use it regularly on applications both large and small. A large application will start faster if you only need to load the code necessary to start it up. As you access more features of your application, the code will load automatically. Even a small application benefits from auto loading because it encourages you to keep commonly used code in procedure libraries.

Interactive Conveniences

The `unknown` command provides a few other conveniences. These are used only when you are typing commands directly. They are disabled once execution enters a procedure or if the Tcl shell is not being used interactively. The convenience features are automatic execution of programs, command history, and command abbreviation. These options are tried, in order, if a command implementation cannot be loaded from a script library.

Auto Execute

The `unknown` procedure implements a second feature: automatic execution of external programs. This makes a Tcl shell behave more like other UNIX shells that are used to execute programs. The search for external programs is done using the standard `PATH` environment variable that is used by other shells to find programs. If you want to disable the feature all together, set the `auto_noexec` variable:

```
set auto_noexec anything
```

History

The history facility described in Chapter 13 is implemented by the `unknown` procedure.

Abbreviations

If you type a unique prefix of a command, `unknown` recognizes it and executes the matching command for you. This is done after automatic program execution is attempted and history substitutions are performed.

Tcl Shell Library Environment

Tcl searches for its script library directory when it starts up. In early versions of Tcl you had to compile in the correct location, set a Windows registry value, or set the TCL_LIBRARY environment variable to the correct location. Recent versions of Tcl use a standard searching scheme to locate the script library. The search understands the standard installation and build environments for Tcl, and it should eliminate the need to use the TCL_LIBRARY environment variable. On Windows the search for the library used to depend on registry values, but this has also been discontinued in favor of a standard search. In summary, "it should just work." However, this section explains how Tcl finds its script library so that you can troubleshoot problems.

Locating the Tcl Script Library

The default library location is defined when you configure the source distribution, which is explained on page 732. At this time an initial value for the `auto_path` variable is defined. (This default value appears in `tcl_pkgPath`, but changing this variable has no effect once Tcl has started. I just pretend `tcl_pkgPath` does not exist.) These values are just hints; Tcl may use other directories depending on what it finds in the file system.

When Tcl starts up, it searches for a directory that contains its `init.tcl` startup script. You can short-circuit the search by defining the `TCL_LIBRARY` environment variable. If this is defined, Tcl uses it only for its script library directory. However, you should not need to define this with normal installations of Tcl 8.0.5 or later. In my environment I'm often using several different versions of Tcl for various applications and testing purposes, so setting `TCL_LIBRARY` is never correct for all possibilities. If I find myself setting this environment variable, I know something is wrong with my Tcl installations!

The standard search starts with the default value that is compiled into Tcl (e.g., `/usr/local/lib/tcl8.4`.) After that, the following directories are examined for an `init.tcl` file. These example values assume Tcl version 8.4 and patch level 8.4.1:

```
../lib/tcl8.4
../../lib/tcl8.4
../library
../../tcl8.4.1/library
../../../tcl8.4.1/library
```

The first two directories correspond to the standard installation directories, while the last three correspond to the standard build environment for Tcl or Tk. The first directory in the list that contains a valid `init.tcl` file becomes the Tcl script library. This directory location is saved in the `tcl_library` global variable, and it is also returned by the `info library` command.

The primary thing defined by `init.tcl` is the implementation of the `unknown` procedure. It also initializes `auto_path` to contain `$tcl_library` and the parent directory of `$tcl_library`. There may be additional directories added to `auto_path` depending on the compiled in value of `tcl_pkgPath`.

tcl_findLibrary

A generalization of this search is implemented by `tcl_findLibrary`. This procedure is designed for use by extensions like Tk and [incr Tcl]. Of course, Tcl cannot use `tcl_findLibrary` itself because it is defined in `init.tcl`!

The `tcl_findLibrary` procedure searches relative to the location of the main program (e.g., *tclsh* or *wish)* and assumes a standard installation or a standard build environment. It also supports an override by an environment variable, and it takes care of sourcing an initialization script. The usage of `tcl_findLibrary` is:

```
tcl_findLibrary base version patch script enVar varName
```

The *base* is the prefix of the script library directory name. The *version* is the main version number (e.g., "8.0"). The *patch* is the full patch level (e.g., "8.0.3"). The *script* is the initialization script to source from the directory. The *enVar* names an environment variable that can be used to override the default search path. The *varName* is the name of a variable to set to name of the directory found by `tcl_findLibrary`. A side effect of `tcl_findLibrary` is to source the script from the directory. An example call is:

```
tcl_findLibrary tk 8.0 8.0.3 tk.tcl TK_LIBRARY tk_library
```

This call first checks to see whether `TK_LIBRARY` is defined in the environment. If so, it uses its value. Otherwise, it searches the following directories for a file named `tk.tcl`. It sources the script and sets the `tk_library` variable to the directory containing that file. The search is relative to the value returned by `info nameofexecutable`:

```
../lib/tk8.0
../../lib/tk8.0
../library
../../tk8.0.3/library
../../../tk8.0.3/library
```

Tk also adds `$tk_library` to the end of `auto_path`, so the other script files in that directory are available to the application:

```
lappend auto_path $tk_library
```

Coding Style

If you supply a package, you need to follow some simple coding conventions to make your library easier to use by other programmers. You can use the namespace facility introduced in Tcl 8.0. You can also use conventions to avoid name conflicts with other library packages and the main application. This section describes the conventions I developed before namespaces were added to Tcl.

A Module Prefix for Procedure Names

The first convention is to choose an identifying prefix for the procedures in your package. For example, the preferences package in Chapter 45 uses `Pref` as its prefix. All the procedures provided by the library begin with `Pref`. This convention is extended to distinguish between private and exported procedures. An exported procedure has an underscore after its prefix, and it is acceptable to call this procedure from the main application or other library packages. Examples include `Pref_Add`, `Pref_Init`, and `Pref_Dialog`. A private procedure is meant for use only by the other procedures in the same package. Its name does not have the underscore. Examples include `PrefDialogItem` and `PrefXres`.

This naming convention precludes casual names like `doit`, `setup`, `layout`, and so on. Without using namespaces, there is no way to hide procedure names, so you must maintain the naming convention for all procedures in a package.

A Global Array for State Variables

You should use the same prefix on the global variables used by your package. You can alter the capitalization; just keep the same prefix. I capitalize procedure names and use lowercase letters for variables. By sticking with the same prefix you identify what variables belong to the package and you avoid conflict with other packages.

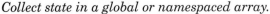
Collect state in a global or namespaced array.

In general, I try to use a single global or namespaced array for a package (namespaces are discussed in Chapter 14). The array provides a convenient place to collect a set of related variables, much as a struct is used in C. For example, the preferences package uses the `pref` array to hold all its state information. It is also a good idea to keep the use of the array private. It is better coding practice to provide exported procedures than to let other modules access your data structures directly. This makes it easier to change the implementation of your package without affecting its clients. When choosing a namespace name, try to make it significant to your application.

If you do need to export a few key variables from your module, use the underscore convention to distinguish exported variables. If you need more than one global variable, just stick with the prefix convention to avoid conflicts, or provide accessor functions instead.

The Official Tcl Style Guide

John Ousterhout has published two programming style guides, one for C programming known as *The Engineering Manual* and one for Tcl scripts known as *The Style Guide*. These describe details about file structure as well as naming conventions for modules, procedures, and variables. The *Tcl Style Guide* conventions use Tcl namespaces to separate packages. Namespaces automatically provide a way to avoid conflict between procedure names. Namespaces also support collections of variables without having to use arrays for grouping.

You can find these style guides on the CD-ROM and also in `ftp://ftp.tcl.tk/pub/tcl/doc`. *The Engineering Manual* is distributed as a compressed tar file, `engManual.tar.Z`, that contains sample files as well as the main document. *The Style Guide* is distributed as `styleGuide.ps` (or `.pdf`).

Reflection and Debugging

This chapter describes commands that give you a view into the interpreter. The `history` command and a simple debugger are useful during development and debugging. The `info` command provides a variety of information about the internal state of the Tcl interpreter. The `time` command measures the time it takes to execute a command. Tcl commands discussed are: `clock`, `info`, `history`, and `time`.

Reflection provides feedback to a script about the internal state of the interpreter. This is useful in a variety of cases, from testing to see whether a variable exists to dumping the state of the interpreter. The `info` command provides lots of different information about the interpreter.

The `clock` command returns the time, formats time values, does time calculations, and parses time strings. It is a great tool all by itself. It also provides high-resolution timer information for precise measurements.

Interactive command history is the third topic of the chapter. The history facility can save you some typing if you spend a lot of time entering commands interactively.

Debugging is the last topic. The old-fashioned approach of adding `puts` commands to your code is often quite useful. For tough problems, however, a real debugger is invaluable. The *Tcl Dev Kit* toolset from ActiveState include a high quality debugger and static code checker. The *thinspect* program is an inspector that lets you look into the state of a Tk application. It can hook up to any Tk application dynamically, so it proves quite useful.

The clock Command

The `clock` command has facilities for getting the current time, formatting time values, and scanning printed time strings to get an integer time value. Table 13–1 summarizes the `clock` command:

Table 13–1 The `clock` command.

`clock clicks ?-milliseconds?`	A high resolution counter. The precision is milliseconds, if specified (Tcl 8.4), or a system-dependent value.
`clock format` *value* `?-format` *str*?	Formats a clock value according to *str*. See Table 13–2.
`clock scan` *string* `?-base` *clock*? `?-gmt` *boolean*?	Parses date *string* and return seconds value. The *clock* value determines the date.
`clock seconds`	Returns the current time in seconds.

The following command prints the current time:

```
clock format [clock seconds]
=> Fri Nov 22 4:09:14 PM PST 2002
```

The `clock seconds` command returns the current time, in seconds since a starting epoch. The `clock format` command formats an integer value into a date string. It takes an optional argument that controls the format. The format strings contains % keywords that are replaced with the year, month, day, date, hours, minutes, and seconds, in various formats. The default string is:

```
%a %b %d %H:%M:%S %Z %Y
```

Tables 13–2 summarizes the `clock` formatting strings:

Table 13–2 `clock format` keywords.

`%%`	Inserts a %.
`%a`	Abbreviated weekday name (Mon, Tue, etc.).
`%A`	Full weekday name (Monday, Tuesday, etc.).
`%b`	Abbreviated month name (Jan, Feb, etc.).
`%B`	Full month name.
`%c`	Locale specific date and time (e.g., `Nov 24 16:00:59 1996`).
`%C`	First two digits of the four-digit year (19 or 20).
`%d`	Day of month (01 – 31).
`%D`	Date as `%m/%d/%y` (e.g., 02/19/97).
`%e`	Day of month (1 – 31), no leading zeros.
`%h`	Abbreviated month name.
`%H`	Hour in 24-hour format (00 – 23).
`%I`	Hour in 12-hour format (01 – 12).
`%j`	Day of year (001 – 366).
`%k`	Hour in 24-hour format, without leading zeros (0 - 23).

Table 13–2 clock format keywords. (Continued)

%l	Hour in 12-hour format, without leading zeros (1 – 12).
%m	Month number (01 – 12).
%M	Minute (00 – 59).
%n	Inserts a newline.
%p	AM/PM indicator.
%r	Time as %I:%M:%S %p (e.g., 02:39:29 PM).
%R	Time as %H:%M (e.g., 14:39).
%s	Seconds since the epoch.
%S	Seconds (00 – 59).
%t	Inserts a tab.
%T	Time as %H:%M:%S (e.g., 14:34:29).
%u	Weekday number (Monday = 1, Sunday = 7).
%U	Week of year (00 – 52) when Sunday starts the week.
%V	Week of year according to ISO-8601 rules (Week 1 contains January 4).
%w	Weekday number (Sunday = 0).
%W	Week of year (00 – 52) when Monday starts the week.
%x	Locale specific date format (e.g., Feb 19 1997).
%X	Locale specific time format (e.g., 20:10:13).
%y	Year without century (00 – 99).
%Y	Year with century (e.g. 1997).
%Z	Time zone name.

The clock clicks command returns the value of the system's highest resolution clock. The units of the clicks is milliseconds if -milliseconds is specified, otherwise it is undefined. The main use of this command is to measure the relative time of different performance tuning trials. The -milliseconds flag was added in Tcl 8.4. Example 13–1 shows how to calibrate the clicks value by counting the clicks per second over 10 seconds, which will vary from system to system:

Example 13–1 Calculating clicks per second.

```
set t1 [clock clicks]
after 10000 ;# See page 228
set t2 [clock clicks]
puts "[expr ($t2 - $t1)/10] Clicks/second"
=> 1001313 Clicks/second
```

The `clock scan` command parses a date string and returns a seconds value. The command handles a variety of date formats. If you leave off the year, the current year is assumed.

Year 2000 Compliance

Tcl implements the standard interpretation of two-digit year values, which is that 70–99 are 1970–1999, 00–69 are 2000–2069. Versions of Tcl before 8.0 did not properly deal with two-digit years in all cases. Note, however, that Tcl is limited by your system's time epoch and the number of bits in an integer. On Windows, Macintosh, and most UNIX systems, the clock epoch is January 1, 1970. A 32-bit integer can count enough seconds to reach forward into the year 2037, and backward to the year 1903. If you try to `clock scan` a date outside that range, Tcl will raise an error because the seconds counter will overflow or underflow. In this case, Tcl is just reflecting limitations of the underlying system. Some 64-bit systems (such as Solaris 8 64-bit) use 64-bit integers for the system clock, which Tcl 8.4 supports. This extends the recognized range into the billions of years.

If you leave out a date, `clock scan` assumes the current date. You can also use the `-base` option to specify a date. The following example uses the current time as the base, which is redundant:

```
clock scan "10:30:44 PM" -base [clock seconds]
=> 2931690644
```

The date parser allows these modifiers: `year`, `month`, `fortnight` (two weeks), `week`, `day`, `hour`, `minute`, `second`. You can put a positive or negative number in front of a modifier as a multiplier. For example:

```
clock format [clock scan "10:30:44 PM 1 week"]
=> Fri Nov 29 10:30:44 PM PST 2002
clock format [clock scan "10:30:44 PM -1 week"]
Fri Nov 15 10:30:44 PM PST 2002
```

You can also use `tomorrow`, `yesterday`, `today`, `now`, `last`, `this`, `next`, and `ago`, as modifiers.

```
clock format [clock scan "3 years ago"]
=> Mon Nov 22 4:18:34 PM PST 1999
```

Both `clock format` and `clock scan` take a `-gmt` option that uses Greenwich Mean Time. Otherwise, the local time zone is used.

```
clock format [clock seconds] -gmt true
=> Sat Nov 23 12:19:13 AM GMT 2002
clock format [clock seconds] -gmt false
=> Fri Nov 22 4:19:35 PM PST 2002
```

The `info` Command

Table 13–3 summarizes the `info` command. The operations are described in more detail later.

Table 13–3 The info command.

info args *procedure*	A list of *procedure*'s arguments.
info body *procedure*	The commands in the body of *procedure*.
info cmdcount	The number of commands executed so far.
info commands ?*pattern*?	A list of all commands, or those matching *pattern*. Includes built-ins and Tcl procedures.
info complete *string*	True if *string* contains a complete Tcl command.
info default *proc arg var*	True if *arg* has a default parameter value in procedure *proc*. The default value is stored into *var*.
info exists *variable*	True if *variable* is defined.
info functions ?*pattern*?	A list of all math functions, or those matching *pattern*. (Tcl 8.4)
info globals ?*pattern*?	A list of all global variables, or those matching *pattern*.
info hostname	The name of the machine. This may be the empty string if networking is not initialized.
info level	The stack level of the current procedure, or 0 for the global scope.
info level *number*	A list of the command and its arguments at the specified level of the stack.
info library	The pathname of the Tcl library directory.
info loaded ?*interp*?	A list of the libraries loaded into the interpreter named *interp*, which defaults to the current one.
info locals ?*pattern*?	A list of all local variables, or those matching *pattern*.
info nameofexecutable	The file name of the program (e.g., of *tclsh* or *wish*).
info patchlevel	The release patch level for Tcl.
info procs ?*pattern*?	A list of all Tcl procedures, or those that match *pattern*.
info script ?*filename*?	The name of the file being processed, or the empty string.
info sharedlibextension	The file name suffix of shared libraries.
info tclversion	The version number of Tcl.
info vars ?*pattern*?	A list of all visible variables, or those matching *pattern*.

Variables

There are three categories of variables: *local*, *global*, and *visible*. Information about these categories is returned by the locals, globals, and vars operations, respectively. The local variables include procedure arguments as well as locally defined variables. The global variables include all variables defined at the global scope. The visible variables include locals, plus any variables made visible via `global` or `upvar` commands. A pattern can be specified to limit the returned list of variables to those that match the pattern. The pattern is interpreted according to the rules of `string match`, which is described on page 53:

```
info globals auto*
=> auto_index auto_noexec auto_path
```

Namespaces, which are the topic of the next chapter, partition global variables into different scopes. You query the variables visible in a namespace with:

```
info vars namespace::*
```

Remember that a variable may not be defined yet even though a `global` or `upvar` command has declared it visible in the current scope. Use the `info exists` command to test whether a variable or an array element is defined or not. An example is shown on page 96.

Procedures

You can find out everything about a Tcl procedure with the `args`, `body`, and `default` operations. This is illustrated in the following `Proc_Show` example. The `puts` commands use the `-nonewline` flag because the newlines in the procedure body, if any, are retained:

Example 13–2 Printing a procedure definition.

```
proc Proc_Show {{namepat *} {file stdout}} {
    foreach proc [info procs $namepat] {
        set space ""
        puts -nonewline $file "proc $proc {"
        foreach arg [info args $proc] {
            if [info default $proc $arg value] {
                puts -nonewline $file "$space{$arg $value}"
            } else {
                puts -nonewline $file $space$arg
            }
            set space " "
        }

        # Double quotes allow substitution
        # of [info body $proc]

        puts $file "} {[info body $proc]}"
    }
}
```

Example 13–3 is a more elaborate example of procedure introspection that comes from the `direct.tcl` file, which is part of the Tcl Web Server described in Chapter 18. This code is used to map URL requests and the associated query data directly into Tcl procedure calls. This is discussed in more detail on page 262. The Web server collects Web form data into an array called `form`. Example 13–3 matches up elements of the `form` array with procedure arguments, and it collects extra elements into an `args` parameter. If a form value is missing, then the default argument value or the empty string is used:

Example 13–3 Mapping form data onto procedure arguments.

```
# cmd is the name of the procedure to invoke
# form is an array containing form values

set cmdOrig $cmd
set params [info args $cmdOrig]

# Match elements of the form array to parameters

foreach arg $params {
    if {![info exists form($arg)]} {
        if {[info default $cmdOrig $arg value]} {
            lappend cmd $value
        } elseif {[string equal $arg "args"]} {
            set needargs yes
        } else {
            lappend cmd {}
        }
    } else {
        lappend cmd $form($arg)
    }
}
# If args is a parameter, then append the form data
# that does not match other parameters as extra parameters

if {[info exists needargs]} {
    foreach {name value} [array get form] {
        if {[lsearch $params $name] < 0} {
            lappend cmd $name $value
        }
    }
}
# Eval the command

set code [catch $cmd result]
```

The `info commands` operation returns a list of all commands, which includes both built-in commands defined in C and Tcl procedures. There is no operation that just returns the list of built-in commands. Example 13–4 finds the built-in commands by removing all the procedures from the list of commands.

Example 13–4 Finding built-in commands.

```
proc Command_Info {{pattern *}} {
    # Create a table of procedures for quick lookup

    foreach p [info procs $pattern] {
        set isproc($p) 1
    }

    # Look for command not in the procedure table
    set result {}
    foreach c [info commands $pattern] {
        if {![info exists isproc($c)]} {
            lappend result $c
        }
    }
    return [lsort $result]
}
```

The Call Stack

The `info level` operation returns information about the Tcl evaluation stack, or *call stack*. The global level is numbered zero. A procedure called from the global level is at level one in the call stack. A procedure it calls is at level two, and so on. The `info level` command returns the current level number of the stack if no level number is specified.

If a positive level number is specified (e.g., `info level 3`), then the command returns the procedure name and argument values at that level in the call stack. If a negative level is specified, then it is relative to the current call stack. Relative level -1 is the level of the current procedure's caller, and relative level 0 is the current procedure. The following example prints the call stack. The `Call_trace` procedure avoids printing information about itself by starting at one less than the current call stack level:

Example 13–5 Getting a trace of the Tcl call stack.

```
proc Call_Trace {{file stdout}} {
    puts $file "Tcl Call Trace"
    for {set x [expr [info level]-1]} {$x > 0} {incr x -1} {
        puts $file "$x: [info level $x]"
    }
}
```

Command Evaluation

If you want to know how many Tcl commands are executed, use the `info cmdcount` command. This counts all commands, not just top-level commands. The counter is never reset, so you need to sample it before and after a test run if you want to know how many commands are executed during a test.

Command tracing provides detailed information about the execution of commands. It is described along with variable tracing on page 193.

The `info complete` operation figures out whether a string is a complete Tcl command. This is useful for command interpreters that need to wait until the user has typed in a complete Tcl command before passing it to `eval`. Example 13–6 defines `Command_Process` that gets a line of input and builds up a command. When the command is complete, the command is executed at the global scope. `Command_Process` takes two *callbacks* as arguments. The `inCmd` is evaluated to get the line of input, and the `outCmd` is evaluated to display the results. Chapter 10 describes callbacks why the curly braces are used with `eval` as they are in this example:

Example 13–6 A procedure to read and evaluate commands.

```
proc Command_Process {inCmd outCmd} {
   global command
   append command(line) [eval $inCmd]
   if {[info complete $command(line)]} {
      set code [catch {uplevel #0 $command(line)} result]
      eval $outCmd {$result $code}
      set command(line) {}
   }
}
proc Command_Read {{in stdin}} {
   if {[eof $in]} {
      if {$in != "stdin"} {
         close $in
      }
      return {}
   }
   return [gets $in]
}
proc Command_Display {file result code} {
   puts stdout $result
}
while {![eof stdin]} {
   Command_Process {Command_Read stdin} \
      {Command_Display stdout}
}
```

Scripts and the Library

The name of the current script file is returned with the `info script` command. For example, if you use the `source` command to read commands from a file, then `info script` returns the name of that file if it is called during execution of the commands in that script. This is true even if the `info script` command is called from a procedure that is not defined in the script.

Use `info script` to find related files.

I often use `info script` to source or process files stored in the same directory as the script that is running. A few examples are shown in Example 13–7.

Example 13–7 Using `info script` to find related files.

```
# Get the directory containing the current script.
set dir [file dirname [info script]]

# Source a file in the same directory
source [file join $dir helper.tcl]

# Add an adjacent script library directory to auto_path
# The use of ../lib with file join is cross-platform safe.
lappend auto_path [file join $dir ../lib]
```

The pathname of the Tcl library is stored in the `tcl_library` variable, and it is also returned by the `info library` command. While you could put scripts into this directory, it might be better to have a separate directory and use the script library facility described in Chapter 12. This makes it easier to deal with new releases of Tcl and to package up your code if you want other sites to use it.

Version Numbers

Each Tcl release has a version number such as 7.4 or 8.0. This number is returned by the `info tclversion` command. If you want your script to run on a variety of Tcl releases, you may need to test the version number and take different actions in the case of incompatibilities between releases.

The Tcl release cycle starts with one or two alpha and beta releases before the final release, and there may even be a patch release after that. The `info patchlevel` command returns a qualified version number, like 8.0b1 for the first beta release of 8.0. We switched from using "p" (e.g., 8.0p2) to a three-level scheme (e.g., 8.0.3) for patch releases. The patch level is zero for the final release (e.g., 8.2.0). In general, you should be prepared for feature changes during the beta cycle, but there should only be bug fixes in the patch releases. Another rule of thumb is that the Tcl script interface remains quite compatible between releases; feature additions are upward compatible.

Execution Environment

The file name of the program being executed is returned with `info nameofexecutable`. This is more precise than the name in the `argv0` variable, which could be a relative name or a name found in a command directory on your command search path. It is still possible for `info nameofexecutable` to return a relative pathname if the user runs your program as `./foo`, for example. The following construct always returns the absolute pathname of the current program. If `info nameofexecutable` returns an absolute pathname, then the value of the current directory is ignored. The `pwd` command is described on page 122:

```
file join [pwd] [info nameofexecutable]
```

A few operations support dynamic loading of shared libraries, which are described in Chapter 47. The `info sharedlibextension` returns the file name suffix of dynamic link libraries. The `info loaded` command returns a list of libraries that have been loaded into an interpreter. Multiple interpreters are described in Chapter 19.

Cross-Platform Support

Tcl is designed so that you can write scripts that run unchanged on UNIX, Macintosh, and Windows platforms. In practice, you may need a small amount of code that is specific to a particular platform. You can find out information about the platform via the `tcl_platform` variable. This is an array with these elements defined:

- `tcl_platform(platform)` is one of `unix`, `macintosh`, or `windows`.
- `tcl_platform(os)` identifies the operating system. Examples include `MacOS`, `Solaris`, `Linux`, `Win32s` (Windows 3.1 with the Win32 subsystem), `Windows 95`, `Windows NT`, and `SunOS`.
- `tcl_platform(osVersion)` gives the version number of the operating system.
- `tcl_platform(machine)` identifies the hardware. Examples include `ppc` (Power PC), `68k` (68000 family), `sparc`, `intel`, `mips`, and `alpha`.
- `tcl_platform(byteOrder)` identifies the byte order of this machine and is one of `littleEndian` or `bigEndian`.
- `tcl_platform(wordSize)` identifies the size of the native machine word in bytes. This was introduced in Tcl 8.4.
- `tcl_platform(isWrapped)` indicates that the application has been wrapped up into a single executable with *TclPro Wrapper*. This is not defined in normal circumstances.
- `tcl_platform(user)` gives the login name of the current user.
- `tcl_platform(debug)` indicates that Tcl was compiled with debugging symbols.
- `tcl_platform(threaded)` indicates that Tcl was compiled with thread support enabled.

On some platforms a *hostname* is defined. If available, it is returned with the `info hostname` command. This command may return an empty string.

One of the most significant areas affected by cross-platform portability is the file system and the way files are named. This topic is discussed on page 110.

Tracing Variables and Commands

The `trace` command registers a command to be called whenever a variable is accessed, modified, or unset. Tcl 8.4 introduced an updated `trace` command which includes support for command tracing. The original (and still supported) form of the command applies only to variable traces:

II. Advanced Tcl

```
trace variable name ops command
trace vdelete name ops command
trace vinfo name
```

The *name* is a Tcl variable name, which can be a simple variable, an array, or an array element. If a whole array is traced, the trace is invoked when any element is used according to *ops*. The *ops* argument is one or more of the letters r, for read traces, w, for write traces, u, for unset traces, and a for array traces. The *command* is executed when one of these events occurs. It is invoked as:

```
command name1 name2 op
```

The *name1* argument is the variable or array name. The *name2* argument is the name of the array index, or null if the trace is on a simple variable. If there is an unset trace on an entire array and the array is unset, *name2* is also null. The value of the variable is not passed to the procedure. The traced variable is one level up the Tcl call stack. The upvar, uplevel, or global commands need to be used to make the variable visible in the scope of *command*. These commands are described in more detail in Chapter 7.

A read trace is invoked before the value of the variable is returned, so if it changes the variable itself, the new value is returned. A write trace is called after the variable is modified. The unset trace is called after the variable is unset. The array trace, which was added in Tcl 8.4, is called before the array command (e.g., array names) is used on the variable. A variable trace is automatically deleted when the variable is unset.

Command Tracing

The new form of trace supports both variable and command tracing:

```
trace add type name ops command
trace remove type name ops command
trace info type name
```

The *type* is one of command, execution or variable. For command, *ops* is a list and may contain rename, to trace the renaming of a Tcl command, or delete, to trace the deletion of a command. Command tracing cannot be used to prevent the actual deletion of a command, it just receives the notification. No command traces are triggered when an interpreter is deleted. The *command* is invoked as:

```
command oldName newName op
```

For execution, the *ops* may be any of enter, leave, enterstep, and leavestep. enter invokes *command* immediately before the command *name* is executed, and leave will invoke command immediately following each execution. enterstep and leavestep are similar but they operate on the Tcl procedure *name*, invoking *command* for each Tcl command inside the procedure. In order to do this, they prevent the bytecode compilation of that procedure. This allows you to create a simple debugger in pure Tcl. The enter and enterstep operations invoke *command* as:

```
command command-string op
```

The `leave` and `leavestep` operations invoke *command* as:

```
command command-string code result op
```

The *command-string* is the current command being executed, *code* is the result code of the execution and *result* is the result string. Example 6–16 on page 84 illustrates the different result codes.

For `variable` tracing, the *ops* may be one or more of `read`, `write`, `unset`, or `array`. This is an alternate way to set up the variable traces described earlier.

Read-Only Variables

Example 13–8 uses traces to implement a read-only variable. A variable is modified before the trace procedure is called, so the `ReadOnly` variable is needed to preserve the original value. When a variable is unset, the traces are automatically removed, so the unset trace action reestablishes the trace explicitly. Note that the `upvar` alias (e.g., `var`) cannot be used to set up the trace. Instead, `uplevel` is used to create the trace in the original context of the variable. In general, essentially all traces are on global or namespace variables.

Example 13–8 Tracing variables.

```
proc ReadOnlyVar {varName} {
    upvar 1 $varName var
    global ReadOnly
    set ReadOnly($varName) $var
    uplevel 1 [list trace variable $varName wu ReadOnlyTrace]
}
proc ReadOnlyTrace { varName index op } {
    global ReadOnly
    upvar 1 $varName var
    switch $op {
        w {
            set var $ReadOnly($varName)
        }
        u {
            set var $ReadOnly($varName)
            # Re-establish the trace using the true name
            uplevel 1 [list ReadOnlyVar $varName]
        }
    }
}
```

This example merely overrides the new value with the saved value. Another alternative is to raise an error with the `error` command. This will cause the command that modified the variable to return the error. Another common use of `trace` is to update a user interface widget in response to a variable change. Several of the Tk widgets have this feature built into them.

If more than one trace is set on a variable, then they are invoked in reverse order; the most recent trace is executed first. If there is a trace on an array and on an array element, then the trace on the array is invoked first.

Creating an Array with Traces

Example 13–9 uses an array trace to dynamically create array elements:

Example 13–9 Creating array elements with array traces.

```
# make sure variable is an array
set dynamic() {}
trace variable dynamic r FixupDynamic
proc FixupDynamic {name index op} {
    upvar 1 $name dynArray
    if {![info exists dynArray($index)]} {
        set dynArray($index) 0
    }
}
```

Information about traces on a variable is returned with the `vinfo` option:

```
trace vinfo dynamic
=> {r FixupDynamic}
```

A trace is deleted with the `vdelete` option, which has the same form as the `variable` option. The trace in the previous example can be removed with the following command:

```
trace vdelete dynamic r FixupDynamic
```

Interactive Command History

Table 13–4 The `history` command.

`history`	Short for `history info` with no *count*.
`history add command ?exec?`	Adds the command to the history list. If `exec` is specified, then execute the command.
`history change new ?event?`	Changes the command specified by *event* to *new* in the command history.
`history event ?event?`	Returns the command specified by *event*.
`history info ?count?`	Returns a formatted history list of the last *count* commands, or of all commands.
`history keep count`	Limits the history to the last *count* commands.
`history nextid`	Returns the number of the next event.
`history redo ?event?`	Repeats the specified command.

The Tcl shell programs keep a log of the commands that you type by using a history facility. The log is controlled and accessed via the `history` command. The history facility uses the term *event* to mean an entry in its history log. The events are just commands, and they have an event ID that is their index in the log. You can also specify an event with a negative index that counts backwards from the end of the log. Event -1 is the previous event. Table 13–4 summarizes the Tcl `history` command. In the table, *event* defaults to -1.

In practice you will want to take advantage of the ability to abbreviate the history options and even the name of the `history` command itself. For the command, you need to type a unique prefix, and this depends on what other commands are already defined. For the options, there are unique one-letter abbreviations for all of them. For example, you could reuse the last word of the previous command with [`history w $`]. This works because a `$` that is not followed by alphanumerics or an open brace is treated as a literal `$`.

Several of the history operations update the history list. They remove the actual `history` command and replace it with the command that resulted from the history operation. The `event` and `redo` operations all behave in this manner. This makes perfect sense because you would rather have the actual command in the history, instead of the history command used to retrieve the command.

History Syntax

Some extra syntax is supported when running interactively to make the history facility more convenient to use. Table 13–5 shows the special history syntax supported by `tclsh` and `wish`.

Table 13–5 Special `history` syntax.

`!!`	Repeats the previous command.
`!n`	Repeats command number *n*. If *n* is negative it counts backward from the current command. The previous command is event -1.
`!prefix`	Repeats the last command that begins with *prefix*.
`!pattern`	Repeats the last command that matches *pattern*.
`^old^new`	Globally replaces *old* with *new* in the last command.

The next example shows how some of the history operations work:

Example 13–10 Interactive `history` usage.

```
% set a 5
5
% set a [expr $a+7]
12
% history
    1 set a 5
    2 set a [expr $a+7]
    3 history
% !2
19
```

```
% !!
26
% ^7^13
39
% !h
   1 set a 5
   2 set a [expr $a+7]
   3 history
   4 set a [expr $a+7]
   5 set a [expr $a+7]
   6 set a [expr $a+13]
   7 history
```

A Comparison to C Shell History Syntax

The history syntax shown in the previous example is simpler than the history syntax provided by the C shell. Not all of the history operations are supported with special syntax. The substitutions (using ^old^new) are performed globally on the previous command. This is different from the quick-history of the C shell. Instead, it is like the !:gs/old/new/ history command. So, for example, if the example had included ^a^b in an attempt to set b to 39, an error would have occurred because the command would have used b before it was defined:

```
set b [expr $b+7]
```

If you want to improve the history syntax, you will need to modify the unknown command, which is where it is implemented. This command is discussed in more detail in Chapter 12. Here is the code from the unknown command that implements the extra history syntax. The main limitation in comparison with the C shell history syntax is that the ! substitutions are performed only when ! is at the beginning of the command:

Example 13–11 Implementing special history syntax.

```
# Excerpts from the standard unknown command
# uplevel is used to run the command in the right context
if {$name == "!!"} {
   set newcmd [history event]
} elseif {[regexp {^!(.+)$} $name dummy event]} {
   set newcmd [history event $event]
} elseif {[regexp {^\^([^^]*)\^([^^]*)\^?$} $name x old new]} {
   set newcmd [history event -1]
   catch {regsub -all -- $old $newcmd $new newcmd}
}
if {[info exists newcmd]} {
   history change $newcmd 0
   return [uplevel $newcmd]
}
```

Debugging

The rapid turnaround with Tcl coding means that it is often sufficient to add a few `puts` statements to your script to gain some insight about its behavior. This solution doesn't scale too well, however. A slight improvement is to add a `Debug` procedure that can have its output controlled better. You can log the information to a file, or turn it off completely. In a Tk application, it is simple to create a text widget to hold the contents of the log so that you can view it from the application. Here is a simple `Debug` procedure. To enable it you need to set the `debug(enable)` variable. To have its output go to your terminal, set `debug(file)` to `stderr`.

Example 13–12 A `Debug` procedure.

```
proc Debug { args } {
    global debug
    if {![info exists debug(enabled)]} {
        # Default is to do nothing
        return
    }
    puts $debug(file) [join $args " "]
}
proc DebugOn {{file {}}} {
    global debug
    set debug(enabled) 1
    if {[string length $file] == 0} {
        set debug(file) stderr
    } else {
        if [catch {open $file w} fileID] {
            puts stderr "Cannot open $file: $fileID"
            set debug(file) stderr
        } else {
            puts stderr "Debug info to $file"
            set debug(file) $fileID
        }
    }
}
proc DebugOff {} {
    global debug
    if {[info exists debug(enabled)]} {
        unset debug(enabled)
        flush $debug(file)
        if {$debug(file) != "stderr" &&
            $debug(file) != "stdout"} {
            close $debug(file)
            unset debug(file)
        }
    }
}
```

Tcl Dev Kit

Tcl Dev Kit is a commercial development environment for Tcl based on the original *TclPro* created by Scriptics. *TclPro* was released to the open-source community in November 2001. ActiveState has enhanced *Tcl Dev Kit* with new tools and more features. The development environment includes *ActiveTcl*[*], which is an extended Tcl platform that includes [incr Tcl], Expect, and TclX. These extensions and Tcl/Tk are distributed in source and binary form for Windows and a variety of UNIX platforms. More information is available at this URL:

```
http://www.activestate.com/Tcl
```

The current version of the *Tcl Dev Kit* contains these tools:

Debugger with Coverage

The *Debugger* provides a nice graphical user interface with all the features you expect from a traditional debugger. You can set breakpoints, single step, examine variables, and look at the call stack. It understands a subtle issue that can arise from using the update command: nested call stacks. It is possible to launch a new Tcl script as a side effect of the update command, which pushes the current state onto the execution stack. This shows up clearly in the debugger stack trace. It maintains project state, so it will remember breakpoint settings and other preference items between runs. One of the most interesting features is that it can debug remotely running applications. The debugger also has built-in code coverage and hotspot profiling analysis. I use it regularly to debug Tcl code running inside the Tcl Web Server.

Checker

The *Checker* is a static code checker. This is a real win for large program development. It examines every line of your program looking for syntax errors and dubious coding practices. It has detailed knowledge of Tcl, Tk, Expect, [incr Tcl], and TclX commands and validates your use of them. It checks that you call Tcl procedures with the correct number of arguments, and can cross-check large groups of Tcl files. It knows about changes between Tcl versions, and it can warn you about old code that needs to be updated.

Compiler

The *Compiler* is really just a reader and writer for the byte codes that the Tcl byte-code compiler generates internally. It lets you precompile scripts and save the results, and then load the byte-code later instead of raw source. This provides a great way to hide your source code, if that is important to you. It turns out to save less time than you might think, however. By the time it reads the file from disk, decodes it, and builds the necessary Tcl data structures, it is not much faster than reading a source file and compiling it on the fly.

---

[*] ActiveTcl is a trademark of ActiveState Corporation.

TclApp

TclApp assembles a collection of Tcl scripts, data files, and a Tcl/Tk interpreter into Starkits and Starpacks, which are described in Chapter 22. *TclApp* provides a more friendly user interface than the *sdx* command line tool described in that Chapter. The *Tcl Dev Kit* comes with pre-built Starkit runtimes that include Metakit, Expect, [incr Tcl], and TclX.

Tcl Service Manager

The *Tcl Service Manager* helps you turn your Tcl application into a service for Windows NT/2000/XP. Services have to implement special OS interfaces that are not supported by *tclsh* or *wish*. You can create services that use the DLLs and scripts from an existing Tcl/Tk installation, or create stand alone services that have no external dependencies.

Inspector

The *Inspector* is an improved version of the *thinspect* application that lets you look at the state of other Tk applications. It displays procedures, variables, and the Tk widget hierarchy. You can issue commands to another application to change variables or test out commands. This turns out to be a very useful way to debug Tk applications. The original *thinspect* was written by Sam Shen.

Other Tools

The Tcl community has built many interesting and useful tools to help your Tcl development. Only two of them are mentioned below, but you can find many more at the Tcl Resource Center:

```
http://www.tcl.tk/resource/
```

The tkcon Console

Tkcon is an enhanced Tk console application written purely in Tcl. It includes many useful interactive control features, and may be embedded in other Tcl applications. It was written by Jeff Hobbs and you can find it at:

```
http://tkcon.sourceforge.net/
```

Critcl

Critcl is a tool that lets you mix C code right into your Tcl scripts. When the `cproc` command encounters its code for the first time, it automatically compiles it with *gcc* and loads it into your application. This provides an easy way to recode small parts of your application in C to get a performance boost. It's home page is:

```
http://www.equi4.com/critcl
```

II. Advanced Tcl

The bgerror Command

When a Tcl script encounters an error during background processing, such as handling file events or during the command associated with a button, it signals the error by calling the bgerror procedure. A default implementation displays a dialog and gives you an opportunity to view the Tcl call stack at the point of the error. You can supply your own version of bgerror. For example, when my exmh mail application gets an error it offers to send mail to me with a few words of explanation from the user and a copy of the stack trace. I get interesting bug reports from all over the world!

The bgerror command is called with one argument that is the error message. The global variable errorInfo contains the stack trace information. There is an example tkerror implementation in the on-line sources associated with this book.

The tkerror Command

The bgerror command used to be called tkerror. When event processing shifted from Tk into Tcl with Tcl 7.5 and Tk 4.1, the name tkerror was changed to bgerror. Backwards compatibility is provided so that if tkerror is defined, then tkerror is called instead of bgerror. I have run into problems with the compatibility setup and have found it more reliable to update my applications to use bgerror instead of tkerror. If you have an application that runs under either Tk 4.0 or Tk 4.1, you can simply define both:

```
proc bgerror [info args tkerror] [info body tkerror]
```

Performance Tuning

The time command measures the execution time of a Tcl command. It takes an optional parameter that is a repetition count:

```
time {set a "Hello, World!"} 1000
=> 28 microseconds per iteration
```

If you need the result of the command being timed, use set to capture the result:

```
puts $log "command: [time {set result [command]}]"
```

An extensive benchmark suite that compares various Tcl versions is available at:

```
http://wiki.tcl.tk/Tcl%20Benchmarks
```

Time stamps in a Log

Another way to gain insight into the performance of your script is to generate log records that contain time stamps. The clock seconds value is too coarse, but you can couple it with the clock clicks value to get higher resolution measurements. Use the code shown in Example 13–1 on page 185 to calibrate the clicks per second on your system. Example 13–13 writes log records that contain the current time and the number of clicks since the last record. There will be occasional glitches in the clicks value when the system counter wraps around or is reset by the system clock, but it will normally give pretty accurate results. The Log procedure adds overhead, too, so you should take several measurements in a tight loop to see how long each Log call takes:

Example 13–13 Time Stamps in log records.

```
proc Log {args} {
    global log
    if [info exists log(file)] {
        set now [clock clicks]
        puts $log(file) [format "%s (%d)\t%s" \
            [clock format [clock seconds]] \
            [expr $now - $log(last)] \
            [join $args " "]]
        set log(last) $now
    }
}
proc Log_Open {file} {
    global log
    catch {close $log(file)}
    set log(file) [open $file w]
    set log(last) [clock clicks]
}
proc Log_Flush {} {
    global log
    catch {flush $log(file)}
}
proc Log_Close {} {
    global log
    catch {close $log(file)}
    catch {unset log(file)}
}
```

A more advanced profile command is part of the Extended Tcl (TclX) package. The TclX profile command monitors the number of calls, the CPU time, and the elapsed time spent in different procedures.

The Tcl Compiler

The built-in Tcl compiler improves performance in the following ways:

- Tcl scripts are converted into an internal byte-code format that is efficient to process. The byte codes are saved so that cost of compiling is paid only the first time you execute a procedure or loop. After that, execution proceeds much faster. Compilation is done as needed, so unused code is never compiled. If you redefine a procedure, it is recompiled the next time it is executed.

II. Advanced Tcl

- Variables and command arguments are kept in a native format as long as possible and converted to strings only when necessary. There are several native types, including integers, floating point numbers, Tcl lists, byte codes, and arrays. There are C APIs for implementing new types. Tcl is still dynamically typed, so a variable can contain different types during its lifetime.

- Expressions and control structures are compiled into special byte codes, so they are executed more efficiently. Because `expr` does its own round of substitutions, the compiler generates better code if you group expressions with braces. This means that expressions go through only one round of substitutions. The compiler can generate efficient code because it does not have to worry about strange code like:

```
set subexpr {$x+$y}
expr 5 * $subexpr
```

The previous expression is not fully defined until runtime, so it has to be parsed and executed each time it is used. If the expression is grouped with braces, then the compiler knows in advance what operations will be used and can generate byte codes to implement the expression more efficiently.

The operation of the compiler is essentially transparent to scripts, but there are some differences in lists and expressions. These are described in Chapter 54. With lists, the good news is that large lists are more efficient. The problem is that lists are parsed more aggressively, so syntax errors at the end of a list will be detected even if you access only the beginning of the list. There were also some bugs in the code generator in the widely used Tcl 8.0p2 release. Most of these were corner cases like unbraced expressions in `if` and `while` commands. Most of these bugs were fixed in the 8.0.3 patch release, and the rest were cleaned up in Tcl 8.1 with the addition of a new internal parsing package.

The internal compiler continues to improve over time, with 8.4 extending the core instruction table to significantly improve performance over previous versions.

Namespaces

Namespaces group procedures and variables into separate name spaces. Namespaces were added in Tcl 8.0. This chapter describes the `namespace` and `variable` commands.

Namespaces provide new scopes for procedures and global variables. Originally Tcl had one global scope for shared variables, local scopes within procedures, and one global namespace for procedures. The single global scope for procedures and global variables can become unmanageable as your Tcl application grows. I describe some simple naming conventions on page 181 that I have used successfully in large programs. The namespace facility is a more elegant solution that partitions the global scope for procedure names and global variables.

Namespaces help structure large Tcl applications, but they add complexity. In particular, command callbacks may have to be handled specially so that they execute in the proper namespace. You choose whether or not you need the extra structure and learning curve of namespaces. If your applications are small, then you can ignore the namespace facility. If you are developing library packages that others will use, you should pick a namespace for your procedures and data so that they will not conflict with the applications in which they are used.

Using Namespaces

Namespaces add new syntax to procedure and variable names. A double colon, ::, separates the namespace name from the variable or procedure name. You use this syntax to reference procedures and variables in a different namespace. The `namespace import` command lets you name things in other namespaces without the extra syntax. Namespaces can be nested, so you can create a hierarchy of scopes. These concepts are explained in more detail in the rest of this chapter.

One feature not provided by namespaces is any sort of protection, or a way to enforce access controls between different namespaces. This sort of thing is awkward, if not impossible, to provide in a dynamic language like Tcl. For example, you are always free to use `namespace eval` to reach into any other namespace. Instead of providing strict controls, namespaces are meant to provide structure that enables large scale programming.

The package facility described in Chapter 12 was designed before namespaces. This chapter illustrates a style that ties the two facilities together, but they are not strictly related. It is possible to create a package named A that implements a namespace B, or to use a package without namespaces, or a namespace without a package. However, it makes sense to use the facilities together.

Example 14–1 repeats the random number generator from Example 7–4 on page 91 using namespaces. The standard naming style conventions for namespaces use lowercase:

Example 14–1 Random number generator using namespaces.

```
package provide random 1.0

namespace eval random {
    # Create a variable inside the namespace
    variable seed [clock seconds]

    # Make the procedures visible to namespace import
    namespace export init random range

    # Create procedures inside the namespace
    proc init { value } {
        variable seed
        set seed $value
    }
    proc random {} {
        variable seed
        set seed [expr {($seed*9301 + 49297) % 233280}]
        return [expr {$seed/double(233280)}]
    }
    proc range { range } {
        expr {int([random]*$range)}
    }
}
```

Example 14–1 defines three procedures and a variable inside the namespace `random`. From inside the namespace, you can use these procedures and variables directly. From outside the namespace, you use the `::` syntax for namespace qualifiers. For example, the state variable is just `seed` within the namespace, but you use `random::seed` to refer to the variable from outside the namespace. Using the procedures looks like this:

```
random::random
=> 0.3993355624142661
random::range 10
=> 4
```

If you use a package a lot you can *import* its procedures. A namespace declares what procedures can be imported with the `namespace export` command. Once you import a procedure, you can use it without a qualified name:

```
namespace import random::random
random
=> 0.54342849794238679
```

Importing and exporting are described in more detail later.

Namespace Variables

The `variable` command defines a variable inside a namespace. It is like the `set` command because it can define a value for the variable. You can declare several namespace variables with one `variable` command. The general form is:

```
variable name ?value? ?name value? ...
```

If you have an array, do not assign a value in the `variable` command. Instead, use regular Tcl commands after you declare the variable. You can put any commands inside a `namespace` block:

```
namespace eval foo {
    variable arr
    array set arr {name value name2 value2}
}
```

A namespace variable is similar to a global variable because it is outside the scope of any procedures. Procedures use the `variable` command or qualified names to reference namespace variables. For example, the `random` procedure has a `variable` command that brings the namespace variable into the current scope:

```
variable seed
```

If a procedure has a `variable` command that names a new variable, it is created in the namespace when it is first `set`.

Watch out for conflicts with global variables.

You need to be careful when you use variables inside a namespace block. If you declare them with a `variable` command, they are clearly namespace variables. However, if you forget to declare them, then they will either become namespace variables, or latch onto an existing global variable by the same name. Consider the following code:

```
namespace eval foo {
    variable table
    for {set i 1} {$i <= 256} {incr i} {
     set table($i) [format %c $i]
    }
}
```

If there is already a global variable i, then the for loop will use that variable. Otherwise, it will create the foo::i variable. I found this behavior surprising, but it does make it easier to access global variables like env without first declaring them with global inside the namespace block.

Qualified Names

A fully qualified name begins with ::, which is the name for the global namespace. A fully qualified name unambiguously names a procedure or a variable. The fully qualified name works anywhere. If you use a fully qualified variable name, it is *not* necessary to use a global command. For example, suppose namespace foo has a namespace variable x, and there is also a global variable x. The global variable x can be named with this:

```
::x
```

The :: syntax does not affect variable substitutions. You can get the value of the global variable x with $::x. Name the namespace variable x with this:

```
::foo::x
```

A partially qualified name does not have a leading ::. In this case the name is resolved from the current namespace. For example, the following also names the namespace variable x:

```
foo::x
```

You can use qualified names with global. Once you do this, you can access the variable with its short name:

```
global ::foo::x
set x 5
```

 Declaring variables is more efficient than using qualified names.

The Tcl byte-code compiler generates faster code when you declare namespace and global variables. Each procedure context has its own table of variables. The table can be accessed by a direct slot index, or by a hash table lookup of the variable name. The hash table lookup is slower than the direct slot access. When you use the variable or global command, then the compiler can use a direct slot access. If you use qualified names, the compiler uses the more general hash table lookup.

Command Lookup

A command is looked up first in the current name space. If it is not found there, then it is looked up in the global namespace. This means that you can use all the built-in Tcl commands inside a namespace with no special effort.

You can play games by redefining commands within a namespace. For example, a namespace could define a procedure named set. To get the built-in set you could use ::set, while set referred to the set defined inside namespace. Obviously you need to be quite careful when you do this.

You can use qualified names when defining procedures. This eliminates the need to put the `proc` commands inside a `namespace` block. However, you still need to use `namespace eval` to create the namespace before you can create procedures inside it. Example 14–2 repeats the random number generator using qualified names. `random::init` does not need a `variable` command because it uses a qualified name for `seed`:

Example 14–2 Random number generator using qualified names.

```
namespace eval random {
    # Create a variable inside the namespace
    variable seed [clock seconds]
}
# Create procedures inside the namespace
proc random::init { seed } {
    set ::random::seed $seed
}
proc random::random {} {
    variable seed
    set seed [expr {($seed*9301 + 49297) % 233280}]
    return [expr {$seed/double(233280)}]
}
proc random::range { range } {
    expr {int([random]*$range)}
}
```

Nested Namespaces

Namespaces can be nested inside other namespaces. Example 14–3 shows three namespaces that have their own specific variable x. The fully qualified names for these variables are `::foo::x`, `::bar::x`, and `::bar::foo::x`.

Example 14–3 Nested namespaces.

```
namespace eval foo {
    variable x 1      ;# ::foo::x
}
namespace eval bar {
    variable x 2      ;# ::bar::x
    namespace eval foo {
        variable x 3  ;# ::bar::foo::x
    }
    puts $foo::x       ;# prints 3
}
puts $foo::x           ;# prints 1
```

Partially qualified names can refer to two different objects.

In Example 14–3 the partially qualified name `foo::x` can reference one of two variables depending on the current namespace. From the global scope the name `foo::x` refers to the namespace variable `x` inside `::foo`. From the `::bar` namespace, `foo::x` refers to the variable `x` inside `::bar::foo`.

If you want to unambiguously name a variable in the current namespace, you have two choices. The simplest is to bring the variable into scope with the `variable` command:

```
variable x
set x something
```

If you need to give out the name of the variable, then you have two choices. The most general solution is to use the `namespace current` command to create a fully qualified name:

```
trace variable [namespace current]::x r \
    [namespace current]::traceproc
```

However, it is simpler to just explicitly write out the namespace as in:

```
trace variable ::myname::x r ::myname::traceproc
```

The drawback of this approach is that it litters your code with references to `::myname::`, which might be subject to change during program development.

Importing and Exporting Procedures

Commands can be imported from namespaces to make it easier to name them. An imported command can be used without its namespace qualifier. Each namespace specifies exported procedures that can be the target of an import. Variables cannot be imported. Note that importing is only a convenience; you can always use qualified names to access any procedure. As a matter of style, I avoid importing names, so I know what package a command belongs to when I'm reading code.

The `namespace export` command goes inside the namespace block, and it specifies what procedures a namespace exports. The specification is a list of `string match` patterns that are compared against the set of commands defined in a namespace. The export list can be defined before the procedures being exported. You can do more than one `namespace export` to add more procedures, or patterns, to the export list for a namespace. Use the `-clear` flag if you need to reset the export list.

```
namespace export ?-clear? ?pat? ?pat? ...
```

Only exported names appear in package indexes.

When you create the `pkgIndex.tcl` package index file with `pkg_mkIndex`, which is described Chapter 12, you should be aware that only exported names appear in the index. Because of this, I often resort to exporting everything. I never plan to import the names, but I do rely on automatic code loading based on the index files. This exports everything:

```
namespace export *
```

The `namespace import` command makes commands in another namespace visible in the current namespace. An `import` can cause conflicts with commands in the current namespace. The `namespace import` command raises an error if there is a conflict. You can override this with the -force option. The general form of the command is:

```
namespace import ?-force? namespace::pat ?namespace::pat?...
```

The *pat* is a string match type pattern that is matched against *exported* commands defined in *namespace*. You cannot use patterns to match *namespace*. The *namespace* can be a fully or partially qualified name of a namespace.

If you are lazy, you can import all procedures from a namespace:

```
namespace import random::*
```

The drawback of this approach is that random exports an init procedure, which might conflict with another module you import in the same way. It is safer to import just the procedures you plan on using:

```
namespace import random::random random::range
```

A namespace import takes a snapshot.

If the set of procedures in a namespace changes, or if its export list changes, then this has no effect on any imports that have already occurred from that namespace.

Callbacks and Namespaces

Commands like after, bind, and button take arguments that are Tcl scripts that are evaluated later. These *callback* commands execute later in the global scope by default. If you want a callback to be evaluated in a particular namespace, you can construct the callback with namespace code. This command does not execute the callback. Instead, it generates a Tcl command that will execute in the current namespace scope when it is evaluated later. For example, suppose ::current is the current namespace. The namespace code command determines the current scope and adds that to the namespace inscope command it generates:

```
set callback [namespace code {set x 1}]
=> namespace inscope ::current {set x 1}
# sometime later ...
eval $callback
```

When you evaluate $callback later, it executes in the ::current namespace because of the namespace inscope command. In particular, if there is a namespace variable ::current::x, then that variable is modified. An alternative to using namespace code is to name the variable with a qualified name:

```
set callback {set ::current::x 1}
```

The drawback of this approach is that it makes it tedious to move the code to a different namespace.

If you need substitutions to occur on the command when you define it, use list to construct it. Using list is discussed in more detail on pages 131 and 455. Example 14–4 wraps up the list and the namespace inscope into the code procedure, which is handy because you almost always want to use list when constructing callbacks. The uplevel in code ensures that the correct namespace is captured; you can use code anywhere:

Example 14–4 The code procedure to wrap callbacks.

```
proc code {args} {
    set namespace [uplevel {namespace current}]
    return [list namespace inscope $namespace $args]
}
namespace eval foo {
    variable y "y value" x {}
    set callback [code set x $y]
    => namespace inscope ::foo {set x {y value}}
}
```

The example defines a callback that will set `::foo::x` to `y value`. If you want to set `x` to the value that `y` has at the time of the callback, then you do not want to do any substitutions. In that case, the original `namespace code` is what you want:

```
set callback [namespace code {set x $y}]
=> namespace inscope ::foo {set x $y}
```

If the callback has additional arguments added by the caller, `namespace inscope` correctly adds them. For example, the scrollbar protocol described on page 501 adds parameters to the callback that controls a scrollbar.

Introspection

The `info commands` operation returns all the commands that are currently visible. It is described in more detail on page 190. You can limit the information returned with a `string match` pattern. You can also include a namespace specifier in the pattern to see what is visible in a namespace. Remember that global commands and imported commands are visible, so `info commands` returns more than just what is defined by the namespace. Example 14–5 uses `namespace origin`, which returns the original name of imported commands, to sort out the commands that are really defined in a namespace:

Example 14–5 Listing commands defined by a namespace.

```
proc Namespace_List {{namespace {}}} {
    if {[string length $namespace] == 0} {
        # Determine the namespace of our caller
        set namespace [uplevel {namespace current}]
    }
    set result {}
    foreach cmd [info commands ${namespace}::*] {
        if {[namespace origin $cmd] == $cmd} {
            lappend result $cmd
        }
    }
    return [lsort $result]
}
```

The namespace Command

Table 14–1 summarizes the namespace operations:

Table 14–1 The namespace command.

namespace current	Returns the current namespace.
namespace children ?*name*? ?*pat*?	Returns names of nested namespaces. *name* defaults to current namespace. *pat* is a string match pattern that limits what is returned.
namespace code *script*	Generates a namespace inscope command that will eval *script* in the current namespace.
namespace delete *name* ?*name*? ...	Deletes the variables and commands from the specified namespaces.
namespace eval *name* *cmd* ?*args*? ...	Concatenates *args*, if present, onto *cmd* and evaluates it in *name* namespace.
namespace exists *name*	Returns 1 if namespace *name* exists, 0 otherwise. (Tcl 8.4)
namespace export ?-clear? ?*pat*? ?*pat*? ...	Adds patterns to the export list for current namespace. Returns export list if no patterns.
namespace forget *pat* ?*pat*? ...	Undoes the import of names matching patterns.
namespace import ?-force? *pat* ?*pat*? ...	Adds the names matching the patterns to the current namespace.
namespace inscope *name* *cmd* ?*args*? ...	Appends *args*, if present, onto *cmd* as list elements and evaluates it in *name* namespace.
namespace origin *cmd*	Returns the original name of *cmd*.
namespace parent ?*name*?	Returns the parent namespace of *name*, or of the current namespace.
namespace qualifiers *name*	Returns the part of *name* up to the last :: in it.
namespace which ?*flag*? *name*	Returns the fully qualified version of *name*. The *flag* is one of -command, -variable, or -namespace.
namespace tail *name*	Returns the last component of *name*.

Converting Existing Packages to use Namespaces

Suppose you have an existing set of Tcl procedures that you want to wrap in a namespace. Obviously, you start by surrounding your existing code in a namespace eval block. However, you need to consider three things: global variables, exported procedures, and callbacks.

II. Advanced Tcl

- Global variables remain global until you change your code to use `variable` instead of `global`. Some variables may make sense to leave at the global scope. Remember that the variables that Tcl defines are global, including `env`, `tcl_platform`, and the others listed in Table 2–2 on page 31. If you use the `upvar #0` trick described on page 92, you can adapt this to namespaces by doing this instead:

```
upvar #0 [namespace current]::$instance state
```

- Exporting procedures makes it more convenient for users of your package. It is not strictly necessary because they can always use qualified names to reference your procedures. An export list is a good hint about which procedures are expected to be used by other packages. Remember that the export list determines what procedures are visible in the index created by `pkg_mkIndex`.

- Callbacks execute at the global scope. If you use variable traces and variables associated with Tk widgets, these are also treated as global variables. If you want a callback to invoke a namespace procedure, or if you give out the name of a namespace variable, then you must construct fully qualified variable and procedure names. You can hardwire the current namespace:

```
button .foo -command ::myname::callback \
    -textvariable ::myname::textvar
```

or you can use `namespace current`:

```
button .foo -command [namespace current]::callback \
    -textvariable [namespace current]::textvar
```

[incr Tcl] Object System

The Tcl namespace facility does not provide classes and inheritance. It just provides new scopes and a way to hide procedures and variables inside a scope. There are Tcl C APIs that support hooks in variable name and command lookup for object systems so that they can implement classes and inheritance. By exploiting these interfaces, various object systems can be added to Tcl as shared libraries.

The Tcl namespace facility was proposed by Michael McLennan based on his experiences with [incr Tcl], which is the most widely used object-oriented extension for Tcl. [incr Tcl] provides classes, inheritance, and protected variables and commands. If you are familiar with C++, [incr Tcl] should feel similar. A complete treatment of [incr Tcl] is not made in this book. *[incr Tcl] From The Ground Up* (Chad Smith, Osborn-McGraw Hill, 1999) is an excellent source of information. You can find a version of [incr Tcl] on the CD-ROM. The [incr Tcl] home page is:

```
http://www.tcltk.com/itcl/
```

The [incr Tcl] sources are maintained on SourceForge:

```
http://incrtcl.sourceforge.net/
```

xotcl Object System

Xotcl is a more recently developed object-oriented extension that blends object-orientation and scripting in a way that preserves the benefits of both. It includes features such as dynamic object aggregation, per-object mixins, filters, dynamic component loading and more. The xotcl home page is:

```
http://www.xotcl.org/
```

Notes

The final section of this chapter touches on a variety of features of the namespace facility.

Names for Widgets, Images, and Interpreters

There are a number of Tcl extensions that are not affected by the namespaces described in this chapter, which apply only to commands and variable names. For example, when you create a Tk widget, a Tcl command is also created that corresponds to the Tk widget. This command is always created in the global command namespace even when you create the Tk widget from inside a `namespace eval` block. Other examples include Tcl interpreters, which are described in Chapter 19, and Tk images, which are described in Chapter 41.

The `variable` command at the global scope

It turns out that you can use `variable` like the `global` command if your procedures are not inside a namespace. This is consistent because it means "this variable belongs to the current namespace," which might be the global namespace.

Auto Loading and `auto_import`

The following sequence of commands can be used to import commands from the `foo` package:

```
package require foo
namespace import foo::*
```

However, because of the default behavior of packages, there may not be anything that matches `foo::*` after the `package require`. Instead, there are entries in the `auto_index` array that will be used to load those procedures when you first use them. The auto loading mechanism is described in Chapter 12. To account for this, Tcl calls out to a hook procedure called `auto_import`. This default implementation of this procedure searches `auto_index` and forcibly loads any pending procedures that match the import pattern. Packages like [incr Tcl] exploit this hook to implement more elaborate schemes. The `auto_import` hook was first introduced in Tcl 8.0.3.

Namespaces and `uplevel`

Namespaces affect the Tcl call frames just like procedures do. If you walk the call stack with `info level`, the namespace frames are visible. This means that you can get access to all variables with `uplevel` and `upvar`. Level #0 is still the absolute global scope, outside any namespace or procedure. Try out `Call_Trace` from Example 13–5 on page 190 on your code that uses namespaces to see the effect.

Naming Quirks

When you name a namespace, you are allowed to have extra colons at the end. You can also have two or more colons as the separator between namespace name components. These rules make it easier to assemble names by adding to the value returned from `namespace current`. These all name the same namespace:

```
::foo::bar
::foo::bar::
::foo:::::::bar
```

The name of the global namespace can be either `::` or the empty string. This follows from the treatment of `::` in namespace names.

When you name a variable or command, a trailing `::` is significant. In the following command a variable inside the `::foo::bar` namespace is modified. The variable has an empty string for its name!

```
set ::foo::bar:: 3
namespace eval ::foo::bar { set {} }
=> 3
```

If you want to embed a reference to a variable just before two colons, use a backslash to turn off the variable name parsing before the colons:

```
set x xval
set y $x\::foo
=> xval::foo
```

Miscellaneous

You can remove names you have imported:

```
namespace forget random::init
```

You can `rename` imported procedures to modify their names:

```
rename range Range
```

You can even move a procedure into another namespace with `rename`:

```
rename random::init myspace::init
```

Internationalization

This chapter describes features that support text processing for different
character sets such as ASCII and Japanese. Tcl can read and write data
in various character set encodings, but it processes data in a standard
character set called Unicode. Tcl has a message catalog that lets you
generate different versions of an application for different languages. Tcl
commands described are: `encoding` and `msgcat`.

*D*ifferent languages use different alpha-
bets, or *character sets*. An *encoding* is a standard way to represent a character
set. Tcl hides most of the issues associated with encodings and character sets,
but you need to be aware of them when you write applications that are used in
different countries. You can also write an application using a *message catalog* so
that the strings you display to users can be in the language of their choice. Using
a message catalog is more work, but Tcl makes it as easy as possible.

Most of the hard work in dealing with character set encodings is done
"under the covers" by the Tcl C library. The Tcl C library underwent substantial
changes to support international character sets. Instead of using 8-bit bytes to
store characters, Tcl uses a 16-bit character set called Unicode, which is large
enough to encode the alphabets of all languages. There is also plenty of room left
over to represent special characters like ♥ and ⊗.

In spite of all the changes to support Unicode, there are few changes visible
to the Tcl script writer. Scripts written for Tcl 8.0 and earlier continue to work
fine with Tcl 8.1 and later versions. You only need to modify scripts if you want
to take advantage of the features added to support internationalization.

This chapter begins with a discussion of what a character set is and why
different codings are used to represent them. It concludes with a discussion of
message catalogs.

Character Sets and Encodings

If you are from the United States, you've probably never thought twice about character sets. Most computers use the ASCII encoding, which has 127 characters. That is enough for the 26 letters in the English alphabet, upper case and lower case, plus numbers, various punctuation characters, and control characters like tab and newline. ASCII fits easily in 8-bit characters, which can represent 256 different values.

European alphabets include accented characters like è, ñ, and ä. The ISO Latin-1 encoding is a superset of ASCII that encodes 256 characters. It shares the ASCII encoding in values 0 through 127 and uses the "high half" of the encoding space to represent accented characters as well as special characters like ©. There are several ISO Latin encodings to handle different alphabets, and these share the trick of encoding ASCII in the lower half and other characters in the high half. You might see these encodings referred to as `iso8859-1`, `iso8859-2`, and so on.

Asian character sets are simply too large to fit into 8-bit encodings. There are a number of 16-bit encodings for these languages. If you work with these, you are probably familiar with the "Big 5" or ShiftJIS encodings.

Unicode is an international standard character set encoding. There are both 16-bit Unicode and 32-bit Unicode standards, but Tcl and just about everyone else use the 16-bit standard. Unicode has the important property that it can encode all the important character sets without conflicts and overlap. By converting all characters to the Unicode encoding, Tcl can work with different character sets simultaneously. As of 8.4, Tcl is compliant with Unicode v3.1. For more information on Unicode, see `http://www.unicode.org/`

The System Encoding

Computer systems are set up with a standard system encoding for their files. If you always work with this encoding, then you can ignore character set issues. Tcl will read files and automatically convert them from the system encoding to Unicode. When Tcl writes files, it automatically converts from Unicode to the system encoding. If you are curious, you can find out the system encoding with:

```
encoding system
=> cp1252
```

The "cp" is short for "code page," the term that Windows uses to refer to different encodings. On my Unix system, the system encoding is `iso8859-1`.

Do not change the system encoding.

You could also change the system encoding with:

```
encoding system encoding
```

But this is not a good idea. It immediately changes how Tcl passes strings to your operating system, and it is likely to leave Tcl in an unusable state. Tcl automatically determines the system encoding for you. Don't bother trying to set it yourself.

The `encoding names` command lists all the encodings that Tcl knows about. The encodings are kept in files stored in the `encoding` directory under the Tcl script library. They are loaded automatically the first time you use an encoding.

```
lsort [encoding names]
=> ascii big5 cp1250 cp1251 cp1252 cp1253 cp1254 cp1255
cp1256 cp1257 cp1258 cp437 cp737 cp775 cp850 cp852 cp855
cp857 cp860 cp861 cp862 cp863 cp864 cp865 cp866 cp869
cp874 cp932 cp936 cp949 cp950 dingbats euc-cn euc-jp euc-
kr gb12345 gb1988 gb2312 identity iso2022 iso2022-jp
iso2022-kr iso8859-1 iso8859-2 iso8859-3 iso8859-4
iso8859-5 iso8859-6 iso8859-7 iso8859-8 iso8859-9
jis0201 jis0208 jis0212 ksc5601 macCentEuro macCroatian
macCyrillic macDingbats macGreek macIceland macJapan
macRoman macRomania macThai macTurkish macUkraine
shiftjis symbol unicode utf-8
```

The encoding names reflect their origin. The "cp" refers to the "code pages" that Windows uses to manage encodings. The "mac" encodings come from the Macintosh. The "iso," "euc," "gb," and "jis" encodings come from various standards bodies.

File Encodings and `fconfigure`

The conversion to Unicode happens automatically in the Tcl C library. When Tcl reads and writes files, it translates from the current system encoding into Unicode. If you have files in different encodings, you can use the `fconfigure` command to set the encoding. For example, to read a file in the standard Russian encoding (`iso8859-7`):

```
set in [open README.russian]
fconfigure $in -encoding iso8859-7
```

Example 15–1 shows a simple utility I use in `exmh`,[*] a MIME-aware mail reader. MIME has its own convention for specifying the character set encoding of a mail message that differs slightly from Tcl's naming convention. The procedure launders the name and then sets the encoding. Exmh was already aware of MIME character sets, so it could choose fonts for message display. Adding this procedure and adding two calls to it was all I had to do to adapt *exmh* to Unicode.

Example 15–1 MIME character sets and file encodings.

```
proc Mime_SetEncoding {file charset} {
    regsub -all {(iso|jis|us)-} $charset {\1} charset
    set charset [string tolower charset]
    regsub usascii $charset ascii charset
    fconfigure $file -encoding $charset
}
```

[*] The `exmh` home page is http://www.beedub.com/exmh/. It is a wonderful tool that helps me manage tons of email. It is written in Tcl/Tk, of course, and relies on the MH mail system, which limits it to UNIX.

Scripts in Different Encodings

If you have scripts that are not in the system encoding, then you cannot use source to load them. However, it is easy to read the files yourself under the proper encoding and use eval to process them. Example 15–2 adds a -encoding flag to the source command. This is likely to become a built-in feature in future versions of Tcl so that commands like info script will work properly:

Example 15–2 Using scripts in nonstandard encodings.

```
proc Source {args} {
    set file [lindex $args end]
    if {[llength $args] == 3 &&
            [string equal -encoding [lindex $args 0]]} {
        set encoding [lindex $args 1]
        set in [open $file]
        fconfigure $in -encoding $encoding
        set script [read $in]
        close $in
        return [uplevel 1 $script]
    } elseif {[llength $args] == 1} {
        return [uplevel 1 [list source $file]]
    } else {
        return -code error \
            "Usage: Source ?-encoding encoding? file?"
    }
}
```

Unicode and UTF-8

UTF-8 is an encoding for Unicode. While Unicode represents all characters with 16 bits, the UTF-8 encoding uses either 8, 16, or 24 bits to represent one Unicode character. This variable-width encoding is useful because it uses 8 bits to represent ASCII characters. This means that a pure ASCII string, one with character codes all less than 128, is also a UTF-8 string. Tcl uses UTF-8 internally to make the transition to Unicode easier. It allows interoperability with Tcl extensions that have not been made Unicode-aware. They can continue to pass ASCII strings to Tcl, and Tcl will interpret them correctly.

As a Tcl script writer, you can mostly ignore UTF-8 and just think of Tcl as being built on Unicode (i.e., full 16-bit character set support). If you write Tcl extensions in C or C++, however, the impact of UTF-8 and Unicode is quite visible. This is explained in more detail in Chapter 47.

Tcl lets you read and write files in UTF-8 encoding or directly in Unicode. This is useful if you need to use the same file on systems that have different system encodings. These files might be scripts, message catalogs, or documentation. Instead of using a particular native format, you can use Unicode or UTF-8 and read the files the same way on any of your systems. Of course, you will have to set the encoding properly by using fconfigure as shown earlier.

The Binary Encoding

If you want to read a data file and suppress all character set transformations, use the `binary` encoding:

```
fconfigure $in -encoding binary
```

Under the binary encoding, Tcl reads in each 8-bit byte and stores it into the lower half of a 16-bit Unicode character with the high half set to zero. During binary output, Tcl writes out the lower byte of each Unicode character. You can see that reading in binary and then writing it out doesn't change any bits. Watch out if you read something in one encoding and then write it out in binary. Any information in the high byte of the Unicode character gets lost!

Tcl actually handles the binary encoding more efficiently than just described, but logically the previous description is still accurate. As described in Chapter 47, Tcl can manage data in several forms, not just strings. When you read a file in binary format, Tcl stores the data as a `ByteArray` that is simply 8 bits of data in each byte. However, if you ask for this data as a string (e.g., with the `puts` command), Tcl automatically converts from 8-bit bytes to 16-bit Unicode characters by setting the high byte to all zeros.

The `binary` command also manipulates data in `ByteArray` format. If you read a file with the binary encoding and then use the `binary` command to process the data, Tcl will keep the data in an efficient form.

The string command also understands the `ByteArray` format, so you can do operations like `string length`, `string range`, and `string index` on binary data without suffering the conversion cost from a `ByteArray` to a UTF-8 string.

Conversions Between Encodings

The `encoding` command lets you convert strings between encodings. The `encoding convertfrom` command converts data in some other encoding into a Unicode string. The `encoding convertto` command converts a Unicode string into some other encoding. For example, the following two sequences of commands are equivalent. They both read data from a file that is in Big5 encoding and convert it to Unicode:

```
fconfigure $input -encoding gb12345
set unicode [read $input]
```

or

```
fconfigure $input -encoding binary
set unicode [encoding convertfrom gb12345 [read $input]]
```

In general, you can lose information when you go from Unicode to any other encoding, so you ought to be aware of the limitations of the encodings you are using. In particular, the `binary` encoding may not preserve your data if it starts out from an arbitrary Unicode string. Similarly, an encoding like `iso8859-2` may simply not have a representation of a given Unicode character.

The encoding Command

Table 15–1 summarizes the encoding command:

Table 15–1 The encoding command.

encoding convert-
    from ?*encoding*?
    data
	Converts binary *data* from the specified *encoding*, which defaults to the system encoding, into Unicode.

encoding convertto ?*encoding*? *string*	Converts *string* from Unicode into data in the *encoding* format, which defaults to the system encoding.
encoding names	Returns the names of known encodings.
encoding system ?*encoding*?	Queries or change the system encoding.

Message Catalogs

A *message catalog* is a list of messages that your application will display. The main idea is that you can maintain several catalogs, one for each language you support. Unfortunately, you have to be explicit about using message catalogs. Everywhere you generate output or display strings in Tk widgets, you need to change your code to go through a message catalog. Fortunately, Tcl uses a nice trick to make this fairly easy and to keep your code readable. Instead of using keys like "message42" to get messages out of the catalog, Tcl just uses the strings you would use by default. For example, instead of this code:

```
puts "Hello, World!"
```

A version that uses message catalogs looks like this:

```
puts [msgcat::mc "Hello, World!"]
```

If you have not already loaded your message catalog, or if your catalog doesn't contain a mapping for "Hello, World!", then msgcat::mc just returns its argument. Actually, you can define just what happens in the case of unknown inputs by defining your own msgcat::mcunknown procedure, but the default behavior is quite good.

The message catalog is implemented in Tcl in the msgcat package. You need to use package require to make it available to your scripts:

```
package require msgcat
```

In addition, all the procedures in the package begin with "mc," so you can use namespace import to shorten their names further. I am not a big fan of namespace import, but if you use message catalogs, you will be calling the msgcat::mc function a lot, so it may be worthwhile to import it:

```
namespace import msgcat::mc
puts [mc "Hello, World!"]
```

Specifying a Locale

A *locale* identifies a language or language dialect to use in your output. A three-level scheme is used in the locale identifier:

```
language_country_dialect
```

The language codes are defined by the ISO-3166 standard. For example, "en" is English and "es" is Spanish. The country codes are defined by the ISO-639 standard. For example, US is for the United States and UK is for the United Kingdom. The dialect is up to you. The country and dialect parts are optional. Finally, the locale specifier is case insensitive. The following examples are all valid locale specifiers:

```
es
en
en_US
en_us
en_UK
en_UK_Scottish
en_uk_scottish
```

Users can set their initial locale with the LANG and LOCALE environment variables. If there is no locale information in the environment, then the "c" locale is used (i.e., the C programming language.) You can also set and query the locale with the msgcat::mclocale procedure:

```
msgcat::mclocale
=> c
msgcat::mclocale en_US
```

The msgcat::mcpreferences procedure returns a list of the user's locale preferences from most specific (i.e., including the dialect) to most general (i.e., only the language). For example:

```
msgcat::mclocale en_UK_Scottish
msgcat::mcpreferences
=> en_UK_Scottish en_UK en
```

Managing Message Catalog Files

A message catalog is simply a Tcl source file that contains a series of msgcat::mcset commands that define entries in the catalog. The syntax of the msgcat::mcset procedure is:

```
msgcat::mcset locale src-string ?dest-string?
```

The *locale* is a locale description like es or en_US_Scottish. The *src-string* is the string used as the key when calling msgcat::mc. The *dest-string* is the result of msgcat::mc when the *locale* is in force.

The msgcat::mcload procedure should be used to load your message catalog files. It expects the files to be named according to their locale (e.g., en_US_Scottish.msg), and it binds the message catalog to the current namespace.

II. Advanced Tcl

The `msgcat::mcload` procedure loads files that match the `msgcat::mcpref-` `erences` and have the `.msg` suffix. For example, with a locale of `en_UK_Scottish`, `msgcat::mcload` would look for these files:

    en_UK_Scottish.msg en_UK.msg en.msg

The standard place for message catalog files is in the `msgs` directory below the directory containing a package. With this arrangement you can call `msg-` `cat::mcload` as shown below. The use of `info script` to find related files is explained on page 192.

    msgcat::mcload [file join [file dirname [info script]] msgs]

The message catalog file is sourced, so it can contain any Tcl commands. You might find it convenient to import the `msgcat::mcset` procedure. Be sure to use `-force` with `namespace import` because that command might already have been imported as a result of loading other message catalog files. Example 15–3 shows three trivial message catalog files:

Example 15–3 Three sample message catalog files.

```
## en.msg
namespace import -force msgcat::mcset

mcset en Hello Hello_en
mcset en Goodbye Goodbye_en
mcset en String String_en
# end of en.msg

## en_US.msg
namespace import -force msgcat::mcset

mcset en_US Hello Hello_en_US
mcset en_US Goodbye Goodbye_en_US
# end of en_US.msg

## en_US_Texan.msg
namespace import -force msgcat::mcset

mcset en_US_Texan Hello Howdy!
# end of en_US_Texan.msg
```

Assuming the files from Example 15–3 are all in the `msgs` directory below your script, you can load all these files with these commands:

    msgcat::mclocale en_US_Texan
    msgcat::mcload [file join [file dirname [info script]] msgs]

The dialect has the highest priority:

    msgcat::mc Hello
    => *Howdy!*

If the dialect does not specify a mapping, then the country mapping is checked:

```
msgcat::mc Goodbye
=> Goodbye_en_US
```

Finally, the lowest priority is the language mapping:

```
msgcat::mc String
=> String_en
```

Message Catalogs and Namespaces

What happens if two different library packages have conflicting message catalogs? Suppose the `foo` package contains this call:

```
msgcat::set fr Hello Bonjour
```

But the `bar` package contains this conflicting definition:

```
msgcat::mcset fr Hello Ello
```

What happens is that `msgcat::mcset` and `msgcat::mc` are sensitive to the current Tcl namespace. Namespaces are described in detail in Chapter 14. If the `foo` package loads its message catalog while inside the `foo` namespace, then any calls to `msgcat::mc` from inside the `foo` namespace will see those definitions. In fact, if you call `msgcat::mc` from inside any namespace, it will find only message catalog definitions defined from within that namespace.

If you want to share message catalogs between namespaces, you will need to implement your own version of `msgcat::mcunknown` that looks in the shared location. Example 15–4 shows a version that looks in the global namespace before returning the default string.

Example 15–4 Using `msgcat::mcunknown` to share message catalogs.

```
proc msgcat::mcunknown {local src} {
    variable insideUnknown
    if {![info exist insideUnknown]} {

        # Try the global namespace, being careful to note
        # that we are already inside this procedure.

        set insideUnknown true
        set result [namespace eval :: [list \
            msgcat::mc $src \
        ]]
        unset insideUnknown
        return $result
    } else {

        # Being called because the message isn't found
        # in the global namespace

        return $src
    }
}
```

The `msgcat` package

Table 15–2 summarizes the `msgcat` package.

Table 15–2   The `msgcat` package

`msgcat::mc` *src*	Returns the translation of *src* according to the current locale and namespace.
`msgcat::mclocale` *?locale?*	Queries or set the current *locale*.
`msgcat::mcmax ?`*src-string* `src-string ...?`	Returns the length of the longest *src-string* after translation. (Tcl 8.3)
`msgcat::mcpreferences`	Returns a list of locale preferences ordered from the most specific to the most general.
`msgcat::mcload` *directory*	Loads message files for the current locale from *directory*.
`msgcat::mcset` *locale src translation*	Defines a mapping for the *src* string in *locale* to the *translation* string. (Tcl 8.3)
`msgcat::mcmset` *src-trans-list*	Define multiple *src-translation* pairs in a single call.
`msgcat::mcunknown` *locale src*	This procedure is called to resolve unknown translations. Applications can provide their own implementations.

## CHAPTER 16

Event-Driven Programming

This chapter describes event-driven programming using timers and asynchronous I/O facilities. The `after` command causes Tcl commands to occur at a time in the future, and the `fileevent` command registers a command to occur in response to file input/output (I/O). Tcl commands discussed are: `after`, `fblocked`, `fconfigure`, `fileevent`, and `vwait`.

*E*vent-driven programming is used in long-running programs like network servers and graphical user interfaces. This chapter introduces event-driven programming in Tcl. Tcl provides an easy model in which you register Tcl commands, and the system then calls those commands when a particular event occurs. The `after` command is used to execute Tcl commands at a later time, and the `fileevent` command is used to execute Tcl commands when the system is ready for I/O. The `vwait` command is used to wait for events. During the wait, Tcl automatically calls Tcl commands that are associated with different events.

The event model is also used when programming user interfaces using Tk. Originally, event processing was associated only with Tk. The event loop moved from Tk to Tcl in the Tcl 7.5/Tk 4.1 release.

The Tcl Event Loop

An event loop is built into Tcl, which checks for events and calls out to handlers that have been registered for different types of events. Some of the events are processed internally to Tcl. You can register Tcl commands to be called in response to events. There are also C APIs for the event loop, which are described on page 781. Event processing is active all the time in Tk applications. If you do not use Tk, you can start the event loop with the `vwait` command as shown in Example 16–2 on page 230. The four event classes are handled in the following order:

- Window events. These include keystrokes and button clicks. Handlers are set up for these automatically by the Tk widgets, and you can register window event handlers with the `bind` command described in Chapter 29.
- File and socket I/O events. The `fileevent` command registers handlers for these events.
- Timer events. The `after` command registers commands to occur at specific times.
- Idle events. These events are processed when there is nothing else to do. The Tk widgets use idle events to display themselves. The `after idle` command registers a command to run at the next idle time.

The `after` Command

The `after` command sets up commands to happen in the future. In its simplest form, it pauses the application for a specified time, in milliseconds. The example below waits for half a second:

```
after 500
```

During this time, the application *does not* process events. You can use the `vwait` command as shown on page 230 to keep the Tcl event loop active during the waiting period. The `after` command can register a Tcl command to occur after a period of time, in milliseconds:

```
after milliseconds cmd arg arg...
```

The `after` command treats its arguments like `eval`; if you give it extra arguments, it concatenates them to form a single command. If your argument structure is important, use `list` to build the command. The following example always works, no matter what the value of `myvariable` is:

```
after 500 [list puts $myvariable]
```

The return value of `after` is an identifier for the registered command. You can cancel this command with the `after cancel` operation. You specify either the identifier returned from `after`, or the command string. In the latter case, the event that matches the command string exactly is canceled.

Table 16–1 summarizes the `after` command:

Table 16–1 The `after` command.

`after milliseconds`	Pauses for `milliseconds`.
`after ms arg ?arg...?`	Concatenates the `args` into a command and executes it after `ms` milliseconds. Immediately returns an ID.
`after cancel id`	Cancels the command registered under `id`.
`after cancel command`	Cancels the registered `command`.
`after idle command`	Runs `command` at the next idle moment.
`after info ?id?`	Returns a list of IDs for outstanding `after` events, or the command associated with `id`.

The `fileevent` Command

The `fileevent` command registers a procedure that is called when an I/O channel is ready for read or write events. For example, you can open a pipeline or network socket for reading, and then process the data from the pipeline or socket using a command registered with `fileevent`. The advantage of this approach is that your application can do other things, like update the user interface, while waiting for data from the pipeline or socket. Network servers use `fileevent` to manage connections to many clients. You can use `fileevent` on `stdin` and `stdout`, too. Using network sockets is described in Chapter 17.

The command registered with `fileevent` uses the regular Tcl commands to read or write data on the I/O channel. For example, if the pipeline generates line-oriented output, you should use `gets` to read a line of input. If you try and read more data than is available, your application may block waiting for more input. For this reason, you should read one line in your `fileevent` handler, assuming the data is line-oriented. If you know the pipeline will generate data in fixed-sized blocks, then you can use the `read` command to read one block.

The `fconfigure` command, which is described on page 232, can put a channel into nonblocking mode. This is not strictly necessary when using `fileevent`. The pros and cons of nonblocking I/O are discussed later.

End of file makes a channel readable.

You should check for end of file in your read handler because it will be called when end of file occurs. It is important to close the channel inside the handler because closing the channel automatically unregisters the handler. If you forget to close the channel, your read event handler will be called repeatedly.

Example 16–1 shows a read event handler. A pipeline is opened for reading and its command executes in the background. The `Reader` command is invoked when data is available on the pipe. When end of file is detected a variable is set, which signals the application waiting with `vwait`. Otherwise, a single line of input is read and processed. The `vwait` command is described on the next page. Example 24–1 on page 378 also uses `fileevent` to read from a pipeline.

Example 16–1 A read event file handler.

```
proc Reader { pipe } {
    global done
    if {[eof $pipe]} {
        catch {close $pipe}
        set done 1
        return
    }
    gets $pipe line
    # Process the line here...
}
set pipe [open "|some command"]
fileevent $pipe readable [list Reader $pipe]
vwait done
```

There can be at most one read handler and one write handler for an I/O channel. If you register a handler and one is already registered, then the old registration is removed. If you call `fileevent` without a command argument, it returns the currently registered command, or it returns the empty string if there is none. If you register the empty string, it deletes the current file handler. Table 16–2 summarizes the `fileevent` command.

Table 16–2 The `fileevent` command.

`fileevent` *fileId* `readable` *?command?*	Queries or registers *command* to be called when *fileId* is readable.
`fileevent` *fileId* `writable` *?command?*	Queries or registers *command* to be called when *fileId* is writable.

The `vwait` Command

The `vwait` command waits until a variable is modified. For example, you can set variable x at a future time, and then wait for that variable to be set with `vwait`.

```
set x 0
after 500 {set x 1}
vwait x
```

Waiting with `vwait` causes Tcl to enter the event loop. Tcl will process events until the variable x is modified. The `vwait` command completes when some Tcl code runs in response to an event and modifies the variable. In this case the event is a timer event, and the Tcl code is simply:

```
set x 1
```

In some cases `vwait` is used only to start the event loop. Example 16–2 sets up a file event handler for `stdin` that will read and execute commands. Once this is set up, `vwait` is used to enter the event loop and process commands until the input channel is closed. The process exits at that point, so the `vwait` variable `Stdin(wait)` is not used:

Example 16–2 Using `vwait` to activate the event loop.

```
proc Stdin_Start {prompt} {
    global Stdin
    set Stdin(line) ""
    puts -nonewline $prompt
    flush stdout
    fileevent stdin readable [list StdinRead $prompt]
    vwait Stdin(wait)
}
proc StdinRead {prompt} {
    global Stdin
    if {[eof stdin]} {
        exit
    }
```

```
        append Stdin(line) [gets stdin]
        if {[info complete $Stdin(line)]} {
            catch {uplevel #0 $Stdin(line)} result
            puts $result
            puts -newline $prompt
            flush stdout
            set Stdin(line) {}
        } else {
            append Stdin(line) \n
        }
    }
```

The `fconfigure` Command

The `fconfigure` command sets and queries several properties of I/O channels.
The default settings for channels are suitable for most cases. If you do event-
driven I/O you may want to set your channel into nonblocking mode. If you handle binary data, you should turn off end of line and character set translations.
You can query the channel parameters like this:

```
fconfigure stdin
=> -blocking 1 -buffering none -buffersize 4096 -encoding
iso8859-1 -eofchar {} -translation lf
```

Table 16–3 summarizes the properties controlled by `fconfigure`, not
including properties for serial lines.

Table 16–3 I/O channel properties controlled by `fconfigure`.

`-blocking`	Blocks until I/O channel is ready: 0 or 1.
`-buffering`	Buffer mode: `none`, `line`, or `full`.
`-buffersize`	Number of characters in the buffer.
`-encoding`	The character set encoding.
`-eofchar`	Special end of file character. Control-z (`\x1a`) for DOS. Null otherwise.
`-lasterror`	Returns the last POSIX error message associated with a channel.
`-translation`	End of line translation: `auto`, `lf`, `cr`, `crlf`, `binary`.
`-peername`	Sockets only. IP address of remote host.
`-peerport`	Sockets only. Port number of remote host.

Serial lines have many additional properties. Before Tcl 8.4, you could only
control the baud rate, parity and number of bits using the `-mode` property. Many
new properties for serial line control were added in Tcl 8.4. Table 16–4 lists the
serial line properties set by `fconfigure`.

Table 16–4 Serial line properties controlled by `fconfigure`.

`-mode`	Format: *baud,parity,data,stop*.
`-queue`	Returns a list of two integers representing the current number of bytes in the input and output queues. Tcl 8.4.
`-timeout`	Specifies the timeout in milliseconds for blocking reads. Tcl 8.4.
`-ttycontrol`	Sets up the handshake output lines. Tcl 8.4.
`-ttystatus`	Returns the current serial line status. Tcl 8.4.
`-xchar`	Specifies the software handshake characters. Tcl 8.4.
`-handshake`	Specifies one of *rtscts*, *xonxoff* or (Windows only) *dtrdsr*. Tcl 8.4.
`-pollinterval`	Sets the maximum time for polling of fileevents (Windows only.) Tcl 8.4.
`-sysbuffer`	Specifies the size of system buffers for a serial channel. (Windows only.) Tcl 8.4.

Nonblocking I/O

By default, I/O channels are *blocking*. A `gets` or `read` will wait until data is available before returning. A `puts` may also wait if the I/O channel is not ready to accept data. This behavior is all right if you are using disk files, which are essentially always ready. If you use pipelines or network sockets, however, the blocking behavior can hang up your application.

The `fconfigure` command can set a channel into *nonblocking mode*. A `gets` or `read` command may return immediately with no data. This occurs when there is no data available on a socket or pipeline. A `puts` to a nonblocking channel will accept all the data and buffer it internally. When the underlying device (i.e., a pipeline or socket) is ready, then Tcl automatically writes out the buffered data. Nonblocking channels are useful because your application can do something else while waiting for the I/O channel. You can also manage several nonblocking I/O channels at once. Nonblocking channels should be used with the `fileevent` command described earlier. The following command puts a channel into nonblocking mode:

```
fconfigure fileID -blocking 0
```

It is not strictly necessary to put a channel into nonblocking mode if you use `fileevent`. However, if the channel is in blocking mode, then it is still possible for the `gets` or `read` done by your `fileevent` procedure to block. For example, an I/O channel might have some data ready, but not a complete line. In this case, a `gets` would block, unless the channel is nonblocking. Perhaps the best motivation for a nonblocking channel is the buffering behavior of a nonblocking `puts`. You can even `close` a channel that has buffered data, and Tcl will automatically write out the buffers as the channel becomes ready. For these reasons, it is common to use a nonblocking channel with `fileevent`. Example 16–3 shows a `fileevent` handler for a nonblocking channel. As described above, the `gets` may not find a complete line, in which case it doesn't read anything and returns -1.

Example 16–3 A read event file handler for a nonblocking channel.

```
set pipe [open "|some command"]
fileevent $pipe readable [list Reader $pipe]
fconfigure $pipe -blocking 0
proc Reader { pipe } {
    global done
    if {[eof $pipe]} {
        catch {close $pipe}
        set done 1
        return
    }
    if {[gets $pipe line] < 0} {
        # We blocked anyway because only part of a line
        # was available for input
    } else {
        # Process one line
    }
}
vwait done
```

The fblocked Command

The `fblocked` command returns 1 if a channel does not have data ready. Normally the `fileevent` command takes care of waiting for data, so I have seen `fblocked` useful only in testing channel implementations.

Buffering

By default, Tcl buffers data, so I/O is more efficient. The underlying device is accessed less frequently, so there is less overhead. In some cases you may want data to be visible immediately and buffering gets in the way. The following turns off all buffering:

```
fconfigure fileID -buffering none
```

Full buffering means that output data is accumulated until a buffer fills; then a write is performed. For reading, Tcl attempts to read a whole buffer each time more data is needed. The read-ahead for buffering will not block. The `-buffersize` parameter controls the buffer size:

```
fconfigure fileID -buffering full -buffersize 8192
```

Line buffering is used by default on `stdin` and `stdout`. Each newline in an output channel causes a write operation. Read buffering is the same as full buffering. The following command turns on line buffering:

```
fconfigure fileID -buffering line
```

End of Line Translations

On UNIX, text lines end with a newline character (\n). On Macintosh they end with a carriage return (\r). On Windows they end with a carriage return, newline sequence (\r\n). Network sockets also use the carriage return, newline sequence. By default, Tcl accepts any of these, and the line terminator can even change within a channel. All of these different conventions are converted to the UNIX style so that once read, text lines always end with a newline character (\n). Both the `read` and `gets` commands do this conversion. By default, text lines are generated in the platform-native format during output.

The default behavior is almost always what you want, but you can control the translation with `fconfigure`. Table 16–5 shows settings for `-translation`:

Table 16–5   End of line translation modes.

`binary`	No translation at all.
`lf`	UNIX-style, which also means no translations.
`cr`	Macintosh style. On input, carriage returns are converted to newlines. On output, newlines are converted to carriage returns.
`crlf`	Windows and Network style. On input, carriage return, newline is converted to a newline. On output, a newline is converted to a carriage return, newline.
`auto`	The default behavior. On input, all end of line conventions are converted to a newline. Output is in native format.

End of File Character

In DOS file systems, there may be a Control-z character (\x1a) at the end of a text file. By default, this character is ignored on the Windows platform if it occurs at the end of the file, and this character is output when you close the file. You can turn this off by specifying an empty string for the end of file character:

```
fconfigure fileID -eofchar {}
```

In Tcl 8.4 the end-of-file character trick is used by `Tcl_EvalFile` and `source` to allow *Tclkit* and other tools to append non-script data to script files. This is enabled by default, and should not normally interfere with your scripts.

Serial Devices

The `-mode` attribute specifies the baud rate, parity mode, the number of data bits, and the number of stop bits:

```
set tty [open /dev/ttya]
fconfigure $tty -mode
=> 9600,0,8,2
```

Tcl 8.4 added the enhanced control of serial channels for Windows and Unix systems. The options are listed in Table 16–4.

Windows has some special device names that always connect you to the serial line devices when you use `open`. They are `com1` through `com9`. To access com devices above 9, use this form: `{\\.\comXX}`. The Windows system console is named `con`. The Windows null device is `nul`.

UNIX has names for serial devices in `/dev`. The serial devices are `/dev/ttya`, `/dev/ttyb`, and so on. The system console is `/dev/console`. The current terminal is `/dev/tty`. The null device is `/dev/null`.

Macintosh needs a special command to open serial devices. This is provided by a third-party extension that you can find at the Tcl Resource Center under:

```
http://www.tcl.tk/resource/software/extensions/macintosh/
```

Character Set Encodings

Tcl automatically converts various character set encodings into Unicode internally. It cannot automatically detect the encoding for a file or network socket, however, so you need to use `fconfigure -encoding` if you are reading data that is not in the system's default encoding. Character set issues are explained in more detail in Chapter 15.

Configuring Read-Write Channels

If you have a channel that is used for both input and output, you can set the channel parameters independently for input and output. In this case, you can specify a two-element list for the parameter value. The first element is for the input side of the channel, and the second element is for the output side of the channel. If you specify only a single element, it applies to both input and output. For example, the following command forces output end of line translations to be `crlf` mode, leaves the input channel on automatic, and sets the buffer size for both input and output:

```
fconfigure pipe -translation {auto crlf} -buffersize 4096
```

II. Advanced Tcl

Socket Programming

This chapter shows how to use sockets for programming network clients and servers. Advanced I/O techniques for sockets are described, including nonblocking I/O and control over I/O buffering. Tcl commands discussed are: socket, fconfigure, *and* http::geturl.

Sockets are network communication channels. The sockets described in this chapter use the TCP network protocol, although you can find Tcl extensions that create sockets using other protocols. TCP provides a reliable byte stream between two hosts connected to a network. TCP handles all the issues about routing information across the network, and it automatically recovers if data is lost or corrupted along the way. TCP is the basis for other protocols like Telnet, FTP, and HTTP.

A Tcl script can use a network socket just like an open file or pipeline. Instead of using the Tcl open command, you use the socket command to open a socket. Then you use gets, puts, and read to transfer data. The close command closes a network socket.

Network programming distinguishes between clients and servers. A server is a process or program that runs for long periods of time and controls access to some resource. For example, an FTP server governs access to files, and an HTTP server provides access to hypertext pages on the World Wide Web. A client typically connects to the server for a limited time in order to gain access to the resource. For example, when a Web browser fetches a hypertext page, it is acting as a client. The extended examples in this chapter show how to program the client side of the HTTP protocol.

Networking Extensions for Tcl

This chapter describes the basic programming techniques for sockets. Socket programing in Tcl is pretty easy, and a variety of extensions have been created to handle common protocols. This section reviews some of the packages that are available, and then the rest of the chapter describes how to program sockets yourself.

Scotty

The Scotty extension supports many network protocols.

The Scotty Tcl extension provides access to other network protocols like UDP, DNS, and RPC. It also supports the SNMP network management protocol and the MIB database associated with SNMP. Scotty is a great extension package that is widely used for network management applications. It is a C-level extension, so you have to compile it yourself or find a binary distribution. Its home page is:

```
http://wwwsnmp.cs.utwente.nl/~schoenw/scotty/
```

Standard Tcl Library

The Standard Tcl Library (*tcllib*) has several packages that support widely used TCP-based protocols. These are all pure-Tcl implementations. There are packages for:

- DNS client. Map between hostnames and IP addresses.
- FTP client. Open FTP connections and download files from FTP servers.
- FTP server. Implement a simple, extensible FTP server.
- IRC client. Implement a chat client.
- NNTP client. Fetch news from a news server.
- POP3 client. Post Office Protocol lets you fetch email from mail servers.
- POP3 server. Implement a mail server.
- SMTP client. Send email via the SMTP protocol.
- SMTP server. Accept incoming email via SMTP.
- URI manipulation. Package for parsing URLs.
  There is good on-line documentation for these packages at:
  ```
  http://tcllib.sourceforge.net/tcllib/doc/
  ```

HTTP

The Tcl distribution includes an HTTP client, which is described on page 251. You don't need to add *tcllib* to get this. In addition, there is a nice web server built in Tcl, which is the topic of Chapter 18.

Client Sockets

A client opens a socket by specifying the *host address* and *port number* for the server of the socket. The host address gives the network location (i.e., which computer), and the port selects a particular server from all the possible servers that may be running on that host. For example, HTTP servers typically use port 80, while FTP servers use port 20. The following example shows how to open a client socket to a Web server:

```
set s [socket www.tcl.tk 80]
```

There are two forms for host names. The previous example uses a *domain name*: `www.tcl.tk`. You can also specify raw IP addresses, which are specified with four dot-separated integers (e.g., 192.220.75.86). A domain name is mapped into a raw IP address by the system software, and it is almost always a better idea to use a domain name in case the IP address assignment for the host changes. This can happen when hosts are upgraded or they move to a different part of the network.

Some systems also provide symbolic names for well-known port numbers. For example, instead of using `20` for the FTP service, you can use `ftp`. On UNIX systems, the well-known port numbers are listed in the file named `/etc/services`.

Client Socket Options

The `socket` command accepts some optional arguments when opening the client-side socket. The general form of the command is:

```
socket ?-async? ?-myaddr address? ?-myport myport? host port
```

Ordinarily the address and port on the client side are chosen automatically. If your computer has multiple network interfaces, you can select one with the `-myaddr` option. The `address` value can be a domain name or an IP address. If your application needs a specific client port, it can choose one with the `-myport` option. If the port is in use, the `socket` command will raise an error.

The `-async` option causes connection to happen in the background, and the `socket` command returns immediately. The socket becomes writable when the connection completes, or fails. You can use `fileevent` to get a callback when this occurs. This is shown in Example 17–1. If you use the socket before the connection completes, and the socket is in blocking mode, then Tcl automatically blocks and waits for the connection to complete. If the socket is in nonblocking mode, attempts to use the socket return immediately. The `gets` and `read` commands would return -1, and `fblocked` would return 1 in this situation.

In some cases, it can take a long time to open the connection to the server. Usually this occurs when the server host is down, and it may take longer than you want for the connection to time out. The following example sets up a timer with `after` so that you can choose your own timeout limit on the connection:

II. Advanced Tcl

Example 17–1 Opening a client socket with a timeout.

```
proc Socket_Client {host port timeout} {
    global connected
    after $timeout {set connected timeout}
    set sock [socket -async $host $port]
    fileevent $sock w {set connected ok}
    vwait connected
    fileevent $sock w {}
    if {$connected == "timeout"} {
        return -code error timeout
    } else {
        return $sock
    }
}
```

Server Sockets

A TCP server socket allows multiple clients. The way this works is that the socket command creates a *listening socket*, and then new sockets are created when clients make connections to the server. Tcl takes care of all the details and makes this easy to use. You simply specify a port number and give the socket command a *callback* to execute when a client connects to your server socket. The callback is just a Tcl command. A simple example is shown below:

Example 17–2 Opening a server socket.

```
set listenSocket [socket -server Accept 2540]
proc Accept {newSock addr port} {
    puts "Accepted $newSock from $addr port $port"
}
vwait forever
```

The Accept command is the callback made when clients connect to the server. Tcl adds additional arguments to the callback before it calls it. The arguments are the new socket connection, and the host and port number of the remote client. In this simple example, Accept just prints out its arguments.

The vwait command puts Tcl into its event loop so that it can do the background processing necessary to accept connections. The vwait command will wait until the forever variable is modified, which won't happen in this simple example. The key point is that Tcl processes other events (e.g., network connections and other file I/O) while it waits. If you have a Tk application (e.g., *wish*), then it already has an event loop to handle window system events, so you do not need to use vwait. The Tcl event loop is discussed on page 227.

Server Socket Options

By default, Tcl lets the operating system choose the network interface used for the server socket, and you simply supply the port number. If your computer has multiple interfaces, you may want to specify a particular one. Use the -myaddr option for this. The general form of the command to open server sockets is:

```
socket -server callback ?-myaddr address? port
```

The last argument to the socket command is the server's port number. For your own unofficial servers, you'll need to pick port numbers higher than 1024 to avoid conflicts with existing services. UNIX systems prevent user programs from opening server sockets with port numbers less than 1024. If you use 0 as the port number, then the operating system will pick the listening port number for you. You must use fconfigure to find out what port you have:

```
fconfigure $sock -sockname
=> ipaddr hostname port
```

The Echo Service

Example 17–3 The echo service.

```
proc Echo_Server {port} {
    global echo
    set echo(main) [socket -server EchoAccept $port]
}
proc EchoAccept {sock addr port} {
    global echo
    puts "Accept $sock from $addr port $port"
    set echo(addr,$sock) [list $addr $port]
    fconfigure $sock -buffering line
    fileevent $sock readable [list Echo $sock]
}
proc Echo {sock} {
    global echo
    if {[eof $sock] || [catch {gets $sock line}]} {
        # end of file or abnormal connection drop
        close $sock
        puts "Close $echo(addr,$sock)"
        unset echo(addr,$sock)
    } else {
        if {[string compare $line "quit"] == 0} {
            # Prevent new connections.
            # Existing connections stay open.
            close $echo(main)
        }
        puts $sock $line
    }
}
```

The echo server accepts connections from clients. It reads data from the clients and writes that data back. The example uses `fileevent` to wait for data from the client, and it uses `fconfigure` to adjust the buffering behavior of the network socket. You can use Example 17–3 as a template for more interesting services.

The `Echo_Server` procedure opens the socket and saves the result in `echo(main)`. When this socket is closed later, the server stops accepting new connections but existing connections won't be affected. If you want to experiment with this server, start it and wait for connections like this:

```
Echo_Server 2540
vwait forever
```

The `EchoAccept` procedure uses the `fconfigure` command to set up line buffering. This means that each `puts` by the server results in a network transmission to the client. The importance of this will be described in more detail later. A complete description of the `fconfigure` command is given in Chapter 16. The `EchoAccept` procedure uses the `fileevent` command to register a procedure that handles I/O on the socket. In this example, the `Echo` procedure will be called whenever the socket is readable. Note that it is not necessary to put the socket into nonblocking mode when using the `fileevent` callback. The effects of nonblocking mode are discussed on page 232.

`EchoAccept` saves information about each client in the `echo` array. This is used only to print out a message when a client closes its connection. In a more sophisticated server, however, you may need to keep more interesting state about each client. The name of the socket provides a convenient handle on the client. In this case, it is used as part of the array index.

The `Echo` procedure first checks to see whether the socket has been closed by the client or there is an error when reading the socket. The `if` expression only performs the `gets` if the `eof` does not return true:

```
if {[eof $sock] || [catch {gets $sock line}]} {
```

Closing the socket automatically clears the `fileevent` registration. If you forget to close the socket upon the end of file condition, the Tcl event loop will invoke your callback repeatedly. It is important to close it when you detect end of file.

Example 17–4 A client of the echo service.

```
proc Echo_Client {host port} {
    set s [socket $host $port]
    fconfigure $s -buffering line
    return $s
}
set s [Echo_Client localhost 2540]
puts $s "Hello!"
gets $s
=> Hello!
```

In the normal case, the server simply reads a line with `gets` and then writes it back to the client with `puts`. If the line is "quit," then the server closes its main socket. This prevents any more connections by new clients, but it doesn't affect any clients that are already connected.

Example 17–4 shows a sample client of the `Echo` service. The main point is to ensure that the socket is line buffered so that each `puts` by the client results in a network transmission. (Or, more precisely, each newline character results in a network transmission.) If you forget to set line buffering with `fconfigure`, the client's `gets` command will probably hang because the server will not get any data; it will be stuck in buffers on the client.

Fetching a URL with HTTP

The HyperText Transport Protocol (HTTP) is the protocol used on the World Wide Web. This section presents a procedure to fetch pages or images from a server on the Web. Items in the Web are identified with a Universal Resource Location (URL) that specifies a host, port, and location on the host. The basic outline of HTTP is that a client sends a URL to a server, and the server responds with some header information and some content data. The header information describes the content, which can be hypertext, images, postscript, and more.

Example 17–5 Opening a connection to an HTTP server.

```
proc Http_Open {url} {
    global http
    if {![regexp -nocase {^(http://)?([^:/]+)(:([0-9]+))?(/.*)} \
            $url x protocol server y port path]} {
        error "bogus URL: $url"
    }
    if {[string length $port] == 0} {
        set port 80
    }
    set sock [socket $server $port]
    puts $sock "GET $path HTTP/1.0"
    puts $sock "Host: $server"
    puts $sock "User-Agent: Tcl/Tk Http_Open"
    puts $sock ""
    flush $sock
    return $sock
}
```

The `Http_Open` procedure uses `regexp` to pick out the server and port from the URL. This regular expression is described in detail on page 159. The leading `http://` is optional, and so is the port number. If the port is left off, then the standard port 80 is used. If the regular expression matches, then a `socket` command opens the network connection.

The protocol begins with the client sending a line that identifies the command (GET), the path, and the protocol version. The path is the part of the URL after the server and port specification. The rest of the request is lines in the following format:

```
key: value
```

The Host identifies the server, which supports servers that implement more than one server name. The User-Agent identifies the client program, which is often a browser like *Netscape Navigator*, *Mozilla*, or *Internet Explorer*. The key-value lines are terminated with a blank line. This data is flushed out of the Tcl buffering system with the flush command. The server will respond by sending the URL contents back over the socket. This is described shortly, but first we consider proxies.

Proxy Servers

A *proxy* is used to get through firewalls that many organizations set up to isolate their network from the Internet. The proxy accepts HTTP requests from clients inside the firewall and then forwards the requests outside the firewall. It also relays the server's response back to the client. The protocol is nearly the same when using the proxy. The difference is that the complete URL is passed to the GET command so that the proxy can locate the server. Example 17–6 uses a proxy if one is defined:

Example 17–6 Opening a connection through a HTTP proxy.

```
# Http_Proxy sets or queries the proxy
proc Http_Proxy {{new {}}} {
    global http
    if ![info exists http(proxy)] {
        return {}
    }
    if {[string length $new] == 0} {
        return $http(proxy):$http(proxyPort)
    } else {
        regexp {^([^:]+):([0-9]+)$} $new x \
            http(proxy) http(proxyPort)
    }
}

proc Http_Open {url {cmd GET} {query {}}} {
    global http
    if {![regexp -nocase {^(http://)?([^:/]+)(:([0-9]+))?(/.*)} \
            $url x protocol server y port path]} {
        error "bogus URL: $url"
    }
    if {[string length $port] == 0} {
        set port 80
    }
```

```
        if {[info exists http(proxy)] &&
                [string length $http(proxy)]} {
            set sock [socket $http(proxy) $http(proxyPort)]
            puts $sock "$cmd http://$server:$port$path HTTP/1.0"
        } else {
            set sock [socket $server $port]
            puts $sock "$cmd $path HTTP/1.0"
        }
        puts $sock "User-Agent: Tcl/Tk Http_Open"
        puts $sock "Host: $server"
        if {[string length $query] > 0} {
            puts $sock "Content-Length: [string length $query]"
            puts $sock ""
            puts $sock $query
        }
        puts $sock ""
        flush $sock
        fconfigure $sock -blocking 0
        return $sock
}
```

The HEAD Request

In Example 17–6, the Http_Open procedure takes a cmd parameter so that the user of Http_Open can perform different operations. The GET operation fetches the contents of a URL. The HEAD operation just fetches the description of a URL, which is useful to validate a URL. The POST operation transmits query data to the server (e.g., values from a form) and also fetches the contents of the URL. All of these operations follow a similar protocol. The reply from the server is a status line followed by lines that have key-value pairs. This format is similar to the client's request. The reply header is followed by content data with GET and POST operations. Example 17–7 implements the HEAD command, which does not involve any reply data:

Example 17–7 Http_Head validates a URL.

```
proc Http_Head {url} {
    upvar #0 $url state
    catch {unset state}
    set state(sock) [Http_Open $url HEAD]
    fileevent $state(sock) readable [list HttpHeader $url]
    # Specify the real name, not the upvar alias, to vwait
    vwait $url\(status)
    catch {close $state(sock)}
    return $state(status)
}
proc HttpHeader {url} {
    upvar #0 $url state
    if {[eof $state(sock)]} {
        set state(status) eof
        close $state(sock)
```

```
        return
    }
    if {[[catch {gets $state(sock) line} nbytes]} {
        set state(status) error
        lappend state(headers) [list error $nbytes]
        close $state(sock)
        return
    }
    if {$nbytes < 0} {
        # Read would block
        return
    } elseif {$nbytes == 0} {
        # Header complete
        set state(status) head
    } elseif {![info exists state(headers)]} {
        # Initial status reply from the server
        set state(headers) [list http $line]
    } else {
        # Process key-value pairs
        regexp {^([^:]+): *(.*)$} $line x key value
        lappend state(headers) [string tolower $key] $value
    }
}
```

The `Http_Head` procedure uses `Http_Open` to contact the server. The `HttpHeader` procedure is registered as a `fileevent` handler to read the server's reply. A global array keeps state about each operation. The URL is used in the array name, and `upvar` is used to create an alias to the name (`upvar` is described on page 92):

```
    upvar #0 $url state
```

You cannot use the `upvar` alias as the variable specified to `vwait`. Instead, you must use the actual name. The backslash turns off the array reference in order to pass the name of the array element to `vwait`, otherwise Tcl tries to reference `url` as an array:

```
    vwait $url\(status)
```

The `HttpHeader` procedure checks for special cases: end of file, an error on the `gets`, or a short read on a nonblocking socket. The very first reply line contains a status code from the server that is in a different format than the rest of the header lines:

```
    code message
```

The code is a three-digit numeric code. `200` is OK. Codes in the `400`'s and `500`'s indicate an error. The codes are explained fully in RFC 1945 that specifies HTTP 1.0. The first line is saved with the key `http`:

```
    set state(headers) [list http $line]
```

The rest of the header lines are parsed into key-value pairs and appended onto `state(headers)`. This format can be used to initialize an array:

```
    array set header $state(headers)
```

When `HttpHeader` gets an empty line, the header is complete and it sets the `state(status)` variable, which signals `Http_Head`. Finally, `Http_Head` returns the status to its caller. The complete information about the request is still in the global array named by the URL. Example 17–8 illustrates the use of `Http_Head`:

Example 17–8 Using `Http_Head`.

```
set url http://www.sun.com/
set status [Http_Head $url]
=> eof
upvar #0 $url state
array set info $state(headers)
parray info
info(http)             HTTP/1.0 200 OK
info(server)           Apache/1.1.1
info(last-modified)    Nov ...
info(content-type)     text/html
```

The GET and POST Requests

Example 17–9 shows `Http_Get`, which implements the GET and POST requests. The difference between these is that POST sends query data to the server after the request header. Both operations get a reply from the server that is divided into a descriptive header and the content data. The `Http_Open` procedure sends the request and the query, if present, and reads the reply header. `Http_Get` reads the content.

The descriptive header returned by the server is in the same format as the client's request. One of the key-value pairs returned by the server specifies the `Content-Type` of the URL. The content-types come from the MIME standard, which is described in RFC 1521. Typical content-types are:

- `text/html` — HyperText Markup Language (HTML), which is introduced in Chapter 3.
- `text/plain` — plain text with no markup.
- `image/gif` — image data in GIF format.
- `image/jpeg` — image data in JPEG format.
- `application/postscript` — a postscript document.
- `application/x-tcl` — a Tcl program! This type is discussed in Chapter 20.

Example 17–9 `Http_Get` fetches the contents of a URL.

```
proc Http_Get {url {query {}}} {
    upvar #0 $url state          ;# Alias to global array
    catch {unset state}          ;# Aliases still valid.
    if {[string length $query] > 0} {
        set state(sock) [Http_Open $url POST $query]
    } else {
        set state(sock) [Http_Open $url GET]
    }
```

```
    set sock $state(sock)
    fileevent $sock readable [list HttpHeader $url]

    # Specify the real name, not the upvar alias, to vwait
    vwait $url\(status)
    set header(content-type) {}
    set header(http) "500 unknown error"
    array set header $state(headers)

    # Check return status.
    # 200 is OK, other codes indicate a problem.
    regsub "HTTP/1.. " $header(http) {} header(http)
    if {![string match 2* $header(http)]} {
        catch {close $sock}
        if {[info exists header(location)] &&
                [string match 3* $header(http)]} {
            # 3xx is a redirection to another URL
            set state(link) $header(location)
            return [Http_Get $header(location) $query]
        }
        return -code error $header(http)
    }
    # Set up to read the content data
    switch -glob -- $header(content-type) {
        text/*     {
            # Read HTML into memory
            fileevent $sock readable [list HttpGetText $url]
        }
        default    {
            # Copy content data to a file
            fconfigure $sock -translation binary
            set state(filename) [File_TempName http]
            if [catch {open $state(filename) w} out] {
                set state(status) error
                set state(error) $out
                close $sock
                return $header(content-type)
            }
            set state(fd) $out
            fcopy $sock $out -command [list HttpCopyDone $url]
        }
    }
    vwait $url\(status)
    return $header(content-type)
}
```

Http_Get uses Http_Open to initiate the request, and then it looks for errors. It handles redirection errors that occur if a URL has changed. These have error codes that begin with 3. A common case of this error is when a user omits the trailing slash on a URL (e.g., http://www.tcl.tk). Most servers respond with:

```
302 Document has moved
Location: http://www.tcl.tk/
```

If the `content-type` is text, then `Http_Get` sets up a `fileevent` handler to read this data into memory. The socket is in nonblocking mode, so the read handler can read as much data as possible each time it is called. This is more efficient than using `gets` to read a line at a time. The text will be stored in the `state(body)` variable for use by the caller of `Http_Get`. Example 17–10 shows the `HttpGetText fileevent` handler:

Example 17–10 `HttpGetText` reads `text` URLs.

```
proc HttpGetText {url} {
    upvar #0 $url state
    if {[eof $state(sock)]} {
        # Content complete
        set state(status) done
        close $state(sock)
    } elseif {[catch {read $state(sock)} block]} {
        set state(status) error
        lappend state(headers) [list error $block]
        close $state(sock)
    } else {
        append state(body) $block
    }
}
```

The content may be in binary format. This poses a problem for Tcl 7.6 and earlier. A null character will terminate the value, so values with embedded nulls cannot be processed safely by Tcl scripts. Tcl 8.0 supports strings and variable values with arbitrary binary data. Example 17–9 uses `fcopy` to copy data from the socket to a file without storing it in Tcl variables. This command was introduced in Tcl 7.5 as `unsupported0`, and became `fcopy` in Tcl 8.0. It takes a callback argument that is invoked when the copy is complete. The callback gets additional arguments that are the bytes transferred and an optional error string. In this case, these arguments are added to the `url` argument specified in the `fcopy` command. Example 17–11 shows the `HttpCopyDone` callback:

Example 17–11 `HttpCopyDone` is used with `fcopy`.

```
proc HttpCopyDone {url bytes {error {}}} {
    upvar #0 $url state
    if {[string length $error]} {
        set state(status) error
        lappend state(headers) [list error $error]
    } else {
        set state(status) ok
    }
    close $state(sock)
    close $state(fd)
}
```

The user of `Http_Get` uses the information in the `state` array to determine the status of the fetch and where to find the content. There are four cases to deal with:

- There was an error, which is indicated by the `state(error)` element.
- There was a redirection, in which case, the new URL is in `state(link)`. The client of `Http_Get` should change the URL and look at its state instead. You can use `upvar` to redefine the alias for the `state` array:

  ```
  upvar #0 $state(link) state
  ```
- There was text content. The content is in `state(body)`.
- There was another content-type that was copied to `state(filename)`.

The `fcopy` Command

The `fcopy` command can do a complete copy in the background. It automatically sets up `fileevent` handlers, so you do not have to use `fileevent` yourself. It also manages its buffers efficiently. The general form of the command is:

```
fcopy input output ?-size size? ?-command callback?
```

The `-command` argument makes `fcopy` work in the background. When the copy is complete or an error occurs, the `callback` is invoked with one or two additional arguments: the number of bytes copied, and, in the case of an error, it is also passed an error string:

```
fcopy $in $out -command [list CopyDone $in $out]
proc CopyDone {in out bytes {error {}} {
    close $in ; close $out
}
```

With a background copy, the `fcopy` command transfers data from *input* until end of file or *size* bytes have been transferred. If no `-size` argument is given, then the copy goes until end of file. It is not safe to do other I/O operations with *input* or *output* during a background `fcopy`. If either *input* or *output* gets closed while the copy is in progress, the current copy is stopped. If the *input* is closed, then all data already queued for *output* is written out.

Without a `-command` argument, the `fcopy` command reads as much as possible depending on the blocking mode of *input* and the optional *size* parameter. Everything it reads is queued for output before `fcopy` returns. If *output* is blocking, then `fcopy` returns after the data is written out. If *input* is blocking, then `fcopy` can block attempting to read *size* bytes or until end of file.

The `fcopy` command had a bug which ignored the encoding on the channels which was corrected in 8.3.4.

The `http` Package

The standard Tcl library includes an `http` package that is based on the code I wrote for this chapter. This section documents the package, which has a slightly different interface. The library version uses namespaces and combines the `Http_Get`, `Http_Head`, and `Http_Post` procedures into a single `http::geturl` procedure. The examples in this chapter are still interesting, but you should use the standard `http` package for your production code.

`http::config`

The `http::config` command is used to set the proxy information, timeouts, and the `User-Agent` and `Accept` headers that are generated in the HTTP request. You can specify the proxy host and port, or you can specify a Tcl command that is run to determine the proxy. With no arguments, `http::config` returns the current settings:

```
http::config
=> -accept */* -proxyfilter http::ProxyRequired
-proxyhost {} -proxyport {}
-useragent {Tcl http client package 2.4}
```

If you specify just one option, its value is returned:

```
http::config -proxyfilter
=> http::ProxyRequired
```

You can set one or more options:

```
http::config -proxyhost webcache.eng -proxyport 8080
```

The default proxy filter just returns the `-proxyhost` and `-proxyport` values if they are set. You can supply a smarter filter that picks a proxy based on the host in the URL. The proxy filter is called with the hostname and should return a list of two elements, the proxy host and port. If no proxy is required, return an empty list.

`http::geturl`

The `http::geturl` procedure does a GET, POST, or HEAD transaction depending on its arguments. By default, `http::geturl` blocks until the request completes and it returns a token that represents the transaction. As described below, you use the token to get the results of the transaction. If you supply a `-command` *callback* option, then `http::geturl` returns immediately and invokes *callback* when the transaction completes. The callback is passed the token that represents the transaction.

For simple applications you can simply block on the transaction:

```
set token [http::geturl www.beedub.com/index.html]
=> http::1
```

The leading `http://` in the URL is optional. The return value is a token that represents the transaction. There are other `http::` commands that return information when passed the token. The token is also the name of an array that contains state about the transaction. Make sure to clean up this array to free memory when you are done:

```
http::cleanup $token
```

If you need to access the array directly, use `upvar` to create an alias:

```
upvar #0 $token data
```

Table 17–1 lists the options to `http::geturl`.

Table 17–1 Options to the `http::geturl` command.

`-binary boolean`	Specifies whether we should do a binary transfer of the data. (Tcl 8.3)
`-blocksize num`	Block size when copying to a channel.
`-channel fileID`	The `fileID` is an open file or socket. The URL data is copied to this channel instead of saving it in memory.
`-command callback`	Calls `callback` when the transaction completes. The token from `http::geturl` is passed to `callback`.
`-handler command`	Called from the event handler to read data from the URL.
`-headers list`	The `list` specifies a set of headers that are included in the HTTP request. The list alternates between header keys and values.
`-progress command`	Calls `command` after each block is copied to a channel. It gets called with three parameters: `command token totalsize currentsize`
`-query codedstring`	Issues a POST request with the `codedstring` form data.
`-queryblocksize num`	Block size when copying to the query channel.
`-querychannel fileID`	The `fileID` is an open file or socket. The query data is copied from this channel instead of passed in a string.
`-queryprogress command`	Calls `command` after each block is copied from the query channel. It gets called with three parameters: `command token totalsize currentsize`
`-timeout msec`	Aborts the request after `msec` milliseconds have elapsed.
`-type mime-type`	Use `mime-type` as the Content-Type value during a POST operation.
`-validate bool`	If `bool` is true, a HEAD request is made.

Table 17–2 lists the access functions to the state array.

Table 17–2 The http support procedures.

`http::cleanup $token`	Unsets the state array named by `$token`.
`http::code $token`	Returns `state(http)`.
`http::data $token`	Returns `state(body)`.
`http::error $token`	Returns `state(error)`.
`http::ncode $token`	Returns the numeric return code contained in `state(http)`.
`http::size $token`	Return the number of bytes read from the URL so far.
`http::status $token`	Returns `state(status)`.
`http::wait $token`	Blocks until the transaction completes.

The array elements are listed in Table 17–3:

Table 17–3 Elements of the `http::geturl` state array.

`body`	The contents of the URL.
`charset`	The value of the charset attribute from the Content-Type meta-data value. If none was specified, this defaults to the RFC standard iso8859-1.
`coding`	A copy of the Content-Encoding meta-data value.
`currentsize`	The current number of bytes transferred.
`error`	An explanation of why the transaction was aborted.
`http`	The HTTP reply status.
`meta`	A list of the keys and values in the reply header.
`posterror`	An explanation of why the transaction was aborted when writing post query data, if any.
`status`	The current status: `pending`, `ok`, `eof`, or `reset`.
`totalsize`	The expected size of the returned data.
`type`	The content type of the returned data.
`url`	The URL of the request.

You can take advantage of the asynchronous interface by specifying a command that is called when the transaction completes. The callback is passed the token returned from `http::geturl` so that it can access the transaction state:

```
http::geturl $url -command [list Url_Display $text $url]
proc Url_Display {text url token} {
    upvar #0 $token state
    # Display the url in text
}
```

You can have `http::geturl` copy the URL to a file or socket with the
`-channel` option. This is useful for downloading large files or images. In this
case, you can get a progress callback so that you can provide user feedback during the transaction. Example 17–12 shows a simple downloading script:

Example 17–12 Downloading files with `http::geturl`.

```
#!/usr/local/bin/tclsh8.4
if {$argc < 2} {
    puts stderr "Usage: $argv0 url file"
    exit 1
}
package require http
set url [lindex $argv 0]
set file [lindex $argv 1]
set out [open $file w]
proc progress {token total current} {
    puts -nonewline "."
}
http::config -proxyhost webcache.eng -proxyport 8080
set token [http::geturl $url -progress progress \
    -headers {Pragma no-cache} -channel $out]
close $out
# Print out the return header information
puts ""
upvar #0 $token state
puts $state(http)
foreach {key value} $state(meta) {
    puts "$key: $value"
}
exit 0
```

http::formatQuery

If you specify form data with the `-query` option, then `http::geturl` does a
POST transaction. You need to encode the form data for safe transmission. The
`http::formatQuery` procedure takes a list of keys and values and encodes them
in `x-www-url-encoded` format. Pass this result as the query data:

```
http::formatQuery name "Brent Welch" title "Tcl Programmer"
=> name=Brent+Welch&title=Tcl+Programmer
```

`http::register` and `http::unregister`

The `http::register` procedure registers a protocol handler for URL protocols other than HTTP. The `http::unregister` procedure removes the handler registration. The primary application is to provide secure web access via HTTPS and the TLS extension.

```
package require tls
http::register https 443 ::tls::socket
set token [http::geturl https://my.secure.site/]
```

`http::reset`

You can cancel an outstanding transaction with `http::reset`:

```
http::reset $token
```

This is done automatically when you setup a `-timeout` with `http::config`.

`http::cleanup`

When you are done with the data returned from `http::geturl`, use the `http::cleanup` procedure to unset the state variable used to store the data.

Basic Authentication

Web pages are often password protected. The most common form of this uses a protocol called Basic Authentication, which is not very strong, but easy to implement. With this scheme, the server responds to an HTTP request with a 401 error status and a `Www-Authenticate` header, which specifies the authentication protocol the server wants to use. For example, the server response can contain the following information:

```
HTTP/1.0 401 Authorization Required
Www-Authenticate: Basic realm="My Pages"
```

The *realm* is meant to be an authentication domain. In practice, it is used in the string that gets displayed to the user as part of the password prompt. For example, a Web browser will display this prompt:

```
Enter the password for My Pages at www.beedub.com
```

After getting the user name and password from the user, the Web browser tries its HTTP request again. This time it includes an `Authorization` header that contains the user name and password encoded with *base64 encoding*. There is no encryption at all — anyone can decode the string, which is why this is not a strong form of protection. The Standard Tcl Library includes a `base64` package that has `base64::encode` and `base64::decode` procedures. Example 17–13 illustrates the Basic Authentication protocol. It uses the `-headers` option to `http::geturl` that lets you pass additional headers in the request.

Example 17–13 Basic Authentication using `http::geturl`.

```
package require base64
package require http
proc BasicAuthentication {url promptProc} {
    set token [http::geturl $url]
    http::wait $token
    if {[string match *401* [http::code $token]]} {
        upvar #0 $token data

        # Extract the realm from the Www-Authenticate line

        array set reply $data(meta)
        if {[regexp {realm=(.*)} $reply(Www-Authenticate) \
                x realm]} {

            # Call back to prompt for username, password

            set answer [$promptProc $realm]
            http::cleanup $token

            # Encode username:password and pass this in
            # the Authorization header

            set auth [base64::encode \
                [lindex $answer 0]:[lindex $answer 1]]
            set token [http::geturl $url -headers \
                [list Authorization "Basic $auth"]]
            http::wait $token
        }
    }
    return $token
}
```

Example 17–13 takes a `promptProc` argument that is the name of a procedure to call to get the username and password. This procedure could display a Tk dialog box, or prompt for user input from the terminal. In practice, you probably already know the username and password. In this case, you can skip the initial challenge–response steps and simply supply the `Authorization` header on the first request:

```
http::geturl $url -headers \
    [list Authorization \
        "Basic [base64::encode $username:$password]"]
```

TclHttpd Web Server

This chapter describes TclHttpd, a Web server built entirely in Tcl. The Web
server can be used as a standalone server, or it can be embedded into
applications to Web-enable them. TclHttpd provides a Tcl+HTML
template facility that is useful for maintaining site-wide look and feel, and
an Application Direct URL that invokes a Tcl procedure in an application.

TclHttpd started out as about 175 lines of
Tcl that could serve up HTML pages and images. The Tcl `socket` and I/O commands make this easy, and the C language implementation of the Tcl runtime
library makes the server surprisingly fast. Of course, there are lots of features in
Web servers like Apache or Netscape that were not present in the first prototype.
Steve Uhler took my prototype, refined the HTTP handling, and aimed to keep
the basic server under 250 lines. I went the other direction, setting up a modular
architecture, adding in features found in other Web servers, and adding some
interesting ways to connect TclHttpd to Tcl applications.

Today TclHttpd is used both as a general-purpose Web server, and as a
framework for building server applications. It implements www.tcl.tk and a
number of other general purpose Web sites. It is also built into several commercial applications such as license servers and mail spam filters. The server is
freely available, just like Tcl itself, and you can use it in any application without
restriction or license fees. Instructions for setting up the TclHttpd on your platform are given toward the end of the chapter, on page 284. It works on Unix,
Windows, and Macintosh. Using TclHttpd, you can have your own Web server up
and running quickly.

This chapter provides an overview of the server and several examples of
how you can use it. The chapter is not an exhaustive reference to every feature.
Instead, it concentrates on a very useful subset of server features that I use the
most.

Integrating TclHttpd with Your Application

The bulk of this chapter describes the various ways you can extend the server and integrate it into your application. TclHttpd is interesting because, as a Tcl script, it is easy to add to your application. Suddenly your application has an interface that is accessible to Web browsers in your company's intranet or the global Internet. The Web server provides several ways you can connect it to your application:

- *Static pages* — As a "normal" Web server, you can serve static documents that describe your application.
- *Domain handlers* — You can arrange for all URL requests in a section of your Web site to be handled by your application. This is a very general interface where you interpret what the URL means and what sort of pages to return to each request. For example, http://www.tcl.tk/resource is implemented this way. The URL past /resource selects an index in a simple database, and the server returns a page describing the pages under that index.
- *Application Direct URLs* — This is a domain handler that maps URLs onto Tcl procedures. The form query data that is part of the HTTP GET or POST request is automatically mapped onto the parameters of the Application Direct procedure. The procedure simply computes the page as its return value. This is an elegant and efficient alternative to the CGI interface. For example, in TclHttpd, the URLs under /status report various statistics about the Web server's operation.
- *Document handlers* — You can define a Tcl procedure that handles all files of a particular type. For example, the server has a handler for CGI scripts, HTML files, image maps, and HTML+Tcl template files.
- *HTML+Tcl Templates* — These are Web pages that mix Tcl and HTML markup. The server replaces the Tcl using the subst command and returns the result. The server can cache the result in a regular HTML file to avoid the overhead of template processing on future requests. Templates are a great way to maintain the common look and feel to a family of Web pages, as well as to implement more advanced dynamic HTML features like self-checking forms.

TclHttpd Architecture

You may find it helpful to read the code to learn more about the features of the server. In this section, there are references to Tcl files in the source, which are in the lib directory of the distribution that is on the CD-ROM.

Figure 18–1 shows the basic components of the server. At the core is the Httpd module (httpd.tcl), which implements the server side of the HTTP protocol. The "d" in Httpd stands for *daemon*, which is the name given to system servers on UNIX. This module manages network requests, dispatches them to the Url module, and provides routines used to return the results to requests.

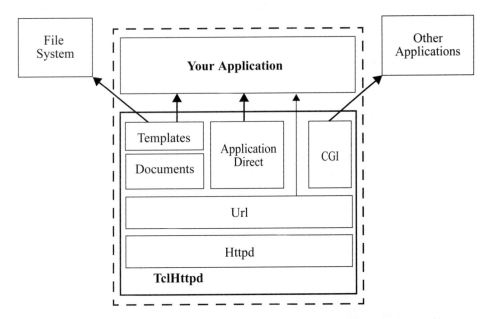

Fig. 18–1 The dotted box represents one application that embeds TclHttpd. Document templates and Application Direct URLs provide direct connections from an HTTP request to your application. You can also implement completely custom URL handlers.

The `Url` module (`url.tcl`) divides the Web site into *domains*, which are subtrees of the URL hierarchy provided by the server. The idea is that different domains may have completely different implementations. For example, the Document domain (`doc.tcl`) maps its URLs into files and directories on your hard disk, while the Application Direct domain (`direct.tcl`) maps URLs into Tcl procedure calls within your application. The CGI domain (`cgi.tcl`) maps URLs onto other programs that compute Web pages.

Adding Code to TclHttpd

The TclHttpd distribution, which is described in more detail starting at page 284, is set up so you can easily add code for your application into the server. For simple applications, you simply put your files into a special directory for custom code, and the server loads them automatically upon startup. These files should define Tcl procedures and register them as Domain Handlers, Direct URL handlers, or Document handlers. Example 18–1 implements `/hello/world`:

Example 18–1 The `hello.tcl` file implements `/hello/world`.

```
Direct_Url /hello Hello
proc Hello/world {} {
    return "<b>Hello, World!</b>"
}
```

II. Advanced Tcl

Suppose you put that file into the directory `/tmp/tclhttpd_test`. Then you can start the server like this:

```
tclsh8.3 bin/httpd.tcl -library /tmp/tclhttpd_test -debug 1
```

Now access this URL:

```
http://localhost:8015/hello/world
```

Custom Main Programs

The TclHttpd main program, `bin/httpd.tcl`, may conflict with the main program of your existing application. For those applications that embed Tcl interpreters in a more custom manner, you will need to modify `bin/httpd.tcl` for use with your application. That script is not very big, and it is well-commented. The key elements are the `Httpd_Server` call that opens the listening socket for the Web server, and the `vwait` at the very end that activates the event loop. The rest is all about argument parsing and initializing the various modules that support the server. It is those aspects that may differ for your custom server application.

Domain Handlers

You can implement new kinds of domains that provide your own interpretation of a URL. This is the most flexible interface available to extend the Web server. You provide a callback that is invoked to handle every request in a domain, or subtree, of the URL hierarchy. The callback interprets the URL, computes the page content, and returns the data using routines from the `Httpd` module.

Example 18–2 defines a simple domain that always returns the same page to every request. The domain is registered with the `Url_PrefixInstall` command. The arguments to `Url_PrefixInstall` are the URL prefix and a callback that is called to handle all URLs that match that prefix. In the example, all URLs that have the prefix `/simple` are dispatched to the `SimpleDomain` procedure.

The `SimpleDomain` handler illustrates several properties of domain handlers. The `sock` and `suffix` arguments to `SimpleDomain` are appended by `Url_Dispatch` when it invokes the domain handler. The `sock` is the socket connection to the client. The `suffix` parameter is the part of the URL after the prefix. For example, if the server receives a request for the URL `/simple/page`, then the prefix is `/simple` and the suffix is `/page`.

The `prefix` argument is defined when the callback is registered with `Url_PrefixInstall`. You can specify whatever information you need to pass to the domain handler. In this simple example, we probably don't need the prefix, but if you implement several different URL domains with the same handler, then you can pass in the prefix to distinguish them.

Example 18–2 A simple URL domain.

```
Url_PrefixInstall /simple [list SimpleDomain /simple]

proc SimpleDomain {prefix sock suffix} {
    upvar #0 Httpd$sock data

    # Generate page header

    set html "<title>A simple page</title>\n"
    append html "<h1>$prefix$suffix</h1>\n"
    append html "<h1>Date and Time</h1>\n"
    append html [clock format [clock seconds]]

    # Display connection state

    append html "<h1>Connection State</h1>"
    append html [html::tableFromArray data border=1]

    # Display query data

    if {[info exist data(query)]} {
        append html "<h1>Query Data</h1>\n"
        append html [html::tableFromList [ncgi::nvlist] border=1]
    }
    Httpd_ReturnData $sock text/html $html
}
```

Connection State and Query Data

The `sock` parameter is a handle on the socket connection to the remote client. This variable is also used to name a state variable that the `Httpd` module maintains about the connection. The name of the state array is `Httpd$sock`. In some cases, you may need access to this information, and the standard idiom is to use `upvar` to get a more convenient name for this array (i.e., `data`):

```
upvar #0 Httpd$sock data
```

The `html` and `ncgi` Packages

The `html` package provides many procedures useful for generating fragments of HTML. The `html::tableFromArray` procedure is used to dump out the connection state in the `data` array. Its cousin, `html::tableFromList`, is used to dump out the query data. The query data is obtained with the `ncgi::nvlist` procedure. TclHttpd initializes the `ncgi` module so you can use `ncgi::nvlist`, `ncgi::value`, and other procedures to access query data in your domain handlers. *Note*: it is not necessary to call `ncgi::parse` as you would from a CGI script. The `html` package has some other features, which are described later, that are very useful when generating HTML forms. These packages are part of the Standard Tcl Library, *tcllib*, which can be found along with Tcl and TclHttpd.

Returning Results

Finally, once the page has been computed, the `Httpd_ReturnData` procedure is used to return the page to the client. This takes care of the HTTP protocol as well as returning the data. There are three related procedures, `Httpd_ReturnFile`, `Httpd_Error`, and `Httpd_Redirect`. These are summarized in Table 18–1 on page 277.

Application Direct URLs

The Application Direct domain implementation provides the simplest way to extend the Web server. It hides the details associated with query data, decoding URL paths, and returning results. All you do is define Tcl procedures that correspond to URLs. Their arguments are automatically matched up to the query data, as shown in Example 13–3 on page 189. The Tcl procedures compute a string that is the result data, which is usually HTML. That's all there is to it.

The name of the Tcl procedure that implements an Application Direct URL is related to the name of the URL. This way, TclHttpd can automatically look up the Tcl procedure that should implement a given URL. The Tcl procedure name and the URL have distinct prefixes, but the suffix is the same. For example, if the Tcl procedure prefix is `Demo` and the URL prefix is `/demo`, then the `Demo/time` Tcl procedure implements the `/demo/time` URL. The `Direct_Url` procedure sets up the correspondence between the procedures and URLs. This is shown in Example 18–3:

Example 18–3 Application Direct URLs.

```
Direct_Url /demo Demo
proc Demo {} {
    return "<html><head><title>Demo page</title></head>\n\
        <body><h1>Demo page</h1>\n\
        <a href=/demo/time>What time is it?</a>\n\
        <form action=/demo/echo>\n\
        Data: <input type=text name=data>\n\
        <br>\n\
        <input type=submit name=echo value='Echo Data'>\n\
        </form>\n\
        </body></html>"
}
proc Demo/time {{format "%H:%M:%S"}} {
    return [clock format [clock seconds] -format $format]
}
proc Demo/echo {args} {
    # Compute a page that echoes the query data
    set html "<head><title>Echo</title></head>\n"
    append html "<body>"
    append html [html::tableFromList $args "border=1"]
    return $html
}
```

Example 18–3 defines `/demo` as an Application Direct URL domain that is implemented by procedures that begin with `Demo`. There are just three URLs defined:

```
/demo
/demo/time
/demo/echo
```

The `/demo` page displays a hypertext link to the `/demo/time` page and a simple form that will be handled by the `/demo/echo` page. This page is static, so there is just one `return` command in the procedure body. Each line of the string ends with:

```
\n\
```

This is just a formatting trick to let me indent each line in the procedure, without having the line indented in the resulting string. Actually, the \-newline will be replaced by one space, so each line will be indented one space. You can leave those off and the page will display the same in the browser, but when you view the page source, you'll see the indenting. Or you could not indent the lines in the string, but then your code looks somewhat odd.

The `/demo/time` procedure just returns the result of `clock format`. It doesn't even bother adding `<html>`, `<head>`, or `<body>` tags, which you can get away with in today's browsers. A simple result like this is also useful if you are using programs to fetch information via HTTP requests to your application.

Using Query Data

Application Direct URL handlers have their parameters automatically assigned to values from the query data. Like any Tcl procedure, your Application Direct URL procedure can have named parameters, named parameters with default values, and the `args` parameter. The server matches the names of form values with names of your procedure parameters in order to assign their values. There are three cases:

- The name of the procedure parameter matches the name of a query data item. The query value is assigned to the parameter.
- The name of the procedure parameter does not appear in the query data. The parameter is assigned the empty string or its default value, if it has one. The `/demo/time` procedure is defined with an optional `format` argument. If a `format` value is present in the query data, then it overrides the default value given in the procedure definition.
- The query data item does not match any of the parameters. If the procedure has an `args` parameter as its last parameter, then the name and value of the query data item are appended to the `args` value. Otherwise, the query value is simply ignored. For example, the `/demo/echo` procedure's `args` parameter gets filled in with a name-value list of all query data.

You can see that missing arguments or extra arguments do not cause errors. If you want to do strict parameter checking, then just use `args` and check the name-value query list yourself.

Here is another example to illustrate the different ways that form data is assigned to procedure parameters. Suppose you have an Application Direct procedure declared like this:

```
proc Demo/param { a b {c cdef} args} { body }
```

You could create an HTML form that had elements named a, b, and c, and specified /demo/param for the ACTION parameter of the FORM tag. Or you could type the following into your browser to embed the query data right into the URL:

```
/demo/param?a=5&b=7&c=red&d=%7ewelch&e=two+words
```

The `?` separates the query data from the URL, and each query item is separated by `&`. In this case, when your procedure is called, a is 5, b is 7, c is red, and the `args` parameter becomes a list of:

```
d ~welch e {two words}
```

The `%7e` and the `+` are special codes for nonalphanumeric characters in the query data. The `+` becomes a space, and the `%xx` sequence is replaced by the character with character code xx (e.g., `%7e` becomes ~). Normally, this encoding is taken care of automatically by the Web browser when it gets data from a form and passes it to the Web server. However, if you type query data directly or format URLs with complex query data in them, then you need to encode special values as we did here. Use the `Url_Encode` procedure to encode URLs that you put into Web pages. The Web server automatically decodes the values as it makes the assignments to the Application Direct URL procedure parameters.

If a parameter does not match the query data, it gets its default value from the procedure definition, or it gets the empty string. Consider this example:

```
/demo/param?b=5
```

In this case, a is `""`, b is 5, c is cdef, and `args` is an empty list.

Returning Other Content Types

The default content type for Application Direct URLs is `text/html`. You can specify other content types by using a global variable with the same name as your procedure. (Yes, this is a crude way to craft an interface.) Example 18–4 shows part of the `faces.tcl` file that implements an interface to a database of picons — personal icons — that is organized by user and domain names. The idea is that the database contains images corresponding to your email correspondents. The `Faces_ByEmail` procedure, which is not shown, looks up an appropriate image file. The Application Direct procedure is `Faces/byemail`, and it sets the global variable `Faces/byemail` to the correct `Content-Type` value based on the filename extension. The mapping from extension to content type is implemented by the `Mtype` procedure (`mtype.tcl`). MIME is the multimedia content standard for email, and it originated the various content types now also used in HTTP, hence the term "MIME type."

Example 18–4 Alternate types for Application Direct URLs.

```
Direct_Url /faces Faces
proc Faces/byemail {email} {
    global Faces/byemail
    set filename [Faces_ByEmail $email]
    set Faces/byemail [Mtype $filename]
    set in [open $filename]
    fconfigure $in -translation binary
    set X [read $in]
    close $in
    return $X
}
```

Document Types

The Document domain (`doc.tcl`) maps URLs onto files and directories. It provides more ways to extend the server by registering different document type handlers. You can make up new types to support your application. Example 18–5 shows the pieces needed to create a handler for a fictitious document type `application/myjunk` that is invoked to handle files with the `.junk` suffix. Use the `Mtype_Add` procedure to register the mapping from file suffix to document type:

Example 18–5 A sample document type handler.

```
# Register the mapping from suffix to MIME type
Mtype_Add application/myjunk .junk

# Define the document handler procedure
#    path is the name of the file on disk
#    suffix is part of the URL after the domain prefix
#    sock is the handle on the client connection

proc Doc_application/myjunk {path suffix sock} {
    upvar #0 Httpd$sock data
    # data(url) is more useful than the suffix parameter.

    # Use the contents of file $path to compute a page
    set contents [somefunc $path]

    # Determine your content type
    set type text/html

    # Return the page
    Httpd_ReturnData $sock $type $data
}
```

The server finds the document handler in a two-step process. First, the type of a file is determined by its suffix. The `mime.types` file contains a map from suffixes to MIME types such as text/html or image/gif. This map is controlled by the Mtype module in mtype.tcl. Second, the server checks for a Tcl procedure with the appropriate name:

    Doc_mimetype

The matching procedure, if any, is called to handle the URL request. The procedure should use routines in the Httpd module to return data for the request. If there is no matching Doc_mimetype procedure, then the default document handler uses Httpd_ReturnFile and specifies the Content Type based on the file extension. This is the heart of the default document handler:

    Httpd_ReturnFile $sock [Mtype $path] $path

As another example, the HTML+Tcl templates use the .tml suffix that is mapped to the application/x-tcl-template type. You can find the document handler Doc_application/x-tcl-template in doc.tcl. The TclHttpd distribution also includes support for files with a .snmp extension that implements a template-based Web interface to the Scotty SNMP Tcl extension.

HTML + Tcl Templates

The template system uses HTML pages that embed Tcl commands and Tcl variable references. The server replaces these using the subst command and returns the results. The server comes with a general template system, but using subst is so easy you could create your own template system. The TclHttpd template framework has these components:

- Each page.html can have a corresponding page.tml template file. This feature is enabled with the Doc_CheckTemplates command in the server's configuration file. Normally, the server returns the page.html file unless the corresponding page.tml file has been modified more recently. In this case, the server processes the template with subst, caches the result in the page.html file, and returns the result.
- A dynamic template (e.g., a form handler) must be processed each time it is requested. If you put the Doc_Dynamic command into your page, it turns off the caching of the result in the page.html page. The server responds to a request for a page.html page by processing the page.tml page. Or you can just reference the page.tml file directly and the server will always processes the template.
- The server creates a page global Tcl variable that has context about the page being processed. Table 18–6 lists the elements of the page array.
- The server initializes the env global Tcl variable with similar information, but in the standard way for CGI scripts. Table 18–7 lists the elements of the env array that are set by Cgi_SetEnv in cgi.tcl.
- The server initializes the ncgi module so you can use the ncgi procedures to access query data.

- The server supports per-directory .tml files that contain Tcl source code. These files are designed to contain procedure definitions and variable settings that are shared among pages. The name of the file is simply ".tml", with nothing before the period. This is a standard way to hide files in UNIX, but it can be confusing to talk about the per-directory .tml files and the *page*.tml templates that correspond to *page*.html pages. Before processing each *page*.tml file, the server will source the .tml files in all directories leading down to the directory containing the template file. The server compares the modify time of these files against the template file and will process the template if these .tml files are newer than the cached *page*.html file. So, by modifying the .tml file in the root of your URL hierarchy, you invalidate all the cached *page*.html files.

Where to Put Your Tcl Code

There are three places you can put the code of your application: directly in your template pages, in the per-directory .tml files, or in the library directory. There are pros and cons to each:

- The library directory is where you should put most of your code. The library directory is specified with the -library command line argument, and the server loads all files in the library upon startup. The advantage of putting procedure definitions in the library is that they are defined one time but executed many times. This works well with the Tcl byte-code compiler. The disadvantage is that if you modify procedures in these files, you have to explicitly source them into the server for these changes to take effect. You can restart the server, or you can use the /debug/source URL described on page 282 to reload source files into the running server.
- The .tml files are best for variable definitions that you want to share among pages in a directory, or as a staging area for procedures during development. The advantage of putting code into the per-directory .tml files is that changes are picked up immediately with no effort on your part. The server automatically checks if these files are modified and sources them each time it processes your templates. However, using .tml files tends to scatter your code around the URL tree and can make it harder to maintain.
- I try to put as little code as possible directly in my *page*.tml template files. It is awkward to put lots of code there, and you cannot share procedures and variable definitions easily with other pages. Instead, my goal is to have only procedure calls in the template files, and put the procedure definitions elsewhere. If you want control structures in your page, such as if and foreach, you may want to use the version of those commands provided by the html package, as described on page 277.

II. Advanced Tcl

Templates for Site Structure

The next few examples show a simple template system used to maintain a common "look and feel" across the pages of a site. The key to a successful template system is a data structure that defines the structure of the site, and some procedures that generate standard navigational HTML structure for your pages. Once you do this, then you can easily add new pages by updating your data structure. The template procedures automatically reformat your site to include the new pages. Example 18–6 shows a simple one-level site definition that is kept in the root `.tml` file. This structure lists the title and URL of each page in the site:

Example 18–6 A one-level site structure.

```
set site(pages) {
    Home                    /index.html
    "Ordering Computers"/ordering.html
    "New Machine Setup" /setup.html
    "Adding a New User" /newuser.html
    "Network Addresses" /network.html
}
```

Of course, your Web site is likely to have more pages and a more elaborate structure. For example, you might have several main sections, each with a collection of pages, or even a three-level hierarchy of pages. Example 18–7 shows another simple data structure to define a two-level structure. The `site(sections)` variable stores the names and URLs of the main sections. For each section, there is an element of `site` that lists the pages in that section. Only the `About` section is shown in the example:

Example 18–7 A two-level site structure.

```
set site(sections) {
    About       /about
    Products    /products
    Support     /support
}
set site(About) {
    Company     company.html
    Contacts    contacts.html
    Directions   directions.html
}
```

In practice, you may want to include more information in your data structure to help you generate HTML. For example, if you have graphics for the main sections, you may need to record their size. Whatever you need, collect it into your data structures and then generate the HTML from procedures. You can quickly give your whole site a face lift with new graphics by changing the template procedures that generate your pages. In contrast, if you hand-code all your pages, it can take months instead of days.

Example 18–8 shows a sample template file for the one-level structure shown in Example 18–6. Each page includes two commands, SitePage and Site-Footer, that generate HTML for the navigational part of the page. Between these commands is regular HTML for the page content:

Example 18–8 A HTML + Tcl template file.

```
[SitePage "New Machine Setup"]
This page describes the steps to take when setting up a new
computer in our environment. See
[SiteLink "Ordering Computers"]
for instructions on ordering machines.
<ol>
<li>Unpack and setup the machine.
<li>Use the Network control panel to set the IP address
and hostname.
<!-- Several steps omitted -->
<li>Reboot for the last time.
</ol>
[SiteFooter]
```

The SitePage procedure takes the page title as an argument. It generates HTML to implement a standard navigational structure. Example 18–9 has a simple implementation of SitePage:

Example 18–9 SitePage template procedure, version 1.

```
proc SitePage {title} {
    global site
    set html "<html><head><title>$title</title></head>\n"
    append html "<body bgcolor=white text=black>\n"
    append html "<h1>$title</h1>\n"
    set sep ""
    foreach {label url} $site(pages) {
        append html $sep
        if {[string compare $label $title] == 0} {
            append html "$label"
        } else {
            append html "<a href='$url'>$label</a>"
        }
        set sep " | "
    }
    return $html
}
```

The foreach loop that computes the simple menu of links turns out to be useful in many places. Example 18–10 splits out the loop and uses it in a new version of SitePage along with the SiteFooter procedure. This version of the templates creates a left column for the navigation and a right column for the page content. The example also puts a few more visual elements (e.g., page background color) into the site array so you can easily maintain them:

Example 18–10 `SiteMenu` and `SiteFooter` template procedures.

```
array set site {
    bg          white
    fg          black
    mainlogo    /images/mainLogo.gif
}
proc SitePage {title} {
    global site
    set html "<html><head><title>$title</title></head>\n\
        <body bgcolor=$site(bg) text=$site(fg)>\n\
        <!-- Two Column Layout -->\n\
        <table cellpadding=0>\n\
        <tr><td>\n\
        <!-- Left Column -->\n\
        <img src='$site(mainlogo)'>\n\
        <font size=+1>\n\
        [SiteMenu <br> $site(pages)]\n\
        </font>\n\
        </td><td>\n\
        <!-- Right Column -->\n\
        <h1>$title</h1>\n\
        <p>\n"
    return $html
}
proc SiteFooter {} {
    global site
    set html "<p><hr>\n\
        <font size=-1>[SiteMenu | $site(pages)]</font>\n\
        <!-- Close Right Column -->\n\
        </td></tr></table>\n"
    return $html
}
proc SiteMenu {sep list} {
    global page
    set s ""
    set html ""
    foreach {label url} $list {
        if {[string compare $page(url) $url] == 0} {
            append html $s$label
        } else {
            append html "$s<a href='$url'>$label</a>"
        }
        set s $sep
    }
    return $html
}
```

There are many other applications for "macros" that make repetitive HTML coding chores easy. For example, take the `SiteLink` procedure call in Example

18–8. Instead of hand-coding the <A> tag with the link to /ordering.html, the page uses the SiteLink procedure to format the link with a consistent label for the link. Using the procedure also means that the page will automatically get updated if you change the URL associated with the ordering page by modifying site(pages). Example 18–11 shows SiteLink:

Example 18–11 The SiteLink procedure.

```
proc SiteLink {label} {
    global site
    array set map $site(pages)
    if {[info exist map($label)]} {
        return "<a href='$map($label)'>$label</a>"
    } else {
        return $label
    }
}
```

Using Variables for Important Site Information

Another useful feature of templates is the ability to embed variable references in your pages. Instead of hard coding the sales phone number, or the current product version number, or even the product name, you can put variables into your pages. For example, SiteLink and SitePage take a parameter that is the page title. Instead of hard coding your page titles, you could keep all of your page titles in an array, and use array references everywhere. That puts all the text in one place and makes it easy to change. The array definition would look something like this:

```
array set title {
    Home Home
    Order "Ordering Computers"
    Setup "New Machine Setup"
    AddUser "Adding a New User"
    Network "Network Addresses"
}
```

And the calls to SitePage or SiteLink could be made like this:

```
[SitePage $title(Order)]
```

The .tml pages are a good place to define the variables because the definitions are shared by all pages in that directory, and in any subdirectories. Also, the definitions in the per-directory .tml override any definitions that come from the top-level .tml file at the root of your URL tree. Changing the definition of the variable in the .tml file immediately updates all the pages that share it.

The main drawback to variable references is the clash with $ in pricing. If you put $10 into a page.tml file, it will raise an error (unless the variable 10 is defined). It turns out that you want to generate prices from some database anyway, so you should avoid hard coding prices into your pages anyway. It is much better to put [price T-shirt] or $price(T-shirt) into your page than $10, although if you must do that, just quote the $ with a backslash, \$10.

Form Handlers

HTML forms and form-handling programs go together. The form is presented to the user on the client machine. The form handler runs on the server after the user fills out the form and presses the submit button. The form presents input widgets like radiobuttons, checkbuttons, selection lists, and text entry fields. Each of these widgets is assigned a name, and each widget gets a value based on the user's input. The form handler is a program that looks at the names and values from the form and computes the next page for the user to read.

CGI is a standard way to hook external programs to Web servers for the purpose of processing form data. CGI has a special encoding for values so that they can be transported safely. The encoded data is either read from standard input or taken from the command line. The CGI program decodes the data, processes it, and writes a new HTML page on its standard output. Chapter 3 describes writing CGI scripts in Tcl.

TclHttpd provides alternatives to CGI that are more efficient because they are built right into the server. This eliminates the overhead that comes from running an external program to compute the page. Another advantage is that the Web server can maintain state between client requests in Tcl variables. If you use CGI, you must use some sort of database or file storage to maintain information between requests.

Application Direct Handlers

The server comes with several built-in form handlers that you can use with little effort. The /mail/forminfo URL will package up the query data and mail it to you. You use form fields to set various mail headers, and the rest of the data is packaged up into a Tcl-readable mail message. Example 18–12 shows a form that uses this handler. Other built-in handlers are described starting at page 281.

Example 18–12 Mail form results with /mail/forminfo.

```
<form action=/mail/forminfo method=post>
    <input type=hidden name=sendto value=mailreader@my.com>
    <input type=hidden name=subject value="Name and Address">
    <table>
        <tr><td>Name</td><td><input name=name></td></tr>
        <tr><td>Address</td><td><input name=addr1></td></tr>
        <tr><td> </td><td><input name=addr2></td></tr>
        <tr><td>City</td><td><input name=city></td></tr>
        <tr><td>State</td><td><input name=state></td></tr>
        <tr><td>Zip/Postal</td><td><input name=zip></td></tr>
        <tr><td>Country</td><td><input name=country></td></tr>
    </table>
</form>
```

The mail message sent by /mail/forminfo is shown in Example 18–13.

Example 18–13 Mail message sent by `/mail/forminfo`.

```
To: mailreader@my.com
Subject: Name and Address

data {
    name    {Joe Visitor}
    addr1   {Acme Company}
    addr2   {100 Main Street}
    city    {Mountain View}
    state   California
    zip     12345
    country    USA
}
```

The email message is designed to be easily processed by a Tcl program. You can use a mail processor like *procmail* to filter all mail with a given Subject or To field to a program for processing. It is easy to write a script that strips the headers, defines a `data` procedure, and uses `eval` to process the message body. Whenever you send data via email, if you format it with Tcl list structure, you can process it quite easily. The basic structure of such a mail reader procedure is shown in Example 18–14:

Example 18–14 Processing mail sent by `/mail/forminfo`.

```
# Assume the mail message is on standard input

set X [read stdin]

# Strip off the mail headers, when end with a blank line
if {[regsub {.*?\n\ndata} $X {data} X] != 1} {
    error "Malformed mail message"
}
proc data {fields} {
    foreach {name value} $fields {
        # Do something
    }
}
# Process the message.
eval $X
```

The raw `eval` in the mail handler is dangerous. It will be fine if the only source of email to that program is the `/mail/forminfo` URL handler. However, an attacker could send you an email that results in arbitrary Tcl commands being evaluated by your mail processor. The safe way to process the email is with a safe interpreter, which is described in Chapter 19. Example 18–15 adds just a few commands to create a safe interpreter for processing the incoming data. The `data` command is evaluated in the trusted interpreter by the alias mechanism. All other commands in the email are evaluated in the safe interpreter, and any malicious commands simply raise Tcl errors but cause no harm:

Example 18–15 Processing mail sent by /mail/forminfo, Safe-Tcl version.

```
# Assume the mail message is on standard input

set X [read stdin]

# Strip off the mail headers, when end with a blank line
if {[regsub {.*?\n\ndata} $X {data} X] != 1} {
    error "Malformed mail message"
}
proc data {fields} {
    foreach {name value} $fields {
        # Do something
    }
}
# Create the safe interpreter
set i [interp create -safe]

# Link the data command in the safe interpreter to the
# data procedure in this interpreter
interp alias $i data {} data

# Process the message in the safe interpreter
interp eval $i $X
```

Template Form Handlers

The drawback of using Application Direct URL form handlers is that you must modify their Tcl implementation to change the resulting page. Another approach is to use templates for the result page that embed a command that handles the form data. The Mail_FormInfo procedure, for example, mails form data. It takes no arguments. Instead, it looks in the query data for sendto and subject values, and if they are present, it sends the rest of the data in an email. It returns an HTML comment that flags that mail was sent.

When you use templates to process form data, you need to turn off result caching because the server must process the template each time the form is submitted. To turn off caching, embed the Doc_Dynamic command into your form handler pages, or set the page(dynamic) variable to 1. Alternatively, you can simply post directly to the file.tml page instead of to the file.html page.

Self-Posting Forms

This section illustrates a self-posting form. This is a form on a page that posts the form data to back to the same page. The page embeds a Tcl command to check its own form data. Once the data is correct, the page triggers a redirect to the next page in the flow. This is a powerful technique that I use to create complex page flows using templates. Of course, you need to save the form data at each step. You can put the data in Tcl variables, use the data to control your application, or store it into a database. TclHttpd comes with a Session module,

which is one way to manage this information. For details, you should scan the
`session.tcl` file in the distribution.

Example 18–16 shows the `Form_Simple` procedure that generates a simple
self-checking form. Its arguments are a unique ID for the form, a description of
the form fields, and the URL of the next page in the flow. The field description is
a list with three elements for each field: a required flag, a form element name,
and a label to display with the form element:

Example 18–16 A self-checking form procedure.

```
proc Form_Simple {id fields nextpage} {
    global page
    if {![html::varEmpty formid]} {
        # Incoming form values, check them
        set check 1
    } else {
        # First time through the page
        set check 0
    }
    set html "<!-- Self-posting. Next page is $nextpage -->\n"
    append html "<form action=\"$page(url)\" method=post>\n"
    append html "<input type=hidden name=formid value=$id>\n"
    append html "<table border=1>\n"
    foreach {required key label} $fields {
        append html "<tr><td>"
        if {$check && $required && [html::varEmpty $key]} {
            lappend missing $label
            append html "<font color=red>*</font>"
        }
        append html "</td><td>$label</td>\n"
        append html "<td><input [html::formValue $key]></td>\n"
        append html "</tr>\n"
    }
    append html "</table>\n"
    if {$check} {
        if {![info exist missing]} {

            # No missing fields, so advance to the next page.
            # In practice, you must save the existing fields
            # at this point before redirecting to the next page.

            Doc_Redirect $nextpage
        } else {
            set msg "<font color=red>Please fill in "
            append msg [join $missing ", "]
            append msg "</font>"
            set html <p>$msg\n$html
        }
    }
    append html "<input type=submit>\n</form>\n"
    return $html
}
```

II. Advanced Tcl

The `Form_Simple` procedure does two things at once: it computes the HTML form, and it also checks if the required fields are present. It uses some procedures from the `html` module to generate form elements that retain values from the previous page. If all the required fields are present, then it triggers a redirect by calling `Doc_Redirect`. Example 18–17 shows a page template that calls `Form_Simple` with the required field description:

Example 18–17 A page with a self-checking form.

```
<html><head>
    <title>Name and Address Form</title>
</head>
<body bgcolor=white text=black>
    <h1>Name and Address</h1>
    Please enter your name and address.
    [Form_Simple nameaddr {
        1 name    "Name"
        1 addr1   "Address"
        0 addr2"  "Address"
        1 city    "City"
        0 state   "State"
        1 zip     "Zip Code"
        0 country "Country"
    } nameok.html]
</body></html>
```

The html Package

The Standard Tcl Library, *tcllib*, includes an `html` package that is designed to support page generation and self-posting forms. The `html` package works in conjunction with the `ncgi` package, which was introduced in Chapter 3. The `Form_Simple` procedure uses `html::varEmpty` to test if particular form values are present in the query data. For example, it tests to see whether the `formid` field is present so that the procedure knows whether or not to check for the rest of the fields. The `html::formValue` procedure is useful for constructing form elements on self-posting form pages. It returns:

```
name="name" value="value"
```

The *value* is the value of form element *name* based on incoming query data, or just the empty string if the query value for *name* is undefined. As a result, the form can post to itself and retain values from the previous version of the page. It is used like this:

```
<input type=text [html::formValue name]>
```

The `html::checkValue` and `html::radioValue` procedures are similar to `html::formValue`, but are designed for checkbuttons and radio buttons. The `html::select` procedure formats a selection list and highlights the selected values.

The `html` package includes a versions of `foreach` and `if` that are designed for use in templates. These commands perform a `subst` on their body instead of evaluating it. This lets you put HTML with variable and command references into the body to build up results. Example 18–18 shows the `html::foreach` procedure used to generate a table with several rows. Note that you don't have to worry about the `$` in the prices because they are inside the braces of the `html::foreach` value list:

Example 18–18 Generating a table with `html::foreach`.

```
<TABLE BORDER=1>
[html::foreach {product price} {
    T-Shirt    $10.00
    YoYo       $7.50
    Footbag    $15.00
} {
    <TR>
        <TD>$product</TD>
        <TD ALIGN=RIGHT><FONT FACE=courier>$price</FONT></TD>
    </TR>
}
</TABLE>
```

Programming Reference

This section summarizes many of the more useful functions defined by the server. These tables are not complete, however. You are encouraged to read through the code to learn more about the features offered by the server. A simple naming convention is used to distinguish procedures that are private to a file (e.g., `HttpdEvent`) and procedures that are meant to be used by other modules or by the main application (e.g., `Httpd_Server`). The underscore after the module prefix indicates that the procedure is public.

This section does not detail the `ncgi` and `html` packages, which are quite useful to the TclHttpd programmer. There are doc files that come with tcllib, and you can find man pages for the tcllib packages in the `www.tcl.tk` manual section.

Table 18–1 shows `Httpd` functions used when returning pages to the client.

Table 18–1 `Httpd` support procedures.

`Httpd_Error sock code`	Returns a simple error page to the client. The *code* is a numeric error code such as 404 or 500.
`Httpd_ReturnData sock type data`	Returns a page with Content-Type *type* and content *data*.
`Httpd_ReturnFile sock type file`	Returns a *file* with Content-Type *type*.
`Httpd_Redirect newurl sock`	Generates a 302 error return with a Location of *newurl*.
`Httpd_SelfUrl url`	Expands *url* to include the proper `http://` *server:port* prefix to reference the current server.

Table 18–2 summarizes a few useful procedures provided by the `Url` module (`url.tcl`). The `Url_DecodeQuery` is used to decode query data into a Tcl-friendly list. The `Url_Encode` procedure is useful when encoding values directly into URLs. URL encoding is discussed in more detail on page 262.

Table 18–2 `Url` support procedures.

`Url_DecodeQuery` *query*	Decodes a `www-url-encoded` query string and returns a name, value list. *Depreciated*. This is equivalent to `ncgi::nvlist`, which takes no arguments.
`Url_Encode` *value*	Returns *value* encoded according to the www-url-encoded standard.
`Url_PrefxInstall` *prefix* *handler ?-thread bool?* *?-callback cmd?* *?-readpost bool?*	Registers *handler* as the handler for all URLs that begin with *prefix*. The handler is invoked with two additional arguments: *sock*, the handle to the client, and *suffix*, the part of the URL after *prefix*. Use `-thread 1` to have the handler run in a worker thread. Use `-callback cmd` to register a callback invoked at the very end of URL processing. Use `-readpost 0` to disable pre-reading post data.

The `Doc` module procedures for configuration are listed in Table 18–3.

Table 18–3 `Doc` procedures for configuration.

`Doc_Root ?`*directory*`?`	Sets or queries the *directory* that corresponds to the root of the URL hierarchy.
`Doc_AddRoot` *virtual* *directory*	Maps the file system *directory* into the URL subtree starting at *virtual*.
`Doc_ErrorPage` *file*	Specifies a *file* relative to the document root used as a simple template for error messages. This is processed by `DocSubstSystem` file in `doc.tcl`.
`Doc_CheckTemplates` *how*	If *how* is 1, then `.html` files are compared against corresponding `.tml` files and regenerated, if necessary.
`Doc_IndexFile` *pattern*	Registers a file name *pattern* that will be searched for the default index file in directories.
`Doc_NotFoundPage` *file*	Specifies a *file* relative to the document root used as a simple template for page not found messages. This is processed by `DocSubstSystem` file in `doc.tcl`.
`Doc_PublicHtml` *dirname*	Defines the directory used for each user's home directory. When a URL such as `~user` is specified, the *dirname* under their home directory is accessed.
`Doc_TemplateLibrary` *directory*	Adds *directory* to the `auto_path` so that the source files in it are available to the server.

Table 18–3 Doc procedures for configuration. (Continued)

`Doc_TemplateInterp interp`	Specifies an alternate interpreter in which to process document templates (i.e., `.tml` files.)
`Doc_Webmaster ?email?`	Sets or queries the *email* for the Webmaster.

The Doc module procedures for generating results are listed in Table 18–4.

Table 18–4 Doc procedures for generating responses.

`Doc_Error sock errorInfo`	Generates a 500 response on *sock* based on the template registered with `Doc_ErrorPage`. *errorInfo* is a copy of the Tcl error trace after the error.
`Doc_NotFound sock`	Generates a 404 response on *sock* by using the template registered with `Doc_NotFoundPage`.
`Doc_Subst sock file ?interp?`	Performs a `subst` on the file and return the resulting page on *sock*. *interp* specifies an alternate Tcl interpreter.

The Doc module also provides procedures for cookies and redirects that are useful in document templates. These are described in Table 18–5.

Table 18–5 Doc procedures that support template processing.

`Doc_Coookie name`	Returns the cookie *name* passed to the server for this request, or the empty string if it is not present.
`Doc_Dynamic`	Turns off caching of the HTML result. Meant to be called from inside a page template.
`Doc_IsLinkToSelf url`	Returns 1 if the *url* is a link to the current page.
`Doc_Redirect newurl`	Raises a special error that aborts template processing and triggers a page redirect to *newurl*.
`Doc_SetCookie -name name -value value -path path -domain domain -expires date`	Sets cookie *name* with the given *value* that will be returned to the client as part of the response. The *path* and *domain* restrict the scope of the cooke. The *date* sets an expiration date.

Table 18–6 shows the initial elements of the page array that are defined during the processing of a template.

Table 18–6 Elements of the page array.

`query`	The decoded query data in a name, value list. Also available through `ncgi`.
`dynamic`	If 1, the results of processing the template are not cached in the corresponding `.html` file.

Table 18–6 Elements of the `page` array. (Continued)

`filename`	The file system pathname of the requested file (e.g., `/usr/local/htdocs/tclhttpd/index.html`).
`template`	The file system pathname of the template file (e.g., `/usr/local/htdocs/tclhttpd/index.tml`).
`url`	The part of the URL after the server name (e.g., `/tclhttpd/index.tml`).
`root`	A relative path from the template file back to the root of the URL tree.

Table 18–7 shows the elements of the `env` array. These are defined during CGI requests, Application Direct URL handlers, and page template processing:

Table 18–7 Elements of the `env` array.

`AUTH_TYPE`	Authentication protocol (e.g., `Basic`).
`CONTENT_LENGTH`	The size of the query data.
`CONTENT_TYPE`	The type of the query data.
`DOCUMENT_ROOT`	File system pathname of the document root.
`GATEWAY_INTERFACE`	Protocol version, which is `CGI/1.1`.
`HTTP_ACCEPT`	The Accept headers from the request.
`HTTP_AUTHORIZATION`	The Authorization challenge from the request.
`HTTP_COOKIE`	The cookie from the request.
`HTTP_FROM`	The From: header of the request.
`HTTP_REFERER`	The Referer indicates the previous page.
`HTTP_USER_AGENT`	An ID string for the Web browser.
`PATH_INFO`	Extra path information after the template file.
`PATH_TRANSLATED`	The extra path information appended to the document root.
`QUERY_STRING`	The form query data.
`REMOTE_ADDR`	The client's IP address.
`REMOTE_USER`	The remote user name specified by Basic authentication.
`REQUEST_METHOD`	GET, POST, or HEAD.
`REQUEST_URI`	The complete URL that was requested.
`SCRIPT_NAME`	The name of the current file relative to the document root.
`SERVER_NAME`	The server name, e.g., `www.beedub.com`.
`SERVER_PORT`	The server's port, e.g., 80.
`SERVER_PROTOCOL`	The protocol (e.g., `http` or `https`).
`SERVER_SOFTWARE`	A software version string for the server.

Standard Application Direct URLs

The server has several modules that provide Application Direct URLs. These Application Direct URLs let you control the server or examine its state from any Web browser. You can look at the implementation of these modules as examples for your own application.

Status

The `/status` URL is implemented in the `status.tcl` file. The status module implements the display of hit counts, document hits, and document misses (i.e., documents not found). The `Status_Url` command enables the Application Direct URLs and assigns the top-level URL for the status module. The default configuration file contains this command:

```
Status_Url /status
```

Table 18–8 shows the URLs implemented by the status module:

Table 18–8 Status Application Direct URLs.

`/status`	Main status page showing summary counters and hit count histograms.
`/status/doc`	Shows hit counts for each page. This page lets you sort by name or hit count, and limit files by patterns.
`/status/domain`	Shows hit counts for each domain in the server.
`/status/hello`	A trivial URL that returns "hello".
`/status/notfound`	Shows miss counts for URLs that users tried to fetch.
`/status/size`	Displays an estimated size of Tcl code and Tcl data used by the TclHttpd program.
`/status/text`	This is a version of the main status page that doesn't use the graphical histograms of hit counts.

Debugging

The `/debug` URL is implemented in the `debug.tcl` file. The debug module has several useful URLs that let you examine variable values and other internal state. It is turned on with this command in the default configuration file:

```
Debug_Url /debug
```

Table 18–9 lists the `/debug` URLs. These URLs often require parameters that you can specify directly in the URL. For example, the `/debug/echo` URL echoes its query parameters:

```
http://yourserver:port/debug/echo?name=value&name2=val2
```

Note: The debug URL is active in the default configuration. If it makes you nervous, then delete the call to `Debug_Url` from the `httpdthread.tcl` file.

The sample URL tree that is included in the distribution includes the file
`htdocs/hacks.html`. This file has several small forms that use the /debug URLs
to examine variables and source files. It may seem dangerous to have these facilities, but I reason that because my source directories are under my control, it
cannot hurt to reload any source files. In general, the library scripts contain only
procedure definitions and no global code that might reset state inappropriately.
In practice, the ability to tune (i.e., fix bugs) in the running server has proven
useful to me on many occasions. It lets you evolve your application without
restarting it!

Table 18–9 Debug Application Direct URLs.

/debug/after	Lists the outstanding after events.
/debug/dbg	Connects to *TclPro Debugger*. This takes a host and port parameter. You need to install prodebug.tcl from *TclPro* into the server's script library directory.
/debug/echo	Echoes its query parameters. Accepts a title parameter.
/debug/errorInfo	Displays the errorInfo variable along with the server's version number and Webmaster email. Accepts title and errorInfo arguments.
/debug/parray	Displays a global array variable. The name of the variable is specified with the aname parameter.
/debug/pvalue	A more general value display function. The name of the variable is specified with the aname parameter. This can be a variable name, an array name, or a pattern that matches several variable names.
/debug/raise	Raises an error (to test error handling). Any parameters become the error string.
/debug/source	Sources a file from either the server's main library directory or the Doc_TemplateLibrary directory. The file is specified with the source parameter.

Example 18–19 shows the implementation of /debug/source. You can see
that it limits the files to the main script library and to the script library associated with document templates.

Example 18–19 The /debug/source Application Direct URL implementation.

```
proc Debug/source {source} {
    global Httpd Config errorInfo
    set source [file tail $source]
    set dirlist $Httpd(library)    ;# TclHttpd implementation
    lappend dirlist $Config(lib)   ;# Application custom code
    foreach dir $dirlist {
        set file [file join $dir $source]
        if {[file exists $file]} break
    }
```

```
    set error [catch {uplevel #0 [list source $file]} result]
    set html "<title>Source $source</title>\n"
    if {$error} {
        append html "<H1>Error in $source</H1>\n"
        append html "<pre>$result<p>$errorInfo</pre>"
    } else {
        append html "<H1>Reloaded $source</H1>\n"
        append html "<pre>$result</pre>"
    }
    return $html
}
```

Sending Email

The `/mail` URL is implemented in the `mail.tcl` file. The mail module implements various form handlers that email form data. Currently, it is UNIX-specific because it uses `/usr/lib/sendmail` to send the mail. It is turned on with this command in the default configuration file:

```
Mail_Url /mail
```

The Application Direct URLs shown in Table 18–10 are useful form handlers. You can specify them as the ACTION parameter in your `<FORM>` tags. The

Table **18–10** Application Direct URLS that email form results.

`/mail/bugreport`	Sends email with the `errorInfo` from a server error. It takes an `email` parameter for the destination address and an `error-Info` parameter. Any additional arguments get included into the message.
`/mail/forminfo`	Sends email containing form results. It requires these parameters: `sendto` for the destination address, `subject` for the mail subject, `href` and `label` for a link to display on the results page. Any additional arguments are formatted with the Tcl `list` command for easy processing by programs that read the mail.
`/mail/formdata`	This is an older form of `/mail/forminfo` that doesn't format the data into Tcl lists. It requires only the `email` and `subject` parameters. The rest are formatted into the message body.

mail module provides two Tcl procedures that are generally useful. The `MailInner` procedure is the one that sends mail. It is called like this:

```
MailInner sendto subject from type body
```

The `sendto` and `from` arguments are email addresses. The `type` is the MIME type (e.g., `text/plain` or `text/html`) and appears in a `Content-Type` header. The `body` contains the mail message without any headers.

The `Mail_FormInfo` procedure is designed for use in HTML+Tcl template files. It takes no arguments but instead looks in current query data for its parameters. It expects to find the same arguments as the `/mail/forminfo` direct

URL. Using a template with `Mail_FormInfo` gives you more control over the result page than posting directly to `/mail/forminfo`, and is illustrated in Example 18–12 on page 272.

The TclHttpd Distribution

Get the TclHttpd distribution from the CD-ROM, or find it on the Internet at:

```
ftp://ftp.tcl.tk/pub/tcl/httpd/
http://www.tcl.tk/software/tclhttpd/
http://www.sourceforge.net/projects/tclhttpd
```

Quick Start

Unpack the tar file or the zip file, and you can run the server from the `httpd.tcl` script in the `bin` directory. On UNIX:

```
tclsh bin/httpd.tcl -port 80
```

This command will start the Web server on the standard port (80). On UNIX, you need to be root to run a server on this port. By default TclHttpd uses port 8015 instead. If you run it with the `-help` flag, it will tell you what command line options are available. If you use *wish* instead of *tclsh,* then a simple Tk user interface is displayed that shows how many hits the server is getting.

On Windows, you can double-click the `httpd.tcl` script to start the server. It will use *wish* and display the user interface. Again it will start on port 8015. You will need to create a shortcut that passes the `-port` argument, or edit the associated configuration file to change this. Configuring the server is described later.

Once you have the server running, you can connect to it from your Web browser. Use this URL if you are running on the default (nonstandard) port:

```
http://hostname:8015/
```

If you are running without a network connection, you may need to specify `127.0.0.1` for the hostname. This is the "localhost" address and will bypass the network subsystem.

```
http://127.0.0.1:8015/
```

Inside the Distribution

The TclHttpd distribution is organized into the following directories:

- `bin` — This has sample start-up scripts and configuration files. The `httpd.tcl` script runs the server. The `tclhttpd.rc` file is the standard configuration file.
- `bin/mini` — This has a few tiny versions of the server that provide a basic server in about 300 lines of code. Use these as a starting point by modifying the `HttpdRespond` procedure.

- `bin/test` — This has a number of test scripts, including the `torture.tcl` file that can fetch many URLs at once from a server.
- `certs` — This has sample certificates you can use to test a secure server for `https` URLs. If you have your own server certificates, put the `server.pem` file here.
- `config` — This contains autoconf support used by C extensions you can build with the server.
- `custom` — This is where you put your own custom code. Files here are automatically loaded by the server on startup. This contains a few samples.
- `doc` — This has a UNIX-style manual page for how to run the server.
- `htaccess` — This has sample access control files.
- `htdocs` — This is a sample URL tree that demonstrates the features of the Web server. There is also some documentation there. One directory to note is `htdocs/libtml`, which is the standard place to put site-specific Tcl scripts used with the Tcl+HTML template facility.
- `lib` — This has all the Tcl sources. In general, each file provides a package. You will see the `package require` commands partly in `bin/httpd.tcl` and partly in `bin/httpdthread.tcl`.
- `src` — There are a few C source files for a some optional packages. These have been precompiled for some platforms, and you can find the compiled libraries under `src/Solaris` and `src/Linux`.

Server Configuration

TclHttpd configures itself with two main steps: setting configuration parameters and loading packages. The configuration step uses a configuration file and command line arguments to set basic configuration parameters. The default configuration file is named `tclhttpd.rc` in the same directory as the start-up script (i.e., `bin/tclhttpd.rc`). Specify an alternate configuration file with the `-config` command line argument. You can override the configuration file with additional command line arguments, which are described in Table 18–11. The configuration values from the file and the command line are copied into the `Config` Tcl array.

Package loading is split into two parts. The main `bin/httpd.tcl` script loads some core packages. The rest are loaded in the `bin/httpdthread.tcl` script. The reason for the split is to try to isolate the core of the server from application-specific functions. In addition, in the threaded version of the server, every thread loads and runs the `bin/httpdthread.tcl` script. You can specify an alternate package loading script with the `-main` command line argument.

For example, to start the server for the document tree under `/usr/local/htdocs` and your own email address as Webmaster, you can execute this command to start the server:

```
tclsh httpd.tcl -docRoot /usr/local/htdocs -webmaster welch
```

If you are using the Tclkit version described in Chapter 22:

```
tclkit tclhttpd.kit -docRoot /usr/local/htdocs -webmaster welch
```

Alternatively, you can put these settings into a configuration file, and start the server with that configuration file:

```
tclsh httpd.tcl -config mytclhttpd.rc
```

Command Line Arguments

There are several parameters you may need to set for a standard Web server. These are shown below in Table 18–11. The command line values are mapped into the `Config` array by the `httpd.tcl` startup script.

Table **18–11** Basic TclHttpd parameters.

Parameter	Command Option	Config Variable
Port number. The default is 8015.	`-port number`	`Config(port)`
Server name. The default is `[info hostname]`.	`-name name`	`Config(name)`
IP address. The default is 0, for "any address".	`-ipaddr address`	`Config(ipaddr)`
Directory of the root of the URL tree. The default is the `htdocs` directory.	`-docRoot directory`	`Config(docRoot)`
User ID of the TclHttpd process. The default is 50. (UNIX only.)	`-uid uid`	`Config(uid)`
Group ID of the TclHttpd process. The default is 100. (UNIX only.)	`-gid gid`	`Config(gid)`
Webmaster email. The default is `webmaster`.	`-webmaster email`	`Config(webmaster)`
Configuration file. The default is `tclhttpd.rc`.	`-config filename`	`Config(file)`
Directory containing custom code. The server loads all files found in this directory.	`-library directory`	`Config(library)`

Server Name and Port

The name and port parameters define how your server is known to Web browsers. The URLs that access your server begin with:

```
http://name:port/
```

If the port number is 80, you can leave out the port specification. The call that starts the server using these parameters is found in `httpd.tcl` as:

```
Httpd_Server $Config(name) $Config(port) $Config(ipaddr)
```

Specifying the IP address is necessary only if you have several network interfaces (or several IP addresses assigned to one network interface) and want the server to listen to requests on a particular network address. Otherwise, by default, the server accepts requests from any network interface.

User and Group ID

The user and group IDs are used on UNIX systems with the `setuid` and `setgid` system calls. This lets you start the server as root, which is necessary to listen on port 80, and then switch to a less privileged user account. If you use Tcl+HTML templates that cache the results in HTML files, then you need to pick an account that can write those files. Otherwise, you may want to pick a very unprivileged account.

The `setuid` function is available through the TclX (Extended Tcl) `id` command, or through a `setuid` extension distributed with TclHttpd under the src directory. If either of these facilities is not available, then the attempt to change user ID gracefully fails. See the README file in the `src` directory for instructions on compiling and installing the extensions found there.

Webmaster Email

The Webmaster email address is used for automatic error reporting in the case of server errors. This is defined in the configuration file with the following command:

```
Doc_Webmaster $Config(webmaster)
```

If you call `Doc_Webmaster` with no arguments, it returns the email address you previously defined. This is useful when generating pages that contain `mailto:` URLs with the Webmaster address.

Document Root

The document root is the directory that contains the static files, templates, CGI scripts, and so on that make up your Web site. By default, the httpd.tcl script uses the *htdocs* directory next to the directory containing *httpd.tcl*. It is worth noting the trick used to locate this directory:

```
file join [file dirname [info script]] ../htdocs
```

The `info script` command returns the full name of the `http.tcl` script, `file dirname` computes its directory, and `file join` finds the adjacent directory. The path `../htdocs` works with `file join` on any platform. The default location of the configuration file is found in a similar way:

```
file join [file dirname [info script]] tclhttpd.rc
```

The configuration file initializes the document root with this call:

```
Doc_Root $Config(docRoot)
```

If you need to find out what the document root is, you can call `Doc_Root` with no arguments and it returns the directory of the document root. If you want to add additional document trees into your Web site, you can do that with a call like this in your configuration file:

```
Doc_AddRoot directory urlprefix
```

Other Document Settings

The `Doc_IndexFile` command sets a pattern used to find the index file in a directory. The command used in the default configuration file is:

```
Doc_IndexFile index.{htm,html,tml,subst}
```

If you invent other file types with different file suffixes, you can alter this pattern to include them. This pattern will be used by the Tcl `glob` command.

The `Doc_PublicHtml` command is used to define "home directories" on your HTML site. If the URL begins with `~username`, then the Web server will look under the home directory of the user for a particular directory. The command in the default configuration file is:

```
Doc_PublicHtml public_html
```

For example, if my home directory is `/home/welch`, then the URL `~welch` maps to the directory `/home/welch/public_html`. If there is no `Doc_PublicHtml` command, then this mapping does not occur.

You can register two special pages that are used when the server encounters an error and when a user specifies an unknown URL. The default configuration file has these commands:

```
Doc_ErrorPage error.html

Doc_NotFoundPage notfound.html
```

These files are treated like templates in that they are passed through `subst` in order to include the error information or the URL of the missing page. These are pretty crude templates compared to the templates described earlier. You can count only on the `Doc` and `Httpd` arrays being defined. Look at the `Doc_SubstSystemFile` in `doc.tcl` for the truth about how these files are processed.

Document Templates

The template mechanism has two main configuration options. The first specifies an additional library directory that contains your application-specific scripts. This lets you keep your application-specific files separate from the TclHttpd implementation. The command in the default configuration file specifies the libtml directory of the document tree:

```
Doc_TemplateLibrary [file join $Config(docRoot) libtml]
```

You can also specify an alternate Tcl interpreter in which to process the templates. The default is to use the main interpreter, which is named {} according to the conventions described in Chapter 19.

```
Doc_TemplateInterp {}
```

Log Files

The server keeps standard format log files. The `Log_SetFile` command defines the base name of the log file. The default configuration file uses this command:

```
Log_SetFile /tmp/log$Config(port)_
```

By default, the server rotates the log file each night at midnight. Each day's log file is suffixed with the current date (e.g., `/tmp/log`*port*`_990218`.) The error log, however, is not rotated, and all errors are accumulated in `/tmp/log`*port*`_error`.

The log records are normally flushed every few minutes to eliminate an extra I/O operation on each HTTP transaction. You can set this period with `Log_FlushMinutes`. If minutes is 0, the log is flushed on every HTTP transaction. The default configuration file contains:

```
Log_FlushMinutes 1
```

CGI Directories

You can register a directory that contains CGI programs with the `Cgi_Directory` command. This command has the interesting effect of forcing all files in the directory to be executed as CGI scripts, so you cannot put normal HTML files there. The default configuration file contains:

```
Cgi_Directory /cgi-bin
```

This means that the `cgi-bin` directory under the document root is a CGI directory. If you supply another argument to `Cgi_Directory`, then this is a file system directory that gets mapped into the URL defined by the first argument. You can also put CGI scripts into other directories and use the `.cgi` suffix to indicate that they should be executed as CGI scripts.

The `cgi.tcl` file has some additional parameters that you can tune only by setting some elements of the `Cgi` Tcl array. See the comments in the beginning of that file for details.

Multiple Interpreters and Safe-Tcl

This chapter describes how to create more than one Tcl interpreter in your application. A child interpreter can be made safe so that it can execute untrusted scripts without compromising your application or your computer. Command aliases, hidden commands, and shared I/O channels enable communication among interpreters. Tcl command described is: `interp`.

Safe-Tcl was invented by Nathaniel Borenstein and Marshall Rose so that they could send Tcl scripts via email and have the recipient safely execute the script without worry of viruses or other attacks. Safe-Tcl works by removing dangerous commands like `exec` and `open` that would let an untrusted script damage the host computer. You can think of this restricted interpreter as a "padded cell" in which it is safe to execute untrusted scripts. To continue the analogy, if the untrusted code wants to do anything potentially unsafe, it must ask permission. This works by adding additional commands, or *aliases*, that are implemented by a different Tcl interpreter. For example, a `safeopen` command could be implemented by limiting file space to a temporary directory that is deleted when the untrusted code terminates.

The key concept of Safe-Tcl is that there are two Tcl interpreters in the application, a trusted one and an untrusted (or "safe") one. The trusted interpreter can do anything, and it is used for the main application (e.g., the Web browser or email user interface). When the main application receives a message containing an untrusted script, it evaluates that script in the context of the untrusted interpreter. The restricted nature of the untrusted interpreter means that the application is safe from attack. This model is much like user mode and kernel mode in a multiuser operating system like UNIX or Windows/NT. In these systems, applications run in user mode and trap into the kernel to access resources like files and the network. The kernel implements access controls so that users cannot read and write each other's files, or hijack network services. In Safe-Tcl the application implements access controls for untrusted scripts.

The dual interpreter model of Safe-Tcl has been generalized in Tcl 7.5 and made accessible to Tcl scripts. A Tcl script can create other interpreters, destroy them, create command aliases among them, share I/O channels among them, and evaluate scripts in them.

The `interp` Command

The `interp` command is used to create and manipulate interpreters. The interpreter being created is called a *slave*, and the interpreter that creates it is called the *master*. The master has complete control over the slave. The `interp` command is summarized in Table 19–1.

Table 19–1 The `interp` command.

`interp aliases slave`	Lists aliases that are defined in `slave`.
`interp alias slave cmd1`	Returns target command and arguments for the alias `cmd1` in `slave`.
`interp alias slave cmd1 master cmd2 arg ...`	Defines `cmd1` in `slave` that is an alias to `cmd2` in `master` with additional `args`.
`interp create ?-safe? slave`	Creates an interpreter named `slave`.
`interp delete slave`	Destroys interpreter `slave`.
`interp eval slave cmd args ...`	Evaluates `cmd` and `args` in `slave`.
`interp exists slave`	Returns 1 if `slave` is an interpreter, else 0.
`interp expose slave cmd`	Exposes hidden command `cmd` in `slave`.
`interp hide slave cmd`	Hides `cmd` from `slave`.
`interp hidden slave`	Returns the commands hidden from `slave`.
`interp invokehidden slave cmd arg ...`	Invokes hidden command `cmd` and `args` in `slave`.
`interp issafe slave`	Returns 1 if `slave` was created with `-safe` flag.
`interp marktrusted slave`	Clears the `issafe` property of `slave`.
`interp recursionlimit slave ?limit?`	Set or get the interpreter recursion limit for `slave`. (Tcl 8.4)
`interp share master file slave`	Shares the I/O descriptor named `file` in `master` with `slave`.
`interp slaves master`	Returns the list of slave interpreters of `master`.
`interp target slave cmd`	Returns the name of the interpreter that is the target of alias `cmd` in `slave`.
`interp transfer master file slave`	Transfers the I/O descriptor named `file` from `master` to `slave`.

Creating Interpreters

Here is a simple example that creates an interpreter, evaluates a couple of commands in it, and then deletes the interpreter:

Example 19–1 Creating and deleting an interpreter.

```
interp create foo
=> foo
interp eval foo {set a 5}
=> 5
set sum [interp eval foo {expr {$a + $a}}]
=> 10
interp delete foo
```

In Example 19–1 the interpreter is named foo. Two commands are evaluated in the foo interpreter:

```
set a 5
expr {$a + $a}
```

Note that curly braces are used to protect the commands from any interpretation by the main interpreter. The variable a is defined in the foo interpreter and does not conflict with variables in the main interpreter. The set of variables and procedures in each interpreter is completely independent.

The Interpreter Hierarchy

A slave interpreter can itself create interpreters, resulting in a hierarchy. The next examples illustrates this, and it shows how the grandparent of an interpreter can reference the grandchild by name. The example uses interp slaves to query the existence of child interpreters.

Example 19–2 Creating a hierarchy of interpreters.

```
interp create foo
=> foo
interp eval foo {interp create bar}
=> bar
interp create {foo bar2}
=> foo bar2
interp slaves
=> foo
interp slaves foo
=> bar bar2
interp delete bar
=> interpreter named "bar" not found
interp delete {foo bar}
```

The example creates `foo`, and then it creates two children of `foo`. The first one is created by `foo` with this command:

```
interp eval foo {interp create bar}
```

The second child is created by the main interpreter. In this case, the grand-child must be named by a two-element list to indicate that it is a child of a child. The same naming convention is used when the grandchild is deleted:

```
interp create {foo bar2}
interp delete {foo bar2}
```

The `interp slaves` operation returns the names of child (i.e., slave) inter-preters. The names are relative to their parent, so the slaves of `foo` are reported simply as `bar` and `bar2`. The name for the current interpreter is the empty list, or `{}`. This is useful in command aliases and file sharing described later. For secu-rity reasons, it is not possible to name the master interpreter from within the slave.

The Interpreter Name as a Command

After interpreter *slave* is created, a new command is available in the main interpreter, also called *slave*, that operates on the child interpreter. The follow-ing two forms are equivalent most operations:

```
slave operation args ...
interp operation slave args ...
```

For example, the following are equivalent commands:

```
foo eval {set a 5}
interp eval foo {set a 5}
```

And so are these:

```
foo issafe
interp issafe foo
```

However, the operations `delete`, `exists`, `share`, `slaves`, `target`, and `transfer` cannot be used with the per interpreter command. In particular, there is no `foo delete` operation; you must use `interp delete foo`.

If you have a deep hierarchy of interpreters, the command corresponding to the slave is defined only in the parent. For example, if a master creates `foo`, and `foo` creates `bar`, then the master must operate on `bar` with the `interp` command. There is no "`foo bar`" command defined in the master.

Use `list` with `interp eval`

The `interp eval` command treats its arguments like `eval`. If there are extra arguments, they are all concatenated together first. This can lose important structure, as described in Chapter 10. To be safe, use `list` to construct your com-mands. For example, to safely define a variable in the slave, you should do this:

```
interp eval slave [list set var $value]
```

Safe Interpreters

A child can be created either safe (i.e., untrusted) or fully functional. In the examples so far, the children have been trusted and fully functional; they have all the basic Tcl commands available to them. An interpreter is made safe by eliminating certain commands. Table 19–2 lists the commands removed from safe interpreters. As described later, these commands can be used by the master on behalf of the safe interpreter. To create a safe interpreter, use the `-safe` flag:

```
interp create -safe untrusted
```

Table 19–2 Commands hidden from safe interpreters.

cd	Changes directory.
exec	Executes another program.
exit	Terminates the process.
fconfigure	Sets modes of an I/O stream.
file	Queries file attributes.
glob	Matches on file name patterns.
load	Dynamically loads object code.
open	Opens files and process pipelines.
pwd	Determines the current directory.
socket	Opens network sockets.
source	Loads scripts.

A safe interpreter does not have commands to manipulate the file system and other programs (e.g., cd, open, and `exec`). This ensures that untrusted scripts cannot harm the host computer. The `socket` command is removed so that untrusted scripts cannot access the network. The `exit`, `source`, and `load` commands are removed so that an untrusted script cannot harm the hosting application. Note that commands like `puts` and `gets` are *not* removed. A safe interpreter can still do I/O, but it cannot create an I/O channel. We will show how to pass an I/O channel to a child interpreter on page 299.

The initial state of a safe interpreter is very safe, but it is too limited. The only thing a safe interpreter can do is compute a string and return that value to the parent. By creating command aliases, a master can give a safe interpreter controlled access to resources. A *security policy* implements a set of command aliases that add controlled capabilities to a safe interpreter. We will show, for example, how to provide limited network and file system access to untrusted slaves. Tcl provides a framework to manage several security policies, which is described in Chapter 20.

Command Aliases

A *command alias* is a command in one interpreter that is implemented by a command in another interpreter. The master interpreter installs command aliases in its slaves. The command to create an alias has the following general form:

```
interp alias slave cmd1 target cmd2 ?arg arg ...?
```

This creates `cmd1` in `slave` that is an alias for `cmd2` in `target`. When `cmd1` is invoked in `slave`, `cmd2` is invoked in `target`. The alias mechanism is transparent to the slave. Whatever `cmd2` returns, the slave sees as the return value of `cmd1`. If `cmd2` raises an error, the error is propagated to the slave.

Name the current interpreter with `{}`.

If `target` is the current interpreter, name it with `{}`. The empty list is the way to name yourself as the interpreter. This is the most common case, although `target` can be a different slave. The `slave` and `target` can even be the same interpreter.

The arguments to `cmd1` are passed to `cmd2`, after any additional arguments to `cmd2` that were specified when the alias was created. These hidden arguments provide a safe way to pass extra arguments to an alias. For example, it is quite common to pass the name of the slave to the alias. In Example 19–3, `exit` in the interpreter `foo` is an alias that is implemented in the current interpreter (i.e., `{}`). When the slave executes `exit`, the master executes:

```
interp delete foo
```

Example 19–3 A command alias for `exit`.

```
interp create foo
interp alias foo exit {} interp delete foo
interp eval foo exit
# Child foo is gone.
```

Alias Introspection

You can query what aliases are defined for a child interpreter. The `interp aliases` command lists the aliases; the `interp alias` command can also return the value of an alias, and the `interp target` command tells you what interpreter implements an alias. These are illustrated in the following examples:

Example 19–4 Querying aliases.

```
proc Interp_ListAliases {name out} {
    puts $out "Aliases for $name"
    foreach alias [interp aliases $name] {
        puts $out [format "%-20s => (%s) %s" $alias \
                [interp target $name $alias] \
                [interp alias $name $alias]]
    }
}
```

Example 19–4 generates output in a human readable format. Example 19–5 generates the aliases as Tcl commands that can be used to re-create them later:

Example 19–5 Dumping aliases as Tcl commands.

```
proc Interp_DumpAliases {name out} {
    puts $out "# Aliases for $name"
    foreach alias [interp aliases $name] {
        puts $out [format "interp alias %s %s %s %s" \
            $name $alias [list [interp target $name $alias]] \
            [interp alias $name $alias]]
    }
}
```

Hidden Commands

The commands listed in Table 19–2 are *hidden* instead of being completely removed. A hidden command can be invoked in a slave by its master. For example, a master can load Tcl scripts into a slave by using its hidden `source` command:

```
interp create -safe slave
interp invokehidden slave source filename
```

Without hidden commands, the master has to do a bit more work to achieve the same thing. It must open and read the file and `eval` the contents of the file in the slave. File operations are described in Chapter 9.

```
interp create -safe slave
set in [open filename]
interp eval slave [read $in]
close $in
```

Hidden commands were added in Tcl 7.7 in order to better support the Tcl/Tk browser plug-in described in Chapter 20. In some cases, hidden commands are strictly necessary; it is not possible to simulate them any other way. The best examples are in the context of Safe-Tk, where the master creates widgets or does potentially dangerous things on behalf of the slave. These will be discussed in more detail later.

A master can hide and expose commands using the `interp hide` and `interp expose` operations, respectively. You can even hide Tcl procedures. However, the commands inside the procedure run with the same privilege as that of the slave. For example, if you are really paranoid, you might not want an untrusted interpreter to read the clock or get timing information. You can hide the `clock` and `time` commands:

```
interp create -safe slave
interp hide slave clock
interp hide slave time
```

You can remove commands from the slave entirely like this:

```
interp eval slave [list rename clock {}]
interp eval slave [list rename time {}]
```

Substitutions

You must be aware of Tcl parsing and substitutions when commands are invoked in other interpreters. There are three cases corresponding to `interp eval`, `interp invokehidden`, and command aliases.

With `interp eval` the command is subject to a complete round of parsing and substitutions in the target interpreter. This occurs after the parsing and substitutions for the `interp eval` command itself. In addition, if you pass several arguments to `interp eval`, those are concatenated before evaluation. This is similar to the way the `eval` command works as described in Chapter 19. The most reliable way to use `interp eval` is to construct a list to ensure the command is well structured:

```
interp eval slave [list cmd arg1 arg2]
```

With hidden commands, the command and arguments are taken directly from the arguments to `interp invokehidden`, and there are no substitutions done in the target interpreter. This means that the master has complete control over the command structure, and nothing funny can happen in the other interpreter. For this reason you should not create a list. If you do that, the whole list will be interpreted as the command name! Instead, just pass separate arguments to `interp invokehidden` and they are passed straight through to the target:

```
interp invokehidden slave command arg1 arg2
```

Never `eval` *alias arguments.*

With aliases, all the parsing and substitutions occur in the slave before the alias is invoked in the master. The alias implementation should never `eval` or `subst` any values it gets from the slave to avoid executing arbitrary code.

For example, suppose there is an alias to open files. The alias does some checking and then invokes the hidden `open` command. An untrusted script might pass `[exit]` as the name of the file to open in order to create mischief. The untrusted code is hoping that the master will accidentally `eval` the filename and cause the application to exit. This attack has nothing to do with opening files; it just hopes for a poor alias implementation. Example 19–6 shows an alias that is not subject to this attack:

Example 19–6 Substitutions and hidden commands.

```
interp alias slave open {} safeopen slave
proc safeopen {slave filename {mode r}} {
    # do some checks, then...
    interp invokehidden $slave open $filename $mode
}
interp eval slave {open \[exit\]}
```

The command in the slave starts out as:

```
open \[exit\]
```

The master has to quote the brackets in its `interp eval` command or else the slave will try to invoke `exit` because of command substitution. Presumably `exit` isn't defined, or it is defined to terminate the slave. Once this quoting is done, the value of `filename` is `[exit]` and it is not subject to substitutions. It is safe to use `$filename` in the `interp invokehidden` command because it is only substituted once, in the master. The hidden `open` command also gets `[exit]` as its filename argument, which is never evaluated as a Tcl command.

I/O from Safe Interpreters

A safe child interpreter cannot open files or network sockets directly. An alias can create an I/O channel (i.e., open a file or socket) and give the child access to it. The parent can share the I/O channel with the child, or it can transfer the I/O channel to the child. If the channel is shared, both the parent and the child can use it. If the channel is transferred, the parent no longer has access to the channel. In general, transferring an I/O channel is simpler, but sharing an I/O channel gives the parent more control over an unsafe child. The differences are illustrated in Example 19–7 and Example 19–9.

There are three properties of I/O channels that are important to consider when choosing between sharing and transferring: the name, the seek offset, and the reference count.

- The name of the I/O channel (e.g., `file4`) is the same in all interpreters. If a parent transfers a channel to a child, it can close the channel by evaluating a `close` command in the child. Although names are shared, an interpreter cannot attempt I/O on a channel to which it has not been given access.
- The seek offset of the I/O channel is shared by all interpreters that share the I/O channel. An I/O operation on the channel updates the seek offset for all interpreters that share the channel. This means that if two interpreters share an I/O channel, their output will be cleanly interleaved in the channel. If they both read from the I/O channel, they will get different data. Seek offsets are explained in more detail on page 121.
- A channel has a reference count of all interpreters that share the I/O channel. The channel remains open until all references are closed. When a parent transfers an I/O channel, the reference count stays the same. When a parent shares an I/O channel, the reference count increments by one. When an interpreter closes a channel with `close`, the reference count is decremented by one. When an interpreter is deleted, all of its references to I/O channels are removed.

The syntax of commands to share or transfer an I/O channel is:

```
interp share interp1 chanName interp2
interp transfer interp1 chanName interp2
```

II. Advanced Tcl

In these commands, *chanName* exists in *interp1* and is being shared or transferred to *interp2*. As with command aliases, if *interp1* is the current interpreter, name it with {}.

The following example creates a temporary file for an unsafe interpreter. The file is opened for reading and writing, and the slave can use it to store data temporarily.

Example 19–7 Opening a file for an unsafe interpreter.

```
proc TempfileAlias {slave} {
    set i 0
    while {[file exists Temp$slave$i]} {
        incr i
    }
    set out [open Temp$slave$i w+]
    interp transfer {} $out $slave
    return $out
}
proc TempfileExitAlias {slave} {
    foreach file [glob -nocomplain Temp$slave*] {
        file delete -force $file
    }
    interp delete $slave
}
interp create -safe foo
interp alias foo Tempfile {} TempfileAlias foo
interp alias foo exit {} TempfileExitAlias foo
```

The `TempfileAlias` procedure is invoked in the parent when the child interpreter invokes `Tempfile`. `TempfileAlias` returns the name of the open channel, which becomes the return value from `Tempfile`. `TempfileAlias` uses `interp transfer` to pass the I/O channel to the child so that the child has permission to access the I/O channel. In this example, it would also work to invoke the hidden `open` command to create the I/O channel directly in the slave.

Example 19–7 is not fully safe because the unsafe interpreter can still overflow the disk or create a million files. Because the parent has transferred the I/O channel to the child, it cannot easily monitor the I/O activity by the child. Example 19–9 addresses these issues.

The Safe Base

An safe interpreter created with `interp create -safe` has no script library environment and no way to source scripts. Tcl provides a *safe base* that extends a raw safe interpreter with the ability to source scripts and packages which are described in Chapter 12. The safe base also defines an `exit` alias that terminates the slave like the one in Example 19–7. The safe base is implemented as Tcl scripts that are part of the standard Tcl script library. Create an interpreter that uses the safe base with `safe::interpCreate`:

```
safe::interpCreate foo
```

The safe base has `source` and `load` aliases that only access directories on an *access path* defined by the master interpreter. The master has complete control over what files can be loaded into a slave. In general, it would be all right to source any Tcl program into an untrusted interpreter. However, untrusted scripts might learn things from the error messages they get by sourcing arbitrary files. The safe base also has versions of the `package` and `unknown` commands that support the library facility. Table 19–3 lists the Tcl procedures in the safe base:

Table 19–3 The safe base master interface.

`safe::interpCreate ?slave?` `?options?`	Creates a safe interpreter and initialize the security policy mechanism.
`safe::interpInit slave` `?options?`	Initializes a safe interpreter so it can use security policies.
`safe::interpConfigure slave` `?options?`	Options are `-accessPath pathlist`, `-nostatics`, `-deleteHook script`, `-nestedLoadOk`.
`safe::interpDelete slave`	Deletes a safe interpreter.
`safe::interpAddToAccessPath` `slave directory`	Adds a directory to the slave's access path.
`safe::interpFindInAccessPath`	Maps from a directory to the token visible in the slave for that directory.
`safe::setLogCmd ?cmd arg ... ?`	Sets or queries the logging command used by the safe base.

Table 19–4 lists the aliases defined in a safe interpreter by the safe base.

Table 19–4 The safe base slave aliases.

`source`	Loads scripts from directories in the access path.
`load`	Loads binary extensions from the slaves access path.
`file`	Only the `dirname`, `join`, `extension`, `root`, `tail`, `pathname`, and `split` operations are allowed.
`exit`	Destroys the slave interpreter.

Security Policies

A *security policy* defines what a safe interpreter can do. Designing security policies that are secure is difficult. If you design your own, make sure to have your colleagues review the code. Give out prizes to folks who can break your policy. Good policy implementations are proven with lots of review and trial attacks.

The good news is that Safe-Tcl security policies can be implemented in relatively small amounts of Tcl code. This makes them easier to analyze and get correct. Here are a number of rules of thumb:

- Small policies are better than big, complex policies. If you do a lot of complex processing to allow or disallow access to resources, chances are there are holes in your policy. Keep it simple.
- Never `eval` arguments to aliases. If an alias accepts arguments that are passed by the slave, you must avoid being tricked into executing arbitrary Tcl code. The primary way to avoid this is never to `eval` arguments that are passed into an alias. Watch your expressions, too. The `expr` command does an extra round of substitutions, so brace all your expressions so that an attacker cannot pass `[exit]` where you expect a number!
- Security policies do not compose. Each time you add a new alias to a security policy, it changes the nature of the policy. Even if *alias1* and *alias2* are safe in isolation, there is no guarantee that they cannot be used together to mount an attack. Each addition to a security policy requires careful review.

Limited Socket Access

The `Safesock` security policy provides limited socket access. The policy is designed around a simple table of allowed hosts and ports. An untrusted interpreter can connect only to addresses listed in the table. For example, I would never let untrusted code connect to the *sendmail, ftp,* or *telnet* ports on my hosts. There are just too many attacks possible on these ports. On the other hand, I might want to let untrusted code fetch a URL from certain hosts, or connect to a database server for an intranet application. The goal of this policy is to have a simple way to specify exactly what hosts and ports a slave can access. Example 19–8 shows a simplified version of the `Safesock` security policy that is distributed with Tcl 8.0.

Example 19–8 The `Safesock` security policy.

```
# The index is a host name, and the
# value is a list of port specifications, which can be
# an exact port number
# a lower bound on port number: N-
# a range of port numbers, inclusive: N-M
array set safesock {
    sage.eng      3000-4000
    www.sun.com   80
    webcache.eng  {80 8080}
    bisque.eng    {80 1025-}
}
proc Safesock_PolicyInit {slave} {
    interp alias $slave socket {} SafesockAlias $slave
}
```

```
proc SafesockAlias {slave host port} {
    global safesock
    if ![info exists safesock($host)] {
        error "unknown host: $host"
    }

    foreach portspec $safesock($host) {
        set low [set high ""]
        if {[regexp {^([0-9]+)-([0-9]*)$} $portspec x low high]} {
            if {($low <= $port && $high == "") ||
                    ($low <= $port && $high >= $port)} {
                set good $port
                break
            }
        } elseif {$port == $portspec} {
            set good $port
        }
    }

    if [info exists good] {
        set sock [interp invokehidden $slave socket $host $good]
        interp invokehidden $slave fconfigure $sock \
            -blocking 0
        return $sock
    }
    error "bad port: $port"
}
```

The policy is initialized with `Safesock_PolicyInit`. The name of this procedure follows a naming convention used by the safe base. In this case, a single alias is installed. The alias gives the slave a `socket` command that is implemented by `SafesockAlias` in the master.

The alias checks for a port that matches one of the port specifications for the host. If a match is found, then the `invokehidden` operation is used to invoke two commands in the slave. The `socket` command creates the network connection, and the `fconfigure` command puts the socket into nonblocking mode so that `read` and `gets` by the slave do not block the application:

```
set sock [interp invokehidden $slave socket $host $good]
interp invokehidden $slave fconfigure $sock -blocking 0
```

The `socket` alias in the slave does not conflict with the hidden `socket` command. There are two distinct sets of commands, hidden and exposed. It is quite common for the alias implementation to invoke the hidden command after various permission checks are made.

The Tcl Web browser plug-in ships with a slightly improved version of the `Safesock` policy. It adds an alias for `fconfigure` so that the `http` package can set end of line translations and buffering modes. The `fconfigure` alias does not let you change the blocking behavior of the socket. The policy has also been extended to classify hosts into trusted and untrusted hosts based on their address. A different table of allowed ports is used for the two classes of hosts. The classification is done with two tables: One table lists patterns that match trusted hosts, and the other table lists hosts that should not be trusted even though they match the first table. The improved version also lets a downloaded script connect to the Web server that it came from. The Web browser plug-in is described in Chapter 20.

Limited Temporary Files

Example 19–9 improves on Example 19–7 by limiting the number of temporary files and the size of the files. It is written to work with the safe base, so it has a `Tempfile_PolicyInit` that takes the name of the slave as an argument. `TempfileOpenAlias` lets the child specify a file by name, yet it limits the files to a single directory.

The example demonstrates a shared I/O channel that gives the master control over output. `TempfilePutsAlias` restricts the amount of data that can be written to a file. By sharing the I/O channel for the temporary file, the slave can use commands like `gets`, `eof`, and `close`, while the master does the `puts`. The need for shared I/O channels is somewhat reduced by hidden commands, which were added to Safe-Tcl more recently than shared I/O channels. For example, the `puts` alias can either write to a shared channel after checking the file size, or it can invoke the hidden `puts` in the slave. This alternative is shown in Example 19–10.

Example 19–9 The `Tempfile` security policy.

```
# Policy parameters:
#   directory is the location for the files
#   maxfile is the number of files allowed in the directory
#   maxsize is the max size for any single file.

array set tempfile {
    maxfile         4
    maxsize         65536
}
# tempfile(directory) is computed dynamically based on
# the source of the script

proc Tempfile_PolicyInit {slave} {
    global tempfile
    interp alias $slave open {} \
        TempfileOpenAlias $slave $tempfile(directory) \
            $tempfile(maxfile)
    interp alias $slave puts {} TempfilePutsAlias $slave \
        $tempfile(maxsize)
    interp alias $slave exit {} TempfileExitAlias $slave
}
proc TempfileOpenAlias {slave dir maxfile name {m r} {p 0777}} {
    global tempfile
    # remove sneaky characters
    regsub -all {|/:} [file tail $name] {} real
    set real [file join $dir $real]
```

```
        # Limit the number of files
        set files [glob -nocomplain [file join $dir *]]
        set N [llength $files]
        if { ($N >= $maxfile) && (\
                [lsearch -exact $files $real] < 0)} {
            error "permission denied"
        }
        if [catch {open $real $m $p} out] {
            return -code error "$name: permission denied"
        }
        lappend tempfile(channels,$slave) $out
        interp share {} $out $slave
        return $out
    }
proc TempfileExitAlias {slave} {
    global tempfile
    interp delete $slave
    if [info exists tempfile(channels,$slave)] {
        foreach out $tempfile(channels,$slave) {
            catch {close $out}
        }
        unset tempfile(channels,$slave)
    }
}
# See also the puts alias in Example 24-4 on page 389
proc TempfilePutsAlias {slave max chan args} {
    # max is the file size limit, in bytes
    # chan is the I/O channel
    # args is either a single string argument,
    # or the -nonewline flag plus the string.

    if {[llength $args] > 2} {
        error "invalid arguments"
    }
    if {[llength $args] == 2} {
        if {![string match -n* [lindex $argv 0]]} {
            error "invalid arguments"
        }
        set string [lindex $args 1]
    } else {
        set string [lindex $args 0]\n
    }
    set size [expr [tell $chan] + [string length $string]]
    if {$size > $max} {
        error "File size exceeded"
    } else {
        puts -nonewline $chan $string
    }
}
```

The `TempfileAlias` procedure is generalized in Example 19–9 to have parameters that specify the directory, name, and a limit to the number of files allowed. The `directory` and `maxfile` limit are part of the alias definition. Their existence is transparent to the slave. The slave specifies only the name and

II. Advanced Tcl

access mode (i.e., for reading or writing.) The `Tempfile` policy can be used by different slave interpreters with different parameters.

The master is careful to restrict the files to the specified directory. It uses `file tail` to strip off any leading pathname components that the slave might specify. The `tempfile(directory)` definition is not shown in the example. The application must choose a directory when it creates the safe interpreter. The `Browser` security policy described on page 317 chooses a directory based on the name of the URL containing the untrusted script.

The `TempfilePutsAlias` procedure implements a limited form of `puts`. It checks the size of the file with `tell` and measures the output string to see if the total exceeds the limit. The limit comes from a parameter defined when the alias is created. The file cannot grow past the limit, at least not by any action of the child interpreter. The `args` parameter is used to allow an optional `-nonewline` flag to `puts`. The value of `args` is checked explicitly instead of using the `eval` trick described in Example 10–3 on page 136. Never `eval` arguments to aliases or else a slave can attack you with arguments that contain embedded Tcl commands.

The master and slave share the I/O channel. The name of the I/O channel is recorded in `tempfile`, and `TempfileExitAlias` uses this information to close the channel when the child interpreter is deleted. This is necessary because both parent and child have a reference to the channel when it is shared. The child's reference is automatically removed when the interpreter is deleted, but the parent must close its own reference.

The shared I/O channel lets the master use `puts` and `tell`. It is also possible to implement this policy by using hidden `puts` and `tell` commands. The reason `tell` must be hidden is to prevent the slave from implementing its own version of `tell` that lies about the seek offset value. One advantage of using hidden commands is that there is no need to clean up the tempfile state about open channels. You can also layer the puts alias on top of any existing puts implementation. For example, a script may define `puts` to be a procedure that inserts data into a text widget. Example 19–10 shows the difference when using hidden commands.

Example 19–10 Restricted `puts` using hidden commands.

```
proc Tempfile_PolicyInit {slave} {
    global tempfile
    interp alias $slave open {} \
        TempfileOpenAlias $slave $tempfile(directory) \
            $tempfile(maxfile)
    interp hide $slave tell
    interp alias $slave tell {} TempfileTellAlias $slave
    interp hide $slave puts
    interp alias $slave puts {} TempfilePutsAlias $slave \
        $tempfile(maxsize)
    # no special exit alias required
}
```

```
proc TempfileOpenAlias {slave dir maxfile name {m r} {p 0777}} {
    # remove sneaky characters
    regsub -all {|/:} [file tail $name] {} real
    set real [file join $dir $real]
    # Limit the number of files
    set files [glob -nocomplain [file join $dir *]]
    set N [llength $files]
    if {($N >= $maxfile) && (\
            [lsearch -exact $files $real] < 0)} {
        error "permission denied"
    }
    if [catch {interp invokehidden $slave \
            open $real $m $p} out] {
        return -code error "$name: permission denied"
    }
    return $out
}
proc TempfileTellAlias {slave chan} {
    interp invokehidden $slave tell $chan
}
proc TempfilePutsAlias {slave max chan args} {
    if {[llength $args] > 2} {
        error "invalid arguments"
    }
    if {[llength $args] == 2} {
        if {![string match -n* [lindex $args 0]]} {
            error "invalid arguments"
        }
        set string [lindex $args 1]
    } else {
        set string [lindex $args 0]\n
    }
    set size [interp invokehidden $slave tell $chan]
    incr size [string length $string]
    if {$size > $max} {
        error "File size exceeded"
    } else {
        interp invokehidden $slave \
            puts -nonewline $chan $string
    }
}
```

Safe after Command

The after command is unsafe because it can block the application for an arbitrary amount of time. This happens if you only specify a time but do not specify a command. In this case, Tcl just waits for the time period and processes no events. This will stop all interpreters, not just the one doing the after command. This is a kind of *resource attack*. It doesn't leak information or damage anything, but it disrupts the main application.

Example 19–11 defines an alias that implements after on behalf of safe interpreters. The basic idea is to carefully check the arguments, and then do the

after in the parent interpreter. As an additional feature, the number of outstanding after events is limited. The master keeps a record of each after event
scheduled. Two IDs are associated with each event: one chosen by the master
(i.e., myid), and the other chosen by the after command (i.e., id). The master
keeps a map from myid to id. The map serves two purposes: The number of map
entries counts the number of outstanding events. The map also hides the real
after ID from the slave, which prevents a slave from attempting mischief by
specifying invalid after IDs to after cancel. The SafeAfterCallback is the procedure scheduled. It maintains state and then invokes the original callback in
the slave.

Example 19–11 A safe after command.

```
# SafeAfter_PolicyInit creates a child with
# a safe after command

proc SafeAfter_PolicyInit {slave max} {
    # max limits the number of outstanding after events
    global after
    interp alias $slave after {} SafeAfterAlias $slave $max
    interp alias $slave exit {} SafeAfterExitAlias $slave
    # This is used to generate after IDs for the slave.
    set after(id,$slave) 0
}

# SafeAfterAlias is an alias for after. It disallows after
# with only a time argument and no command.

proc SafeAfterAlias {slave max args} {
    global after
    set argc [llength $args]
    if {$argc == 0} {
        error "Usage: after option args"
    }
    switch -- [lindex $args 0] {
        cancel {
            # A naive implementation would just
            # eval after cancel $args
            # but something dangerous could be hiding in args.
            set myid [lindex $args 1]
            if {[info exists after(id,$slave,$myid)]} {
                set id $after(id,$slave,$myid)
                unset after(id,$slave,$myid)
                after cancel $id
            }
            return ""
        }
        default {
            if {$argc == 1} {
                error "Usage: after time command args..."
            }
            if {[llength [array names after id,$slave,*]]\
```

```
                        >= $max} {
               error "Too many after events"
            }
            # Maintain concat semantics
            set command [concat [lrange $args 1 end]]
            # Compute our own id to pass the callback.
            set myid after#[incr after(id,$slave)]
            set id [after [lindex $args 0] \
                [list SafeAfterCallback $slave $myid $command]]
            set after(id,$slave,$myid) $id
            return $myid
        }
    }
}

# SafeAfterCallback is the after callback in the master.
# It evaluates its command in the safe interpreter.

proc SafeAfterCallback {slave myid cmd} {
    global after
    unset after(id,$slave,$myid)
    if [catch {
        interp eval $slave $cmd
    } err] {
        catch {interp eval $slave bgerror $error}
    }
}

# SafeAfterExitAlias is an alias for exit that does cleanup.

proc SafeAfterExitAlias {slave} {
    global after
    foreach id [array names after id,$slave,*] {
        after cancel $after($id)
        unset after($id)
    }
    interp delete $slave
}
```

Safe-Tk and
the Browser Plugin

This chapter describes Safe-Tk that lets untrusted scripts display and manipulate graphical user interfaces. The main application of Safe-Tk is the Tcl/Tk plugin for Web browsers like Netscape Navigator and Internet Explorer.

Safe-Tk supports network applets that display user interfaces. The main vehicle for Safe-Tk is a plugin for Netscape Navigator, Mozilla and Internet Explorer. The plugin supports Tcl applets, or *Tclets*, that are downloaded from the Web server and execute inside a window in a Web browser. For the most part, Tcl/Tk applications can run unchanged in the plugin. However, security policies place some restrictions on Tclets. The plugin supports multiple security policies, so Tclets can do a variety of interesting things in a safe manner.

You can configure the plugin to use an existing *wish* application to host the Tcl applets if you require a newer version of Tk, or the plugin can load the Tcl/Tk shared libraries and everything runs in the browser process. You can use a custom *wish* that has extensions built in or dynamically loaded. This gives intranet applications of the plugin the ability to access databases and other services that are not provided by the Tcl/Tk core. With the security policy mechanism you can still provide mediated access to these resources. This chapter describes how to set up the plugin.

Jeff Hobbs recently updated the plugin to use Tcl/Tk 8.4. Compiled versions of the plugin are available as part of the *Tcl Dev Kit* from ActiveState. The source code of the plugin is freely available. You can recompile the plugin against newer versions of Tcl/Tk, or build custom plugins that have your own Tcl extensions built in. You can find its sources at:

```
http://tclplugin.sourceforge.net/
```

Tk in Child Interpreters

A child interpreter starts out with just the core Tcl commands. It does not include Tk or any other extensions that might be available to the parent interpreter. This is true whether or not the child interpreter is declared safe. You add extensions to child interpreters by using a form of the `load` command that specifies an interpreter:

```
load {} Tk child
```

Normally, `load` takes the name of the library file that contains the extension. In this case, the Tk package is a *static package* that is already linked into the program (e.g., *wish* or the plugin), so the file name is the empty string. The `load` command calls the Tk initialization procedure to register all the Tcl commands provided by Tk.

Embedding Tk Windows

By default, a slave interpreter that loads Tk gets a new top-level window. *Wish* supports a `-use` command line option that directs Tk to use an existing window as dot. You can use this to embed an application within another. For example, the following commands run a copy of *Wish* that uses the `.embed` toplevel as its main window:

```
toplevel .embed
exec wish -use [winfo id .embed] somescript.tcl &
```

More often, embedding is used with child interpreters. If the interpreter is *not* safe, you can set the `argv` and `argc` variables in the slave before loading Tk:

```
interp create trustedTk
interp eval trustedTk \
    [list set argv [list -use [winfo id .embed]]]
interp eval trustedTk [list set argc 2]
load {} Tk trustedTk
```

If the child interpreter is safe, then you cannot set `argv` and `argc` directly. The easiest way to pass `-use` to a safe interpreter is with the `safe::loadTk` command:

```
safe::interpCreate safeTk
safe::loadTk safeTk -use [winfo id .embed]
```

When Tk is loaded into a safe interpreter, it calls back into the master interpreter and evaluates the `safe::TkInit` procedure. The job of this procedure is to return the appropriate `argv` value for the slave. The `safe::loadTk` procedure stores its additional arguments in the `safe::tkInit` variable, and this value is retrieved by the `safe::TkInit` procedure and returned to the slave. This protocol is used so that a safe interpreter cannot attempt to hijack the windows of its master by constructing its own `argv` variable!

Safe-Tk Restrictions

When Tk is loaded into a safe interpreter, it hides several Tk commands. Primarily these are hidden to prevent *denial of service* attacks against the main process. For example, if a child interpreter did a global `grab` and never released it, all input would be forever directed to the child. Table 20–1 lists the Tk commands hidden by default from a safe interpreter. The Tcl commands that are hidden in safe interpreters are listed on page 295.

Table 20–1 Tk commands omitted from safe interpreters.

`bell`	Rings the terminal bell.
`clipboard`	Accesses the CLIPBOARD selection.
`grab`	Directs input to a specified widget.
`menu`	Creates and manipulates menus, because menus need `grab`.
`selection`	Manipulates the selection.
`send`	Executes a command in another Tk application.
`tk appname`	Sets the application name.
`tk_chooseColor`	Color choice dialog.
`tk_chooseDirectory`	Directory chooser dialog.
`tk_getOpenFile`	File open dialog.
`tk_getSaveFile`	File save dialog.
`tk_messageBox`	Simple dialog boxes.
`toplevel`	Creates a detached window.
`wm`	Controls the window manager.

If you find these restrictions limiting, you can restore commands to safe interpreters with the `interp expose` command. For example, to get menus and toplevels working, you could do:

```
interp create -safe safeTk
foreach cmd {grab menu menubutton toplevel wm} {
    interp expose safeTk $cmd
}
```

Instead of exposing the command directly, you can also construct aliases that provide a subset of the features. For example, you could disable the `-global` option to grab. Aliases are described in detail in Chapter 19.

The Browser plugin defines a more elaborate configuration system to control what commands are available to slave interpreters. You can have lots of control, but you need to distribute the *security policies* that define what Tclets can do in the plugin. Configuring security policies for the plugin is described later.

II. Advanced Tcl

The Browser Plugin

The HTML EMBED tag is used to put various objects into a Web page, including a Tcl program. Example 20–1 shows the EMBED tag used to insert a Tclet:

Example 20–1 Using EMBED to insert a Tclet.

```
<EMBED
    TYPE="application/x-tcl"
    PLUGINSPAGE="http://www.tcl.tk/plugin/"
    WIDTH="400"
    HEIGHT="300"
    SRC="eval.tcl"
</EMBED>
```

The width and height are interpreted by the plugin as the size of the embedded window. The src specifies the URL of the program. These parameter names (e.g., width) are case sensitive and should be lowercase. In the above example, eval.tcl is a relative URL, so it should be in the same directory as the HTML file that has the EMBED tag. The window size is fixed in the browser, which is different from normal toplevels in Tk. The plugin turns off geometry propagation on your main window so that your Tclet stays the size allocated.

There are also "full window" Tclets that do not use an EMBED tag at all. Instead, you just specify the .tcl file directly in the URL. In this case, the plugin occupies the whole browser window and will resize as you resize the browser window.

The embed_args and plugin Variables

The parameters in the EMBED tag are available to the Tcl program in the embed_args variable, which is an array with the parameter names as the index values. For example, the string for a ticker-tape Tclet can be passed in the EMBED tag as the string parameter, and the Tclet will use $embed_args(string) as the value to display:

```
<EMBED src=ticker.tcl width=400 height=50 string="Hello World">
```

Note that HTML tag parameters are case sensitive. Your Tclet may want to map all the parameter names to lowercase for convenience:

```
foreach {name value} [array get embed_args] {
    set embed_args([string tolower $name]) $value
}
```

The plugin array has version, patchLevel, and release elements that identify the version and release date of the plugin implementation.

Example Plugins

The plugin home page is a great place to find Tclet examples. There are sev-

eral plugins done by the Tcl/Tk team at Sunlabs, plus links to a wide variety of
Tclets done on the Net.

> `http://www.tcl.tk/plugin/`

My first plugin was calculator for the effective wheel diameter of multigear
bicycles. Brian Lewis, who built the Tcl 8.0 byte-code compiler, explained to me
the concept and how important this information is to bicycle enthusiasts. The
Tclet that displays the gear combinations on a Tk canvas and lets you change the
number of gears and their size. You can find the result at:

> `http://www.beedub.com/plugin/bike.html`

Setting Up the plugin

There are plugin versions for UNIX, Windows, and Macintosh. The installation details vary somewhat between platforms and between releases of the plugin. The following components make up the plugin installation:

- The plugin shared libraries (i.e., DLLs). The Web browser dynamically loads
  the plugin implementation when it needs to execute a Tclet embedded in a
  Web page. There is a standard directory that the browser scans for the
  libraries that implement plugins.
- The Tcl/Tk script libraries. The plugin needs the standard script libraries
  that come with Tcl and Tk, plus it has its own scripts that complete its
  implementation. Each platform has a plugin script directory with these
  subdirectories: `tcl`, `tk`, `plugin`, `config`, `safetcl`, and `utils`. The plugin
  implementation is in the `plugin` directory.
- The security policies. These are kept in a `safetcl` directory that is a peer of
  the Tcl script library.
- The trust configuration. This defines what Tclets can use which security
  policies. This is in a `config` directory that is a peer of the Tcl script library.
- Local hooks. Local customization is supported by two hooks, `siteInit` and
  `siteSafeInit`. The `siteInit` procedure is called from the plugin when it
  first loads, and `siteSafeInit` is called when each applet is initialized. It is
  called with the name of the slave interpreter and the list of arguments from
  the `<EMBED>` tag. You can provide these as scripts that get loaded from the
  `auto_path` of the master interpreter. Chapter 12 describes how to manage
  script libraries found in the `auto_path`. The plugin also sources a personal
  start up script in which you can define `siteInit` and `siteSafeInit`. This
  script is `~/.pluginrc` on UNIX and `plugin/tclplugin.rc` on Windows and
  Macintosh.

Security Policies and Browser Plugin

Tclets run in a safe interpreter that is set up with the *safe base* facilities
described on page 300. This limits a Tclet to a display-only application. To do
something more interesting, you must grant the Tclet more privilege. The extra

functions are bundled together into a *security policy*, which is implemented as a set of command aliases. Unlike a Java applet, a Tclet can choose from different security policies. A few standard security policies are distributed with the plugin, and these are described below. You can also create custom security policies to support intranet applications. You can even choose to grant certain Tclets the full power of Tcl/Tk. The `policy` command is used to request a security policy:

> `policy` *name*

The policies that are part of the standard plugin distribution are described below. The `home`, `inside`, and `outside` policies all provide limited network access. They differ in what set of hosts are accessible. The default trust configuration lets any Tclet request the `home`, `inside`, or `outside` policy.

- `home`. This provides a `socket` and `fconfigure` commands that are limited to connecting to the host from which the Tclet was downloaded. You can specify an empty string for the host argument to `socket` to connect back to the home host. This policy also supports `open` and `file delete` that are similar to the `Tempfile` policy shown in Example 19–9 on page 304. This provides limited local storage that is inside a directory that is, by default, private to the Tclet. Files in the private directory persist after the Tclet exits, so it can maintain long term state. Tclets from the same server can share the directory by putting the same `prefix=`*partialurl* argument in their `EMBED` tag. The *partialurl* must be a prefix of the Tclet's URL. Finally, the `home` policy automatically provides a `browser` package that is described later.

- `inside`. This is just like the `home` policy, except that the site administrator controls a table of hosts and ports to which untrusted slaves can connect with `socket`. A similar set of tables control what URLs can be accessed with the `browser` package. This is similar to the `Safesock` policy shown in Example 19–8 on page 302. The set of hosts is supposed to be inside the firewall. The local file storage used by this policy is distinct from that used by the `home` and `outside` policies. This is true even if Tclets try to share by using the `prefix=`*partialurl* parameter.

- `outside`. This is just like the `home` and `inside` policies, except that the set of hosts is configured to be outside the firewall. The local file storage used by this policy is distinct from that used by the `home` and `inside` policies.

- `trusted`. This policy restores all features of Tcl and Tk. This policy lets you launch all your Tcl and Tk applications from the Web browser. The default trust map settings do not allow this for any Tclet. The trust map configuration is described later.

- `javascript`. This policy provides a superset of the `browser` package that lets you invoke arbitrary Javascript and to write HTML directly to frames. This does not have the limited socket or temporary file access that the `home`, `inside`, and `outside` policies have. However, the `javascript` policy places no restrictions on the URLs you can fetch, plus it lets Tclets execute Javascript, which may have its own security risks. The default trust map settings do not allow this for any Tclet.

The Browser Package

The `browser` package is bundled with several of the security policies. It makes many features of the Web browser accessible to Tclets. They can fetch URLs and display HTML in frames. However, the `browser` package has some risks associated with it. HTTP requests can be used to transmit information, so a Tclet using the policy could leak sensitive information if it can fetch a URL outside the firewall. To avoid information leakage, the `inside`, `outside`, and `home` policies restrict the URL that can be fetched with `browser::getURL`. Table 20–2 lists the aliases defined by the `browser` package.

Table 20–2 Aliases defined by the `browser` package.

`browser::status` *string*	Displays *string* in the browser status window.
`browser::getURL` *url* *?timeout? ?newcallback? ?writecallback? ?endcallback?*	Fetches *url*, if allowed by the security policy. The *callbacks* occur before, during, and after the *url* data is returned.
`browser::displayURL` *url* *frame*	Causes the browser to display *url* in *frame*.
`browser::getForm` *url data* *?raw? ?timeout? ?newcallback? ?writecallback? ?endcallback?*	Posts data to url. The callbacks are the same as for browser::getURL. If *raw* is 0, then data is a name value list that gets encoded automatically. Otherwise, it is assumed to be encoded already.
`browser::displayForm` *url* *frame data ?raw?*	Posts *data* to *url* and displays the result in *frame*. The *raw* argument is the same as in `browser::getForm`.

The `browser::getURL` function uses the browser's built-in functions, so it understands proxies and supports `ftp:`, `http:`, and `file:` urls. Unfortunately, the `browser::getURL` interface is different from the `http::geturl` interface. It uses a more complex callback scheme that is due to the nature of the browser's built-in functions. If you do not specify any callbacks, then the call blocks until all the data is received, and then that data is returned. The callback functions are described in Table 20–3.

Table 20–3 The `browser::getURL` callbacks.

`newcallback` *name stream url mimetype datemodified size*	This is called when data starts to arrive from *url*. The *name* identifies the requesting Tclet, and the *stream* identifies the connection. The *mimetype*, *datemodified*, and *size* parameters are attributes of the returned data.
`writecallback` *name stream size data*	This is called when *size* bytes of *data* arrive for Tcllet *name* over *stream*.

Table 20–3 The `browser::getURL` callbacks. (Continued)

`endcallback` *name stream* *reason data*	This is called when the request has completed, although there may be some final bytes in `data`. The reason is one of: `EOF`, `NETWOR_ERROR`, `USER_BREAK`, or `TIMEOUT`.

Configuring Security Policies

There are three aspects to the plugin security policy mechanism: *policies*, *features*, and *trust maps*. A policy is an umbrella for a set of features that are allowed for certain Tclets based on the trust map. A feature is a set of commands and aliases that are defined for a safe interpreter that requests a policy. The trust map is a filter based on the URL of the Tclet. In the future, trust may bet determined by digital signatures instead of URLs. The trust map determines whether a Tclet can request a given policy.

Security Policies are configured for each client.

Remember that the configuration files affect the client machine, which is the workstation that runs the Web browser. If you create Tclets that require custom security policies, you have the burden of distributing the configuration files to clients that will use your Tclets. You also have the burden of convincing them that your security policy is safe!

The `config/plugin.cfg` File

The main configuration file is the `config/plugin.cfg` file in the plugin distribution. This file lists what features are supported by the plugin, and it defines the URL filters for the trust map.

The configuration file is defined into sections with a `section` command. The policies section defines which Tclets can use which security policies. For example, the default configuration file contains these lines in the policies section:

```
section policies
    allow home
    disallow intercom
    disallow inside
    disallow outside
    disallow trusted
    allow javascript ifallowed trustedJavaScriptURLS \
        $originURL
```

This configuration grants all Tclets the right to use the `home` policy, disallows all Tclets from using the `intercom`, `inside`, `outside`, and `trusted` policies, and grants limited access to the `javascript` policy. If you are curious, the configuration files are almost Tcl, but not quite. I lost an argument about that one, so these are stylized configuration files that follow their own rules. For example, the `originURL` variable is not defined in the configuration file but is a value that is tested later when the Tclet is loaded. I'll just give examples here and you can peer under the covers if you want to learn how they are parsed.

The `ifallowed` clause depends on another section to describe the trust mapping for that policy. For the `javascript` policy, the `config/plugin.cfg` file contains:

```
section trustedJavascriptURLs
    allow http://sunscript.sun.com:80/plugin/javascript/*
```

Unfortunately, this server isn't running anymore, so you may want to add the Scriptics Web server to your own configuration:

```
    allow http://www.tcl.tk:80/plugin/javascript/*
```

You can use a combination of `allow` and `disallow` rules in a section. The arguments to `allow` and `disallow` are URL `string match` patterns, and they are processed in order. For example, you could put a liberal `allow` rule followed by `disallow` rules that restrict access, or vice versa. It is probably safest to explicitly list each server that you trust.

Policy Configuration Files

Each security policy has a configuration file associated with it. For example, the `outside` policy uses the file `outside.cfg` file in the `config` directory. This file specifies what hosts and ports are accessible to Tclets using the outside policy. For the `inside` and `outside` policies, the configuration files are similar in spirit to the `safesock` array used to configure the `Safesock` security policy shown on page 302. There are a set of allowed hosts and ports, and a set of excluded hosts. The excluded hosts are an exception list. If a host matches the included set but also matches the excluded set, it is not accessible. There is an included and excluded set for URLs that affect `browser::geturl`. The settings from the `Tempfile` policy shown on page 304 are also part of the `home`, `inside`, and `outside` configuration files. The configuration files are well commented, and you should read through them to learn about the configuration options for each security policy.

Security Policy Features

The aliases that make up a security policy are organized into sets called *features*. The features are listed in the main `config/plugin.cfg` configuration file:

```
    variable featuresList {url stream network persist unsafe}
```

In turn, each security policy configuration file lists what features are part of the policy. For example, the `config/home.cfg` file lists these features:

```
section features
    allow url
    allow network
    allow persist unless {[string match {UNKNOWN *} \
        [getattr originURL]]}
```

Each feature is implemented in a file in the `safetcl` directory of the distribution. For example, the url feature is implemented in `safetcl/url.tcl`. The code in these files follows some conventions in order to work with the configuration mechanism. Each one is implemented inside a namespace that is a child of the `safefeature` namespace (e.g., `safefeature::url`). It must implement an `install` procedure that is called to initialize the feature for a new Tclet. It is inside this procedure that the various allow/disallow rules are checked. The `cfg::allowed` command supports the rule language used in the `.cfg` files.

Creating New Security Policies

This book does not describe the details of the configuration language or the steps necessary to create a new security policy. There are several manual pages distributed with the plugin that explain these details. They can be found on the Web at:

```
http://www.tcl.tk/plugin/man/
```

If you are serious about tuning the existing security policies or creating new ones, you should read the existing feature implementations in detail. As usual, modifying a working example is the best way to proceed! I think it is a very nice property of the plugin that its security policies are implemented in Tcl source code that is clearly factored out from the rest of the Tcl/Tk and plugin implementation. With a relatively small amount of code, you can create custom security policies that grant interesting abilities to Tclets.

Multi-Threaded Tcl Scripts

This chapter describes the `Thread` extension for creating multi-threaded Tcl scripts.

Thread support, a key feature of many languages, is a recent addition to Tcl. That's because the Tcl event loop supports features implemented by threads in most other languages, such as graphical user interface management, multi-client servers, asynchronous communication, and scheduling and timing operations. However, although Tcl's event loop can replace the need for threads in many circumstances, there are still some instances where threads can be a better solution:

- Long-running calculations or other processing, which can "starve" the event loop
- Interaction with external libraries or processes that don't support asynchronous communication
- Parallel processing that doesn't adapt well to an event-driven model
- Embedding Tcl into an existing multi-threaded application

What are Threads?

Traditionally, processes have been limited in that they can do only one thing at a time. If your application needed to perform multiple tasks in parallel, you designed the application to create multiple processes. However, this approach has its drawbacks. One is that processes are relatively "heavy" in terms of the resources they consume and the time it takes to create them. For applications that frequently create new processes — for example, servers that create a new process to handle each client connection — this can lead to decreased response time. And widely parallel applications that create many processes can consume so many system resources as to slow down the entire system. Another drawback is that passing information between processes can be slow because most inter-process communication mechanisms — such as files, pipes, and sockets — involve intermediaries such as the file system or operating system, as well as requiring a context switch from one running process to another.

Threads were designed as a light-weight alternative. Threads are multiple flows of execution within the same process. All threads within a process share the same memory and other resources. As a result, creating a thread requires far fewer resources than creating a separate process. Furthermore, sharing information between threads is much faster and easier than sharing information between processes.

The operating system handles the details of thread creation and coordination. On a single-processor system, the operating system allocates processor time to each of an application's threads, so a single thread doesn't block the rest of the application. On multi-processor systems, the operating system can even run threads on separate processors, so that threads truly can run simultaneously.

The drawback to traditional multi-threaded programming is that it can be difficult to design a *thread-safe* application — that is, an application in which one thread doesn't corrupt the resources being used by another thread. Because all resources are shared in a multi-threaded application, you need to use various locking and scheduling mechanisms to guard against multiple threads modifying resources concurrently.

Thread Support in Tcl

Tcl added support for multi-threaded programming in version 8.1. The Tcl core was made thread-safe. Furthermore, new C functions exposed "platform-neutral" thread functionality. However, no official support was provided for multi-threaded scripting. Since then, the `Thread` extension — originally written by Brent Welch and currently maintained by Zoran Vasiljevic — has become the accepted mechanism for creating multi-threaded Tcl scripts. The most recent version of the `Thread` extension as this was being written was 2.5. In general, this version requires Tcl 8.3 or later, and several of the commands provided require Tcl 8.4 or later.

At the C programming level, Tcl's threading model requires that a Tcl interpreter be managed by only one thread. However, each thread can create as many Tcl interpreters as needed running under its control. As is the case in even a single-threaded application, each Tcl interpreter has its own set of variables and procedures. A thread can execute commands in another thread's Tcl interpreter only by sending special messages to that interpreter's event queue. Those messages are handled in the order received along with all other types of events.

Obtaining a Thread-Enabled Tcl Interpreter

Most binary distributions of Tcl are not thread-enabled, because the default options for building the Tcl interpreters and libraries do not enable thread support. Thread safety adds overhead, slowing down single-threaded Tcl applications, which constitute the vast majority of Tcl applications. Also, many Tcl extensions aren't thread safe, and naively trying to use them in a multi-threaded application can cause errors or crashes.

Unless you can obtain a thread-enabled binary distribution of Tcl, you must compile your own from the Tcl source distribution. This requires running the `configure` command with the `--enable-threads` option during the build process. (See Chapter 48, "Compiling Tcl and Extensions" for more information.)

You can test whether a particular Tcl interpreter is thread-enabled by checking for the existence of the `tcl_platform(threaded)` element. This element exists and contains a Boolean true value in thread-enabled interpreters, whereas it doesn't exist in interpreters without thread support.

Using Extensions in Multi-Threaded Scripts

Because each interpreter has its own set of variables and procedures, you must explicitly load an extension into each thread that wants to use it. Only the `Thread` extension itself is automatically loaded into each interpreter.

You must be careful when using extensions in multi-threaded scripts. Many Tcl extensions aren't thread-safe. Attempting to use them in multi-threaded scripts often results in crashes or corrupted data.

Tcl-only extensions are generally thread-safe. Of course, they must make no use of other commands or extensions that aren't thread-safe. But otherwise, multi-threaded operation doesn't add any new issues that don't already affect single-threaded scripts.

You should always assume that a binary extension is not thread-safe unless its documentation explicitly says that it is. And even thread-safe binary extensions must be compiled with thread support enabled for you to use them in multi-threaded applications. (The default compilation options for most binary extensions don't include thread support.)

Tk isn't truly thread-safe.

Most underlying display libraries (such as X Windows) aren't thread safe — or at least aren't typically compiled with thread-safety enabled. However, significant work has gone into making the Tk core thread-safe. The result is that you can safely use Tk in a multi-threaded Tcl application as long as only one thread uses Tk commands to manage the interface. Any other thread that needs to update the interface should send messages to the thread controlling the interface.

Getting Started with the Thread Extension

You start a thread-enabled `tclsh` or `wish` the same as you would a non-threaded `tclsh` or `wish`. When started, there is only one thread executing, often referred to as the *main thread*, which contains a single Tcl interpreter. If you don't create any more threads, your application runs like any other single-threaded application.

Make sure that the main thread is the last one to terminate.

The main thread has a unique position in a multi-threaded Tcl script. If it exits, then the entire application terminates. Also, if the main thread terminates while other threads still exist, Tcl can sometimes crash rather than exiting cleanly. Therefore, you should always design your multi-threaded applications so that your main thread waits for all other threads to terminate before it exits.

Before accessing any threading features from your application, you must load the `Thread` extension:

```
package require Thread
```

The `Thread` extension automatically loads itself into any new threads your application creates with `thread::create`. All other extensions must be loaded explicitly into each thread that needs to use them. The `Thread` extension creates commands in three separate namespaces:

- The `thread` namespace contains all of the commands for creating and managing threads, including inter-thread messaging, mutexes, and condition variables.
- The `tsv` namespace contains all of the commands for creating and managing thread shared variables.
- The `tpool` namespace contains all of the commands for creating and managing thread pools.

Creating Threads

The `thread::create` command creates a new thread containing a new Tcl interpreter. Any thread can create another thread at will; you aren't limited to starting threads from only the main thread. The `thread::create` command returns immediately, and its return value is the ID of the thread created. The ID is a unique token that you use to interact with and manipulate the thread, in much the same way as you use a channel identifier returned by `open` to interact with and manipulate that channel. There are several commands available for introspection on thread IDs: `thread::id` returns the ID of the current thread; `thread::names` returns a list of threads currently in existence; and `thread::exists` tests for the existence of a given thread.

The `thread::create` command accepts a Tcl script as an argument. If you provide a script, the interpreter in the newly created thread executes it and then terminates the thread. Example 21–1 demonstrates this by creating a thread to perform a recursive search for files in a directory. For a large directory structure, this could take considerable time. By performing the search in a separate thread, the main thread is free to perform other operations in parallel. Also note how the "worker" thread loads an extension and opens a file, completely independent of any extensions loaded or files opened in other threads.

Example 21–1 Creating a separate thread to perform a lengthy operation.

```
package require Thread

# Create a separate thread to search the current directory
# and all its subdirectories, recursively, for all files
# ending in the extension ".tcl". Store the results in the
# file "files.txt".

thread::create {
    # Load the Tcllib fileutil package to use its
    # findByPattern procedure.

    package require fileutil

    set files [fileutil::findByPattern [pwd] *.tcl]

    set fid [open files.txt w]
    puts $fid [join $files \n]
    close $fid
}

# The main thread can perform other tasks in parallel...
```

If you don't provide a script argument to `thread::create`, the thread's interpreter enters its event loop. You then can use the `thread::send` command, described on page 328, to send it scripts to evaluate. Often though, you'd like to perform some initialization of the thread before having it enter its event loop. To do so, use the `thread::wait` command to explicitly enter the event loop after performing any desired initialization, as shown in Example 21–2. You should always use `thread::wait` to cause a thread to enter its event loop, rather than `vwait` or `tkwait`, for reasons discussed in "Preserving and Releasing Threads" on page 330.

Example 21–2 Initializing a thread before entering its event loop.

```
set httpThread [thread::create {
    package require http
    thread::wait
}]
```

After creating a thread, never assume that it has started executing.

There is a distinction between creating a thread and starting execution of a thread. When you create a thread, the operating system allocates resources for the thread and prepares it to run. But after creation, the thread might not start execution immediately. It all depends on when the operating system allocates execution time to the thread. Be aware that the `thread::create` command returns when the thread is *created*, not necessarily when it has *started*. If your application has any inter-thread timing dependencies, always use one of the thread synchronization techniques discussed in this chapter.

Creating Joinable Threads

Remember that the main thread must be the last to terminate. Therefore you often need some mechanism for determining when it's safe for the main thread to exit. Example 21–3 shows one possible approach: periodically checking `thread::names` to see if the main thread is the only remaining thread.

Example 21–3 Creating several threads in an application.

```
package require Thread

puts "*** I'm thread [thread::id]"

# Create 3 threads

for {set thread 1} {$thread <= 3} {incr thread} {
    set id [thread::create {

        # Print a hello message 3 times, waiting
        # a random amount of time between messages

        for {set i 1} {$i <= 3} {incr i} {
            after [expr { int(500*rand()) }]
            puts "Thread [thread::id] says hello"
        }

    }] ;# thread::create

    puts "*** Started thread $id"
} ;# for

puts "*** Existing threads: [thread::names]"

# Wait until all other threads are finished

while {[llength [thread::names]] > 1} {
    after 500
}

puts "*** That's all, folks!"
```

A better approach in this situation is to use *joinable* threads, which are supported in Tcl 8.4 or later. A joinable thread allows another thread to wait upon its termination with the `thread::join` command. You can use thread::join only with joinable threads, which are created by including the thread::create -joinable option. Attempting to join a thread not created with -joinable results in an error. Failing to join a joinable thread causes memory and other resource leaks in your application. Example 21–4 revises the program from Example 21–3 to use joinable threads.

Example 21–4 Using joinable threads to detect thread termination.

```
package require Thread

puts "*** I'm thread [thread::id]"

# Create 3 threads

for {set thread 1} {$thread <= 3} {incr thread} {
    set id [thread::create -joinable {

        # Print a hello message 3 times, waiting
        # a random amount of time between messages

        for {set i 1} {$i <= 3} {incr i} {
            after [expr { int(500*rand()) }]
            puts "Thread [thread::id] says hello"
        }

    }] ;# thread::create

    puts "*** Started thread $id"

    lappend threadIds $id

} ;# for

puts "*** Existing threads: [thread::names]"

# Wait until all other threads are finished

foreach id $threadIds {
    thread::join $id
}

puts "*** That's all, folks!"
```

The thread::join *command blocks.*

Be aware that thread::join blocks. While the thread is waiting for thread::join to return, it can't perform any other operations, including servicing its event loop. Therefore, make sure that you don't use thread::join in situations where a thread must be responsive to incoming events.

Sending Messages to Threads

The `thread::send` command sends a script to another thread to execute. The target thread's main interpreter receives the script as a special type of event added to the end of its event queue. A thread evaluates its messages in the order received along with all other types of events. Obviously, a thread must be in its event loop for it to detect and respond to messages. As discussed on page 324, a thread enters its event loop if you don't provide a script argument to `thread::create`, or if you include the `thread::wait` command in the thread's initialization script.

Synchronous Message Sending

By default, `thread::send` blocks until the target thread finishes executing the script. The return value of `thread::send` is the return value of the last command executed in the script. If an error occurs while evaluating the script, the error condition is "reflected" into the sending thread; `thread::send` generates the same error code, and the target thread's stack trace is included in the value of the `errorInfo` variable of the sending thread:

Example 21–5 Examples of synchronous message sending.

```
set t [thread::create]   ;# Create a thread
=> 1572
set myX 42   ;# Create a variable in the main thread
=> 42
# Copy the value to a variable in the worker thread
thread::send $t [list set yourX $myX]
=> 42
# Perform a calculation in the worker thread
thread::send $t {expr { $yourX / 2 } }
=> 21
thread::send $t {expr { $yourX / 0 } }
=> divide by zero
catch {thread::send $t {expr { $yourX / 0 } } } ret
=> 1
puts $ret
=> divide by zero
puts $errorInfo
=> divide by zero
        while executing
    "expr { $yourX / 0 } "
        invoked from within
    "thread::send $t {expr { $yourX / 0 } } "
```

If you also provide the name of a variable to a synchronous `thread::send`, then it behaves analogously to a `catch` command; `thread::send` returns the return code of the script, and the return value of the last command executed in the script — or the error message — is stored in the variable. Tcl stores the target thread's stack trace in the sending thread's `errorInfo` variable.

Example 21–6 Using a return variable with synchronous message sending.

```
thread::send $t {incr yourX 2} myY
=> 0
puts $myY
=> 44
thread::send $t {expr { acos($yourX) } } ret
=> 1
puts $ret
=> domain error: argument not in valid range
puts $errorInfo
=> domain error: argument not in valid range
        while executing
    "expr { acos($yourX) } "
```

While the sending thread is waiting for a synchronous `thread::send` to return, it can't perform any other operations, including servicing its event loop. Therefore, synchronous sending is appropriate only in cases where:

- you want a simple way of getting a value back from another thread;
- you don't mind blocking your thread if the other thread takes a while to respond; or
- you need a response from the other thread before proceeding.

Watch out for deadlock conditions with synchronous message sending.

If Thread A performs a synchronous `thread::send` to Thread B, and while evaluating the script Thread B performs a synchronous `thread::send` to Thread A, then your application is deadlocked. Because Thread A is blocked in its `thread::send`, it is not servicing its event loop, and so can't detect Thread B's message.

This situation arises most often when the script you send calls procedures in the target thread, and those procedures contain `thread::send` commands. Under these circumstances, it might not be obvious that the script sent will trigger a deadlock condition. For this reason, you should be cautious about using synchronous `thread::send` commands for complex actions. Sending in asynchronous mode, described in the next section, avoids potential deadlock situations like this.

Asynchronous Message Sending

With the `-async` option, `thread::send` sends the script to the target thread in asynchronous mode. In this case, `thread::send` returns immediately.

By default, an asynchronous `thread::send` discards any return value of the script. However, if you provide the name of a variable as an additional argument to `thread::send`, the return value of the last command executed in the script is stored as the value of the variable. You can then either `vwait` on the variable or create a write trace on the variable to detect when the target thread responds. For example:

```
thread::send -async $t [list ProcessValues $vals] result
vwait result
```

In this example, the `thread::send` command returns immediately; the sending thread could then continue with any other operations it needed to perform. In this case, it executes a `vwait` on the return variable to wait until the target thread finishes executing the script. However, while waiting for the response, it can detect and process incoming events. In contrast, the following synchronous `thread::send` blocks, preventing the sending thread from processing events until it receives a response from the target thread:

```
thread::send $t [list ProcessValues $vals] result
```

Preserving and Releasing Threads

A thread created with a script not containing a `thread::wait` command terminates as soon as the script finishes executing. But if a thread enters its event loop, it continues to run until its event loop terminates. So how do you terminate a thread's event loop?

Each thread maintains an internal reference count. The reference count is set initially to 0, or to 1 if you create the thread with the `thread::create -preserved` option. Any thread can increment the reference count afterwards by executing `thread::preserve`, and decrement the reference count by executing `thread::release`. These commands affect the reference count of the current thread unless you specify the ID of another thread. If a call to `thread::release` results in a reference count of 0 or less, the thread is marked for termination.

The use of thread reference counts allows multiple threads to preserve the existence of a worker thread until all of the threads release the worker thread. But the majority of multi-threaded Tcl applications don't require that degree of thread management. In most cases, you can simply create a thread and then later use `thread::release` to terminate it:

```
set worker [thread::create]
thread::send -async $worker $script
# Later in the program, terminate the worker thread
thread::release $worker
```

A thread marked for termination accepts no further messages and discards any pending events. It finishes processing any message it might be executing currently, then exits its event loop. If the thread entered its event loop through a call to `thread::wait`, any other commands following `thread::wait` are executed before thread termination, as shown in Example 21–7. This can be useful for performing "clean up" tasks before terminating a thread.

Example 21-7 Executing commands after `thread::wait` returns.

```
set t [thread::create {
    puts "Starting worker thread"
    thread::wait
    # This is executed after the thread is released
    puts "Exiting worker thread"
}]
```

Note that if a thread is executing a message script when `thread::release` is called (either by itself or another thread), the thread finishes executing its message script before terminating. So, if a thread is stuck in an endless loop, calling `thread::release` has no effect on the thread. In fact, there is no way to kill such a "runaway thread."

Always use `thread::wait` *to enter a thread's event loop.*

This system for preserving and releasing threads works only if you use the `thread::wait` command to enter the thread's event loop (or if you did not provide a creation script when creating the thread). If you use `vwait` or `tkwait` to enter the event loop, `thread::release` cannot terminate the thread.

Error Handling

If an error occurs while a thread is executing its creation script (provided by `thread::create`), the thread dies. In contrast, if an error occurs while processing a message script (provided by `thread::send`), the default behavior is for the thread to stop execution of the message script, but to return to its event loop and continue running. To cause a thread to die when it encounters an uncaught error, use the `thread::configure` command to set the thread's `-unwindonerror` option to true:

```
thread::configure $t -unwindonerror 1
```

Error handling is determined by the thread creating the thread or sending the message. If an error occurs in a script sent by a synchronous `thread::send`, then the error condition is "reflected" to the sending thread, as described in "Synchronous Message Sending" on page 328. If an error occurs during thread creation or an asynchronous `thread::send`, the default behavior is for Tcl to send a stack trace to the standard error channel. Alternatively, you can specify the name of your own custom error handling procedure with `thread::errorproc`. Tcl automatically calls your procedure whenever an "asynchronous" error occurs, passing it two arguments: the ID of the thread generating the error, and the stack trace. (This is similar to defining your own `bgerror` procedure, as described in "The `bgerror` Command" on page 202.) For example, the following code logs all uncaught errors to the file `errors.txt`:

Example 21–8 Creating a custom thread error handler.

```
set errorFile [open errors.txt a]

proc logError {id error} {
    global errorFile
    puts $errorFile "Error in thread $id"
    puts $errorFile $error
    puts $errorFile ""
}

thread::errorproc logError
```

Shared Resources

The present working directory is a resource shared by all interpreters in all threads. If one thread changes the present working directory, then that change affects all interpreters and all threads. This can pose a significant problem, as some library routines temporarily change the present working directory during execution, and then restore it before returning. But in a multi-threaded application, another thread could attempt to access the present working directory during this period and get incorrect results. Therefore, the safest approach if your application needs to access the present working directory is to store this value in a global or thread-shared variable before creating any other threads. The following example uses `tsv::set` to store the current directory in the `pwd` element of the `application` shared variable:

```
package require Thread
# Save the pwd in a thread-shared variable
tsv::set application pwd [pwd]
set t [thread::create {#...}]
```

Environment variables are another shared resource. If one thread makes a change to an environment variable, then that change affects all threads in your application. This might make it tempting to use the global `env` array as a method for sharing information between threads. However, you should not do so, because it is far less efficient than thread-shared variables, and there are subtle differences in the way environment variables are handled on different platforms. If you need to share information between threads, you should instead use thread-shared variables, as discussed in "Shared Variables" on page 337.

The `exit` *command kills the entire application.*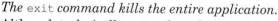

Although technically not a shared resource, it's important to recognize that the `exit` command kills the entire application, no matter which thread executes it. Therefore, you should never call `exit` from a thread when your intention is to terminate only that thread.

Managing I/O Channels

Channels are shared resources in most programming languages. But in Tcl, channels are implemented as a per-interpreter resource. Only the standard I/O channels (stdin, stdout, and stderr) are shared.

Be careful with standard I/O channel on Windows and Macintosh.

When running wish on Windows and Macintosh prior to OS X, you don't have real standard I/O channels, but simulated stdout and stderr channels direct output to the special console window. As of Thread 2.5, these simulated channels appear in the main thread's channel list, but not in any other thread's channel list. Therefore, you'll cause an error if you attempt to access these channels from any thread other than the main thread.

Accessing Files from Multiple Threads

In a multi-threaded application, avoid having the same file open in multiple threads. Having the same file open for read access in multiple threads is safe, but it is more efficient to have only one thread read the file and then share the information with other threads as needed. Opening the same file in multiple threads for write or append access is likely to fail. Operating systems typically buffer information written to a disk on a per-channel basis. With multiple channels open to the same file, it's likely that one thread will end up overwriting data written by another thread. If you need multiple threads to have write access to a single file, it's far safer to have one thread responsible for all file access, and let other threads send messages to the thread to write the data. Example 21–9 shows the skeleton implementation of a logging thread. Once the log file is open, other threads can call the logger's AddLog procedure to write to the log file.

Example 21–9 A basic implementation of a logging thread.

```
set logger [thread::create {
    proc OpenLog {file} {
        global fid
        set fid [open $file a]
    }
    proc CloseLog {} {
        global fid
        close $fid
    }
    proc AddLog {msg} {
        global fid
        puts $fid $msg
    }
    thread::wait
}]
```

II. Advanced Tcl

Transferring Channels between Threads

As long as you're working with Tcl 8.4 or later, the `Thread` extension gives you the ability to transfer a channel from one thread to another with the `thread::transfer` command. After the transfer, the initial thread has no further access to the channel. The symbolic channel ID remains the same in the target thread, but you need some method of informing the target thread of the ID, such as a thread-shared variable. The `thread::transfer` command blocks until the target thread has incorporated the channel. The following shows an example of transferring a channel, and simply duplicating the value of the channel ID in the target thread rather than using a thread-shared variable:

```
set fid [open myfile.txt r]
# ...
set t [thread::create]
thread::transfer $t $fid
# Duplicate the channel ID in the target thread
thread::send $t [list set fid $fid]
```

Another option for transferring channels introduced in `Thread 2.5` is `thread::detach`, which detaches a channel from a thread, and `thread::attach`, which attaches a previously detached channel to a thread. The advantage to this approach is that the thread relinquishing the channel doesn't need to know which thread will be acquiring it. This is useful when your application uses thread pools, which are described on page 342.

The ability to transfer channels between threads is a key feature in implementing a multi-thread server, in which a separate thread is created to service each client connected. One thread services the listening socket. When it receives a client connection, it creates a new thread to service the client, then transfers the client's communication socket to that thread.

Transferring socket channels requires special handling.

A complication arises in that you can't perform the transfer of the communication socket directly from the connection handler, like this:

```
socket -server ClientConnect 9001
proc ClientConnect {sock host port} {
    set t [thread::create { ... }]
    # The following command fails
    thread::transfer $t $sock
}
```

The reason is that Tcl maintains an internal reference to the communication socket during the connection callback. The `thread::transfer` command (and the `thread::detach` command) cannot transfer the channel while this additional reference is in place. Therefore, we must use the `after` command to defer the transfer until after the connection callback returns, as shown in Example 21–10.

Example 21–10 Deferring socket transfer until after the connection callback.

```
proc _ClientConnect {sock host port} {
    after 0 [list ClientConnect $sock $host $port]
}

proc ClientConnect {sock host port} {
    # Create the client thread and transfer the channel
}
```

One issue in early versions of Tcl 8.4 was a bug that failed to initialize Tcl's socket support when a socket channel was transferred into a thread. The workaround for this bug is to explicitly create a socket in the thread (which can then be immediately closed) to initialize the socket support, and then transfer the desired socket. This bug has been fixed, but Example 21–11 illustrates how you can perform extra initialization in a newly created thread before it enters its event loop:

Example 21–11 Working around Tcl's socket transfer bug by initializing socket support.

```
set t [thread::create {
    # Initialize socket support by opening and closing
    # a server socket.

    close [socket -server {} 0]

    # Now sockets can be transferred safely into this thread.

    thread::wait
}]
```

Example 21–12 integrates all of these techniques to create a simple multi-threaded echo server. Note that the server still uses event-driven interaction in each client thread. Technically, this isn't necessary for such a simple server, because once a client thread starts it doesn't expect to receive messages from any other thread. If a thread needs to respond to messages from other threads, it must be in its event loop to detect and service such messages. Because this requirement is common, this application demonstrates the event-driven approach.

Example 21–12 A multi-threaded echo server.

```
package require Tcl 8.4
package require Thread 2.5

if {$argc > 0} {
    set port [lindex $argv 0]
} else {
    set port 9001
}
```

```
    socket -server _ClientConnect $port

proc _ClientConnect {sock host port} {

    # Tcl holds a reference to the client socket during
    # this callback, so we can't transfer the channel to our
    # worker thread immediately. Instead, we'll schedule an
    # after event to create the worker thread and transfer
    # the channel once we've re-entered the event loop.

    after 0 [list ClientConnect $sock $host $port]
}

proc ClientConnect {sock host port} {

    # Create a separate thread to manage this client. The
    # thread initialization script defines all of the client
    # communication procedures and puts the thread in its
    # event loop.

    set thread [thread::create {
        proc ReadLine {sock} {
            if {[catch {gets $sock line} len] || [eof $sock]} {
                catch {close $sock}
                thread::release
            } elseif {$len >= 0} {
                EchoLine $sock $line
            }
        }

        proc EchoLine {sock line} {
            if {[string equal -nocase $line quit]} {
                SendMessage $sock \
                    "Closing connection to Echo server"
                catch {close $sock}
                thread::release
            } else {
                SendMessage $sock $line
            }
        }

        proc SendMessage {sock msg} {
            if {[catch {puts $sock $msg} error]} {
                puts stderr "Error writing to socket: $error"
                catch {close $sock}
                thread::release
            }
        }


        # Enter the event loop

        thread::wait

    }]
```

```
        # Release the channel from the main thread. We use
        # thread::detach/thread::attach in this case to prevent
        # blocking thread::transfer and synchronous thread::send
        # commands from blocking our listening socket thread.


        thread::detach $sock

        # Copy the value of the socket ID into the
        # client's thread

        thread::send -async $thread [list set sock $sock]

        # Attach the communication socket to the client-servicing
        # thread, and finish the socket setup.

        thread::send -async $thread {
            thread::attach $sock
            fconfigure $sock -buffering line -blocking 0
            fileevent $sock readable [list ReadLine $sock]
            SendMessage $sock "Connected to Echo server"
        }
    }

    vwait forever
```

Shared Variables

Standard Tcl variables are a per-interpreter resource; an interpreter has no access to variables in another interpreter. For the simple exchange of information between threads, you can substitute the *values* of variables into a script that you send to another thread, and obtain the return value of a script evaluated by another thread. But this technique is inadequate for sharing information among multiple threads, and inefficient when transferring large amounts of information.

The `Thread` extension supports the creation of *thread-shared variables*, which are accessible by all threads in an application. Thread-shared variables are stored independent of any interpreter, so if the thread that originally created a shared variable terminates, the shared variable continues to exist. Shared variables are stored in collections called *arrays*. The term is somewhat unfortunate, because while shared variable arrays are similar to standard Tcl arrays, they do not use the same syntax. Your application can contain as many shared variable arrays as you like.

Because of the special nature of shared variables, you cannot use the standard Tcl commands to create or manipulate shared variables, or use standard variable substitution syntax to retrieve their values. (This also means that you cannot use shared variables as a widget's -textvariable or -listvariable, with `vwait` or `tkwait`, or with variable traces.) All commands for interacting with shared variables are provided by the `Thread` extension in the `tsv` namespace. Most of the `tsv` commands are analogous to Tcl commands for creating and manipulating standard Tcl variables. Table 21–3 on page 346 describes all of the `tsv` commands.

You create a shared variable with `tsv::set`, specifying the array name, the variable name (sometimes also referred to as the shared array *element*), and the value to assign to it. For example:

```
tsv::set application timeout 10
```

To retrieve the value of a shared variable, either use `tsv::set` without a value or call `tsv::get`. The two commands shown below are equivalent:

```
tsv::set application timeout
tsv::get application timeout
```

All shared variable commands are guaranteed to be *atomic*. A thread locks the variable during the entire command. No other thread can access the variable until the command is complete; if a thread attempts to do so, it blocks until the variable is unlocked. This simplifies the use of shared variables in comparison to most other languages, which require explicit locking and unlocking of variables to prevent possible corruption from concurrent access by multiple threads.

This locking feature is particularly useful in the class of `tsv` commands that manipulate lists. Standard Tcl commands like `linsert` and `lreplace` take a list value as input, and then return a new list as output. Modifying the value of a list stored in a standard Tcl variable requires a sequence like this:

```
set states [linsert $states 1 California Nevada]
```

Doing the same with shared variables is problematic:

```
tsv::set common cities \
    [linsert [tsv::get common cities] 1 Yreka Winnemucca]
```

After reading the shared variable with `tsv::get`, another thread could modify the value of the variable before the `tsv::set` command executes, resulting in data corruption. For this reason, the `tsv` commands that manipulate list values actually modify the value of the shared variable. Data corruption by another thread won't occur because the shared variable is locked during the entire execution of the command:

```
tsv::linsert common cities 1 Yreka Winnemucca
```

Mutexes and Condition Variables

Mutexes and condition variables are thread synchronization mechanisms. Although they are used frequently in other languages, they aren't needed as often in Tcl because of Tcl's threading model and the atomic nature of all shared variable commands. All mutex and condition variable commands are provided by the Thread extension in the thread namespace.

Mutexes

A *mutex*, which is short for *mutual exclusion*, is a locking mechanism. You use a mutex to protect shared resources — such as shared variables, serial ports, databases, etc. — from concurrent access by multiple threads. Before accessing the shared resource, the thread attempts to *lock* the mutex. If no other thread currently holds the mutex, the thread successfully locks the mutex and can access the resource. If another thread already holds the mutex, then the attempt to lock the mutex blocks until the other thread releases the mutex.

This sequence is illustrated in Example 21–13. The first step is creating a mutex with the thread::mutex create operation, which returns a unique token representing the mutex. The same token is used in all threads, and so you must make this token available (for example, through a shared variable) to all threads that access the shared resource.

Example 21–13 Using a mutex to protect a shared resource.

```
# Create the mutex, storing the mutex token in a shared
# variable for other threads to access.

tsv::set db mutex [thread::mutex create]

# ...

# Lock the mutex before accessing the shared resource.

thread::mutex lock [tsv::get db mutex]

# Use the shared resource, and then unlock the mutex.

thread::mutex unlock [tsv::get db mutex]

# Lather, rinse, repeat as needed...

thread::mutex destroy [tsv::get db mutex]
```

Mutexes rely on threads being "good citizens."
Mutexes work only if all threads in an application use them properly. A "rogue" thread can ignore using a mutex and access the shared resource directly. Therefore, you should be very careful to use your mutexes consistently when designing and implementing your application.

Condition Variables

A *condition variable* is a synchronization mechanism that allows one or more threads to sleep until they receive notification from another thread. A condition variable is associated with a mutex and a boolean condition known as a *predicate*. A thread uses the condition variable to wait until the boolean predicate is true. A different thread changes the state of the predicate to true, and then notifies the condition variable. The mutex synchronizes thread access to the data used to compute the predicate value. The general usage pattern for the signalling thread is:

- Lock the mutex
- Change the state so the predicate is true
- Notify the condition variable
- Unlock the mutex

The pattern for a waiting thread is:

- Lock the mutex
- Check the predicate
- If the predicate is false, wait on the condition variable until notified
- Do the work
- Unlock the mutex

In practice, a waiting thread should always check the predicate inside a `while` loop, because multiple threads might be waiting on the same condition variable. A waiting thread automatically releases the mutex when it waits on the condition variable. When the signalling thread notifies the condition variable, all threads waiting on that condition variable compete for a lock on the mutex. Then when the signalling thread releases the mutex, one of the waiting threads gets the lock. It is quite possible for that thread then to change the state so that the predicate is no longer true when it releases the lock. For example, several worker threads forming a *thread pool* might wait until there is some type of job to process. Upon notification, the first worker thread takes the job, leaving nothing for the other worker threads to process.

This sequence for using a condition variable sounds complex, but is relatively easy to code. Example 21–14 shows the sequence for the signalling thread. The first step is creating a condition variable with the `thread::cond create` operation, which returns a unique token representing the condition variable. As with mutexes, the same token is used in all threads, and so you must make this token available (for example, through a shared variable) to all threads that access the condition variable. When the thread is ready to update the predicate, it first locks the associated mutex. Then it notifies the condition variable with `thread::cond notify` and finally unlocks the mutex.

Example 21–14 Standard condition variable use for a signalling thread.

```
# Create the condition variable and accompanying mutex.
# Use shared variables to share these tokens with all other
# threads that need to access them.

set cond [tsv::set tasks cond [thread::cond create]]
set mutex [tsv::set tasks mutex [thread::mutex create]]

# When we're ready to update the state of the predicate, we
# must first obtain the mutex protecting it.

thread::mutex lock $mutex

# Now update the predicate. In this example, we'll just set a
# shared variable to true. In practice, the predicate can be
# more complex, such as the length of a list stored in a
# shared variable being greater than 0.

tsv::set tasks predicate 1

# Notify the condition variable, waking all waiting threads.
# Each thread will block until it can lock the mutex.

thread::cond notify $cond

# Unlock the mutex.

thread::mutex unlock $mutex
```

Example 21–15 shows the sequence for a waiting thread. When a thread is ready to test the predicate, it must first lock the mutex protecting it. If the predicate is true, the thread can continue processing, unlocking the mutex when appropriate. If the predicate is false, the thread executes `thread::cond wait` to wait for notification. The `thread::cond wait` command atomically unlocks the mutex and puts the thread into a wait state. Upon notification, the thread atomically locks the mutex (blocking until it can obtain it) and returns from the `thread::cond wait` command. It then tests the predicate, and repeats the process until the predicate is true.

Example 21–15 Standard condition variable use for a waiting thread.

```
set mutex [tsv::get tasks mutex]
set cond [tsv::get tasks cond]

# Lock the mutex before testing the predicate.

thread::mutex lock $mutex

# Test the predicate, if necessary waiting until it is true.
```

```
while {![tsv::get tasks predicate]} {
    # Wait for notification on the condition variable.
    # thread::cond wait internally unlocks the mutex,
    # blocks until it receives notification, then locks
    # the mutex again before returning.

    thread::cond wait $cond $mutex
}

# We now hold the mutex and know the predicate is true. Do
# whatever processing is desired, and unlock the mutex when
# it is no longer needed.

thread::mutex unlock $mutex
```

Tcl's threading model greatly reduces the need for condition variables. It's usually much simpler to place a thread in its event loop with `thread::wait`, and then send it messages with `thread::send`. And for applications where you want a thread pool to handle jobs on demand, the `Thread` extension's built-in thread pool implementation is far easier than creating your own with condition variables.

Thread Pools

A *thread pool* is a common multi-threaded design pattern. A thread pool consists of several worker threads that wait for jobs to perform. When a job is sent to the thread pool, one of the available worker threads processes it. If all worker threads are busy, either additional worker threads are created to handle the incoming jobs, or the jobs are queued until worker threads are available.

The `tpool` namespace of the `Thread` extension provides several commands for creating and managing thread pools. Using these commands is much easier than trying to build your own thread pools from scratch using mutexes, condition variables, etc. Thread pool support was added to the `Thread` extension in version 2.5.

The `tpool::create` command creates a thread pool, returning the ID of the new thread pool. There are several options to `tpool::create` that allow you to configure the behavior of the thread pool. The `-minthreads` option specifies the minimum number of threads in the pool. This number of threads is created when the thread pool is created, and as worker threads in the pool terminate, new worker threads are created to bring the number up to this minimum. The `-maxthreads` option specifies the maximum number of worker threads allowed. If a job is posted to the thread pool and there are no idle worker threads available, a new worker thread is created to handle the job only if the number of worker threads won't exceed the maximum number. If the maximum has been reached, the job is queued until a worker thread is available. The `-idletime` option specifies the number of seconds that a worker thread waits for a new job before terminating itself to preserve system resources. And the `-initcmd` and `-exitcmd` options provide scripts to respectively initialize newly created worker threads and clean up exiting worker threads.

Once you have created a thread pool, you send *jobs* to it with the `tpool::post` command. A job consists of an arbitrary Tcl script to execute. The job is executed by the first available worker thread in the pool. If there are no idle worker threads, a new worker thread is created, as long as the number of worker threads doesn't exceed the thread pool maximum. If a new worker thread can't be created, the `tpool::post` command blocks until a worker thread can handle the job, but while blocked the posting thread still services its event loop.

The return value of `tpool::post` is a job ID. To receive notification that a job is complete, your thread must call `tpool::wait`. The `tpool::wait` command blocks, but continues to service the thread's event loop while blocked. Additionally, the `tpool::wait` command can wait for several jobs simultaneously, returning when any of the jobs are complete. The return value of `tpool::wait` is a list of completed job IDs.

After `tpool::wait` reports that a job is complete, you can call `tpool::get` to retrieve the result of the job, which is the return value of the last command executed in the job script. If the job execution resulted in an error, the error is "reflected" to the posting thread: `tpool::get` raises an error and the values of `errorInfo` and `errorCode` are updated accordingly.

Finally, a thread pool can be preserved and released in much the same way as an individual thread. Each thread pool maintains an internal reference count, which is initially set to 0 upon creation. Any thread can increment the reference count afterwards by executing `tpool::preserve`, and decrement the reference count by executing `tpool::release`. If a call to `tpool::release` results in a reference count of 0 or less, the thread pool is marked for termination. Any further reference to a thread pool once it is marked for termination results in an error.

The Thread Package Commands

The commands of the `Thread` extension are grouped into three separate namespaces, based on their functionality. This section summarizes the commands found in each namespace.

The thread Namespace

The `thread` namespace contains all of the commands for creating and managing threads, including inter-thread messaging, mutexes, and condition variables. Table 21–1 describes all of the commands contained in the `thread` namespace.

Table 21–1 The commands of the `thread` namespace.

`thread::attach` *channel*	Attaches the previously detached *channel* into current interpreter of the current thread.
`thread::cond create`	Returns a token for a newly created condition variable.
`thread::cond destroy` *cond*	Destroys the specified condition variable.
`thread::cond notify` *cond*	Wakes up all threads waiting on the specified condition variable.
`thread::cond wait` *cond mutex* ?*ms*?	Blocks until the specified condition variable is signaled by another thread with `thread::cond notify`, or until the optional timeout in milliseconds specified by *ms* expires. The *mutex* must be locked by the calling thread before calling `thread::cond wait`. While waiting on the *cond*, the command releases *mutex*. Before returning to the calling thread, the command re-acquires *mutex* again.
`thread::configure` *id* ?*option* ?*value*? ?*option value*...?	Queries or sets thread configuration options, as described in Table 21–2.
`thread::create` ?-joinable? ?-preserved? ?*script*?	Creates a thread, returning the thread's ID. The -joinable flag allows another thread to wait for termination of this thread with `thread::join`. The -preserved flag sets the thread's initial reference count to 1, rather than the default of 0. (See `thread::preserve` and `thread::release`.) If provided, the thread executes the *script*, then exits; otherwise, it enters an events loop to wait for messages.
`thread::detach` *channel*	Detaches the specified *channel* from the current thread so that it no longer has access to it. Any single thread can then `thread::attach` the channel to gain access to it.
`thread::errorproc` ?*proc*?	Registers a procedure to handle errors that occur when performing asynchronous `thread::send` commands. When called, *proc* receives two argument: the ID of the thread that generated the error, and the value of that thread's `errorInfo` variable.
`thread::eval` ?-lock *mutex*? *arg* ?*arg*...?	Concatenates the arguments and evaluates the resulting script under the *mutex* protection. If no *mutex* is specified, an internal static one is used for the duration of the evaluation.
`thread::exists` *id*	Returns boolean indicating whether or not the specified thread exists.
`thread::id`	Returns the current thread's ID.

Table 21–1 The commands of the `thread` namespace. (Continued)

`thread::join id`	Blocks until the target thread terminates. (Available only with Tcl 8.4 or later.)
`thread::mutex create`	Returns a token for a newly created mutex.
`thread::mutex destroy mutex`	Destroys the `mutex`.
`thread::mutex lock mutex`	Locks the `mutex`, blocking until it can gain exclusive access.
`thread::mutex unlock mutex`	Unlocks the `mutex`.
`thread::names`	Returns a list of the IDs of all running threads.
`thread::preserve ?id?`	Increments the reference count of the indicated thread, or the current thread if no `id` is given.
`thread::release ?-wait? ?id?`	Decrements the reference count of the indicated thread, or the current thread if no `id` is given. If the reference count is 0 or less, mark the thread for termination. If `-wait` is specified, the command blocks until the target thread terminates.
`thread::send ?-async? id script ?varname?`	Sends the `script`, to thread `id`. If `-async` is specified, do not wait for `script` to complete. Stores the result of `script` in `varname`, if provided.
`thread::transfer id channel`	Transfers the open `channel` from the current thread to the main interpreter of the target thread. This command blocks until the target thread incorporates the channel. (Available only with Tcl 8.4 or later.)
`thread::unwind`	Terminates a prior `thread::wait` to cause a thread to exit. Deprecated in favor of `thread::release`.
`thread::wait`	Enters the event loop.

The `thread::configure` command allows an application to query and set thread configuration options, in much the same way as the `fconfigure` command configures channels. Table 21–2 lists the available thread configuration options.

Table 21–2 Thread configuration options.

`-eventmark int`	Specifies the maximum number of pending scripts sent with `thread::send` that the thread accepts. Once the maximum is reached, subsequent `thread::send` messages to this script block until the number of pending scripts drops below the maximum. A value of 0 (default) allows an unlimited number of pending scripts.
`-unwindonerror boolean`	If true, the thread "unwinds" (terminates its event loop) on uncaught errors. Default is false.

II. Advanced Tcl

The `tsv` Namespace

The `tsv` namespace contains all of the commands for creating and managing thread shared variables. Table 21–3 describes all of the commands contained in the `tsv` namespace.

Table 21–3 The commands of the `tsv` namespace.

`tsv::append` *array element value ?value ...?*	Appends to the shared variable like `append`.
`tsv::exists` *array ?element?*	Returns boolean indicating whether the given *element* exists, or if no *element* is given, whether the shared *array* exists.
`tsv::get` *array element ?varname?*	Returns the value of the shared variable. If *varname* is provided, the value is stored in the variable, and the command returns 1 if the *element* existed, 0 otherwise.
`tsv::incr` *array element ?increment?*	Increments the shared variable like `incr`.
`tsv::lappend` *array element value ?value ...?*	Appends elements to the shared variable like `lappend`.
`tsv::lindex` *array element index*	Returns the indicated element from the shared variable, similar to `lindex`.
`tsv::linsert` *array element index value ?value ...?*	Atomically inserts elements into the shared variable, similar to `linsert`, but actually modifying the variable.
`tsv::llength` *array element*	Returns the number of elements in the shared variable, similar to `llength`.
`tsv::lock` *array arg ?arg ...?*	Concatenates the *args* and evaluates the resulting script. During script execution, the command locks the specified shared *array* with an internal mutex.
`tsv::lpop` *array element ?index?*	Atomically deletes the value at the *index* list position from the shared variable and returns the value deleted. The default *index* is 0.
`tsv::lpush` *array element value ?index?*	Atomically inserts the *value* at the *index* list position in the shared variable. The default *index* is 0.
`tsv::lrange` *array element first last*	Returns the indicated range of elements from the shared variable, similar to `lrange`.
`tsv::lreplace` *array element value ?value ...?*	Atomically replaces elements in the shared variable, similar to `lreplace`, but actually modifying the variable.
`tsv::lsearch` *array element ?mode? pattern*	Returns the index of the first element in the shared variable matching the *pattern*, similar to `lsearch`. Supported modes are: `-exact`, `-glob` (default), and `-regexp`.

Table 21–3 The commands of the `tsv` namespace. (Continued)

`tsv::move array old new`	Atomically renames the shared variable from *old* to *new*.
`tsv::names ?pattern?`	Returns a list of all shared variable arrays, or those whose names match the optional glob pattern.
`tsv::object array element`	Creates and returns the name of an accessor command for the shared variable. Other `tsv` commands are available as subcommands of the accessor to manipulate the shared variable.
`tsv::pop array element`	Atomically returns the value of the shared variable and deletes the *element*.
`tsv::set array element ?value?`	Sets the *value* of the shared variable, creating it if necessary. If *value* is omitted, the current value is returned.
`tsv::unset array ?element?`	Deletes the shared variable, or the entire *array* if no *element* is specified.

The tpool Namespace

The `tpool` namespace contains all of the commands for creating and managing thread pools. Table 21–4 describes all of the commands contained in the `tpool` namespace.

Table 21–4 The commands of the `tpool` namespace.

`tpool::create ?options?`	Creates a thread pool, returning the thread pool's ID. Table 21–5 describes supported configuration options.
`tpool::post tpoolId script`	Sends a Tcl *script* to the specified thread pool for execution, returning the ID of the posted job. This command blocks (entering the event loop to service events) until a worker thread can service the job
`tpool::wait tpoolId jobList ?varName?`	Blocks (entering the event loop to service events) until one or more of the jobs whose IDs are given by the *jobList* argument are completed. Returns a list of completed jobs from *jobList*. If provided, *varName* is set to a list of jobs from *jobList* that are still pending.
`tpool::get tpoolId jobId`	Returns the result of the specified *jobId*. `tpool::wait` must have reported previously that the job is complete. If no error occurred in the job, the result is the return value of the last command executed in the job script. Any error encountered in job execution is in turn thrown by `tpool::get`, with the `errorCode` and `errorInfo` variables set appropriately.

Table 21–4 The commands of the `tpool` namespace. (Continued)

`tpool::names`	Returns a list of existing thread pool IDs.
`tpool::preserve` *tpoolId*	Increments the reference count of the indicated thread pool.
`tpool::release` *tpoolId*	Decrements the reference count of the indicated thread pool. If the reference count is 0 or less, mark the thread pool for termination.

The `tpool::create` command supports several options for configuring thread pools. Table 21–5 lists the available thread pool configuration options.

Table 21–5 Thread pool configuration options.

`-minthreads` *number*	The minimum number of threads. If the number of live threads in the thread pool is less than this number (including when the thread pool is created initially), new threads are created to bring the number up to the minimum. Default is 0.
`-maxthreads` *number*	The maximum number of threads. When a job is posted to the thread pool, if there are no idle threads and the number of existing worker threads is at the maximum, the thread posting the job blocks (in its event loop) until a worker thread is free to handle the job. Default is 4.
`-idletime` *seconds*	The maximum idle time, in seconds, before a worker thread exits (as long as the number of threads doesn't drop below the `-minthreads` limit). Default value is 0, meaning idle threads wait forever.
`-initcmd` *script*	A script that newly created worker threads execute.
`-exitcmd` *script*	A script that worker threads execute before exiting.

Tclkit and Starkits

Tclkit is a version of the Tcl/Tk interpreter that is designed to make packaging and deployment of Tcl applications easy. Tclkit includes Tcl/Tk, [incr Tcl], the Metakit database, and TclVFS. A Starkit is a special file that contains all the scripts and supporting files you need for your Tcl application. This chapter describes how to package and deploy your application as a Starkit.

*T*clkit was created by Jean-Claude Wippler as a way to make deploying Tcl applications easier. Tclkit is an extended Tcl interpreter that includes the Metakit database, the [incr Tcl] object-oriented system, and a Virtual File System (VFS). The database is cleverly stored as part of the Tclkit application itself, and the VFS interface is used to make the database look like a private filesystem. Tclkit puts all the scripts normally associated with Tcl and its extensions into this database. The result is a self-contained, single file distribution of Tcl that includes extensions for your GUI, object-oriented programming, a database, and a few other goodies.

Metakit is a fast, transactional database with a simple programming API. Like Tcl, Metakit is a compact, efficient library designed to be embedded into applications. The Tcl interface to Metakit gives you a simple, easy way to manipulate persistent data. Although you do not have to program Metakit directly when using Starkits, this Chapter does provide a short introduction to using Metakit to store data for your application.

A Starkit is a Metakit database file that stores your application. The VFS interface makes this transparent. Tclkit processes the Starkit just like *tclsh* or *wish*, and your application doesn't even have to know it is packaged inside a Starkit.

The original Tclkit used an early version of VFS created by Matt Newman. TclVFS was ported to the Tcl core in version 8.4.1 by Vince Darley. Today you can build Tclkit using unmodified Tcl sources. The ActiveTcl distribution includes Metakit, TclVFS and tools to create Starkits, too.

Getting Started with Tclkit

Using Tclkit is easy. Just copy the version for your platform (e.g., Linux, Windows or Solaris) into a convenient location under the name *tclkit* (or *tclkit.exe* on Windows.) The CD-ROM has builds for lots of platforms, and you can find more at the Tclkit home page:

```
http://www.equi4.com/tclkit
```

You can use the *tclkit* application just like *tclsh*. Run with no arguments, it prints a prompt and you can type Tcl commands interactively. If you pass a file argument, then it sources that file just as *tclsh* would. To use *tclkit* like *wish*, you must add this to your scripts:

```
package require Tk
```

Although you can use *tclkit* to source .tcl files, *tclkit* is normally used to interpret Starkits, which have a .kit suffix. On UNIX, Starkits use the #! header to associate themselves with *tclkit*. Make sure that *tclkit* is in a directory named in your PATH environment variable. On Windows, you can associate *tclkit.exe* with the .kit extension. Mac OS X behaves like UNIX (yay!). On Mac Classic systems you can use the File Source menu to source .kit files. Creating Starkits is described on page 352.

Inside a Starkit

Tclkit uses the Virtual Filesystem extension to make records in a Metakit database look like files and directories to your application. Through a simple packaging step described shortly, you can easily put all of the Tcl scripts and other supporting files that make up your application into a single database file. The Virtual Filesystem (VFS) extension lets you transparently access these files through the regular file system interface (e.g., open, gets, source, even cd.)

A *Starkit* is a Metakit database that stores an application. The great thing about a Starkit is that it is a single file so it is easy to manage. There is no need to unpack files or run an installer to set things up. Instead, you can distribute your application as two files: the Tclkit interpreter and the Starkit file. Both of these embed a virtual file system that include all the bits and pieces needed for Tcl/Tk and your application. The Tclkit file is platform-specific because it contains Tcl and all the other extensions in a compiled form. There are pre-compiled Tclkits for Windows, Macintosh, and many flavors of Unix. The Starkit file is platform-independent. You can use it with the appropriate Tclkit interpreter on different platforms.

Deploying Applications as Starkits

The key benefit of Tclkit and Starkits is easy deployment. Users just copy *tclkit* and your Starkits onto their system; there is no special installation step. You can even have different versions of *tclkit* and they don't interfere with each other. If users get tired of your application, they just remove the files.

Creating Starkits is made easy with the *sdx* application, which was created by Steve Landers and Jean-Claude Wippler. You organize your collection of application scripts, data files, binary graphics, and online documentation into a file system directory structure. Then you use *sdx* to wrap that into a Starkit. Creating your own Starkits is described on page 352.

You can include binary extensions in a Starkit and dynamically load them. The `load` command automatically copies the shared library out of the VFS to a temporary location, and loads the library from that location. The temporary file is necessary because the host OS cannot find the library inside the Starkit. Binary extensions make the Starkit platform-specific, but it is possible to put libraries for different platforms into the Starkit. For example, the `kitten.kit` Starkit includes extensions for Windows, Linux, and Solaris.

You can combine Tclkit and a Starkit into a *Starpack*. The advantage of this is that it reduces deployment to a single file. The main drawback is that the Starpack file is relatively large, and it is platform-specific. Use *sdx* to create Starpacks as described later.

The Starkit archive contains a growing collection of Starkits that include applications, games, development tools, a Wiki, tutorials and documentation bundles. There is a copy of the archive on the CD-ROM, and its home page is:

```
http://mini.net/sdarchive/
```

Virtual File Systems

The key concept in Tclkit and Starkits is the virtual file system (VFS). You may be familiar with the file system interface inside a Unix operating system that makes everything look the same (files, tape drives, network sockets, pipes). The nice thing about Unix is that a system programmer can use the same APIs to access all of these things. The goal of the Tcl VFS interface is similar in spirit: use the regular Tcl file system interface to make things like embedded databases, FTP servers, and zip files available to the Tcl programmer. The VFS layer in Tcl 8.4 is implemented below the Tcl C APIs for file system access (e.g., `Tcl_CreateChannel`, `Tcl_FSDeleteFile`). The result is that scripting commands (e.g., `open`, `file`, `glob`) and any C extensions that use these APIs automatically access any Virtual File Systems that are part of the Starkit.

The virtual file system is *mounted* on a regular file; by default it is mounted on the Starkit. For example, if the Starkit is named `foo.kit`, and its virtual file system contains a file named `main.tcl`, then it is visible to the Tcl application as `foo.kit/main.tcl`. The VFS can contain a whole directory structure (e.g., `foo.kit/lib/httpd.tcl` or `foo.kit/htdocs/help/index.html`.)

The next section explores some simple Starkits and their file system structure. The main idea is that the Starkit file itself is the root of the virtual file system hierarchy, and everything in the virtual file system is visible to Tcl via the regular scripting commands. If the VFS supports it, you can create and write files as well as read them.

II. Advanced Tcl

Tclkit includes the TclVFS extension that exposes the ability to implement new file systems in Tcl. Ordinarily you do not need to use the `vfs` API directly when using a Starkit. However, the TclVFS project has created a number of VFS implementations that let you access web sites, FTP sites, zip files, tar files, and more through the filesystem interface. Tclkit does not include all of these, but you can get them as part of the TclVFS extension. Its home page is

```
http://sourceforge.net/projects/tclvfs
```

Accessing a Zip File Through a VFS

Tclkit includes a *zipvfs* package that lets you mount a compressed ZIP file archive and read its contents. This is currently limited to read-only access. Example 22–1 uses the `vfs::zip::Mount` command to set up the VFS access. If you use other VFS types supplied by the TclVFS extension, you will find that each supplies its own `vfs::vfs_type::Mount` API:

Example 22–1 Accessing a Zip file through a VFS

```
package require vfs::zip
=> 1.0
# Mount the zip file on "xyz"
vfs::zip::Mount c:/downloads/tclhttpd343.zip xyz
=> filecb15a8
# Examine the contents
glob xyz/*
=> xyz/tclhttpd3.4.3
# Open and read file inside the zip archive
set in [open xyz/tclhttpd3.4.3/README]
=> rechan16
gets $in
This HTTPD is written in Tcl and Tk.
```

Using *sdx* to Bundle Applications

Sdx, which stands for Starkit Developer eXtension, is an application that you run from the Unix, Windows, or MacOS command line to create and manipulate Starkits. It is itself a Starkit, of course. The *sdx* application is on the CD-ROM, and you can find a link to it from the Starkit home page:

```
http://www.equi4.com/starkit/
```

Creating a Simple Starkit

Creating a Starkit amounts to creating a directory structure that contains the files you need, and then wrapping them up with *sdx*. Create files under *kitname.vfs*, and wrap them into the *kitname.kit* Starkit with:

```
sdx wrap kitname.kit
```

In simple cases, *sdx* will create the directory structure for you. For example, if you have a self-contained Tcl script called `hello.tcl`, then you can turn it into a Starkit like this:

```
sdx qwrap hello.tcl
```

The `qwrap` operation (i.e., "quick wrap") creates a new Starkit, `hello.kit`, that includes the original `hello.tcl` script organized into a virtual file system hierarchy with some additional support files. You run the Starkit like this:

```
tclkit hello.kit
```

On Unix systems you can also execute the Starkit directly. The file uses the `#!` syntax to specify that *tclkit* should run the file. On Windows, you can achieve the same effect by associating *tclkit.exe* with files that end in `.kit`.

Examining a Starkit

There are two ways to look at a Starkit. You can get a listing of the files with the `sdx lsk` operation, or you can use `sdx unwrap` to extract the files from the Starkit into a `kitname.vfs` directory. Example 22–2 shows the `lsk` output for `hello.kit`. The dates are in `YY/MM/DD` format:

Example 22–2 The output of `sdx lsk hello.kit`.

```
hello.kit:
                        dir   lib/
        67   02/11/08 12:07   main.tcl
hello.kit/lib:
                        dir   app-hello/
hello.kit/lib/app-hello:
        43   02/11/08 12:10   hello.tcl
        72   02/11/08 12:07   pkgIndex.tcl
```

Standard Package Organization

The `qwrap` operation turns the `hello.tcl` script into the `app-hello` package. If necessary, *sdx* adds a `package provide app-hello 1.0` command to the `hello.tcl` script. It also creates a short `main.tcl` script that initializes the Starkit system and invokes `hello.tcl` by doing a `package require`. Example 22–3 shows `main.tcl`:

Example 22–3 The main program of a Starkit.

```
package require starkit
starkit::startup
package require app-hello
```

When you run the Starkit, its Metakit database is mounted into a Virtual File System that is visible to the Tcl application. Tclkit sources the `main.tcl` script it finds in the VFS. The `starkit::startup` procedure updates the `auto_path` to contain the Starkit's `lib` directory, so any packages stored there are available to the package mechanism. By convention, the application is put into a package with the name `app-`*kitname*. Example 22–4 shows the `pkgIn-dex.tcl`, which causes the `package require app-hello` command to source `hello.tcl`.

Example 22–4 The `pkgIndex.tcl` in a Starkit.

```
package ifneeded app-hello 1.0 \
    [list source [file join $dir hello.tcl]]
```

The `dir` variable is set by the package mechanism to be the directory containing the `pkgIndex.tcl` file. That the `lib` directory happens to be inside the virtual file system is completely transparent to the package mechanism. The package mechanism is described in more detail in Chapter 12.

Creating a Starpack

A Starpack contains a copy of Tclkit and your Starkit. Use *sdx* to create Starpacks. The `-runtime` flag specifies which Tclkit application you want to merge with your Starkit. For example, to build a Windows Starpack out of our `hello.tcl` application:

```
sdx wrap hello.kit -runtime tclkit-win32.exe
```

To build a Starkit for Linux, use the appropriate runtime:

```
sdx wrap hello.kit -runtime tclkit-linux-x86
```

There are 4 variations of the Windows Tclkit. One option uses *zlib* to automatically compress Tclkit and the Metakit database. These have .upx in their name. The other creates a console-mode application that does not include Tk. These have `-sh` in their name. The smallest Tclkit, `tclkit-win32-sh.upx.exe`, is only 450 K. Even `tclkit-win32.upx.exe` is only 907 K, so you really can create complete applications that fit easily onto a floppy disk!

The auto-compress variation is also available on the Linux x86 builds as the `tclkit-linux-x86.upx.bin` runtime file. Check the Tclkit home page for the latest set of Tclkit builds:

```
http://www.equi4.com/tclkit
```

Exploring the Virtual File System in a Starkit

Example 22–2 introduces the standard, recommended VFS structure for a Starkit that makes everything into a package, even the main application. However, in this section we are going to show a Starkit without packages in order to get a feel for how the VFS works. For example, instead of doing the `package require hello`, the `main.tcl` script of Example 22–3 could `source` the `hello.tcl` file directly:

```
source hello.kit/lib/app-hello/hello.tcl
```

However, this only works if you are in the directory containing the `hello.kit` file.

Use `starkit::topdir` to find things in the Starkit Virtual File System.

The `starkit::topdir` variable is set by `starkit::startup` to be the file name of the Starkit, which is also the root of the Virtual File System inside the Starkit. The value of `starkit::topdir` is an absolute pathname, so it is always valid. Example 22–5 shows a Starkit that manipulates its virtual file system.

Example 22–5 A Starkit that examines its Virtual File System.

```
package require starkit
starkit::startup

puts "Contents of VFS before"
foreach f [glob [file join $starkit::topdir *]] {
    puts "[file size $f] $f"
}
puts "Reading data file"
set in [open [file join starkit::topdir data]]
set X [read $in]
puts $X
close $in
set out [open [file join $starkit::topdir data.new w]]
puts $out $X
close $out
puts "Contents of VFS after"
foreach f [glob [file join $starkit::topdir *]] {
    puts "[file size $f] $f"
}
```

Create the Starkit by putting the code in Example 22–5 into a file named `main.tcl` in the `write.vfs` directory. Then use *sdx* as shown in Example 22–6:

Example 22–6 Creating a simple Starkit.

```
# These are UNIX shell commands
mkdir write.vfs
cp 22_5.tcl write.vfs/main.tcl
sdx wrap write.kit
tclkit write.kit
```

If you run the `write.kit` file more than once you will notice that the `write.kit/data.new` file does not persist between runs. This is because, by default, the Metakit database is modified in main memory and it is not written out to the Starkit file. If you want to store files long term, use the `-writable` flag to *sdx*:

```
sdx wrap write.kit -writable
```

Creating `tclhttpd.kit`

The Tcl Web Server, TclHttpd, has its source tree organized so you can run the server without any installation steps. This makes it very easy to put into a Starkit. For our first version, which we will refine later, all we need is a copy of the TclHttpd source code and a copy of the Standard Tcl Library, *tcllib*. I used the `tcllib1.3` directory that was installed in the main lib directory of my desktop Tcl environment, and the `tclhttpd3.4.3` source distribution. Example 22–7 shows the contents of the `tclhttpd.vfs` directory:

Example 22–7 The contents of the `tclhttpd.vfs` directory, version 1.

```
main.tcl
tclhttpd3.4.3/bin/httpd.tcl
tclhttpd3.4.3/bin/httpdthread.tcl
tclhttpd3.4.3/bin/tclhttpd.rc
tclhttpd3.4.3/lib/ (lots of files)
tclhttpd3.4.3/htdocs/ (lots of files)
tcllib1.3 (copy of /usr/local/lib/tcllib1.3)
```

Example 22–8 shows the short `main.tcl` script used to start up the Starkit. The first two lines are common to all Starkits. The `starkit::autoextend` command is used to add the `tcllib1.3` directory to the `auto_path` so the Standard Tcl Library packages are available. The last line uses `starkit::topdir` to find the TclHttpd startup script, `bin/httpd.tcl`.

Example 22–8 The main program for the TclHttpd Starkit, version 1.

```
package require starkit
starkit::startup
starkit::autoextend [file join $starkit::topdir tcllib1.3]
source [file join $starkit::topdir tclhttpd3.4.3/bin/httpd.tcl]
```

The Starkit is created and used as shown below, assuming `tclhttpd.vfs` is in the current directory. Note that command line options are passed through, so you can also use this Starkit to host an `htdocs` directory outside the Starkit. If you don't specify one, the `htdocs` tree inside the Starkit is used:

```
sdx wrap tclhttpd.kit
tclkit tclhttpd.kit -port 8080 -docRoot /my/htdocs
```

The standard structure introduced in Example 22–2 organizes packages under a `lib` directory. By convention, the version numbers are dropped from the package directory names. Because everything is self contained, there really isn't any need to have explicit version numbers in the directory names. The file system for the second version of `tclhttpd.kit` is shown in Example 22–9.

Example 22–9 Contents of the `tclhttpd.vfs` directory, version 2.

```
main.tcl
bin/httpd.tcl
bin/httpdthread.tcl
bin/tclhttpd.rc
lib/tclhttpd/pkgIndex.tcl
lib/tclhttpd/*.tcl (lots of files)
lib/tcllib/pkgIndex.tcl
lib/tcllib/* (lots of subdirectories)
```

The `main.tcl` file is shown in Example 22–10. There is no need to adjust the `auto_path` because `starkit::startup` ensures that the `lib` directory is on it.

Example 22–10 The main program for the TclHttpd Starkit, version 2.

```
package require starkit
starkit::startup
source [file join $starkit::topdir bin/httpd.tcl]
```

One of the first things I noticed about the `tclhttpd.vfs` was that *tcllib* took up far more space than the rest of TclHttpd. TclHttpd only uses a few of the many modules in *tcllib*. I ended up only adding the modules I needed in order to keep the Starkit smaller. Another way to solve this problem is to use the `tcllib.kit` Starkit that can be shared among applications. Creating shared Starkits is the topic of the next section.

Creating a Shared Starkit

Starkits can be used to create modules that are shared by other applications. For example, the `kitten.kit` Starkit contains about 50 popular extensions, and several of them are binary extensions. It is over 4 MB in size, and so it is a great candidate for sharing. You can find `kitten.kit` on the CD-ROM or in the Starkit archive. By organizing each shared module into a Starkit with the appropriate structure, it is a simple matter to share them.

Whenever a Starkit is sourced, *Tclkit* mounts its VFS and looks for its `main.tcl` file. This is true for shared Starkits as well as the main Starkit of an application. If `main.tcl` calls `starkit::startup`, then the `lib` directory in the VFS is automatically added to the `auto_path`. Any libraries organized under `lib` will be automatically accessible to the application that sourced the Starkit.

You can add a little logic to make your package behave differently if it is run as the main Starkit or sourced into another application. For example, this is done in the *tcllib* Starkit, which starts a stand-alone Wiki that describes the Standard Tcl Library APIs if run as its own Starkit. Otherwise it just sets up *tcllib* to be shared by the main application. Example 22–11 shows the `main.tcl` of `tcllib.kit`. It has to explicitly add the `tcllib` directory to the `auto_path` because it has both a `lib` and `tcllib` directory in its VFS:

Example 22–11 The Standard Tcl Library Starkit `main.tcl` file.

```
package require starkit
if {[starkit::startup] eq "starkit"} {
    # Do application startup
    package require app-tcllib
} else {
    # Set up to be used as a library
    set vfsroot [file dirname [file normalize [info script]]]
    lappend auto_path [file join $vfsroot tcllib]
}
```

Another side effect of `starkit::startup` is to set `starkit::topdir`. However, this variable is only set once. If you source other Starkits that call `starkit::startup`, then the `starkit::topdir` value is not disturbed.

This behavior changed in Tclkit 8.4.2. In earlier versions, `starkit::topdir` was set by each Starkit, so you had to worry about saving its value if you loaded other Starkits. If you source `tcllib.kit` and cannot `package require` its packages, check its `main.tcl`. If it uses `starkit::topdir` in the non-Starkit case, then it is an older version. Simply unwrap it, make its `main.tcl` look like Example 22–11, and wrap it back up to fix the problem.

The `starkit::startup` procedure determines the environment of the application by making a series of tests against the script environment. Its return value helps your `main.tcl` script distinguish between starting out as the main Starkit, or being loaded into another Starkit as a library. Table 22–1 lists the return values of the `starkit::startup` procedure in the order they are checked:

Table 22–1 Return values of the `starkit::startup` procedure.

`starpack`	The Starkit was bundled with *tclkit* to make a Starpack.
`starkit`	The Starkit was run by itself.
`unwrapped`	The Starkit was run out of its unpacked vfs directory.
`tclhttpd`	The Starkit was sourced into TclHttpd.
`plugin`	The Starkit was sourced in the browser plugin.
`service`	The Starkit was run in an NT service.
`sourced`	The Starkit was sourced by another Starkit.

The easiest way to organize your shared Starkits is to put them into the same directory. Example 22–12 shows how the TclHttpd Starkit is modified to load the *tcllib* Starkit from the same directory.

Example 22–12 The main program for TclHttpd Starkit, version 3.

```
package require starkit
starkit::startup
set dir [file dirname $starkit::topdir]
if {![file exists [file join $dir tcllib.kit]]} {
    puts stderr "Please install tcllib.kit in $dir"
    exit 1
}
source [file join $dir tcllib.kit]
source [file join $starkit::topdir tclhttpd/bin/httpd.tcl]
```

Metakit

This section provides a short overview of the Metakit database that is used by Starkits to store their data. You do not need to program Metakit directly to use Starkits because of the transparent VFS interface. However, Metakit is an easy-to-use database that provides more power than storing data in flat files, but not as much power (or overhead) as a full SQL database engine. Metakit has a simple, flexible programming API and an efficient implementation. By storing your application data in a Metakit table, you can have persistent data that lives with your application. You can store the data in a file separate from your application, or right inside the application Starkit itself.

This Chapter gives a few introductory examples and explains some of the other features that are available. This Chapter does not provide a complete reference. The following URLs are excellent guides to the Tcl interface for Metakit. The first URL is also on the CD as sdarchive/doc/mk4dok.kit.

```
http://www.equi4.com/metakit/tcl.html
http://www.equi4.com/metakit/wiki.cgi/mk4tcl
http://www.markroseman.com/tcl/mktcl.html
```

Metakit Data Model

The Metakit data model is table-oriented. A *view* is like a table with rows of values. Each row in a view has an *index*, which is an integer that counts from 0. The elements (i.e., columns or fields) of a row are called *properties*. A property might itself be a view, which leads to nested views (i.e., nested tables). All the rows in a view have the same properties, and the properties of a view can be changed dynamically. You can directly relate (view, row, property) to (table, row, field) when thinking about Metakit views.

A Metakit data file has one or more views within it. When you open a Metakit file, you specify a *tag*. Views are specified as *tag.view*. Row N of a view is specified as *tag.view!N*. Such a position within a view is called a *cursor*, and there are operations to create cursor variables and move them through a view. If a property is a nested view, then you can specify a row in the nested view with *tag.view!N.subview!M*.

Examining a Metakit Database

Our first exercise is to open up a Starkit and look at the Metakit database views inside. The `mk::file` command implements several operations. The `open` operation opens a database and associates it with a tag. The `views` operation lists the views in the database identified by the tag. The `close` operation commits any outstanding modifications to the database. The other `mk::file` operations are used to control the commit behavior and to save or restore the database to an external file. Example 22–13 illustrates how to open a Metakit database and examine the views it contains:

Example 22–13 Examining the views in a Metakit database.

```
package require Mk4tcl
=> 2.4.8
mk::file open tclhttpd tclhttpd.kit
=> tclhttpd
mk::file views tclhttpd
=> dirs
```

The `mk::view` command has several operations to inspect and manipulate views. The `layout` operation queries or sets the properties of a view. Given only a view, the `layout` operation returns the properties defined for the view. Each property has a type, and nested views are represented as a nested list of the property name and its list of properties. Given a set of properties, the `layout` operation defines new properties for a view. This may involve adding or deleting properties from any existing rows in the table. Example 22–14 shows the layout of the `dirs` view in a Starkit. The `files` property is a nested view, which provides a natural way to represent a hierarchical filesystem. The example gets the `name` property of `tclhttpd.dirs!0.files!0`, which is the first file in the first directory in the view:

Example 22–14 Examining data in a Metakit view.

```
mk::view layout tclhttpd.dirs
=> name parent:I {files {name size:I date:I contents:B}}
mk::view size tclhttpd.dirs
=> 48
mk::get tclhttpd.dirs!0
=> name <root> parent -1
mk::get tclhttpd.dirs!1
=> name tcllib1.3 parent 0
mk::get tclhttpd.dirs!1 name
=> tcllib1.3
mk::get tclhttpd.dirs!0.files!0 name
=> main.tcl
```

Of course, real applications will want to query views for values that have certain properties. The `mk::select` command returns the row numbers for rows that match given criteria, or all the row numbers if no matching criteria are given. You can match on multiple properties, and there are flags that control how the match is done. For example, you can do numeric comparisons, regular expression or glob matches, and min/max comparisons.

Example 22–15 shows two forms of `mk::select`. The `KitWalk` procedure enumerates the files in a given directory, which is the view `$tag.dirs!$dir.files`. Then it queries the row indices for the `$tag.dirs` view whose `parent` property equals `$dir`, and calls itself recursively to process the child directories. `KitWalk` provides a similar function to `sdx lsk`:

Example 22–15 Selecting data with `mk::select`.

```
proc KitWalk {tag dir {indent 0}} {
    set prefix [string repeat " " $indent]
    puts "$prefix[mk::get $tag.dirs!$dir name]/"
    incr indent 2

    # List the plain files in the directory, if any

    foreach j [mk::select $tag.dirs!$dir.files] {
        puts "$prefix  [mk::get $tag.dirs!$dir.files!$j name]"
    }

    # Recursively process directories where $dir is the parent

    foreach i [mk::select $tag.dirs parent $dir] {
        KitWalk $tag $i $indent
    }
}
proc KitInit {starkit} {
    mk::file open starkit $starkit
    if {[mk::file views starkit] != "dirs"} {
        mk::file close $starkit
        error "This database is not a starkit"
    }
    return starkit           ;# db tag
}
proc KitTest {} {
    set tag [KitInit tclhttpd.kit]
    KitWalk $tag 0
}
```

Creating a Metakit View

Creating a new view is simple. Example 22–16 opens a database file `mydb.tkd` and creates a view `test` with three properties: `name`, `blob`, and `i`. If the file does not exist, then it gets created automatically. If the `test` view doesn't exist, it gets created. If it already exists, it is reformatted to have the new properties. The `name` property has the default type, which is a null-terminated string. The `blob` property is a binary value (B) which can store anything, including null characters. The i property is a 32-bit integer (I). Other types include 64-bit integer (L), 32-bit floating point (F), 64-bit double-precision floating point (D), and null-terminated string (S), which is the default and needn't be specified.

Example 22–16 Creating a new view.

```
mk::file open mydb mydb.tkd
=> mydb
mk::view layout mydb.test {name blob:B i:I}
=> mydb.test
mk::file close mydb
```

The mk::set command sets property values, and the mk::row command modifies rows. Example 22–17 adds a few values to the test view. Note that you can insert into rows beyond the end of the view and it is automatically extended. If you only define some properties for a row, the other properties get default values. Other mk::row operations include insert, replace, and delete.

Example 22–17 Adding data to a view.

```
mk::set mydb.test!0 name hello
=> mydb.test!0
mk::get mydb.test!0
=> hello {} 0
mk::row append mydb.test "line two" 0x0 65
=> mydb.test!1
mk::view size mydb.test
=> 2
mk::set mydb.test!100 i 1234
=> mydb.test!100
mk::view size mydb.test
=> 101
```

Storing Application Data in a Starkit

Your application can create new views in a Starkit to store persistent data. Remember to wrap your application with the -writable flag. You can determine the name of the Starkit from $starkit::topdir, and then define a new view within it. Of course, remember that Starkits use dirs view to store files, but you can create any number of other views within your Starkits. This is illustrated in Example 22–18, which records each time the application was run in a simple audit view.

Example 22–18 is careful to find the existing Metakit handle that is already opened by Tclkit. The vfs::filesystem info command returns an alternating list of VFS names and their Metakit database handle. The example extracts the handle and saves it in the $db variable. This is important because opening the same Metakit file twice (for writing) can cause corruption:

Example 22–18 Storing data in a Starkit.

```
package require starkit
starkit::startup
set db [lindex [vfs::filesystem info [$starkit::topdir]] 1]
mk::view layout $db.audit {action timestamp:I}
mk::row append $db.audit "Run as pid [pid]" [clock seconds]
puts "$argv0 has been run [mk::view size $db.audit] times"
```

To test this, put this example into the `main.tcl` of a trivial Starkit. When you create the Starkit, remember the `-writable` option with *sdx*:

```
mkdir bundle.vfs
cp 22_18.tcl bundle.vfs/main.tcl
sdx wrap bundle.kit -writable-
```

Wikit and the Tcler's Wiki

The alternative to storing data in the Starkit file is to have a separate Metakit data file. This is the approach taken by *Wikit*. The `wikit.kit` file is the Wikit application, and the `wikit.tkd` file is a Metakit database file that stores all the pages in the Wiki. (Creating a new Wiki is simple, just specify a different `.tkd` file name.) The advantage of having a separate Metakit file is that you can easily maintain your application by unwrapping and wrapping your application Starkit. Otherwise, if you put the application data directly into the Starkit you have to extract it and restore it as an additional maintenance step. In that case, you must use the `mk::file save` and `load` operations to save and restore your Metakit views to a file.

A Wiki is a web site that users can easily edit using a simplified markup syntax. Wikit is a Wiki implementation in Tcl using Metakit to store pages. It can run as a stand-alone Tk application, a GGI script, as its own little web server, or embedded into another application as a documentation bundle. There is a copy of `wikit.tkd` on the CD-ROM. For example, you run a stand alone copy of the Tcler's Wiki as:

```
tclkit wikit.kit wikit.tkd
```

The live Wiki is at `wiki.tcl.tk`[*], and you can find out more about Wikit at:

```
http://wiki.tcl.tk/wikit
```

More Ideas

This Chapter has provided a brief introduction to Tclkit, Starkits, and Metakit. This should be enough to help you get started creating your own Starkits and using Metakit for persistent storage. You should consult the documentation on the Web for more detailed reference material.

---

[*] http://wiki.tcl.tk is an alias for http://mini.net/tcl.

Document Bundles

The Starkit archive includes a number of documentation bundles. For example, `mk4dok.kit` is a Starkit that contains all the MetaKit documentation. These document bundles are all based on Wikit. It is very easy to create Wiki-style documentation for your application and then bundle it up as a Metakit file. You can load `wikit.kit` and your `.tkd` document bundle into your application and use the "local" Wikit interface to display your documentation. For example, the *critcl* Starkit displays its help with this simple command:

```
Wikit::init [file join $::starkit::topdir doc critcl.tkd]
```

Self-Updating Applications

The client in a client-server application is an ideal candidate for a self-updating application. The front-end client is a Starkit with some simple startup logic that connects to a server via HTTP and displays a pretty splash screen. The server, which is often based on TclHttpd, delivers code updates to the client. The client caches the code in the VFS inside the Starkit. The application is maintained on the server, and clients automatically get updated as they are used.

This scenario has the same deployment advantage as browser-based applications: you deploy a "thin-client" to desktops that rarely, if ever, changes and you update the application code on the server. In addition, this application structure lets you create a nice client front-end that uses Tcl/Tk instead of HTML, yet still have the benefit of an easy to manage server-side installation of the application code. This design pattern is being used for a number of large-scale commercial application deployments with considerable success.

A similar system is used with the Starkit archive. If you do:

```
sdx update tclhttpd.kit
```

The *sdx* application contacts the web server running the archive and checks for any updates available for the Starkit. Only the differences are transmitted, so updates are quick, and they are automatically applied to your copy of the Starkit. This should work for all the Starkits in the snapshot of the archive on the CD-ROM.

Simple Installers

In some cases you simply must install a collection of files as part of your application. It is very easy to include those files in the VFS, and then extract them into the local file system the first time your application runs. Or, you can create a traditional "installer" that unpacks the entire application from the Starkit (or Starpack).

Tk Basics

Part III introduces Tk, the toolkit for building graphical user interfaces. The Tcl command interface to Tk makes it quick and easy to build powerful user interfaces. Tk is portable and your user interface code can work unchanged on UNIX, Windows, and the Macintosh.

Chapter 23 describes the basic concepts of Tk and provides an overview of its facilities.

Chapter 24 illustrates Tk with three example programs including a browser for the examples from this book. These examples use facilities that are described in more detail in later chapters.

Geometry managers implement the layout of a user interface. Chapters Chapter 25, Chapter 26, and Chapter 27 describe the `pack`, `grid`, and `place` geometry managers. The packer and gridder are general-purpose managers that use constraints to create flexible layouts with a small amount of code. The placer is a special purpose geometry manager that can be used for special effects. Chapter 28 describes the panedwindow widget, which is also a geometry manager.

Chapter 29 describes event bindings that associate Tcl commands with events like keystrokes and mouse motion.

Tk Fundamentals

This chapter introduces the basic concepts used in the Tk graphical user interface toolkit. Tk adds about 45 Tcl commands that let you create and manipulate widgets in a graphical user interface. Tk works with the X window system, Windows, and Macintosh. The same script can run unchanged on all of these major platforms.

Tk is a toolkit for programming graphical user interfaces. It was designed for the X window system used on UNIX systems, and it was ported later to the Macintosh and Windows environments. Tk shares many concepts with other windowing toolkits, but you do not need to know much about graphical user interfaces to get started with Tk.

Tk provides a set of Tcl commands that create and manipulate *widgets*. A widget is a window in a graphical user interface that has a particular appearance and behavior. The terms *widget* and *window* are often used interchangeably. Widget types include buttons, scrollbars, menus, and text windows. Tk also has a general-purpose drawing widget called a *canvas* that lets you create lighter-weight items such as lines, boxes, and bitmaps. The canvas is extremely powerful, yet very easy to use. The Tcl commands added by Tk are summarized at the end of this chapter.

Tk widgets are organized in a hierarchy. To an application, the window hierarchy means that there is a primary window, and inside that window there can be a number of children windows. The children windows can contain more windows, and so on. Just as a hierarchical file system has directories (i.e., folders) that are containers for files and directories, a hierarchical window system uses windows as containers for other windows. The hierarchy affects the naming scheme used for Tk widgets as described later, and it is used to help arrange widgets on the screen.

Widgets are under the control of a *geometry manager* that controls their size and location on the screen. Until a geometry manager learns about a widget, it will not be mapped onto the screen and you will not see it. Tk has powerful geometry managers that make it very easy to create nice screen layouts. The main trick with any geometry manager is that you use *frame* widgets as containers for other widgets. One or more widgets are created and then arranged in a frame by a geometry manager. By putting frames within frames you can create complex layouts. There are three different geometry managers you can use in Tk: `grid`, `pack`, and `place`, and one widget, the panedwindow, that also acts as a geometry manager. The Tk geometry managers are discussed in detail in Chapters 25, 26, and 27; the panedwindow is discussed in Chapter 28.

A Tk-based application has an *event-driven* control flow, like most window system toolkits. The Tk widgets handle most events automatically, so programming your application remains simple. For specialized behaviors, you use the `bind` command to register a Tcl command that runs when an event occurs. There are lots of events, including mouse motion, keystrokes, window resize, and window destruction. You can also define *virtual events*, like `Cut` and `Paste`, that are caused by different events on different platforms. Bindings are discussed in detail in Chapter 29. Chapter 16 describes I/O events and the Tcl event loop, while Chapter 50 describes C programming and the event loop.

Event bindings are grouped into classes, which are called *bindtags*. The `bindtags` command associates a widget with an ordered set of bindtags. The level of indirection between the event bindings and the widgets creates a flexible and powerful system for managing events. You can create your own bindtags and dynamically change the bindtags for a widget to support mode changes in your application.

A concept related to binding is *focus*. At any given time, one of the widgets has the input focus, and keyboard events are directed to it. There are two general approaches to focusing: give focus to the widget under the mouse, or explicitly set the focus to a particular widget. Tk provides commands to change focus so you can implement either style of focus management. To support modal dialog boxes, you can forcibly *grab* the focus away from other widgets. Chapter 39 describes focus, grabs, and dialogs.

The basic structure of a Tk script begins by creating widgets and arranging them with a geometry manager, and then binding actions to the widgets. After the interpreter processes the commands that initialize the user interface, the event loop is entered and your application begins running.

If you use *wish* interactively, it creates and displays an empty main window and gives you a command-line prompt. With this interface, your keyboard commands are handled by the event loop, so you can build your Tk interface gradually. As we will see, you will be able to change virtually all aspects of your application interactively.

Hello, World! in Tk

Our first Tk script is very simple. It creates a button that prints "Hello, World!" to standard output when you press it. Above the button widget is a title bar that is provided by the window manager, which in this case is *twm* under X windows:

Example 23–1 "Hello, World!" Tk program.

```
#!/usr/local/bin/wish
button .hello -text Hello \
    -command {puts stdout "Hello, World!"}
pack .hello -padx 20 -pady 10
```

The first line identifies the interpreter for the script:

```
#!/usr/local/bin/wish
```

This special line is necessary if the script is in a file that will be used like other UNIX command files. Chapter 2 describes how to set up scripts on different platforms.

There are two Tcl commands in the script: one to create the button, and one to make it visible on the display. The button command creates an instance of a button:

```
button .hello -text Hello \
    -command {puts stdout "Hello, World!"}
=> .hello
```

The name of the button is .hello. The label on the button is Hello, and the command associated with the button is:

```
puts stdout "Hello, World!"
```

The pack command maps the button onto the screen. Some padding parameters are supplied, so there is space around the button:

```
pack .hello -padx 20 -pady 10
```

If you type these two commands into wish, you will not see anything happen when the button command is given. After the pack command, though, you will see the empty main window shrink to be just big enough to contain the button and its padding. The behavior of the packer will be discussed further in Chapters 24 and 25.

Tk uses an object-based system for creating and naming widgets. Associated with each class of widget (e.g., Button) is a command that creates instances of that class of widget. As the widget is created, a new Tcl command is defined that operates on that instance of the widget. Example 23–1 creates a button named .hello, and we can operate on the button using its name as a Tcl command. For example, we can cause the button to highlight a few times:

```
.hello flash
```

Or we can run the command associated with the button:

```
.hello invoke
=> Hello, World!
```

Tk has widget classes and instances, but it is not fully object oriented. It is not possible to subclass a widget class and use inheritance. Instead, Tk provides very flexible widgets that can be configured in many different ways to tune their appearance. The resource database can store configuration information that is shared by many widgets, and new classes can be introduced to group resources. Widget behavior is shared by using binding tags that group bindings. Instead of building class hierarchies, Tk uses composition to assemble widgets with shared behavior and attributes.

Naming Tk Widgets

The period in the name of the button instance, .hello, is required. Tk uses a naming system for the widgets that reflects their position in a hierarchy of widgets. The root of the hierarchy is the main window of the application, and its name is simply a dot (i.e., .). This is similar to the naming convention for directories in UNIX where the root directory is named /, and then / is used to separate components of a file name. Tk uses a dot in the same way. Each widget that is a child of the main window is named something like .foo. A child widget of .foo would be .foo.bar, and so on. Just as file systems have directories that are containers for files and other directories, the Tk window hierarchy uses frame widgets that are containers for widgets and other frames.

Each component of a Tk pathname must start with a lowercase letter or a number. Obviously, a component cannot include a period, either. The lower case restriction avoids a conflict with resource class names that begin with an upper case letter. A resource name can include Tk pathname components and Tk widget classes, and case is used to distinguish them. Chapter 31 describes resources in detail.

Store widget names in variables.

There is one drawback to the Tk widget naming system. If your interface changes enough it can result in some widgets changing their position in the widget hierarchy. In that case they may need to change their name. You can insulate yourself from this programming nuisance by using variables to hold the names of important widgets. Use a variable reference instead of widget pathnames in case you need to change things, or if you want to reuse your code in a different interface. The widget creating commands return the name of the widget:

```
set b [button .hello -text "Hello" -command {puts "Hello!"}]
```

You use $b as a command to operate on the button:

```
$b configure -background green
```

Configuring Tk Widgets

Example 23–1 illustrates a style of named parameter passing that is prevalent in the Tk commands. Pairs of arguments specify the attributes of a widget. The attribute names begin with -, such as -text, and the next argument is the value of that attribute. Even the simplest Tk widget can have a dozen or more attributes that can be specified this way, and complex widgets can have 30 or more attributes. However, the beauty of Tk is that you need to specify only the attributes for which the default value is not good enough. This is illustrated by the simplicity of the Hello, World example.

Finally, each widget instance supports a configure operation, which can be abbreviated to config, that can query and change these attributes. The syntax for config uses the same named argument pairs used when you create the widget. For example, we can change the background color of the button to red even after it has been created and mapped onto the screen:

```
.hello config -background red
```

Widget attributes can be redefined any time, even the text and command that were set when the button was created. The following command changes .hello into a goodbye button:

```
.hello config -text Goodbye! -command exit
```

Widgets have a cget operation to query the current value of an attribute:

```
.hello cget -background
=> red
```

You can find out more details about a widget attribute by using configure without a value:

```
.hello config -background
=> -background background Background #ffe4c4 red
```

The returned information includes the command-line switch, the resource name, the class name, the default value, and the current value, which is last. The class and resource name have to do with the resource mechanism described in Chapter 31. If you only specify configure and no attribute, then a list of the configuration information for all widget attributes is returned. Example 23–2 uses this to print out all the information about a widget:

Example 23–2 Looking at all widget attributes.

```
proc Widget_Attributes {w {out stdout}} {
    puts $out [format "%-20s %-10s %s" Attribute Default Value]
    foreach item [$w configure] {
        puts $out [format "%-20s %-10s %s" \
            [lindex $item 0] [lindex $item 3] \
            [lindex $item 4]]
    }
}
```

Tk Widget Attributes and the Resource Database

A widget attribute can be named three different ways: by its command-line option, by its resource name, and by its resource class. The command-line option is the format you use in Tcl scripts. This form is always all lowercase and prefixed with a hyphen (e.g., -offvalue). The resource name for the attribute has no leading hyphen, and it has uppercase letters at internal word boundaries (e.g., offValue). The resource class begins with an uppercase letter and has uppercase letters at internal word boundaries. (e.g., OffValue).

The tables in this book list widget attributes by their resource name.

You need to know these naming conventions if you specify widget attributes via the resource mechanism. The command-line option can be derived from the resource name by mapping it to all lowercase. The primary advantage of using resources to specify attributes is that you do not have to litter your code with attribute specifications. With just a few resource database entries you can specify attributes for all your widgets. In addition, if attributes are specified with resources, users can provide alternate resource specifications in order to override the values supplied by the application. For attributes like colors and fonts, this feature can be important to users. Resource specifications are described in detail in Chapter 31.

The Tk Manual Pages

This book provides summaries for all the Tk commands, the widget attributes, and the default bindings. However, for the absolute truth, you may need to read the on-line manual pages that come with Tk. They provide a complete reference source for the Tk commands. You should be able to use the UNIX *man* program to read them:

```
% man button
```

The *tkman* program provides a very nice graphical user interface to the UNIX manual pages. On the Macintosh platform, the manual pages are formatted into HTML documents that you can find in the HTML Docs folder of the Tcl/Tk distribution. On Windows, the manual pages are formatted into Help documents. You can find the manual pages on the web at:

```
http://www.tcl.tk/man/
```

There are a large number of attributes that are common across most of the Tk widgets. These are described in a separate man page under the name options. Each man page begins with a STANDARD OPTIONS section that lists which of these standard attributes apply, but you have to look at the options man page for the description. In contrast, the tables in this book always list all widget attributes.

Summary of the Tk Commands

The following tables list the Tcl commands added by Tk. The page number in the table is the primary reference for the command, and there are other references in the index.

Widget Commands

Table 23–1 lists commands that create widgets. There are 18 different widgets in Tk, although 4 of them are variations on a button, and 5 are devoted to different flavors of text display.

Table 23–1 Tk widget-creation commands.

Command	Pg.	Description
button	454	Create a command button.
canvas	557	Create a canvas, which supports lines, boxes, bitmaps, images, arcs, text, polygons, and embedded widgets.
checkbutton	458	Create a toggle button that is linked to a Tcl variable.
entry	507	Create a one-line text entry widget.
frame	485	Create a container widget used with geometry managers.
label	490	Create a read-only, multiline text label.
labelframe	485	Create a container widget used with geometry managers that has extra label attributes. (Tk 8.4)
listbox	519	Create a line-oriented, scrolling text widget.
menu	462	Create a menu.
menubutton	462	Create a button that posts a menu.
message	493	Create a read-only, multiline text message.
panedwindow	429	Create a container widget that controls other widgets in a paned fashion. (Tk 8.4)
radiobutton	458	Create one of a set of radio buttons linked to one variable.
scale	495	Create a scale widget that adjusts the value of a variable.
scrollbar	499	Create a scrollbar that can be linked to another widget.
spinbox	511	Create a spinbox widget that is a composite entry widget with button controls for adjusting the value. (Tk 8.4)
text	531	Create a general-purpose, editable text widget.
toplevel	485	Create a frame that is a new top level window.

III. Tk Basics

Widget Manipulation Commands

Table 23–2 lists commands that manipulate widgets and provide associated functions like input focus, event binding, and geometry management.

Table 23–2 Tk widget-manipulation commands.

Command	Pg.	Description
bell	497	Ring the terminal bell device.
bind	435	Bind a Tcl command to an event.
bindtags	437	Create binding classes and control binding inheritance.
clipboard	594	Manipulate the clipboard .
destroy	605	Delete a widget.
event	446	Define and generate virtual events.
focus	603	Control the input focus.
font	641	Set and query font attributes and measurements.
grab	604	Steal the input focus from other widgets.
grid	419	Arrange widgets into a grid with constraints.
image	626	Create and manipulate images.
lower	409	Lower a window in the stacking order.
option	477	Set and query the resources database.
pack	409	Pack a widget in the display with constraints.
place	427	Place a widget in the display with positions.
raise	409	Raise a window in the stacking order.
selection	593	Manipulate the selection.
send	648	Send a Tcl command to another Tk application.
tk	669	Query or set the application name or global caret.
tkerror	202	Handler for background errors.
tkwait	605	Wait for an event.
update	608	Update the display by going through the event loop.
winfo	663	Query window state.
wm	657	Interact with the window manager.

Support Procedures

Table 23–3 lists several support procedures that implement standard dialogs, option menus, and other facilities.

Table 23–3 Tk support procedures.

Command	Pg.	Description
tk_bisque	621	Install bisque family of colors.
tk_chooseColor	602	Dialog to select a color. (Tk 4.2)
tk_chooseDirectory	600	Dialog to select a directory. (Tk 8.2)
tk_dialog	599	Create simple dialogs.
tk_focusFollowsMouse	603	Install mouse-tracking focus model.
tk_focusNext	604	Focus on next widget in tab order.
tk_focusPrev	604	Focus on previous widget in tab order.
tk_getOpenFile	600	Dialog to open an existing file. (Tk 4.2)
tk_getSaveFile	600	Dialog to open a new file. (Tk 4.2)
tk_messageBox	600	Message dialog. (Tk 4.2)
tk_optionMenu	465	Create an option menu.
tk_popup	465	Create a pop-up menu.
tk_setPalette	621	Set the standard color palette. (Tk 4.2)

Other Widget Sets

This book describes the set of widgets provided by core Tk distribution. There are number of other widget sets for Tk. Some are implemented as Tcl procedures that compose the basic widgets into useful combinations (e.g., BWidgets). Others are C-based toolkits (e.g., Tix and BLT). A few of the more popular widget sets are listed here:

BLT

George Howlett created BLT. It includes a great graph widget that efficiently supports large datasets. It also includes a tabbed notebook and tree view widget. Its busy widget covers your application with a transparent widget that just displays a watch cursor, which is handy when the application is busy doing something and you don't want to accept mouse clicks. This is a C-based toolkit.

```
http://www.sourceforge.net/projects/blt/
```

Tix

Tix was created by Ioi Lam, and is now supported by a team of volunteers. It includes several widgets and an infrastructure for creating new widgets in Tcl. Notable features include balloon help, tabbed windows, paned window, and a hierarchy browser. This is a C-based toolkit, although it includes a number of compound widgets created in Tcl.

    http://tix.sourceforge.net/

[incr Tk] and [incr Widgets]

[incr Tk] is a C-based framework for creating compound widgets using the [incr Tcl] object system. [incr Widgets] is the widget set created using that framework. It includes loads of widgets, from simple labeled-entry widgets up through HTML display widgets. These tools are described in Chad Smith's book, *[incr Tcl] from the Ground Up* (Osborne-McGraw Hill, 1999).

    http://incrtcl.sourceforge.net

BWidgets

BWidgets is a set of Tcl-based widgets. It includes a variety of compound widgets, including a tabbed notebook, combobox, and hierarchy browser. It is hosted at the Standard Tcl Lib (tcllib) web site:

    http://www.sourceforge.net/projects/tcllib

TkTable

TkTable is combination of a gridding geometry manager and several text-oriented widgets. It makes it easy to lay out tabular data like spreadsheets, and it also provides a large amount of control over the formatting of cells and their data.

    http://www.sourceforge.net/projects/tktable

Tk by Example

This chapter introduces Tk through a series of short examples. The ExecLog
runs a program in the background and displays its output. The Example
Browser displays the Tcl examples from the book. The Tcl Shell lets you
type Tcl commands and execute them in a slave interpreter.

Tk provides a quick and fun way to gen-
erate user interfaces. In this chapter we will go through a series of short example
programs to give you a feel for what you can do. Some details are glossed over in
this chapter and considered in more detail later. In particular, the `pack` geometry manager is covered in Chapter 25 and event bindings are discussed in Chapter 29. The Tk widgets are discussed in more detail in later chapters.

ExecLog

Our first example provides a simple user interface to running another program
with the `exec` command. The interface consists of two buttons, `Run it` and `Quit`,
an entry widget in which to enter a command, and a text widget in which to log
the results of running the program. The script runs the program in a pipeline
and uses the `fileevent` command to wait for output. This structure lets the user
interface remain responsive while the program executes. You could use this to
run *make*, for example, and it would save the results in the log. The complete
example is given first, and then its commands are discussed in more detail.

Example 24–1 Logging the output of a program run with exec.

```
#!/usr/local/bin/wish
# execlog - run a program with exec and log the output
# Set window title
wm title . ExecLog

# Create a frame for buttons and entry.

frame .top -borderwidth 10
pack .top -side top -fill x

# Create the command buttons.

button .top.quit -text Quit -command exit
set but [button .top.run -text "Run it" -command Run]
pack .top.quit .top.run -side right

# Create a labeled entry for the command

label .top.l -text Command: -padx 0
entry .top.cmd -width 20 -relief sunken \
    -textvariable command
pack .top.l -side left
pack .top.cmd -side left -fill x -expand true

# Set up key binding equivalents to the buttons

bind .top.cmd <Return> Run
bind .top.cmd <Control-c> Stop
focus .top.cmd

# Create a text widget to log the output

frame .t
set log [text .t.log -width 80 -height 10 \
    -borderwidth 2 -relief raised -setgrid true \
    -yscrollcommand {.t.scroll set}]
```

```
scrollbar .t.scroll -command {.t.log yview}
pack .t.scroll -side right -fill y
pack .t.log -side left -fill both -expand true
pack .t -side top -fill both -expand true

# Run the program and arrange to read its input

proc Run {} {
    global command input log but
    if [catch {open "|$command |& cat"} input] {
        $log insert end $input\n
    } else {
        fileevent $input readable Log
        $log insert end $command\n
        $but config -text Stop -command Stop
    }
}

# Read and log output from the program

proc Log {} {
    global input log
    if [eof $input] {
        Stop
    } else {
        gets $input line
        $log insert end $line\n
        $log see end
    }
}

# Stop the program and fix up the button

proc Stop {} {
    global input but
    catch {close $input}
    $but config -text "Run it" -command Run
}
```

Window Title

The first command sets the title that appears in the title bar implemented by the window manager. Recall that dot (i.e., .) is the name of the main window:

```
wm title . ExecLog
```

The wm command communicates with the window manager. The window manager is the program that lets you open, close, and resize windows. It implements the title bar for the window and probably some small buttons to close or resize the window. Different window managers have a distinctive look; the figure shows a title bar from *twm*, a window manager for X.

III. Tk Basics

A Frame for Buttons

A frame is created to hold the widgets that appear along the top of the interface. The frame has a border to provide some space around the widgets:

```
frame .top -borderwidth 10
```

The frame is positioned in the main window. The default packing side is the top, so -side top is redundant here, but it is used for clarity. The -fill x packing option makes the frame fill out to the whole width of the main window:

```
pack .top -side top -fill x
```

Command Buttons

Two buttons are created: one to run the command, the other to quit the program. Their names, .top.quit and .top.run, imply that they are children of the .top frame. This affects the pack command, which positions widgets inside their parent by default:

```
button .top.quit -text Quit -command exit
set but [button .top.run -text "Run it" \
    -command Run]
pack .top.quit .top.run -side right
```

A Label and an Entry

The label and entry are also created as children of the .top frame. The label is created with no padding in the X direction so that it can be positioned right next to the entry. The size of the entry is specified in terms of characters. The relief attribute gives the entry some looks to set it apart visually on the display. The contents of the entry widget are linked to the Tcl variable command:

```
label .top.l -text Command: -padx 0
entry .top.cmd -width 20 -relief sunken \
    -textvariable command
```

The label and entry are positioned to the left inside the .top frame. The additional packing parameters to the entry allow it to expand its packing space and fill up that extra area with its display. The difference between packing space and display space is discussed in Chapter 25 on page 399:

```
pack .top.l -side left
pack .top.cmd -side left -fill x -expand true
```

Key Bindings and Focus

Key bindings on the entry widget provide an additional way to invoke the functions of the application. The bind command associates a Tcl command with an event in a particular widget. The <Return> event is generated when the user presses the Return key on the keyboard. The <Control-c> event is generated when the letter c is typed while the Control key is already held down. For the events to go to the entry widget, `.top.cmd`, input focus must be given to the widget. By default, an entry widget gets the focus when you click the left mouse button in it. The explicit `focus` command is helpful for users with the focus-follows-mouse model. As soon as the mouse is over the main window the user can type into the entry:

```
bind .top.cmd <Return> Run
bind .top.cmd <Control-c> Stop
focus .top.cmd
```

A Resizable Text and Scrollbar

A text widget is created and packed into a frame with a scrollbar. The width and height of the text widget are specified in characters and lines, respectively. The `setgrid` attribute of the text widget is turned on. This restricts the resize so that only a whole number of lines and average-sized characters can be displayed.

The scrollbar is a separate widget in Tk, and it can be connected to different widgets using the same setup as is used here. The text's `yscrollcommand` updates the display of the scrollbar when the text widget is modified, and the scrollbar's `command` scrolls the associated widget when the user manipulates the scrollbar:

```
frame .t
set log [text .t.log -width 80 -height 10 \
    -borderwidth 2 -relief raised -setgrid true\
    -yscrollcommand {.t.scroll set}]
scrollbar .t.scroll -command {.t.log yview}
pack .t.scroll -side right -fill y
pack .t.log -side left -fill both -expand true
pack .t -side top -fill both -expand true
```

A side effect of creating a Tk widget is the creation of a new Tcl command that operates on that widget. The name of the Tcl command is the same as the Tk pathname of the widget. In this script, the text widget command, `.t.log`, is needed in several places. However, it is a good idea to put the Tk pathname of an important widget into a variable because that pathname can change if you reorganize your user interface. The disadvantage of this is that you must declare the variable with `global` inside procedures. The variable `log` is used for this purpose in this example to demonstrate this style.

The Run Procedure

The `Run` procedure starts the program specified in the command entry. That value is available in the global `command` variable because of the `textvariable` attribute of the entry. The command is run in a pipeline so that it executes in the background. The leading | in the argument to `open` indicates that a pipeline is being created. The `catch` command guards against bogus commands. The variable `input` is set to an error message, or to the normal `open` return that is a file descriptor. The program is started like this:

```
if [catch {open "|$command |& cat"} input] {
```

Trapping errors from pipelines.

The pipeline diverts error output from the command through the *cat* program. If you do not use *cat* like this, then the error output from the pipeline, if any, shows up as an error message when the pipeline is closed. In this example it turns out to be awkward to distinguish between errors generated from the program and errors generated because of the way the `Stop` procedure is implemented. Furthermore, some programs interleave output and error output, and you might want to see the error output in order instead of all at the end.

If the pipeline is opened successfully, then a callback is set up using the `fileevent` command. Whenever the pipeline generates output, then the script can read data from it. The `Log` procedure is registered to be called whenever the pipeline is readable:

```
fileevent $input readable Log
```

The `command` (or the error message) is inserted into the log. This is done using the name of the text widget, which is stored in the `log` variable, as a Tcl command. The value of the command is appended to the log, and a newline is added so that its output will appear on the next line.

```
$log insert end $command\n
```

The text widget's `insert` function takes two parameters: a *mark* and a string to insert at that mark. The symbolic mark `end` represents the end of the contents of the text widget.

The run button is changed into a stop button after the program begins. This avoids a cluttered interface and demonstrates the dynamic nature of a Tk interface. Again, because this button is used in a few different places in the script, its pathname has been stored in the variable `but`:

```
$but config -text Stop -command Stop
```

The Log Procedure

The `Log` procedure is invoked whenever data can be read from the pipeline, and when end of file has been reached. This condition is checked first, and the `Stop` procedure is called to clean things up. Otherwise, one line of data is read and inserted into the log. The text widget's `see` operation is used to position the view on the text so that the new line is visible to the user:

```
if [eof $input] {
    Stop
} else {
    gets $input line
    $log insert end $line\n
    $log see end
}
```

The Stop Procedure

The Stop procedure terminates the program by closing the pipeline. The close is wrapped up with a catch. This suppresses the errors that can occur when the pipeline is closed prematurely on the process. Finally, the button is restored to its run state so that the user can run another command:

```
catch {close $input}
$but config -text "Run it" -command Run
```

In most cases, closing the pipeline is adequate to kill the job. On UNIX, this results in a signal, SIGPIPE, being delivered to the program the next time it does a write to its standard output. There is no built-in way to kill a process, but you can exec the UNIX *kill* program. The pid command returns the process IDs from the pipeline:

```
foreach pid [pid $input] {
    catch {exec kill $pid}
}
```

If you need more sophisticated control over another process, you should check out the *expect* Tcl extension, which is described in the book *Exploring Expect* (Don Libes, O'Reilly & Associates, Inc., 1995). *Expect* provides powerful control over interactive programs. You can write Tcl scripts that send input to interactive programs and pattern match on their output. *Expect* is designed to automate the use of programs that were designed for interactive use.

Cross-Platform Issues

This script will run on UNIX and Windows, but not on Macintosh because there is no exec command. One other problem is the binding for <Control-c> to cancel the job. This is UNIX-like, while Windows users expect <Escape> to cancel a job, and Macintosh users expect <Command-period>. Platform_CancelEvent defines a virtual event, <<Cancel>>, and Stop is bound to it:

Example 24–2 A platform-specific cancel event.

```
proc Platform_CancelEvent {} {
    global tcl_platform
    switch $tcl_platform(platform) {
        unix {
            event add <<Cancel>> <Control-c>
        }
        windows {
            event add <<Cancel>> <Escape>
        }
        macintosh {
            event add <<Cancel>> <Command-period>
        }
    }
}
bind .top.entry <<Cancel>> Stop
```

III. Tk Basics

There are other virtual events already defined by Tk. The event command and virtual events are described on page 446.

The Example Browser

Example 24–3 is a browser for the code examples that appear in this book. The basic idea is to provide a menu that selects the examples, and a text window to display the examples. Before you can use this sample program, you need to edit it to set the proper location of the exsource directory that contains all the example sources from the book. Example 24–4 on page 389 extends the browser with a shell that is used to test the examples.

Example 24–3 A browser for the code examples in the book.

```
#!/usr/local/bin/wish
#   Browser for the Tcl and Tk examples in the book.

# browse(dir) is the directory containing all the tcl files
# Please edit to match your system configuration.

switch $tcl_platform(platform) {
    "unix" {set browse(dir) /cdrom/tclbook2/exsource}
    "windows" {set browse(dir) D:/exsource}
    "macintosh" {set browse(dir) /tclbook2/exsource}
}

wm minsize . 30 5
wm title . "Tcl Example Browser"

# Create a row of buttons along the top

set f [frame .menubar]
pack $f -fill x
button $f.quit -text Quit -command exit
button $f.next -text Next -command Next
button $f.prev -text Previous -command Previous

# The Run and Reset buttons use EvalEcho that
# is defined by the Tcl shell in Example 24-4 on page 389

button $f.load -text Run -command Run
button $f.reset -text Reset -command Reset
pack $f.quit $f.reset $f.load $f.next $f.prev -side right

# A label identifies the current example

label $f.label -textvariable browse(current)
pack $f.label -side right -fill x -expand true

# Create the menubutton and menu
```

```
menubutton $f.ex -text Examples -menu $f.ex.m
pack $f.ex -side left
set m [menu $f.ex.m]

# Create the text to display the example
# Scrolled_Text is defined in Example 33-1 on page 500

set browse(text) [Scrolled_Text .body \
    -width 80 -height 10\
    -setgrid true]
pack .body -fill both -expand true

# Look through the example files for their ID number.

foreach f [lsort -dictionary [glob [file join $browse(dir) *]]] {
    if [catch {open $f} in] {
        puts stderr "Cannot open $f: $in"
        continue
    }
    while {[gets $in line] >= 0} {
        if [regexp {^# Example ([0-9]+)-([0-9]+)} $line \
                x chap ex] {
            lappend examples($chap) $ex
            lappend browse(list) $f
            # Read example title
            gets $in line
            set title($chap-$ex) [string trim $line "# "]
            set file($chap-$ex) $f
            close $in
            break
        }
    }
}

# Create two levels of cascaded menus.
# The first level divides up the chapters into chunks.
# The second level has an entry for each example.

option add *Menu.tearOff 0
set limit 8
set c 0; set i 0
foreach chap [lsort -integer [array names examples]] {
    if {$i == 0} {
        $m add cascade -label "Chapter $chap..." \
            -menu $m.$c
        set sub1 [menu $m.$c]
        incr c
    }
    set i [expr ($i +1) % $limit]
    $sub1 add cascade -label "Chapter $chap" -menu $sub1.sub$i
    set sub2 [menu $sub1.sub$i]
    foreach ex [lsort -integer $examples($chap)] {
        $sub2 add command -label "$chap-$ex $title($chap-$ex)" \
            -command [list Browse $file($chap-$ex)]
```

```
        }
}

# Display a specified file. The label is updated to
# reflect what is displayed, and the text is left
# in a read-only mode after the example is inserted.

proc Browse { file } {
    global browse
    set browse(current) [file tail $file]
    set browse(curix) [lsearch $browse(list) $file]
    set t $browse(text)
    $t config -state normal
    $t delete 1.0 end
    if [catch {open $file} in] {
        $t insert end $in
    } else {
        $t insert end [read $in]
        close $in
    }
    $t config -state disabled
}

# Browse the next and previous files in the list

set browse(curix) -1
proc Next {} {
    global browse
    if {$browse(curix) < [llength $browse(list)] - 1} {
        incr browse(curix)
    }
    Browse [lindex $browse(list) $browse(curix)]
}
proc Previous {} {
    global browse
    if {$browse(curix) > 0} {
        incr browse(curix) -1
    }
    Browse [lindex $browse(list) $browse(curix)]
}

# Run the example in the shell

proc Run {} {
    global browse
    EvalEcho [list source \
        [file join $browse(dir) $browse(current)]]
}

# Reset the slave in the eval server

proc Reset {} {
    EvalEcho reset
}
```

More about Resizing Windows

This example uses the `wm minsize` command to put a constraint on the minimum size of the window. The arguments specify the minimum width and height. These values can be interpreted in two ways. By default they are pixel values. However, if an internal widget has enabled *geometry gridding*, then the dimensions are in grid units of that widget. In this case the text widget enables gridding with its `setgrid` attribute, so the minimum size of the window is set so that the text window is at least 30 characters wide by five lines high:

```
wm minsize . 30 5
```

In older versions of Tk, Tk 3.6, gridding also enabled interactive resizing of the window. Interactive resizing is enabled by default in Tk 4.0 and later.

Managing Global State

The example uses the `browse` array to collect its global variables. This makes it simpler to reference the state from inside procedures because only the array needs to be declared global. As the application grows over time and new features are added, that `global` command won't have to be adjusted. This style also serves to emphasize what variables are important. The `browse` array holds the name of the example directory (`dir`), the Tk pathname of the text display (`text`), and the name of the current file (`current`). The `list` and `curix` elements are used to implement the `Next` and `Previous` procedures.

Searching through Files

The browser searches the file system to determine what it can display. The `tcl_platform(platform)` variable is used to select a different example directory on different platforms. You may need to edit the on-line example to match your system. The example uses `glob` to find all the files in the `exsource` directory. The `file join` command is used to create the file name pattern in a platform-independent way. The result of `glob` is sorted explicitly so the menu entries are in the right order. Each file is read one line at a time with `gets`, and then `regexp` is used to scan for keywords. The loop is repeated here for reference:

```
foreach f [lsort -dictionary [glob -directory $browse(dir) *]] {
    if {[catch {open $f} in]} {
        puts stderr "Cannot open $f: $in"
        continue
    }
    while {[gets $in line] >= 0} {
        if {[regexp {^# Example ([0-9]+)-([0-9]+)} $line \
                x chap ex]} {
            lappend examples($chap) $ex
            lappend browse(list) $f
            # Read example title
            gets $in line
            set title($chap-$ex) [string trim $line "# "]
            set file($chap-$ex) $f
```

```
            close $in
            break
        }
    }
}
```

The example files contain lines like this:

```
# Example 1-1
# The Hello, World! program
```

The `regexp` picks out the example numbers with the `([0-9]+)-([0-9]+)` part of the pattern, and these are assigned to the `chap` and `ex` variables. The `x` variable is assigned the value of the whole match, which is more than we are interested in. Once the example number is found, the next line is read to get the description of the example. At the end of the `foreach` loop the `examples` array has an element defined for each chapter, and the value of each element is a list of the examples for that chapter.

Cascaded Menus

The values in the `examples` array are used to build up a cascaded menu structure. First a menubutton is created that will post the main menu. It is associated with the main menu with its `menu` attribute. The menu must be a child of the menubutton for its display to work properly:

```
menubutton $f.ex -text Examples -menu $f.ex.m
set m [menu $f.ex.m]
```

There are too many chapters to put them all into one menu. The main menu has a `cascade` entry for each group of eight chapters. Each of these submenus has a `cascade` entry for each chapter in the group, and each chapter has a menu of all its examples. Once again, the submenus are defined as a child of their parent menu. Note the inconsistency between menu entries and buttons. Their text is defined with the `-label` option, not `-text`. Other than this they are much like buttons. Chapter 30 describes menus in more detail. The code is repeated here:

```
set limit 8 ; set c 0 ; set i 0
foreach key [lsort -integer [array names examples]] {
    if {$i == 0} {
        $m add cascade -label "Chapter $key..." \
            -menu $m.$c
        set sub1 [menu $m.$c]
        incr c
    }
    set i [expr {($i +1) % $limit}]
    $sub1 add cascade -label "Chapter $key" -menu $sub1.sub$i
    set sub2 [menu $sub1.sub$i]
    foreach ex [lsort -integer $examples($key)] {
        $sub2 add command -label "$key-$ex $title($key-$ex)" \
            -command [list Browse $file($key-$ex)]
    }
}
```

A Read-Only Text Widget

The `Browse` procedure is fairly simple. It sets `browse(current)` to be the name of the file. This changes the main label because of its `textvariable` attribute that links it to this variable. The `state` attribute of the text widget is manipulated so that the text is read-only after the text is inserted. You have to set the `state` to `normal` before inserting the text; otherwise, the `insert` has no effect. Here are a few commands from the body of `Browse`:

```
global browse
set browse(current) [file tail $file]
$t config -state normal
$t insert end [read $in]
$t config -state disabled
```

A Tcl Shell

This section demonstrates the text widget with a simple Tcl shell application. It uses a text widget to prompt for commands and display their results. It uses a second Tcl interpreter to evaluate the commands you type. This dual interpreter structure is used by the console built into the Windows and Macintosh versions of *wish*. The *TkCon* application written by Jeff Hobbs is an even more elaborate console that has many features to support interactive Tcl use:

> http://tkcon.sourceforge.net/

Example 24–4 is written to be used with the browser from Example 24–3 in the same application. The browser's `Run` button runs the current example in the shell. An alternative is to have the shell run as a separate process and use the `send` command to communicate Tcl commands between separate applications. That alternative is shown in Example 43–2 on page 651.

Example 24–4 A Tcl shell in a text widget.

```
#!/usr/local/bin/wish
# Simple evaluator. It executes Tcl in a slave interpreter

set t [Scrolled_Text .eval -width 80 -height 10]
pack .eval -fill both -expand true

# Text tags give script output, command errors, command
# results, and the prompt a different appearance

$t tag configure prompt -underline true
$t tag configure result -foreground purple
$t tag configure error -foreground red
$t tag configure output -foreground blue

# Insert the prompt and initialize the limit mark

set eval(prompt) "tcl> "
$t insert insert $eval(prompt) prompt
```

III. Tk Basics

```
$t mark set limit insert
$t mark gravity limit left
focus $t
set eval(text) $t

# Key bindings that limit input and eval things. The break in
# the bindings skips the default Text binding for the event.

bind $t <Return> {EvalTypein ; break}
bind $t <BackSpace> {
    if {[%W tag nextrange sel 1.0 end] != ""} {
        %W delete sel.first sel.last
    } elseif {[%W compare insert > limit]} {
        %W delete insert-1c
        %W see insert
    }
    break
}
bind $t <Key> {
    if [%W compare insert < limit] {
        %W mark set insert end
    }
}


# Evaluate everything between limit and end as a Tcl command

proc EvalTypein {} {
    global eval
    $eval(text) insert insert \n
    set command [$eval(text) get limit end]
    if [info complete $command] {
        $eval(text) mark set limit insert
        Eval $command
    }
}

# Echo the command and evaluate it

proc EvalEcho {command} {
    global eval
    $eval(text) mark set insert end
    $eval(text) insert insert $command\n
    Eval $command
}

# Evaluate a command and display its result

proc Eval {command} {
    global eval
    $eval(text) mark set insert end
    if [catch {$eval(slave) eval $command} result] {
        $eval(text) insert insert $result error
    } else {
        $eval(text) insert insert $result result
    }
```

```
        if {[$eval(text) compare insert != "insert linestart"]} {
            $eval(text) insert insert \n
        }
        $eval(text) insert insert $eval(prompt) prompt
        $eval(text) see insert
        $eval(text) mark set limit insert
        return
}

# Create and initialize the slave interpreter

proc SlaveInit {slave} {
    interp create $slave
    load {} Tk $slave
    interp alias $slave reset {} ResetAlias $slave
    interp alias $slave puts {} PutsAlias $slave
    return $slave
}

# The reset alias deletes the slave and starts a new one

proc ResetAlias {slave} {
    interp delete $slave
    SlaveInit $slave
}

# The puts alias puts stdout and stderr into the text widget

proc PutsAlias {slave args} {
    if {[llength $args] > 3} {
        error "invalid arguments"
    }
    set newline "\n"
    if {[string match "-nonewline" [lindex $args 0]]} {
        set newline ""
        set args [lreplace $args 0 0]
    }
    if {[llength $args] == 1} {
        set chan stdout
        set string [lindex $args 0]$newline
    } else {
        set chan [lindex $args 0]
        set string [lindex $args 1]$newline
    }
    if [regexp (stdout|stderr) $chan] {
        global eval
        $eval(text) mark gravity limit right
        $eval(text) insert limit $string output
        $eval(text) see limit
        $eval(text) mark gravity limit left
    } else {
        puts -nonewline $chan $string
    }
}
set eval(slave) [SlaveInit shell]
```

Text Marks, Tags, and Bindings

The shell uses a text *mark* and some extra bindings to ensure that users only type new text into the end of the text widget. A mark represents a position in the text that is updated as characters are inserted and deleted. The `limit` mark keeps track of the boundary between the read-only area and the editable area. The `insert` mark is where the cursor is displayed. The `end` mark is always the end of the text. The `EvalTypein` procedure looks at all the text between `limit` and `end` to see if it is a complete Tcl command. If it is, it evaluates the command in the slave interpreter.

The `<Key>` binding checks to see where the `insert` mark is and bounces it to the `end` if the user tries to input text before the `limit` mark. The `puts` alias sets `right` gravity on `limit`, so the mark is pushed along when program output is inserted right at `limit`. Otherwise, the `left` gravity on `limit` means that the mark does not move when the user inserts right at `limit`.

Text *tags* are used to give different regions of text difference appearances. A tag applies to a range of text. The tags are configured at the beginning of the script and they are applied when text is inserted.

Chapter 36 describes the text widget in more detail.

Multiple Interpreters

The `SlaveInit` procedure creates another interpreter to evaluate the commands. This prevents conflicts with the procedures and variables used to implement the shell. Initially, the slave interpreter only has access to Tcl commands. The `load` command installs the Tk commands, and it creates a new top-level window that is "." for the slave interpreter. Chapter 20 describes how you can embed the window of the slave within other frames.

The `shell` interpreter is not created with the `-safe` flag, so it can do anything. For example, if you type `exit`, it will exit the whole application. The `SlaveInit` procedure installs an alias, `reset`, that just deletes the slave interpreter and creates a new one. You can use this to clean up after working in the shell for a while. Chapter 19 describes the `interp` command in detail.

Native Look and Feel

When you run a Tk script on different platforms, it uses native buttons, menus, and scrollbars. The text and entry widgets are tuned to give the application the native look and feel. The following screen shots show the combined browser and shell as it looks on Macintosh, Windows, and UNIX.

Example 24–5 Macintosh look and feel.

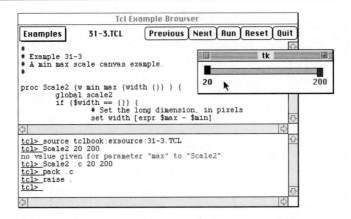

Example 24–6 Windows look and feel.

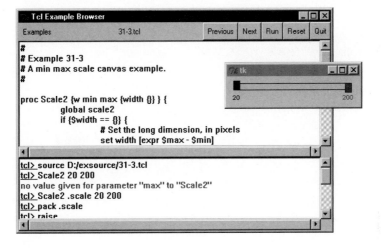

Example 24–7 UNIX look and feel.

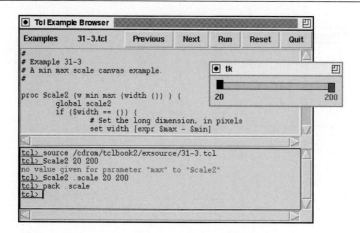

The Pack Geometry Manager

This chapter explores the `pack` geometry manager that positions widgets on the screen.

Geometry managers arrange widgets on the screen. This chapter describes the `pack` geometry manager, which is a constraint-based system. The next two chapters describe the `grid` and `place` geometry managers. The `pack` and `grid` geometry managers are quite general, while `place` is used for special-purpose applications. This book uses `pack` a lot because it was the original geometry manager for Tk. The `grid` geometry manager was added in Tk 4.1.

A geometry manager uses one widget as a *parent*, and it arranges multiple *children* (also called *slaves*) inside the parent. The parent is almost always a frame, but this is not strictly necessary. A widget can only be managed by one geometry manager at a time, but you can use different managers to control different widgets in your user interface. If a widget is not managed, then it doesn't appear on your display at all.

Don't `pack` *and* `grid` *into the same manager widget.*

For each individual manager widget — such as a frame, a labelframe, or a toplevel — you have the choice of using either `pack` or `grid` to manage all of its immediate children. Attempting to use both in the same manager results in an endless loop as both geometry managers try to control the window layout. This restriction applies only to the immediate children of a manager widget; you can use a different geometry manager for "descendents" that aren't immediate children. For example, you can choose to `pack` all of the immediate children of the . toplevel. Then, if one of the children of . is a frame, you can choose to use either `pack` or `grid` to manage the children of that frame.

The packer is a powerful constraint-based geometry manager. Instead of specifying in detail the placement of each window, the programmer defines some constraints about how windows should be positioned, and the packer works out the details. It is important to understand the algorithm the packer uses; otherwise, the constraint-based results may not be what you expect.

This chapter explores the packer through a series of examples. The background of the main window is set to black, and the other frames are given different colors so you can identify frames and observe the effect of the different packing parameters. When consecutive examples differ by a small amount, the added command or option is printed in **bold courier** to highlight the addition.

Packing toward a Side

The following example creates two frames and packs them toward the top side of the main window. The upper frame, .one, is not as big and the main window shows through on either side. The children are packed toward the specified side in order, so .one is on top. The four possible sides are: top, right, bottom, and left. The top side is the default.

Example 25–1 Two frames packed inside the main frame.

```
# Make the main window black
. config -bg black
# Create and pack two frames
frame .one -width 40 -height 40 -bg white
frame .two -width 100 -height 50 -bg grey50
pack .one .two -side top
```

Shrinking Frames and pack propagate

In the previous example, the main window shrank down to be just large enough to hold its two children. In most cases this is the desired behavior. If not, you can turn it off with the pack propagate command. Apply this to the parent frame, and it will not adjust its size to fit its children:

Example 25–2 Turning off geometry propagation.

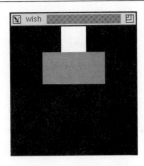

```
frame .one -width 40 -height 40 -bg white
frame .two -width 100 -height 50 -bg grey50
pack propagate . false
pack .one .two -side top
```

Horizontal and Vertical Stacking

In general, you use either horizontal or vertical stacking within a frame. If you
mix sides such as left and top, the effect might not be what you expect. Instead,
you should introduce more frames to pack a set of widgets into a stack of a different orientation. For example, suppose we want to put a row of buttons inside the
upper frame in the examples we have given so far:

Example 25–3 A horizontal stack inside a vertical stack.

```
frame .one -bg white
frame .two -width 100 -height 50 -bg grey50
# Create a row of buttons
foreach b {alpha beta gamma} {
    button .one.$b -text $b
    pack .one.$b -side left
}
pack .one .two -side top
```

Example 25–4 Even more nesting of horizontal and vertical stacks.

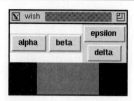

```
frame .one -bg white
frame .two -width 100 -height 50 -bg grey50
foreach b {alpha beta} {
    button .one.$b -text $b
    pack .one.$b -side left
}
# Create a frame for two more buttons
frame .one.right
foreach b {delta epsilon} {
    button .one.right.$b -text $b
    pack .one.right.$b -side bottom
}
pack .one.right -side right
pack .one .two -side top
```

You can build more complex arrangements by introducing nested frames and switching between horizontal and vertical stacking as you go. Within each frame pack all the children with either a combination of -side left and -side right, or -side top and -side bottom.

Example 25–4 replaces the .one.gamma button with a vertical stack of two buttons, .one.right.delta and .one.right.epsilon. These are packed toward the bottom of .one.right, so the first one packed is on the bottom.

The frame .one.right was packed to the right, and in the previous example, the button .one.gamma was packed to the left. Despite the difference, they ended up in the same position relative to the other two widgets packed inside the .one frame. The next section explains why.

The Cavity Model

The packing algorithm is based on a *cavity model* for the available space inside a frame. For example, when the main *wish* window is created, the main frame is empty and there is an obvious space, or cavity, in which to place widgets. The primary rule about the packing cavity is *a widget occupies one whole side of the cavity.* To demonstrate this, pack three widgets into the main frame. Put the first two on the bottom, and the third one on the right:

Example 25–5 Mixing bottom and right packing sides.

```
# pack two frames on the bottom.
frame .one -width 100 -height 50 -bg grey50
frame .two -width 40 -height 40 -bg white
pack .one .two -side bottom
# pack another frame to the right
frame .three -width 20 -height 20 -bg grey75
pack .three -side right
```

When we pack a third frame into the main window with `-side left` or `-side right`, the new frame is positioned inside the cavity, which is above the two frames already packed toward the bottom side. The frame does not appear to the right of the existing frames as you might have expected. This is because the `.two` frame occupies the whole bottom side of the packing cavity, even though its display does not fill up that side.

Can you tell where the packing cavity is after this example? It is to the left of the frame `.three`, which is the last frame packed toward the right, and it is above the frame `.two`, which is the last frame packed toward the bottom. This explains why there was no difference between the previous two examples when `.one.gamma` was packed to the left, but `.one.right` was packed to the right. At that point, packing to the left or right of the cavity had the same effect. However, it will affect what happens if another widget is packed into those two configurations. Try out the following commands after running Example 25–3 and Example 25–4 and compare the difference.[*]

```
button .one.omega -text omega
pack .one.omega -side right
```

Each packing parent has its own cavity, which is why introducing nested frames can help. If you use a horizontal or vertical arrangement inside any given frame, you can more easily simulate the packer's behavior in your head!

Packing Space and Display Space

The packer distinguishes between *packing* space and *display* space when it arranges the widgets. The display space is the area requested by a widget for the purposes of painting itself. The packing space is the area the packer allows for the placement of the widget. Because of geometry constraints, a widget may be allocated more (or less) packing space than it needs to display itself. The extra space, if any, is along the side of the cavity against which the widget was packed.

---

[*] Answer: After Example 25–3 the new button is to the right of all buttons. After Example 25–4 the new button is between `.one.beta` and `.one.right`.

The -fill Option

The -fill packing option causes a widget to fill up the allocated packing space with its display. A widget can fill in the X or Y direction, or both. The default is not to fill, which is why the black background of the main window has shown through in the examples so far:

Example 25–6 Filling the display into extra packing space.

```
frame .one -width 100 -height 50 -bg grey50
frame .two -width 40 -height 40 -bg white
# Pack with fill enabled
pack .one .two -side bottom -fill x
frame .three -width 20 -height 20 -bg red
pack .three -side right -fill x
```

This is just like Example 25–5, except that -fill x has been specified for all the frames. The .two frame fills, but the .three frame does not. This is because the fill does not expand into the packing cavity. In fact, after this example, the packing cavity is the part that shows through in black. Another way to look at this is that the .two frame was allocated the whole bottom side of the packing cavity, so its fill can expand the frame to occupy that space. The .three frame has only been allocated the right side, so a fill in the X direction will not have any effect.

Another use of fill is for a menu bar that has buttons at either end and some empty space between them. The frame that holds the buttons is packed toward the top. The buttons are packed into the left and right sides of the menu bar frame. Without fill, the menu bar shrinks to be just large enough to hold all the buttons, and the buttons are squeezed together. When fill is enabled in the X direction, the menu bar fills out the top edge of the display:

Example 25–7 Using horizontal fill in a menu bar.

```
frame .menubar -bg white
frame .body -width 150 -height 50 -bg grey50
# Create buttons at either end of the menubar
foreach b {alpha beta} {
    button .menubar.$b -text $b
}
```

```
pack .menubar.alpha -side left
pack .menubar.beta -side right
# Let the menu bar fill along the top
pack .menubar -side top -fill x
pack .body
```

Internal Padding with -ipadx and -ipady

Another way to get more fill space is with the -ipadx and -ipady packing options that request more display space in the X and Y directions, respectively. Due to other constraints the request might not be offered, but in general you can use this to give a widget more display space. The next example is just like the previous one except that some internal padding has been added:

Example 25–8 The effects of internal padding (-ipady).

```
# Create and pack two frames
frame .menubar -bg white
frame .body -width 150 -height 50 -bg grey50
# Create buttons at either end of the menubar
foreach b {alpha beta} {
    button .menubar.$b -text $b
}
pack .menubar.alpha -side left -ipady 10
pack .menubar.beta -side right -ipadx 10
# Let the menu bar fill along the top
pack .menubar -side top -fill x -ipady 5
pack .body
```

The alpha button is taller and the beta button is wider because of the internal padding. The frame has internal padding, which reduces the space available for the packing cavity, so the .menubar frame shows through above and below the buttons.

Some widgets have attributes that result in more display space. For example, it would be hard to distinguish a frame with width 50 and no internal padding from a frame with width 40 and a -ipadx 5 packing option. The packer would give the frame 5 more pixels of display space on either side for a total width of 50.

Buttons have their own -padx and -pady options that give them more display space, too. This padding provided by the button is used to keep its text away from the edge of the button. The following example illustrates the difference. The -anchor e button option positions the text as far to the right as possible. Example 40–5 on page 617 provides another comparison of these options:

III. Tk Basics

Example 25–9 Button padding vs. packer padding.

```
# Foo has internal padding from the packer
button .foo -text Foo -anchor e -padx 0 -pady 0
pack .foo -side right -ipadx 10 -ipady 10
# Bar has its own padding
button .bar -text Bar -anchor e -pady 10 -padx 10
pack .bar -side right -ipadx 0 -ipady 0
```

In all cases, you can specify the amount of padding using any type of screen distance recognized by Tk. A simple numeric value is interpreted as pixels. You can also follow a number with one of i, m, c, or p, which is interpreted as inches, millimeters, centimeters, or typographic points, respectively.

External Padding with -padx and -pady

The packer can provide external padding that allocates packing space that cannot be filled. The space is outside of the border that widgets use to implement their 3D reliefs. Example 40–2 on page 614 shows the different reliefs. The look of a default button is achieved with an extra frame and some padding:

Example 25–10 The look of a default button.

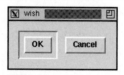

```
. config -borderwidth 10
# OK is the default button
frame .ok -borderwidth 2 -relief sunken
button .ok.b -text OK
pack .ok.b -padx 5 -pady 5
# Cancel is not
button .cancel -text Cancel
pack .ok .cancel -side left -padx 5 -pady 5
```

The .ok.b button looks the same even if it is packed with -fill both. The child widgets do not fill the external padding provided by the packer.

Example 25–10 handcrafts the look of a default button. Tk 8.0 added a -default attribute for buttons that gives them the right appearance for the default button on the current platform. It looks somewhat like this on UNIX, but the appearance is different on Macintosh and Windows.

Tk 8.4 added the ability to specify asymmetric padding as a list of two screen distances. For example, the following adds 5 pixels of padding to the left and right of the widgets, 3 pixels above them, and 6 pixels below them:

```
pack .ok .cancel -side left -padx 5 -pady {3 6}
```

Resizing and -expand

The -expand true packing option lets a widget expand its packing space into unclaimed space in the packing cavity. Example 25–6 could use this on the small frame on top to get it to expand across the top of the display, even though it is packed to the right side. The more common case occurs when you have a resizable window. When the user makes the window larger, the widgets have to be told to take advantage of the extra space. Suppose you have a main widget like a text, listbox, or canvas that is in a frame with a scrollbar. That frame has to be told to expand into the extra space in its parent (e.g., the main window) and then the main widget (e.g., the canvas) has to be told to expand into its parent frame. Example 24–1 on page 378 does this.

In nearly all cases the -fill both option is used along with -expand true so that the widget actually uses its extra packing space for its own display. The converse is not true. There are many cases where a widget should fill extra space but not attempt to expand into the packing cavity. The examples below show the difference.

Now we can investigate what happens when the window is made larger. The next example starts like Example 25–7 on page 400, but the size of the main window is increased:

Example 25–11 Resizing without the expand option.

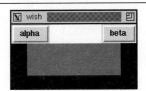

```
# Make the main window black
. config -bg black
# Create and pack two frames
frame .menubar -bg white
frame .body -width 150 -height 50 -bg grey50
# Create buttons at either end of the menubar
foreach b {alpha beta} {
    button .menubar.$b -text $b
}
pack .menubar.alpha -side left
pack .menubar.beta -side right
# Let the menu bar fill along the top
pack .menubar -side top -fill x
pack .body
# Resize the main window to be bigger
wm geometry . 200x100
# Allow interactive resizing
wm minsize . 100 50
```

The only widget that claims any of the new space is .menubar because of its -fill x packing option. The .body frame needs to be packed properly:

III. Tk Basics

Example 25–12 Resizing with expand turned on.

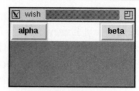

```
# Use all of Example 25-11 then repack .body
pack .body -expand true -fill both
```

If more than one widget inside the same parent is allowed to expand, then the packer shares the extra space between them proportionally. This is probably not the effect you want in the examples we have built so far. The .menubar, for example, is not a good candidate for expansion.

Example 25–13 More than one expanding widget.

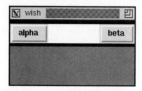

```
# Use all of Example 25-11 then repack .menubar and .body
pack .menubar -expand true -fill x
pack .body -expand true -fill both
```

Anchoring

If a widget is left with more packing space than display space, you can position it within its packing space using the -anchor packing option. The default anchor position is center. The other options correspond to points on a compass: n, ne, e, se, s, sw, w, and nw:

Example 25–14 Setup for anchor experiments.

```
# Make the main window black
. config -bg black
# Create two frames to hold open the cavity
frame .prop -bg white -height 80 -width 20
frame .base -width 120 -height 20 -bg grey50
```

```
pack .base -side bottom
# Float a label and the prop in the cavity
label .foo -text Foo
pack .prop .foo -side right -expand true
```

The .base frame is packed on the bottom. Then the .prop frame and the .foo label are packed to the right with expand set but no fill. Instead of being pressed up against the right side, the expand gives each of these widgets half of the extra space in the X direction. Their default anchor of center results in the positions shown. The next example shows some different anchor positions:

Example 25–15 The effects of noncenter anchors.

```
. config -bg black
# Create two frames to hold open the cavity
frame .prop -bg white -height 80 -width 20
frame .base -width 120 -height 20 -bg grey50
pack .base -side bottom
# Float the label and prop
# Change their position with anchors
label .foo -text Foo
pack .prop -side right -expand true -anchor sw
pack .foo -side right -expand true -anchor ne
```

The label has room on all sides, so each of the different anchors will position it differently. The .prop frame only has room in the X direction, so it can only be moved into three different positions: left, center, and right. Any of the anchors w, nw, and sw result in the left position. The anchors center, n, and s result in the center position. The anchors e, se, and ne result in the right position.

If you want to see all the variations, type in the following commands to animate the different packing anchors. The update idletasks forces any pending display operations. The after 500 causes the script to wait for 500 milliseconds:

Example 25–16 Animating the packing anchors.

```
foreach anchor {center n ne e se s sw w nw center} {
    pack .foo .prop -anchor $anchor
    # Update the display
    update idletasks
    # Wait half a second
    after 500
}
```

III. Tk Basics

Packing Order

The packer maintains an order among the children that are packed into a frame. By default, each new child is appended to the end of the packing order. The most obvious effect of the order is that the children first in the packing order are closest to the side they are packed against. You can control the packing order with the -before and -after packing options, and you can reorganize widgets after they have already been packed:

Example 25–17 Controlling the packing order.

```
# Create five labels in order
foreach label {one two three four five} {
    label .$label -text $label
    pack .$label -side left -padx 5
}
# ShuffleUp moves a widget to the beginning of the order
proc ShuffleUp { parent child } {
    set first [lindex [pack slaves $parent] 0]
    pack $child -in $parent -before $first
}
# ShuffleDown moves a widget to the end of the order
proc ShuffleDown { parent child } {
    pack $child -in $parent
}
ShuffleUp . .five
ShuffleDown . .three
```

Introspection

The pack slaves command returns the list of children in their packing order. The ShuffleUp procedure uses this to find out the first child so that it can insert another child before it. The ShuffleDown procedure is simpler because the default is to append the child to the end of the packing order.

When a widget is repacked, then it retains all its packing parameters that have already been set. If you need to examine the current packing parameters for a widget, use the pack info command.

```
pack info .five
=> -in . -anchor center -expand 0 -fill none -ipadx 0 \
      -ipady 0 -padx 0 -pady 0 -side left
```

Pack the Scrollbar First

The packing order also determines what happens when the window is made too small. If the window is made small enough the packer will clip children that come later in the packing order. This is why, when you pack a scrollbar and a text widget into a frame, you should pack the scrollbar first. Otherwise, when the window is made smaller the `text` widget takes up all the space and the scrollbar is clipped.

Choosing the Parent for Packing

In nearly all of the examples in this chapter, a widget is packed into its parent frame. In general, it is possible to pack a widget into any descendent of its parent. For example, the `.a.b` widget could be packed into `.a`, `.a.c` or `.a.d.e.f`. The `-in` packing option lets you specify an alternate packing parent. One motivation for this is that the frames introduced to get the arrangement right can cause cluttered names for important widgets. In Example 25–4 on page 398, the buttons have names like `.one.alpha` and `.one.right.delta`, which is not consistent. Here is an alternate implementation of the same example that simplifies the button names and gives the same result:

Example 25–18 Packing into other relatives.

```
# Create and pack two frames
frame .one -bg white
frame .two -width 100 -height 50 -bg grey50
# Create a row of buttons
foreach b {alpha beta} {
    button .$b -text $b
    pack .$b -in .one -side left
}
# Create a frame for two more buttons
frame .one.right
foreach b {delta epsilon} {
    button .$b -text $b
    pack .$b -in .one.right -side bottom
}
pack .one.right -side right
pack .one .two -side top
```

When you do this, remember that the order in which you create widgets is important. Create the frames first, then create the widgets. The stacking order for windows will cause the later windows to obscure the windows created first. The following is a common mistake because the frame obscures the button:

```
button .a -text hello
frame .b
pack .a -in .b
```

If you cannot avoid this problem scenario, then you can use the `raise` command to fix things up. Stacking order is also discussed on page 409.

```
raise .a
```

Unpacking a Widget

The `pack forget` command removes a widget from the packing order. The widget gets unmapped, so it is not visible. If you unpack a parent frame, the packing structure inside it is maintained, but all the widgets inside the frame get unmapped. Unpacking a widget is useful if you want to suppress extra features of your interface. You can create all the parts of the interface, and just delay packing them in until the user requests to see them. Then you can pack and unpack them dynamically.

Packer Summary

Keep these rules in mind about the packer:

- Pack vertically (`-side top` and `-side bottom`) or horizontally (`-side left` and `-side right`) within a frame. Only rarely will a different mixture of packing directions work out the way you want. Add frames to build more complex structures.
- By default, the packer puts widgets into their parent frame, and the parent frame must be created before the children that are packed into it.
- If you put widgets into other relatives, remember to create the frames first so the frames stay underneath the widgets packed into them.
- By default, the packer ignores `-width` and `-height` attributes of frames that have widgets packed inside them. It shrinks frames to be just big enough to allow for its border width and to hold the widgets inside them. Use `pack propagate` to turn off the shrink-wrap behavior.
- The packer distinguishes between packing space and display space. A widget's display might not take up all the packing space allocated to it.
- The `-fill` option causes the display to fill up the packing space in the X or Y directions, or both.
- The `-expand true` option causes the packing space to expand into any room in the packing cavity that is otherwise unclaimed. If more than one widget in the same frame wants to expand, then they share the extra space.
- The `-ipadx` and `-ipady` options allocate more display space inside the border, if possible.
- The `-padx` and `-pady` options allocate more packing space outside the border, if possible. The widget never fills this space. These values may be specified as a list of two values to get asymmetric padding (Tk 8.4.)

The pack Command

Table 25–1 summarizes the `pack` command. Table 25–2 summarizes the packing options for a widget. These are set with the `pack configure` command, and the current settings are returned by the `pack info` command.

Table 25–1 The `pack` command.

pack *win* ?*win ..*? ?*options*?	This is just like `pack configure`.
pack configure *win* ?*win ...*? ?*options*?	Packs one or more widgets according to the *options,* which are given in Table 25–2.
pack forget *win* ?*win...*?	Unpacks the specified windows.
pack info *win*	Returns the packing parameters of *win*.
pack propagate *win* ?*bool*?	Queries or sets the geometry propagation of *win,* which has other widgets packed inside it.
pack slaves *win*	Returns the list of widgets managed by *win*.

Table 25–2 Packing options.

-after *win*	Packs after *win* in the packing order.
-anchor *anchor*	Anchors: center, n, ne, e, se, s, sw, w, or nw.
-before *win*	Packs before *win* in the packing order.
-expand *boolean*	Controls expansion into the unclaimed packing cavity.
-fill *style*	Controls fill of packing space. Style: x, y, both, or none.
-in *win*	Packs inside *win*.
-ipadx *amount*	Horizontal internal padding, in screen units.
-ipady *amount*	Vertical internal padding, in screen units.
-padx *amount*	Horizontal external padding, in screen units. May be a list of two screen units for asymmetric padding (Tk 8.4).
-pady *amount*	Vertical external padding, in screen units. May be a list of two screen units for asymmetric padding (Tk 8.4).
-side *side*	Sides: top, right, bottom, or left.

Window Stacking Order

The `raise` and `lower` commands control the window stacking order. The stacking order controls the display of windows. Windows higher in the stacking order obscure windows lower in the stacking order. By default, new windows are created at the top of the stacking order so they obscure older windows. Consider this sequence of commands:

III. Tk Basics

```
button .one
frame .two
pack .one -in .two
```

If you do this, you do not see the button. The problem is that the frame is higher in the stacking order so it obscures the button.

You can change the stacking order with the `raise` command:

```
raise .one .two
```

This puts `.one` just above `.two` in the stacking order. If `.two` was not specified, then `.one` would be put at the top of the stacking order.

The `lower` command has a similar form. With one argument, it puts that window at the bottom of the stacking order. Otherwise, it puts it just below another window in the stacking order.

You can use `raise` and `lower` on top-level windows to control their stacking order among all other top-level windows. For example, if a user requests a dialog that is already displayed, use `raise` to make it pop to the foreground of their cluttered desktop. To determine the stacking order of toplevel windows, use the `wm stackorder` command. (See "Toplevel Size, Placement, and Decoration" on page 658.)

The Grid Geometry Manager

This chapter explores the `grid` geometry manager that positions widgets on a
grid that automatically adjusts its size. Grid was added in Tk 4.1.

The `grid` geometry manager arranges
widgets on a grid with variable-sized rows and columns. You specify the rows
and columns occupied by each widget, and the grid is adjusted to accommodate
all the widgets it contains. This is ideal for creating table-like layouts. The manager also has sophisticated facilities for controlling row and column sizes and the
dynamic resize behavior. By introducing subframes with grids of their own, you
can create arbitrary layouts.

Don't `pack` *and* `grid` *into the same manager widget.*

As discussed on page 395, you can use a combination of `pack` and `grid` to
create your display. But for each individual manager widget, you must use only
one of `pack` or `grid` to manage all of its immediate children.

A Basic Grid

Example 26–1 uses `grid` to lay out a set of labels and frames in two parallel columns. It takes advantage of the relative placement feature of `grid`. Instead of
specifying rows and columns, the order of `grid` commands and their arguments
implies the layout. Each `grid` command starts a new row, and the order of the
widgets in the `grid` command determines the column. In the example, there are
two columns, and each iteration of the loop adds a new row. `grid` makes each column just wide enough to hold the biggest widget. Widgets that are smaller are
centered in their cell. That's why the labels appear centered in their column:

Example 26–1 A basic grid.

```
foreach color {red orange yellow green blue purple} {
    label .l$color -text $color -bg white
    frame .f$color -background $color -width 100 -height 2
    grid .l$color .f$color
}
```

The -sticky Setting

If a grid cell is larger than the widget inside it, you can control the size and position of the widget with the -sticky option. The -sticky option combines the functions of -fill and -anchor used with the pack geometry manager. You specify to which sides of its cell a widget sticks. You can specify any combination of n, e, w, and s to stick a widget to the top, right, left, and bottom sides of its cell. You can concatenate these letters together (e.g., news) or uses spaces or commas to separate them (e.g., n,e,w,s). Example 26–2 uses -sticky w to left justify the labels, and -sticky ns to stretch the color frames to the full height of their row:

Example 26–2 A grid with sticky settings.

```
foreach color {red orange yellow green blue purple} {
    label .l$color -text $color -bg white
    frame .f$color -background $color -width 100 -height 2
    grid .l$color .f$color
    grid .l$color -sticky w
    grid .f$color -sticky ns
}
```

Example 26–2 uses `grid` in two ways. The first `grid` in the loop fixes the positions of the widgets because it is the first time they are assigned to the master. The next `grid` commands modify the existing parameters; they just adjust the `-sticky` setting because their row and column positions are already known.

You can specify row and column positions explicitly with the `-row` and `-column` attributes. This is generally more work than using the relative placement, but it is necessary if you need to dynamically move a widget into a different cell. Example 26–3 keeps track of rows and columns explicitly and achieves the same layout as Example 26–2:

Example 26–3 A grid with row and column specifications.

```
set row 0
foreach color {red orange yellow green blue purple} {
    label .l$color -text $color -bg white
    frame .f$color -background $color -width 100
    grid .l$color -row $row -column 0 -sticky w
    grid .f$color -row $row -column 1 -sticky ns
    incr row
}
```

External Padding with **-padx** and **-pady**

You can keep a widget away from the edge of its cell with the `-padx` and `-pady` settings. Example 26–4 uses external padding to shift the labels away from the left edge, and to keep some blank space between the color bars:

Example 26–4 A grid with external padding.

```
foreach color {red orange yellow green blue purple} {
    label .l$color -text $color -bg white
    frame .f$color -background $color -width 100 -height 2
    grid .l$color .f$color
    grid .l$color -sticky w -padx 3
    grid .f$color -sticky ns -pady 1
}
```

Tk 8.4 added the ability to specify asymmetric padding as a list of two screen distances. For example, `-padx {0.125i 0.25i}` adds 1/8 inch of padding to the left and 1/4 inch padding to the right of a widget.

Internal Padding with `-ipadx` and `-ipady`

You can give a widget more display space than it normally needs with internal padding. The internal padding increases the size of the grid. In contrast, a `-sticky` setting might stretch a widget, but it will not change the size of the grid. Example 26–5 makes the labels taller with `-ipady`:

Example 26–5 A grid with internal padding.

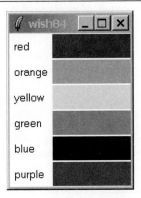

```
foreach color {red orange yellow green blue purple} {
    label .l$color -text $color -bg white
    frame .f$color -background $color -width 100 -height 2
    grid .l$color .f$color
    grid .l$color -sticky w -padx 3 -ipady 5
    grid .f$color -sticky ns -pady 1
}
```

Multiple Widgets in a Cell

Example 26–6 shows all possible `-sticky` settings. It uses the ability to put more than one widget into a grid cell. A large square frame is put in each cell, and then a label is put into the same cell with a different `-sticky` setting. It is important to create the frame first so it is below the label. Window stacking is discussed on page 409. External padding is used to keep the labels away from the edge so that they do not hide the `-ridge` relief of the frames.

Example 26–6 All combinations of `-sticky` settings.

```
set index 0
foreach x {news ns ew  " " new sew wsn esn nw ne sw se n s w e} {
    frame .f$x -borderwidth 2 -relief ridge -width 40 -height 40
    grid .f$x -sticky news \
        -row [expr {$index/4}] -column [expr {$index%4}]
    label .l$x -text $x -background white
    grid .l$x -sticky $x -padx 2 -pady 2 \
        -row [expr {$index/4}] -column [expr {$index%4}]
    incr index
}
```

Spanning Rows and Columns

A widget can occupy more than one cell. The -rowspan and -columnspan attributes indicate how many rows and columns are occupied by a widget. Example 26–7 uses explicit row, column, rowspan, and columnspan specifications:

Example 26–7 Explicit row and column span.

```
. config -bg white
foreach color {888 999 aaa bbb ccc fff} {
    frame .$color -bg #$color -width 40 -height 40
}
grid .888 -row 0 -column 0 -columnspan 3 -sticky news
grid .999 -row 1 -column 0 -rowspan 2 -sticky news
grid .aaa -row 1 -column 1 -columnspan 2 -sticky news
grid .bbb -row 2 -column 2 -rowspan 2 -sticky news
grid .ccc -row 3 -column 0 -columnspan 2 -sticky news
grid .fff -row 2 -column 1 -sticky news
```

You can also use special syntax in grid commands that imply row and column placement. Special characters represent a cell that is spanned or skipped:

- represents a spanned column.
^ represents a spanned row.
x represents a skipped cell.

A nice feature of the implicit row and column assignments is that it is easy to make minor changes to your layout. Example 26–8 achieves the same layout:

Example 26–8 Grid syntax row and column span.

```
. config -bg white
foreach color {888 999 aaa bbb ccc ddd fff} {
    frame .$color -bg #$color -width 40 -height 40
}
grid .888 -       -      -sticky news
grid .999 .aaa    -      -sticky news
grid ^    .fff   .bbb    -sticky news
grid .ccc -       ^      -sticky news
```

Row and Column Constraints

The `grid` manager supports attributes on whole rows and columns that affect their size and resize behavior. The `grid` command has a `rowconfigure` and `columnconfigure` operation to set and query these attributes:

```
grid columnconfigure master col ?attributes?
grid rowconfigure master row ?attributes?
```

With no *attributes*, the current settings are returned. The *row* and *col* specifications can be lists instead of simple indices, so you can configure several rows or columns at once.

Row and Column Padding

The `-pad` attribute increases a row or column size. The initial size of a row or column is determined by the largest widget, and `-pad` adds to this size. This padding can be filled by the widget by using the `-sticky` attribute. Row and column padding works like internal padding because it is extra space that can be occupied by the widget's display. In contrast, the `-padx` and `-pady` attributes on an individual widget act like a spacer that keeps the widget away from the edge of the cell. Example 26–9 shows the difference. The row padding increases the height of the row, but the padding on `.f1` keeps it away from the edge of the cell:

Example 26–9 Row padding compared to cell padding.

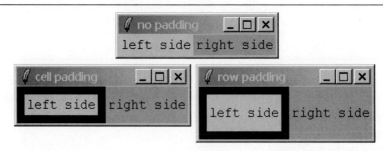

```
. config -bg black
label .f1 -text left -bg #ccc
label .f2 -text right -bg #aaa
grid .f1 .f2 -sticky news          ;# no padding
grid .f1 -padx 10 -pady 10         ;# cell padding
grid rowconfigure . 0 -pad 20      ;# row padding
```

Minimum Size

The -minsize attribute restricts a column or row to be a minimum size. The row or column can grow bigger if its widget requests it, but they will not get smaller than the minimum. One useful application of -minsize is to create empty rows or columns, which is more efficient than creating an extra frame.

Managing Resize Behavior

If the master frame is bigger than the required size of the grid, it shrinks to be just large enough to contain the grid. You can turn off the shrink-wrap behavior with grid propagate. If geometry propagation is off, then the grid is centered inside the master. If the master frame is too small to fit the grid, then the grid is anchored to the upper-left corner of the master and clipped on the bottom-right.

By default, rows and columns do not resize when you grow the master frame. You enable resizing by specifying a -weight for a row or column that is an integer value greater than zero. Example 26–10 grids a text widget and two scrollbars. The protocol between the scrollbar and the text widget is described on page 501. The text widget is in row 0, column 0, and both of these can expand. The vertical scrollbar is in row 0, column 1, so it only grows in the Y direction. The horizontal scrollbar is in row 1, column 0, so it only grows in the X direction:

Example 26–10 Gridding a text widget and scrollbar.

```
text .text -yscrollcommand ".yscroll set" \
    -xscrollcommand ".xscroll set"-width 40 -height 10
scrollbar .yscroll -command ".text yview" -orient vertical
scrollbar .xscroll -command ".text xview" -orient horizontal
grid .text .yscroll -sticky news
grid .xscroll -sticky ew
grid rowconfigure . 0 -weight 1
grid columnconfigure . 0 -weight 1
```

You can use different weights to let different rows and columns grow at different rates. However, there are some tricky issues because the resize behavior applies to extra space, not total space. For example, suppose there are four columns that have widths 10, 20, 30, and 40 pixels, for a total of 100. If the master frame is grown to 140 pixels wide, then there are 40 extra pixels. If each column has weight 1, then each column gets an equal share of the extra space, or 10 more pixels. Now suppose column 0 has weight 0, columns 1 and 2 have weight 1, and column 3 has weight 2. Column 0 will not grow, columns 1 and 2 will get 10 more pixels, and column 3 will get 20 more pixels. In most cases, weights of 0 or 1 make the most sense.

Weight works in reverse when shrinking.

If a row or column has to shrink, the weights are applied in reverse. A row or column with a higher weight will shrink more. For example, put two equal sized frames in columns with different weights. When the user makes the window bigger, the frame in the column with more weight gets larger more quickly. When the window is made smaller, that frame gets smaller more quickly.

Uniform Columns

The `-uniform` attribute makes it easy to create columns (or rows) that are the same width (or height). Use the `-uniform` attribute to create a group of columns (or rows). The value of the attribute can by anything (e.g., `xyz`). All columns (or rows) with the same `-uniform` attribute are in the same group. If they all have the same `-weight` value, then they are all the same size. If one column (or row) in a group has a `-weight` that is twice what the other columns (or rows) have, then it is twice as big. This is illustrated in Example 26–11.

Example 26–11 Uniform column width.

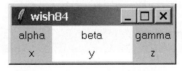

```
foreach x {alpha beta gamma x y z} {
    label .$x -text $x
}
.beta config -bg white
.y config -bg white
grid .alpha .beta .gamma -sticky news
grid .x .y .z -sticky news
grid columnconfigure . "0 1 2" -uniform group1 -weight 1
grid columnconfigure . 1 -weight 2
```

The grid Command

Table 26–1 summarizes the usage of the grid command. Table 26–2 summarizes the options for a widget set with the grid configure command.

Table 26–1 The grid command.

grid bbox *master ?c1 r1? ?c2 r2?*	Returns the bounding box, of the whole grid, the cell at *c1*, *r1*, or the cells from *c1*, *r1* to *c2*, *r2*.
grid columnconfigure *master col ?options?*	Sets or queries the configuration of *col*. Options are -minsize, -weight, -pad, and -uniform.
grid configure *win ?win ...? ?options?*	Grids one or more widgets according to the *options*, which are given in Table 26–2.
grid forget *win ?win...?*	Unmaps the specified windows.
grid info *win*	Returns the grid options of *win*.
grid location *master x y*	Returns the cell column and row under the point *x*, *y* in *master*.
grid propagate *master ?boolean?*	Enables or disables shrink-wrapping of *master*.
grid rowconfigure *master row ?options?*	Sets or queries the configuration of *row*. Options are -minsize, -weight, -pad, and -uniform.
grid remove *slave*	Unmaps *slave*, but remember its configuration.
grid size master	Returns the number of columns and rows.
grid slaves *win ?-row r? ?-column c?*	Returns the list of widgets managed by *win*, or just those in the specified row or column.

Table 26–2 Grid widget options.

-in *win*	Places inside *win*.
-column *col*	Column position. Columns count from zero.
-columnspan *n*	Spans *n* columns.
-ipadx *pixels*	Internal widget padding in the X direction, in screen units.
-ipady *pixels*	Internal widget padding in the Y direction, in screen units.
-padx *pixels*	External widget padding in the X direction, in screen units. May be a list of two screen units for asymmetric padding (Tk 8.4).
-pady *pixels*	External widget padding in the Y direction, in screen units. May be a list of two screen units for asymmetric padding (Tk 8.4).
-row *row*	Row position. Rows count from zero.
-rowspan *n*	Spans *n* rows.
-sticky *how*	Positions widget next to any combination of north (n), south (s), east (e), and west (w) sides of the cell. Use { } for center.

III. Tk Basics

The Place Geometry Manager

This chapter explores the `place` geometry manager that positions widgets on the screen.

*T*he `place` geometry manager is much simpler than `pack` and `grid`. You specify the exact position and size of a window, or you specify the relative position and relative size of a widget. This is useful in a few situations, but it rapidly becomes tedious if you have to position lots of windows. The best application of `place` is to create special-purpose geometry managers using its relative constraints. A standard application of `place` is to adjust the boundary between two adjacent windows.

place Basics

The `place` command lets you specify the width and height of a window, and the X and Y locations of the window's anchor point. The size and location can be specified in absolute or relative terms. Relative specifications are more powerful. Example 27–1 uses `place` to center a window in its parent. You can use this command to position dialogs that you do not want to be detached top-level windows:

Example 27–1 Centering a window with `place`.

```
place $w -in $parent -relx 0.5 -rely 0.5 -anchor center
```

The `-relx` and `-rely` specify the relative X and Y positions of the anchor point of the widget `$w` in `$parent`. A relative X (or Y) value of zero corresponds to the left (or top) edge of $parent. A value of one corresponds to the right (or bottom) edge of $parent. A value of 0.5 specifies the middle. The anchor point determines what point in $w is positioned according to the specifications. In Example 27–1 the center anchor point is used so that the center of $w is centered in $parent.

The relative height and width settings are used to base a widget's size on another widget. Example 27–2 completely covers one window with another window. It uses the default anchor point for windows, which is their upper-left hand corner (nw):

Example 27–2 Covering a window with place.

```
place $w -in $parent -relwidth 1 -relheight 1 -x 0 -y 0
```

The absolute and relative size and position parameters are additive (e.g., -width and -relwidth). You can make a window slightly larger or smaller than the parent by specifying both parameters. In Example 27–3, a negative width and height are used to make a window smaller than another one:

Example 27–3 Combining relative and absolute sizes.

```
place $w -in $parent -relwidth 1 -relheight 1 -x 0 -y 0 \
    -width -4 -height -4
```

It is not necessary for $parent to actually be the parent widget of $w. The requirement is that $parent be the parent, or a descendant of the parent, of $w. It also has to be in the same top-level window. This guarantees that $w is visible whenever $parent is visible. These are the same restrictions imposed by the pack geometry manager.

It is not necessary to position a widget inside another widget, either. Example 27–4 positions a window five pixels above a sibling widget. If $sibling is repositioned, then $w moves with it. This approach is useful when you decorate a resizable window by placing other widgets at its corners or edges. When the window is resized, the decorations automatically move into place:

Example 27–4 Positioning a window above a sibling with place.

```
place $w -in $sibling -relx 0.5 -y -5 -anchor s \
    -bordermode outside
```

The -bordermode outside option is specified so that any decorative border in $sibling is ignored when positioning $w. In this case the position is relative to the outside edge of $sibling. By default, the border is taken into account to make it easy to position widgets inside their parent's border.

The parent widget does not have to be a frame. Example 27–1 can be used to place a dialog in the middle of a text widget. In Example 27–4, $sibling and $w can both be label widgets.

The Pane Manager

The relative size and placement parameters of the `place` command can be used to create custom geometry managers. Example 27–5 shows a paned layout manager. Two frames, or panes, are placed inside another frame. A small third frame represents a grip that is used to adjust the boundary between the two panes.

Note that Tk 8.4 added a `panedwindow` widget, which can manage an arbitrary number of horizontal or vertical panes. See Chapter 28 for information on how to use the `panedwindow` widget.

Example 27–5 `Pane_Create` sets up vertical or horizontal panes.

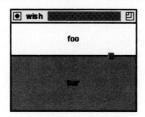

```
proc Pane_Create {f1 f2 args} {

    # Map optional arguments into array values
    set t(-orient) vertical
    set t(-percent) 0.5
    set t(-in) [winfo parent $f1]
    array set t $args

    # Keep state in an array associated with the master frame
    set master $t(-in)
    upvar #0 Pane$master pane
    array set pane [array get t]

    # Create the grip and set placement attributes that
    # will not change. A thin divider line is achieved by
    # making the two frames one pixel smaller in the
    # adjustable dimension and making the main frame black.

    set pane(1) $f1
    set pane(2) $f2
    set pane(grip) [frame $master.grip -background gray50 \
        -width 10 -height 10 -bd 1 -relief raised \
        -cursor crosshair]
    if {[string match vert* $pane(-orient)]} {
        set pane(D) Y;# Adjust boundary in Y direction
        place $pane(1) -in $master -x 0 -rely 0.0 -anchor nw \
            -relwidth 1.0 -height -1
        place $pane(2) -in $master -x 0 -rely 1.0 -anchor sw \
            -relwidth 1.0 -height -1
        place $pane(grip) -in $master -anchor c -relx 0.8
    } else {
```

```
    set pane(D) X ;# Adjust boundary in X direction
    place $pane(1) -in $master -relx 0.0 -y 0 -anchor nw \
        -relheight 1.0 -width -1
    place $pane(2) -in $master -relx 1.0 -y 0 -anchor ne \
        -relheight 1.0 -width -1
    place $pane(grip) -in $master -anchor c -rely 0.8
}
$master configure -background black

# Set up bindings for resize, <Configure>, and
# for dragging the grip.

bind $master <Configure> [list PaneGeometry $master]
bind $pane(grip) <ButtonPress-1> \
    [list PaneDrag $master %$pane(D)]
bind $pane(grip) <B1-Motion> \
    [list PaneDrag $master %$pane(D)]
bind $pane(grip) <ButtonRelease-1> \
    [list PaneStop $master]

# Do the initial layout

PaneGeometry $master
}
```

Parsing Arguments and Maintaining State

The `Pane_Create` procedure is given two widgets to manage, and an optional set of parameters. The general syntax of `Pane_Create` is:

```
Pane_Create f1 f2 ?-orient xy? ?-percent p? ?-in master?
```

All the optional arguments are available in `$args`. Its attribute-value structure is used to initialize a temporary array `t`. Default values are set before the assignment from `$args`. The following code is compact but doesn't check errors in the optional arguments.

```
set t(-orient) vertical
set t(-percent) 0.5
set t(-in) [winfo parent $f1]
array set t $args
```

Global state about the layout is kept in an array whose name is based on the master frame. The name of the master frame isn't known until after arguments are parsed, which is why `t` is used. After the `upvar` the argument values are copied from the temporary array into the global state array:

```
set master $t(-in)
upvar #0 Pane$master pane
array set pane [array get t]
```

Sticky Geometry Settings

Example 27–5 sets several `place` parameters on the frames when they are created. These are remembered, and other parameters are adjusted later to dynamically adjust the boundary between the frames. All Tk geometry managers retain settings like this. The initial settings for the vertical layout is shown here:

```
place $pane(1) -in $parent -x 0 -rely 0.0 -anchor nw \
    -relwidth 1.0 -height -1
place $pane(2) -in $parent -x 0 -rely 1.0 -anchor sw \
    -relwidth 1.0 -height -1
place $pane(grip) -in $parent -anchor c -relx 0.8
```

The position of the upper and lower frames is specified with an absolute X and a relative Y position, and the anchor setting is chosen to keep the frame visible inside the main frame. For example, the lower frame is positioned at the bottom-left corner of the container with `-x 0` and `-rely 1.0`. The `-anchor sw` attaches the lower-left corner of the frame to this position.

The size of the contained frames is also a combination of absolute and relative values. The width is set to the full width of the container with `-relwidth 1.0`. The height is set to minus one with `-height -1`. This value gets added to a relative height that is determined later. It will leave a little space between the two contained frames.

The resize grip is just a small frame positioned at the boundary. Initially it is just placed over toward one size with `-relx 0.8`. It gets positioned on the boundary with a `-rely` setting later. It has a different cursor to indicate it is active.

Event Bindings

The example uses some event bindings that are described in more detail in Chapter 29. The `<Configure>` event occurs when the containing frame is resized by the user. When the user presses the mouse button over the grip and drags it, there is a `<ButtonPress-1>` event, one or more `<B1-Motion>` events, and finally a `<ButtonRelease-1>` event. Tcl commands are bound to these events:

```
bind $parent <Configure> [list PaneGeometry $parent]
bind $pane(grip) <ButtonPress-1> \
    [list PaneDrag $parent %$pane(D)]
bind $pane(grip) <B1-Motion> \
    [list PaneDrag $parent %$pane(D)]
bind $pane(grip) <ButtonRelease-1> [list PaneStop $parent]
```

Managing the Layout

The code is set up to work with either horizontal or vertical layouts. The `pane(D)` variable is either `X`, for a horizontal layout, or `Y`, for a vertical layout. This value is used in the bindings to get `%X` or `%Y`, which are replaced with the X and Y screen positions of the mouse when the bindings fire. This value is passed to `PaneDrag` as the parameter `D`. The `PaneDrag` procedure remembers the previous position in `pane(lastD)` and uses that to update the percentage split between the two contained panes:

Example 27–6 `PaneDrag` adjusts the percentage.

```
proc PaneDrag {master D} {
    upvar #0 Pane$master pane
    if [info exists pane(lastD)] {
        set delta [expr double($pane(lastD) - $D) \
                               / $pane(size)]
        set pane(-percent) [expr $pane(-percent) - $delta]
        if {$pane(-percent) < 0.0} {
            set pane(-percent) 0.0
        } elseif {$pane(-percent) > 1.0} {
            set pane(-percent) 1.0
        }
        PaneGeometry $master
    }
    set pane(lastD) $D
}
proc PaneStop {master} {
    upvar #0 Pane$master pane
    catch {unset pane(lastD)}
}
```

The `PaneGeometry` procedure adjusts the positions of the frames. It is called when the main window is resized, so it updates `pane(size)`. It is also called as the user drags the grip. For a vertical layout, the grip is moved by setting its relative Y position. The size of the two contained frames is set with a relative height. Remember that this is combined with the fixed height of -1 to get some space between the two frames:

Example 27–7 `PaneGeometry` updates the layout.

```
proc PaneGeometry {master} {
    upvar #0 Pane$master pane
    if {$pane(D) == "X"} {
        place $pane(1) -relwidth $pane(-percent)
        place $pane(2) -relwidth [expr 1.0 - $pane(-percent)]
        place $pane(grip) -relx $pane(-percent)
        set pane(size) [winfo width $master]
    } else {
        place $pane(1) -relheight $pane(-percent)
        place $pane(2) -relheight [expr 1.0 - $pane(-percent)]
        place $pane(grip) -rely $pane(-percent)
        set pane(size) [winfo height $master]
    }
}
```

```
proc PaneTest {{p .p} {orient vert}} {
    catch {destroy $p}
    frame $p -width 200 -height 200
    label $p.1 -bg blue -text foo
    label $p.2 -bg green -text bar
    pack $p -expand true -fill both
    pack propagate $p off
    Pane_Create $p.1 $p.2 -in $p -orient $orient -percent 0.3
}
```

The place Command

Table 27–1 summarizes the usage of the place command.

Table 27–1 The place command.

place win ?win ..? ?options?	This is just like place configure.
place configure win ?win ...? ?options?	Places one or more widgets according to the options, which are given Table 27–2.
place forget win ?win...?	Unmaps the specified windows.
place info win	Returns the placement parameters of win.
place slaves win	Returns the list of widgets managed by win.

Table 27–2 summarizes the placement options for a widget, which you set with the place configure command and retrieve with the place info command.

Table 27–2 Placement options.

-in win	Places inside (or relative to) win.
-anchor where	Anchors: center, n, ne, e, se, s, sw, w, or nw. Default: nw.
-x coord	X position, in screen units, of the anchor point.
-relx offset	Relative X position. 0.0 is the left edge. 1.0 is the right edge.
-y coord	Y position, in screen units, of the anchor point.
-rely offset	Relative Y position. 0.0 is the top edge. 1.0 is the bottom edge.
-width size	Width of the window, in screen units.
-relwidth size	Width relative to parent's width. 1.0 is full width.
-height size	Height of the window, in screen units.
-relheight size	Height relative to the parent's height. 1.0 is full height.
-bordermode mode	If mode is inside, then size and position are inside the parent's border. If mode is outside, then size and position are relative to the outer edge of the parent. The default is inside.

The Panedwindow Widget

The panedwindow widget, introduced in Tk 8.4, displays widgets in resizable
horizontal or vertical panes.

A panedwindow contains any number of
panes, arranged horizontally or vertically. Each pane contains one widget, and
each pair of panes is separated by a moveable sash, which causes the widgets on
either side of the sash to be resized. When a panedwindow is resized externally
— for example, if the user resizes the toplevel containing the panedwindow —
space is added or subtracted from the last pane (right-most or bottom-most pane)
in the widget.

Using the Panedwindow

The panedwindow is a relatively simple widget, requiring little configuration or
programming in most applications. The most frequently used configuration
attribute is `orient`, which determines whether the widget has a `horizontal` or
`vertical` arrangement of panes. The other frequently used configuration
attribute is `showHandle`. The handle is a small square drawn on the sashes, giving users another visual cue that the sashes are interactive. The default value of
`showHandle` is False on Windows to match its native look and feel. Most other
configuration attributes control the size, positioning, and appearance of the handles, the sashes, and the widget in general.

Manipulating the Pane Contents

Once you've created the panedwindow, you add widgets to it with the `add` operation. You can add multiple widgets with a single `add` operation. The panedwindow displays each widget added in its own pane, separated by sashes. By default, the widgets are arranged in the order added. However, you can override this behavior with the `-after` and `-before` options to insert widgets after or before currently managed widgets. You can add horizontal and vertical padding to the widgets in the panes with `-padx` and `-pady` options, just like with other geometry managers. The `-minsize` attribute allows you to specify a minimum size for managed widgets (in any screen units supported by Tk.) You can also control the position of a widget within its pane with the `-sticky` attribute, which operates similarly to `grid`'s `-sticky` attribute. The panedwindow's default `-sticky` setting is `nsew`, causing the managed widget to resize to completely fill its pane in both directions.

Don't `pack`, `grid`, or `place` the widgets in a panedwindow.

A panedwindow widget is not only a container for other widgets, but it is also a geometry manager. It controls the size and position of the widgets that it manages. Therefore, don't use the `pack`, `grid`, or `place` commands to control the widgets that you add to a panedwindow.

Of course, for more complex interfaces, you can add frames as the managed widgets of a panedwindow, and then `pack`, `grid`, or `place` other widgets within those frames. As an example, consider a layout with two text widgets. We'd like each text widget to have horizontal and vertical scrollbars, which is a natural application of `grid`. But then we want the entire layout managed by a 2-pane vertical panedwindow. In this case, we'll use a labelframe widget to contain each gridded text-and-scrollbar assembly, and then add each labelframe as a managed widget of our panedwindow. The result is shown in Example 28–1.

Example 28–1 A panedwindow with complex managed widgets.

```
# Create the panedwindow to manage the entire display

panedwindow .p -orient vertical -showhandle 1
pack .p -expand yes -fill both

# Create 2 labelframe widgets, each containing a
# gridded text and scrollbar assembly.

foreach {w label} {code "Code:" notes "Notes:"} {
    set f [labelframe .p.$w -text $label]
    text $f.t -height 10 -width 40 \
        -wrap none -font {courier 12} \
        -xscrollcommand [list $f.xbar set] \
        -yscrollcommand [list $f.ybar set]
    scrollbar $f.xbar -orient horizontal \
        -command [list $f.t xview]
    scrollbar $f.ybar -orient vertical \
        -command [list $f.t yview]
```

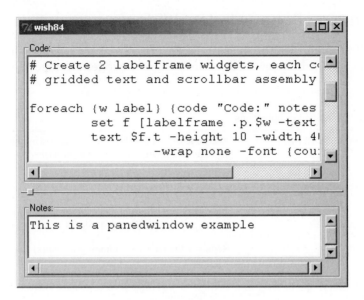

```
grid $f.t -row 0 -column 0 -sticky news -padx 2 -pady 2
grid $f.ybar -row 0 -column 1 -sticky ns -padx 2 -pady 2
grid $f.xbar -row 1 -column 0 -sticky ew -padx 2 -pady 2
grid columnconfigure $f 0 -weight 1
grid rowconfigure $f 0 -weight 1

# Add the frame assembly to the panedwindow

.p add $f -minsize 1i -padx 4 -pady 6
}
```

The `forget` operation removes widgets from a panedwindow. The widgets aren't destroyed, but they are no longer managed by the paned window, and the pane they formerly occupied is removed from the panedwindow. You can also get a list of the widgets currently managed by a panedwindow (in the order in which they appear) with the `panes` operation.

Create the managed widgets as children of the panedwindow.

For best results, create the widgets managed by a panedwindow as children of that panedwindow. Tk then automatically handles the stacking order for windows so that the child appears on top of the panedwindow. If you don't create the managed widget as a child of the panedwindow, you either need to create the managed widget after the panedwindow, or else use the `raise` command to raise the managed widget above the panedwindow, as discussed in "Window Stacking Order" on page 409.

Programming Panedwindow Widgets

Table 28–1 summarizes the operations for programming a panedwindow. In the table, $w is a panedwindow widget and win is a widget managed by the panedwindow.

Table 28–1 Panedwindow operations.

`$w add win ?win...? ?option value...?`	Adds one or more widgets to the panedwindow, each in a separate pane, with *options* as described in Table 28–2.
`$w cget option`	Returns the value of the configuration *option* as described in Table 28–3.
`$w configure ?option value...?`	Queries or modifies the panedwindow configuration, with *options* as described in Table 28–3.
`$w forget win ?win...?`	Removes the pane(s) containing widget(s) from the panedwindow.
`$w identify x y`	Identifies the panedwindow component underneath the specified point.
`$w panecget win option`	Returns the value of the widget's configuration *option* as described in Table 28–2.
`$w paneconfigure index ?option? ?value? ?...?`	Queries or modifies the widget's configuration *options* as described in Table 28–2.
`$w panes`	Returns an ordered list of the widgets managed by the panedwindow.
`$w proxy coord`	Returns the current x and y coordinate pair for the sash proxy, used for rubberband-style pane resizing.
`$w proxy forget`	Removes the sash proxy from the display.
`$w proxy place x y`	Places the sash proxy at the given coordinates.
`$w sash coord index`	Returns the current x and y coordinate pair for the sash indicated by *index*.
`$w sash dragto index x y`	Moves the sash from the previous mark position.
`$w sash mark index x y`	Starts a sash movement operation. *index* is the sash to move, and x and y are widget-relative screen coordinates.
`$w sash place index x y`	Places the indicated sash at the given coordinates.

Table 28–2 summarizes the panedwindow options for managed widgets. These are set when adding a widget to the paned window with the add operation or afterwards with paneconfigure operation. The current settings are returned by the panecget operation.

Table 28–2 Panedwindow managed widget options.

-after *win*	Inserts the widget after the specified *win*.
-before *win*	Inserts the widget before the specified *win*.
-height *size*	Height of the widget, including its border, in screen units. The actual widget height may vary based on -sticky settings, panedwindow resizing, and sash movement.
-minsize *size*	Minimum widget size of the widget in the paned dimension, specified in screen units.
-padx *size*	External widget padding in the X direction, in screen units.
-pady *size*	External widget padding in the Y direction, in screen units.
-sticky *how*	Positions the widget next to any combination of north (n), south (s), east (w), and west (e) sides of the pane. Use { } for center. If opposing directions are specified (e.g., ns), the widget stretches to fill in those directions. Default: nsew.
-width *size*	Width of the widget, including its border, in screen units. The actual widget width may vary based on -sticky settings, panedwindow resizing, and sash movement.

Panedwindow Attributes

Table 28–3 lists the panedwindow widget attributes. The table uses the resource name for the attribute, which has capitals at internal word boundaries. In Tcl commands these options are specified with a dash and all lowercase.

Table 28–3 Panedwindow attributes.

background	Background color (also bg).
borderWidth	Extra space around the edge of the widget, in screen units.
cursor	Cursor to display when mouse is over the widget.
handlePad	When sash handles are drawn, the distance in screen units from the top or left end of the sash (depending on the orientation) at which to draw the handle.
handleSize	The size of a sash handle, in screen units. Handles are always drawn as squares.
height	Height of the widget in screen units.
opaqueResize	Boolean. True indicates the panes should resize as a sash is moved. False (default) indicates resizing is deferred until the sash is placed.
orient	horizontal or vertical
relief	flat, sunken, raised, groove, solid, or ridge.
sashCursor	Cursor to display over a sash. Defaults to a double-sided arrow.

III. Tk Basics

Table 28–3 Panedwindow attributes. (Continued)

sashPad	Padding on both sides of a sash.
sashRelief	Relief style for sashes. flat, sunken, raised (default), groove, solid, or ridge.
sashWidth	Width of each sash, in screen units.
showHandle	Boolean, whether or not to show the sash handles. Defaults to False on Windows, and True on other platforms.
width	Width of the widget in screen units.

Binding Commands to Events

This chapter introduces the event binding mechanism in Tk. Bindings associate a Tcl command with an event like a mouse click or a key stroke. There are also facilities to define virtual events like <<Cut>> and <<Paste>> that are associated with different keystrokes on different platforms. Tcl commands discussed are: bind, bindtags, and event.

*B*indings associate a Tcl command with a sequence of events from the window system. Events include key press, key release, button press, button release, mouse entering a window, mouse leaving, window changing size, window open, window close, focus in, focus out, and widget destroyed. The bindings are defined on *binding tags*, and each widget is associated with an ordered set of binding tags. The binding tags provide a level of indirection between bindings and widgets that creates a flexible and powerful system.

Virtual events are used to support a different look and feel on different platforms. A virtual event is a higher-level name, like <<Copy>>, for a lower-level event name like <Control-c> or <Key-F6>. A virtual event hides the different keystrokes used on different platforms for the same logical operation. Tk defines a few virtual events, and applications can define their own.

The bind Command

The bind command creates event bindings, and it returns information about current bindings. The general form of the command is:

> bind *bindingTag* ?*eventSequence*? ?*command*?

If all arguments are present, a binding from *eventSequence* to *command* is defined for *bindingTag*. The *bindingTag* is typically a widget class name (e.g., Button) or a widget instance name (e.g., .buttons.foo). Binding tags are described in more detail later. Called with a single argument, a binding tag, `bind` returns the events for which there are command bindings:

```
bind Menubutton
=> <Key-Return> <Key-space> <ButtonRelease-1>
    <B1-Motion> <Motion> <Button-1> <Leave> <Enter>
```

The events in this example are keystroke and mouse events. `<Button-1>` is the event generated when the user presses the first, or left-hand, mouse button. `<B1-Motion>` is generated when the user moves the mouse while holding down the first mouse button. The `<Key-space>` event occurs when the user presses the space bar. The surrounding angle brackets delimit a single event, and you can define bindings for a sequence of events. The event syntax is described on page 439, and event sequences are described on page 445.

If `bind` is given a binding tag and an event sequence, it returns the Tcl command bound to that event sequence:

```
bind Menubutton <B1-Motion>
=> tk::MbMotion %W down %X %Y
```

The Tcl commands in event bindings support an additional syntax for event keywords. These keywords begin with a percent sign and have one more character that identifies some attribute of the event. The keywords are substituted with event-specific data before the Tcl command is evaluated. For example, `%W` is replaced with the widget's pathname. The `%X` and `%Y` keywords are replaced with the coordinates of the event relative to the screen. The `%x` and `%y` keywords are replaced with the coordinates of the event relative to the widget. The event keywords are summarized on page 448.

The `%` substitutions are performed throughout the entire command bound to an event, without regard to other quoting schemes. You must use `%%` to obtain a single percent sign. For this reason you should make your binding commands short, adding a new procedure if necessary (e.g., `tk::MbMotion`), instead of littering percent signs throughout your code.

A new binding is created by specifying a binding tag, an event sequence, and a command:

```
bind Menubutton <B1-Motion> {tk::MbMotion %W down %X %Y}
```

If the first character of the binding command is +, the command (without the +) is added to the commands, if any, for that event and binding tag:

```
bind bindingTag event {+ command args}
```

To delete a binding for an event, bind the event to the null string:

```
bind bindingTag event {}
```

Bindings execute in the global scope.

When a binding is triggered, the command is evaluated at the global scope. A very common mistake is to confuse the scope that is active when the `bind` command creates a binding, and the scope that is active when the binding is triggered. The same problem crops up with the commands associated with buttons, and it is discussed in more detail at the beginning of Chapter 30.

The `bindtags` Command

A binding tag groups related bindings, and each widget is associated with an ordered set of binding tags. The level of indirection between widgets and bindings lets you group functionality on binding tags and compose widget behavior from different binding tags.

For example, the `all` binding tag has bindings on `<Tab>` that change focus among widgets. The `Text` binding tag has bindings on keystrokes that insert and edit text. Only text widgets use the `Text` binding tag, but all widgets share the `all` binding tag. You can introduce new binding tags and change the association of widgets to binding tags dynamically. The result is a powerful and flexible way to manage bindings.

The `bindtags` command sets or queries the binding tags for a widget. The general form of the `bindtags` command is:

```
bindtags widget ?tagList?
```

The following command returns the binding tags for text widget `.t`:

```
bindtags .t
=> .t Text . all
```

You can change the binding tags and their order. The `tagList` argument to `bindtags` must be a proper Tcl list. The following command reorders the binding tags for `.t` and eliminates the `.` binding tag:

```
bindtags .t [list all Text .t]
```

By default, all the Tk widgets, except a toplevel, have four binding tags in the following order:

- The widget's Tk pathname (e.g., `.t`). Use this binding tag to provide special behavior to a particular widget. There are no bindings on this bindtag by default.
- The widget's class (e.g., `Text`). The class for a widget is derived from the name of the command that creates it. A button widget has the class `Button`, a text has the class `Text`, and so on. The Tk widgets define their default behavior with bindings on their class.
- The Tk pathname of the widget's toplevel window (e.g., `.`). This is redundant in the case of a toplevel widget, so it is not used twice. There are no bindings on this bindtag by default. The bindings on a toplevel window can be used in dialog boxes to handle keyboard accelerators.
- The global binding tag `all`. The default bindings on `all` are used to change focus among widgets. They are described on page 604.

When there is more than one binding tag on a widget, then one binding from each binding tag can match an event. The bindings are processed in the order of the binding tags. By default, the most specific binding tag comes first, and the most general binding tag comes last.

Example 29–1 has two frame widgets that have the following behavior. When the mouse enters them, they turn red. They turn white when the mouse leaves. When the user types `<Control-c>`, the frame under the mouse is destroyed. One of the frames, `.two`, reports the coordinates of mouse clicks.

438   Binding Commands to Events   Chap. 29

Example 29–1 Bindings on different binding tags.

```
frame .one -width 30 -height 30
frame .two -width 30 -height 30
bind Frame <Enter> {%W config -bg red}
bind Frame <Leave> {%W config -bg white}
bind .two <Button> {puts "Button %b at %x %y"}
pack .one .two -side left
bind all <Control-c> {destroy %W}
bind all <Enter> {focus %W}
```

The `Frame` class has a binding on `<Enter>` and `<Leave>` that changes a frame's background color when the mouse moves in and out of the window. This binding is shared by all the frames. There is also a binding on `all` for `<Enter>` that sets the keyboard focus. Both bindings will trigger when the mouse enters a frame.

Focus and Key Events

The binding on `<Control-c>` is shared by all widgets. The binding destroys the target widget. Because this is a keystroke, it is important to get the keyboard *focus* directed at the proper widget. By default, focus is on the main window, and destroying it terminates the entire application. The global binding for `<Enter>` gives focus to a widget when you move the mouse over the widget. In this example, moving the mouse into a widget and then typing `<Control-c>` destroys the widget. Bind the `focus` command to `<Button>` instead of `<Enter>` if you prefer a click-to-type focus model. Focus is described in Chapter 39.

Using `break` and `continue` in Bindings

The `break` and `continue` commands control the progression through the set of binding tags. The `break` command stops the current binding and suppresses the bindings from any remaining tags in the binding set order. The `continue` command in a binding stops the current binding and continues with the command from the next binding tag.

For example, the `Entry` binding tag has bindings that insert and edit text in a one-line entry widget. You can put a binding on `<Return>` that executes a Tcl command using the value of the widget. The following example runs *Some Command* before the \r character is added to the entry widget. The binding is on the name of the widget, which is first in the set of binding tags, so the `break` suppresses the `Entry` binding that inserts the character:

```
bind .entry <Return> {Some Command ; break}
```

Note that you cannot use the `break` or `continue` commands inside a procedure that is called by the binding. This is because the procedure mechanism will not propagate the `break` or `continue` signal. Instead, you could use the `-code` option to `return`, which is described on page 86:

```
return -code break
```

Defining New Binding Tags

You introduce new binding tags just by using them in a `bind` or `bindtags` command. Binding tags are useful for grouping bindings into different sets, such as specialized bindings for different modes of an editor. One way to emulate the *vi* editor, for example, is to use two bind tags, one for insert mode and one for command mode. The user types `i` to enter insert mode, and they type `<Escape>` to enter command mode:

```
bindtags $t [list ViInsert Text $t all]
bind ViInsert <Escape> {bindtags %W {ViCmd %W all}}
bind ViCmd <Key-i> {bindtags %W {ViInsert Text %W all}}
```

The `Text` class bindings are used in insert mode. The command to put the widget into command mode is put on a new binding tag, `ViInsert`, instead of changing the default `Text` bindings. The `bindtag` command changes the mode by changing the set of binding tags for the widget. The `%W` is replaced with the name of the widget, which is the same as `$t` in this example. Of course, you need to define many more bindings to fully implement all the *vi* commands.

Event Syntax

The `bind` command uses the following syntax to describe events:

```
<modifier-modifier-type-detail>
<<Event>>
```

The first form is for physical events like keystrokes and mouse motion. The second form is for *virtual events* like Cut and Paste, which correspond to different physical events on different platforms. Physical events are described in this section. Virtual events are described in more detail on page 446.

The primary part of the description is the *type*, (e.g., `Button` or `Motion`). The *detail* is used in some events to identify keys or buttons, (.e.g., `Key-a` or `Button-1`). A *modifier* is another key or button that is already pressed when the event occurs, (e.g., `Control-Key-a` or `B2-Motion`). There can be multiple modifiers (e.g., `Control-Shift-x`) . The `<` and `>` delimit a single event.

Table 29–1 lists all physical event types. When two event types are listed together (e.g., `ButtonPress` and `Button`) they are equivalent.

Table 29–1 Event types.

Activate	The application has been activated. (Macintosh)
ButtonPress, Button	A button is pressed (down).
ButtonRelease	A button is released (up).
Circulate	The stacking order of the window changed.
CirculateRequest	An application request to change its window stacking order. (Used by window managers.)
Colormap	The color map has changed.

III. Tk Basics

Table 29–1 Event types. (Continued)

Configure	The window changed size, position, border, or stacking order.
ConfigureRequest	An application request to change its window configuration. (Used by window managers.)
Create	An application request to create a window. (Used by window managers.)
Deactivate	The application has been deactivated. (Macintosh)
Destroy	The window has been destroyed.
Enter	The mouse has entered the window.
Expose	The window has been exposed.
FocusIn	The window has received focus.
FocusOut	The window has lost focus.
Gravity	The window has moved because of a change in size of its parent window.
KeyPress, Key	A key is pressed (down).
KeyRelease	A key is released (up).
Leave	The mouse is leaving the window.
Map	The window has been mapped (opened).
MapRequest	An application request to map a window. (Used by window managers.)
Motion	The mouse is moving in the window.
MouseWheel	The scrolling mouse wheel has moved.
Property	A property on the window has been changed or deleted.
Reparent	A window has been reparented.
ResizeRequest	An application request to resize window. (Used by window managers.)
Unmap	The window has been unmapped (iconified).
Visibility	The window has changed visibility.

Keyboard Events

The KeyPress type is distinguished from KeyRelease so that you can have different bindings for each of these events. KeyPress can be abbreviated Key, and Key can be left off altogether if a detail is given to indicate what key. Finally, as a special case for KeyPress events, the angle brackets can also be left out. The following are all equivalent event specifications:

```
<KeyPress-a>
<Key-a>
<a>
a
```

The detail for a key is also known as the *keysym*, which refers to the graphic printed on the key of the keyboard. For punctuation and non-printing characters, special keysyms are defined. Case is significant in keysyms, but unfortunately there is no consistent scheme. In particular `BackSpace` has a capital `B` and a capital `S`. Commonly encountered keysyms include: `Return`, `Escape`, `BackSpace`, `Tab`, `Up`, `Down`, `Left`, `Right`, `comma`, `period`, `dollar`, `asciicircum`, `numbersign`, `exclam`. Starting in Tk 8.3.2, the online documentation includes a new `keysym` reference page that documents all standard keysyms.

Finding out what keysyms are generated by your keyboard.

There are times when you do not know what keysym is generated by a special key on your keyboard. The keysyms are defined by the window system implementation, and on UNIX systems they are affected by a dynamic keyboard map, the X modmap. You may find the next binding useful to determine just what the keysym for a particular key is on your system:

```
bind $w <KeyPress> {puts stdout {%%K=%K %%A=%A}}
```

The `%K` keyword is replaced with the keysym from the event. The `%A` is replaced with the printing character that results from the event and any modifiers like `Shift`. The `%%` is replaced with a single percent sign. Note that these substitutions occur in spite of the curly braces used for grouping. If the user types a capital `Q`, there are two `KeyPress` events, one for the `Shift` key, and one for the `q` key. The output is:

```
%K=Shift_R %A={}
%K=Q %A=Q
```

The `Shift_R` keysym indicates the right-hand shift key was pressed. The `%A` keyword is replaced with `{}` when modifier keys are pressed. You can check for this in `<KeyPress>` bindings to avoid doing anything if only a modifier key is pressed. On Macintosh, there is no event at all when the modifier keys are pressed. The following can be used with a text widget. The double quotes are necessary to force a string comparison:

```
bind $w <KeyPress> {
    if {"%A" != "{}"} {%W insert insert %A}
}
```

Mouse Events

Button events also distinguish between `ButtonPress`, (or `Button`), and `ButtonRelease`. `Button` can be left off if a detail specifies a button by number. The following are equivalent:

```
<ButtonPress-1>
<Button-1>
<1>
```

Note: The event `<1>` implies a `ButtonPress` event, while the event `1` implies a `KeyPress` event. To avoid confusion, always specify the `Key` or `Button` type.

The mouse is tracked by binding to the `Enter`, `Leave`, and `Motion` events. `Enter` and `Leave` are triggered when the mouse comes into and exits out of the widget, respectively. A `Motion` event is generated when the mouse moves within a widget.

The coordinates of the mouse event are represented by the `%x` and `%y` keywords in the binding command. The coordinates are widget-relative, with the origin at the upper-left hand corner of a widget's window. The keywords `%X` and `%Y` represent the coordinates relative to the screen:

```
bind $w <Enter>  {puts stdout "Entered %W at %x %y"}
bind $w <Leave>  {puts stdout "Left %W at %x %y"}
bind $w <Motion> {puts stdout "%W %x %y"}
```

A mouse drag event is a `Motion` event that occurs when the user holds down a mouse button. In this case the mouse button is a modifier, which is discussed in more detail on page 443. The binding looks like this:

```
bind $w <B1-Motion> {puts stdout "%W %x %y"}
```

Other Events

The `<Map>` and `<Unmap>` events are generated when a window is opened and closed, or when a widget is packed or unpacked by its geometry manager.

The `<Activate>` and `<Deactivate>` events are generated when an application is activated by the operating system. This applies to Macintosh systems, and it occurs when the user clicks in the application window.

The `<Configure>` event is generated when the window changes size. A canvas that computes its display based on its size can bind a redisplay procedure to the `<Configure>` event, for example. The `<Configure>` event can be caused by interactive resizing. It can also be caused by a `configure` widget command that changes the size of the widget. You should not reconfigure a widget's size while processing a `<Configure>` event to avoid an indefinite sequence of these events.

The `<Destroy>` event is generated when a widget is destroyed. You can intercept requests to delete windows, too. See also the description of the `wm` command on page 657.

The `<MouseWheel>` event is generated on Windows by the small scrolling wheel built into the Microsoft Mouse. It reports a delta value using the `%D` keyword. Currently the delta is an integer multiple of 120, where positive values indicate a scroll up, and negative values indicate a scroll down. Note that most Unix systems don't report `<MouseWheel>` events, but some do report mousewheel movement via `<ButtonPress-4>` and `<ButtonPress-5>` events.

Chapter 39 presents some examples that use the `<FocusIn>` and `<FocusOut>` events. The remaining events in Table 29–1 have to do with dark corners of the X protocol, and they are seldom used. More information can be found on these events in the Event Reference section of the *Xlib Reference Manual* (Adrian Nye, O'Reilly & Associates, Inc., 1992).

Bindings on Top-level Windows

Bindings on toplevels are shared by widgets they contain.

Be careful when binding events to toplevel windows because their name is used as a binding tag on all the widgets contained in them. For example, the following binding fires when the user destroys the main window, which means the application is about to exit:

```
bind . <Destroy> {puts "goodbye"}
```

Unfortunately, all widgets inside the main window are destroyed as a side effect, and they all share the name of their toplevel widget as a binding tag. So this binding fires when every widget inside the main window is destroyed. Typically you only want to do something one time. The following binding checks the identity of the widget before doing anything:

```
bind . <Destroy> {if {"%W" == "."} {puts "goodbye"}}
```

Modifiers

A modifier indicates that another key or button is being held down at the time of the event. Typical modifiers are the `Shift` and `Control` keys. The mouse buttons can also be used as modifiers. If an event does not specify any modifiers, the presence of a modifier key is ignored by the event dispatcher. However, if there are two possible matching events, the more accurate match will be used. For example, consider these three bindings:

```
bind $w <KeyPress> {puts "key=%A"}
bind $w <Key-c> {puts "just a c"}
bind $w <Control-Key-c> {exit}
```

The last event is more specific than the others. Its binding will be triggered when the user types c with the `Control` key held down. If the user types c with the `Meta` key held down, the second binding will be triggered. The `Meta` key is ignored because it does not match any binding. If the user types something other than a c, the first binding is triggered. If the user presses the `Shift` key, then the keysym that is generated is C, not c, so the last two events do not match.

There are eight possible modifier keys. The `Control`, `Shift`, and `Lock` modifiers are found on nearly all keyboards. The `Meta` and `Alt` modifiers tend to vary from system to system, and they may not be defined at all. They are commonly mapped to be the same as `Mod1` or `Mod2`, and Tk will try to determine how the mappings are set. The Macintosh has a `Command` modifier that corresponds to the clover-leaf or apple key. The remaining modifiers, `Mod3` through `Mod5`, are sometimes mapped to other special keys. In OpenLook environments, for example, the `Paste` function key is also mapped to the `Mod5` modifier.

The button modifiers, `B1` through `B5`, are most commonly used with the `Motion` event to distinguish different mouse dragging operations. For example, `<B1-Motion>` is the event generated when the user drags the mouse with the first mouse button held down.

Double-click warning.

The Double, Triple, and Quadruple events match on repetitions of an event within a short period of time. These are commonly used with mouse events. Be careful: The binding for the regular press event will match on the first press of the Double. Then the command bound to the Double event will match on the second press. Similarly, a Double event will match on the first two presses of a Triple event, and so on. Verify this by trying out the following bindings:

```
bind . <1> {puts stdout 1}
bind . <Double-1> {puts stdout 2}
bind . <Triple-1> {puts stdout 3}
```

If you click the first mouse button several times quickly, you will see a 1, 2, and then a few 3's output. Your bindings must take into consideration that more than one binding might match a Double, Triple, or Quadruple event. This effect is compatible with an interface that selects an object with the first click, and then operates on the selected object with a Double event. In an editor, character, word, line, and paragraph selection on a single, double, triple, and quadruple click, respectively, is a good example.*

Table 29–2 summarizes the modifiers.

Table 29–2 Event modifiers.

Control	The control key.
Shift	The shift key.
Lock	The caps-lock key.
Command	The command key. (Macintosh)
Meta, M	Defined to be what ever modifier (M1 through M5) is mapped to the Meta_L and Meta_R keysyms.
Alt	Defined to be the modifier mapped to Alt_L and Alt_R.
Mod1, M1	The first modifier.
Mod2, M2, Alt	The second modifier.
Mod3, M3	Another modifier.
Mod4, M4	Another modifier.
Mod5, M5	Another modifier.
Button1, B1	The first mouse button (left).
Button2, B2	The second mouse button (middle).

* If you really want to disable this, you can experiment with using after to postpone processing of one event. The time constant in the bind implementation of <Double> is 500 milliseconds. At the single-click event, schedule its action to occur after 600 milliseconds, and verify at that time that the <Double> event has not occurred.

Table 29–2 Event modifiers. (Continued)

Button3, B3	The third mouse button (right).
Button4, B4	The fourth mouse button.
Button5, B5	The fifth mouse button.
Double	Matches double-press event.
Triple	Matches triple-press event.
Quadruple	Matches quadruple-press event.
Any	Matches any combination of modifiers. (Before Tk 4.0)

The UNIX *xmodmap* program returns the current mappings from keys to these modifiers. The first column of its output lists the modifier. The rest of each line identifies the keysym(s) and low-level keycodes that are mapped to each modifier. The *xmodmap* program can also be used to change mappings. The following example shows the mappings on my system. Your setup may be different.

Example 29–2 Output from the UNIX *xmodmap* program.

```
xmodmap: up to 3 keys per modifier,
        (keycodes in parentheses):
shift Shift_L (0x6a), Shift_R (0x75)
lock Caps_Lock (0x7e)
control Control_L (0x53)
mod1 Meta_L (0x7f), Meta_R (0x81)
mod2 Mode_switch (0x14)
mod3 Num_Lock (0x69)
mod4 Alt_L (0x1a)
mod5 F13 (0x20), F18 (0x50), F20 (0x68)
```

Event Sequences

The bind command accepts a sequence of events in a specification, and most commonly this is a sequence of key events. In the following examples, the Key events are abbreviated to just the character detail, and so abc is a sequence of three Key events:

```
bind . a {puts stdout A}
bind . abc {puts stdout C}
```

With these bindings in effect, both bindings are executed when the user types abc. The binding for a is executed when a is pressed, even though this event is also part of a longer sequence. This is similar to the behavior with Double and Triple event modifiers. For this reason you must be careful when binding sequences. You can use break in the binding for the prefix to ensure that it does not do anything:

```
bindtags $w [list $w Text [winfo toplevel $w] all]
bind $w <Control-x> break
bind $w <Control-x><Control-s> {Save ; break}
bind $w <Control-x><Control-c> {Quit ; break}
```

The `break` ensures that the default `Text` binding that inserts characters does not trigger. This trick is embodied by `BindSequence` in the next example. If a sequence is detected, then a `break` binding is added for the prefix. The procedure also supports the *emacs* convention that `<Meta-x>` is equivalent to `<Escape>x`. This convention arose because `Meta` is not that standard across keyboards. There is no meta key at all on Windows and Macintosh keyboards. The `regexp` command is used to pick out the detail from the `<Meta>` event.

Example 29–3 Emacs-like binding convention for `Meta` and `Escape`.

```
proc BindSequence { w seq cmd } {
    bind $w $seq $cmd
    # Double-bind Meta-key and Escape-key
    if [regexp {<Meta-(.*)>} $seq match letter] {
        bind $w <Escape><$letter> $cmd
    }
    # Make leading keystroke harmless
    if [regexp {(<.+>)<.+>} $seq match prefix] {
        bind $w $prefix break
    }
}
```

The use of `break` and `continue` in bindings is not supported in Tk 3.6 and earlier. This is because only a single binding tag can match an event. To make a prefix of a sequence harmless in Tk 3.6, bind a space to it:

```
bind $w $prefix { }
```

This installs a binding for the widget, which suppresses the class binding in Tk 3.6. The space is different than a null string, `{}`. Binding to a null string deletes the current binding instead of replacing it with a harmless one.

Virtual Events

A virtual event corresponds to one or more event sequences. When any of the event sequences occurs, then the virtual event occurs. Example 29–4 shows the cut, copy, and paste virtual events for each platform:

Example 29–4 Virtual events for cut, copy, and paste.

```
switch $tcl_platform(platform) {
    "unix" {
        event add <<Cut>> <Control-Key-x> <Key-F20>
        event add <<Copy>> <Control-Key-c> <Key-F16>
        event add <<Paste>> <Control-Key-v> <Key-F18>
    }
```

```
    "windows" {
        event add <<Cut>> <Control-Key-x> <Shift-Key-Delete>
        event add <<Copy>> <Control-Key-c> <Control-Key-Insert>
        event add <<Paste>> <Control-Key-v> <Shift-Key-Insert>
    }
    "macintosh" {
        event add <<Cut>> <Control-Key-x> <Key-F2>
        event add <<Copy>> <Control-Key-c> <Key-F3>
        event add <<Paste>> <Control-Key-v> <Key-F4>
    }
}
```

You can define more than one physical event that maps to the same virtual event:

```
event add <<Cancel>> <Control-c> <Escape> <Command-period>
```

With this definition any of the physical events will trigger a `<<Cancel>>`. This would be convenient if the same user commonly used your application on different platforms. However, it is also possible that the physical bindings on different platforms overlap in conflicting ways.

By default, virtual event definitions add to existing definitions for the same virtual event. The previous command could be replaced with these three:

```
event add <<Cancel>> <Control-c>
event add <<Cancel>> <Escape>
event add <<Cancel>> <Command-period>
```

Several widgets use virtual events as a notification mechanism. They generate virtual events in response to various conditions so that you can create bindings to respond to those conditions. For example, the listbox widget generates a `<<ListboxSelect>>` virtual event whenever the listbox selection changes. The easiest way to respond to changes to the listbox selection is to bind to this virtual event, for example:

```
bind .lbox <<ListboxSelect>> {ListboxChanged %W}
```

Generating Events

Your application can use the `event generate` command to programmatically generate events, in essence emulating user interaction. You can generate either standard windowing events or virtual events. However, you can generate events only for the current application; you can't send events to other applications running on your system. (In other words, you can't use the `event generate` command to have your application control another application.)

The first argument to `event generate` is the target widget for the event. You may provide either the path name of the widget, or the window identifier (such as returned by `winfo id`) as long as it is for a window in the current application.

The second argument is an event specification, using the same syntax as for creating event bindings. (See "Event Syntax" on page 439.) However, you can't generate an event sequence (such as `<KeyPress-Escape><KeyPress-a>`), only single events.

As an example, the following command delivers a `ButtonPress-3` event to a widget:

```
event generate .b <ButtonPress-3>
```

A widget must have focus to receive key events.

Remember that a widget must have keyboard focus to receive `KeyPress` or `KeyRelease` events. You can use the `focus` command to assign keyboard focus to a widget:

```
focus .e1
event generate .e1 <KeyPress-a>
```

The `event generate` command also accepts options to specify additional attributes of the event, such as the x and y mouse position. Table 29–4 lists the `event generate` options. Of note is the `-warp` option, added in Tk 8.3. If you provide a `-warp` value of True, then the mouse pointer moves to the x and y coordinates of the generated event; otherwise, the mouse pointer remains at its current location. For example, the following commands moves the mouse pointer to the point 10,20 relative to the top-left corner of the main window:

```
event generate . <Motion> -x 10 -y 20 -warp 1
```

Event Summary

Event Command Syntax

The `event` command is summarized in Table 29–3.

Table 29–3 The `event` command.

`event add virt phys1 phy2 ...`	Adds a mapping from one or more physical events to virtual event `virt`.
`event delete virt`	Deletes virtual event `virt`.
`event info`	Returns the defined virtual events.
`event info virt`	Returns the physical events that map to `virt`.
`event generate win event ?opt val? ...`	Generates `event` for window `win`. The options are listed in Table 29–4.

Event Keywords

Table 29–4 lists the percent keywords and the corresponding option to the `event generate` command. Remember that keyword substitutions occur throughout the command, regardless of other Tcl quoting conventions. Keep your binding commands short, introducing procedures if needed. For the details about various event fields, consult the *Xlib Reference Manual* (O'Reilly & Associates, Inc.). The string values for the keyword substitutions are listed after a short description of the keyword. If no string values are listed, the keyword has an integer value like a coordinate or a window ID.

Table 29–4 A summary of the `event` keywords.

`%%`		Use this to get a single percent sign. All events.
`%#`	`-serial` *num*	The serial number for the event. All events.
`%a`	`-above` *win*	The above field from the event. `Configure` event.
`%b`	`-button` *num*	Button number. Events: `ButtonPress` and `ButtonRelease`.
`%c`	`-count` *num*	The count field. Events: `Expose` and `Map`.
`%d`	`-detail` *value*	The detail field. Values: `NotifyAncestor`, `NotifyNonlinearVirtual`, `NotifyDetailNone`, `NotifyPointer`, `NotifyInferior`, `NotifyPointerRoot`, `NotifyNonlinear`, or `NotifyVirtual`. Events: `Enter`, `Leave`, `FocusIn`, and `FocusOut`.
`%f`	`-focus` *boolean*	The focus field (0 or 1). Events: `Enter` and `Leave`.
`%h`	`-height` *num*	The height field. Events: `Configure` and `Expose`.
`%i`		The window field from the event, represented as a hexadecimal integer. All events.
`%k`	`-keycode` *num*	The keycode field. Events: `KeyPress` and `KeyRelease`.
`%m`	`-mode` *value*	The mode field. Values: `NotifyNormal`, `NotifyGrab`, `NotifyUngrab`, or `NotifyWhileGrabbed`. Events: `Enter`, `Leave`, `FocusIn`, and `FocusOut`.
`%o`	`-override` *boolean*	The override_redirect field. Events: `Map`, `Reparent`, and `Configure`.
`%p`	`-place` *value*	The place field. Values: `PlaceOnTop`, `PlaceOnBottom`. `Circulate` event.
`%s`	`-state` *value*	The state field. A decimal string for events: `ButtonPress`, `ButtonRelease`, `Enter`, `Leave`, `KeyPress`, `KeyRelease`, and `Motion`. Values for the `Visibility` event: `VisibilityUnobscured`, `VisibilityPartiallyObscured`, or `VisibilityFullyObscured`.
`%t`	`-time` *num*	The time field. All events.
`%v`		The value_mask field. `Configure` event.
`%w`	`-width` *num*	The width field. Events: `Configure` and `Expose`.
`%x`	`-x` *pixel*	The X coordinate, widget relative. Mouse events.
`%y`	`-y` *pixel*	The Y coordinate, widget relative. Mouse events.

Table 29–4 A summary of the `event` keywords. (Continued)

`%A`		The printing character from the event, or `{ }`. Events: `KeyPress` and `KeyRelease`.
`%B`	`-borderwidth num`	The border width. `Configure` event.
`%D`	`-delta value`	The delta value. `MouseWheel` event.
`%E`	`-sendevent bool`	The send_event field. All events.
`%K`	`-keysym symbol`	The keysym from the event. Events: `KeyPress` and `KeyRelease`.
`%N`		The keysym as a decimal number. Events: `KeyPress` and `KeyRelease`.
`%P`		The atom name for the property being changed or deleted. `Property` event.
`%R`	`-root win`	The root window ID. All events.
`%S`	`-subwindow win`	The subwindow ID. All events.
`%T`		The type field. All events.
`%W`		The Tk pathname of the widget receiving the event. All events.
`%X`	`-rootx pixel`	The x_root field. Relative to the (virtual) root window. Events: `ButtonPress`, `ButtonRelease`, `KeyPress`, `KeyRelease`, and `Motion`.
`%Y`	`-rooty pixel`	The y_root field. Relative to the (virtual) root window. Events: `ButtonPress`, `ButtonRelease`, `KeyPress`, `KeyRelease`, and `Motion`.

P A R T   IV

Tk Widgets

Part IV describes the Tk widgets. These are the components you use to build up your graphical user interface. Tk widgets are simple to use, so you can rapidly develop your interface. At the same time, they have sophisticated features that you can use to fine-tune your interface in response to user feedback.

Chapter 30 describes buttons and menus. Tk 8.0 adds native look and feel to these widgets, so a single script will look different depending on the platform it is running on.

Associated with the widgets is a resource database that stores settings like colors and fonts. Chapter 31 describes the resource database and generalizes it to store button and menu configurations.

Chapter 32 describes a few simple widgets. The frame, labelframe, and toplevel are containers for other widgets. The label displays a text string. The message formats a long text string onto multiple lines. The scale represents a numeric value. The bell command rings the terminal bell.

Chapter 33 describes scrollbars, which can be attached in a general way to other widgets.

Chapter 34 describes entry widgets, which provide one line of editable text and spinboxes, which allow users to select from multiple values by "spinning" through selections.

Chapter 35 describes the listbox widget that displays several lines of text. The lines are manipulated as units.

Chapter 36 describes the general-purpose text widget. It can display multiple fonts and have binding tags on ranges of text.

Chapter 37 describes the canvas widget. The canvas manages objects like lines, boxes, images, arcs, and text labels. You can have binding tags on these objects and classes of objects.

IV. Tk Widgets

Buttons and Menus

Buttons and menus are the primary way that applications expose functions to users. This chapter describes how to create and manipulate buttons and menus.

A button widget is associated with a Tcl command that invokes an action in the application. The checkbutton and radiobutton widgets affect an application indirectly by controlling a Tcl variable. A menu elaborates on this concept by organizing button-like items into related sets, including cascaded menus. The menubutton widget is a special kind of button that displays a menu when you click on it.

Tk 8.0 provides a cross-platform menu bar facility. The menu bar is really just a menu that is displayed horizontally along the top of your application's main window. On the Macintosh, the menu bar appears at the top of the screen. You define the menu bar the same on all platforms. Tk 8.0 also uses native button and menu widgets on the Windows and Macintosh platforms. This contributes to a native look and feel for your application. In earlier versions, Tk displayed the widgets identically on all platforms.

Associating a command to a button is usually quite simple, as illustrated by the Tk "Hello, World!" example:

```
button .hello -command {puts stdout "Hello, World!"}
```

This chapter describes a few useful techniques for setting up the commands in more general cases. If you use variables inside button commands, you have to understand the scoping rules that apply. This is the first topic of the chapter. Once you get scoping figured out, then the other aspects of buttons and menus are quite straightforward.

IV. Tk Widgets

Button Commands and Scope Issues

Perhaps the trickiest issue with button commands has to do with variable scoping. A button command is executed at the global scope, which is outside of any procedure. If you create a button while inside a procedure, then the button command executes in a different scope later. The commands used in event bindings also execute later at the global scope.

I think of this as the "now" (i.e., button definition) and "later" (i.e., button use) scope problem. For example, you may want to use the values of some variables when you define a button command but use the value of other variables when the button command is used. When these two contexts are mixed, it can be confusing. The next example illustrates the problem. The button's command involves two variables: x and val. The global variable x is needed later, when the button's command executes. The local variable val is needed now, in order to define the command. Example 30–1 shows this awkward mixture of scopes:

Example 30–1 A troublesome button command.

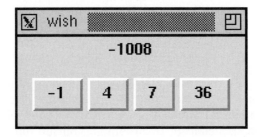

```
proc Trouble {args} {
    set b 0
    # Display the value of x, a global variable
    label .label -textvariable x
    set f [frame .buttons -borderwidth 10]
    # Create buttons that multiply x by their value
    foreach val $args {
        button $f.$b -text $val \
            -command "set x \[expr \$x * $val\]"
        pack $f.$b -side left
        incr b
    }
    pack .label $f
}
set x 1
Trouble -1 4 7 36
```

The example uses a label widget to display the current value of x. The tex-tvariable attribute is used so that the label displays the current value of the variable, which is always a global variable. It is not necessary to have a global command inside Trouble because the value of x is not used there. The button's command is executed later at the global scope.

The definition of the button's command is ugly, though. The value of the loop variable val is needed when the button is defined, but the rest of the substitutions need to be deferred until later. The variable substitution of $x and the command substitution of expr are suppressed by quoting with backslashes:

```
set x \[expr \$x * $val\]
```

In contrast, the following command assigns a constant expression to x each time the button is clicked, and it depends on the current value of x, which is not defined the first time through the loop. Clearly, this is incorrect:

```
button $f.$b -text $val \
     -command "set x [expr $x * $val]"
```

Another incorrect approach is to quote the whole command with braces. This defers too much, preventing the value of val from being used at the correct time.

Use procedures for button commands.

The general technique for dealing with these sorts of scoping problems is to introduce Tcl procedures for use as the button commands. Example 30–2 introduces a little procedure to encapsulate the expression:

Example 30–2 Fixing the troublesome situation.

```
proc LessTrouble { args } {
    set b 0
    label .label -textvariable x
    set f [frame .buttons -borderwidth 10]
    foreach val $args {
        button $f.$b -text $val \
            -command "UpdateX $val"
        pack $f.$b -side left
        incr b
    }
    pack .label $f
}
proc UpdateX { val } {
    global x
    set x [expr $x * $val]
}
set x 1
LessTrouble -1 4 7 36
```

It may seem just like extra work to introduce the helper procedure, UpdateX. However, it makes the code clearer in two ways. First, you do not have to struggle with backslashes to get the button command defined correctly. Second, the code is much clearer about the function of the button. Its job is to update the global variable x.

You can generalize UpdateX to work on any variable by passing the name of the variable to update. Now it becomes much like the incr command:

```
button $f.$b -text $val -command "Update x $val"
```

IV. Tk Widgets

The definition of Update uses upvar, which is explained on page 91, to manipulate the named variable in the global scope:

```
proc Update {varname val} {
    upvar #0 $varname x
    set x [expr $x * $val]
}
```

Double quotes are used in the button command to allow $val to be substituted. Whenever you use quotes like this, you have to be aware of the possible values for the substitutions. If you are not careful, the command you create may not be parsed correctly. The safest way to generate the command is with list:

```
button $f.$b -text $val -command [list UpdateX $val]
```

Using list ensures that the command is a list of two elements, UpdateX and the value of val. This is important because UpdateX takes only a single argument. If val contained white space, then the resulting command would be parsed into more words than you expected. Of course, in this case we plan to always call LessTrouble with an integer value, which does not contain white space.

Example 30–3 provides a more straightforward application of procedures for button commands. In this case the advantage of the procedure MaxLine-Length is that it creates a scope for the local variables used during the button action. This ensures that the local variables do not accidentally conflict with global variables used elsewhere in the program. There is also the standard advantage of a procedure, which is that you may find another use for the action in another part of your program.

Example 30–3 A button associated with a Tcl procedure.

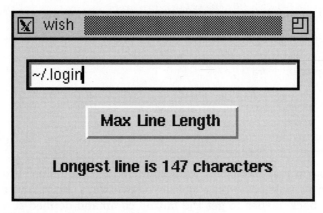

```
proc MaxLineLength { file } {
    set max 0
    if [catch {open $file} in] {
        return $in
    }
```

```
    foreach line [split [read $in] \n] {
        set len [string length $line]
        if {$len > $max} {
            set max $len
        }
    }
    return "Longest line is $max characters"
}
# Create an entry to accept the file name,
# a label to display the result
# and a button to invoke the action
. config -borderwidth 10
entry .e -width 30 -bg white -relief sunken
button .doit -text "Max Line Length" \
    -command {.label config -text [MaxLineLength [.e get]]}
label .label -text "Enter file name"
pack .e .doit .label -side top -pady 5
```

The example is centered around the MaxLineLength procedure. This opens a file and loops over the lines finding the longest one. The file open is protected with catch in case the user enters a bogus file name. In that case, the procedure returns the error message from open. Otherwise, the procedure returns a message about the longest line in the file. The local variables in, max, and len are hidden inside the scope of the procedure.

The user interface has three widgets: an entry for user input, the button, and a label to display the result. These are packed into a vertical stack, and the main window is given a border. Obviously, this simple interface can be improved in several ways. There is no Quit button, for example.

All the action happens in the button command:

```
.label config -text [MaxLineLength [.e get]]
```

Braces are used when defining the button command so that the command substitutions all happen when the button is clicked. The value of the entry widget is obtained with .e get. This value is passed into MaxLineLength, and the result is configured as the text for the label. This command is still a little complex for a button command. For example, suppose you wanted to invoke the same command when the user pressed <Return> in the entry. You would end up repeating this command in the entry binding. It might be better to introduce a one-line procedure to capture this action so that it is easy to bind the action to more than one user action. Here is how that might look:

```
proc Doit {} {
    .label config -text [MaxLineLength [.e get]]
}
button .doit -text "Max Line Length" -command Doit
bind .e <Return> Doit
```

Chapter 29 describes the bind command in detail, Chapter 32 describes the label widget, and Chapter 35 describes the entry widget.

IV. Tk Widgets

Buttons Associated with Tcl Variables

The checkbutton and radiobutton widgets are associated with a global Tcl variable. When one of these buttons is clicked, a value is assigned to the Tcl variable. In addition, if the variable is assigned a value elsewhere in the program, the appearance of the checkbutton or radiobutton is updated to reflect the new value. A set of radiobuttons all share the same global variable. The set represents a choice among mutually exclusive options. In contrast, each checkbutton has its own global variable.

The ShowChoices example uses a set of radiobuttons to display a set of mutually exclusive choices in a user interface. The ShowBooleans example uses checkbutton widgets:

Example 30–4 Radiobuttons and checkbuttons.

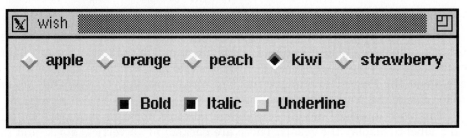

```
proc ShowChoices { parent varname args } {
    set f [frame $parent.choices -borderwidth 5]
    set b 0
    foreach item $args {
        radiobutton $f.$b -variable $varname \
            -text $item -value $item
        pack $f.$b -side left
        incr b
    }
    pack $f -side top
}
proc ShowBooleans { parent args } {
    set f [frame $parent.booleans -borderwidth 5]
    set b 0
    foreach item $args {
        checkbutton $f.$b -text $item -variable $item
        pack $f.$b -side left
        incr b
    }
    pack $f -side top
}
set choice kiwi
ShowChoices {} choice apple orange peach kiwi strawberry
set Bold 1 ; set Italic 1
ShowBooleans {} Bold Italic Underline
```

The `ShowChoices` procedure takes as arguments the parent frame, the name of a variable, and a set of possible values for that variable. If the parent frame is null, `{}`, then the interface is packed into the main window. `ShowChoices` creates a radiobutton for each value, and it puts the value into the text of the button. It also has to specify the value to assign to the variable when the button is clicked because the default value associated with a radiobutton is the empty string.

The `ShowBooleans` procedure is similar to `ShowChoices`. It takes a set of variable names as arguments, and it creates a checkbutton for each variable. The default values for the variable associated with a checkbutton are zero and one, which is fine for this example. If you need particular values, you can specify them with the `-onvalue` and `-offvalue` options.

Radiobuttons and checkbuttons can have commands associated with them, just like ordinary buttons. The command is invoked after the associated Tcl variable has been updated. Remember that the Tcl variable associated with the button is defined in the global scope. For example, you could log the changes to variables as shown in the next example.

Example 30–5 A command on a radiobutton or checkbutton.

```
proc PrintByName { varname } {
    upvar #0 $varname var
    puts stdout "$varname = $var"
}
checkbutton $f.$b -text $item -variable $item \
    -command [list PrintByName $item]
radiobutton $f.$b -variable $varname \
    -text $item -value $item \
    -command [list PrintByName $varname]
```

Button Attributes

Table 30–1 lists the attributes for the button, checkbutton, menubutton, and radiobutton widgets. Unless otherwise indicated, the attributes apply to all of these widget types. Chapters 40, 41, and 42 discuss many of these attributes in more detail. Some attributes are ignored on the Windows and Macintosh platforms because they are not supported by the native button widgets.

The table uses the resource name for the attributes, which has capitals at internal word boundaries. In Tcl commands, the attributes are specified with a dash and they are all lowercase. Compare:

```
option add *Menubutton.activeBackground: red
.mb configure -activebackground red
```

The first command defines a resource database entry that covers all menubuttons and gives them a red active background. This only affects menubuttons created after the database entry is added. The second command changes an existing menubutton (.mb) to have a red active background. Note the difference in capitalization of background in the two commands. The resource database is introduced on page 372, and Chapter 31 explains how to use the resource database in more detail.

Table 30–1 Resource names of attributes for all button widgets.

activeBackground	Background color when the mouse is over the button.
activeForeground	Text color when the mouse is over the button.
anchor	Anchor point for positioning the text.
background	The normal background color.
bitmap	A bitmap to display instead of text.
borderWidth	Width of the border around the button.
command	Tcl command to invoke when button is clicked.
compound	Where the image or bitmap should be placed relative to the text: bottom, center, left, right, top or none (default). (Tk 8.4)
cursor	Cursor to display when mouse is over the widget.
default	active displays as a default button. normal and disabled display as normal button. See page 809 (Tk 8.0).
direction	up, down, left, right, active. Offset direction for posting menus. menubutton. (Tk 8.0).
disabledForeground	Foreground (text) color when button is disabled.
font	Font for the text.
foreground	Foreground (text) color. (Also fg).
height	Height, in lines for text, or screen units for images.
highlightBackground	Focus highlight color when widget does not have focus.
highlightColor	Focus highlight color when widget has focus.
highlightThickness	Width of highlight border.
image	Image to display instead of text or bitmap.
indicatorOn	Boolean that controls if the indicator is displayed. checkbutton, menubutton, and radiobutton.
justify	Text justification: center, left, or right.
menu	Menu posted when menubutton is clicked.
offRelief	Alternate relief style when the widget is deselected. checkbutton and radiobutton. (Tk 8.4)

Table 30–1 Resource names of attributes for all button widgets. (Continued)

offValue	Value for Tcl variable when checkbutton is not selected.
onValue	Value for Tcl variable when checkbutton is selected.
overRelief	Alternate relief style when mouse is over the widget. button, checkbutton, and radiobutton. (Tk 8.4)
padX	Extra space to the left and right of the button text.
padY	Extra space above and below the button text.
relief	flat, sunken, raised, groove, solid or ridge.
repeatDelay	The number of milliseconds a button or key must be held down before it begins to auto-repeat. For button only. (Tk 8.4)
repeatInterval	The number of milliseconds between auto-repeats. For button only. (Tk 8.4)
selectColor	Color for selector. checkbutton or radiobutton.
selectImage	Alternate graphic image for selector: checkbutton or radiobutton.
state	normal (enabled), disabled (deactivated), or active (when the mouse pointer is over the button).
takeFocus	Control focus changes from keyboard traversal.
text	Text to display in the button.
textVariable	Tcl variable that has the value of the text.
underline	Index of text character to underline.
value	Value for Tcl variable when radiobutton is selected.
variable	Tcl variable associated with the button: checkbutton or radiobutton.
width	Width in characters for text, or screen units for image. As of Tk 8.4, on Windows only, a negative value is treated as a minimum width for button widgets only.
wrapLength	Maximum character length before text is wrapped, *in screen units.*

IV. Tk Widgets

Button Operations

Table 30–2 summarizes the operations on button widgets. In the table, $w is a button, checkbutton, radiobutton, or menubutton, except when noted. For the most part, these operations are used by the script libraries that implement the bindings for buttons. The cget and configure operations are the most commonly used by applications.

Table 30–2 Button operations.

`$w cget` *option*	Returns the value of the specified attribute.
`$w configure ?`*option*`?` `?`*value*`? ...`	Queries or manipulates the configuration information for the widget.
`$w deselect`	Deselects the `radiobutton` or `checkbutton`. Set the `radiobutton` variable to the null string. Set the `checkbutton` variable to the off value.
`$w flash`	Redisplays the button several times in alternate colors.
`$w invoke`	Invokes the command associated with the button.
`$w select`	Selects the `radiobutton` or `checkbutton`, setting the associated variable appropriately.
`$w toggle`	Toggles the state of the `checkbutton`, setting the associated variable appropriately.

Menus and Menubuttons

A menu presents a set of button-like *menu entries* to users. A menu entry is not a full fledged Tk widget. Instead, you create a menu widget and then add entries to the menu as shown in the following examples. There are several kinds of menu entries:

- Command entries are like buttons.
- Check entries are like checkbuttons.
- Radio entries are like radiobuttons.
- Separator entries are used to visually set apart entries.
- Cascade entries are used to post submenus.
- Tear-off entries are used to detach a menu from its menu button so that it becomes a new top-level window.

A menubutton is a special kind of button that posts (i.e., displays) a menu when you press it. If you click on a menubutton, then the menu is posted and remains posted until you click on a menu entry to select it, or click outside the menu to dismiss it. If you press and hold the menubutton, then the menu is unposted when you release the mouse. If you release the mouse over the menu, it selects the menu entry that was under the mouse.

You can have a command associated with a menubutton, too. The command is invoked *before* the menu is posted, which means you can compute the menu contents when the user presses the menubutton.

Our first menu example creates a sampler of the different entry types:

Example 30–6 A menu sampler.

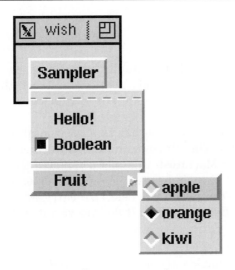

```
menubutton .mb -text Sampler -menu .mb.menu
pack .mb -padx 10 -pady 10
set m [menu .mb.menu -tearoff 1]
$m add command -label Hello! -command {puts "Hello, World!"}
$m add check -label Boolean -variable foo \
    -command {puts "foo = $foo"}
$m add separator
$m add cascade -label Fruit -menu $m.sub1
set m2 [menu $m.sub1 -tearoff 0]
$m2 add radio -label apple -variable fruit -value apple
$m2 add radio -label orange -variable fruit -value orange
$m2 add radio -label kiwi -variable fruit -value kiwi
```

The example creates a menubutton and two menus. The main menu
.mb.menu is a child of the menubutton .mb. This relationship is necessary so that
the menu displays correctly when the menubutton is selected. Similarly, the cascaded submenu .mb.menu.sub1 is a child of the main menu. The first menu entry
is represented by the dashed line. This is a tear-off entry that, when selected,
makes a copy of the menu in a new top-level window. This is useful if the menu
operations are invoked frequently. The -tearoff 0 argument is used when creating the submenu to eliminate its tear-off entry.

The command, radio, and check entries are similar to the corresponding
button types. The configuration options for menu entries are similar to those for
buttons. The main difference is that the text string in the menu entry is defined
with the -label option, not -text. Table 30–6 gives the complete set of options
for menu entries.

The cascade menu entry is associated with another menu. It is distinguished by the small right arrow in the entry. When you select the entry, the
submenu is posted. It is possible to have several levels of cascaded menus. There

IV. Tk Widgets

is no limit to the number of levels, except that your users will complain if you nest too many menus.

A Menu Bar

You can create a menu bar manually by packing several menubuttons into a frame. The default bindings on menubuttons are such that you can drag your mouse over the menu bar and the different menus will display as you drag over their menubutton.

Tk 8.0 lets you create a menu bar as a horizontal menu that is associated with a top-level window. On Windows and UNIX the menu is displayed along the top of the window. On Macintosh this menu replaces the main menu along the top of the screen when the window is activated. The menu bar menu should have all cascade entries so that when you select an entry, another menu is displayed. This is illustrated in Example 30–7. It defines variables that store the names of the menu widgets:

```
set $m [menu .menubar.m$m]
```

This creates a variable named `File`, `Edit`, and `Help` that store the names of the menu widgets. This trick is generalized on page 470 in a package that hides the menu widget names.

Example 30–7 A menu bar in Tk 8.0.

```
menu .menubar
# attach it to the main window
. config -menu .menubar
# Create more cascade menus
foreach m {File Edit Help} {
    set $m [menu .menubar.m$m]
    .menubar add cascade -label $m -menu .menubar.m$m
}
$File add command -label Quit -command exit
# add more menu items...
```

System Menus

The Tk 8.0 menu bar implementation can add entries to the Windows system menu, the Macintosh Apple menu, and the Help menu on all platforms. This works by recognizing special names. For example, if the menu bar is `.menubar`, then the special names are `.menubar.system`, `.menubar.apple`, and `.menubar.help`. The Help menu is right justified on all platforms. The Apple menu is normally used by applications for their `About...` entry. The entries you add to the Apple menu are added to the top of the menu. The System menu appears in the Windows title bar and has entries such as `Close` and `Minimize`.

Pop-Up Menus

A pop-up menu is not associated with a menubutton. Instead, it is posted in response to a keystroke or other event in the application. The `tk_popup` command posts a pop-up menu:

```
tk_popup menu x y ?entry?
```

The last argument specifies the entry to activate when the menu is posted. It is an optional parameter that defaults to 1, which avoids the tear-off entry in position zero. The menu is posted at the specified X and Y coordinates in its parent widget.

Option Menus

An option menu represents a choice with a set of radio entries, and it displays the current choice in the text of the menubutton. The `tk_optionMenu` command creates a menubutton and a menu full of radio entries:

```
tk_optionMenu w varname firstValue ?value value ...?
```

The first argument is the pathname of the menubutton to create. The second is the variable name. The third is the initial value for the variable, and the rest are the other choices for the value. The menubutton displays the current choice and a small symbol, the indicator, to indicate it is an option menu.

Multicolumn Palette Menus

Tk 8.0 adds a `-columnbreak` menu entry attribute that puts the entry at the top of a new column. This is most useful when the menu consists of several images that are arranged as a palette. Set the entry's image with the `-image` attribute. You can create checkbutton and radiobutton entries that have images and no indicator by using the `-hidemargin` attribute. In this case, a selected entry is indicated by drawing a solid rectangle around it.

Menu Bindings and Events

Keyboard Traversal

The default bindings for menus allow for keyboard selection of menu entries. The selection process is started by pressing `<Alt-x>`, where x is the distinguishing letter for a menubutton or a menu bar's cascade entry. The `underline` attribute is used to highlight the appropriate letter. The `underline` value is a number that specifies a character position, and the count starts at zero. For example, a `File` menu with a highlighted F is created for a menubutton like this:

```
menubutton .menubar.file -text File -underline 0 \
    -menu .menubar.file.m
```

IV. Tk Widgets

If the `File` menu is implemented as a menu bar cascade, you create the traversal highlight like this:

```
menu .mbar
. configure -menu .mbar
.mbar add cascade -label File -underline 0 \
    -menu .mbar.file
```

When the user types `<Alt-f>` over the main window, the menu is posted. The case of the highlighted letter is not important.

After a menu is posted, the arrow keys change the selected entry. The `<Up>` and `<Down>` keys move within a menu, and the `<Left>` and `<Right>` keys move between adjacent menus. The bindings assume that you create your menus from left to right.

If any of the menu entries have a letter highlighted with the `-underline` option, typing that letter invokes that menu entry. For example, an `Export` entry that is invoked by typing `x` can be created like this:

```
.menubar.file.m add command -label Export -underline 1 \
    -command File_Export
```

The `<space>` and `<Return>` keys invoke the menu entry that is currently selected. The `<Escape>` key aborts the menu selection and removes the menu.

Menu Virtual Events

As of Tk 8.0, a menu widget generates a `<<MenuSelect>>` virtual event whenever the menu's active entry changes. The event is fired after the menu selection has changed, so the binding action can access the new selection. The easiest way to be aware of changes to the menu selection is to bind to this virtual event, as shown in Example 30–8. Notification like this is useful for features such as context-sensitive help.

Example 30–8 Using the `<<MenuSelect>>` virtual event.

```
proc MenuChanged {w} {
    puts "Menu $w selection: [$w entrycget active -label]"
}
bind .mbar.file <<MenuSelect>> {MenuChanged %W}
```

Manipulating Menus and Menu Entries

There are a number of operations that apply to menu entries. We have already introduced the `add` operation. The `entryconfigure` operation is similar to the `configure` operation for widgets. It accepts the same attribute-value pairs used when the menu entry was added. The `delete` operation removes a range of menu entries. The rest of the operations are used by the library scripts that implement the standard bindings for menus.

A menu entry is referred to by an *index*. The index can be numerical, counting from zero, or symbolic. Table 30–3 summarizes the index formats. One of the most useful indices is a pattern that matches the `label` in the menu entry. The pattern matching is done with the rules of `string match`. Using a pattern eliminates the need to keep track of the numerical indices.

Table 30–3 Menu entry index keywords

index	A numerical index counting from zero.
active	The activated entry, either because it is under the mouse or has been activated by keyboard traversal.
end	The last menu entry.
last	The same as end.
none	No entry at all.
@*ycoord*	The entry under the given Y coordinate. Use @%y in bindings.
pattern	A string match pattern to match the label of a menu entry.

Table 30–4 summarizes the complete set of menu operations. In the table, $w is a menu widget.

Table 30–4 Menu operations.

$w activate *index*	Highlights the specified entry.
$w add *type ?option value? ...*	Adds a new menu entry of the specified type with the given values for various attributes.
$w cget *option*	Returns the value for the configuration *option*.
$w clone	Makes a linked copy of the menu. This is used to implement tear-offs and menu bars.
$w configure *?option? ?value? ...*	Returns the configuration information for the menu.
$w delete *i1 ?i2?*	Deletes the menu entries from index *i1* to *i2*.
$w entrycget *index option*	Returns the value of *option* for the specified entry.
$w entryconfigure *index ?option? ?value? ...*	Queries or modifies the configuration information for the specified menu entry.
$w index *index*	Returns the numerical value of *index*.
$w insert *type index ?option value? ...*	Like add, but inserts the new entry after the specified *index*.
$w invoke *index*	Invokes the command associated with the entry.

IV. Tk Widgets

Table 30–4 Menu operations. (Continued)

`$w post x y`	Displays the menu at the specified coordinates.
`$w postcascade index`	Displays the cascade menu from entry *index*.
`$w type index`	Returns the type of the entry at *index*.
`$w unpost`	Unmaps the menu.
`$w yposition index`	Returns the Y coordinate of the top of the entry.

Menu Attributes

A menu has a few global attributes, and then each menu entry has many button-like attributes that describe its appearance and behavior. Table 30–5 specifies the attributes that apply globally to the menu, unless overridden by a per-entry attribute. The table uses the X resource names, which may have a capital at interior word boundaries. In Tcl commands, use all lowercase and a leading dash.

Table 30–5 Menu attribute resource names.

`activeBackground`	Background color when the mouse is over a menu entry.
`activeBorderWidth`	Width of the raised border around active entries.
`activeForeground`	Text color when the mouse is over a menu entry.
`background`	The normal background color for menu entries.
`borderWidth`	Width of the border around the menu (except on systems where native menus are used, such as Windows).
`cursor`	Cursor to display when mouse is over the menu.
`disabledForeground`	Foreground (text) color when menu entries are disabled.
`font`	Default font for the text.
`foreground`	Foreground color. (Also `fg`).
`postCommand`	Tcl command to run just before the menu is posted.
`relief`	The relief style of the menu (except on systems where native menus are used such, as Windows).
`selectColor`	Color for selector in check and radio type entries.
`takeFocus`	Control focus changes from keyboard traversal.
`tearOff`	True if menu should contain a tear-off entry.
`tearOffCommand`	Command to execute when menu is torn off. Two arguments are added: the original menu and the new tear-off.

Table 30–5 Menu attribute resource names. (Continued)

`title`	Title for the window created when the menu is torn off. If this is an empty string (default), the title is the text of the menubutton or cascade item from which this menu was torn off. (Tk 8.0)
`type`	(Read-only) `normal`, `menubar`, or `tearoff`. (Tk 8.0).

Table 30–6 describes the attributes for menu entries, as you would use them in a Tcl command (i.e., all lowercase with a leading dash.) The attributes for menu entries are not supported directly by the resource database. However, Example 31–6 on page 481 describes how you can use the resource database for menu entries.

Table 30–6 Attributes for menu entries.

`-activebackground`	Background color when the mouse is over the entry.
`-activeforeground`	Foreground (text) color with mouse is over the entry.
`-accelerator`	Text to display as a reminder about keystroke binding.
`-background`	The normal background color.
`-bitmap`	A bitmap to display instead of text.
`-columnbreak`	Puts the entry at the start of a new column. (Tk 8.0).
`-command`	Tcl command to invoke when entry is invoked.
`-compound`	Where the image or bitmap should be placed relative to the text: `bottom`, `center`, `left`, `right`, `top` or `none` (default). (Tk 8.4)
`-font`	Default font for the text.
`-foreground`	Foreground color. (Also `fg`).
`-hidemargin`	Suppresses the margin reserved for button indicators. (Tk 8.0).
`-image`	Image to display instead of text or bitmap.
`-indicatoron`	Boolean that controls if the indicator is displayed: `check` and `radio` entries.
`-label`	Text to display in the menu entry.
`-menu`	Menu posted when `cascade` entry is invoked.
`-offvalue`	Variable value when `check` entry is not selected.
`-onvalue`	Value for Tcl variable when `check` entry is selected.
`-selectcolor`	Color for selector: `check` and `radio` entries.
`-selectimage`	Alternate image to use when entry is selected: `check` and `radio` entries.

IV. Tk Widgets

Table 30–6 Attributes for menu entries. (Continued)

`-state`	The state: `normal`, `active`, or `disabled`
`-underline`	Index of text character to underline.
`-value`	Value for Tcl variable when `radiobutton` entry is selected.
`-variable`	Tcl variable associated with the `check` or `radio` entry.

A Menu by Name Package

If your application supports extensible or user-defined menus, it can be tedious to expose all the details of the Tk menus. The examples in this section create a little package that lets users refer to menus and entries by name. In addition, the package keeps keystroke accelerators for menus consistent with bindings.

The `Menu_Setup` procedure initializes the package. It creates a frame to hold the set of menu buttons, and it initializes some state variables: the frame for the menubuttons and a counter used to generate widget pathnames. All the global state for the package is kept in the array called `menu`.

The `Menu` procedure creates a menubutton and a menu. It records the association between the text label of the menubutton and the menu that was created for it. This mapping is used throughout the rest of the package so that the client of the package can refer to the menu by its label (e.g., `File`) as opposed to the internal Tk pathname, (e.g., `.top.menubar.file.menu`).

Example 30–9 A simple menu by name package.

```
proc Menu_Setup { menubar } {
    global menu
    frame $menubar
    pack $menubar -side top -fill x
    set menu(menubar) $menubar
    set menu(uid) 0
}
proc Menu { label } {
    global menu
    if [info exists menu(menu,$label)] {
        error "Menu $label already defined"
    }
    # Create the menubutton and its menu
    set name $menu(menubar).mb$menu(uid)
    set menuName $name.menu
    incr menu(uid)
    set mb [menubutton $name -text $label -menu $menuName]
    pack $mb -side left
    menu $menuName -tearoff 1
    # Remember the name to menu mapping
    set menu(menu,$label) $menuName
}
```

These procedures are repeated in Example 30–10, except that they use the Tk 8.0 menu bar mechanism. The rest of the procedures in the package are the same with either version of menu bars.

Example 30–10 Using the Tk 8.0 menu bar facility.

```
proc Menu_Setup { menubar } {
    global menu
    menu $menubar
    # Associated menu with its main window
    set top [winfo parent $menubar]
    $top config -menu $menubar
    set menu(menubar) $menubar
    set menu(uid) 0
}
proc Menu { label } {
    global menu
    if [info exists menu(menu,$label)] {
        error "Menu $label already defined"
    }
    # Create the cascade menu
    set menuName $menu(menubar).mb$menu(uid)
    incr menu(uid)
    menu $menuName -tearoff 1
    $menu(menubar) add cascade -label $label -menu $menuName
    # Remember the name to menu mapping
    set menu(menu,$label) $menuName
}
```

Once the menu is set up, the `menu` array is used to map from a menu name, like `File`, to the Tk widget name such as `.menubar.mb3`. Even though this can be done with a couple of lines of Tcl code, the mapping is put inside the `MenuGet` procedure to hide the implementation. `MenuGet` uses `return -code error` if the menu name is unknown, which changes the error reporting slightly as shown in Example 6–19 on page 86. If the user specifies a bogus menu name, the undefined variable error is caught and a more informative error is raised instead. `MenuGet` is private to the package, so it does not have an underscore in its name.

Example 30–11 `MenuGet` maps from name to menu.

```
proc MenuGet {menuName} {
    global menu
    if [catch {set menu(menu,$menuName)} m] {
        return -code error "No such menu: $menuName"
    }
    return $m
}
```

IV. Tk Widgets

The procedures `Menu_Command`, `Menu_Check`, `Menu_Radio`, and `Menu_Separator` are simple wrappers around the basic menu commands. They use `MenuGet` to map from the menu label to the Tk widget name.

Example 30–12 Adding menu entries.

```
proc Menu_Command { menuName label command } {
    set m [MenuGet $menuName]
    $m add command -label $label -command $command
}

proc Menu_Check { menuName label var { command {} } } {
    set m [MenuGet $menuName]
    $m add check -label $label -command $command \
        -variable $var
}

proc Menu_Radio { menuName label var {val {}} {command {}} }
{
    set m [MenuGet $menuName]
    if {[string length $val] == 0} {
        set val $label
    }
    $m add radio -label $label -command $command \
        -value $val -variable $var
}

proc Menu_Separator { menuName } {
    [MenuGet $menuName] add separator
}
```

Creating a cascaded menu also requires saving the mapping between the label in the cascade entry and the Tk pathname for the submenu. This package imposes a restriction that different menus, including submenus, cannot have the same label.

Example 30–13 A wrapper for cascade entries.

```
proc Menu_Cascade { menuName label } {
    global menu
    set m [MenuGet $menuName]
    if [info exists menu(menu,$label)] {
        error "Menu $label already defined"
    }
    set sub $m.sub$menu(uid)
    incr menu(uid)
    menu $sub -tearoff 0
    $m add cascade -label $label -menu $sub
    set menu(menu,$label) $sub
}
```

Creating the sampler menu with this package looks like this:

Example 30–14 Using the menu by name package.

```
Menu_Setup .menubar
Menu_Sampler
Menu_Command Sampler Hello! {puts "Hello, World!"}
Menu_Check Sampler Boolean foo {puts "foo = $foo"}
Menu_Separator Sampler
Menu_Cascade Sampler Fruit
Menu_Radio Fruit apple fruit
Menu_Radio Fruit orange fruit
Menu_Radio Fruit kiwi fruit
```

Menu Accelerators

The final touch on the menu package is to support accelerators in a consistent way. A menu entry can display another column of information that is assumed to be a keystroke identifier to remind users of a binding that also invokes the menu entry. However, there is no guarantee that this string is correct, or that if the user changes the binding that the menu will be updated. Example 30–15 shows the `Menu_Bind` procedure that takes care of this.

Example 30–15 Keeping the accelerator display up to date.

```
proc Menu_Bind { what sequence accText menuName label } {
    variable menu
    set m [MenuGet $menuName]
    if {[catch {$m index $label} index]} {
        error "$label not in menu $menuName"
    }
    bind $what $sequence [list MenuInvoke $m $index]
    $m entryconfigure $index -accelerator $accText
}
proc MenuInvoke {m index} {
    set state [$m entrycget $index -state]
    if {[string equal $state normal]} {
        $m invoke $index
    }
}
```

The `Menu_Bind` command uses the `index` operation to find out what menu entry has the given label. It sets up a binding for the key sequence that will invoke the menu operation, and it updates the display of the accelerator using the `entryconfigure` operation. This approach has the advantage of keeping the keystroke command consistent with the menu command, as well as updating the display.

The `MenuInvoke` procedure is used for the binding. We could use `entrycget` to fetch the command, and then bind directly to that. However, that wouldn't honor the state of the menu entry, which could be temporarily disabled. In addition, the `invoke` operation on the menu handles any special cases such as updating radiobutton variables associated with the entry.

To try `Menu_Bind`, add an empty frame to the sampler example, and bind a keystroke to it and one of the menu commands, like this:

```
frame .body -width 100 -height 50
pack .body ; focus .body
Menu_Bind .body <Control-q> Ctrl-Q Sampler Hello!
```

The Resource Database

This chapter describes the use of the resource database, and how users can define buttons and menus via resource specifications. This chapter describes the `option` command.

Tk supports a resource database that holds specifications of widget attributes such as fonts and colors. You can control all attributes of the Tk widgets through the resource database. It can also be used as a more general database of application-specific parameter settings.

Because a Tk application can use Tcl for customization, it might not seem necessary to use the resource database. The resource database is, however, a useful tool for your Tk application. A developer can make global changes with just a few database entries. In addition, it lets users and site administrators customize applications without modifying the code.

An Introduction to Resources

When a Tk widget is created, its attributes are set by one of three sources. It is important to note that Tcl command specifications have priority over resource database specifications:

- The most evident source of attributes are the options in Tcl commands, such as the `-text quit` attribute specification for a button.
- If an attribute is not specified on the command line, then the resource database is queried as described later.
- If there is nothing in the resource database, then a hard-coded value from the widget implementation is used.

IV. Tk Widgets

475

The resource database consists of a set of keys and values. Unlike many other databases, however, the keys are patterns that are matched against the names of widgets and attributes. This makes it possible to specify attribute values for a large number of widgets with just a few database entries. In addition, the resource database can be shared by many applications, so users and administrators can define common attributes for their whole set of applications.

The resource database is maintained in main memory by the Tk toolkit. On UNIX the database is initialized from the RESOURCE_MANAGER property on the root window, or the .Xdefaults file in your home directory. On Windows and Macintosh, there are a few resources added by the tk.tcl library file. Additional files can be explicitly loaded with the option readfile command, and individual database entries are added with the option add Tcl command.

The initialization of the database is different from the Xt toolkit, which loads specifications from as many as five different files to allow per-user, per-site, per-application, per-machine, and per-user-per-application specifications. You can achieve the same effect in Tk, but you must do it yourself. Example 45–1 on page 672 gives a partial solution.

Resource Patterns

The pattern language for the keys is related to the naming convention for Tk widgets. Recall that a widget name reflects its position in the hierarchy of windows. You can think of the resource names as extending the hierarchy one more level at the bottom to account for all the attributes of each individual widget. There is also a new level of the hierarchy at the top to specify the application by name. For example, the database could contain an entry like the following in order to define a font for the quit button in a frame called .buttons:

    Exmh.buttons.quit.font: fixed

The leading Exmh. matches the class name for the Tcl/Tk application. The class name of the application is set from the name of the script file, with the first character capitalized. For example, if the script is /usr/local/bin/foobar, then the class is set to Foobar. You could also specify an asterisk to match any application:

    *buttons.quit.font: fixed

Resource keys can also specify *classes* of widgets and attributes as opposed to individual instances. The quit button, for example, is an instance of the Button class. Class names for widgets are the same as the Tcl command used to create them, except for a leading capital letter. A class-oriented specification that would set the font for all buttons in the .buttons frame would be:

    Exmh.buttons.Button.font: fixed

Don't use widget names for script names.

The application class name becomes the class name for the main toplevel window. For example, if you use a script name like button.tcl, the class for . becomes Button. This causes it to inherit all the standard Button bindings and attribute values, which can cause problems in your application.

Patterns let you replace one or more components of the resource name with an asterisk (*). For example, to set the font for all the widgets packed into the .buttons frame, you can use the resource name *buttons*font, or you can specify the font for all buttons with the pattern *Button.font. In these examples, we have replaced the leading Tk. with an asterisk as well. It is the ability to collapse several layers of the hierarchical name with a single asterisk that makes it easy to specify attributes for many widgets with just a few database entries.

The tables in this book list attributes by their resource name. The resource names use a capital letter at the internal word boundaries. For example, if the command line switch is -offvalue, then the corresponding resource name is offValue. There are also class names for attributes, which are distinguished with a leading capital (e.g., OffValue).

Warning: Order is Important!

The matching between a widget name and the patterns in the database can be ambiguous, with multiple patterns matching the same widget. The order of database entries determines which pattern is used, with later entries taking precedence. (This is different from the Xt toolkit, in which longer matching patterns have precedence, and instance specifications have priority over class specifications.) Suppose the database contained just two entries, in this order:

```
*Text*foreground: blue
*foreground: red
```

Despite the more specific *Text*foreground entry, all widgets will have a red foreground, even text widgets. For this reason you should list your most general patterns early in your resource files and give the more specific patterns later.

Tk also supports different priorities among resources, as described in the next section. The ordering precedence described here applies to all resources with the same priority.

Loading Option Database Files

The option command manipulates the resource database. The first form of the command loads a file containing database entries:

```
option readfile filename ?priority?
```

The *priority* distinguishes different sources of resource information and gives them different priorities. Priority levels are numeric, from 0 to 100. However, symbolic names are defined for standard priorities. From lowest to highest, the standard priorities are widgetDefault (20), startupFile (40), userDefault (60), and interactive (80). These names can be abbreviated. The default priority is interactive.

Example 31–1 Reading an option database file.

```
if [file exists $appdefaults] {
    if [catch {option readfile $appdefaults startup} err] {
        puts stderr "error in $appdefaults: $err"
    }
}
```

The format of the entries in the file is:

    key: *value*

The key has the pattern format previously described. The value can be anything, and there is no need to group multiword values with any quoting characters. In fact, quotes will be picked up as part of the value.

Comment lines are introduced by the exclamation mark (!).

Example 31–2 A file containing resource specifications.

```
!
! Grey color set
! These values match those used by the Tk widgets on UNIX
!
*background:          #d9d9d9
*foreground:          black
*activeBackground:    #ececec
*activeForeground:    black
*selectColor:         #b03060
*selectBackground:    #c3c3c3
*troughColor:         #c3c3c3
*disabledforeground:#a3a3a3
```

The example resource file specifies the color scheme for the Tk widget set on UNIX that is based on a family of gray levels. Color highlighting shows up well against this backdrop. These colors are applied generically to all the widgets. The hexadecimal values for the colors specify two digits (eight bits) each for red, green, and blue. Chapter 41 describes the use of color in detail.

Adding Individual Database Entries

You can enter individual database entries with the option add Tcl command. This is appropriate to handle special cases, or if you do not want to manage a separate per application resource specification file. The command syntax is:

        option add *pattern value ?priority?*

The *priority* is the same as that used with option readfile. The *pattern* and *value* are the same as in the file entries, except that the key does not have a trailing colon when specified in an option add command. If *value* contains spaces or special characters, you will need to group it like any other argument to a Tcl command. Some of the specifications from the last example could be added as follows:

        option add *foreground black
        option add *selectBackground #bfdfff

You can clear the option database:

        option clear

However, on UNIX the database will be initialized from your `~/.Xdefaults` file, or the `RESOURCE_MANAGER` property on the root window, the next time the database is accessed.

Accessing the Database

Often, it is sufficient just to set up the database and let the widget implementations use the values. However, it is also possible to record application-specific information in the database. To fetch a resource value, use `option get`:

```
option get window name class
```

The `window` is a Tk widget pathname. The `name` is a resource name. In this case, it is not a pattern or a full name. Instead, it is the resource name as specified in the tables in this book. Similarly, the `class` is a simple class name. It is possible to specify a null name or class. If there is no matching database entry, `option get` returns the empty string.

It is not possible to enumerate the database, nor can you detect the difference between a value that is the empty string and the absence of a value. You can work around this by introducing well-known resource names that list other resources. This trick is used in the next section.

User-Defined Buttons

Suppose you want users to be able to define a set of their own buttons for frequently executed commands. Or perhaps users can augment the application with their own Tcl code. The following scheme, which is based on an idea from John LoVerso, lets them define buttons to invoke their own code or their favorite commands.

The application creates a special frame to hold the user-defined buttons and places it appropriately. Assume the frame is created like this:

```
frame .user -class User
```

The class specification for the frame means that we can name resources for the widgets inside the frame relative to `*User`. Users specify the buttons that go in the frame via a personal file containing resource specifications.

The first problem is that there is no means to enumerate the database, so we must create a resource that lists the names of the user-defined buttons. We use the name `buttonlist` and make an entry for `*User.buttonlist` that specifies which buttons are being defined. It is possible to use artificial resource names (e.g., `buttonlist`), but they must be relative to an existing Tk widget.

Example 31–3 Using resources to specify user-defined buttons.

```
*User.buttonlist: save search justify quit
*User.save.text: Save
*User.save.command: File_Save
*User.search.text: Search
```

```
*User.search.command: Edit_Search
*User.justify.text: Justify
*User.justify.command: Edit_Justify
*user.quit.text: Quit
*User.quit.command: File_Quit
*User.quit.background: red
```

In Example 31–3, we have listed four buttons and specified some of the attributes for each, most importantly the text and command attributes. We are assuming, of course, that the application manual publishes a set of commands that users can invoke safely. In this simple example, the commands are all one word, but there is no problem with multiword commands. There is no interpretation done of the value, so it can include references to Tcl variables and nested command calls. Example 31–4 uses these resource specifications to define the buttons:

Example 31–4 Resource_ButtonFrame defines buttons based on resources.

```
proc Resource_ButtonFrame { f class } {
    frame $f -class $class -borderwidth 2
    pack $f -side top -fill x
    foreach b [option get $f buttonlist {}] {
        if [catch {button $f.$b}] {
            button $f.$b -font fixed
        }
        pack $f.$b -side right
    }
}
```

The catch phrase is introduced to handle a common problem with fonts and widget creation. If the user's resources specify a bogus or missing font, then the widget creation command will fail. The catch phrase guards against this case by falling back to the fixed font, which is guaranteed to exist. This problem is fixed in Tk 8.0 because the font mechanism will search for alternate fonts.

Example 31–5 assumes that the resource specifications from Example 31–2 are in the file button.resources. It creates the user-defined buttons in the .users frame.

Example 31–5 Using Resource_ButtonFrame.

```
option readfile button.resources
Resource_ButtonFrame .user User
```

User-Defined Menus

User-defined menus can be set up with a similar scheme. However, it is more complex because there are no resources for specific menu entries. We must use more artificial resources to emulate this. We use `menulist` to name the set of menus. Then, for each of these, we define an `entrylist` resource. Finally, for each entry we define a few more resources. The name of the entry has to be combined with some type information, which leads to the following convention:

- `l_entry` is the label for the entry.
- `t_entry` is the type of the entry.
- `c_entry` is the command associated with the entry.
- `v_entry` is the variable associated with the entry.
- `m_entry` is the menu associated with the entry.

Example 31–6 Specifying menu entries via resources.

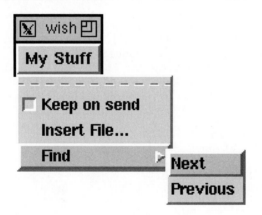

```
*User.menulist: stuff
*User.stuff.text: My stuff
*User.stuff.m.entrylist: keep insert find
*User.stuff.m.l_keep: Keep on send
*User.stuff.m.t_keep: check
*User.stuff.m.v_keep: checkvar
*User.stuff.m.l_insert: Insert File...
*User.stuff.m.c_insert: InsertFileDialog
*User.stuff.m.l_find: Find
*User.stuff.m.t_find: cascade
*User.stuff.m.m_find: find
*User.stuff.m.find.entrylist: next prev
*User.stuff.m.find.tearoff: 0
*User.stuff.m.find.l_next: Next
*User.stuff.m.find.c_next: Find_Next
*User.stuff.m.find.l_prev: Previous
*User.stuff.m.find.c_prev: Find_Previous
```

In Example 31–6, .user.stuff is a Tk menubutton. It has a menu as its child, .user.stuff.m, where the menu .m is set by convention. You will see this later in the code for Resource_Menubar. The entrylist for the menu is similar in spirit to the buttonlist resource. For each entry, however, we have to be a little creative with the next level of resource names. The following does not work:

```
*User.stuff.m.keep.label: Keep on send
```

The problem is that Tk does not directly support resources for menu entries, so it assumes .stuff.m.keep is a widget pathname, but it is not. You can add the resource, but you cannot retrieve it with option get. Instead, we must combine the attribute information (i.e., label) with the name of the entry:

```
*User.stuff.m.l_keep: Keep on send
```

You must do something similar if you want to define resources for items on a canvas, too, because that is not supported directly by Tk. The code to support menu definition by resources is shown in the next example:

Example 31–7 Defining menus from resource specifications.

```
proc Resource_Menubar { f class } {
    set f [frame $f -class $class]
    pack $f -side top
    foreach b [option get $f menulist {}] {
        set cmd [list menubutton $f.$b -menu $f.$b.m \
                    -relief raised]
        if [catch $cmd t] {
            eval $cmd {-font fixed}
        }
        if [catch {menu $f.$b.m}] {
            menu $f.$b.m -font fixed
        }
        pack $f.$b -side left
        ResourceMenu $f.$b.m
    }
}
proc ResourceMenu { menu } {
    foreach e [option get $menu entrylist {}] {
        set l [option get $menu l_$e {}]
        set c [option get $menu c_$e {}]
        set v [option get $menu v_$e {}]
        switch -- [option get $menu t_$e {}] {
            check {
                $menu add checkbutton -label $l -command $c \
                    -variable $v
            }
            radio {
                $menu add radiobutton -label $l -command $c \
                    -variable $v -value $l
            }
            separator {
                $menu add separator
            }
            cascade {
                set sub [option get $menu m_$e {}]
```

```
                    if {[string length $sub] != 0} {
                        set submenu [menu $menu.$sub]
                        $menu add cascade -label $l -command $c \
                            -menu $submenu
                        ResourceMenu $submenu
                    }
                }
                default {
                    $menu add command -label $l -command $c
                }
            }
        }
    }
}
```

Application and User Resources

The examples presented here are a subset of a package I use in some large applications, *exmh* and *webtk*. The applications define nearly every button and menu via resources, so users and site administrators can redefine them. The `buttonlist`, `menulist`, and `entrylist` resources are generalized into user, site, and application lists. The application uses the application lists for the initial configuration. The site and user lists can add and remove widgets. For example:

- `buttonlist` – the application list of buttons
- `l-buttonlist` – the site-specific list of buttons to remove
- `lbuttonlist` – the site-specific list of buttons to add
- `u-buttonlist` – the per-user list of buttons to remove
- `ubuttonlist` – the per-user list of buttons to add

This idea and the initial implementation was contributed to *exmh* by Achim Bonet. The `Resource_GetFamily` procedure merges five sets of resources shown above. It can replace the `option get` commands for the `buttonlist`, `menulist`, and `entrylist` resources in Examples 31–4 and 31–7:

Example 31–8 `Resource_GetFamily` merges user and application resources.

```
proc Resource_GetFamily { w resname } {
    set res    [option get $w $resname {}]
    set lres   [option get $w l$resname {}]
    set ures   [option get $w u$resname {}]
    set l-res  [option get $w l-$resname {}]
    set u-res  [option get $w u-$resname {}]
    # Site-local deletions from application resources
    set list [lsubtract $res ${l-res}]
    # Site-local additions
    set list [concat $list $lres]
    # Per-user deletions
    set list [lsubtract $list ${u-res}]
    # Per-user additions
    return [concat $list $ures]
}
```

```
proc lsubtract { orig nuke } {
    # Remove elements in $nuke from $orig
    foreach x $nuke {
        set ix [lsearch $orig $x]
        if {$ix >= 0} {
            set orig [lreplace $orig $ix $ix]
        }
    }
    return $orig
}
```

Expanding Variables

If the command resource contains substitution syntax like $ and [], then these are evaluated later when the command is invoked by the button or menu. This is because there is no interpretation of the command value when the widgets are created. However, it may be that you want variables substituted when the buttons and menus are defined. You can use the subst command to do this:

```
set cmd [$button cget -command]
$button config -command [subst $cmd]
```

Choosing the scope for the subst can be tricky. The previous command does the subst in the current scope. If this is the Resource_ButtonFrame procedure, then there are no interesting application-specific variables defined. The next command uses uplevel to do the subst in the scope of the caller of Resource_ButtonFrame. The list is necessary so that uplevel preserves the structure of the original subst command.

```
$button config -command [uplevel [list subst $cmd]]
```

If you do a subst in ResourceMenu, then you need to keep track of the recursion level to get back to the scope of the caller of Resource_Menubar. The next few lines show what changes in ResourceMenu:

```
proc ResourceMenu { menu {level 1} } {
    foreach e [option get $menu entrylist {}] {
        # code omitted
        set c [option get $menu c_$e {}]
        set c [uplevel $level [list subst $c]]
        # And the recursive call is
        ResourceMenu $submenu [expr $level+1]
        # more code omitted
    }
}
```

If you want the subst to occur in the global scope, use this:

```
$button config -command [uplevel #0 [list subst $cmd]]
```

However, the global scope may not be much different when you define the button than when the button is invoked. In practice, I have used subst to capture variables defined in the procedure that calls Resource_Menubar.

Simple Tk Widgets

This chapter describes several simple Tk widgets: the `frame`, `label`, `labelframe`, `message`, `scale`, and `toplevel`. In general, these widgets require minimal setup to be useful in your application. The `bell` command rings the terminal bell.

*T*his chapter describes six simple widgets and the `bell` command.

IV. Tk Widgets

- The `frame` is a building block for widget layout.
- A `labelframe` is an enhanced frame that also supports the display of a label along its border.
- A `toplevel` is a frame that is detached from the main window.
- The `label` displays read-only text or an image.
- The `message` provides a read-only block of text that gets formatted onto several lines.
- The `scale` is a slider-like widget used to set a numeric value.
- The `bell` command rings the terminal bell.

Chapters 40, 41, and 42 go into more detail about some of the generic widget attributes shared by the widgets presented in this chapter. The examples in this chapter use the default widget attributes in most cases.

Frames, Labelframes, and Toplevel Windows

Frames have been introduced before for use with the geometry managers. There is not much to a frame, except for its background color and border. You can also specify a colormap and visual type for a frame. Chapter 41 describes visual types and colormaps on page 624.

485

The labelframe widget, introduced in Tk 8.4, is a frame that can also display a widget along its border. The labelframe widget can create its own internal label, if needed, or it can automatically position a label widget that you create separately.

A toplevel widget is like a frame, except that it is created as a new main window. That is, it is not positioned inside the main window of the application. This is useful for dialog boxes, for example. A toplevel has the same attributes as a frame, plus `screen` and `menu` attributes. The `menu` attribute is used to create menubars along the top edge of a toplevel. This feature was added in Tk 8.0, and it is described on page 464. On UNIX, the `screen` option lets you put the toplevel on any X display. The value of the `screen` option has the following format:

     host:display.screenNum

For example, I have one X server on my workstation `sage` that controls two screens. My two screens are named `sage:0.0` and `sage:0.1`. If the *screenNum* specifier is left off, it defaults to `0`.

Attributes for Frames, Labelframes, and Toplevels

Table 32–1 lists the attributes for the frame, labelframe, and toplevel widgets. The attributes are named according to their resource name, which includes a capital letter at internal word boundaries. When you specify an attribute in a Tcl command when creating or reconfiguring a widget, however, you specify the attribute with a dash and all lowercase letters. Chapter 31 explains how to use resource specifications for attributes. Chapters 40, 41, and 42 discuss many of these attributes in more detail.

Table 32–1 Attributes for frame, labelframe, and toplevel widgets.

`background`	Background color (also `bg`).
`borderWidth`	Extra space around the edge of the frame.
`class`	Resource class and binding class name.
`colormap`	The value is `new` or the name of a window.
`container`	If `true`, frame embeds another application.
`cursor`	Cursor to display when mouse is over the frame.
`font`	The font to use for the label. Labelframe only.
`foreground`	The text color for the label. Labelframe only.
`height`	Height, in screen units.
`highlightBackground`	Focus highlight color when widget does not have focus.
`highlightColor`	Focus highlight color when widget has focus.
`highlightThickness`	Thickness of focus highlight rectangle.

Table 32–1 Attributes for frame, labelframe, and toplevel widgets. (Continued)

labelAnchor	Position of the embedded label; clockwise: nw (default), n, ne, en, e, es, se, s, sw, ws, w, wn. Labelframe only.
labelWidget	Pathname of a widget to use as a label, overriding any -text option. The label must already exist. Labelframe only.
menu	The menu to use for the menubar. Toplevel only.
padX	Extra internal space to the left and right.
padY	Extra internal space above and below.
relief	flat, sunken, raised, groove, solid or ridge.
screen	An X display specification. (Toplevel only, and this cannot be specified in the resource database).
takeFocus	Controls focus changes from keyboard traversal.
text	The text of the embedded label. Labelframe only.
use	A window ID from winfo id. This embeds the frame or toplevel into the specified window.
visual	Type: staticgrey, greyscale, staticcolor, pseudocolor, directcolor, or truecolor.
width	Width, in screen units.

You cannot change the class, colormap, visual, or screen attributes after the frame, labelframe, or toplevel has been created. These settings are so fundamental that you need to destroy the frame and start over if you must change them.

Using Labelframe Widgets

Labelframe widgets, which were added in Tk 8.4, function identically to simple frame widgets in most respects. However, they also have the ability to display a label along its border — either one that you create separately or an internal one created automatically by the labelframe. Another minor difference is that a labelframe has a default borderWidth of 2 and relief of groove, in comparison with the simple frame's default borderWidth of 0 and relief of flat. The rationale for this difference is that labelframes are used typically to set off distinct areas of a user interface, whereas frames are often used solely to group together other widgets for layout.

In many cases, you can simply set the text attribute of the labelframe to display a textual label in the upper-left hand corner of the frame. Example 32–1 shows a labelframe around a group of radio buttons:

IV. Tk Widgets

Example 32–1 Labelframe example.

```
labelframe .s -text Sizes
radiobutton .s.small -text Small -variable size -value small
radiobutton .s.med -text Medium -variable size -value medium
radiobutton .s.large -text Large -variable size -value large
.s.large select
pack .s.small .s.med .s.large -anchor w -padx 2 -pady 1
pack .s
```

You can change the appearance of the label's text by setting the font and foreground attributes as desired. The labelAnchor attribute accepts a map direction which controls the position of the label along the frame's border. The default, nw, places the label on the north (top) border on the west (left) side. In contrast, setting the labelAnchor to wn places the label on the west (left) border towards the north (top) side, as shown in Example 32–2:

Example 32–2 Using the labelAnchor option to position a labelframe's anchor.

```
-labelanchor wn          -labelanchor s          -labelanchor ne
```

You also have the option of creating a separate label widget, configuring it in any way that you like, and then associating it with a labelframe through the labelWidget attribute. The labelWidget attribute overrides any text value already set for the labelframe. Example 32–3 shows a label with a bitmap as the frame decoration:

Example 32–3 Associating an existing label widget with a labelframe.

```
label .l -bitmap question
.s configure -labelwidget .l -labelanchor wn
```

Embedding Other Applications

The `container` and `use` attributes support application embedding. Embedding puts another application's window into a Tk frame or puts a Tk frame into another application. The `use` attribute specifies the ID of a window that will contain a Tk frame. *Wish* supports a `-use` command line argument that is used for the same purpose. Set the `container` attribute if you want to embed another window. For example, here is how to run another *wish* application and embed its window in one of your frames:

```
frame .embed -container 1 -bd 4 -bg red
exec wish somescript.tcl -use [winfo id .embed] &
```

Toplevel Window Styles

On Windows and Macintosh there are several styles of toplevel windows. They differ in their appearance and their behavior. On UNIX, toplevel windows are usually decorated by the window manager, which is a separate application. Chapter 44 describes how to interact with the window manager.

On Macintosh, Tk has an `unsupported1` command that you can use to set the window style:

```
unsupported1 style window style
```

The possible values for *style* include `documentProc`, `dBoxProc`, `plainDBox`, `altDBoxProc`, `movableDBoxProc`, `zoomDocProc`, `rDocProc`, `floatProc`, `floatZoomProc`, `floatSideProc`, or `floatSideZoomProc`. The `dBoxProc`, `plainDBox`, and `altDBoxProc` styles have no title bar, so there is no close box on them. The other styles have different title bars, a close box, and possibly a full-sized zoom box. The default style is `documentProc`. I used the following code to see what each looked like:

Example 32–4 Macintosh window styles.

```
set x {documentProc dBoxProc plainDBox altDBoxProc \
    movableDBoxProc zoomDocProc rDocProc floatProc \
    floatZoomProc floatSideProc floatSideZoomProc}
```

```
foreach y $x {
    toplevel .$y
    label .$y.l -text $y
    pack .$y.l -padx 40 -pady 20
    if [catch {unsupported1 style .$y $y} err] {
        puts "$y: $err"
    }
}
```

This feature may appear as part of the `wm` command in future releases of Tk. On Windows you can get a couple different styles by using `transient` and `overrideredirect` windows, as well as with options to the `wm attributes` command, all of which are described starting on page 663.

The Label Widget

The label widget provides a read-only text label, and it has attributes that let you control the position of the label within the display space. Most commonly, however, you just need to specify the text for the label:

```
label .version -text "MyApp v1.0"
```

The text can be specified indirectly by using a Tcl variable to hold the text. In this case the label is updated whenever the value of the Tcl variable changes. The variable is used from the global scope, even if there happens to be a local variable by the same name when you create the widget inside a procedure:

```
set version "MyApp v1.0"
label .version -textvariable version
```

You can change the appearance of a label dynamically by using the `configure` widget operation. If you change the text or font of a label, you are liable to change the size of the widget, and this causes the packer to shuffle window positions. You can avoid this by specifying a width for the label that is large enough to hold all the strings you plan to display in it. The width is specified in characters, not screen coordinates:

Example 32–5 A label that displays different strings.

```
proc FixedWidthLabel { name values } {
    # name is a widget name to be created
    # values is a list of strings
    set maxWidth 0
    foreach value $values {
        if {[string length $value] > $maxWidth} {
            set maxWidth [string length $value]
        }
    }
```

```
      # Use -anchor w to left-justify short strings
      label $name -width $maxWidth -anchor w \
         -text [lindex $values 0]
      return $name
  }
```

The `FixedWidthLabel` example is used to create a label with a width big enough to hold a set of different strings. It uses the `-anchor w` attribute to left-justify strings that are shorter than the maximum. You can change the text for the label later by using the `configure` widget operation, which can be abbreviated to `config`:

```
      FixedWidthLabel .status {OK Busy Error}
      .status config -text Busy
```

A label can display a bitmap or image instead of a text string, which is described in Chapter 41 and the section on *Bitmaps and Images*.

This example could use the font metrics facilities of Tk 8.0 to get more accurate sizes of the text for different strings. It is possible, for example, that a three-character string like **OOO** is wider than a four-character string like **llll** in a variable-width font. The `font metrics` command is described on page 640.

Label Width and Wrap Length

When a label is displaying text, its `width` attribute is interpreted as a number of characters. The label is made wide enough to hold this number of averaged width characters in the label's font. However, if the label is holding a bitmap or an image, then the `width` is in pixels or another screen unit.

The `wrapLength` attribute determines when a label's text is wrapped onto multiple lines. *The wrap length is always screen units.* If you need to compute a `wrapLength` based on the font metrics, then you can use the `font metrics` command. If you use Tk 4.2 or earlier, then you have to measure text using a `text` widget with the same font. Chapter 36 describes the `text` widget operations that return size information for characters.

You can force line breaks by including newlines (\n) in the label's text. This lets you create labels that have multiple lines of text.

Label Attributes

Table 32–2 lists the widget attributes for the label widget. The attributes are named according to their resource name, which includes a capital letter at internal word boundaries. When you specify an attribute as an option in a Tcl command when creating or reconfiguring a widget, however, you specify the attribute with a dash and all lowercase letters. Chapter 31 explains how to use resource specifications for attributes. Chapters 40, 41, and 42 discuss many of these attributes in more detail.

Table 32–2 Label Attributes.

`activeBackground`	Background color when the label is in the `active` state. (Tk 8.3.2)
`activeForeground`	Text color when the label is in the `active` state. (Tk 8.3.2)
`anchor`	Relative position of the label within its packing space.
`background`	Background color (also `bg`).
`bitmap`	Name of a bitmap to display instead of a text string.
`borderWidth`	Extra space around the edge of the label.
`compound`	Where the image or bitmap should be placed relative to the text: `bottom`, `center`, `left`, `none` (**default**), `right` and `top`. (Tk 8.4)
`cursor`	Cursor to display when mouse is over the label.
`disabledForeground`	Foreground (text) color when the label is disabled. (Tk 8.3.1)
`font`	Font for the label's text.
`foreground`	Foreground color (also `fg`).
`height`	In screen units for bitmaps, in lines for text.
`highlightBackground`	Focus highlight color when widget does not have focus.
`highlightColor`	Focus highlight color when widget has focus.
`highlightThickness`	Thickness of focus highlight rectangle.
`image`	Specifies image to display instead of bitmap or text.
`justify`	Text justification: `left`, `right`, or `center`.
`padX`	Extra space to the left and right of the label.
`padY`	Extra space above and below the label.
`relief`	`flat`, `sunken`, `raised`, `groove`, `solid` or `ridge`.
`state`	`normal` (**enabled**), `disabled` (**deactivated**), or `active`. (Tk 8.3.1)
`takeFocus`	Controls focus changes from keyboard traversal.
`text`	Text to display.
`textVariable`	Name of Tcl variable. Its value is displayed.
`underline`	Index of character to underline.
`width`	Width. In characters for text labels.
`wrapLength`	Length at which text is wrapped *in screen units*.

The Message Widget

The message widget displays a long text string by formatting it onto several lines. It is designed for use in dialog boxes. It can format the text into a box of a given width, in screen units, or a given *aspect ratio*. The aspect ratio is defined to be the ratio of the width to the height, times 100. The default is 150, which means that the text will be one and a half times as wide as it is high.

Example 32–6 creates a message widget with one long line of text. Backslashes are used to continue the text string without embedding any newlines. (You can also just type a long line into your script.) Note that backslash-newline collapses white space after the newline into a single space.

Example 32–6 The message widget formats long lines of text.

```
message .msg -justify center -text "This is a very long text\
    line that will be broken into many lines by the\
    message widget"
pack .msg
```

A newline in the string forces a line break in the message display. You can retain exact control over the formatting by putting newlines into your string and specifying a very large aspect ratio. In Example 32–7, grouping with double quotes is used to continue the string over more than one line. The newline character between the quotes is included in the string, and it causes a line break:

Example 32–7 Controlling the text layout in a message widget.

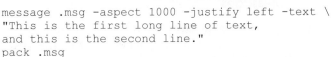

```
message .msg -aspect 1000 -justify left -text \
"This is the first long line of text,
and this is the second line."
pack .msg
```

One disadvantage of a message widget is that, by default, you cannot select the text it displays. Chapter 38 describes how to define custom selection handlers, so you could define one that returned the message string. The message widget predates the text widget, which has many more features and can emulate the message widget. If selections, multiple fonts, and other formatting are important, use a text widget instead of a message widget. Text widgets are described in Chapter 36.

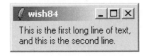

IV. Tk Widgets

Message Attributes

Table 32–3 lists the attributes for the message widget. The table lists the resource name, which has capitals at internal word boundaries. In Tcl commands these options are specified with a dash and all lowercase:

Table 32–3 Message Attributes

anchor	Relative position of the text within its packing space.
aspect	100 * width / height. Default 150.
background	Background color (also bg).
borderWidth	Extra space around the edge of the text.
cursor	Cursor to display when mouse is over the widget.
font	Font for the message's text.
foreground	Foreground color (also fg).
highlightBackground	Focus highlight color when widget does not have focus.
highlightColor	Focus highlight color when widget has focus.
highlightThickness	Thickness of focus highlight rectangle.
justify	Justification: left, center, or right.
padX	Extra space to the left and right of the text.
padY	Extra space above and below the text.
relief	flat, sunken, raised, groove, solid or ridge.
takeFocus	Controls focus changes from keyboard traversal.
text	Text to display.
textVariable	Name of Tcl variable. Its value is displayed.
width	Width, in screen units.

Arranging Labels and Messages

Both the label and message widgets have attributes that control the position of their text in much the same way that the packer controls the position of widgets within a frame. These attributes are padX, padY, anchor, and border-Width. The anchor takes effect when the size of the widget is larger than the space needed to display its text. This happens when you specify the -width attribute or if you pack the widget with fill enabled and there is extra room. See Chapter 40 and the section on *Padding and Anchors* for more details.

The Scale Widget

The scale widget displays a *slider* in a *trough*. The trough represents a range of numeric values, and the slider position represents the current value. The scale can have an associated label, and it can display its current value next to the slider. The value of the scale can be used in three different ways:

- Explicitly get and set the value with widget commands.
- Associate the scale with a Tcl variable. The variable is kept in sync with the value of the scale, and changing the variable affects the scale.
- Register a Tcl command to be executed after the scale value changes. You specify the initial part of the Tcl command, and the scale implementation adds the current value as another argument to the command.

Example 32–8 A scale widget.

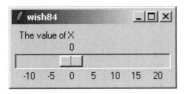

```
scale .scale -from -10 -to 20 -length 200 -variable x \
    -orient horizontal -label "The value of X" \
    -tickinterval 5 -showvalue true
pack .scale
```

Example 32–8 shows a scale for a variable that ranges in value from -10 to +20. The variable x is defined at the global scope. The tickinterval option results in the labels across the bottom, and the showvalue option causes the current value to be displayed. The length of the scale is in screen units (i.e., pixels).

Scale Bindings

Table 32–4 lists the bindings for scale widgets. You must direct focus to a scale explicitly for the key bindings like <Up> and <Down> to take effect.

Table 32–4 Bindings for scale widgets.

<Button-1>	Clicking on the trough moves the slider by one unit of resolution toward the mouse click.
<Control-Button-1>	Clicking on the trough moves the slider all the way to the end of the trough toward the mouse click.
<Left> <Up>	Moves the slider toward the left (top) by one unit.
<Control-Left> <Control-Up>	Moves the slider toward the left (top) by the value of the bigIncrement attribute.

IV. Tk Widgets

Table 32–4 Bindings for scale widgets. (Continued)

`<Right> <Down>`	Moves the slider toward the right (bottom) one unit.
`<Control-Right>` `<Control-Down>`	Moves the slider toward the right (bottom) by the value of the `bigIncrement` attribute.
`<Home>`	Moves the slider all the way to the left (top).
`<End>`	Moves the slider all the way to the right (bottom).

Scale Attributes

Table 32–5 lists the scale widget attributes. The table uses the resource name, which has capitals at internal word boundaries. In Tcl commands the attributes are specified with a dash and all lowercase.

Table 32–5 Attributes for scale widgets.

`activeBackground`	Background color when the mouse is over the slider.
`background`	The background color (also `bg` in commands).
`bigIncrement`	Coarse grain slider adjustment value.
`borderWidth`	Extra space around the edge of the widget.
`command`	Command to invoke when the value changes. The current value is appended as another argument
`cursor`	Cursor to display when mouse is over the widget.
`digits`	Number of significant digits in scale value.
`from`	Minimum value. The left or top end of the scale.
`font`	Font for the label.
`foreground`	Foreground color (also `fg`).
`highlightBackground`	Focus highlight color when widget does not have focus.
`highlightColor`	Focus highlight color when widget has focus.
`highlightThickness`	Thickness of focus highlight rectangle.
`label`	A string to display with the scale.
`length`	The length, in screen units, of the long axis of the scale.
`orient`	`horizontal` or `vertical`.
`relief`	`flat`, `sunken`, `raised`, `groove`, `solid` or `ridge`.
`repeatDelay`	Delay before keyboard auto-repeat starts. Auto-repeat is used when pressing `<Button-1>` on the trough.
`repeatInterval`	Time period between auto-repeat events.
`resolution`	The value is rounded to a multiple of this value.

Table 32–5 Attributes for scale widgets. (Continued)

showValue	If true, value is displayed next to the slider.
sliderLength	The length, in screen units, of the slider.
sliderRelief	The relief of the slider.
state	normal, active, or disabled.
takeFocus	Controls focus changes from keyboard traversal.
tickInterval	Spacing between tick marks. Zero means no marks.
to	Maximum value. Right or bottom end of the scale.
troughColor	The color of the bar on which the slider sits.
variable	Name of Tcl variable. Changes to the scale widget are reflected in the Tcl variable value, and changes in the Tcl variable are reflected in the scale display.
width	Width of the trough, or slider bar.

Programming Scales

The scale operations are primarily used by the default bindings and you do not need to program the scale directly. Table 32–6 lists the operations supported by the scale. In the table, $w is a scale widget.

Table 32–6 Operations on the scale widget.

$w cget *option*	Returns the value of the configuration option.
$w configure ...	Queries or modifies the widget configuration.
$w coords ?*value*?	Returns the coordinates of the point in the trough that corresponds to *value*, or the scale's value.
$w get ?x y?	Returns the value of the scale, or the value that corresponds to the position given by *x* and *y*.
$w identify *x y*	Returns trough1, slider, or trough2 to indicate what is under the position given by *x* and *y*.
$w set *value*	Sets the value of the scale.

The `bell` Command

The `bell` command rings the terminal bell. The bell is associated with the display; even if you are executing your program on a remote machine, the bell is heard by the user. If your application has windows on multiple displays, you can direct the bell to the display of a particular window with the `-displayof` option. The syntax for the `bell` command is given below:

```
bell ?-displayof window? ?-nice?
```

UNIX has an *xset* program that controls the bell's duration, pitch, and volume. The volume is in percent of a maximum, for example, 50. In practice, many keyboard bells only support a variable duration; the pitch and volume are fixed. The arguments of *xset* that control the bell are shown below.

```
exec xset b ?volume? ?hertz? ?milliseconds?
```

The b argument by itself resets the bell to the default parameters. You can turn the bell off with -b, or you can use the on or off arguments.

```
exec xset -b
exec xset b ?on? ?off?
```

The bell command has the side effect on most systems of resetting the screen saver for the screen, which usually makes the screen visible again. In Tk 8.4, a -nice option was added to prevent the bell command from resetting the screen saver.

## CHAPTER 33

Scrollbars

This chapter describes the Tk `scrollbar`. Scrollbars have a general protocol
that is used to attach them to one or more other widgets.

$\mathcal{S}$crollbars control other widgets through a
standard protocol based around Tcl commands. A scrollbar uses a Tcl command
to ask a widget to display part of its contents. The scrollable widget uses a Tcl
command to tell the scrollbar what part of its contents are visible. The Tk widgets designed to work with scrollbars are: entry, listbox, text, and canvas. The
scrollbar protocol is general enough to use with new widgets, or collections of
widgets. This chapter explains the protocol between scrollbars and the widgets
they control, but you don't need to know the details to use a scrollbar. All you
need to know is how to set things up, and then these widgets take care of themselves.

Using Scrollbars

The following commands create a text widget and two scrollbars that scroll it
horizontally and vertically:

```
scrollbar .yscroll -command {.text yview} -orient vertical
scrollbar .xscroll -command {.text xview} -orient horizontal
text .text -yscrollcommand {.yscroll set} \
    -xscrollcommand {.xscroll set}
```

The scrollbar's `set` operation is designed to be called from other widgets
when their display changes. The scrollable widget's `xview` and `yview` operations
are designed to be called by the scrollbar when the user manipulates them. Addi-

tional parameters are passed to these operations as described later. In most cases you can ignore the details of the protocol and just set up the connection between the scrollbar and the widget.

Example 33–1 A text widget and two scrollbars.

```
 wish84                                              _ □ ×
# colors.tcl --
#
# This demonstration script creates a li
# many of the colors from the X color da
# a color to change the application's pa
#
# RCS: @(#) $Id: colors.tcl,v 1.2 1998/0
◄                                                    ►
```

```
proc Scrolled_Text { f args } {
    frame $f
    eval {text $f.text -wrap none \
        -xscrollcommand [list $f.xscroll set] \
        -yscrollcommand [list $f.yscroll set]} $args
    scrollbar $f.xscroll -orient horizontal \
        -command [list $f.text xview]
    scrollbar $f.yscroll -orient vertical \
        -command [list $f.text yview]
    grid $f.text $f.yscroll -sticky news
    grid $f.xscroll -sticky news
    grid rowconfigure $f 0 -weight 1
    grid columnconfigure $f 0 -weight 1
    return $f.text
}
set t [Scrolled_Text .f -width 40 -height 8 \
    -font {courier 12}]
pack .f -side top -fill both -expand true
set in [open [file join $tk_library demos colors.tcl]]
$t insert end [read $in]
close $in
```

Example 33–1 defines Scrolled_Text that creates a text widget with two scrollbars. It reads and inserts one of the Tk demo files into the text widget. There is not enough room to display all the text, and the scrollbars indicate how much text is visible. Chapter 36 describes the text widget in more detail.

The list command constructs the -command and -xscrollcommand values. Even though one could use double quotes here, you should make a habit of using list when constructing values that are used later as Tcl commands. Example 33–1 uses args to pass through extra options to the text widget. The use of eval and args is explained in Example 10–3 on page 136. The scrollbars and the text widget are lined up with the grid geometry manager as explained in Example 26–10 on page 417.

The Scrollbar Protocol

When the user manipulates the scrollbar, it calls its registered `command` with some additional parameters that indicate what the user said to do. The associated widget responds to this command (e.g., its `xview` operation) by changing its display. After the widget changes its display, it calls the scrollbar by using its registered `xscrollcommand` or `yscrollcommand` (e.g., the `set` operation) with some parameters that indicate the new relative size and position of the display. The scrollbar updates its appearance to reflect this information.

The protocol supports widgets that change their display by themselves, such as when more information is added to the widget. Scrollable widgets also support a binding to `<B2-Motion>` (i.e., "middle drag") that scrolls the widget. When anything happens to change the view on a widget, the scrollable widgets use their scroll commands to update the scrollbar.

The Scrollbar `set` Operation

The scrollbar `set` operation takes two floating point values between zero and one, *first* and *last*, that indicate the relative position of the top and bottom (or left and right) of the widget's display. The scrollable widget adds these values when they use their `yscrollcommand` or `xscrollcommand`. For example, the text widget would issue the following command to indicate that the first quarter of the widget is displayed:

```
.yscroll set 0.0 0.25
```

If the two values are 0.0 and 1.0, it means that the widget's contents are fully visible, and a scrollbar is not necessary. You can monitor the protocol by using a Tcl wrapper, `Scroll_Set`, instead of the `set` operation directly. `Scroll_Set` waits for the scrollbar to be necessary before mapping it with a geometry manager command. It is not safe to unmap the scrollbar because that can change the size of the widget and create the need for a scrollbar. That leads to an infinite loop.

Example 33–2 `Scroll_Set` manages optional scrollbars.

```
proc Scroll_Set {scrollbar geoCmd offset size} {
    if {$offset != 0.0 || $size != 1.0} {
        eval $geoCmd      ;# Make sure it is visible
    }
    $scrollbar set $offset $size
}
```

`Scroll_Set` takes a geometry management command as an argument, which it uses to make the scrollbar visible. Example 33–3 uses `Scroll_Set` with a listbox. Note that it does not grid the scrollbars directly. Instead, it lets `Scroll_Set` do the geometry command the first time it is necessary.

Example 33–3 Listbox with optional scrollbars.

```
proc Scrolled_Listbox { f args } {
    frame $f
    listbox $f.list \
        -xscrollcommand [list Scroll_Set $f.xscroll \
            [list grid $f.xscroll -row 1 -column 0 -sticky we]] \
        -yscrollcommand [list Scroll_Set $f.yscroll \
            [list grid $f.yscroll -row 0 -column 1 -sticky ns]]
    eval {$f.list configure} $args
    scrollbar $f.xscroll -orient horizontal \
        -command [list $f.list xview]
    scrollbar $f.yscroll -orient vertical \
        -command [list $f.list yview]
    grid $f.list -sticky news
    grid rowconfigure $f 0 -weight 1
    grid columnconfigure $f 0 -weight 1
    return $f.list
}

set l [Scrolled_Listbox .f -listvariable fonts]
pack .f -expand yes -fill both
set fonts [lsort -dictionary [font families]]
```

`Scrolled_Listbox` takes optional parameters for the listbox. It uses `eval` to configure the listbox with these arguments. The style of using `eval` shown here is explained in Example 10–3 on page 136. Example 46–4 on page 686 associates two listboxes with one scrollbar.

The **xview** and **yview** Operations

The `xview` and `yview` operations are designed to be called from scrollbars, and they work the same for all scrollable widgets. You can use them to scroll the widgets for any reason, not just when the scrollbar is used. The following examples use a text widget named `.text` for illustration.

The `xview` and `yview` operations return the current *first* and *last* values that would be passed to a scrollbar `set` command:

```
.text yview
=> 0.2 0.55
```

When the user clicks on the arrows at either end of the scrollbar, the scrollbar adds `scroll num units` to its command, where *num* is positive to scroll down, and negative to scroll up. Scrolling up one line is indicated with this command:

```
.text yview scroll -1 units
```

When the user clicks above or below the elevator of the scrollbar, the scrollbar adds `scroll num pages` to its command. Scrolling down one page is indicated with this command:

```
.text yview scroll 1 pages
```

You can position a widget so that the top (or left) edge is at a particular offset from the beginning of the widget's contents. The offset is expressed as a floating point value between zero and one. To view the beginning of the contents:

```
.text yview moveto 0.0
```

If the offset is 1.0, the last part of the widget content's is displayed. The Tk widgets always keep the end of the widget contents at the bottom (or right) edge of the widget, unless the widget is larger than necessary to display all the contents. You can exploit this with the one-line entry widget to view the end of long strings:

```
.entry xview moveto 1.0
```

The Scrollbar Widget

Tk 8.0 uses native scrollbar widgets on Macintosh and Windows. While the use of scrollbars with other widgets is identical on all platforms, the interpretation of the attributes and the details of the bindings vary across platforms. This section describes the Tk scrollbar on UNIX. The default bindings and attributes are fine on all platforms, so the differences should not be important.

The scrollbar is made up of five components: `arrow1`, `trough1`, `slider`, `trough2`, and `arrow2`. The arrows are on either end, with `arrow1` being the arrow to the left for horizontal scrollbars, or the arrow on top for vertical scrollbars. The slider represents the relative position of the information displayed in the associated widget, and the size of the slider represents the relative amount of the information displayed. The two trough regions are the areas between the slider and the arrows. If the slider covers all of the trough area, you can see all the information in the associated widget.

Scrollbar Bindings

Table 33–1 lists the default bindings for scrollbars on UNIX. Button 1 and button 2 of the mouse have the same bindings. You must direct focus to a scrollbar explicitly for the key bindings like <Up> and <Down> to take effect.

Table 33–1 Bindings for the scrollbar widget.

`<Button-1> <Button-2>`	Clicking on the arrows scrolls by one unit. Clicking on the trough moves by one screenful.
`<B1-Motion> <B2-Motion>`	Dragging the slider scrolls dynamically.
`<Control-Button-1>` `<Control-Button-2>`	Clicking on the trough or arrow scrolls all the way to the beginning (end) of the widget.
`<Up> <Down>`	Scrolls up (down) by one unit.
`<Control-Up>` `<Control-Down>`	Scrolls up (down) by one screenful.
`<Left> <Right>`	Scrolls left (right) by one unit.
`<Control-Left>` `<Control-Right>`	Scrolls left (right) by one screenful.
`<Prior> <Next>`	Scrolls back (forward) by one screenful.
`<Home>`	Scrolls all the way to the left (top).
`<End>`	Scrolls all the way to the right (bottom).

Scrollbar Attributes

Table 33–2 lists the scrollbar attributes. The table uses the resource name for the attribute, which has capitals at internal word boundaries. In Tcl commands, the attributes are specified with a dash and all lowercase.

There is no `length` attribute for a scrollbar. Instead, a scrollbar is designed to be packed next to another widget with a fill option that lets the `scrollbar` display grow to the right size. Only the relief of the active element can be set. The `background` color is used for the slider, the arrows, and the border. The slider and arrows are displayed in the `activeBackground` color when the mouse is over them. The trough is always displayed in the `troughColor`.

Table 33–2 Attributes for the scrollbar widget.

`activeBackground`	Color when the mouse is over the slider or arrows.
`activeRelief`	Relief of slider and arrows when mouse is over them.
`background`	The background color (also `bg` in commands).
`borderWidth`	Extra space around the edge of the scrollbar.
`command`	Prefix of the command to invoke when the scrollbar changes. Typically this is a `xview` or `yview` operation.
`cursor`	Cursor to display when mouse is over the widget.
`elementBorderWidth`	Border width of arrow and slider elements.
`highlightBackground`	Focus highlight color when widget does not have focus.

Table 33–2 Attributes for the scrollbar widget. (Continued)

`highlightColor`	Focus highlight color when widget has focus.
`highlightThickness`	Thickness of focus highlight rectangle.
`elementBorderWidth`	Width of 3D border on arrows and slider.
`jump`	If true, dragging the elevator does not scroll dynamically. Instead, the display jumps to the new position.
`orient`	Orientation: `horizontal` or `vertical`.
`repeatDelay`	Milliseconds before auto-repeat starts. Auto-repeat is used when pressing `<Button-1>` on the trough or arrows.
`repeatInterval`	Milliseconds between auto-repeat events.
`troughColor`	The color of the bar on which the slider sits.
`width`	Width of the narrow dimension of the scrollbar.

Programming Scrollbars

The scrollbar operations are primarily used by the default bindings. Table 33–3 lists the operations supported by the scrollbar. In the table, `$w` is a scrollbar widget.

Table 33–3 Operations on the scrollbar widget.

`$w activate ?element?`	Queries or sets the active element, which can be `arrow1`, `arrow2`, or `slider`.
`$w cget option`	Returns the value of the configuration option.
`$w configure ...`	Queries or modifies the widget configuration.
`$w delta dx dy`	Returns the change in the *first* argument to `set` required to move the scrollbar slider by *dx* or *dy*.
`$w fraction x y`	Returns a number between 0 and 1 that indicates the relative location of the point in the trough.
`$s get`	Returns *first* and *last* from the `set` operation.
`$w identify x y`	Returns `arrow1`, `trough1`, `slider`, `trough2`, or `arrow2`, to indicate what is under the point.
`$w set first last`	Sets the scrollbar parameters. *first* is the relative position of the top (left) of the display. *last* is the relative position of the bottom (right) of the display.

The Entry and Spinbox Widgets

The entry widget provides a single line of text for use as a data entry field. The string in the entry can be linked to a Tcl variable. A spinbox is an extended entry that also allows the user to move, or "spin," through a fixed set of values.

*E*ntry widgets are specialized text widgets that display a single line of editable text. They have a subset of the functionality of the general-purpose text widget described in Chapter 36. The entry is commonly used in dialog boxes when values need to be filled in, or as a simple command entry widget. A very useful feature of the entry is the ability to link it to a Tcl variable. The entry displays that variable's value, and editing the contents of the entry changes the Tcl variable.

Spinbox widgets, introduced in Tk 8.4, are entry widgets that include up and down arrows, allowing the user to "spin" through a fixed set of values such as dates or times. A spinbox normally allows a user to type any arbitrary text into the text area, but you can also configure a spinbox so that users can only spin through the valid choices.

Using Entry Widgets

The entry widget supports editing, scrolling, and selections, which make it more complex than label or message widgets. Fortunately, the default settings for an entry widget make it usable right away. You click with the left button to set the insert point and then type in text. Text is selected by dragging out a selection with the left button. The entry can be scrolled horizontally by dragging with the middle mouse button.

One common use of an entry widget is to associate a label with it, and a command to execute when `<Return>` is pressed in the entry. The grid geometry manager is ideal for lining up several entries and their labels. This is implemented in the following example:

Example 34–1 Associating entry widgets with variables and commands.

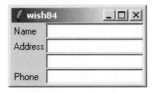

```
foreach {field label} {name Name address1 Address
         address2 {} phone Phone} {
    label .l$field -text $label -anchor w
    entry .e$field -textvariable address($field) -relief sunken
    grid .l$field .e$field -sticky news
    bind .e$field <Return> UpdateAddress
}
```

Example 34–1 creates four entries that are linked to variables with the `textvariable` attribute. The variables are elements of the `address` array. The `-relief sunken` for the entry widget sets them apart visually. Widget relief is described in more detail on page 614. The Tcl command `UpdateAddress` is bound to the `<Return>` keystroke. The `UpdateAddress` procedure, which is not shown, can get the current values of the entry widgets through the global array `address`.

Validating Entry Contents

As of Tk 8.3, entry widgets gained several new options that make it easy to prevent users from entering invalid text into an entry.

The `validate` attribute determines when validation should take place. A value of `none` (the default) disables validation. Other supported values are: `focusin` (receiving keyboard focus), `focusout` (losing focus), `focus` (gaining or losing focus), `key` (any keypress), and `all`.

For validation to take effect, you must also provide a value for the `validateCommand` (or `-vcmd`) attribute. This is a Tcl script to execute whenever validation takes place. If the script returns a Boolean True, the proposed change to the widget is accepted; if the script returns a Boolean False, the proposed change is rejected and the widget's text remains the same.

Optionally, you can also assign a Tcl script to the `invalidCommand` attribute. This script executes if the validation script returns False.

The `validateCommand` validation script can contain "percent substitutions," just like in an event binding. These substitutions occur before executing the script, whenever validation is triggered. Table 34–1 lists the validation substitutions:

Table 34–1 Entry and spinbox validation substitutions.

%d	The type of action that triggered validation: 1 for insert; 0 for delete; -1 for focus, forced or textvariable validation.
%i	Index of the character string to be inserted or deleted, if any; otherwise -1.
%P	The value of the widget should the change occur.
%s	The current value before the proposed change.
%v	The type of validation currently set (that is, the current value of the validate attribute).
%V	The type of validation that triggered the callback: key, focusin, focusout, forced.
%W	The name of the widget that triggered the validation.

Example 34–2 demonstrates using validation to allow a user to enter only integer values into an entry.

Example 34–2 Restricting entry text to integer values.

```
proc ValidInt {val} {
    return [ expr {[string is integer $val]
        || [string match {[-+]} $val]} ]
}

entry .e -validate all -vcmd {ValidInt %P}
pack .e
```

Validation errors turn off validation.

If an uncaught error occurs during the validation callback, then the validate attribute is set to none, preventing further validation from taking place. Additionally, if the return value of the validation callback is anything other than a Boolean value, validation is also disabled. Therefore, you should take care not to raise errors or return non-Boolean values from your validation callback.

Be careful with textvariables and validation.

Using textvariables for read-only purposes never causes a problem. However, you can run into trouble if you try to change the value of an entry using its textvariable. If you set the textvariable to a value that wouldn't be accepted by the validation script (that is, it would return False), then Tk allows the change to occur, but disables further validation by setting validate to none. So in general, you should use textvariables only to read an entry's value if you also have validation enabled.

Changing a widget's value during validation disables future validation.

IV. Tk Widgets

The other caveat to validation is that if you change the value of the widget while evaluating either the validation script or the `invalidCommand` script, `validate` is set to `none`, disabling further validations. The intent is to prevent the change from triggering yet another validation check, which could attempt to change the widget and trigger another validation, and so on in an endless cycle.

For most validation applications, this is not a major restriction. In most cases, you simply want to prevent an invalid change from taking place, which you accomplish simply by returning Boolean False from your validation script.

But some sophisticated validation schemes might require edits to the widget's text. If you need to change the value of the entry from either the `validateCommand` or `invalidCommand` script, the script should also schedule an idle task to reset the `validate` attribute back to its previous value. Example demonstrates this with a validation command that ensures all letters inserted into an entry are upper case, by converting all characters to upper case as they are inserted. As this example modifies the value of the widget directly, it must reestablish validation in an idle task.

Example 34–3 Reestablishing validation using an idle task.

```
proc Upper {w validation action new} {
    if {$action == 1} {
        $w insert insert [string toupper $new]
        after idle [list $w configure -validate $validation]
    }
    return 1
}

entry .e -validate all -vcmd {Upper %W %v %d %S}
pack .e
```

Tips for Using Entry Widgets

If you are displaying long strings in an entry, you can use the following command to keep the end of the string in view. The command requests that all the string be off screen to the left, but the widget implementation fills up the display; the scrolling is limited so that the tail of the string is visible:

```
$entry xview moveto 1.0
```

The `show` attribute is useful for entries that accept passwords or other sensitive information. If `show` is not empty, it is used as the character to display instead of the real value:

```
$entry config -show *
```

The `state` attribute determines if the contents of an entry can be modified. Set the `state` to `disabled` to prevent modification and set it to `normal` to allow modification.

```
$entry config -state disabled ;# read-only
$entry config -state normal   ;# editable
```

Tcl 8.4 added a new state, `readonly`, in which the contents of the widget can't be edited, just like `disabled`. However, the `readonly` state allows the user to select and copy the widget contents. If the widget is a spinbox, the user can also use the up and down spinbuttons to change the value displayed while the widget is in `readonly` state (but not if it is in the `disabled` state).

The middle mouse button (`<Button-2>`) is overloaded with two functions. If you click and release the middle button, the selection is inserted at the insert cursor. The location of the middle click does not matter. If you press and hold the middle button, you can scroll the contents of the entry by dragging the mouse to the left or right.

Using Spinbox Widgets

The spinbox widget is based on the entry widget, and therefore all of the options and operations available for an entry are also available for a spinbox. Additional options and operations give access to the spinbox's enhanced functionality.

In addition to the text entry field, a spin box has up and down arrow buttons, allowing the user to "spin" through a fixed set of values such as dates or times. A spinbox normally allows a user to type any arbitrary text into the text area, but you can also configure a spinbox so that users can only spin through the valid choices.

There are two ways to set the range of values for a spinbox. The first is to set numerical minimum, maximum, and increment values with the `from`, `to`, and `increment` attributes, respectively. Each time the user clicks the up or down arrow, the spinbox adjusts the displayed value by the increment. For example, the spinbox in Example 34–4 has a range of -10 to 10, and uses the default increment of 1.

Example 34–4 A simple spinbox with calculated values.

```
spinbox .s1 -from -10 -to 10
pack .s1
```

Particularly if you start using floating-point values and increments, you might need to specify the format for displaying the value. You do so by setting a value for the `format` attribute in the form %*<pad>*.*<pad>*f, as used with the `format` command. (Note that no other `format`-like conversion specifiers are supported by the spinbox.) Example 34–5 demonstrates using the `format` attribute.

Example 34–5 Formatting numeric values in a spinbox.

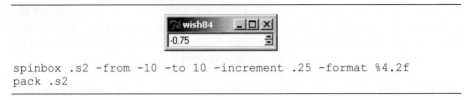

```
spinbox .s2 -from -10 -to 10 -increment .25 -format %4.2f
pack .s2
```

Another option for specifying values for a spinbox is to enumerate them. Simply provide the spinbox's `values` attribute a list of values. If you set a spinbox's `values` attribute, it ignores its `from`, `to`, and `increment` attributes.

Additionally, if you set the `wrap` attribute of a spinbox to True, then the spinbox wraps around from the last value to the first (or vice versa) while spinning through the values. With the default `wrap` setting of False, the spinbox stops spinning values once it reaches the beginning or end. You can use the wrap feature with either enumerated values (`values`) or value ranges (`from` and `to`).

Example 34–6 demonstrates both using enumerated values and wrapping in a spinbox.

Example 34–6 Enumerating spinbox values and wrapping.

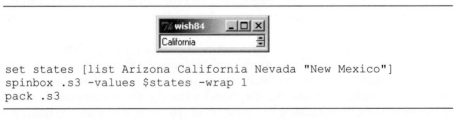

```
set states [list Arizona California Nevada "New Mexico"]
spinbox .s3 -values $states -wrap 1
pack .s3
```

In all of the spinbox examples shown so far, the user is free to type any arbitrary text into the entry portion, rather than selecting one of the spinbox values. In some applications this is acceptable, and you could use standard validation features to ensure reasonable values. (See "Validating Entry Contents" on page 508.) However, sometimes you want to allow a user to select only one of the preset spinbox values. The easiest way to accomplish this is to set the spinbox `state` attribute to `readonly`. Unlike the `disabled` state, which makes the widget insensitive to user actions and prevents programmatic changes to the widget's contents, the `readonly` state allows a user to spin through the values. You can also programmatically change the contents of the spinbox with the `set` operation, and even change the values while the spinbox is in the `readonly` state.

Example 34–7 shows an example of using the `readonly` state for several spinboxes, allowing the user to select a date. The spinboxes are linked by text-variables to elements in a global array, so that after the user selects the date, you can easily retrieve the values from the array.

Example 34–7 Using the spinbox readonly state.

```
set months {Jan Feb Mar Apr May Jun Jul Aug Sep Oct Nov Dec}

spinbox .month -values $months -textvariable date(month) \
    -state readonly -width 8
spinbox .date -from 1 -to 31 -textvariable date(date) \
    -state readonly -width 8
spinbox .year -from 2003 -to 2010 -textvariable date(year) \
    -state readonly -width 8

label .l_month -text "Month:"
label .l_date -text "Date:"
label .l_year -text "Year:"

grid .l_month .month
grid .l_date .date
grid .l_year .year
grid .l_month .l_date .l_year -padx 2 -sticky e
grid .month .date .year -sticky ew
```

Entry and Spinbox Bindings

Table 34–2 gives the bindings for entry and spinbox widgets. When the table lists
two sequences, they are equivalent.

Table 34–2 Entry and spinbox bindings.

`<Button-1>`	Sets the insert point and starts a selection.
`<B1-Motion>`	Drags out a selection.
`<Double-Button-1>`	Selects a word.
`<Triple-Button-1>`	Selects all text in the widget.
`<Shift-B1-Motion>`	Adjusts the ends of the selection.
`<Control-Button-1>`	Sets insert point, leaving selection as is.
`<Button-2>`	Pastes selection at the insert cursor.
`<B2-Motion>`	Scrolls horizontally.
`<Up>`	"Spins" up to the next value. Spinbox only.
`<Down>`	"Spins" down to the previous value. Spinbox only.

Table 34–2 Entry and spinbox bindings. (Continued)

`<Left>` `<Control-b>`	Moves insert cursor one character left and starts the selection.
`<Shift-Left>`	Moves cursor left and extends the selection.
`<Control-Left>` `<Meta-b>`	Moves cursor left one word and starts the selection.
`<Control-Shift-Left>`	Moves cursor left one word and extends the selection.
`<Right>` `<Control-f>`	Moves right one character and starts the selection.
`<Shift-Right>`	Moves cursor right and extends the selection.
`<Control-Right>` `<Meta-f>`	Moves right one word and starts the selection.
`<Control-Shift-Right>`	Moves cursor right one word and extends the selection.
`<Home>` `<Control-a>`	Moves cursor to beginning of widget.
`<Shift-Home>`	Moves cursor to beginning and extends the selection.
`<End>` `<Control-e>`	Moves cursor to end of widget.
`<Shift-End>`	Moves cursor to end and extends the selection.
`<Select>` `<Control-Space>`	Anchors the selection at the insert cursor.
`<Shift-Select>` `<Control-Shift-Space>`	Adjusts the selection to the insert cursor.
`<Control-slash>`	Selects all the text in the entry.
`<Control-backslash>`	Clears the selection in the entry.
`<Delete>`	Deletes the selection or deletes next character.
`<Backspace>` `<Control-h>`	Deletes the selection or deletes previous character.
`<Control-d>`	Deletes next character.
`<Meta-d>`	Deletes next word.
`<Control-k>`	Deletes to the end of the entry.
`<Control-t>`	Transposes characters.
`<<Cut>>` `<Control-x>`	Deletes the section, if it exists.
`<<Copy>>` `<Control-c>`	Copies the selection to the clipboard.
`<<Paste>>` `<Control-v>`	Inserts the clipboard contents at the position of the insertion cursor.

Entry and Spinbox Attributes

Table 34–3 lists the entry and spinbox widget attributes. The table lists the resource name, which has capitals at internal word boundaries. In Tcl commands these options are specified with a dash and are all lowercase.

Table 34–3 Entry and spinbox attribute resource names.

`activeBackground`	Background color for active elements. Spinbox only. (Tk 8.4)
`background`	Background color (also `bg`).
`borderWidth`	Extra space around the edge of the text (also `bd`).
`buttonBackground`	Background color for up and down buttons. Spinbox only. (Tk 8.4)
`command`	Tcl script to invoke whenever a spinbutton is invoked. The script can include the percent substitutions as described in Table 34–1. Spinbox only. (Tk 8.4)
`cursor`	Cursor to display when mouse is over the widget.
`disabledBackground`	Background color when the widget is disabled. (Tk 8.4)
`disabledForeground`	Foreground color when the widget is disabled. (Tk 8.4)
`exportSelection`	If true, selected text is exported via the X selection mechanism.
`font`	Font for the text.
`foreground`	Foreground color (also `fg`).
`format`	Alternate format for spinbox numeric values, used only when `-from` and `-to` are specified. Must be of the form `%<pad>.<pad>f`, as used with the `format` command. Spinbox only. (Tk 8.4)
`from`	Floating-point value corresponding to the lowest value for a spinbox, used in conjunction with -to and `-increment`. Spinbox only. (Tk 8.4)
`highlightBackground`	Focus highlight color when widget does not have focus.
`highlightColor`	Focus highlight color when widget has focus.
`highlightThickness`	Thickness of focus highlight rectangle.
`increment`	Floating-point value specifying the increment. When used with `-from` and `-to`, the value in the widget will be adjusted by `-increment` when a spin button is pressed. Spinbox only. (Tk 8.4)
`insertBackground`	Background for area covered by insert cursor.
`insertBorderWidth`	Width of cursor border. Non-zero for 3D effect.
`insertOffTime`	Time, in milliseconds the insert cursor blinks off.

IV. Tk Widgets

Table 34–3 Entry and spinbox attribute resource names. (Continued)

insertOnTime	Time, in milliseconds the insert cursor blinks on.
insertWidth	Width of insert cursor. Default is 2.
invalidCommand	Tcl script to execute when the -validatecommand script returns 0.
justify	Text justification: left, right, center.
readonlyBackground	Background color when the widget is read-only. (Tk 8.4)
relief	flat, sunken, raised, groove, solid or ridge.
repeatDelay	The number of milliseconds a spin button must be held down before it begins to auto-repeat. Spinbox only. (Tk 8.4)
repeatInterval	The number of milliseconds between auto-repeats. Spinbox only. (Tk 8.4)
selectBackground	Background color of selection.
selectForeground	Foreground color of selection.
selectBorderWidth	Width of selection border. Nonzero for 3D effect.
show	A character (e.g., *) to display instead of contents. Entry only.
state	State: normal, disabled (value unchangeable and non-responsive to user interaction) or readonly (value unchangeable, but the user can select and copy widget contents).
takeFocus	Controls focus changes from keyboard traversal.
textVariable	Name of Tcl variable whose value will be synchronized with the widget.
to	Floating-point value corresponding to the highest value for a spinbox, used in conjunction with -from and -increment. Spinbox only. (Tk 8.4)
validate	When validation should occur: none (default), focus, focusin, focusout, key, or all. (Tk 8.3)
validateCommand	Tcl script to execute to validate widget contents. Must return 1 if new widget value is valid or 0 if new widget value is invalid, in which case the widget contents don't change. (Tk 8.3)
values	List of spinbox values. Overrides any -from and -to settings. (Tk 8.4)
width	Width, in characters.
wrap	Boolean value. True causes the spinbox to wrap values of data in the widget. Default is False. Spinbox only. (Tk 8.4)
xScrollCommand	Connects entry to a scrollbar.

Programming Entry and Spinbox Widgets

The default bindings for entry and spinbox widgets are fairly good. However, you can completely control the entry with a set of widget operations for inserting, deleting, selecting, and scrolling. The operations involve addressing character positions called *indices*. The indices count from zero. The entry defines some symbolic indices such as `end`. The index corresponding to an X coordinate is specified with @*xcoord*, such as `@26`. Table 34–4 lists the formats for indices.

Table 34–4 Entry and spinbox indices.

0	Index of the first character.
anchor	The index of the anchor point of the selection.
end	Index just after the last character.
number	Index a character, counting from zero.
insert	The character right after the insertion cursor.
sel.first	The first character in the selection.
sel.last	The character just after the last character in the selection.
@*xcoord*	The character under the specified X coordinate.

Table 34–5 summarizes the operations on entry and spinbox widgets. In the table, `$w` is an entry or spinbox widget.

Table 34–5 Entry and spinbox operations.

$w bbox *index*	Returns a list of 4 numbers describing the bounding box of the character given by *index*.
$w cget *option*	Returns the value of the configuration option.
$w configure ...	Queries or modifies the widget configuration.
$w delete *first* ?*last*?	Deletes the characters from *first* to *last*, not including the character at *last*. The character at *first* is deleted if *last* is not specified.
$w get	Returns the string in the entry.
$w icursor *index*	Moves the insert cursor.
$w identify *x y*	Identifies the spinbox element at the given *x/y* coordinate: none, buttondown, buttonup, entry. Spinbox only. (Tk 8.4)
$w index *index*	Returns the numerical index corresponding to *index*.
$w insert *index string*	Inserts the *string* at the given *index*.

IV. Tk Widgets

Table 34–5 Entry and spinbox operations. (Continued)

`$w invoke element`	Invokes the spinbox `element`, either `button-down` or `buttonup`, triggering the action associated with it. Spinbox only. (Tk 8.4)
`$w scan mark x`	Starts a scroll operation. `x` is a screen coordinate.
`$w scan dragto x`	Scrolls from previous mark position.
`$w selection adjust index`	Moves the boundary of an existing selection.
`$w selection clear`	Clears the selection.
`$w selection element ?element?`	Sets or gets the currently selected spinbox element. Spinbox only. (Tk 8.4)
`$w selection from index`	Sets the anchor position for the selection.
`$w selection present`	Returns 1 if there is a selection in the entry.
`$w selection range start end`	Selects the characters from `start` to the one just before `end`.
`$w select to index`	Extends the selection.
`$w set ?value?`	Gets or sets the *value* of the spinbox, triggering validation if it is on. Spinbox only. (Tk 8.4)
`$w validate`	Force an evaluation of the `-validatecommand` script, returning 0 or 1. (Tk 8.3)
`$w xview`	Returns the offset and span of visible contents. These are both real numbers between 0 and 1.0.
`$w xview index`	Shifts the display so the character at `index` is at the left edge of the display.
`$w xview moveto fraction`	Shifts the display so that `fraction` of the contents are off the left edge of the display.
`$w xview scroll num what`	Scrolls the contents by the specified number of `what`, which can be `units` or `pages`.

For example, the binding for `<Button-1>` includes the following commands:

```
%W icursor @%x
%W select from @%x
if {[%W cget -state] == "normal"} {focus %W}
```

Recall that the `%` triggers substitutions in binding commands, and that `%W` is replaced with the widget pathname and `%x` is replaced with the X coordinate of the mouse event. Chapter 29 describes bindings and these substitutions in detail. These commands set the insert point to the point of the mouse click by using the `@%x` index, which will be turned into something like `@17` when the binding is invoked. The binding also starts a selection. If the entry is not in the disabled state, then keyboard focus is given to the entry so that it gets `KeyPress` events.

The Listbox Widget

The listbox provides a scrollable list of text lines. The listbox supports
selections of one or more lines.

Listbox widgets display a set of text lines
in a scrollable display. The basic text unit is a line. There are operations to
insert, select, and delete lines, but there are no operations to modify the characters in a line. As such, the listbox is suitable for displaying a set of choices, such
as in a file selection dialog. By default a user can select one item from a listbox,
but you can select multiple items by setting the selection mode attribute.

Using Listboxes

Manipulating Listbox Contents

The lines in a listbox are indexed from zero. The keyword index `end`
addresses the last line. Other indices are described on page 520. The most common programming task for a listbox is to insert text. If your data is in a list, you
can loop through the list and insert each element at the end:

```
foreach item $list {
    $listbox insert end $item
}
```

You can insert several items at once. The next command uses `eval` to concatenate the list onto a single `insert` command:

```
eval {$listbox insert end} $list
```

The `delete` operation deletes items from a listbox. You can delete either a single item or a range of items:

```
$listbox delete 0      ;# Delete the first item
$listbox delete 3 5    ;# Delete items 3-5, inclusive
```

The listbox widget gained a `listvariable` option in Tk 8.3, which works analogously to `textvariable` attributes in other widgets. You give `listvariable` the name of a variable that contains a list value. Tk then keeps the value of the variable and the listbox contents synchronized, so that each element in the variable's value is a line in the listbox. Example 35–1 shows a simple example of modifying a listbox through its linked listvariable.

Example 35–1 Using -listvariable to link a listbox and variable.

```
listbox .choices -height 5 -width 20 -listvariable states
pack .choices
lappend states Arizona
lappend states California "New Mexico"
```

Programming Listboxes

It is also common to react to mouse clicks on a listbox, although the default bindings handle most of the details of selecting items. The `nearest` operation finds the listbox entry that is closest to a mouse event. If the mouse is clicked beyond the last element, the index of the last element is returned:

```
set index [$list nearest $y]
```

Example 35–2 displays two listboxes. The `Scrolled_Listbox` procedure on page 502 is used to put scrollbars on the listboxes. When the user clicks on an item in the first listbox, it is copied into the second listbox. When an item in the second listbox is selected, it is removed. This example shows how to manipulate items selected from a listbox:

Example 35–2 Choosing items from a listbox.

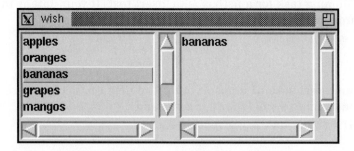

```
proc List_Select { parent values } {
    # Create two lists side by side
    frame $parent
    set choices [Scrolled_Listbox $parent.choices \
        -width 20 -height 5 ]
    set picked [Scrolled_Listbox $parent.picked \
        -width 20 -height 5]
    pack $parent.choices $parent.picked -side left \
        -expand true -fill both

    # Selecting in choices moves items into picked
    bind $choices <ButtonRelease-1> \
        [list ListTransferSel %W $picked]

    # Selecting in picked deletes items
    bind $picked <ButtonRelease-1> \
        {ListDeleteSel %W %y}

    # Insert all the choices
    foreach x $values {
        $choices insert end $x
    }
}
proc ListTransferSel {src dst} {
    foreach i [$src curselection] {
        $dst insert end [$src get $i]
    }
}
proc ListDeleteSel {w y} {
    foreach i [lsort -integer -decreasing [$w curselection]] {
        $w delete $i
    }
}
proc List_SelectValues {parent} {
    set picked $parent.picked.list
    set result {}
    foreach i [$w curselection] {
        lappend result [$w get $i]
    }
}
List_Select .f {apples oranges bananas \
            grapes mangos peaches pears}
pack .f -expand true -fill both
```

Bindings are created to move items from $choices to $picked, and to delete items from $picked. Most of the work of selecting things in the listbox is done by the built-in bindings on the Listbox binding tag. The different selection models are described on page 525. Those bindings are on <ButtonPress-1> and <B1-Motion>. The selection is complete by the time the <ButtonRelease-1> event occurs. Consider the <ButtonRelease-1> binding for $choices:

```
bind $choices <ButtonRelease-1> \
        [list ListTransferSel %W $picked]
```

The `list` command is used to construct the Tcl command because we need to expand the value of `$picked` at the time the binding is created. The command will be evaluated later at the global scope, and `picked` will not be defined after the `List_Select` procedure returns. Or, worse yet, an existing global variable named `picked` will be used, which is unlikely to be correct!

Short procedures are used to implement the binding commands. This style has two advantages. First, it confines the `%` substitutions done by `bind` to a single command. Second, if there are any temporary variables, such as the loop counter `i`, they are hidden within the scope of the procedure.

The `ListTransferSel` gets the list of all the selected items and loops over this list to insert them into the other list. The `ListDeleteSel` procedure is similar. However, it sorts the selection indices in reverse order. It deletes items from the bottom up so the indices remain valid throughout the process.

The Listbox Widget

The listbox operations use indices to reference lines in the listbox. The lines are numbered starting at zero. Keyword indices are also used for some special lines. The listbox keeps track of an *active* element, which is displayed with underlined text. There is also a selection *anchor* that is used when adjusting selections. Table 35–1 summarizes the keywords used for indices.

Table 35–1   Listbox indices.

0	Index of the first line.
active	The index of the activated line.
anchor	The index of the anchor point of the selection.
end	Index of the last line.
number	Index a line, counting from zero.
@*x,y*	The line closest to the specified X and Y coordinates.

Table 35–2 presents the operations for programming a listbox. In the table, `$w` is a listbox widget. Most of the operations have to do with the selection, and these operations are already programmed by the default bindings for the `Listbox` widget class:

Table 35–2   Listbox operations.

`$w activate` *index*	Activates the specified line.
`$w bbox` *index*	Returns the bounding box of the text in the specified line in the form: *xoff yoff width height*.
`$w cget` *option*	Returns the value of the configuration option.

Table 35–2 Listbox operations. (Continued)

`$w configure ...`	Queries or modifies the widget configuration.
`$w curselection`	Returns a list of indices of the selected lines.
`$w delete first ?last?`	Deletes the lines from `first` to `last`, including the line at `last`. The line at `first` is deleted if `last` is not given.
`$w get first ?last?`	Returns the lines from `first` to `last` as a list.
`$w index index`	Returns the numerical index corresponding to `index`.
`$w insert index ?string string string ...?`	Inserts the `string` items before the line at `index`. If `index` is end, then append the items.
`$w itemcget index option`	Returns the current value of the item's configuration option. (Tk 8.3)
`$w itemconfigure index ?option? ?value? ?...?`	Queries or modifies the item's configuration options. (Tk 8.3)
`$w nearest y`	Returns the index of the line closest to the widget-relative Y coordinate.
`$w scan mark x y`	Starts a scroll operation. `x` and `y` are widget-relative screen coordinates.
`$w scan dragto x y`	Scrolls from previous mark position.
`$w see index`	Adjusts the display so the line at `index` is visible.
`$w selection anchor index`	Anchors the selection at the specified line.
`$w selection clear start ?end?`	Clears the selection.
`$w selection includes index`	Returns 1 if the line at `index` is in the selection.
`$w selection set start ?end?`	Selects the lines from `start` to `end`.
`$w size`	Returns the number of items in the listbox.
`$w xview`	Returns the offset and span of visible contents. These are both real numbers between 0 and 1.
`$w xview index`	Shifts the display so the character at `index` is at the left edge of the display.
`$w xview moveto fraction`	Shifts the display so that `fraction` of the contents are off the left edge of the display.
`$w xview scroll num what`	Scrolls the contents horizontally by the specified number of `what`, which can be units or pages.
`$w yview`	Returns the offset and span of visible contents. These are both real numbers between 0 and 1.

IV. Tk Widgets

Table 35–2 Listbox operations. (Continued)

`$w yview` *index*	Shifts the display so the line at *index* is at the top edge of the display.
`$w yview moveto` *fraction*	Shifts the display so that *fraction* of the contents are off the top of the display.
`$w yview scroll` *num what*	Scrolls the contents vertically by the specified number of *what*, which can be `units` or `pages`.

As of Tk 8.3, the `itemcget` and `itemconfigure` operations allow you to control the appearance of individual items in the listbox, overriding the listbox's defaults. Table 35–3 lists the configuration options supported for individual items. Note that there is no direct support for setting these values through the option resource database; you can set them only through the listbox's `itemconfigure` operation.

Table 35–3 Listbox item configuration options.

`-background` *color*	Background color for the item.
`-foreground` *color*	Foreground color for the item.
`-selectbackground` *color*	Background color for the item when it's selected.
`-selectforeground` *color*	Foreground color for the item when it's selected.

Listbox Bindings and Events

A listbox has an *active* element and it may have one or more *selected* elements. The active element is highlighted according to the `-activestyle` options (by default, with an underline), and the selected elements are highlighted with a different color. There are a large number of key bindings for listboxes. You must set the input focus to the listbox for the key bindings to work. Chapter 39 describes focus. There are four selection modes for a listbox, and the bindings vary depending what mode the listbox is in. Table 35–4 lists the four possible `selectMode` settings:

Table 35–4 The values for the `selectMode` of a listbox.

`single`	A single element can be selected.
`browse`	A single element can be selected, and the selection can be dragged with the mouse. This is the default.
`multiple`	More than one element can be selected by toggling the selection state of items, but you only select or deselect one line at a time.
`extended`	More than one element can be selected by dragging out a selection with the shift or control keys.

Browse Select Mode

In `browse` selection mode, `<Button-1>` selects the item under the mouse and dragging with the mouse moves the selection, too. Table 35–5 gives the bindings for `browse` mode.

Table 35–5 Bindings for `browse` selection mode.

`<Button-1>`	Selects the item under the mouse. This becomes the active element, too.
`<B1-Motion>`	Same as `<Button-1>`, the selection moves with the mouse.
`<Shift-Button-1>`	Activates the item under the mouse. The selection is not changed.
`<Key-Up> <Key-Down>`	Moves the active item up (down) one line, and selects it.
`<Control-Home>`	Activates and select the first element of the listbox.
`<Control-End>`	Activates and select the last element of the listbox.
`<space> <Select>` `<Control-slash>`	Selects the active element.

Single Select Mode

In `single` selection mode, `<Button-1>` selects the item under the mouse, but dragging the mouse does not change the selection. When you release the mouse, the item under that point is activated. Table 35–6 specifies the bindings for `single` mode:

Table 35–6 Bindings for `single` selection mode.

`<ButtonPress-1>`	Selects the item under the mouse.
`<ButtonRelease-1>`	Activates the item under the mouse.
`<Shift-Button-1>`	Activates the item under the mouse. The selection is not changed.
`<Key-Up> <Key-Down>`	Moves the active item up (down) one line. The selection is not changed.
`<Control-Home>`	Activates and selects the first element of the listbox.
`<Control-End>`	Activates and selects the last element of the listbox.
`<space> <Select>` `<Control-slash>`	Selects the active element.
`<Control-backslash>`	Clears the selection.

Extended Select Mode

In `extended` selection mode, multiple items are selected by dragging out a selection with the first mouse button. Hold down the `Shift` key to adjust the ends of the selection. Use the `Control` key to make a disjoint selection. The `Control` key works in a toggle fashion, changing the selection state of the item under the mouse. If this starts a new part of the selection, then dragging the mouse extends the new part of the selection. If the toggle action cleared the selected item, then dragging the mouse continues to clear the selection. The extended mode is quite intuitive once you try it. Table 35–7 specifies the complete set of bindings for `extended` mode:

Table 35–7   Bindings for `extended` selection mode.

`<Button-1>`	Selects the item under the mouse. This becomes the anchor point for adjusting the selection.
`<B1-Motion>`	Sweeps out a selection from the anchor point.
`<ButtonRelease-1>`	Activates the item under the mouse.
`<Shift-Button-1>`	Adjusts the selection from the anchor item to the item under the mouse.
`<Shift-B1-Motion>`	Continues to adjust the selection from the anchor.
`<Control-Button-1>`	Toggles the selection state of the item under the mouse, and makes this the anchor point.
`<Control-B1-Motion>`	Sets the selection state of the items from the anchor point to the item under the mouse to be the same as the selection state of the anchor point.
`<Key-Up> <Key-Down>`	Moves the active item up (down) one line, and starts a new selection with this item as the anchor point.
`<Shift-Up> <Shift-Down>`	Moves the active element up (down) and extends the selection to include this element.
`<Control-Home>`	Activates and selects the first element of the listbox.
`<Control-Shift-Home>`	Extends the selection to the first element.
`<Control-End>`	Activates and selects the last element of the listbox.
`<Control-Shift-End>`	Extends the selection to the last element.
`<space> <Select>`	Selects the active element.
`<Escape>`	Cancels the previous selection action.
`<Control-slash>`	Selects everything in the listbox.
`<Control-backslash>`	Clears the selection.

Multiple Select Mode

In `multiple` selection mode you can select more than one item, but you can add or remove only one item at a time. Dragging the mouse does not sweep out a selection. If you click on a selected item it is deselected. Table 35–8 specifies the complete set of bindings for `multiple` selection mode.

Table 35–8 Bindings for `multiple` selection mode.

`<Button-1>`	Selects the item under the mouse.
`<ButtonRelease-1>`	Activates the item under the mouse.
`<Key-Up> <Key-Down>`	Moves the active item up (down) one line, and starts a new selection with this item as the anchor point.
`<Shift-Up> <Shift-Down>`	Moves the active element up (down).
`<Control-Home>`	Activates and selects the first element of the listbox.
`<Control-Shift-Home>`	Activates the first element of the listbox.
`<Control-End>`	Activates and selects the last element of the listbox.
`<Control-Shift-End>`	Activates the last element of the listbox.
`<space> <Select>`	Selects the active element.
`<Control-slash>`	Selects everything in the listbox.
`<Control-backslash>`	Clears the selection.

Scroll Bindings

There are several bindings that scroll the display of the listbox. In addition to the standard middle-drag scrolling, there are some additional key bindings for scrolling. Table 35–9 summarizes the scroll-related bindings:

Table 35–9 Listbox scroll bindings.

`<Button-2>`	Marks the start of a scroll operation.
`<B2-Motion>`	Scrolls vertically *and* horizontally.
`<MouseWheel>`	Scrolls vertically.
`<Button-4>`	Mousewheel support on Unix only; scrolls up. (Tk 8.3)
`<Button-5>`	Mousewheel support on Unix only; scrolls down. (Tk 8.3)
`<Left> <Right>`	Scrolls horizontally by one character.
`<Control-Left> <Control-Right>` `<Control-Prior> <Control-Next>`	Scrolls horizontally by one screen width.

Table 35–9 Listbox scroll bindings. (Continued)

`<Prior> <Next>`	Scrolls vertically by one screen height.
`<Home> <End>`	Scrolls to left and right edges of the screen, respectively.

Listbox Virtual Events

As of Tk 8.1, the listbox widget generates a `<<ListboxSelect>>` virtual event whenever the listbox selection changes. The event fires after the selection has changed, so the binding action can access the new selection. The easiest way to be aware of changes to the listbox selection is to bind to this virtual event, as shown in Example 35–3:

Example 35–3 Using the `<<ListboxSelect>>` virtual event.

```
proc ListboxChanged {w} {
    puts -nonewline "Listbox $w selection is now: "
    foreach index [$w curselection] {
        puts -nonewline "[$w get $index] "
    }
    puts ""
}
bind .lbox <<ListboxSelect>> {ListboxChanged %W}
```

Listbox Attributes

Table 35–10 lists the listbox widget attributes. The table uses the resource name for the attribute, which has capitals at internal word boundaries. In Tcl commands these options are specified with a dash and all lowercase.

Table 35–10 Listbox attribute resource names.

`activeStyle`	Display style of the active element: `dotbox`, `underline` (default), or `none`. (Tk 8.4)
`background`	Background color (also `bg`).
`borderWidth`	Extra space around the edge of the text.
`cursor`	Cursor to display when mouse is over the widget.
`disabledForeground`	Foreground color when the widget is disabled. (Tk 8.4)
`exportSelection`	If `true`, then the selected text is exported via the X selection mechanism.
`font`	Font for the text.
`foreground`	Foreground color (also `fg`).

Table 35–10 Listbox attribute resource names. (Continued)

`height`	Number of lines in the listbox.
`highlightBackground`	Focus highlight color when widget does not have focus.
`highlightColor`	Focus highlight color when widget has focus.
`highlightThickness`	Thickness of focus highlight rectangle.
`listVariable`	Name of Tcl variable containing a list whose value is synchronized with the widget, where each list element is a line of the listbox. (Tk 8.3)
`relief`	`flat`, `sunken`, `raised`, `groove`, `solid`, or `ridge`.
`selectBackground`	Background color of selection.
`selectForeground`	Foreground color of selection.
`selectBorderWidth`	Width of selection border. Nonzero for 3D effect.
`selectMode`	Mode: `browse`, `single`, `extended`, or `multiple`.
`setGrid`	Boolean. Set gridding attribute.
`state`	Widget state: `normal` or `disabled`. (Tk 8.4)
`takeFocus`	Controls focus changes from keyboard traversal.
`width`	Width, in average character sizes.
`xScrollCommand`	Connects listbox to a horizontal scrollbar.
`yScrollCommand`	Connects listbox to a vertical scrollbar.

Geometry Gridding

The `setGrid` attribute affects interactive resizing of the window containing the listbox. By default, a window can be resized to any size. If gridding is turned on, the size is restricted so that a whole number of lines and a whole number of average-width characters is displayed. Gridding affects the user feedback during an interactive resize. Without gridding the size is reported in pixel dimensions. When gridding is turned on, then the size is reported in gridded units.

IV. Tk Widgets

The Text Widget

Tk text widget is a general-purpose editable text widget with features for line
spacing, justification, tags, marks, and embedded windows.

*T*he Tk text widget is versatile, simple to
use for basic text display and manipulation, and has many advanced features to
support sophisticated applications. The line spacing and justification can be controlled on a line-by-line basis. Fonts, sizes, and colors are controlled with *tags*
that apply to ranges of text. Edit operations use positional *marks* that keep track
of locations in text, even as text is inserted and deleted.

Tags are the most important feature of the text widget. You can define
attributes like font and justification for a tag. When that tag is applied to a range
of text, the text uses those attributes. Text can pick up attributes from any number of tags, so you can compose different tags for justification, font, line spacing,
and more. You can also define bindings for tags so that ranges of text can
respond to the mouse. Any interesting application of the text widget uses tags
extensively.

Text Indices

The characters in a text widget are addressed by their line number and the character position within the line. Lines are numbered starting at one, while characters are numbered starting at zero. The numbering for lines was chosen to be
compatible with other programs that number lines starting at one, like compilers
that generate line-oriented error messages. Here are some examples of text indices:

1.0	The first character.
1.1	The second character on the first line.
2.end	The newline character on the second line.

There are also symbolic indices. The `insert` index is the position at which new characters are normally inserted when the user types in characters. You can define new indices called *marks*, too, as described later. Table 36–1 summarizes the various forms for a text index.

Table 36–1 Text indices.

line.char	Lines count from 1. Characters count from 0.
@*x,y*	The character under the specified screen position.
current	The character currently under the mouse.
end	Just after the very last character.
image	The position of the embedded *image*.
insert	The position right after the insert cursor.
mark	Just after the named *mark*.
tag.first	The first character in the range tagged with *tag*.
tag.last	Just after the last character tagged with *tag*.
window	The position of the embedded *window*.

Inserting and Deleting Text

You add text with the `insert` operation (`$t` is a text widget):

```
$t insert index string ?tagList? ?string tagList? ...
```

The *index* can be any of the forms listed in the table, or it can be an index expression as described in a moment. The tags, if any, are added to the newly inserted text. Otherwise, *string* picks up any tags present on both sides of *index*. Tags are described on page 535. Multiple strings with different tags can be inserted with one command.

The most common index at which to insert text is the `insert` index, which is where the insert cursor is displayed. The default bindings insert text at `insert` when you type. You must include a newline character explicitly to force a line break:

```
$t insert insert "Hello, World\n"
```

The `delete` operation deletes text. If only one index is given, the character at that position is deleted. If there are two indices, all the characters up to the second index are deleted. The character at the second index is not deleted. For example, you can delete the first line with this command:

```
$t delete 1.0 2.0
```

As of Tk 8.4, you can delete multiple ranges of text with a single `delete` operation. For example, to delete the first, fourth, and eighth lines:

```
$t delete 1.0 2.0 4.0 5.0 8.0 9.0
```

Index Arithmetic

The text widget supports a simple sort of arithmetic on indices. You can specify "the end of the line with this index" and "three characters before this index," and so on. This is done by grouping a modifying expression with the index. For example, the `insert` index can be modified like this:

```
"insert lineend"
"insert -3 chars"
```

The interpretation of indices and their modifiers is designed to operate well with the `delete` and `tag add` operations of the `text` widget. These operations apply to a range of text defined by two indices. The second index refers to the character just after the end of the range. For example, the following command deletes the word containing the insert cursor:

```
$t delete "insert wordstart" "insert wordend"
```

If you want to delete a whole line, including the trailing newline, you need to use a `"lineend +1 char"` modifier. Otherwise, the newline remains and you are left with a blank line. If you supply several modifiers to an index, they are applied in left to right order:

```
$t delete "insert linestart" "insert lineend +1 char"
```

Table 36–2 summarizes the set of index modifiers.

Table 36–2 Index modifiers for text widgets.

+ *count* chars	*count* characters past the index.
- *count* chars	*count* characters before the index.
+ *count* lines	*count* lines past the index, retaining character position.
- *count* lines	*count* lines before the index, retaining character position.
linestart	The beginning of the line.
lineend	The end of the line (i.e., the newline character).
wordstart	The first character of a word.
wordend	Just after the last character of a word.

Comparing Indices

The `compare` operation compares two text indices and index expressions. You must use `compare` for reliable comparisons because, for example, index 1.3 is less than index 1.13. If you try to compare indices as numbers, you get the wrong answer. The general form of the `compare` operation is:

```
$t compare ix1 op ix2
```

The comparison operator can be one of <, <=, ==, >=, >, or !=. The indices can be simple indices in the forms listed in Table 36–1, and they can be index expressions. Example 36–6 on page 546 uses the `compare` operation.

Text Marks

A mark is a symbolic name for a position between two characters. Marks have the property that when text is inserted or deleted they retain their logical position, not their numerical index position. Marks are persistent: If you delete the text surrounding a mark, it remains intact. Marks are created with the `mark set` operation and must be explicitly deleted with the `mark unset` operation. Once defined, a mark can be used in operations that require indices. The following commands define a mark at the beginning of the word containing the insert cursor and delete from there up to the end of the line:

```
$t mark set foobar "insert wordstart"
$t delete foobar "foobar lineend"
$t mark unset foobar
```

When a mark is defined, it is set to be just before the character specified by the index expression. In the previous example, this is just before the first character of the word where the insert cursor is. When a mark is used in an operation that requires an index, it refers to the character just after the mark. So, in many ways the mark seems associated with the character right after it, except that the mark remains even if that character is deleted.

You can use almost any string for the name of a mark. However, do not use pure numbers and do not include spaces, plus (+) or minus (-). These characters are used in index arithmetic and may cause problems if you put them into mark names. The `mark names` operation returns a list of all defined marks.

The `insert` mark defines where the insert cursor is displayed. The `insert` mark is treated specially: you cannot remove it with the `mark unset` operation. Attempting to do so does not raise an error, though, so the following is a quick way to unset all marks. The `eval` is necessary to join the list of mark names into the `mark unset` command:

```
eval {$t mark unset} [$t mark names]
```

Mark Gravity

Each mark has a *gravity* that determines what happens when characters are inserted at the mark. The default gravity is `right`, which means that the mark sticks to the character that is to its right. Inserting text at a mark with `right` gravity causes the mark to be pushed along so it is always after the inserted text. With `left` gravity the mark stays with the character to its left, so inserted text goes after the mark and the mark does not move. In versions of Tk before 4.0, marks had only right gravity, which made some uses of marks awkward. The `mark gravity` operation is used to query and modify the gravity of a mark:

```
$t mark gravity foobar
=> right
$t mark gravity foobar left
```

Text Tags

A tag is a symbolic name that is associated with one or more ranges of characters. A tag has attributes that affect the display of text that is tagged with it. These attributes include fonts, colors, tab stops, line spacing and justification. A tag can have event bindings so you can create hypertext. A tag can also be used to represent application-specific information. The `tag names` and `tag ranges` operations described later tell you what tags are defined and where they are applied.

You can use almost any string for the name of a tag. However, do not use pure numbers, and do not include spaces, plus (+) or minus (-). These characters are used in index arithmetic and may cause problems if you use them in tag names.

A tag is added to a range with the `tag add` operation. The following command applies the tag `everywhere` to all the text in the widget:

```
$t tag add everywhere 1.0 end
```

You can add one or more tags when text is inserted, too:

```
$t insert insert "new text" {someTag someOtherTag}
```

If you do not specify tags when text is inserted, then the text picks up any tags that are present on the characters on both sides of the insertion point. (Before Tk 4.0, tags from the left-hand character were picked up.) If you specify tags in the `insert` operation, only those tags are applied to the text.

A tag is removed from a range of text with the `tag remove` operation. However, even if there is no text labeled with a tag, its attribute settings are remembered. All information about a tag can be removed with the `tag delete` operation:

```
$t tag remove everywhere 3.0 6.end
$t tag delete everywhere
```

Tag Attributes

The attributes for a tag are defined with the `tag configure` operation. For example, a tag for blue text is defined with the following command:

```
$t tag configure blue -foreground blue
```

Table 36–3 specifies the set of attributes for tags. Some attributes can only be applied with tags; there is no global attribute for `-bgstipple`, `-elide`,

-fgstipple, -justify, -lmargin1, -lmargin2, -offset, -overstrike, -rmargin, and -underline. Table 36–10 on page 554 lists the attributes for the text widget as a whole.

The -relief and -borderwidth attributes go together. If you only specify a relief, there is no visible effect. The default relief is flat, too, so if you specify a border width without a relief you won't see any effect either.

The stipple attributes require a bitmap argument. Bitmaps and colors are explained in more detail in Chapter 41. For example, to "grey out" text you could use a foreground stipple of gray50:

        $t tag configure disabled -fgstipple gray50

The -elide attribute, added in Tk 8.3, controls whether or not the text is displayed. It can be quite useful to set the -elide attribute to True to hide embedded information, such as HTML or XML tags or URLs for hotlinks.

Table 36–3 Attributes for text tags.

-background *color*	The background color for text.
-bgstipple *bitmap*	A stipple pattern for the background color.
-borderwidth *pixels*	The width for 3D border effects.
-elide *boolean*	If True, then the text is not displayed. (Tk 8.3)
-fgstipple *bitmap*	A stipple pattern for the foreground color.
-font *font*	The font for the text.
-foreground *color*	The foreground color for text.
-justify *how*	Justification: left, right, or center.
-lmargin1 *pixels*	Normal left indent for a line.
-lmargin2 *pixels*	Indent for the part of a line that gets wrapped.
-offset *pixels*	Baseline offset. Positive for superscripts.
-overstrike *boolean*	Draw text with a horizontal line through it.
-relief *what*	flat, sunken, raised, groove, solid or ridge.
-rmargin *pixels*	Right-hand margin.
-spacing1 *pixels*	Additional space above a line.
-spacing2 *pixels*	Additional space above wrapped part of line.
-spacing3 *pixels*	Additional space below a line.
-tabs *tabstops*	Specifies tab stops.
-underline *boolean*	If true, the text is underlined.
-wrap *mode*	Line wrap: none, char, or word.

Configure tags early.

You can set up the appearance (and bindings) for tags once in your application, even before you have labeled any text with the tags. The attributes are retained until you explicitly delete the tag. If you are going to use the same appearance over and over again, then it is more efficient to do the setup once so that Tk can retain the graphics context.

On the other hand, if you change the configuration of a tag, any text with that tag will be redrawn with the new attributes. Similarly, if you change a binding on a tag, all tagged characters are affected immediately.

Example 36–1 defines a few tags for character styles you might see in an editor. The example uses the font naming system added in Tk 8.0, which is described on page 636.

Example 36–1 Tag configurations for basic character styles.

```
proc TextStyles { t } {
    $t tag configure bold -font {times 12 bold}
    $t tag configure italic -font {times 12 italic}
    $t tag configure fixed -font {courier 12}
    $t tag configure underline -underline true
    $t tag configure super -offset 6 -font {helvetica 8}
    $t tag configure sub -offset -6 -font {helvetica 8}
}
```

Mixing Attributes from Different Tags

A character can be labeled with more than one tag. For example, one tag could determine the font, another could determine the background color, and so on. If different tags try to supply the same attribute, a priority ordering is taken into account. The latest tag added to a range of text has the highest priority. The ordering of tags can be controlled explicitly with the `tag raise` and `tag lower` commands.

You can achieve interesting effects by composing attributes from different tags. In a mail reader, for example, the listing of messages in a mail folder can use one color to indicate messages that are marked for delete, and it can use another color for messages that are marked to be moved into another folder. The tags might be defined like this:

```
$t tag configure deleted -background grey75
$t tag configure moved -background yellow
```

These tags conflict, but they are never used on the same message. However, a selection could be indicated with an underline, for example:

```
$t tag configure select -underline true
```

You can add and remove the `select` tag to indicate what messages have been selected, and the underline is independent of the background color determined by the `moved` or `deleted` tag. If you look at the *exmh* implementation, the `ftocColor.tcl` file defines several text tags that are composed like this.

Line Spacing and Justification

The spacing and justification for text have several attributes. These settings are complicated by wrapped text lines. The text widget distinguishes between the first *display line* and the remaining display lines for a given text line. For example, if a line in the text widget has 80 characters but the window is only wide enough for 30, then the line may be wrapped onto three display lines. See Table 36–10 on page 554 for a description of the text widget's `wrap` attribute that controls this behavior.

Spacing is controlled with three attributes, and there are global spacing attributes as well as per-tag spacing attributes. The `-spacing1` attribute adds space above the first display line, while `-spacing2` adds space above the subsequent display lines that exist because of wrapping. The `-spacing3` attribute adds space below the last display line, which could be the same as the first display line if the line is not wrapped.

The margin settings also distinguish between the first and remaining display lines. The `-lmargin1` attribute specifies the indent for the first display line, while the `-lmargin2` attribute specifies the indent for the rest of the display lines, if any. There is only a single attribute, `-rmargin`, for the right indent. These margin attributes are only tag attributes. The closest thing for the text widget as a whole is the `-padx` attribute, but this adds an equal amount of spacing on both sides:

Example 36–2 Line spacing and justification in the text widget.

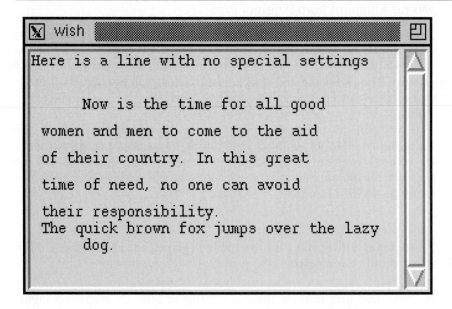

```
proc TextExample { f } {
    frame $f
    pack $f -side top -fill both -expand true
    set t [text $f.t -setgrid true -wrap word \
        -width 42 -height 14 \
        -yscrollcommand "$f.sy set"]
    scrollbar $f.sy -orient vert -command "$f.t yview"
    pack $f.sy -side right -fill y
    pack $f.t -side left -fill both -expand true

    $t tag configure para -spacing1 0.25i -spacing2 0.1i \
        -lmargin1 0.5i -lmargin2 0.1i -rmargin 0.5i
    $t tag configure hang -lmargin1 0.1i -lmargin2 0.5i

    $t insert end "Here is a line with no special settings\n"
    $t insert end "Now is the time for all good women and men
to come to the aid of their country. In this great time of
need, no one can avoid their responsibility.\n"
    $t insert end "The quick brown fox jumps over the lazy dog."

    $t tag add para 2.0 2.end
    $t tag add hang 3.0 3.end
}
```

The example defines two tags, para and hang, that have different spacing and margins. The -spacing1 setting for para causes the white space before the second line. The -spacing2 setting causes the white space between the wrapped portions of the second paragraph. The hang tag has no spacing attributes, so the last paragraph starts right below the previous paragraph. You can also see the difference between the -lmargin1 and -lmargin2 settings.

The newline characters are inserted explicitly. Each newline character defines a new line for the purposes of indexing, but not necessarily for display, as this example shows. In the third line there is no newline. This means that if more text is inserted at the end mark, it will be on line three.

The values for the spacing and margin parameters are in screen units. Because different fonts are different sizes, you may need to compute the spacings as a function of the character sizes. The bbox operation returns the bounding box (x, y, width, height) for a given character:

```
$t insert 1.0 "ABCDE"
$t bbox 1.0
=> 4 4 8 12
```

The Tk 8.0 font metrics command, which is described on page 640, also gives detailed measurements:

```
font metrics {times 12}
-ascent 9 -descent 3 -linespace 12 -fixed 0
```

Text justification is limited to three styles: left, right, or center. There is no setting that causes the text to line up on both margins, which would have to be achieved by introducing variable spacing between words.

IV. Tk Widgets

Tab Stops

Text widgets have adjustable tab stops. The `tabs` attribute is a list of tab stops, which are specified with a screen unit and optionally a keyword that indicates justification. The tab justification keywords are `left`, `right`, `center`, and `numeric`, and these can be abbreviated. The default is `left`. The following resource specification defines tab stops at 2-centimeter intervals with different justification:

```
*Text.tabs: 2c left 4c right 6c center 8c numeric
```

The `tabs` attribute applies to the whole text widget or to a tag. The last tab stop is extrapolated as needed. The following command defines a tag that has left justified tab stops every half inch:

```
$t tag configure foo -tabs ".5i left"
```

The Selection

The selection is implemented with a predefined tag named `sel`. If the application tags characters with `sel`, those characters are added to the selection. This is done as part of the default bindings on the text widget.

The `exportSelection` attribute of a text widget controls whether or not selected text is exported by the selection mechanism to other applications. By default the selection is exported. In this case, when another widget or application asserts ownership of the selection then the `sel` tag is removed from any characters that are tagged with it. Chapter 38 describes the selection mechanism in more detail.

You cannot delete the `sel` tag with the `tag delete` operation. However, it is not an error to do so. You can delete all the tags on the text widget with the following command. The `eval` command is used to join the list of tag names into the `tag delete` command:

```
eval {$t tag delete} [$t tag names]
```

Tag Bindings

You can associate a tag with bindings so that when the user clicks on different areas of the text display, different things happen. The syntax for the `tag bind` command is similar to that of the main Tk `bind` command. You can both query and set the bindings for a tag. Chapter 29 describes the `bind` command and the syntax for events in detail.

The only events supported by the `tag bind` command are `Enter`, `Leave`, `ButtonPress`, `ButtonRelease`, `Motion`, `KeyPress`, and `KeyRelease`. `ButtonPress` and `KeyPress` can be shorted to `Button` and `Key` as in the regular `bind` command. The `Enter` and `Leave` events are triggered when the mouse moves in and out of characters with a tag, which is different from when the mouse moves in and out of the window.

If a character has multiple tags, then the bindings associated with all the tags will be invoked, in the order from lowest priority tag to highest priority tag. After all the tag bindings have run, the binding associated with the main widget is run, if any. The `continue` and `break` commands work inside tag bindings in a similar fashion as they work with regular command bindings. See Chapter 29 for the details.

Example 36–3 defines a text button that has a highlighted relief and an action associated with it. The example generates a new tag name so that each text button is unique. The relief and background are set for the tag to set it apart visually. The `winfo visual` command is used to find out if the display supports color before adding a colored background to the tag. On a black and white display, the button is displayed in reverse video (i.e., white on black.) The command is bound to `<Button-1>`, which is the same as `<ButtonPress-1>`.

The cursor is changed when the mouse is over the tagged area by binding to the `<Enter>` and `<Leave>` events. Upon leaving the tagged area, the cursor is restored. Another tag is used to remember the previous setting for the cursor. You could also use a global variable, but it is often useful to decorate the text with tags for your own purposes.

Example 36–3 An active text button.

```
proc TextButton { t start end command } {
    global textbutton
    if ![info exists textbutton(uid)] {
        set textbutton(uid) 0
    } else {
        incr textbutton(uid)
    }
    set tag button$textbutton(uid)
    $t tag configure $tag -relief raised -borderwidth 2
    if {[regexp color [winfo visual $t]]} {
        $t tag configure $tag -background thistle
    } else {
        $t tag configure $tag -background [$t cget -fg]
        $t tag configure $tag -foreground [$t cget -bg]
    }
    # Bind the command to the tag
    $t tag bind $tag <Button-1> $command
    $t tag add $tag $start $end
    # use another tag to remember the cursor
    $t tag bind $tag <Enter> \
        [list TextButtonChangeCursor %W $start $end tcross]
    $t tag bind $tag <Leave> {TextButtonRestoreCursor %W}
}
proc TextButtonChangeCursor {t start end cursor} {
    $t tag add cursor=[$t cget -cursor] $start $end
    $t config -cursor $cursor
}
```

IV. Tk Widgets

```
proc TextButtonRestoreCursor {t} {
    regexp {cursor=([^ ]*)} [$t tag names] x cursor
    $t config -cursor $cursor
}
```

To behave even more like a button, the action should trigger upon <Button-Release-1>, and the appearance should change upon <ButtonPress-1>. If this is important to you, you can always embed a real Tk button. Embedding widgets is described later.

Searching Text

The search operation scans the text widget for a string that matches a pattern. The index of the text that matches the pattern is returned. The search starts at an index and covers all the text widget unless a stop index is supplied. You can use end as the stop index to prevent the search from wrapping back to the beginning of the document. The general form of the search operation is this:

$t search ?*options*? *pattern index* ?*stopIndex*?

Table 36–4 summarizes the *options* to the search operation:

Table 36–4 Options to the search operation.

-forward	Searches forward from *index*. This is the default.
-backward	Searches backward from *index*.
-exact	Matches *pattern* exactly. This is the default.
-regexp	Uses regular expression pattern matching.
-nocase	Lowercase letters in *pattern* can match upper case letters.
-count *varName*	Returns in *varName* the number of characters that matched *pattern*.
--	Ends the options. Necessary if *pattern* begins with -.

If you use a regular expression to match a pattern, you may be interested in how much text matched so you can highlight the match. The -count option specifies a variable that gets the number of matching characters:

```
set start [$t search -count cnt -regexp -- $pattern 1.0 end]
$t tag add sel $start "$start +$cnt chars"
```

Embedded Widgets

The text widget can display embedded widgets as well as text. You can include a picture, for example, by constructing it in a canvas and then inserting the canvas into the text widget. An embedded widget takes up one character in terms of indices. You can address the widget by its index position or by the Tk pathname of the widget.

For example, suppose `$t` names a text widget. The following commands create a button and insert it into the text widget. The button behaves normally, and in this case it invokes the `Help` command when the user clicks on it:

```
button $t.help -bitmap questhead -command Help
$t window create end -window $t.help
```

By default an embedded widget is centered vertically on its text line. You can adjust this with the `-align` option to the `window create` command. This setting only takes effect if the window is smaller than the text in the line. I find that windows are usually larger than the text line, and in that case the `-align` setting has no effect. This setting is also used with images, however, where it is more common to have small images (e.g., for special bullets). Table 36–5 describes the window and image alignment settings:

Table 36–5 Window and image alignment options.

top	Top lines up with top of text line.
center	Center lines up with center of text line.
baseline	Bottom lines up with text baseline.
bottom	Bottom lines up with bottom of text line.

You can postpone the creation of the embedded widget by specifying a Tcl command that creates the window, instead of specifying the `-window` option. The delayed creation is useful if you have lots of widgets embedded in your text. In this case the Tcl command is evaluated just before the text widget needs to display the widget. In other words, when the user scrolls the text so the widget will appear, the Tcl command is run to create the widget:

Example 36–4 Delayed creation of embedded widgets.

```
$t window create end -create [list MakeGoBack $t]
proc MakeGoBack { t } {
    button $t.goback -text "Go to Line 1" \
        -command [list $t see 1.0]
}
```

The `MakeGoBack` procedure is introduced to eliminate potential quoting problems. If you need to execute more than one Tcl command to create the widget or if the embedded button has a complex command, the quoting can quickly get out of hand.

Table 36–6 gives the complete set of options for creating embedded widgets. You can change these later with the `window configure` operation. For example:

IV. Tk Widgets

```
$t window configure $t.goback -padx 2
```

Table 36–6 Options to the `window create` operation.

`-align` *where*	**Alignment:** `top`, `center`, `bottom`, **or** `baseline`.
`-create` *command*	Tcl command to create the widget.
`-padx` *pixels*	Padding on either side of the widget.
`-pady` *pixels*	Padding above and below the widget.
`-stretch` *boolean*	If true, the widget is stretched vertically to match the spacing of the text line.
`-window` *pathname*	Tk pathname of the widget to embed.

You can specify the window to reconfigure by its pathname or the index where the window is located. In practice, naming the widget by its pathname is much more useful. Note that `end` is not useful for identifying an embedded window because the text widget treats `end` specially. You can insert a window at `end`, but `end` is always updated to be after the last item in the widget. Thus `end` will never name the position of an existing window.

Embedded Images

Tk 8.0 added embedded images that are much like embedded windows. They provide a more efficient way to add images than creating a canvas or label widget to hold the image. You can also put the same image into a text widget many times. Example 36–5 uses an image for the bullets in a bulleted list:

Example 36–5 Using embedded images for a bulleted list.

```
proc BList_Setup { t imagefile } {
    global blist
    set blist(image) [image create photo -file $imagefile]
    $t tag configure bulletlist -tabs ".5c center 1c left" \
        -lmargin1 0 -lmargin2 1c
}
proc BList_Item { t text {mark insert}} {
    global blist
    # Assume we are at the beginning of the line
    $t insert $mark \t bulletlist
    $t image create $mark -image $blist(image)
    $t insert $mark \t$text bulletlist
}
```

In Example 36–5, tabs are used to line up the bullet and the left edges of the text. The first tab centers the bullet over a point 0.5 centimeters from left margin. The second tab stop is the same as the -lmargin2 setting so the text on the first line lines up with the text that wraps onto more lines.

If you update the image dynamically, all the instances of that image in the text widget are updated, too. This follows from the image model used in Tk, which is described in Chapter 41 on page 625.

The options for embedded images are mostly the same as those for embedded windows. One difference is that images have a -name option so you can reference an image without remembering its position in the text widget. You cannot use the image name directly because the same image can be embedded many times in the text widget. If you do not choose a name, the text widget assigns a name for you. The image create operation returns this name:

```
$t image create 1.0 -image image1
=> image1
$t image create end -image image1
=> image1#1
```

Table 36–7 gives the complete set of options for creating embedded images. You can change these later with the image configure operation.

Table 36–7 Options to the image create operation.

-align *where*	Alignment: top, center, bottom, or baseline. Only has effect if *image* is shorter than the line height. See Table 36–5.
-image *image*	The Tk image to add to the text widget.
-name *name*	A name for this instance of the image. A #*num* may be appended to generate a unique name.
-padx *pixels*	Padding on either side of the image.
-pady *pixels*	Padding above and below the image.

Looking inside the Text Widget

The text widget has several operations that let you examine its contents. The simplest is get, which returns of text from the widget. If only one index is given, the character at that position is returned. If there are two indices, all the characters up to but not including the second index are returned. For example, you can get all the text with this command:

```
$t get 1.0 end
```

As of Tk 8.4, you can get multiple ranges of text with a single get operation; the result in this case is a list of the range contents. For example, to retrieve the first and third lines, without the trailing newlines, as a two-element list:

```
$t get 1.0 1.end 3.0 3.end
```

IV. Tk Widgets

Looking at Tags

The `tag names` command returns all the tag names, or the names of the tags at a specified index:

```
$t tag names ?index?
```

A text tag can be applied to many different ranges of text. The `tag ranges` operation returns a list of indices that alternate between the start and end of tag ranges. The `foreach` command with two loop variables makes it easy to iterate through all the ranges:

```
foreach {start end} [$t tag ranges $tag] {
    # start is the beginning of a range
    # end is the end of a range
}
```

The `tag nextrange` and `tag prevrange` operations return two indices that delimit the next and previous range of a tag. They take a starting index and an optional ending index. The `tag nextrange` operation skips to the next range if the tag is present at the starting index, unless the starting index is right at the start of a range. The `tag prevrange` operation is complementary. It does not skip the current range, unless the starting index is at the beginning of the range. These rules are used in Example 36–6 that defines a procedure to return the current range:

Example 36–6 Finding the current range of a text tag.

```
proc Text_CurrentRange { t tag mark } {
    set range [$t tag prevrange $tag $mark]
    set end [lindex $range 1]
    if {[llength $range] == 0 || [$t compare $end < $mark]} {
        # This occurs when the mark is at the
        # very beginning of the node
        set range [$t tag nextrange $tag $mark]
        if {[llength $range] == 0 ||
                [$t compare $mark < [lindex $range 0]]} {
            return {}
        }
    }
    return $range
}
```

Looking at Marks

The `mark names` operation returns the names of all the marks. Unlike `tag names`, you cannot supply an index to find out if there are marks there. You must use the `dump` operation described later. The `mark next` and `mark previous` operations search from a given index for a mark. The `mark next` operation will find a mark if it is at the starting index.

Dumping the Contents

The `dump` operation provides the most general way to examine the contents of the text widget. The general form of the command is:

```
$t dump ?options? ix1 ?ix2?
```

The `dump` operation returns information for the elements from *ix1* to *ix2*, or just for the elements at *ix1* if *ix2* is not specified. You can limit what information is returned with options that indicate what to return: `-text`, `-mark`, `-tag`, `-image`, `-window`, or `-all`.

Three pieces of information are returned for each element of the text widget: the type, the value, and the index. The possible types are `text`, `tagon`, `tagoff`, `mark`, `image`, and `window`. The information reflects the way the text widget represents its contents. Tags are represented as `tagon` and `tagoff` elements. Text is stored in segments that do not include any marks, tag elements, windows, or images. In addition, a newline ends a text segment.

Example 36–7 prints out the contents of the text widget:

Example 36–7 Dumping the text widget.

```
proc Text_Dump {t {start 1.0} {end end}} {
    foreach {key value index} [$t dump $start $end] {
        if {$key == "text"} {
            puts "$index \"$value\""
        } else {
            puts "$index $key $value"
        }
    }
}
```

Instead of having `dump` return all the information, you can have it call a Tcl command to process each element. The command gets passed three pieces of information for each element: the type, the value, and the index. Example 36–8 shows another way to print out the text widget contents:

Example 36–8 Dumping the text widget with a command callback.

```
proc Text_Dump {t {start 1.0} {end end}} {
    $t dump -command TextDump $start $end
}
proc TextDump {key value index} {
    if {$key == "text"} {
        puts "$index \"$value\""
    } else {
        puts "$index $key $value"
    }
}
```

IV. Tk Widgets

The Undo Mechanism

Beginning in Tk 8.4, the text widget supports an unlimited undo and redo mechanism. You enable the undo mechanism by setting the text widget's `undo` attribute to True. The `undo` attribute has a default value of False for backward compatibility.

When enabled, each `insert` and `delete` action, whether performed by the user or programmatically, is recorded on an undo stack. You can programmatically undo an edit with the `edit undo` operation. The undone changes are then moved to the redo stack, so that an undone edit can be redone again with the with the `edit redo` operation. The redo stack is cleared whenever new edit actions are recorded on the undo stack. (Both the `edit undo` and `edit redo` operations generate error conditions if the undo or redo stack is empty, respectively.) The text widget also has default undo and redo bindings; by default, undo is `<Control-z>` and redo is `<Control-y>` on Windows, `<Control-Z>` on all other platforms. (See "Text Bindings" on page 549.)

Each `edit undo` operation undoes the last *action*, which is defined as all of the insert and delete commands that are recorded on the undo stack in between two *separators*. When the `autoSeparators` attribute is True (the default), a separator is automatically placed on the stack whenever:

- the mode changes from insertion to deletion, or vice versa
- the user moves the insert mark using the keyboard or the mouse
- the user presses the `<Return>` key

If you set the `autoSeparators` attribute to False, you are responsible for programmatically placing separators on the stack with the `edit separator` operation. By turning the autoseparators off and inserting them at the desired points, you can define compound actions, such as search and replace. The default paste binding is an example of such an action, such that overwriting selected text by pasting from the clipboard is considered an atomic action.

As of Tk 8.4, only `insert` and `delete` operations are handled by the undo mechanism. In particular, tag operations, such as applying a tag to text, are not actions captured by the undo mechanism, even if the tag was applied as part of an `insert` operation. As an example, consider the following insertion:

```
$t insert end "Let's insert some " {} \
    "special" blue " text." {}
```

If this operation were undone and then redone, the text would be reinserted, but without applying the `blue` tag on the word "special".

Text Bindings and Events

Text Bindings

There is an extensive set of default bindings for text widgets. In general, the commands that move the insertion cursor also clear the selection. Often you can hold the Shift key down to extend the selection, or hold the Control key down to move the insertion cursor without affecting the selection. Table 36–8 lists the default bindings for the text widget:

Table 36–8 Bindings for the text widget.

`<Any-Key>`	Inserts normal printing characters.
`<Button-1>`	Sets the insert point, clears the selection, sets focus.
`<Control-Button-1>`	Sets the insert point without affecting the selection.
`<B1-Motion>`	Sweeps out a selection from the insert point.
`<Double-Button-1>`	Selects the word under the mouse.
`<Triple-Button-1>`	Selects the line under the mouse.
`<Shift-Button-1>`	Adjusts the end of selection closest to the mouse.
`<Shift-B1-Motion>`	Continues to adjust the selection.
`<Button-2>`	Pastes the selection, or sets the scrolling anchor.
`<B2-Motion>`	Scrolls the window.
`<MouseWheel>`	Scrolls vertically.
`<Button-4>`	Mousewheel support on Unix only; scrolls up. (Tk 8.3)
`<Button-5>`	Mousewheel support on Unix only; scrolls down. (Tk 8.3)
`<Key-Left> <Control-b>`	Moves the cursor left one character and clears the selection.
`<Shift-Left>`	Moves the cursor and extends the selection.
`<Control-Left>`	Moves the cursor by words. Clears the selection.
`<Control-Shift-Left>`	Moves the cursor by words. Extends selection.
`<Key-Right> <Control-f>`	`Right` bindings are analogous to `Left` bindings.
`<Meta-b> <Meta-f>`	Same as `<Control-Left>`, `<Control-Right>`.
`<Key-Up> <Control-p>`	Moves the cursor up one line. Clears the selection.
`<Shift-Up>`	Moves the cursor up one line. Extends the selection.

IV. Tk Widgets

Table 36–8 Bindings for the text widget. (Continued)

`<Control-Up>`	Moves the cursor up by paragraphs, which are a group of lines separated by a blank line.
`<Control-Shift-Up>`	Moves the cursor up by paragraph. Extends the selection.
`<Key-Down> <Control-n>`	All `Down` bindings are analogous to `Up` bindings.
`<Next> <Prior>`	Moves the cursor by one screen. Clears the selection.
`<Shift-Next>` `<Shift-Prior>`	Moves the cursor by one screen. Extends the selection.
`<Home> <Control-a>`	Moves the cursor to line start. Clears the selection.
`<Shift-Home>`	Moves the cursor to line start. Extends the selection.
`<End> <Control-e>`	Moves the cursor to line end. Clears the selection.
`<Shift-End>`	Moves the cursor to line end. Extends the selection.
`<Control-Home>` `<Meta-less>`	Moves the cursor to the beginning of text. Clears the selection.
`<Control-End>` `<Meta-greater>`	Moves the cursor to the end of text. Clears the selection.
`<Select>` `<Control-space>`	Sets the selection anchor to the position of the cursor.
`<Shift-Select>` `<Control-Shift-space>`	Adjusts the selection to the position of the cursor.
`<Control-slash>`	Selects everything in the text widget.
`<Control-backslash>`	Clears the selection.
`<Delete>`	Deletes the selection, if any. Otherwise, deletes the character to the right of the cursor.
`<BackSpace> <Control-h>`	Deletes the selection, if any. Otherwise, deletes the character to the left of the cursor.
`<Control-d>`	Deletes character to the right of the cursor.
`<Meta-d>`	Deletes word to the right of the cursor.
`<Control-k>`	Deletes from cursor to end of the line. If you are at the end of line, deletes the newline character.
`<Control-o>`	Inserts a newline but does not advance the cursor.
`<Meta-Delete>` `<Meta-BackSpace>`	Deletes the word to the left of the cursor.
`<Control-t>`	Transposes the characters on either side of the cursor.
`<<Cut>> <Control-x>`	Copies the selection to the clipboard.

Table 36–8 Bindings for the text widget. (Continued)

`<<Copy>> <Control-c>`	Cuts the selection and saves it on the clipboard.
`<<Paste>> <Control-v>`	Pastes from the clipboard.
`<<Undo>> <Control-z>`	Undoes the last edit action if the `undo` attribute is true. (Tk 8.4)

`<<Redo>>`
`<Control-Z> (Unix & Mac)`
`<Control-y> (Windows)`
	Reapplies the last undone edit action if the `undo` attribute is true. (Tk 8.4)

Text Virtual Events

As of Tk 8.4, a text widget generates a `<<Modified>>` virtual event whenever text is inserted into or deleted from the text widget. The event is fired after the text widget has changed, so the binding action can access the new text values. The easiest way to be aware of changes to the menu selection is to bind to this virtual event, for example:

```
bind .t <<Modified>> {ContentsChanged %W}
```

Also added in Tk 8.4 is the `<<Selection>>` virtual event, which is generated whenever the text widget's selection changes. The event is fired after the selection has changed, so the binding action can access the new selection.

Text Operations

Table 36–9 describes the text widget operations, including some that are not discussed in this chapter. In the table, `$t` is a text widget:

Table 36–9 Operations for the text widget.

`$t bbox index`	Returns the bounding box of the character at `index`. Four numbers are returned: `x y width height`.
`$t cget option`	Returns the value of the configuration option.
`$t compare i1 op i2`	Performs index comparison. `i1` and `i2` are indexes. `op` is one of `< <= == >= > !=`
`$t configure ...`	Queries or sets configuration options.
`$t debug boolean`	Enables consistency checking for B-tree code.
`$t delete i1 ?i2? ?...?`	Deletes from `i1` up to, but not including `i2`. Just deletes the character at `i1` if `i2` is not specified. Deletes multiple ranges if specified.
`$t dlineinfo index`	Returns the bounding box, in pixels, of the display for the line containing index. Five numbers are returned: `x y width height baseline`.

Table 36–9 Operations for the text widget. (Continued)

`$t dump ?`*`options`*`? i1 ?i2?`	Returns the marks, tags, windows, images, and text contained in the widget. Options are `-all`, `-command` *`command`*, `-image`, `-mark`, `-tag`, `-text`, and `-window`.
`$t edit modified ?`*`bool-ean`*`?`	Queries or sets the widget's modified flag. (Tk 8.4)
`$t edit redo`	Reapplies the last undone edit action if the `undo` attribute is true. (Tk 8.4)
`$t edit reset`	Clears the undo and redo stacks. (Tk 8.4)
`$t edit separator`	Inserts a separator on the undo stack if the `undo` attribute is true. (Tk 8.4)
`$t edit undo`	Undoes the last edit action if the `undo` attribute is true. (Tk 8.4)
`$t get i1 ?i2? ?...?`	Returns the text from `i1` to `i2`, or just the character at `i1` if `i2` is not specified. Returns multiple ranges as a list, if specified.
`$t image cget` *`option`*	Returns the value of the image *`option`*.
`$t image configure ?`*`options`*`?`	Queries or sets the configuration of an embedded image.
`$t image create` *`option`* *`value`* `...`	Creates an embedded image. Options are described in Table 36–7 on page 545.
`$t image names`	Returns the names of all embedded images.
`$t index` *`index`*	Returns the numerical value of *`index`*.
`$t insert` *`index`* *`chars`* `?`*`tags`*`? ?`*`chars tags`*`? ...`	Inserts *`chars`* at the specified *`index`*. If *`tags`* are specified, they are added to the new characters.
`$t mark gravity` *`name`* `?`*`direction`*`?`	Queries or assigns a gravity direction to the mark *`name`*. *`direction`*, if specified, is `left` or `right`.
`$t mark names`	Returns a list of defined marks.
`$t mark next` *`index`*	Returns the mark after *`index`*.
`$t mark previous` *`index`*	Returns the mark before *`index`*.
`$t mark set` *`name`* *`index`*	Defines a mark *`name`* at the given *`index`*.
`$t mark unset` *`name1`* `?`*`name2`* `...?`	Deletes the named mark, or marks.
`$t scan mark x y`	Anchors a scrolling operation.
`$t scan dragto x y`	Scrolls based on a new position.
`$t search ?`*`switches`*`? pat-tern index ?stopIndex?`	Searches for *`pattern`* starting at *`index`*. The index of the start of the match is returned. Switches are described in Table 36–4 on page 542.

Table 36–9 Operations for the text widget. (Continued)

`$t see index`	Positions the display to view *index*.
`$t tag add name i1 ?i2? ?i1 i2? ?i1 i2? ...`	Adds the tag to *i1* through, but not including *i2*, or just the character at *i1* if *i2* is not given.
`$t tag bind name ?sequence? ?script?`	Queries or defines bindings for the tag *name*.
`$t tag cget name option`	Returns the value of *option* for tag *name*.
`$t tag configure name ...`	Sets or queries the configuration of tag *name*.
`$t tag delete tag1 ?tag2 ...?`	Deletes information for the named tags.
`$t tag lower tag ?below?`	Lowers the priority of *tag* to the lowest priority or to just below tag *below*.
`$t tag names ?index?`	Returns the names of the tags at the specified *index*, or in the whole widget, sorted from lowest to highest priority.
`$t tag nextrange tag i1 ?i2?`	Returns a list of two indices that are the next range of text with tag that starts at or after *i1* and before index *i2*, or the end.
`$t tag prevrange tag i1 ?i2?`	Returns a list of two indices that are the previous range of text with tag that ends at or before *i1* and at or after index *i2*, or 1.0.
`$t tag raise tag ?above?`	Raises the priority of *tag* to the highest priority, or to just above the priority of tag *above*.
`$t tag ranges tag`	Returns a list describing all the ranges of tag.
`$t tag remove tag i1 ?i2? ?i1 i2? ?i1 i2? ...`	Removes *tag* from the range *i1* up to, but not including *i2*, or just at *i1* if *i2* is not specified.
`$t window cget win option`	Returns the value of *option* for *win*.
`$t window config win ...`	Queries or modifies the configuration of the embedded window. *win* is a Tk pathname or an index.
`$t window create ix args`	Creates an embedded window at *ix*.
`$t window names`	Returns a list of windows embedded in `$t`.
`$t xview`	Returns two fractions between zero and one that describe the amount of text off-screen to the left and the amount of text displayed.
`$t xview moveto fraction`	Positions the text so *fraction* of the text is off screen to the left.
`$t xview scroll num what`	Scrolls *num* of *what*, which is *units* or *pages*.

Table 36–9 Operations for the text widget. (Continued)

`$t yview`	Returns two fractions between zero and one that describe the amount of text off-screen toward the beginning and the amount of text displayed.
`$t yview moveto` *fraction*	Positions the text so *fraction* of the text is off-screen toward the beginning.
`$t yview scroll` *num what*	Scrolls *num* of *what*, which is *units* or *pages*.
`$t yview ?-pickplace?` *ix*	Obsolete. Use the `see` operation, which is similar.
`$t yview` *num*	Obsolete. Position line *num* at the top of screen.

Text Attributes

Table 36–10 lists the attributes for the text widget. The table uses the resource name, which has capitals at internal word boundaries. In Tcl commands, the attributes are specified with a dash and all lowercase:

Table 36–10 Text attribute resource names.

`autoSeparators`	Boolean: True (default) automatically insert undo separators after each `insert` or `delete` operation; False requires the use of the `undo separator` operation to insert separators. (Tk 8.4)
`background`	Background color (also `bg`).
`borderWidth`	Extra space around the edge of the text.
`cursor`	Cursor to display when mouse is over the widget.
`exportSelection`	If true, selected text is exported to the selection.
`font`	Default font for the text.
`foreground`	Foreground color (also `fg`).
`height`	Height, in text lines.
`highlightBackground`	Focus highlight color when widget does not have focus.
`highlightColor`	Color for input focus highlight border.
`highlightThickness`	Width of highlight border.
`insertBackground`	Color for the insert cursor.
`insertBorderWidth`	Size of 3D border for insert cursor.
`insertOffTime`	Milliseconds insert cursor blinks off.
`insertOnTime`	Milliseconds insert cursor blinks on.
`insertWidth`	Width of the insert cursor.

Table 36–10 Text attribute resource names. (Continued)

maxUndo	The maximum number of undo actions on the undo stack. A zero or a negative value implies an unlimited undo stack. (Tk 8.4)
padX	Extra space to the left and right of the text.
padY	Extra space above and below the text.
relief	flat, sunken, raised, groove, ridge, or solid.
selectBackground	Background color of selected text.
selectForeground	Foreground color of selected text.
selectBorderWidth	Size of 3D border for selection highlight.
setGrid	Enable/disable geometry gridding.
spacing1	Extra space above each unwrapped line.
spacing2	Space between parts of a line that have wrapped.
spacing3	Extra space below an unwrapped line.
state	Editable (normal) or read-only (disabled).
tabs	Tab stops.
takeFocus	Control focus changes from keyboard traversal.
undo	Boolean: True enables and False (default) disables the undo mechanism. (Tk 8.4)
width	Width, in characters, of the text display.
wrap	Line wrap mode: none, char, or word.
xScrollCommand	Tcl command prefix for horizontal scrolling.
yScrollCommand	Tcl command prefix for vertical scrolling.

IV. Tk Widgets

The Canvas Widget

The canvas widget is a general-purpose widget that you can program to display a variety of objects including arcs, images, lines, ovals, polygons, rectangles, text, and embedded windows.

*C*anvas widgets display objects such as lines and images, and each object can have bindings that respond to user input, or be animated under program control. The objects can be labeled with *tags*, and the tags can be configured with display attributes and event bindings. This chapter describes all the predefined canvas object types. Chapter 50 outlines the C programming interface for creating new canvas objects.

Canvas Coordinates

The coordinate space of the canvas has 0, 0 at the top left corner. Larger X coordinates are to the right, and larger Y coordinates are downward. The position and possibly the size of a canvas object is determined by a set of coordinates. Different objects are characterized by different numbers of coordinates. For example, text objects have two coordinates, $x1$ $y1$, that specify their anchor point. A line can have many pairs of coordinates that specify the end points of its segments. The coordinates are set when the object is created, and they can be updated later with the `coords` operation. By default, coordinates are in pixels. Append a coordinate with one of the following letters to change the units:

```
c    centimeters
i    inches
m    millimeters
p    printer points (1/72 inches)
```

The tk scale command, which is described on page 669, changes the mapping from pixels to other screen measures. Use it before creating the canvas.

The width and height attributes of the canvas determine the size of the viewable area. The scrollRegion attribute of the canvas determines the boundaries of the canvas. Its value is four numbers that specify the upper-left and lower-right coordinates of the canvas. If you do not specify a scroll region, it defaults to the size of the viewable area. Example 37–1 creates a canvas that has a 1000 by 400 scrolling region, and a 300 by 200 viewing area. The canvas is connected to two scrollbars to provide horizontal and vertical scrolling:

Example 37–1 A large scrolling canvas.

```
proc Scrolled_Canvas { c args } {
    frame $c
    eval {canvas $c.canvas \
        -xscrollcommand [list $c.xscroll set] \
        -yscrollcommand [list $c.yscroll set] \
        -highlightthickness 0 \
        -borderwidth 0} $args
    scrollbar $c.xscroll -orient horizontal \
        -command [list $c.canvas xview]
    scrollbar $c.yscroll -orient vertical \
        -command [list $c.canvas yview]
    grid $c.canvas $c.yscroll -sticky news
    grid $c.xscroll -sticky ew
    grid rowconfigure $c 0 -weight 1
    grid columnconfigure $c 0 -weight 1
    return $c.canvas
}
Scrolled_Canvas .c -width 300 -height 200 \
    -scrollregion {0 0 1000 400}
=> .c.canvas
pack .c -fill both -expand true
```

Borders are drawn in the canvas.

The highlight thickness and border width are set to 0 in Example 37–1. Otherwise, these features occupy some of the canvas viewable area. If you want a raised border for your canvas, either use another frame, or remember to offset your positions to avoid having objects clipped by the borders.

Hello, World!

Example 37–2 creates an object that you can drag around with the mouse. It introduces the use of tags to classify objects. In this case the movable tag gets bindings that let you drag the item, so any item with the movable tag shares this behavior. The example uses Scrolled_Canvas from Example 37–1. When you use a scrolled canvas, you must map from the view coordinates reported by bindings to the canvas coordinates used to locate objects:

Example 37–2 The canvas "Hello, World!" example.

```
proc CanvasHello {} {
    set can [Scrolled_Canvas .c -width 400 -height 100 \
        -scrollregion {0 0 800 400}]
    pack .c -fill both -expand true
    # Create a text object on the canvas
    $can create text 50 50 -text "Hello, World!" -tag movable
    # Bind actions to objects with the movable tag
    $can bind movable <Button-1> {CanvasMark %x %y %W}
    $can bind movable <B1-Motion> {CanvasDrag %x %y %W}
}
proc CanvasMark { x y can} {
    global canvas
    # Map from view coordinates to canvas coordinates
    set x [$can canvasx $x]
    set y [$can canvasy $y]
    # Remember the object and its location
    set canvas($can,obj) [$can find closest $x $y]
    set canvas($can,x) $x
    set canvas($can,y) $y
}
proc CanvasDrag { x y can} {
    global canvas
    # Map from view coordinates to canvas coordinates
    set x [$can canvasx $x]
    set y [$can canvasy $y]
    # Move the current object
    set dx [expr $x - $canvas($can,x)]
    set dy [expr $y - $canvas($can,y)]
    $can move $canvas($can,obj) $dx $dy
    set canvas($can,x) $x
    set canvas($can,y) $y
}
```

Example 37–2 creates a text object and gives it a tag named movable:

```
.c create text 50 50 -text "Hello, World!" -tag movable
```

The first argument after create specifies the type, and the remaining arguments depend on the type of object being created. Each canvas object requires some coordinates, optionally followed by attribute value pairs. The coordinates can be provided as separate arguments or, beginning in Tk 8.3, as a single-argument list. The complete set of attributes for canvas objects are presented later in this chapter. A text object needs two coordinates for its location.

Canvas Tags

The create operation returns an ID for the object being created, which would have been 1 in this case. However, the code manipulates the canvas objects by specifying a *tag* instead of an object ID. A tag is a more general handle on canvas objects. Many objects can have the same tag, and an object can have

IV. Tk Widgets

more than one tag. You can define bindings on tags, and you can define attributes for tags that will be picked up by objects with those tags.

A tag name can be almost any string, but you should avoid spaces that can cause parsing problems and pure numbers that get confused with object IDs. There are two predefined tags: `current` and `all`. The `current` tag applies to whatever object is under the mouse. The `all` tag applies to all the objects on the canvas.

Many of the canvas operations take an argument that identifies objects. The value can be a tag name, or it can be the numerical object identifier returned by the `create` operation. Also, beginning in Tk 8.3, you can specify (as a single argument) a logical combination of tags using the operators `&&` (and), `||` (or), `^` (exclusive or), `!` (not), and parenthesized subexpressions. For example, to change the fill color to red on all objects with a tag of `highlight` or `warning`, you could execute the following:

```
$can itemconfigure {highlight || warning} -fill red
```

To move all the objects with the tag `plot1` or `plot2`, but that don't also include the tag `fixed`:

```
$can move {(plot1 || plot2) && !fixed} 50 0
```

Example 37–2 on page 559 defines behavior for objects with the `movable` tag. Pressing button 1 starts a drag, and dragging with the mouse button down moves the object. The pathname of the canvas (`%W`) is passed to `CanvasMark` and `CanvasDrag` so these procedures can be used on different canvases. The `%x` and `%y` keywords get substituted with the X and Y coordinate of the event:

```
$can bind movable <Button-1> {CanvasMark %x %y %W}
$can bind movable <B1-Motion> {CanvasDrag %x %y %W}
```

The `CanvasMark` and `CanvasDrag` procedures let you drag the object around the canvas. Because `CanvasMark` is applied to any object with the `movable` tag, it must first find the object that was clicked on. First, the view coordinates are mapped into the canvas coordinates with the `canvasx` and `canvasy` operations:

```
set x [$can canvasx x]
set y [$can canvasy y]
```

Once you do this, you can use the `find` operation:

```
set canvas($can,obj) [$can find closest $x $y]
```

The actual moving is done in `CanvasDrag` with the `move` operation:

```
$can move $canvas($can,obj) $dx $dy
```

Try creating a few other object types and dragging them around, too:

```
$can create rect 10 10 30 30 -fill red -tag movable
$can create line 1 1 40 40 90 60 -width 2 -tag movable
$can create poly 1 1 40 40 90 60 -fill blue -tag movable
```

The `CanvasMark` and `CanvasDrag` procedures can be used with any canvas. They use the global array `canvas` to keep their state, and they parameterize the indices with the canvas pathname to avoid conflict if there is more that one canvas in the application. If you get into this coding habit early, then you will find it easy to write reusable code.

Canvas tags are not persistent.

Canvas tags do not work exactly like tags in the text widget. In the text widget, a tag is completely independent of the text. You can configure a text tag before it is applied to text, and the tag configuration is remembered even if you remove it from the text. A canvas tag, in contrast, must be applied to an object before you can configure it. If you configure a canvas tag that is not applied to any objects, those settings are forgotten. If you remove all the objects that share a tag, any settings associated with those tags are forgotten.

The Min Max Scale Example

This section presents Example 37–3, which constructs a scale-like object with two sliders. The sliders represent the minimum and maximum values for some parameter. Clearly, the minimum cannot be greater than the maximum, and vice versa. The example creates three rectangles on the canvas. One rectangle forms the long axis of the slider that represents the range of possible values. The other two rectangles are markers that represent the values. Two text objects float below the markers to give the current values of the minimum and maximum.

The example introduces four canvas operations: `bbox`, `coords`, `scale`, and `move`. The `bbox` operation returns the bounding box of an object or of all objects with a given tag. The `coords` operation sets or queries the coordinates of an object. The `scale` operation stretches an object, and the `move` operation translates the position of an object.

Use tags instead of object IDs.

The thoughtful selection of tag names help to create "self-documenting code." And tags give you more flexibility to change an implementation later on. Example 37–3 does not use object IDs. Instead, it gives each object a symbolic identifier with a tag, plus it introduces more tags to represent classes of objects. The example uses the `all` tag to move all the items and to find out the bounding box of the image. The left box and the left hanging text both have the `left` tag. They can be moved together, and they share the same bindings. Similarly, the `right` tag is shared by the right box and the right hanging text. Each item has its own unique tag, so it can be manipulated individually, too. Those tags are `slider`, `lbox`, `lnum`, `rbox`, and `rnum`:

Example 37–3 A min max scale canvas example.

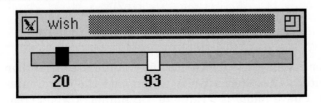

```
proc Scale2 {w min max {width {}} } {
    global scale2
    if {$width == {}} {
        # Set the long dimension, in pixels
        set width [expr $max - $min]
    }
    # Save parameters
    set scale2($w,scale) [expr ($max-$min)/$width.0]
    set scale2($w,min) $min;# Current minimum
    set scale2($w,max) $max
    set scale2($w,Min) $min ;# Lower bound to the scale
    set scale2($w,Max) $max
    set scale2($w,L) 10
    set scale2($w,R) [expr $width+10]

    # Build from 0 to 100, then scale and move it later.
    # Distance between left edges of boxes is 100.
    # The box is 10 wide, therefore the slider is 110 long.
    # The left box sticks up, and the right one hangs down.

    canvas $w
    $w create rect 0 0 110 10 -fill grey -tag slider
    $w create rect 0 -4 10 10 -fill black -tag {left lbox}
    $w create rect 100 0 110 14 -fill red -tag {right rbox}
    $w create text 5 16 -anchor n -text $min -tag {left lnum}
    $w create text 105 16 -anchor n -text $max \
        -tag {right rnum} -fill red

    # Stretch/shrink the slider to the right length
    set scale [expr ($width+10) / 110.0]
    $w scale slider 0 0 $scale 1.0

    # move the right box and text to match new length
    set nx [lindex [$w coords slider] 2]
    $w move right [expr $nx-110] 0
    # Move everything into view
    $w move all 10 10

    # Make the canvas fit comfortably around the image
    set bbox [$w bbox all]
    set height [expr [lindex $bbox 3]+4]
    $w config -height $height -width [expr $width+30]

    # Bind drag actions
    $w bind left  <Button-1> {Scale2Mark %W %x lbox}
    $w bind right <Button-1> {Scale2Mark %W %x rbox}
    $w bind left  <B1-Motion> {Scale2Drag %W %x lbox}
    $w bind right <B1-Motion> {Scale2Drag %W %x rbox}
}
```

The slider is constructed with absolute coordinates, and then it is scaled to the desired width. The alternative is to compute the coordinates based on the desired width. I have found it clearer to use numbers when creating the initial layout as opposed to using `expr` or introducing more variables. The `scale` operation stretches the slider bar to the correct length. The `scale` operation takes a reference point, which in our case is (0, 0), and independent scale factors for the X and Y dimensions. The scale factor is computed from the `width` parameter, taking into account the extra length added (10) so that the distance between the left edge of the slider boxes is `$width`:

```
set scale [expr ($width+10) / 110.0]
$w scale slider 0 0 $scale 1.0
```

The `move` operation repositions the right box and right hanging text. If the marker boxes are scaled, their shape gets distorted. The `coords` operation returns a list of four numbers: *x1 y1 x2 y2*. The distance to move is just the difference between the new right coordinate and the value used when constructing the slider initially. The box and text share the same tag, `right`, so they are both moved with a single `move` operation:

```
set nx [lindex [$w coords slider] 2]
$w move right [expr $nx-110] 0
```

After the slider is constructed, it is shifted away from (0, 0), which is the upper-left corner of the canvas. The `bbox` operation returns four coordinates: *x1 y1 x2 y2*, that define the bounding box of the items with the given tag. In the example, *y1* is zero, so *y2* gives us the height of the image. The information returned by `bbox` can be off by a few pixels, and the example needs a few more pixels of height to avoid clipping the text. The width is computed based on the extra length added for the marker box, the 10 pixels the whole image was shifted, and 10 more for the same amount of space on the right side:

```
set bbox [$w bbox all]
set height [expr [lindex $bbox 3]+4]
$w config -height $height -width [expr $width+30]
```

Bindings are defined for the box and hanging text. The general tags `left` and `right` are used for the bindings. This means that you can drag either the box or the text to move the slider. The pathname of the canvas is passed into these procedures so that you could have more than one double slider in your interface:

```
$w bind left  <Button-1> {Scale2Mark %W %x lbox}
$w bind right <Button-1> {Scale2Mark %W %x rbox}
$w bind left  <B1-Motion> {Scale2Drag %W %x lbox}
$w bind right <B1-Motion> {Scale2Drag %W %x rbox}
```

Example 37–4 Moving the markers for the min max scale.

```
proc Scale2Mark { w x what } {
    global scale2
    # Remember the anchor point for the drag
    set scale2($w,$what) $x
}
```

```
proc Scale2Drag { w x what } {
    global scale2

    # Compute delta and update anchor point
    set x1 $scale2($w,$what)
    set scale2($w,$what) $x
    set dx [expr $x - $x1]

    # Find out where the boxes are currently
    set rx [lindex [$w coords rbox] 0]
    set lx [lindex [$w coords lbox] 0]

    if {$what == "lbox"} {
        # Constrain the movement to be between the
        # left edge and the right marker.
        if {$lx + $dx > $rx} {
            set dx [expr $rx - $lx]
            set scale2($w,$what) $rx
        } elseif {$lx + $dx < $scale2($w,L)} {
            set dx [expr $scale2($w,L) - $lx]
            set scale2($w,$what) $scale2($w,L)
        }
        $w move left $dx 0

        # Update the minimum value and the hanging text
        set lx [lindex [$w coords lbox] 0]
        set scale2($w,min) [expr int($scale2($w,Min) + \
            ($lx-$scale2($w,L)) * $scale2($w,scale))]
        $w itemconfigure lnum -text $scale2($w,min)
    } else {
        # Constrain the movement to be between the
        # right edge and the left marker
        if {$rx + $dx < $lx} {
            set dx [expr $lx - $rx]
            set scale2($w,$what) $lx
        } elseif {$rx + $dx > $scale2($w,R)} {
            set dx [expr $scale2($w,R) - $rx]
            set scale2($w,$what) $scale2($w,R)
        }
        $w move right $dx 0

        # Update the maximum value and the hanging text
        set rx [lindex [$w coords right] 0]
        set scale2($w,max) [expr int($scale2($w,Min) + \
            ($rx-$scale2($w,L)) * $scale2($w,scale))]
        $w itemconfigure rnum -text $scale2($w,max)
    }
}
proc Scale2Value {w} {
    global scale2
    # Return the current values of the double slider
    return [list $scale2($w,min) $scale2($w,max)]
}
```

The Scale2Mark procedure initializes an anchor position, scale2($w,$what), and Scale2Drag uses this to detect how far the mouse has moved. The change in position, dx, is constrained so that the markers cannot move outside their bounds. The anchor is updated if a constraint was used, and this means that the marker will not move until the mouse is moved back over the marker. (Try commenting out the assignments to scale2($w,$what) inside the if statement.) After the marker and hanging text are moved, the value of the associated parameter is computed based on the parameters of the scale. The Scale2Value procedure queries the current values of the double slider.

Canvas Objects

The next several sections describe the built-in object types for the canvas: arc, bitmap, image, line, oval, polygon, rectangle, text, and window. Each object has its own set of attributes, and some attributes are found on most or all object types. Table 37–1 lists the common item attributes found on all or most objects. All -active and -disabled attributes were added in Tk 8.3, as were the -state attribute, the -offset attribute, and those attributes related to dashes.

Table 37–1 Common canvas item attributes.

-dash *pattern* -activedash *pattern* -disableddash *pattern*	The dash pattern of the line or outline when in the normal, active (the mouse over the object), and disabled states. (Tk 8.3)
-dashoffset *offset*	The starting offset distance into the pattern provided by the -dash option. (Tk 8.3)
-fill *color* -activefill *color* -disabledfill *color*	The color of the interior of the object when in the normal, active (the mouse over the object), and disabled states. (Tk 8.3, except -fill)
-stipple *bitmap* -activestipple *bitmap* -disabledstipple *bitmap*	The stipple pattern for the fill when in the normal, active (the mouse over the object), and disabled states. (Tk 8.3, except -stipple)
-offset *offset*	The stipple offset in the form *x,y* or *side*. *side* can be n, ne, e, se, s, sw, w, nw, or center. *x,y* is a distance relative to the canvas origin; putting # in front of the coordinate pair indicates using the toplevel origin instead. (Tk 8.3)
-outline *color* -activeoutline *color* -disabledoutline *color*	The color of the outline when in the normal, active (the mouse over the object), and disabled states. (Tk 8.3, except -outline)

Table 37–1 Common canvas item attributes. (Continued)

`-outlinestipple` *bitmap* `-activeoutlinestipple` *bitmap* `-disabledoutlinestipple` *bitmap*	The stipple pattern for the outline when in the `normal`, active (the mouse over the object), and `disabled` states. (Tk 8.3, except `-outlinestipple`)
`-width` *num* `-activewidth` *num* `-disabledwidth` *num*	Width, in canvas coordinates, of the line or outline when in the `normal`, active (the mouse over the object), and `disabled` states. (Tk 8.3, except `-width`)
`-state` *state*	`normal`, `disabled`, or `hidden`. This overrides the canvas widget's `state` attribute. (Tk 8.3)
`-tags` *tagList*	List of tags for the object.

Every object has a `-tags` attribute used to label the object with a list of symbolic names. Most objects, even `text` objects, specify their color with the `-fill` attribute; only the `bitmap` object uses `-foreground` and `-background`. If the object has a border, the color of the border is specified with `-outline`, and the thickness of the outline is specified with `-width`. Starting in Tk 8.3, lines and objects with borders have a variety of `-dash` attributes for drawing dashed lines and borders.

Canvas Widget and Canvas Object State Options

Tk 8.3 added the `-state` attribute to the canvas widget and all canvas objects. The canvas `state` attribute can be set to `normal` (the default) or `disabled`, which provides a default state for all objects on the canvas. If an individual canvas object's `-state` attribute is the empty string (the default), then it inherits the canvas state. However, you can override the "global" canvas state for an individual object by setting its `-state` attribute to `normal`, `disabled`, or `hidden`.

An object in the `normal` state is visible and any bindings defined for it are fully functional. Additionally, if the mouse is over a `normal` object, it is *activated* and any `-active*` attributes defined for the object take effect. As you would expect, an object in the `hidden` state is not visible, and its bindings are inactive. An object in the disabled state is visible, but its bindings are inactive and it does not activate when the mouse is over it; additionally, any `-disabled*` attributes defined for the object take effect.

Dashed Lines

Tk 8.3 introduced the ability to draw lines and object outlines using dashed lines. The primary object attribute for controlling the dash pattern is `-dash`, although `-activedash` and `-disableddash` attributes are available for controlling the dash pattern in different object states.

Each of these attributes accepts a *dash pattern* as a value. One dash pattern format is a list of integers. Each element represents the number of pixels of a line segment. Only the odd segments are drawn using the -outline color. The other segments are drawn transparent. For example the following command draws a line with 6-pixel dashes separated by 2-pixel spaces:

```
$c create line -dash {6 2}
```

The other dash pattern format is a string containing any combination of the characters shown in Table 37–2.

Table 37–2 Canvas dash pattern characters

.	Dash 1/2 of the length of the following space
,	Dash equal to the length of the following space
–	Dash 1 1/2 times the length of the following space
_	Dash double the length of the following space
space	Doubles the length of the space

For example, the dash pattern {_ . , } is roughly equivalent to {8 4 2 8 4 4}

The main difference of the string-based syntax versus the list-based syntax is that it the string-based syntax is *shape-conserving*. This means that all values in the dash list are multiplied by the line width before display. This assures that "." is always displayed as a dot and "–" as a dash regardless of the line width.

Finally, the -dashoffset attribute specifies the starting offset (in pixels) into the pattern provided by -dash.

Not all dash patterns are supported on all platforms.

On systems that support only a limited set of dash patterns, the dash pattern is displayed as the closest dash pattern that is available. For example, on Windows the dash patterns {.} and {,} and {. } and {, } are displayed identically.

Arc Items

An arc is a section of an oval. The dimensions of the oval are determined by four coordinates that are its bounding box. The arc is then determined by two angles, the start angle and the extent. The region of the oval can be filled or unfilled, and there are three different ways to define the fill region. The pieslice style connects the arc with the center point of the oval. The chord style connects the two end points of the arc. The arc style just draws the arc itself and there is no fill. Example 37–5 shows three arcs with the same bounding box but different styles and angles:

Example 37–5 Canvas `arc` items.

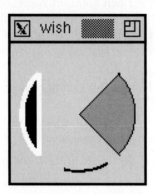

```
# $c is a canvas
$c create arc 10 10 100 100 -start 45 -extent -90 \
    -style pieslice -fill orange -outline black
$c create arc 10 10 100 100 -start 135 -extent 90 \
    -style chord -fill blue -outline white -width 4
$c create arc 10 10 100 100 -start 255 -extent 45 \
    -style arc -outline black -width 3
```

An `arc` object support all of the object attributes listed in Table 37–1. Table 37–3 lists the additional attributes supported by `arc` objects.

Table 37–3 Arc attributes.

`-extent` *degrees*	The length of the arc in the counter-clockwise direction.
`-start` *degrees*	The starting angle of the arc.
`-style` *style*	`pieslice`, `chord`, `arc`.

Bitmap Items

A bitmap is a simple graphic with a foreground and background color. One bit per pixel is used to choose between the foreground and the background. If you do not specify a background color, the background bits are clear and the canvas background shows through. A canvas `bitmap` item is positioned with two coordinates and an anchor position. Its size is determined by the bitmap data. The `bitmap` itself is specified with a symbolic name or by the name of a file that contains its definition. If the name begins with an @, it indicates a file name. The bitmaps built into Tk are shown in the example below. Chapter 50 outlines the C interface for registering bitmaps under a name.

Example 37–6 Canvas `bitmap` items.

```
set o [$c create bitmap 10 10 -bitmap @candle.xbm -anchor nw\
    -background white -foreground blue]
set x [lindex [$c bbox $o] 2] ;# Right edge of bitmap
foreach builtin {error gray12 gray50 hourglass \
            info questhead question warning} {
    incr x 20
    set o [$c create bitmap $x 30 -bitmap $builtin -anchor c]
    set x [lindex [$c bbox $o] 2]
}
```

A `bitmap` object supports only the `-state` and `-tags` attributes listed in Table 37–1. Table 37–4 lists the additional attributes supported by `bitmap` objects.

Table 37–4 Bitmap attributes.

`-anchor` *position*	Anchor: c (default), n, ne, e, se, s, sw, w, or nw.
`-background` *color* `-activebackground` *color* `-disabledbackground` *color*	The background color (for zero bits) when in the normal, active (the mouse over the object), and disabled states. (Tk 8.3, except `-background`)
`-bitmap` *name* `-activebitmap` *name* `-disabledbitmap` *name*	The bitmap to display when in the normal, active (the mouse over the object), and disabled states. (Tk 8.3, except `-bitmap`)
`-foreground` *color* `-activeforeground` *color* `-disabledforeground` *color*	The foreground color (for one bits) when in the normal, active (the mouse over the object), and disabled states. (Tk 8.3, except `-foreground`)

Image Items

The canvas `image` objects use the general image mechanism of Tk. You must first define an image using the `image` command, which is described in Chapter 41 in the section *Bitmaps and Images*. Once you have defined an image, all you need to specify for the canvas is its position, anchor point, and any tags. The size and color information is set when the image is defined. If an image is redefined, anything displaying that image automatically gets updated. Example 37–7 creates one image and puts six instances of it on a canvas:

Example 37–7 Canvas `image` items.

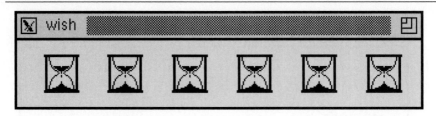

```
image create bitmap hourglass2 \
    -file hourglass.bitmap -maskfile hourglass.mask \
    -background white -foreground blue
for {set x 20} {$x < 300} {incr x 20} {
    $c create image $x 10 -image hourglass2 -anchor nw
    incr x [image width hourglass2]
}
```

An `image` object supports only the `-state` and `-tags` attributes listed in Table 37–1. Table 37–5 lists the additional attributes supported by `image` objects.

Table 37–5 Image attributes.

`-anchor` *position*	Anchor: c (default), n, ne, e, se, s, sw, w, or nw.
`-image` *name* `-activeimage` *name* `-disabledimage` *name*	The name of an image to use when in the `normal`, active (the mouse over the object), and `disabled` states. (Tk 8.3, except `-image`)

Line Items

A line has two or more sets of coordinates, where each set of coordinates defines an end point of a line segment. The segments can be joined in several different styles, and the whole line can be drawn with a spline fit as opposed to straight-line segments. The next example draws a line in two steps. In the first pass, single-segment lines are drawn. When the stroke completes, these are replaced with a single line segment that is drawn with a spline curve.

Example 37–8 A canvas stroke drawing example.

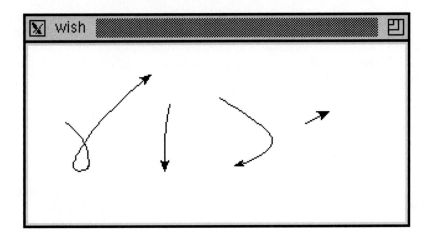

```
proc StrokeInit {} {
    canvas .c ; pack .c
    bind .c <Button-1> {StrokeBegin %W %x %y}
    bind .c <B1-Motion> {Stroke %W %x %y}
    bind .c <ButtonRelease-1> {StrokeEnd %W %x %y}
}
proc StrokeBegin { w x y } {
    global stroke
    catch {unset stroke}
    set stroke(N) 0
    set stroke(0) [list $x $y]
}
proc Stroke { w x y } {
    global stroke
    set coords $stroke($stroke(N))
    lappend coords $x $y
    incr stroke(N)
    set stroke($stroke(N)) [list $x $y]
    # eval gets the coordinates into individual arguments
    eval {$w create line} $coords {-tag segments}
}
proc StrokeEnd { w x y } {
    global stroke
    set coords {}
    for {set i 0} {$i <= $stroke(N)} {incr i} {
        append coords $stroke($i) " "
    }
    $w delete segments
    eval {$w create line} $coords \
        {-tag line -joinstyle round -smooth true -arrow last}
}
```

IV. Tk Widgets

Example 37–8 uses the `stroke` array to hold the points of the line as it builds up the stroke. At the end of the stroke it assembles the points into a list. The `eval` command concatenates this list of points onto the `create line` command. Recall that `eval` uses `concat` if it gets multiple arguments. The other parts of the `create line` command are protected by braces so they get evaluated only once. Chapter 10 describes this trick in more detail on page 134. Note that as of Tk 8.3 this would not be necessary as the `create line` command can now accept a list of coordinates as a single argument.

The arrow attribute adds an arrow head to the end of the stroke. If you try this example you will notice that the arrow is not always aimed as you expect. This is because there are often many points generated close together as you release the mouse button. In fact, the X and Y coordinates seen by `StrokeEnd` are always the same as those seen by the last `Stroke` call. If you add this duplicate point to the end of the list of points, no arrowhead is drawn at all. In practice you might want to make `Stroke` filter out points that are too close together.

A `line` object supports all of the attributes listed in Table 37–1 except for `-offset`, the `-outline` family of attributes, and the `-outlinestipple` family of attributes. Remember that the `-fill` attribute controls the color in which the line is drawn (not the `-outline` attribute, as is common for other canvas items). Table 37–6 lists the additional attributes supported by `line` objects. The `capstyle` affects the way the ends of the line are drawn. The `joinstyle` affects the way line segments are joined together. The `capstyle` and `joinstyle` attributes are from the X window system and may not be implemented on the Macintosh and Windows platforms.

Table 37–6 Line attributes.

`-arrow` *where*	Arrow location: `none`, `first`, `last`, or `both`.
`-arrowshape` *{a b c}*	Three parameters that describe the shape of the arrow. `c` is the width and `b` is the overall length. `a` is the length of the part that touches the line (e.g., `8 10 3`).
`-capstyle` *what*	Line ends: `butt`, `projecting`, or `round`.
`-joinstyle` *what*	Line joints: `bevel`, `miter`, or `round`.
`-smooth` *boolean*	If `true`, a spline curve is drawn.
`-splinesteps` *num*	Number of line segments that approximate the spline.

Oval Items

An `oval` is defined by two sets of coordinates that define its bounding box. If the box is square, a circle is drawn. You can set the color of the interior of the oval as well as the outline of the oval. A sampler of ovals is shown in Example 37–9.

Example 37–9 Canvas `oval` items.

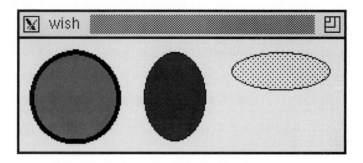

```
$c create oval 10 10 80 80 -fill red -width 4
$c create oval 100 10 150 80 -fill blue -width 0
$c create oval 170 10 250 40 -fill black -stipple gray12
```

An `oval` object support all of the object attributes listed in Table 37–1. There are no additional attributes supported by `oval` objects.

Polygon Items

A `polygon` is a closed shape specified by sets of points, one for each vertex of the polygon. The vertices can be connected with smooth or straight lines. Example 37–10 creates a stop sign. The picture is centered at (0, 0) and then moved fully onto the canvas:

Example 37–10 Canvas `polygon` items.

```
$c create poly 20 -40 40 -20 40 20 20 40 -20 40 \
   -40 20 -40 -20 -20 -40 -fill red \
   -outline white -width 5
$c create text 0 0 -text STOP -fill white \
   -font {helvetica 18 bold}
$c move all 50 50
```

A `polygon` object support all of the object attributes listed in Table 37–1. Table 37–7 lists the additional attributes supported by `polygon` objects

Table 37–7 Polygon attributes.

`-joinstyle` *what*	Line joints: `bevel`, `miter`, or `round`.
`-smooth` *boolean*	If `true`, a spline curve is drawn around the points.
`-splinesteps` *num*	Number of line segments that approximate the spline.

Rectangle Items

A `rectangle` is specified with two coordinates that are its opposite corners. A rectangle can have a fill color and an outline color. If you do not specify a fill, then the background of the canvas (or other objects) shows through. If you stipple the fill, the background also shows through the clear bits of the stipple pattern. You must use a second rectangle if you want the stippled fill to completely hide what is behind it. Example 37–11 drags out a box as the user drags the mouse. All it requires is remembering the last rectangle drawn so that it can be deleted when the next box is drawn:

Example 37–11 Dragging out a box.

```
proc BoxInit {} {
    canvas .c -bg white ; pack .c
    bind .c <Button-1> {BoxBegin %W %x %y}
    bind .c <B1-Motion> {BoxDrag %W %x %y}
}
proc BoxBegin { w x y } {
    global box
    set box($w,anchor) [list $x $y]
    catch {unset box($w,last)}
}
proc BoxDrag { w x y } {
    global box
    catch {$w delete $box($w,last)}
    set box($w,last) [eval {$w create rect} $box($w,anchor) \
        {$x $y -tag box}]
}
```

The example uses `box($w,anchor)` to record the start of the box. This is a list with the X and Y coordinates. The `eval` command is used so that this list can be spliced into the `create rect` command. Note that as of Tk 8.3 this would not be necessary as the `create rect` command can now accept a list of coordinates as a single argument.

A `rectangle` object support all of the object attributes listed in Table 37–1. There are no additional attributes supported by `rectangle` objects.

Text Items

The canvas `text` item provides yet another way to display and edit text. It supports selection, editing, and it can extend onto multiple lines. The position of a `text` item is specified by one set of coordinates and an anchor position. The size of the text is determined by the number of lines and the length of each line. A new line is started if there is a newline in the text string. If a `width` is specified, in screen units, then any line that is longer than this is wrapped onto multiple lines. The wrap occurs before a space character.

The editing and selection operations for `text` items use indices to specify positions within a given text item. These are very similar to those used in the entry widget. Table 37–8 summarizes the indices for canvas `text` items.

Table 37–8 Indices for canvas `text` items.

0	Index of the first character.
end	Index just past the last character.
number	Index a character, where *number* counts from zero.
insert	Index of the character right after the insertion cursor.
sel.first	Index of the first character in the selection.
sel.last	Index of the last character in the selection.
@*x,y*	Index of the character under the specified X and Y coordinate.

There are several canvas operations that manipulate text items. These are similar to some of the operations of the entry widget. The `dchars` and `select to` operations treat the second index differently than the corresponding operations in the entry and text widget. The character at the second index *is* included in the operation (e.g., deleted), while in the entry and text widget it is not.

The canvas text operations are parameterized by the tag or ID of the canvas object being manipulated. If the tag refers to more than one object, then the operations apply to the first object in the display list that supports an insert cursor. The display list is described on page 581. Table 37–9 summarizes the operations on `text` items. In the table `$t` is a text item or tag and `$c` is a canvas.

Table 37–9 Canvas operations that apply to `text` items.

`$c dchars $t` *first* `?`*last*`?`	Deletes the characters from *first* through *last*, or just the character at *first*.
`$c focus ?$t?`	Sets input focus to the specified item, or returns the ID of the item with the focus if it is not given.
`$c icursor $t` *index*	Sets the insert cursor to just before *index*.
`$c index $t` *index*	Returns the numerical value of *index*.

Table 37–9 Canvas operations that apply to `text` items. (Continued)

`$c insert $t index string`	Inserts the string just before *index*.
`$c select adjust $t index`	Moves the boundary of an existing selection.
`$c select clear`	Clears the selection.
`$c select from $t index`	Starts a selection.
`$c select item`	Returns the ID of the selected item, if any.
`$c select to $t index`	Extends the selection to the specified *index*.

There are no default bindings for canvas `text` items. Example 37–12 sets up some basic bindings for canvas text items. The `<Button-1>` and `<Button-2>` bindings are on the canvas as a whole. The rest of the bindings are on items with the `text` tag. You must add the `text` tag to text items that should share the editable text behavior. Small procedures are introduced for each binding to hide the details and any local variables needed in the operations.

Canvas find overlapping vs. find closest.

The `CanvasFocus` procedure uses the canvas `find overlapping` operation to see if a text object has been clicked. This must be used because `find closest` finds an object no matter how far away it is. It also uses the `type` operation to make sure only text objects are given the focus. If you want other object types to respond to key events, you should change that.

The `CanvasPaste` procedure does one of two things. It pastes the selection into the canvas item that has the focus. If no item has the focus, then a new `text` item is created with the selection as its value:

Example 37–12 Simple edit bindings for canvas `text` items.

```
proc Canvas_EditBind { c } {
    bind $c <Button-1> \
        {CanvasFocus %W [%W canvasx %x] [%W canvasy %y]}
    bind $c <Button-2> \
        {CanvasPaste %W [%W canvasx %x] [%W canvasy %y]}
    bind $c <<Cut>> {CanvasTextCopy %W; CanvasDelete %W}
    bind $c <<Copy>> {CanvasTextCopy %W}
    bind $c <<Paste>> {CanvasPaste %W}
    $c bind text <Button-1> \
        {CanvasTextHit %W [%W canvasx %x] [%W canvasy %y]}
    $c bind text <B1-Motion> \
        {CanvasTextDrag %W [%W canvasx %x] [%W canvasy %y]}
    $c bind text <Delete> {CanvasDelete %W}
    $c bind text <Control-d> {CanvasDelChar %W}
    $c bind text <Control-h> {CanvasBackSpace %W}
    $c bind text <BackSpace> {CanvasBackSpace %W}
    $c bind text <Control-Delete> {CanvasErase %W}
    $c bind text <Return> {CanvasNewline %W}
    $c bind text <Any-Key> {CanvasInsert %W %A}
    $c bind text <Key-Right> {CanvasMoveRight %W}
```

```
        $c bind text <Control-f> {CanvasMoveRight %W}
        $c bind text <Key-Left> {CanvasMoveLeft %W}
        $c bind text <Control-b> {CanvasMoveLeft %W}
}
proc CanvasFocus {c x y} {
    focus $c
    set id [$c find overlapping [expr $x-2] [expr $y-2] \
            [expr $x+2] [expr $y+2]]
    if {($id == {}) || ([$c type $id] != "text")} {
        set t [$c create text $x $y -text "" \
            -tags text -anchor nw]
        $c focus $t
        $c select clear
        $c icursor $t 0
    }
}
proc CanvasTextHit {c x y {select 1}} {
    $c focus current
    $c icursor current @$x,$y
    $c select clear
    $c select from current @$x,$y
}
proc CanvasTextDrag {c x y} {
    $c select to current @$x,$y
}
proc CanvasDelete {c} {
    if {[$c select item] != {}} {
        $c dchars [$c select item] sel.first sel.last
    } elseif {[$c focus] != {}} {
        $c dchars [$c focus] insert
    }
}
proc CanvasTextCopy {c} {
    if {[$c select item] != {}} {
        clipboard clear
        set t [$c select item]
        set text [$c itemcget $t -text]
        set start [$c index $t sel.first]
        set end [$c index $t sel.last]
        clipboard append [string range $text $start $end]
    } elseif {[$c focus] != {}} {
        clipboard clear
        set t [$c focus]
        set text [$c itemcget $t -text]
        clipboard append $text
    }
}
proc CanvasDelChar {c} {
    if {[$c focus] != {}} {
        $c dchars [$c focus] insert
    }
}
proc CanvasBackSpace {c} {
    if {[$c select item] != {}} {
        $c dchars [$c select item] sel.first sel.last
```

IV. Tk Widgets

```
        } elseif {[$c focus] != {}} {
            set _t [$c focus]
            $c icursor $_t [expr [$c index $_t insert]-1]
            $c dchars $_t insert
        }
    }
    proc CanvasErase {c} {
        $c delete [$c focus]
    }
    proc CanvasNewline {c} {
        $c insert [$c focus] insert \n
    }
    proc CanvasInsert {c char} {
        $c insert [$c focus] insert $char
    }
    proc CanvasPaste {c {x {}} {y {}}} {
        if {[catch {selection get} _s] &&
            [catch {selection get -selection CLIPBOARD} _s]} {
            return ;# No selection
        }
        set id [$c focus]
        if {[string length $id] == 0 } {
            set id [$c find withtag current]
        }
        if {[string length $id] == 0 } {
            # No object under the mouse
            if {[string length $x] == 0} {
                # Keyboard paste
                set x [expr [winfo pointerx $c] - [winfo rootx $c]]
                set y [expr [winfo pointery $c] - [winfo rooty $c]]
            }
            CanvasFocus $c $x $y
        } else {
            $c focus $id
        }
        $c insert [$c focus] insert $_s
    }

    proc CanvasMoveRight {c} {
        $c icursor [$c focus] [expr [$c index current insert]+1]
    }
    proc CanvasMoveLeft {c} {
        $c icursor [$c focus] [expr [$c index current insert]-1]
    }
```

Of the attributes listed in Table 37–1, text objects support only the -fill family of attributes, the -stipple family of attributes, and the -state and -tags attributes. Table 37–10 specifies the additional attributes for text items. Note that there are no foreground and background attributes. Instead, the fill color specifies the color for the text. It is possible to stipple the text as well. Additionally, the -width attribute is treated differently than for other canvas objects.

Table 37–10 Text attributes

-anchor *position*	Anchor: c (default), n, ne, e, se, s, sw, w, or nw.
-font *font*	The font for the text.
-justify *how*	Justification: left, right, or center.
-text *string*	The string to display.
-width *width*	The width, in screen units, before text is wrapped

Window Items

A window item lets you position other Tk widgets on a canvas. The position is specified by one set of coordinates and an anchor position. You can also specify the width and height, or you can let the widget determine its own size. The following example uses a canvas to provide a scrolling surface for a large set of labeled entries. A frame is created and a set of labeled entry widgets are packed into it. This main frame is put onto the canvas as a single window item. This way we let grid take care of arranging all the labeled entries. The size of the canvas is set up so that a whole number of labeled entries are displayed. The scroll region and scroll increment are set up so that clicking on the scrollbar arrows brings one new labeled entry completely into view.

Example 37–13 Using a canvas to scroll a set of widgets.

```
proc Example37-13 { top title labels } {
    # Create a resizable toplevel window
    toplevel $top
    wm minsize $top 200 100
    wm title $top $title

    # Create a frame for buttons,
    # Only Dismiss does anything useful
    set f [frame $top.buttons -bd 4]
    button $f.quit -text Dismiss -command "destroy $top"
    button $f.save -text Save
    button $f.reset -text Reset
    pack $f.quit $f.save $f.reset -side right
    pack $f -side top -fill x

    # Create a scrolling canvas
    frame $top.c
    canvas $top.c.canvas -width 10 -height 10 \
        -yscrollcommand [list $top.c.yscroll set]
    scrollbar $top.c.yscroll -orient vertical \
        -command [list $top.c.canvas yview]
    pack $top.c.yscroll -side right -fill y
    pack $top.c.canvas -side left -fill both -expand true
    pack $top.c -side top -fill both -expand true

    Scrolled_EntrySet $top.c.canvas $labels
}
```

```
proc Scrolled_EntrySet { canvas labels } {
    # Create one frame to hold everything
    # and position it on the canvas
    set f [frame $canvas.f -bd 0]
    $canvas create window 0 0 -anchor nw -window $f

    # Create and grid the labeled entries
    set i 0
    foreach label $labels {
        label $f.label$i -text $label
        entry $f.entry$i
        grid $f.label$i $f.entry$i
        grid $f.label$i -sticky w
        grid $f.entry$i -sticky we
        incr i
    }
    set child $f.entry0

    # Wait for the window to become visible and then
    # set up the scroll region based on
    # the requested size of the frame, and set
    # the scroll increment based on the
    # requested height of the widgets

    tkwait visibility $child
    set bbox [grid bbox $f 0 0]
    set incr [lindex $bbox 3]
    set width [winfo reqwidth $f]
    set height [winfo reqheight $f]
    $canvas config -scrollregion "0 0 $width $height"
    $canvas config -yscrollincrement $incr
    set max [llength $labels]
    if {$max > 10} {
        set max 10
    }
    set height [expr $incr * $max]
    $canvas config -width $width -height $height
}
Example37-13 .ex "An example" {
    alpha beta gamma delta epsilon zeta eta theta iota kappa
    lambda mu nu xi omicron pi rho sigma tau upsilon
    phi chi psi omega}
```

 The `tkwait visibility` command is important to the example. It causes the script to suspend execution until the top-level window, `$top`, is displayed on the screen. The `tkwait` is necessary so the right information gets returned by the `grid bbox` commands. By waiting for a subframe of the main frame, `$child`, we ensure that grid has gone through all its processing to position the interior widgets. The canvas's scroll region is set to be just large enough to hold the complete frame. The scroll increment is set to the height of one of the grid cells. Each click on the scrollbar arrows brings one new grid row completely into view.

A `window` object supports only the `-state` and `-tags` attributes listed in Table 37–1. Table 37–11 lists the additional attributes supported by `window` objects. Note that the `-width` attribute is treated differently than for other canvas objects.

Table 37–11 Window attributes.

`-anchor` *position*	Anchor: c (default), n, ne, e, se, s, sw, w, or nw.
`-height` *height*	The height, in screen units, for the widget. If the value is an empty string (default), then the window is given whatever height it requests internally.
`-width` *width*	The width, in screen units, for the widget. If the value is an empty string (default), then the window is given whatever width it requests internally.
`-window` *name*	The name of the widget to display within the canvas.

Canvas Operations

Table 37–12 summarizes the operations on canvas widgets. In the table, `$c` is a canvas. `$t` represents a numerical object ID, a canvas tag or — in Tk 8.3 or later — a logical combination of tags using the operators `&&` (and), `||` (or), `^` (exclusive or), `!` (not), and parenthesized subexpressions, grouped as a single argument (for example, `{(plot1 || plot2) && !fixed}`). In some cases, an operation only applies to a single object. In these cases, if a tag or tag expression identifies several objects, the first object in the display list is operated on.

The canvas *display list* refers to the global order among canvas objects. New objects are put at the end of the display list. Objects later in the display list obscure objects earlier in the list. The term *above* refers to objects later in the display list.

Table 37–9 describes several of the canvas operations that only apply to `text` objects. They are `dchars`, `focus`, `index`, `icursor`, `insert`, and `select`. Table 37–12 does not repeat those operations.

Table 37–12 Operations on a `canvas` widget.

`$c addtag` *tag* `above` `$t`	Adds *tag* to the item just above `$t` in the display list.
`$c addtag` *tag* `all`	Adds *tag* to all objects in the canvas.
`$c addtag` *tag* `below` `$t`	Adds *tag* to the item just below `$t` in the display list.

Table 37–12 Operations on a `canvas` widget. (Continued)

`$c addtag tag closest x y ?halo? ?start?`	Adds `tag` to the item closest to the `x` `y` position. If more than one object is the same distance away, or if more than one object is within `halo` pixels, then the last one in the display list (uppermost) is returned. If `start` is specified, the closest object after `start` in the display list is returned.
`$c addtag tag enclosed x1 y1 x2 y2`	Adds `tag` to the items completely enclosed in the specified region. *x1* <= *x2*, *y1* <= *y2*.
`$c addtag tag overlapping x1 y1 x2 y2`	Adds `tag` to the items that overlap the specified region. *x1* <= *x2*, *y1* <= *y2*.
`$c addtag tag withtag $t`	Adds `tag` to the items identified by `$t`.
`$c bbox $t ?tag tag ...?`	Returns the bounding box of the items identified by the tag(s) in the form *x1* *y1* *x2* *y2*
`$c bind $t ?sequence? ?command?`	Sets or queries the bindings of canvas items.
`$c canvasx screenx ?grid?`	Maps from the X screen coordinate `screenx` to the X coordinate in canvas space, rounded to multiples of `grid` if specified.
`$c canvasy screeny ?grid?`	Maps from screen Y to canvas Y.
`$c cget option`	Returns the value of `option` for the canvas.
`$c configure ...`	Queries or updates the attributes of the canvas.
`$c coords $t ?x1 y1 ...?`	Queries or modifies the coordinates of the item. As of Tk 8.3, a list of coordinates can be provided as a single argument.
`$c create type x y ?x2 y2 ...? ?opt value ...?`	Creates a canvas object of the specified `type` at the specified coordinates. As of Tk 8.3, a list of coordinates can be provided as a single argument.
`$c delete $t ?tag ...?`	Deletes the item(s) specified by the tag(s) or ID(s).
`$c dtag $t ?deltag?`	Removes the specified tags from the items identified by `$t`. If `deltag` is omitted, it defaults to `$t`.
`$c find addtagSearch ...`	Returns the IDs of the tags that match the `addtag` search specification: `above`, `all`, `below`, `closest`, `enclosed`, `overlapping` and `withtag`.
`$c gettags $t`	Returns the tags associated with the first item identified by `$t`.
`$c itemcget $t option`	Returns the value of `option` for item `$t`.
`$c itemconfigure $t ...`	Queries or reconfigures item `$t`.
`$c lower $t ?belowThis?`	Moves the items identified by `$t` to the beginning of the display list, or just before `belowThis`.

Table 37–12 Operations on a `canvas` widget. (Continued)

`$c move $t dx dy`	Moves `$t` by the specified amount.
`$c postscript ...`	Generates Postscript. Table 37–13 lists options.
`$c raise $t ?aboveThis?`	Moves the items identified by `$t` to the end of the display list, or just after *aboveThis*.
`$c scale $t x0 y0 xS yS`	Scales the coordinates of the items identified by `$t`. The distance between *x0* and a given X coordinate changes by a factor of *xS*. Similarly for Y.
`$c scan mark x y`	Sets a mark for a scrolling operation.
`$c scan dragto x y`	Scrolls the canvas from the previous mark.
`$c type $t`	Returns the type of the first item identified by `$t`.
`$t xview`	Returns two fractions between zero and one that describes the amount of the canvas off-screen to the left and the amount of the canvas displayed.
`$t xview moveto fraction`	Positions the canvas so that *fraction* of the scroll region is off screen to the left.
`$t xview scroll num what`	Scrolls *num* of *what*, which is *units* or *pages*.
`$t yview`	Returns two fractions between zero and one that describes the amount of the canvas off screen to the top and the amount of the canvas displayed.
`$t yview moveto fraction`	Positions the text so that *fraction* of the canvas scroll region is off screen toward the top.
`$t yview scroll num what`	Scrolls *num* of *what*, which is *units* or *pages*.

Generating Postscript

The `postscript` operation generates Postscript based on the contents of a canvas. One limitation in earlier versions of Tk is that images and embedded windows are not captured in the Postscript output. As of Tk 8.3, images are included in the generated Postscript. Also, as of Tk 8.3 for Unix and Tk 8.4.1 for Windows, embedded windows are included in the generated Postscript if they are currently displayed on the screen (that is, displayed within the canvas's viewport and not obscured by other windows).

Table 37–13 summarizes all the options for generating Postscript.

Table 37–13 Canvas `postscript` options.

`-channel fid`	The channel identifier of a channel already opened for writing. The Postscript is written to that channel, and the channel is left open for further writing at the end of the operation. If `-channel` or `-file` are not specified, the Postscript is returned as the result of the command.
`-colormap varName`	The index of `varName` is a named color, and the contents of each element is the Postscript code to generate the RGB values for that color.
`-colormode mode`	`mode` is one of `color`, `grey`, or `mono`.
`-file name`	The file in which to write the Postscript. If `-file` or `-channel` are not specified, the Postscript is returned as the result of the command.
`-fontmap varName`	The index of `varName` is an X font name. Each element contains a list of two items: a Postscript font name and a point size.
`-height size`	Height of the area to print.
`-pageanchor anchor`	Anchor: c, n, ne, e, se, s, sw, w, or nw.
`-pageheight size`	Height of image on the output. A floating point number followed by c (centimeters), i (inches), m (millimeters), or p (printer points).
`-pagewidth size`	Width of image on the output.
`-pagex position`	The output X coordinate of the anchor point.
`-pagey position`	The output Y coordinate of the anchor point.
`-rotate boolean`	If true, rotates so that X axis is the long direction of the page (landscape orientation).
`-width size`	Width of the area to print.
`-x position`	Canvas X coordinate of left edge of the image.
`-y position`	Canvas Y coordinate of top edge of the image.

You control what region of the canvas is printed with the `-width`, `-height`, `-x`, and `-y` options. You control the size and location of this in the output with the `-pageanchor`, `-pagex`, `-pagey`, `-pagewidth`, and `-pageheight` options. The Postscript is written to the file named by the `-file` option, to a channel already opened for writing whose channel identifier is provided by the `-channel` option, or it is returned as the value of the `postscript` canvas operation.

You control fonts with a mapping from X screen fonts to Postscript fonts. Define an array where the index is the name of the X font and the contents are the name and pointsize of a Postscript font.

Example 37–14 positions a number of text objects with different fonts onto a canvas. For each different X font used, it records a mapping to a Postscript font. The example has a fairly simple font mapping, and in fact the canvas would probably have guessed the same font mapping itself. If you use more exotic screen fonts, you may need to help the canvas widget with an explicit font map.

The example positions the output at the upper-left corner of the printed page by using the -pagex, -pagey, and -pageanchor options. Recall that Postscript has its origin at the lower-left corner of the page.

Example 37–14 Generating Postscript from a canvas.

```
proc Setup {} {
    global fontMap
    canvas .c
    pack .c -fill both -expand true
    set x 10
    set y 10
    set last [.c create text $x $y -text "Font sampler" \
        -font fixed -anchor nw]

    # Create several strings in different fonts and sizes

    foreach family {times courier helvetica} {
        set weight bold
        switch -- $family {
            times { set fill blue; set psfont Times}
            courier { set fill green; set psfont Courier }
            helvetica { set fill red; set psfont Helvetica }
        }
        foreach size {10 14 24} {
            set y [expr 4+[lindex [.c bbox $last] 3]]

            # Guard against missing fonts
            if {[[catch {.c create text $x $y \
                    -text $family-$weight-$size \
                    -anchor nw -fill $fill \
                    -font -*-$family-$weight-*-*-*-$size-*} \
            it] == 0} {
                set fontMap(-*-$family-$weight-*-*-*-$size-*)\
                    [list $psfont $size]
                set last $it
            }
        }
    }
    set fontMap(fixed) [list Courier 12]
}
```

```
proc Postscript { c file } {
    global fontMap
    # Tweak the output color
    set colorMap(blue) {0.1 0.1 0.9 setrgbcolor}
    set colorMap(green) {0.0 0.9 0.1 setrgbcolor}
    # Position the text at the upper-left corner of
    # an 8.5 by 11 inch sheet of paper
    $c postscript -fontmap fontMap -colormap colorMap \
        -file $file \
        -pagex 0.i -pagey 11.i -pageanchor nw
}
```

Canvas Attributes

Table 37–14 lists the attributes for the `canvas` widget. The table uses the resource name, which has capitals at internal word boundaries. In Tcl commands, the attributes are specified with a dash and are all lowercase.

Table 37–14 Canvas attribute resource names.

background	The normal background color.
borderWidth	The width of the border around the canvas.
closeEnough	Distance from mouse to an overlapping object.
confine	Boolean. True constrains the view to the scroll region.
cursor	Cursor to display when mouse is over the widget.
height	Height, in screen units, of canvas display.
highlightBackground	Focus highlight color when widget does not have focus.
highlightColor	Color for input focus highlight border.
highlightThickness	Width of highlight border.
insertBackground	Background for area covered by insert cursor.
insertBorderwidth	Width of cursor border. Nonzero for 3D effect.
insertOffTime	Time, in milliseconds the insert cursor blinks off.
insertOnTime	Time, in milliseconds the insert cursor blinks on.
insertWidth	Width of insert cursor. Default is 2.
relief	flat, sunken, raised, groove, solid, or ridge.
scrollRegion	Left, top, right, and bottom coordinates of the canvas.
selectBackground	Background color of selection.
selectForeground	Foreground color of selection.

Table 37–14 Canvas attribute resource names. (Continued)

`selectBorderWidth`	Width of selection border. Nonzero for 3D effect.
`state`	The default state for canvas objects: `normal` or `disabled`. (Tk 8.3)
`takeFocus`	Controls focus changes from keyboard traversal.
`width`	Width in screen units for viewable area.
`xScrollCommand`	Tcl command prefix for horizontal scrolling.
`xScrollIncrement`	Distance for one scrolling unit in the X direction.
`yScrollCommand`	Tcl command prefix for vertical scrolling.
`yScrollIncrement`	Distance for one scrolling unit in the Y direction.

The scroll region of a canvas defines the boundaries of the canvas coordinate space. It is specified as four coordinates, *x1 y1 x2 y2* where (*x1, y1*) is the top-left corner and (*x2, y2*) is the lower-right corner. If the `confine` attribute is true, then the canvas cannot be scrolled outside this region. It is OK to position canvas objects partially or totally off the scroll region; they just may not be visible. The scroll increment attributes determine how much the canvas is scrolled when the user clicks on the arrows in the scrollbar.

The `closeEnough` attribute indicates how far away a position can be from an object and still be considered to overlap it. This applies to the `overlapping` search criteria.

IV. Tk Widgets

Hints

Screen Coordinates vs. Canvas Coordinates

The `canvasx` and `canvasy` operations map from a screen coordinate to a canvas coordinate. If the scroll region is larger than the display area, then you need to use these operations to map from the X and Y in an event (i.e., `%x` and `%y`) and the canvas coordinates. The typical use is:

```
set id [$c find closest [$c canvasx %x] [$c canvasy %y]]
```

Large Coordinate Spaces

Coordinates for canvas items are stored internally as floating point numbers, so the values returned by the `coords` operation will be floating point numbers. If you have a very large canvas, you may need to adjust the precision with which you see coordinates by setting the `tcl_precision` variable. This is an issue if you query coordinates, perform a computation on them, and then update the coordinates. (Tcl 8.0 changed the default `tcl_precision` from 6 to 12.)

Scaling and Rotation

The `scale` operation scales the coordinates of one or more canvas items. It is not possible to scale the whole coordinate space. The main problem with this is that you can lose precision when scaling and unscaling objects because their internal coordinates are actually changed by the scale operation. For simple cases this is not a problem, but in extreme cases it can show up.

The canvas does not support rotation.

Resources

There is no resource database support built into the canvas and its items. You can, however, define resources and query them yourself. For example, you could define:

```
*Canvas.foreground:    blue
```

This would have no effect by default. However, your code could look for this resource with `option get`, and specify this color directly for the `-fill` attribute of your objects:

```
set fg [option get $c foreground {}]
$c create rect 0 0 10 10 -fill $fg
```

The main reason to take this approach is to let your users customize the appearance of canvas objects without changing your code.

Objects with Many Points

The canvas implementation seems well optimized to handle lots of canvas objects. However, if an object like a line or a polygon has many points that define it, the implementation ends up scanning through these points linearly. This can adversely affect the time it takes to process mouse events in the area of the canvas containing such an item. Apparently any object in the vicinity of a mouse click is scanned to see if the mouse has hit it so that any bindings can be fired.

Selecting Canvas Items

Example 38–5 on page 596 implements cut and paste of canvas objects. The example exchanges the logical description of canvas objects with the selection mechanism.

Tk Details

Part V describes the rest of the Tk toolkit.

Chapter 38 describes the selection mechanism that is used for cut and paste between applications. It includes an example that implements cut and paste of graphical objects on a canvas.

Chapter 39 describes dialogs. Tk has several built-in dialogs that use the native platform look and feel. The chapter also describes how to build your own dialogs.

Chapter 40 is the first of three chapters that explain widget attributes in more detail. It describes size and layout attributes. Chapter 41 describes colors, images, and cursors. It explains how to use the bitmap and color photo image types. The chapter includes a complete map of the cursor font. Chapter 42 describes fonts and other text-related attributes. The extended example is a font selection application.

Chapter 43 describes the Tk send command that lets you send commands among Tk applications. It also presents a socket-based alternative that can be used among applications on different hosts and with the Safe-Tcl mechanism to limit the power of remotely invoked commands.

Chapter 44 explains how to interact with the window manager using the wm command. The chapter describes all the information available through the winfo command.

Chapter 45 builds upon Chapter 31 to create a user preferences package and an associated user interface. The preference package links a Tcl variable used in your application to a resource specification.

Chapter 46 presents a user interface to the binding mechanism. You can browse and edit bindings for widgets and classes with the interface.

Selections and the Clipboard

Cut and paste allows information exchange between applications, and it is built upon a general purpose selection mechanism. The `CLIPBOARD` selection is used to implement cut and paste on all platforms. X Windows applications may also use the `PRIMARY` selection. This chapter describes the `selection` and `clipboard` commands.

Copy and paste is a basic way to transfer data between just about any two applications. In Tk, copy and paste is based on a general selection mechanism where the selection has a name, type, format, and value. For the most part you can ignore these details because they are handled by the Tk widgets. However, you can also control the selection explicitly. This chapter describes the selection model and the `selection` and `clipboard` commands. The last section of this chapter presents an example that implements copy and paste of graphical objects in a canvas.

The Selection Model

The Windows and Macintosh selection model is simpler than the selection model used in X windows. In the Macintosh and Windows there is one selection, although that selection may store different types of data like text or images. Users copy data from an application into a clipboard, and later they paste it into another application.

In X windows the selection model is generalized to support more than one selection, and they are identified by names like `PRIMARY` and `CLIPBOARD`. The `CLIPBOARD` selection is used for copy and paste as in Macintosh and Windows. The `PRIMARY` selection is described later. You could use other selection names, like `SECONDARY` or `FOOBAR`, but that only works if the other applications know about that selection name. The selection data has both a type and a format. These are described briefly later.

V. Tk Details

Data is not copied into a selection. Instead, an application asserts ownership of a selection, and other applications request the value of the selection from
that owner. This model is used on all platforms. The window system keeps track
of ownership, and applications are informed when some other application takes
away ownership. Several of the Tk widgets implement selections and take care of
asserting ownership and returning its value.

The X PRIMARY selection is used in a way that eliminates the explicit copy
step in copy and paste user actions. Whenever you select an object in your application, your application automatically puts that value into the PRIMARY selection.
The Tk entry, listbox, and text widgets do this with their text selections,
although you can turn this off with the exportSelection widget attribute. Users
typically insert the value of the PRIMARY selection by clicking with the middle
mouse button. There is only one instance of the PRIMARY selection across all widgets and all applications. If the user makes a new selection it automatically over-
writes the previous value of the PRIMARY selection.

The CLIPBOARD is cross-platform.

If you want a mechanism that works on all platforms, use the CLIPBOARD
selection. The PRIMARY selection is implemented by Tk on all platforms, and you
can use it within an application, but on Windows and Macintosh the non-Tk
applications do not know about the PRIMARY selection. The main goal of copy and
paste is to provide general interoperability among all applications, so stick with
the CLIPBOARD.

Tk 3.6 and earlier only supported the PRIMARY selection. When Tk 4.0 added
support for the CLIPBOARD, I tried to merge the two selections to "simplify" things
for my users. Example 38–1 implements a Paste function that inserts either the
PRIMARY or CLIPBOARD selection into a text widget. The selection get command
is used to retrieve the selection value:

Example 38–1 Paste the PRIMARY or CLIPBOARD selection.

```
proc Paste { text } {
    if [catch {selection get} sel] {
        if [catch {selection get -selection CLIPBOARD} sel] {
            # no selection or clipboard data
            return
        }
    }
    $text insert insert $sel
}
```

This Paste function can be convenient, but it turns out that users still need
to keep track of the difference between the two selections. If a user only understands the CLIPBOARD, then the use of PRIMARY is only surprising. I learned that
it is best to have a separate paste user action for the two selections. The convention is that <ButtonRelease-2> sets the insert point and inserts the PRIMARY
selection. (This convention is awkward with the one- and two-button mice on
Macintosh and Windows.) The <<Paste>> event (e.g., the Paste key) simply

inserts the CLIPBOARD selection at the current insert point. This convention is shown in Example 38–2, although these bindings are defined automatically for the text and entry widgets:

Example 38–2 Separate paste actions.

```
bind Text <<Paste>> {
    catch {%W insert insert \
        [selection get -selection CLIPBOARD]
    }
}
bind Text <ButtonRelease-2> {
    %W mark set insert @%x,%y
    catch {%W insert insert \
        [selection get -selection PRIMARY]
    }
}
```

The `selection` Command

There are two Tcl commands that deal with selections. The `selection` command is a general-purpose command that can set and get different selections. By default it manipulates the PRIMARY selection. The `clipboard` command is a convenience command for manipulating the CLIPBOARD selection.

The `selection` command exposes the fully general selection model of different selections, types, and formats. You can define selection handlers that return selection values, and you can assert ownership of a selection and find out when you lose ownership to another application. Example 38–5 on page 596 shows a selection handler for a canvas.

A selection can have a type. The default is STRING. The type is different than the name of the selection (e.g., PRIMARY or CLIPBOARD). Each type can have a format, and the default format is STRING. Ordinarily these defaults are fine. If you are dealing with non-Tk applications, however, you may need to ask for their selections by the right type (e.g., FILE_NAME). Formats include UTF8_STRING, STRING, ATOM, and INTEGER. An ATOM is a name that is registered with the X server and identified by number. "Atoms and IDs" on page 667 describes Tk commands for manipulating atoms. It is probably not a good idea to use non-STRING types and formats because it limits what other applications can use the information. The details about X selection types and formats are specified in the *Inter-Client Communication Conventions Manual* (David Rosenthal, Stuart Marks, X Consortium Standard). This is distributed with the X11 sources and can be found on the web at http://tronche.com/gui/x/icccm/.

All of the `selection` operations take a `-selection` option that specifies the name of the selection being manipulated. This defaults to PRIMARY. Some of the operations take a `-displayof` option that specifies what display the selection is on. The value for this option is a Tk pathname of a window, and the selection on that window's display is manipulated. This is useful in X where applications can have their windows on remote displays. The default is to manipulate the selection on the display of the main window. Table 38–1 summarizes the `selection` command:

Table 38–1 The `selection` command.

`selection clear ?-displayof win? ?-selection sel?`	Clears the specified selection.
`selection get ?-displayof win? ?-selection sel? ?-type type?`	Returns the specified selection. The *type* defaults to STRING.
`selection handle ?-selection sel? ?-type type? ?-format format? window command`	Defines *command* to be the handler for selection requests when *window* owns the selection.
`selection own ?-displayof window? ?-selection sel?`	Returns the Tk pathname of the window that owns the selection, if it is in this application.
`selection own ?-command command? ?-selection sel? window`	Asserts that *window* owns the *sel* selection. The *command* is called when ownership of the selection is taken away from *window*.

The `clipboard` Command

The `clipboard` command manipulates values in the CLIPBOARD selection. The CLIPBOARD is meant for values that have been recently or temporarily deleted. It is use for the copy and paste model of selections. Prior to Tk 8.4, you had to use the `selection` command to retrieve values from the CLIPBOARD selection:

```
selection get -selection CLIPBOARD
```

However, Tk 8.4 introduced a `clipboard get` operation as a convenience for retrieving the clipboard value.

Table 38–2 summarizes the `clipboard` command:

Table 38–2 The `clipboard` command.

`clipboard append ?-displayof win? ?-format format? ?-type type? ?--? data`	Appends *data* to the CLIPBOARD with the specified *type* and *format*, which both default to STRING.
`clipboard clear ?-displayof win?`	Clears the CLIPBOARD selection.
`clipboard get ?-displayof win? ?-type type?`	Returns the CLIPBOARD selection. The *type* defaults to STRING.

Selection Handlers

The `selection handle` command registers a Tcl command to handle selection requests. The command is called to return the value of the selection to a requesting application. If the selection value is large, the command might be called several times to return the selection in pieces. The command gets two parameters that indicate the offset within the selection to start returning data, and the maximum number of bytes to return. If the command returns fewer than that many bytes, the selection request is assumed to be completed. Otherwise, the command is called again to get the rest of the data, and the offset parameter is adjusted accordingly.

You can also get a callback when you lose ownership of the selection. At that time it is appropriate to unhighlight the selected object in your interface. The `selection own` command sets ownership and registers a callback for when you lose ownership.

A Canvas Selection Handler

Example 38–3 through Example 38–7 implement cut and paste for a canvas. The `CanvasSelect_Demo` procedure creates a canvas and sets up some bindings for cut and paste:

Example 38–3 Bindings for canvas selection.

```
proc CanvasSelect_Demo { c } {
    canvas $c
    pack $c
    $c create rect 10 10 50 50 -fill red -tag object
    $c create poly 100 100 100 30 140 50 -fill orange \
        -tag object
    # Set up cut and paste bindings
    $c bind object <Button-1> [list CanvasSelect $c %x %y]
    bind $c <Key-Delete> [list CanvasDelete $c]
    bind $c <<Cut>> [list CanvasCut $c]
    bind $c <<Copy>> [list CanvasCopy $c]
    bind $c <<Paste>> [list CanvasPaste $c]
    bind $c <Button-2> [list CanvasPaste $c %x %y]
    # Register the handler for selection requests
    selection handle $c [list CanvasSelectHandle $c]
}
```

The `CanvasSelect` procedure selects an object. It uses the `find closest` canvas operation to find out what object is under the mouse, which works because the binding is on canvas items with the `object` tag. If the binding were on the canvas as a whole, you would use the `find overlapping` operation to limit selection to objects near the mouse click. The `CanvasHighlight` procedure is used to highlight the selected object. It displays small boxes at the corners of the object's bounding box. Finally, the `CanvasSelectLose` procedure is registered to be called when another application asserts ownership of the PRIMARY selection.

V. Tk Details

Example 38–4 Selecting objects.

```
proc CanvasSelect { w x y } {
    # Select an item on the canvas.
    global canvas
    set id [$w find closest $x $y]
    set canvas(select,$w) $id
    CanvasHighlight $w $id
    # Claim ownership of the PRIMARY selection
    selection own -command [list CanvasSelectLose $w] $w
    focus $w
}
proc CanvasHighlight {w id {clear clear}} {
    if {$clear == "clear"} {
        $w delete highlight
    }
    foreach {x1 y1 x2 y2} [$w bbox $id] { # lassign }
    foreach x [list $x1 $x2] {
        foreach y [list $y1 $y2] {
            $w create rectangle [expr $x-2] [expr $y-2] \
                [expr $x+2] [expr $y+2] -fill black \
                -tag highlight
        }
    }
}
proc CanvasSelectLose { w } {
    # Some other app has claimed the selection
    global canvas
    $w delete highlight
    unset canvas(select,$w)
}
```

Once you claim ownership, Tk calls back to the `CanvasSelectHandle` procedure when another application, even yours, requests the selection. This uses `CanvasDescription` to compute a description of the canvas object. It uses canvas operations to query the object's configuration and store that as a command that will create the object:

Example 38–5 A canvas selection handler.

```
proc CanvasSelectHandle { w offset maxbytes } {
    # Handle a selection request
    global canvas
    if ![info exists canvas(select,$w)] {
        error "No selected item"
    }
    set id $canvas(select,$w)
    # Return the requested chunk of data.
    return [string range [CanvasDescription $w $id] \
        $offset [expr $offset+$maxbytes]]
}
proc CanvasDescription { w id } {
    # Generate a description of the object that can
```

```
    # be used to recreate it later.
    set type [$w type $id]
    set coords [$w coords $id]
    set config {}
    # Bundle up non-default configuration settings
    foreach conf [$w itemconfigure $id] {
        # itemconfigure returns a list like
        # -fill {} {} {} red
        set default [lindex $conf 3]
        set value [lindex $conf 4]
        if {[string compare $default $value] != 0} {
            lappend config [lindex $conf 0] $value
        }
    }
    return [concat CanvasObject $type $coords $config]
}
```

The CanvasCopy procedure puts the description of the selected item onto the clipboard with the clipboard append command. The CanvasDelete deletes an object and the highlighting, and CanvasCut is built from CanvasCopy and CanvasDelete:

Example 38–6 The copy and cut operations.

```
proc CanvasCopy { w } {
    global canvas
    if [info exists canvas(select,$w)] {
        set id $canvas(select,$w)
        clipboard clear
        clipboard append [CanvasDescription $w $id]
    }
}
proc CanvasDelete {w} {
    global canvas
    catch {
        $w delete highlight
        $w delete $canvas(select,$w)
        unset canvas(select,$w)
    }
}
proc CanvasCut { w } {
    CanvasCopy $w
    CanvasDelete $w
}
```

The CanvasPaste operation gets the value from the CLIPBOARD selection. The selection value has all the parameters needed for a canvas create operation. It gets the position of the new object from the <Button-2> event, or from the current mouse position if the <<Paste>> event is generated. If the mouse is out of the window, then the object is just put into the middle of the canvas. The original position and the new position are used to compute values for a canvas move:

V. Tk Details

Example 38–7 Pasting onto the canvas.

```
proc CanvasPaste { w {x {}} {y {}}} {
    # Paste the selection from the CLIPBOARD
    if [catch {selection get -selection CLIPBOARD} sel] {
        # no clipboard data
        return
    }
    if {[string length $x] == 0} {
        # <<Paste>>, get the current mouse coordinates
        set x [expr [winfo pointerx $w] - [winfo rootx $w]]
        set y [expr [winfo pointery $w] - [winfo rooty $w]]
        if {$x < 0 || $y < 0 ||
                $x > [winfo width $w] ||
                $y > [winfo height $w]} {
            # Mouse outside the window - center object
            set x [expr [winfo width $w]/2]
            set y [expr [winfo height $w]/2]
        }
    }
    if [regexp {^CanvasObject} $sel] {
        if [catch {eval {$w create} [lrange $sel 1 end]} id] {
            return;
        }
        # look at the first coordinate to see where to
        # move the object. Element 1 is the type, the
        # next two are the first coordinate
        set x1 [lindex $sel 2]
        set y1 [lindex $sel 3]
        $w move $id [expr $x-$x1] [expr $y-$y1]
    }
}
```

There is more you can do for a drawing program, of course. You'd like to be able to select multiple objects, create new ones, and more. The *ImPress* application by Christopher Cox is a full-featured page layout application based on the Tk canvas. You can find it on the Web at:

```
http://www.ntlug.org/~ccox/impress/
```

Focus, Grabs, and Dialogs

Dialog boxes are a standard part of any user interface. Several dialog boxes are built into Tk. This chapter also describes how to build dialogs from scratch, which involves keyboard focus and grabs. Input focus directs keyboard events to different widgets. The grab mechanism lets a widget capture the input focus. This chapter describes the `focus`, `grab`, `tk_dialog`, and `tkwait` commands. Tk 4.2 adds `tk_getOpenFile`, `tk_getSaveFile`, `tk_chooseColor`, and `tk_messageBox`. Tk 8.3 adds `tk_chooseDirectory`.

*D*ialog boxes are a common feature in a user interface. The application needs some user response before it can continue. A dialog box displays some information and some controls, and the user must interact with it before the application can continue. To implement this, the application *grabs* the input focus so that the user can only interact with the dialog box. Tk has several built-in dialog boxes, including standard dialogs for finding files and selecting colors. A standard dialog has the same Tcl interface on all platforms, but it is implemented with platform-specific library routines to provide native look and feel. This chapter describes the dialogs built into Tk and then goes into the details of focus and grabs.

Standard Dialogs

The `tk_dialog` command presents a choice of buttons and returns a number indicating which one was clicked by the user. The general form of the command is:

```
tk_dialog win title text bitmap default ?label? ?label? ...
```

The *title* appears in the title bar, and the *text* appears in the dialog. The *bitmap* appears to the left of the text. Specify { } for the bitmap if you do not want one. The set of built-in bitmaps is given on page 627. The *label* arguments give labels that appear on buttons along the bottom of the dialog. The *default* argument gives the index of the default button, counting from zero. If there is no default, specify { } or -1.

Message Box

The `tk_messageBox` dialog is a limited form of `tk_dialog` that has native implementations on the different platforms. Like `tk_dialog`, it allows for a message, bitmap, and a set of buttons. However, the button sets are predefined, and the bitmaps are limited. The `yesno` button set, for example, displays a `Yes` and a `No` button. The `abortretryignore` button set displays `Abort`, `Retry`, and `Ignore` buttons. The `tk_messageBox` command returns the symbolic name of the selected button (e.g., `yes` or `retry`.) The `yesnocancel` message box could be used when trying to quit with unsaved changes:

```
set choice [tk_messageBox -type yesnocancel -default yes \
        -message "Save changes before quitting?" \
        -icon question]
```

The complete set of options to `tk_messageBox` is listed in Table 39–1:

Table 39–1 Options to `tk_messageBox`.

`-default` *name*	Default button name (e.g., `yes`)
`-icon` *name*	Name: `error`, `info`, `question`, or `warning`.
`-message` *string*	Message to display.
`-parent` *window*	Embeds dialog in *window.*
`-title` *title*	Dialog title (UNIX and Windows)
`-type` *type*	Type: `abortretrycancel`, `ok`, `okcancel`, `retrycancel`, `yesno`, or `yesnocancel`

File and Directory Dialogs

There are two standard file dialogs, `tk_getOpenFile` and `tk_getSaveFile`, and one standard directory dialog, `tk_chooseDirectory`. The `tk_getOpenFile` dialog is used to find an existing file, while `tk_getSaveFile` can be used to find a new file. The `tk_chooseDirectory` dialog, added in Tk 8.3, allows the user to select a directory, rather than a file. These procedures return the selected file or directory name, or the empty string if the user cancels the operation. These procedures take several options that are listed in Table 39–2:

Table 39–2 Options to the standard file and directory dialogs.

`-defaultextension` *ext*	Appends *ext* if an extension is not specified. `tk_getOpenFile` and `tk_getSaveFile` only.
`-filetypes` *typelist*	*typelist* defines a set of file types that the user can select to limit the files displayed in the dialog. `tk_getOpenFile` and `tk_getSaveFile` only.

Table 39–2 Options to the standard file and directory dialogs. (Continued)

`-initialdir` *dir*	Lists contents of *dir* in the initial display. If not provided, then the current working directory is displayed.
`-initialfile` *file*	Default *file*, for `tk_getSaveFile` only.
`-message` *string*	A message to include in the client area of the dialog. (Macintosh, only when Navigation Services are installed.) `tk_getOpenFile` and `tk_getSaveFile` only. (Tk 8.3.1)
`-multiple`	Allows the user to select multiple files, returned as a list. `tk_getOpenFile` only. (Tk 8.4)
`-mustexist` *boolean*	If False (default), the user may specify non-existent directories. `tk_chooseDirectory` only.
`-parent` *window*	Creates the dialog as a child of *window*. The dialog is displayed on top of its parent window.
`-title` *string*	Displays *string* in the title (UNIX and Windows).

The file dialogs can include a listbox that lists different file types. The file types are used to limit the directory listing to match only those types. The *typelist* option specifies a set of file extensions and Macintosh file types that correspond to a named file type. If you do not specify a *typelist*, users just see all the files in a directory. Each item in *typelist* is itself a list of three values:

> *name extensions ?mactypes?*

The *name* is displayed in the list of file types. The *extensions* is a list of file extensions corresponding to that type. The empty extension "" matches files without an extension, and the extension * matches all files. The *mactypes* is an optional list of four-character Macintosh file types, which are ignored on other platforms. On the Macintosh, if you give both *extensions* and *mactypes*, the files must match both. If the *extensions* is an empty list, only the *mactypes* are considered. However, you can repeat *name* in the *typelist* and give *extensions* in one set and *mactypes* in another set. If you do this, then files that match either the *extensions* or *mactypes* are listed.

The following *typelist* matches Framemaker Interchange Files that have both a `.mif` extension *and* a `MIF` type:

```
set typelist {
    {"Maker Interchange Files" {".mif"} {"MIF "}}
}
```

The following typelist matches GIF image files that have either a `.gif` extension *or* the `GIFF` file type. Note that the *mactypes* are optional:

```
set typelist {
    {"GIF Image" {".gif"}}
    {"GIF Image" {} {"GIFF"}}}
}
```

The following typelist puts all these together, along with an entry for all files. The entry that comes first is displayed first:

```
set typelist {
    {"All Files" {*}}
    {"GIF Image" {".gif"}}
    {"GIF Image" {} {"GIFF"}}
    {"Maker Interchange Files" {".mif"} {"MIF "}}
}
```

Color Dialog

The `tk_chooseColor` dialog displays a color selection dialog. It returns a color, or the empty string if the user cancels the operation. The options to `tk_chooseColor` are listed in Table 39–3:

Table 39–3 Options to `tk_chooseColor`.

`-initialcolor` *color*	Initial color to display.
`-parent` *window*	Creates the dialog as an embedded child of *window*.
`-title` *string*	Displays *string* in the title (UNIX and Windows).

Custom Dialogs

When you create your own dialogs, you need to understand keyboard focus, focus grabs, and how to wait for the user to finish with a dialog. Here is the general structure of your code when creating a dialog:

```
# Create widgets, then
focus $toplevel
grab $toplevel
tkwait window $toplevel
```

This sequence of commands directs keyboard focus to the toplevel containing your dialog. The `grab` forces the user to interact with the dialog before using other windows in your application. The `tkwait` command returns when the toplevel window is destroyed, and this automatically releases the grab. This assumes that the button commands in the dialog destroy the toplevel. The following sections explain these steps in more detail, and Example 39–1 on page 606 illustrates a more robust sequence.

Input Focus

The window system directs keyboard events to the toplevel window that currently has the input focus. The application, in turn, directs the keyboard events to one of the widgets within that toplevel window. The `focus` command sets focus to a particular widget, and it is used by the default bindings for Tk widgets. Tk remembers what widget has focus within a toplevel window and automatically gives focus to that widget when the system gives focus to a toplevel window.

On Windows and Macintosh, the focus is given to an application when you click in its window. On UNIX, the window manager application gives focus to different windows, and window managers allow different conventions to shift focus. The click-to-type model is similar to Windows and Macintosh. There is also focus-follows-mouse, which gives focus to the window under the mouse. One thing to note about click-to-type is that the application does not see the mouse click that gives the window focus.

Once the application has focus, you can manage the focus changes among your widgets any way you like. By default, Tk uses a click-to-type model. Text and entry widgets set focus to themselves when you click on them with the left mouse button. You can get the focus-follows-mouse model within your widgets by calling the `tk_focusFollowsMouse` procedure. However, in many cases you will find that an explicit focus model is actually more convenient for users. Carefully positioning the mouse over a small widget can be tedious.

The focus Command

Table 39–4 summarizes the `focus` command. The focus implementation supports multiple displays with a separate focus window on each display. This is useful on UNIX where X supports multiple displays. The `-displayof` option can be used to query the focus on a particular display. The `-lastfor` option finds out what widget last had the focus within the same toplevel as another window. Tk will restore focus to that window if the widget that has the focus is destroyed. The toplevel widget gets the focus if no widget claims it.

Table 39–4 The `focus` command.

`focus`	Returns the widget that currently has the focus on the display of the application's main window.
`focus ?-force? window`	Sets the focus to *window*. The `-force` option ignores the window manger, so use it sparingly.
`focus -displayof win`	Returns the focus widget on the same display as *win*.
`focus -lastfor win`	Returns the name of the last widget to have the focus in the same toplevel as *win*.

V. Tk Details

Keyboard Focus Traversal

Users can change focus among widgets with <Tab> and <Shift-Tab>. The creation order of widgets determines a traversal order for focus that is used by the tk_focusNext and tk_focusPrev procedures. There are global bindings for <Tab> and <Shift-Tab> that call these procedures:

```
bind all <Tab> {tk_focusNext %W}
bind all <Shift-Tab> {tk_focusPrev %W}
```

The Tk widgets highlight themselves when they have the focus. The highlight size is controlled with the highlightThickness attribute, and the color of the highlight is set with the highlightColor attribute. The Tk widgets, even buttons and scrollbars, have bindings that support keyboard interaction. A <space> invokes the command associated with a button, if the button has the input focus.

All widgets have a takeFocus attribute that the tk_focusNext and tk_focusPrev procedures use to determine if a widget will take the focus during keyboard traversal. There are four possible values to the attribute:

- 0 indicates the widget should not take focus.
- 1 indicates the widget should always take focus.
- An empty string means the traversal procedures tk_focusNext and tk_focusPrev should decide based on the widget's state and bindings.
- Otherwise the value is a Tcl command prefix. The command is called with the widget name as an argument, and it should return either 0, 1, or the empty string.

Grabbing the Focus

An input *grab* overrides the normal focus mechanism. For example, a dialog box can grab the focus so that the user cannot interact with other windows in the application. The typical scenario is that the application is performing some task but it needs user input. The grab restricts the user's actions so it cannot drive the application into an inconsistent state. In most cases you only need to use the grab and grab release commands. Note that the grab set command is equivalent to the grab command. Table 39–5 summarizes the grab command.

Table 39–5 The grab command.

grab ?-global? *window*	Sets a grab to a particular window.
grab current ?*window*?	Queries the grabs on the display of *window*, or on all displays if *window* is omitted.
grab release *window*	Releases a grab on *window*.
grab set ?-global? *win*	Sets a grab to a particular window.
grab status *window*	Returns none, local, or global.

A *global grab* prevents the user from interacting with other applications, too, even the window manager. Tk menus use a global grab, for example, which is how they unpost themselves no matter where you click the mouse. When an application prompts for a password, a global grab is also a good idea. This prevents the user from accidentally typing their password into a random window. The next section includes examples that use the `grab` command.

The `tkwait` Command

You wait for the user to interact with the dialog by using the `tkwait` command. The `tkwait` waits for something to happen, and while waiting it allows events to be processed. Like `vwait`, you can use `tkwait` to wait for a Tcl variable to change value. You can also wait for a window to become visible, or wait for a window to be destroyed. Table 39–6 summarizes the `tkwait` command.

Table 39–6 The `tkwait` command.

`tkwait variable` *varname*	Waits for the global variable *varname* to be set. This is just like the `vwait` command.
`tkwait visibility` *win*	Waits for the window *win* to become visible.
`tkwait window` *win*	Waits for the window *win* to be destroyed.

Use `tkwait` with global variables.

The variable specified in the `tkwait variable` command must be a global variable. Remember this if you use procedures to modify the variable. They must declare it global or the `tkwait` command will not notice the assignments.

The `tkwait visibility` waits for the visibility state of the window to change. Most commonly this is used to wait for a newly created window to become visible. For example, if you have any sort of animation in a complex dialog, you could wait until the dialog is displayed before starting the animation.

Destroying Widgets

The `destroy` command deletes one or more widgets. If the widget has children, all the children are destroyed, too. Chapter 44 describes a protocol on page 661 to handle destroy events that come from the window manager. You wait for a window to be deleted with the `tkwait window` command.

The `focus, grab, tkwait` sequence

In practice, I use a slightly more complex command sequence than just `focus`, `grab`, and `tkwait`. You can remember what widget used to have the focus and then restore it after the dialog completes. When you do this, it is more reliable to restore focus before destroying the dialog. This prevents a tug of war between your application and the window manager. This sequence looks like:

```
set old [focus]
focus $toplevel
grab $toplevel
tkwait variable doneVar
grab release $toplevel
focus $old
destroy $toplevel
```

This sequence supports another trick I use, which is to unmap dialogs instead of destroying them. This way the dialogs appear more quickly the next time they are used. This makes creating the dialogs a little more complex because you need to see if the toplevel already exists. Chapter 44 describes the window manager commands used to map and unmap windows on page 661. Example 39–1 shows Dialog_Create, Dialog_Wait, and Dialog_Dismiss that capture all of these tricks:

Example 39–1 Procedures to help build dialogs.

```
proc Dialog_Create {top title args} {
    global dialog
    if [winfo exists $top] {
        switch -- [wm state $top] {
            normal {
                # Raise a buried window
                raise $top
            }
            withdrawn -
            iconic {
                # Open and restore geometry
                wm deiconify $top
                catch {wm geometry $top $dialog(geo,$top)}
            }
        }
        return 0
    } else {
        eval {toplevel $top} $args
        wm title $top $title
        return 1
    }
}
proc Dialog_Wait {top varName {focus {}}} {
    upvar $varName var

    # Poke the variable if the user nukes the window
    bind $top <Destroy> [list set $varName cancel]

    # Grab focus for the dialog
    if {[string length $focus] == 0} {
        set focus $top
    }
    set old [focus -displayof $top]
    focus $focus
    catch {tkwait visibility $top}
```

```
        catch {grab $top}

        # Wait for the dialog to complete
        tkwait variable $varName
        catch {grab release $top}
        focus $old
    }
    proc Dialog_Dismiss {top} {
        global dialog
        # Save current size and position
        catch {
            # window may have been deleted
            set dialog(geo,$top) [wm geometry $top]
            wm withdraw $top
        }
    }
```

The `Dialog_Wait` procedure allows a different focus widget than the toplevel. The idea is that you can start the focus out in the appropriate widget within the dialog, such as the first entry widget. Otherwise, the user has to click in the dialog first.

Grab can fail.

The `catch` statements in `Dialog_Wait` come from my experiences on different platforms. The `tkwait visibility` is sometimes required because `grab` can fail if the dialog is not yet visible. However, on other systems, the `tkwait visibility` itself can fail in some circumstances. Tk reflects these errors, but in this case all that can go wrong is no grab. The user can still interact with the dialog without a grab, so I just ignore these errors.

Prompter Dialog

Example 39–2 A simple dialog.

```
proc Dialog_Prompt { string } {
    global prompt
    set f .prompt
    if [Dialog_Create $f "Prompt" -borderwidth 10] {
        message $f.msg -text $string -aspect 1000
```

```
        entry $f.entry -textvariable prompt(result)
        set b [frame $f.buttons]
        pack $f.msg $f.entry $f.buttons -side top -fill x
        pack $f.entry -pady 5
        button $b.ok -text OK -command {set prompt(ok) 1}
        button $b.cancel -text Cancel \
            -command {set prompt(ok) 0}
        pack $b.ok -side left
        pack $b.cancel -side right
        bind $f.entry <Return> {set prompt(ok) 1 ; break}
        bind $f.entry <Control-c> {set prompt(ok) 0 ; break}
    }
    set prompt(ok) 0
    Dialog_Wait $f prompt(ok) $f.entry
    Dialog_Dismiss $f
    if {$prompt(ok)} {
        return $prompt(result)
    } else {
        return {}
    }
}
Dialog_Prompt "Please enter a name"
```

Example 39-2 shows Dialog_Prompt, which gets a value from the user, returning the value entered, or the empty string if the user cancels the operation. Dialog_Prompt uses the Tcl variable prompt(ok) to indicate the dialog is complete. The variable is set if the user presses the OK or Cancel buttons, or if the user presses <Return> or <Control-c> in the entry widget. The Dialog_Wait procedure waits on prompt(ok), and it grabs and restores focus. If the Dialog_Create procedure returns 1, then the dialog is built: otherwise, it already existed.

Keyboard Shortcuts and Focus

Focus is set on the entry widget in the dialog with Dialog_Wait, and it is convenient if users can use special key bindings to complete the dialog. Otherwise, they need to take their hands off the keyboard and use the mouse. The example defines bindings for <Return> and <Control-c> that invoke the OK and Cancel buttons, respectively. The bindings override all other bindings by including a break command. Otherwise, the Entry class bindings insert the short-cut keystroke into the entry widget.

Animation with the update Command

Suppose you want to entertain your user while your application is busy. By default, the user interface hangs until your processing completes. Even if you change a label or entry widget in the middle of processing, the updates to that widget are deferred until an idle moment. The user does not see your feedback, and the window is not refreshed if it gets obscured and uncovered. The solution is to use the `update` command that forces Tk to go through its event loop and update the display.

The next example shows a `Feedback` procedure that displays status messages. A read-only entry widget displays the messages, and the `update` command ensures that the user sees each new message. An entry widget is used because it won't change size based on the message length, and it can be scrolled by dragging with the middle mouse button. Entry widgets also work better with `update idletasks` as described later:

Example 39–3 A feedback procedure.

```
proc Feedback { message } {
    global feedback
    set e $feedback(entry)
    $e config -state normal
    $e delete 0 end
    $e insert 0 $message
    # Leave the entry in a read-only state
    $e config -state disabled
    # Force a display update
    update idletasks
}
```

The Tk widgets update their display at idle moments, which basically means after everything else is taken care of. This lets them collapse updates into one interaction with the window system. On UNIX, this improves the batching effects that are part of the X protocol. A call to `update idletasks` causes any pending display updates to be processed. Chapter 16 describes the Tk event loop in more detail.

Use `update idletasks` if possible.

The safest way to use `update` is with its `idletasks` option. If you use the `update` command with no options, then all events are processed. In particular, user input events are processed. If you are not careful, it can have unexpected effects because another thread of execution is launched into your Tcl interpreter. The current thread is suspended and any callbacks that result from input events are executed. It is usually better to use the `tkwait` command if you need to process input because it pauses the main application at a well-defined point.

One drawback of `update idletasks` is that in some cases a widget's redisplay is triggered by window system events. In particular, when you change the text of a label, it can cause the size of the label to change. The widget is too clever for us in this case. Instead of scheduling a redisplay at idle time, it requests a different size and then waits for the `<Configure>` event from the window system. The `<Configure>` event indicates a size has been chosen by the geometry manager, and it is at that point that the label schedules its redisplay. So, changing the label's text and doing `update idletasks` does not work as expected.

V. Tk Details

Tk Widget Attributes

Each Tk widget has a number of attributes that affect its appearance and behavior. This chapter describes attributes in general, and covers some of the size and appearance-related attributes. The next two chapters cover the attributes associated with colors, images, and text.

*T*his chapter describes some of the attributes that are in common among many Tk widgets. A widget always provides a default value for its attributes, so you can avoid specifying most of them. If you want to fine-tune things, however, you'll need to know about all the widget attributes.

The native widgets implemented in Tk 8.0 ignore some of the original Tk attributes. This is because there is no support for them in the system widgets. For example, the buttons on Macintosh do not honor the `borderWidth` attribute, and they do not display a highlight focus. The native scrollbars on Windows and Macintosh have similar limitations. This chapter notes these limitations in the discussion of each attribute.

Configuring Attributes

You specify attributes for Tk widgets when you create them. You can also change them dynamically at any time after that. In both cases the syntax uses pairs of arguments. The first item in the pair identifies the attribute, the second provides the value. For example, a button can be created like this:

```
button .doit -text Doit -command DoSomething
```

The name of the button is `.doit`, and two attributes are specified: the `text` and the `command`. You can change the `.doit` button later with the `configure` widget operation:

```
.doit configure -text Stop -command StopIt
```

V. Tk Details

The current configuration of a widget can be queried with another form of the `configure` operation. If you just supply an attribute, the settings associated with that attribute are returned:

```
.doit configure -text
=> -text text Text { } Stop
```

This command returns several pieces of information: the command line switch, the resource name, the resource class, the default value, and the current value. If you don't give any options to configure, then the configuration information for all the attributes is returned. The following loop formats the information:

```
foreach item [$w configure] {
    puts "[lindex $item 0] [lindex $item 4]"
}
```

If you just want the current value, use the `cget` operation:

```
.doit cget -text
=> Stop
```

You can also configure widget attributes indirectly by using the resource database. An advantage of using the resource database is that users can reconfigure your application without touching the code. Otherwise, if you specify attribute values explicitly in the code, they cannot be overridden by resource settings. This is especially important for attributes like fonts and colors.

The tables in this chapter list the attributes by their resource name, which may have a capital letter at an internal word boundary (e.g., `activeBackground`). When you specify attributes in a Tcl command, use all lowercase instead, plus a leading dash. Compare:

```
option add *Button.activeBackground red
$button configure -activebackground red
```

The first command defines a resource that affects all buttons created after that point, and the second command changes an existing button. Command-line settings override resource database specifications. Chapter 31 describes the use of resources in detail.

Size

Most widgets have a `width` and `height` attribute that specifies their desired size, although there are some special cases. For most widgets, if an explicit size isn't specified, or the size provided is 0 or less, then the widget automatically sizes itself to be just large enough to display its contents. As of Tk 8.4, on Windows, the `width` attribute for simple button widgets (not checkbuttons, radiobuttons, or menubuttons) accepts a negative value to specify a *minimum* width, enabling better compliance with native Windows look-and-feel. In all cases, the geometry manager for a widget might modify the size to some degree. The `winfo` operations described on page 659 return the current size of a widget.

Most of the text-related widgets interpret their sizes in units of characters for width and lines for height. All other widgets, including the `message` widget, interpret their dimensions in screen units, which are pixels by default. The tk scale command, which is described on page 669, controls the scale between pixels and the other measures. You can suffix the dimension with a unit specifier to get a particular measurement unit:

c	centimeters
i	inch
m	millimeters
p	printer points (1/72 inches)

Scales and scrollbars can have two orientations as specified by the orient attribute, so width and height are somewhat ambiguous. These widgets do not support a height attribute, and they interpret their width attribute to mean the size of their narrow dimension. The scale has a length attribute that determines its long dimension. Scrollbars do not even have a length. Instead, a scrollbar is assumed to be packed next to the widget it controls, and the fill packing attribute is used to extend the scrollbar to match the length of its adjacent widget. Example 33–1 on page 500 shows how to arrange scrollbars with another widget.

The message widget displays a fixed string on multiple lines, and it uses one of two attributes to constrain its size: its aspect or its width. The aspect ratio is defined to be 100*width/height, and it formats its text to honor this constraint. However, if a width is specified, it just uses that and uses as many lines (i.e., as much height) as needed. Example 32–6 on page 493 shows how message widgets display text. Table 40–1 summarizes the attributes used to specify the size for widgets:

Table 40–1 Size attribute resource names.

aspect	The aspect ratio of a message widget, which is 100 times the ratio of width divided by height.
height	Height, in text lines or screen units. Widgets: button, canvas, checkbutton, frame, label, labelframe, listbox, menubutton, panedwindow, radiobutton, text, and toplevel.
length	The long dimension of a scale.
orient	Orientation for long and narrow widgets, or arrangement of panes in a panedwindow: horizontal or vertical. Widgets: panedwindow, scale, and scrollbar.
width	Width, in characters or screen units. Widgets: button, canvas, checkbutton, entry, frame, label, labelframe, listbox, menubutton, message, panedwindow, radiobutton, scale, scrollbar, spinbox, text, and toplevel.

It is somewhat unfortunate that text-oriented widgets only take character- and line-oriented dimensions. These sizes change with the font used, and if you want a precise size you might be frustrated. Both pack and grid let the widgets

V. Tk Details

decide how big to be. One trick is to put each widget, such as a label, in its own frame. Specify the size you want for the frame, and then pack the label and turn off size propagation. For example:

Example 40–1 Equal-sized labels.

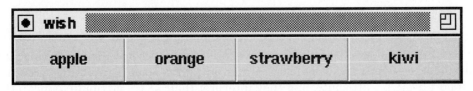

```
proc EqualSizedLabels { parent width height strings args } {
    set l 0
    foreach s $strings {
        frame $parent.$l -width $width -height $height
        pack propagate $parent.$l false
        pack $parent.$l -side left
        eval {label $parent.$l.l -text $s} $args
        pack $parent.$l.l -fill both -expand true
        incr l
    }
}
frame .f ; pack .f
EqualSizedLabels .f 1i 1c {apple orange strawberry kiwi} \
    -relief raised
```

The frames `$parent.$l` are all created with the same size. The `pack` propagate command prevents these frames from changing size when the labels are packed into them later. The labels are packed with `fill` and `expand` turned on so that they fill up the fixed-sized frames around them.

Another way to get equal sized widgets is with the `-uniform` column configuration that was added to grid in Tk 8.4. This is described on page 418.

Borders and Relief

Example 40–2 illustrates the different relief options, which control the way the border around a widget is drawn:

Example 40–2 3D relief sampler.

```
frame .f -borderwidth 10
pack .f
foreach relief {raised sunken flat ridge groove solid} {
    label .f.$relief -text $relief -relief $relief \
        -bd 2 -padx 3
    pack .f.$relief -side left -padx 4
}
```

The three-dimensional appearance of widgets is determined by two attributes: borderWidth and relief. The borderWidth adds extra space around the edge of a widget's display, and this area can be displayed in a number of ways according to the relief attribute. The solid relief was added in Tk 8.0 to support the Macintosh look for entry widget, and it works well against white backgrounds. Macintosh buttons do not support different reliefs or honor border width.

The activeBorderWidth attribute defines the border width for the menu entries. The relief of a menu is not configurable. It probably is not worth adjusting the menu border width attributes because the default looks OK. The native menus on Windows and Macintosh do not honor this attribute.

The activeRelief attribute applies to the elements of a scrollbar (the elevator and two arrows) when the mouse is over them. The elementBorderWidth sets the size of the relief on these elements. Changing the activeRelief does not look good. The native scrollbars on Macintosh and Windows do not honor this attribute.

The offRelief and overRelief attributes describe a relief style to use when a widget is in the "off state" and its indicator is not drawn, or the mouse cursor is over the widget. They were added in Tk 8.4 to provide better support for creating toolbars. The overRelief attribute applies to buttons, checkbuttons, and radiobuttons. The offRelief attribute applies only to checkbuttons and radiobuttons. Table 40–2 lists the attributes for borders and relief.

Table 40–2 Border and relief attribute resource names.

activeBorderWidth	The border width for menu entries. UNIX only.
activeRelief	The relief for active scrollbar elements. UNIX only.
borderWidth	The width of the border around a widget, in screen units. All widgets
bd	Short for borderwidth. Tcl commands only.
elementBorderWidth	The width of the border on scrollbar and scale elements.
offRelief	Alternate relief style when the widget is deselected. Widgets: checkbutton and radiobutton. (Tk 8.4)
overRelief	Alternate relief style when mouse is over the widget. Widgets: button, checkbutton, and radiobutton. (Tk 8.4)
relief	The appearance of the border: flat, raised, sunken, ridge, groove, or solid. All widgets.

The Focus Highlight

Each widget can have a focus highlight indicating which widget currently has the input focus. This is a thin rectangle around each widget that is displayed in the highlight background color by default. When the widget gets the input focus, the highlight rectangle is displayed in an alternate color. The addition of the highlight adds a small amount of space outside the border described in the previous section. The attributes in Table 40–3 control the width and color of this rectangle. If the width is zero, no highlight is displayed.

By default, only the widgets that normally expect input focus have a nonzero width highlight border. This includes the `text`, `entry`, and `listbox` widgets. It also includes the `button` and `menu` widgets because there is a set of keyboard traversal bindings that focus input on these widgets, too. You can define nonzero highlight thicknesses for all widgets except Macintosh buttons.

Table 40–3 Highlight attribute resource names.

`highlightColor`	The color of the highlight when the widget has focus.
`highlightBackground`	The highlight color when the widget does not have focus.
`highlightThickness`	The width of the highlight border.

Padding and Anchors

Table 40–4 lists padding and anchor attributes that are similar in spirit to some packing attributes described in Chapter 25. However, they are distinct from the packing attributes, and this section explains how they work together with the packer.

Table 40–4 Layout attribute resource names.

`anchor`	The anchor position of the widget. Values: n, ne, e, se, s, sw, w, nw, or center. Widgets: button, checkbutton, label, menubutton, message, or radiobutton.
`padX, padY`	Padding space in the X or Y direction, in screen units. Widgets: button, checkbutton, frame, label, labelframe, menubutton, message, radiobutton, text, or toplevel.

The padding attributes for a widget define space that is never occupied by the display of the widget's contents. For example, if you create a `label` with the following attributes and pack it into a frame by itself, you will see the text is still centered, despite the `anchor` attribute.

Example 40–3 Padding provided by labels and buttons.

```
label .foo -text Foo -padx 20 -anchor e
pack .foo
```

The `anchor` attribute only affects the display if there is extra room for another reason. One way to get extra room is to specify a `width` attribute that is longer than the text. The following label has right-justified text. You can see the default `padx` value for labels, which is one pixel:

Example 40–4 Anchoring text in a label or button.

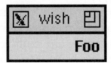

```
label .foo -text Foo -width 10 -anchor e
pack .foo
```

Another way to get extra display space is with the `-ipadx` and `-ipady` packing parameters. The example in the next section illustrates this effect. Chapter 25 has several more examples of the packing parameters.

Putting It All Together

Example 40–5 Borders and padding.

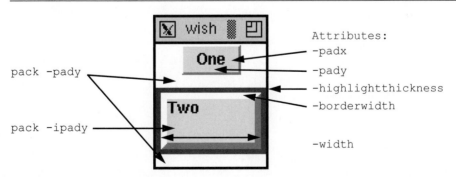

```
frame .f -bg white
label .f.one -text One -relief raised -bd 2 -padx 3m -pady 2m
pack .f.one -side top
label .f.two -text Two \
    -highlightthickness 4 -highlightcolor red \
```

```
    -borderwidth 5 -relief raised \
    -padx 0 -pady 0 \
    -width 10 -anchor nw
pack .f.two -side top -pady 10 -ipady 10 -fill both
focus .f.two
pack .f
```

The number of different attributes that contribute to the size and appearance can be confusing. Example 40–5 uses a label to demonstrate the difference among size, borders, padding, and the highlight. Padding can come from the geometry manager, and it can come from widget attributes.

The first label uses a raised relief, so you can see the two-pixel border. There is no highlight on a label by default. There is internal padding so that the text is spaced away from the edge of the label. The second label adds a highlight rectangle by specifying a nonzero thickness. Widgets like buttons, entries, listboxes, and text have a highlight rectangle by default.

The second label's padding attributes are reduced to zero. The anchor positions the text right next to the border in the upper-left (nw) corner. Note the effect of the padding provided by the packer. There is both external and internal padding in the Y direction. The external padding (from pack -pady) results in unfilled space. The internal packing (pack -ipady) is used by the label for its display. This is different from the label's own -pady attribute, which keeps the text away from the top edge of the widget.

Color, Images, and Cursors

This chapter describes the color attributes shared by the Tk widgets. Images and bitmaps can be displayed instead of text by several widgets. This chapter describes commands that create and manipulate images. The cursor attribute controls the shape and color of the mouse cursor when it is over a particular widget. This chapter includes a figure that shows all the cursors available in Tk.

Color is one of the most fun things to play with in a user interface. However, this chapter makes no attempt to improve your taste in color choices; it just describes the attributes that affect color. The tradition of having users change application colors is stronger in UNIX than on the other platforms. This is because all the X toolkits support color tuning via the resource database. Tk carries this tradition to Windows and Macintosh. However, if native look and feel is important, you should not change the default widget colors. On the other hand, tuning colors can provide a flair to your applications, and knowledge of colors is useful for canvas applications.

This chapter describes images, too. The image facility in Tk lets you create an image and then have other Tk widgets display it. The same image can be displayed by many different widgets, multiple times on a canvas, and multiple times within the text widget. If you redefine an image, its display is updated in whatever widgets are displaying it.

The last topic of the chapter is cursors. All widgets can control what the mouse cursor looks like when it is over them. In addition, the widgets that support text input define another cursor, the insert cursor. Its appearance is controlled with a few related attributes.

Colors

Table 41–1 lists the resource names for color attributes. The table indicates what widgets use the different color attributes. Remember to use all lowercase and a leading dash when specifying attributes in a Tcl command.

Table 41–1 Color attribute resource names.

background	The normal background color. All widgets.
bg	Short for background. Command line only.
foreground	The normal foreground color. Widgets: button, checkbutton, entry, label, listbox, menu, menubutton, message, radiobutton, scale, spinbox, and text.
fg	Short for foreground. Command line only.
activeBackground	The background when a mouse button will take an action. Widgets: button, checkbutton, label, menu, menubutton, radiobutton, scale, scrollbar, and spinbox.
activeForeground	The foreground when the mouse is over an active widget. Widgets: button, checkbutton, entry, label, menu, menubutton, and radiobutton.
disabledBackground	The background when a widget is disabled. Widgets: entry and spinbox.
disabledForeground	The foreground when a widget is disabled. Widgets: button, checkbutton, menu, menubutton, and radiobutton.
highlightBackground	The highlight color when widget does not have focus. All widgets.
highlightColor	The highlight color when the widget has focus. All widgets.
insertBackground	The color of the insert cursor. Widgets: canvas, entry, spinbox, and text.
readonlyBackground	The background when a widget is in the readonly state. Widgets: entry and spinbox.
selectBackground	The background of selected text. Widgets: canvas, entry, listbox, spinbox, and text.
selectColor	The color of the selector indicator. Widgets: checkbutton, menu, and radiobutton.
selectForeground	The foreground of selected text. Widgets: canvas, entry, listbox, spinbox, and text.
troughColor	The trough part of scales and scrollbars.

The `foreground` color is used to draw an element, while the `background` color is used for the blank area behind the element. Text, for example, is painted with the foreground color. There are several variations on foreground and background that reflect different states for widgets or items they are displaying.

Each attribute also has a resource class. This is most useful for the variations on foreground and background colors. For example, Tk does not have a reverse video mode. However, with a couple of resource specifications you can convert a monochrome display into reverse video. The definitions are given in Example 41–1. The `Foreground` and `Background` resource class names are used, and the various foreground and background colors (e.g., `activeBackground`) have the correct resource class so these settings work. You have to set these resources before you create any widgets:

Example 41–1 Resources for reverse video.

```
proc ReverseVideo {} {
    option add *Foreground white
    option add *Background black
}
```

Color Palettes

The `tk_setPalette` command changes colors of existing widgets and installs resource values so new widgets have matching colors. If you give it a single argument, it treats this as the background and then computes new values for the other color resources. For example, if you do not like the standard Tk grey, you can lighten your spirits with a cool blue background:

```
tk_setPalette #0088cc
```

If you liked the light brown color scheme of Tk 3.6, you can restore that palette with the `tk_bisque` command:

```
tk_bisque
```

The `tk_setPalette` command can be used to change any of the color attributes. You can specify a set of name-value pairs, where the names are color resource names and the values are new color values:

```
tk_setPalette activeBackground red activeForeground white
```

Color Values

Color values are specified in two ways: symbolically (e.g., `red`), or by hexadecimal numbers (e.g., `#ff0000`). The leading # distinguishes the hexadecimal representation from the symbolic one. The number is divided into three equal-sized fields that give the red, green, and blue values, respectively. The fields can specify 4, 8, 12, or 16 bits of a color:

```
#RGB               4 bits per color
#RRGGBB            8 bits per color
#RRRGGGBBB         12 bits per color
#RRRRGGGGBBBB      16 bits per color
```

If you specify more resolution than is supported by the display, the low-order bits of each field are discarded. The different display types supported by Tk are described in the next section. Each field ranges from 0, which means no color, to a maximum, which is all ones in binary, or all f in hex, that means full color saturation. For example, pure red can be specified four ways:

```
#f00  #ff0000  #fff000000  #ffff00000000
```

There is a large collection of symbolic color names like "red," "blue," "green," "thistle," "medium sea green," and "yellow4." These names originate from X and UNIX, and Tk supports these colors on all platforms. As of Tk 8.3.2, these color names are documented in the *colors* online reference page. Prior to that, you could find the list in the Tk sources in the xlib/xcolor.c file. Or, run the *xcolors* program that comes with the standard X distribution.

The Windows and Macintosh platforms have a small set of colors that are guaranteed to exist, and Tk defines names for these. The advantage of using these colors is that they are shared by all applications, so the system can manage colors efficiently. Table 41–2 lists the system colors on Windows. Several of these colors map to the same RGB value. Table 41–3 lists the system colors on Macintosh.

Table 41–2 Windows system colors.

system3dDarkShadow	Dark part of button 3D-relief.
system3dLight	Light part of button 3D-relief.
systemActiveBorder	Window border when activated.
systemActiveCaption	Caption (i.e., title bar) when activated.
systemAppWorkspace	Background for MDI workspaces.
systemBackground	Widget background.
systemButtonFace	Button background.
systemButtonHighlight	Lightest part of button 3D-relief.
systemButtonShadow	Darkest part of button 3D-relief.
systemButtonText	Button foreground.
systemCaptionText	Caption (i.e., title bar) text.
systemDisabledText	Text when disabled.
systemGrayText	Grey text color.
systemHighlight	Selection background.

Table 41-2 Windows system colors. (Continued)

systemHighlightText	Selection foreground.
systemInactiveBorder	Window border when not activated.
systemInactiveCaption	Caption background when not activated.
systemInactiveCaptionText	Caption text when not activated.
systemInfoBackground	Help pop-up background.
systemInfoText	Help pop-up text.
systemMenu	Menu background.
systemMenuText	Menu foreground.
systemScrollbar	Scrollbar background.
systemWindow	Text window background.
systemWindowFrame	Text window frame.
systemWindowText	Text window text color.

Table 41-3 Macintosh system colors.

systemHighlight	Selection background.
systemHighlightText	Selection foreground.
systemButtonFace	Button background.
systemButtonFrame	Button frame.
systemButtonText	Button foreground.
systemWindowBody	Widget background.
systemMenuActive	Selected menu item background.
systemMenuActiveText	Selected menu item foreground.
systemMenu	Menu background.
systemMenuDisabled	Disabled menu item background.
systemMenuText	Menu foreground.

Getting RGB values.

The `winfo rgb` command maps from a color name (or value) to three numbers that are its red, green, and blue values. You can use this to compute variations on a color. The `ColorDarken` procedure shown below uses the `winfo rgb` command to get the red, green, and blue components of the input color. It reduces these amounts by 5 percent, and reconstructs the color specification using the `format` command.

Example 41–2 Computing a darker color.

```
proc ColorDarken { win color } {
    set rgb [winfo rgb $win $color]
    return [format "#%03x%03x%03x" \
        [expr round([lindex $rgb 0] * 0.95)] \
        [expr round([lindex $rgb 1] * 0.95)] \
        [expr round([lindex $rgb 2] * 0.95)]]
}
```

Colormaps and Visuals

Computer screens can display only a fixed number of different colors at one time. The best monitors can display 24 million colors, but it is common to find 256 color displays. Really old VGA displays only display 16 colors. If you run several applications at once, it is possible that more colors are requested than can be displayed. The Windows and Macintosh platforms manage this scenario automatically. X provides lower-level facilities that Tk uses on UNIX to do the management. So, for the most part you don't have to worry. However, if you need more control, especially under X, then you need to understand *colormaps* and the different *visual* types.

Each pixel on the screen is represented by one or more bits of memory. There are a number of ways to map from a value stored at a pixel to the color that appears on the screen at that pixel. The mapping is a function of the number of bits at each pixel, which is called the *depth* of the display, and the style of interpretation, or *visual class*. The six visual classes defined by X are listed in Table 41–4:

Table 41–4 Visual classes for displays.

staticgrey	Greyscale with a fixed colormap defined by the system.
greyscale	Greyscale with a writable colormap.
staticcolor	Color with a fixed colormap defined by the system.
pseudocolor	Color values determined by single writable colormap.
truecolor	Color values determined by three colormaps defined by the system: one each for red, green, and blue.
directcolor	Color values determined by three writable colormaps: one each for red, green, and blue.
best	Use the best visual for a given depth.

Some of the visuals use a *colormap* that maps from the value stored at a pixel to a value used by the hardware to generate a color. A colormap enables a compact encoding for a much richer color. For example, a 256-entry colormap can be indexed with 8 bits, but it may contain 24 bits of color information. The UNIX *xdpyinfo* program reports the different visual classes supported by your display.

The frame and toplevel widgets support a `colormap` and `visual` attribute. You can query these attributes on all platforms. On Windows and Macintosh there is only one `visual` type at a time, and users may be able to change it for their whole system. On UNIX, the X server typically supports more than one visual class on the same display, and you can create frames and toplevels that use a particular visual class. The value of the `visual` attribute has two parts, a visual type and the desired depth of the display. The following example requests a greyscale visual with a depth of 4 bits per pixel:

```
toplevel .grey -visual "greyscale 4"
```

You can start *wish* with a `-visual` command line argument:

```
wish -visual "truecolor 24"
```

A visual is associated with a colormap. Windows and Macintosh have a single colormap that is shared by all applications. UNIX allows for private colormaps, which can be useful if you absolutely must have lots of colors. However, the drawback of a private colormap is that the display flashes as the mouse enters windows with their own colormap. This is because the monitor hardware really only has one colormap, so the X server must swap colormaps. Macintosh and Windows manage their colormap more gracefully, although if you use too many colors some flashing can occur. Tk can simulate private colormaps on Windows, but it is probably better to let the system manage the colormap. Tk on the Macintosh always uses a 24-bit `truecolor` visual, which is basically unlimited colors, and lets the operating system dither colors if necessary.

By default a widget inherits the colormap and visual from its parent widget. The value of the `colormap` attribute can be the keyword `new`, in which case the frame or toplevel gets a new private colormap, or it can be the name of another widget, in which case the frame or toplevel shares the colormap of that widget. When sharing colormaps, the other widget must be on the same screen and using the same visual class.

Bitmaps and Images

The label and all the button widgets have an `image` attribute that specifies a graphic image to display. Using an image takes two steps. In the first step the image is created via the `image create` command. This command returns an identifier for the image, and it is this identifier that is passed to widgets as the value of their image attribute.

Example 41–3 Specifying an image for a widget.

```
set im [image create bitmap \
    -file glyph.bitmap -maskfile glyph.mask \
    -background white -foreground blue]
button .foo -image $im
```

V. Tk Details

There are three things that can be displayed by labels and all the buttons: text, bitmaps, and images. If more than one of these attributes are specified, then the image has priority over the bitmap, and the bitmap has priority over the text. You can remove the image or bitmap attribute by specifying a null string for its value:

```
.foo config -image {}
```

Tk 8.4 introduced the `compound` attribute for labels, menu entries, and the various button widgets, which specifies whether the widgets should display both an image (or bitmap) and text, and if so, where the image should be placed relative to the text. For example, the following command would cause a label to display a bitmap on the left, and text to the right:

```
label .warn -text Warning -bitmap warning -compound left
```

The image Command

Table 41–5 summarizes the `image` command.

Table 41–5 Summary of the `image` command.

`image create type ?name? ?options?`	Creates an image of the specified type. If *name* is not specified, one is made up. The remaining arguments depend on the `type` of image being created.
`image delete name`	Deletes the named image.
`image height name`	Returns the height of the image, in pixels.
`image inuse name`	Returns a boolean value indicating whether or not the image given by *name* is in use by any widgets.
`image names`	Returns the list of defined images.
`image type name`	Returns the type of the named image.
`image types`	Returns the list of possible image types.
`image width name`	Returns the width of the image, in pixels.

The exact set of options for `image create` depend on the image type. There are two built-in image types: `bitmap` and `photo`. Chapter 50 describes the C interface for defining new image types.

Bitmap Images

A `bitmap` image has a main image and an optional mask image. The main image is drawn in the foreground color. The mask image is drawn in the background color, unless the corresponding bit is set in the main image. The remaining bits are "clear" and the widget's normal background color shows through. Table 41–6 lists the options supported by the `bitmap` image type:

Table 41–6 Bitmap image options.

`-background` *color*	The background color (*no* `-bg` *equivalent*).
`-data` *string*	The contents of the bitmap as a string.
`-file` *name*	The name of the file containing a bitmap definition.
`-foreground` *color*	The foreground color (*no* `-fg` *equivalent*).
`-maskdata` *string*	The contents of the mask as a string.
`-maskfile` *name*	The name of the file containing the mask data.

The bitmap definition files are stylized C structure definitions that the Tk library parses. The files usually have a `.xbm` file name extension. These are generated by bitmap editors such as *bitmap* program, which comes with the standard X distribution. The `-file` and `-maskfile` options name a file that contains such a definition. The `-data` and `-maskdata` options specify a string in the same format as the contents of one of those files.

The `bitmap` Attribute

The label and all the button widgets also support a `bitmap` attribute, which is a special case of an image. This attribute is a little more convenient than the image attribute because the extra step of creating an image is not required. However, there are some power and flexibility with the `image` command, such as the ability to reconfigure a named image (e.g., for animation) that is not possible with a bitmap.

Example 41–4 Specifying a bitmap for a widget.

```
button .foo -bitmap @glyph.xbm -fg blue
```

The @ syntax for the bitmap attribute signals that a file containing the bitmap is being specified. It is also possible to name built-in bitmaps. The predefined bitmaps are shown in the next figure along with their symbolic name. Chapter 50 describes the C interface for defining built in bitmaps.

Example 41–5 The built-in bitmaps.

```
frame .f -bd 4; frame .g -bd 4 ; pack .f .g -side left
set parent .f ; set next .g
foreach name {error gray12 gray50 hourglass \
            info questhead question warning} {
    frame $parent.$name
    label $parent.$name.l -text $name -width 9 -anchor w
    label $parent.$name.b -bitmap $name
    pack $parent.$name.l -side right
    pack $parent.$name.b -side top
```

V. Tk Details

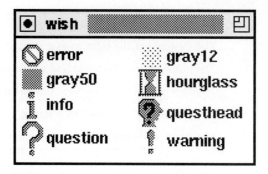

```
    pack $parent.$name -side top -expand true -fill x
    set tmp $parent ; set parent $next ; set next $tmp
}
```

Photo Images

The photo image type was contributed to Tk by Paul Mackerras. It displays full color images and can do dithering and gamma correction. Table 41–7 lists the attributes for photo images. These are specified in the image create photo command.

Table 41–7 Photo image attributes.

-data *string*	The contents of the photo as a base64 encoded or binary string.
-file *name*	The name of the file containing a photo definition.
-format *format*	Specifies the data format for the file or data string.
-gamma *value*	A gamma correction factor, which must be greater than zero. A value greater than one brightens an image.
-height *value*	The height, in screen units.
-palette *spec*	The number of shades of gray or color for the image.
-width *value*	The width of the image, in screen units.

The format indicates what format the data are in. The photo image supports different image formats. Tk has built-in support for the PPM, PGM, and GIF formats. There is a C interface to define new photo formats. The *Img* extension for Tk supports pixmaps and JPEG files. Normally you do not need to specify the format because the photo implementation will try all format handlers until it find one that accepts the data. An explicit format limits what handlers are tried. The format name is treated as a prefix that is compared against the names of handlers. Case is not significant in the format name.

The `palette` setting determines how many colors or graylevels are used when rendering an image. If a single number is specified, the image is rendered in greyscale with that many shades of gray. For full color, three numbers separated by slashes specify the number of shades of red, green, and blue, respectively. The more shades you specify the more room you take up in your colormap. The photo widget will switch to a private colormap if necessary. Multiply the number of red, green, and blue shades to determine how many different colors you use. If you have an 8-bit display, there are only 256 colors available. Reasonable palette settings that do not hog the colormap include `5/5/4` and `6/6/5`. You can use fewer shades of blue because the human eye is less sensitive to blue.

After you create an image you can operate on it. Table 41–8 lists the image instance operations. In the table, `$p` is a photo image handle returned by the `image create photo` command.

Table 41–8 Photo image operations.

`$p blank`	Clears the image. It becomes transparent.
`$p cget option`	Returns the configuration attribute *option*.
`$p configure ...`	Reconfigures the photo image attributes.
`$p copy source ?options?`	Copies another image. Table 41–9 lists the `copy` options.
`$p data ?options?`	Returns image data in the form of a list of rows, where each row is a list of colors in `#rrggbb` format. Table 41–11 lists the `data` options.
`$p get x y`	Returns the pixel value at position *x y*.
`$p put data ?-to x1 y1 x2 y2?`	Inserts *data* into the image. *data* is a list of rows, where each row is a list of colors in `#rrggbb` format.
`$p read file options`	Loads an image from a file. Table 41–10 lists the read options.
`$p redither`	Reapplies the dithering algorithm to the image.
`$p transparency get x y`	Returns a boolean indicating if the specified pixel is transparent
`$p transparency set x y boolean`	Makes the specified pixel transparent if *boolean* is true, or opaque otherwise.
`$p write file ?options?`	Saves the image to *file* according to *options*. Table 41–11 lists the `write` options.

Table 41–9 lists the options available when you copy data from one image to another. The regions involved in the copy are specified by the upper-left and lower-right corners. If the lower-right corner of the source is not specified, then it defaults to the lower-right corner of the image. If the lower-right corner of the

V. Tk Details

destination is not specified, then the size is determined by the area of the source. Otherwise, the source image may be cropped or replicated to fill the destination.

Table 41–9 Copy options for photo images.

`-compositingrule` *rule*	Specifies how transparent pixels in the source image are combined with the destination image. When *rule* is `overlay` (default), the old contents of the destination image remain visible. When *rule* is `set`, the old contents of the destination image are discarded and the source image is used as-is.
`-from` *x1 y1 ?x2 y2?*	Specifies the location and area in the source image. If *x2* and *y2* are not given, they are set to the bottom-right corner.
`-to` *x1 y1 ?x2 y2?*	Specifies the location and area in the destination. If *x2* and *y2* are not given, the size is determined by the source. The source may be cropped or tiled to fill the destination.
`-shrink`	Shrinks the destination so that its bottom right corner matches the bottom right corner of the data copied in. This has no effect if the `width` and `height` have been set for the image.
`-zoom` *x ?y?*	Magnifies the source so each source pixel becomes a block of *x* by *y* pixels. *y* defaults to *x* if it is not specified.
`-subsample` *x ?y?*	Reduces the source by taking every *x*th pixel in the X direction and every *y*th pixel in the Y direction. *y* defaults to *x*.

Table 41–10 lists the `read` options. If not specified, the format is determined automatically. If there are multiple image types that can read the same data, you may specify a read format

Table 41–10 Read options for photo images.

`-format` *format*	Specifies the format of the data. By default, the format is determined automatically.
`-from` *x1 y1 ?x2 y2?*	Specifies a subregion of the source data. If *x2* and *y2* are not given, the size is determined by the data.
`-to` *x1 y1*	Specifies the top-left corner of the new data.
`-shrink`	Shrinks the destination so that its bottom-right corner matches the bottom-right corner of the data read in. This has no effect if the width and height have been set for the image.

Table 41–11 lists the options used for `write` and `data`. When writing to files, the `-format` option is important because if you don't specify it, the first format found is used. On the other hand, you shouldn't use the `-format` option with `data` operation, as `data` returns the image date as a list of rows, where each row is a list of colors in #rrggbb format (suitable as input to the `put` command).

Table 41–11 Write options for photo images.

`-background color`	If specified, all transparent pixels are replaced by the specified *color*.
`-format format`	Specifies the format of the data.
`-from x1 y1 ?x2 y2?`	Specifies a subregion of the data to save. If *x2* and *y2* are not given, they are set to the lower-right corner.
`-grayscale`	If specified, the data is transformed into grayscale.

The Text Insert Cursor

The text, entry, and canvas widgets have a second cursor to mark the text insertion point. The text insert cursor is described by a set of attributes. These attributes can make the insert cursor vary from a thin vertical line to a large rectangle with its own relief. Table 41–12 lists these attributes. The default insert cursor is a two-pixel-wide vertical line. You may not like the look of a wide insert cursor. The cursor is centered between two characters, so a wide one does not look the same as the block cursors found in many terminal emulators. Instead of occupying the space of a single character, it partially overlaps the two characters on either side:

Table 41–12 Cursor attribute resource names.

`cursor`	The mouse cursor. See text for sample formats. All widgets.
`insertBackground`	Color for the text insert cursor. Widgets: `canvas`, `entry`, and `text`.
`insertBorderWidth`	Width for three dimensional appearance. Widgets: `canvas`, `entry`, and `text`.
`insertOffTime`	Milliseconds the cursor blinks off. (Zero disables blinking.) Widgets: `canvas`, `entry`, and `text`.
`insertOnTime`	Milliseconds the cursor blinks on. Widgets: `canvas`, `entry`, and `text`.
`insertWidth`	Width of the text insert cursor, in screen units. Widgets: `canvas`, `entry`, and `text`.

The Mouse Cursor

The cursor attribute defines the mouse cursor. On Unix systems, a foreground and background color for the cursor can be specified. Here are some example cursor specifications:

```
$w config -cursor watch               ;# stop-watch cursor
$w config -cursor {gumby blue}        ;# blue gumby
$w config -cursor {X_cursor red white}  ;# red X on white
```

The other form for the cursor attribute specifies a file that contains the definition of the cursor bitmap. If two file names are specified, then the second specifies the cursor mask that determines what bits of the background get covered up. Bitmap editing programs like *idraw* and *iconedit* can be used to generate these files. Here are some example cursor specification using files. You need to specify a foreground color, and if you specify a mask file, then you also need to specify a background color:

```
$w config -cursor "@timer.xbm black"
$w config -cursor "@timer.xbm timer.mask black red"
```

Example 41–6 on page 633 shows the cursors that come built into Tk. Those shown are from the X cursor font for Unix, which are available on all platforms with Tk. There are some additional platform-specific cursors as noted below, which are not shown. On Windows and Macintosh some of the cursors are mapped to native cursors and appear differently.

On Macintosh, the following cursors are mapped to native cursors: ibeam, xterm, cross, crosshair, plus, watch, arrow. These additional cursors are defined on Macintosh: text and cross-hair.

On Windows the following cursors are mapped to native cursors: arrow, ibeam, icon, crosshair, fleur, sb_v_double_arrow, sb_h_double_arrow, center_ptr, watch, and xterm. These additional cursors are defined on Windows: starting, size, size_ne_sw, size_ns, size_nw_se, size_we, uparrow, and wait. On Windows, use the no cursor to eliminate the cursor.

As of Tk 8.3, when running on Windows you can use Windows system cursors by specifying the name of the appropriate .ani or .cur file. For example:

```
$w config -cursor @C:/WINNT/Cursors/globe.ani
```

Example 41–6 The Tk cursors.

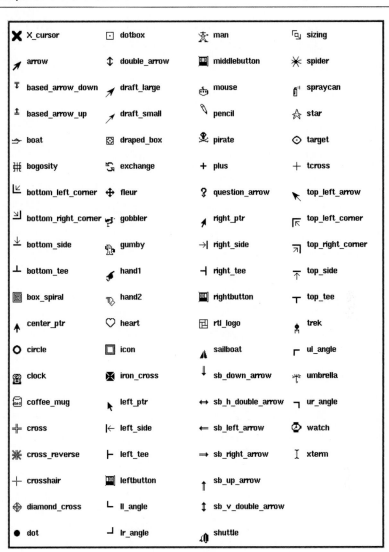

Fonts and Text Attributes

This chapter describes the naming conventions for fonts. Tk has a font object that you can dynamically configure and associate with widgets. This chapter also describes other text-related attributes such as justification, anchoring, and geometry gridding.

Fonts describe how characters look on the screen. Tk widgets like buttons, labels, and listboxes have a `font` attribute that determines which font they use to display their text. The text widget has `font` attributes on tags that are applied to different regions of text. Tk has a platform-independent way to name fonts (e.g., `times 12 bold`), plus it gracefully handles missing fonts. You can define named font objects and then associate those with widgets and text tags. When the font objects are reconfigured, the widgets using them update their display automatically. You can use the resource database to define the fonts used in your interface.

X font names (e.g., `-*-times-bold-r-normal-*-12-*`) were used in versions of Tk before 8.0, and the widgets would raise errors if a font could not be found. The X names have a pattern matching scheme that helps avoid some missing font errors. You can still use X font names in current versions of Tk. However, the Tk font system does not do font substitutions if you use X font names; if you use them, you must be prepared for errors. In general, you should use the platform-independent font names.

After describing fonts, the chapter explains a few of the widget attributes that relate to fonts. This includes justification, anchors, and geometry gridding.

Naming a Font

There are two basic ways to name a font. You can use predefined font names (e.g., `system`), or you can specify a set of font attributes with a platform-independent name:

```
label .foo -text "Hello" -font {times 12 bold}
```

In this form, the font is specified with a three element list. The first element is the font family, the second is the size, in points, and the third is a list of style parameters. The family determines the basic look, such as `courier` or helvetica.

The complete set of style parameters are `normal`, `bold`, `roman`, `italic`, `underline`, and `overstrike`. For example, to specify both **bold** and *italic*:

```
label .foo -text "Hello" -font {times 12 {bold italic}}
```

The font size is points, which are 1/72 inch. Tk maintains a scale factor that maps from points to pixels. The default scale is derived from the screen resolution, and you can change it with the `tk scaling` command, which is described on page 669. You can specify pixel-based sizes with negative numbers. The advantage of points over pixels is that text appears about the same size regardless of the screen resolution. (This works better on Windows and Macintosh than on Unix.) However, sometimes you want to control font size relative to other widget geometry, in which case pixel-based sizes are better.

An alternate way to name font attributes uses name-value pairs. These are summarized in Table 42–1. The format is less compact, but it is useful for changing part of a font configuration because you do not need to specify everything. The same specification can be made like this:

```
label .foo -text "Hello" -font \
    {-family times -size 12 -weight bold -slant italic}
```

Table 42–1 Font attributes.

`-family` *name*	The *name* can be `times`, `courier`, `helvetica`, and others returned by the `font families` command.
`-size` *points*	The font size is given in points, which are 1/72 inch.
`-weight` *value*	The value is `bold` or `normal`.
`-slant` *value*	The value is `roman` or `italic`.
`-underline` *bool*	If *bool* is `true`, an underline is drawn.
`-overstrike` *bool*	If *bool* is `true`, an overstrike line is drawn.

Tk matches a font specification with the fonts available on your system. It will use the best possible font, but it may have to substitute some font parameters. Tk guarantees that the Times, `Courier`, and Helvetica families exist. It also understands the synonyms of `Courier New` for `Courier`, and Arial or Geneva for Helvetica.The `font actual` command returns the parameters chosen to match a font specification:

```
font actual {times 13 bold}
-family Times -size 13 -weight bold -slant roman
    -underline 0 -overstrike 0
```

The Macintosh and Windows platforms have a system-defined default size. You can get this size by specifying a size of 0 in your specification. The system font uses this:

```
font actual system
-family Chicago -size 0 -weight normal -slant roman
    -underline 0 -overstrike 0
```

Named Fonts

You can define your own names for fonts with the `font create` command. Creating a named font provides a level of indirection between the font parameters and the widgets that use the fonts. If you reconfigure a named font, the widgets using it will update their display automatically. This makes it easy to support a user preference for font size. For example, we can define a font name `default` on all platforms:

```
font create default -family times -size 12
```

The `default` font can be made larger at any time with `font configure`. Widgets using the fonts will update automatically:

```
font configure default -size 14
```

System Fonts

The Windows and Macintosh platforms have system-defined fonts that are used by most applications. When you query the configuration of the Tk widgets, you will see the system font names. The parameters for the system fonts can be tuned by the user via the system control panel. You can find out the attributes of the system font with `font actual`. These are the system fonts for each platform:

- The Windows platform supports `system`, `systemfixed`, `ansi`, `ansifixed`, `device`, `oemfixed`. The `fixed` suffix refers to a font where each character is the same size.
- The Macintosh platform has `system` and `application`.
- The UNIX platform has `fixed`. This is the only X font name that is guaranteed to exist. X font names are described in the next section.

Unicode Fonts

Tk does character-by-character font substitution when it displays Unicode characters. This supports mixed display of ASCII and Kanji characters, for example. The great thing about this is that you do not have to worry too much about choosing fonts in the simple case. The problem with font substitution is that it can be slow. In the worst case, Tk will query every font installed in your system to find out whether it can display a particular character. If you know you will be displaying characters in a particular character set, you can optimize your interface by specifying a font that matches what you expect to display.

X Font Names

Fonts can be specified with X font names on all platforms, and you must use X font names in versions of Tk before Tk 8.0. The name `fixed` is an example of a short X font name. Other short names might include `6x12`, `9x15`, or `times12`. However, these aliases are site-dependent. In fact, all X font names are site dependent because different fonts may be installed on different systems. The only font guaranteed to exist on the UNIX platform is named `fixed`.

The more general form of an X font name has several components that describe the font parameters. Each component is separated by a dash, and the asterisk (`*`) is used for unspecified components. Short font names are system-defined aliases for these more complete specifications. Here is an example:

```
-*-times-medium-r-normal-*-18-*-*-*-*-*-iso8859-1
```

The components of X font names are listed in Table 42–2 in the order in which they occur in the font specification. The table gives the possible values for the components. If there is an ellipsis (...), then there are more possibilities, too.

Table 42–2 X Font specification components.

Component	Possible values
foundry	adobe xerox linotype misc ...
family	times helvetica lucida courier symbol ...
weight	bold medium demibold demi normal book light
slant	i r o
swidth	normal sans narrow semicondensed
adstyle	sans
pixels	8 10 12 14 18 24 36 48 72 144 ...
points	0 80 100 120 140 180 240 360 480 720 ...
resx	0 72 75 100
resy	0 72 75 100
space	p m c
avgWidth	73 94 124 ...
registry	iso8859 xerox dec adobe jisx0208.1983 ...
encoding	1 fontspecific dectech symbol dingbats

The most common attributes chosen for a font are its family, weight, slant, and size. The weight is usually **bold** or medium. The slant component is a bit cryptic, but i means *italic*, r means roman (i.e., normal), and o means *oblique*. A given font family might have an italic version, or an oblique version, but not both. Similarly, not all weights are offered by all font families. Size can be specified in pixels (i.e., screen pixels) or points. Points are meant to be independent of the screen resolution. On a 75dpi font, there are about 10 points per pixel. Note: These "points" are different than the printer points Tk uses in screen measurements. When you use X font names, the size of the font is *not* affected by the Tk scaling factor described on page 669.

It is generally a good idea to specify just a few key components and use * for the remaining components. The X server attempts to match the font specification with its set of installed fonts, but it fails if there is a specific component that it cannot match. If the first or last character of the font name is an asterisk, then that can match multiple components. The following selects a 12-pixel times font:

```
*times-medium-r-*-*-12*
```

Two useful UNIX programs that deal with X fonts are *xlsfonts* and *xfontsel*. These are part of the standard X11 distribution. *xlsfonts* simply lists the available fonts that match a given font name. It uses the same pattern matching that the server does. Because asterisk is special to most UNIX shells, you need to quote the font name argument if you run *xlsfonts* from your shell. *xfontsel* has a graphical user interface and displays the font that matches a given font name.

Font Failures before Tk 8.0

Unfortunately, if a font is missing, versions of Tk before 8.0 do not attempt to substitute another font, not even fixed. Current versions of Tk do substitutions only if you use platform-independent font names. Otherwise, the widget creation or reconfiguration command raises an error if the font does not exist. Example 42–1 shows one way to deal with missing fonts, which is to create a wrapper, the FontWidget procedure, around the Tk widget creation routines:

Example 42–1 The FontWidget procedure handles missing fonts.

```
proc FontWidget { args } {
    # args is a Tcl command
    if {[catch $args w]} {
        # Delete the font specified in args, if any
        set ix [lsearch $args -font]
        if {$ix >= 0} {
            set args [lreplace $args $ix [expr $ix+1]]
        }
        # This font overrides the resource database
        # The "fixed" font is UNIX-specific
        set w [eval $args {-font fixed}]
    }
    return $w
}
```

You call `FontWidget` like this:

```
FontWidget button .foo -text Foo -font garbage
```

The `FontWidget` procedure reverts to a default font if the widget creation command fails. It is careful to eliminate the font specified in `args`, if it exists. The explicit font overrides any setting from the resource database or the Tk defaults. Of course, widget creation might fail for some more legitimate reason, but that is allowed to happen in the backup case. Again, the missing font problem disappears when you use platform-independent font names, so you only need to resort to using `FontWidget` in early versions of Tk.

Font Metrics

The `font metrics` command returns measurement information for fonts. It returns general information about all the characters in the font:

```
font metrics {times 10}
-ascent 9 -descent 2 -linespace 11 -fixed 0
```

The `fixed` setting is true for fonts where each character fits into the same-sized bounding box. The `linespace` is the distance between the baselines of successive lines. The `ascent` and `descent` are illustrated in Example 42–2:

Example 42–2 Font metrics.

The `font measure` command returns the width of a string that will be displayed in a given font. The width does not account for heavily slanted letters that overhang their bounding box, nor does it do anything special with tabs or newlines in the string.

The `font` Command

Table 42–3 summarizes the `font` command. In the table, *font* is either a description of font parameters, a logical font name, a system font name, or an X font name. The `-displayof` option applies to X where you can have windows on different displays that can support different fonts. Note that when you delete a logical font name with `font delete`, the font is not really deleted if there are widgets that use that font.

Table 42–3 The `font` command.

`font actual` *font* `?-displayof` *window*? `?`*option*?	Returns the actual parameters of *font*.
`font configure` *fontname* `?`*option*? `?`*value option* *value*?	Sets or queries the parameters for *fontname*.
`font create ?`*fontname*? `?`*option value* `...?`	Defines *fontname* with the specified parameters.
`font delete` *fontname* `?`*name2* `...?`	Removes the definition for the named fonts.
`font families ?-displayof` *win*?	Returns the list of font families supported on the display of *win*.
`font measure` *font* `?-displayof` *win*? *text*	Returns the width of *text* displayed in *win* with *font*.
`font metrics` *font* `?-displayof` *win*? `?`*option*?	The *option* can be `-ascent`, `-descent`, `-linespace`, or `-fixed`.
`font names`	Returns the names of defined fonts.

Text Attributes

Layout

Table 42–4 summarizes two simple text layout attributes: `justify` and `wrapLength`. The `text` widget has several more layout-related attributes, and Chapter 36 describes those in detail. The two attributes described in this section apply to the various button widgets, the label, entry, and message widgets. Those widgets are described in Chapters 30, 32, and 34. The `justify` attribute causes text to be centered, left-justified, or right-justified. The default justification is `center` for all the widgets in the table, except for the entry widget, which is left-justified by default.

The `wrapLength` attribute specifies how long a line of text is before it is wrapped onto another line. It is used to create multiline buttons and labels. This attribute is specified in screen units, however, not string length. It is probably easier to achieve the desired line breaks by inserting newlines into the text for the button or label and specifying a `wrapLength` of 0, which is the default.

Table 42–4 Layout attribute resource names

`justify`	Text line justification. Values: `left`, `center`, or `right`. Widgets: `button`, `checkbutton`, `entry`, `label`, `menubutton`, `message`, and `radiobutton`.
`wrapLength`	Maximum line length for text, in screen units. Widgets: `button`, `checkbutton`, `label`, `menubutton`, and `radiobutton`.

Selection Attributes

Table 42–5 lists the selection-related attributes. The `exportSelection` attribute controls if the selection is exported for cut and paste to other widgets. The colors for selected text are set with `selectForeground` and `selectBackground`. The selection is drawn in a raised relief, and the `selectBorderWidth` attribute affects the 3D appearance. Choose a border width of zero to get a flat relief.

Table 42–5 Selection attribute resource names.

`exportSelection`	Share selection. Widgets: `entry, canvas, listbox, and text.`
`selectForeground`	Foreground of selected text.
`selectBackground`	Background of selected text.
`selectBorderWidth`	Width of 3D raised border for selection highlight.

Gridding, Resizing, and Geometry

The text, listbox, and canvas widgets support geometry gridding. This is an alternate interpretation of the main window geometry that is in terms of grid units, typically characters, as opposed to pixels. The `setGrid` attribute is a boolean that indicates if gridding should be turned on. The listbox and text widgets define a grid size that matches their character size. Example 44–1 on page 658 sets up gridding for a canvas.

When a widget is gridded, its size is constrained to have a whole number of grid units displayed. The height will be constrained to show a whole number of text lines, and the width will be constrained to show a whole number of average width characters. This affects interactive resizing by users, as well as the various window manger commands (`wm`) that relate to geometry. When gridding is turned on, the geometry argument (e.g., `24x80`) is interpreted as grid units; otherwise, it is interpreted as pixels. The window manager geometry commands are summarized in Table 44–1 on page 659.

The following example creates a listbox with gridded geometry enabled. Try resizing the window in the following example with and without the `-setgrid` flag, and with and without the `wm minsize` command, which sets the minimum size of the window. The `Scrolled_Listbox` procedure is defined in Example 33–3 on page 502.

Example 42–3 A gridded, resizable listbox.

```
wm minsize . 5 3
button .quit -text Quit -command exit
pack .quit -side top -anchor e
Scrolled_Listbox .f -width 10 -height 5 -setgrid true
pack .f -side top -fill both -expand true
```

A Font Selection Application

This chapter concludes with an example that lets you select fonts. It is written as a dialog that you can add to your application. The menus are tied to elements of the font array that are used in font configure commands. The actual settings of the font are shown above a sampler of what the font looks like. When the user clicks the OK button, the font configuration is returned:

Example 42–4 Font selection dialog.

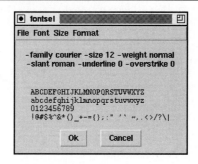

```
proc Font_Select {{top .fontsel}} {
    global font

    # Create File, Font, Size, and Format menus

    toplevel $top -class Fontsel -bd 10
    set menubar [menu $top.menubar]
    $top config -menu $menubar
    foreach x {File Font Size Format} {
        set menu [menu $menubar.[string tolower $x]]
        $menubar add cascade -menu $menu -label $x
    }
    $menubar.file add command -label Reset -command FontReset
    $menubar.file add command -label OK \
        -command {set font(ok) ok}
    $menubar.file add command -label Cancel \
        -command {set font(ok) cancel}

    # The Fonts menu lists the available Font families.

    set allfonts [font families]
    set numfonts [llength $allfonts]
    set limit 20
    if {$numfonts < $limit} {

        # Display the fonts in a single menu

        foreach family $allfonts {
            $menubar.font add radio -label $family \
                -variable font(-family) \
                -value $family \
                -command FontUpdate
```

```
    }
} else {

    # Too many fonts. Create a set of cascaded menus to
    # display all the font possibilities

    set c 0 ; set l 0
    foreach family $allfonts {
        if {$l == 0} {
            $menubar.font add cascade -label $family... \
                -menu $menubar.font.$c
            set m [menu $menubar.font.$c]
            incr c
        }
        $m add radio -label $family \
            -variable font(-family) \
            -value $family \
            -command FontUpdate
        set l [expr ($l +1) % $limit]
    }
}

# Complete the other menus

foreach size {7 8 10 12 14 18 24 36 72} {
    $menubar.size add radio -label $size \
        -variable font(-size) \
        -value $size \
        -command FontUpdate
}
$menubar.size add command -label Other... \
        -command [list FontSetSize $top]
$menubar.format add check -label Bold \
        -variable font(-weight) \
        -onvalue bold -offvalue normal \
        -command FontUpdate
$menubar.format add check -label Italic \
        -variable font(-slant) \
        -onvalue italic -offvalue roman \
        -command FontUpdate
$menubar.format add check -label underline \
    -variable font(-underline) \
    -command FontUpdate
$menubar.format add check -label overstrike \
    -variable font(-overstrike) \
    -command FontUpdate

# FontReset initializes the font array, which causes
# the radio menu entries to get highlighted.

FontReset

# This label displays the current font

label $top.font -textvar font(name) -bd 5
```

```
    # This message displays a sampler of the font.

    message $top.msg -aspect 1000 \
                -borderwidth 10 -font fontsel \
                -text "
ABCDEFGHIJKLMNOPQRSTUVWXYZ
abcdefghijklmnopqrstuvwxyz
0123456789
!@#$%^&*()_+-=[]{};:\"''~,.<>/?\\|
"

    # Lay out the dialog

    pack $top.font $top.msg -side top
    set f [frame $top.buttons]
    button $f.ok -text Ok -command {set font(ok) 1}
    button $f.cancel -text Cancel -command {set font(ok) 0}
    pack $f.ok $f.cancel -padx 10 -side left
    pack $f -side top

    # Dialog_Wait is defined in Example 39-1 on page 606

    set font(ok) cancel
    Dialog_Wait $top font(ok)
    destroy $top
    if {$font(ok) == "ok"} {
        return [array get font -*]
    } else {
        return {}
    }
}

# FontReset recreates a default font

proc FontReset {} {
    catch {font delete fontsel}
    font create fontsel
    FontSet
}

# FontSet initializes the font array with the settings
# returned by the font actual command

proc FontSet {} {
    global font

    # The name is the font configuration information
    # with a line break so it looks nicer

    set font(name) [font actual fontsel]
    regsub -- "-slant" $font(name) "\n-slant" font(name)

    # Save the actual parameters after any font substitutions

    array set font [font actual fontsel]
```

```
    }

    # FontSetSize adds an entry widget to the dialog so you
    # can enter a specific font size.

    proc FontSetSize {top} {
        set f [frame $top.size -borderwidth 10]
        pack $f -side top -fill x
        label $f.msg -text "Size:"
        entry $f.entry -textvariable font(-size)
        bind $f.entry <Return> FontUpdate
        pack $f.msg -side left
        pack $f.entry -side top -fill x
    }

    # FontUpdate is called when any of the font settings
    # are changed, either from the menu or FontSetSize

    proc FontUpdate { } {
        global font

        # The elements of font that have a leading - are
        # used directly in the font configuration command.

        eval {font configure fontsel} [array get font -*]
        FontSet
    }
```

Send

This chapter describes the send command that invokes Tcl commands in other applications. This chapter also presents an alternative to send that uses network sockets.

*T*he send command lets Tk applications on the same display send each other Tcl commands and cooperate in very flexible ways. A large application can be structured as a set of smaller tools that cooperate instead of one large monolith. This encourages reuse, and it exploits your workstation's multiprogramming capabilities.

The send facility provides a name space for Tk applications. The winfo interps command returns the names of all the Tk applications reachable with send. The send communication mechanism is limited to applications running on one display. Multiple screens on one workstation still count as the same display on X. In UNIX, send uses properties on the X display for communication and to record the application names. As of Tk 8.0, send is not yet implemented on Macintosh or Windows. There is an extension for Windows that uses DDE to emulate send.

This chapter also describes an alternative to send that uses network sockets. The facility is not limited to a single display, and can be used in conjunction with safe interpreters to limit the capabilities of remote operations. A number of Tcl extensions provide similar functionality, including *GroupKit* and *Tcl-DP*. Of particular note is the comm package, which is a part of the Standard Tcl Library. The comm package was designed as a sockets-based replacement for send that would work on any platform. You can find more information about comm from the *tcllib* project page on SourceForge:

    http://tcllib.sourceforge.net.

The send Command

The `send` command invokes a Tcl command in another application. The general form of the command is:

```
send options interp arg ?arg...?
```

The `send` command behaves like `eval`; if you give it extra arguments, it concatenates them to form a single command. If your argument structure is important, use `list` to build the command. Table 43–1 lists the options to `send`:

Table 43–1 Options to the `send` command.

`-async`	Does not wait for the remote command to complete.
`-displayof` `window`	Sends to the application on the same display as `window`.
`--`	Delimits options from the `interp` argument. Useful if the `interp` begins with a dash.

The `interp` argument is the name of the other application. An application defines its own name when it creates its main window. The *wish* shell uses as its name the last component of the file name of the script. For example, when *wish* interprets `/usr/local/bin/exmh`, it sets its application name to `exmh`. However, if another instance of the `exmh` application is already running, *wish* chooses the name `exmh #2`, and so on. If *wish* is not executing from a file, its name is just `wish`. You may have noticed `wish #2` or `wish #3` in your window title bars, and this reflects the fact that multiple *wish* applications are running on your display.

A script can find out its own name, so you can pass names around or put them into files in order to set up communications. The `tk appname` command queries or changes the application name:

```
set myname [tk appname]
tk appname aNewName
```

Send and X Authority

The `send` command relies on the X authority mechanism for authorization. A command is rejected by the target interpreter if you do not have X authority set up. There are two ways around this problem. First, you can disable the access check by compiling the `tkSend.c` file with the `-DTK_NO_SECURITY` compile flag. If you must worry about malicious programs that send your programs commands, then you should not do this.

The second option is to start your X server with its `-auth` flag, which initializes the X authority mechanism. The details vary depending on your X server, and most modern X servers do this automatically. The general picture is that you generate a pseudo-random string and store it into a file, which is usually named `~/.Xauthority` and must be readable only by your account. The `-auth` flag specifies the name of this file to the X server. Each X application reads this file and sends the contents to the X server when opening the connection to the server. If the contents match what the server read when it started, then the connection is allowed. The system is slightly more complicated than described here. The file actually contains a sequence of records to support multiple displays and client hosts. Consult your local X guru or the documentation for the details particular to your system.

Your xhost list must be clear.

Tk also requires that the *xhost* list be empty. The *xhost* mechanism is the old, not-so-secure authentication mechanism in X. With *xhost* you allow all programs on a list of hosts to connect to your display. The problem with this is that multiuser workstations allow remote login, so essentially anybody could log in to a workstation on the *xhost* list and gain access to your display. The Xauthority mechanism is much stronger because it restricts access to your account, or to accounts that you explicitly give a secret token to. The problem is that even if Xauthority is set up, the user or a program can turn on *xhosts* and open up access to your display.

If you run the *xhost* program with no argument, it reports the status and what hosts are on the list. The following output is generated when access control is restricted, but programs running on `sage` are allowed to connect to the display:

```
exec xhost
=> Access control enabled: all hosts being restricted
sage
```

This is not good enough for Tk `send`. It will fail because `sage` is on the list. I work in an environment where old scripts and programs are constantly adding things to my *xhost* list for reasons that are no longer valid. I developed a version of `send` that checks for errors and then does the following to clean out the *xhost* list. You have to enable access control and then explicitly remove any hosts on the list. These are reported after an initial line that says whether or not hosts are restricted:

```
xhost - ;# enable access control in general
foreach host [lrange [split [exec xhost] \n] 1 end] {
    exec xhost -$host ;# clear out exceptions
}
```

The Sender Script

The following example is a general-purpose script that reads input and then sends it to another application. You can put this at the end of a pipeline to get a loopback effect to the main application, although you can also use `fileevent` for similar effects. One advantage of `send` over `fileevent` is that the sender and receiver can be more independent. A logging application, for example, can come and go independently of the applications that log error messages:

Example 43–1 The sender application.

```
#!/usr/local/bin/wish
# sender takes up to four arguments:
# 1) the name of the application to send to.
# 2) a command prefix.
# 3) the name of another application to notify
#    after the end of the data.
# 4) the command to use in the notification.

# Hide the unneeded window
wm withdraw .
# Process command line arguments
if {$argc == 0} {
    puts stderr "Usage: send name ?cmd? ?uiName? ?uiCmd?"
    exit 1
} else {
    set app [lindex $argv 0]
}
if {$argc > 1} {
    set cmd [lindex $argv 1]
} else {
    set cmd Send_Insert
}
if {$argc > 2} {
    set ui [lindex $argv 2]
    set uiCmd Send_Done
}
if {$argc > 3} {
    set uiCmd [lindex $argv 3]
}
# Read input and send it to the logger
while {[gets stdin input] >= 0} {
    # Ignore errors with the logger
    catch {send $app [concat $cmd [list $input\n]]}
}
# Notify the controller, if any
if [info exists ui] {
    if [catch {send $ui $uiCmd} msg] {
        puts stderr "send.tcl could not notify $ui\n$msg"
    }
}
# This is necessary to force wish to exit.
exit
```

The *sender* application supports communication with two processes. It sends all its input to a primary "logging" application. When the input finishes, it can send a notification message to another "controller" application. The logger and the controller could be the same application.

Use list to quote arguments to send.

Consider the send command used in the example:

```
send $app [concat $cmd [list $input\n]]
```

The combination of `concat` and `list` is tricky. The `list` command quotes the value of the input line. This quoted value is then appended to the command, so it appears as a single extra argument. Without the quoting by `list`, the value of the input line will affect the way the remote interpreter parses the command. Consider these alternatives:

```
send $app [list $cmd $input]
```

This form is safe, except that it limits `$cmd` to a single word. If `cmd` contains a value like the ones given below, the remote interpreter will not parse it correctly. It will treat the whole multiword value as the name of a command:

```
.log insert end
.log see end ; .log insert end
```

This is the most common wrong answer:

```
send $app $cmd $input
```

The `send` command concatenates `$cmd` and `$input` together, and the result will be parsed again by the remote interpreter. The success or failure of the remote command depends on the value of the input data. If the input included Tcl syntax like `$` or `[ ]`, errors or other unexpected behavior would result.

Communicating Processes

Chapter 24 presented two examples: a browser for the examples in this book, and a simple shell in which to try out Tcl commands. In that chapter they are put into the same application. The two examples shown below hook these two applications together using the `send` command. Example 43–2 changes the `Run` and `Reset` procedures of the browser to send `EvalEcho` commands to the shell.

Example 43–2 Hooking the browser to an `eval` server.

```
# Replace the Run and Reset procedures of the browser in
# Example 24-3 on page 384 with these procedures

# Start up the evalsrv.tcl script.
proc StartEvalServer {} {
    global browse
    # Start the shell and pass it our name.
    exec evalsrv.tcl [tk appname] &
    # Wait for evalsrv.tcl to send us its name
    tkwait variable browse(evalInterp)
}
proc Run {} {
    global browse
    set apps [winfo interps]
    set ix [lsearch -glob $apps evalsrv.tcl*]
    if {$ix < 0} {
        # No evalsrv.tcl application running
        StartEvalServer
    }
```

```
    if {![info exists browse(evalInterp)]} {
        # Hook up to already running eval server
        set browse(evalInterp) [lindex $apps $ix]
    }
    if [catch {send $browse(evalInterp) {info vars}} err] {
        # It probably died - restart it.
        StartEvalServer
    }
    # Send the command asynchronously. The two
    # list commands foil the concat done by send and
    # the uplevel in EvalEcho
    send -async $browse(evalInterp) \
        [list EvalEcho [list source $browse(current)]]
}
# Reset the shell interpreter in the eval server
proc Reset {} {
    global browse
    send $browse(evalInterp) {EvalEcho reset}
}
```

The number of lists created before the send command may seem excessive, but they are all necessary. The send command concatenates its arguments, so instead of letting it do that, we pass it a single list. Similarly, EvalEcho expects a single argument that is a valid command, so list is used to construct that.

The StartEvalServer procedure starts up the shell. Command-line arguments are used to pass the application name of the browser to the shell. The shell completes the connection by sending its own application name back to the browser. The browser stores the name of the shell application in browser(evalInterp). The code that the shell uses is shown in Example 43–3:

Example 43–3 Making the shell into an eval server.

```
# Add this to the shell application shown
# in Example 24-4 on page 389
if {$argc > 0} {
    # Send our application name to the browser
    send [lindex $argv 0] \
        [list set browse(evalInterp) [tk appname]]
}
```

Remote eval through Sockets

Network sockets provide another communication mechanism you can use to evaluate Tcl commands in another application. The "name" of the application is just the host and port for the socket connection. There are a variety of schemes you can use to manage names. A crude, but effective way to manage host and ports for your servers is to record them in a file in your network file system. These examples ignore this problem. The server chooses a port and the client is expected to know what it is.

Example 43–4 implements `Eval_Server` that lets other applications connect and evaluate Tcl commands. The `interp` argument specifies the interpreter in which to evaluate the Tcl commands. If the caller of `Eval_Server` specifies `{}` for the interpreter, then the commands are evaluated in the current interpreter. The `openCmd` is called when the connection is made. It can do whatever setup or authentication is required. If it doesn't like the connection, it can close the socket:

Example 43–4 Remote `eval` using sockets.

```
proc Eval_Server {port {interp {}} {openCmd EvalOpenProc}} {
    socket -server [list EvalAccept $interp $openCmd] $port
}
proc EvalAccept {interp openCmd newsock addr port} {
    global eval
    set eval(cmdbuf,$newsock) {}
    fileevent $newsock readable [list EvalRead $newsock $interp]
    if [catch {
        interp eval $interp $openCmd $newsock $addr $port
    }] {
        close $newsock
    }
}
proc EvalOpenProc {sock addr port} {
    # do authentication here
    # close $sock to deny the connection
}
```

Example 43–5 shows `EvalRead` that reads commands and evaluates them in an interpreter. If the `interp` is `{}`, it causes the commands to execute in the current interpreter. In this case an `uplevel #0` is necessary to ensure the command is executed in the global scope. If you use `interp eval` to execute something in yourself, it executes in the current scope:

Example 43–5 Reading commands from a socket.

```
proc EvalRead {sock interp} {
    global eval errorInfo errorCode
    if [eof $sock] {
        close $sock
    } else {
        gets $sock line
        append eval(cmdbuf,$sock) $line\n
        if {[string length $eval(cmdbuf,$sock)] && \
                [info complete $eval(cmdbuf,$sock)]} {
            set code [catch {
                if {[string length $interp] == 0} {
                    uplevel #0 $eval(cmdbuf,$sock)
                } else {
                    interp eval $interp $eval(cmdbuf,$sock)
                }
```

```
            } result]
            set reply [list $code $result $errorInfo \
                $errorCode]\n
            # Use regsub to count newlines
            set lines [regsub -all \n $reply {} junk]
            # The reply is a line count followed
            # by a Tcl list that occupies that number of lines
            puts $sock $lines
            puts -nonewline $sock $reply
            flush $sock
            set eval(cmdbuf,$sock) {}
        }
    }
}
```

Example 43–6 presents Eval_Open and Eval_Remote that implement the client side of the eval connection. Eval_Open connects to the server and returns a token, which is just the socket. The main task of Eval_Remote is to preserve the information generated when the remote command raises an error

The network protocol is line-oriented. The Eval_Remote command writes the command on the socket. The EvalRead procedure uses info complete to detect the end of the command. The reply is more arbitrary, so server sends a line count and that number of lines. The regsub command counts up all the newlines because it returns the number of matches it finds. The reply is a list of error codes, results, and trace information. These details of the return command are described on page 86.

Example 43–6 The client side of remote evaluation.

```
proc Eval_Open {server port} {
    global eval
    set sock [socket $server $port]
    # Save this info for error reporting
    set eval(server,$sock) $server:$port
    return $sock
}
proc Eval_Remote {sock args} {
    global eval
    # Preserve the concat semantics of eval
    if {[llength $args] > 1} {
        set cmd [concat $args]
    } else {
        set cmd [lindex $args 0]
    }
    puts $sock $cmd
    flush $sock
    # Read return line count and the result.
    gets $sock lines
    set result {}
    while {$lines > 0} {
        gets $sock x
        append result $x\n
```

```
        incr lines -1
    }
    set code [lindex $result 0]
    set x [lindex $result 1]
    # Cleanup the end of the stack
    regsub "\[^\n]+$" [lindex $result 2] \
        "*Remote Server $eval(server,$sock)*" stack
    set ec [lindex $result 3]
    return -code $code -errorinfo $stack -errorcode $ec $x
}
proc Eval_Close {sock} {
    close $sock
}
```

If an error occurs in the remote command, then a stack trace is returned. This includes the command used inside `EvalRead` to invoke the command, which is either the `uplevel` or `interp eval` command. This is the very last line in the stack that is returned, and `regsub` is used to replace this with an indication of where control transferred to the remote server:

```
catch [Eval_Remote sock6 set xx]
=> 1
set errorInfo
=> can't read "xx": no such variable
    while executing
"set xx
"
    ("uplevel" body line 1)
    invoked from within
*Remote Server sage:4000*
    invoked from within
"catch [Eval_Remote sock6 set xx]"
```

Window Managers and Window Information

The window manager controls the size and location of other applications' windows. The window manager is built into Windows and Macintosh, while it is a separate application on UNIX. The wm command provides an interface to the window manager. The winfo command returns information about windows. The tk command provides miscellaneous information about Tk and the windowing system.

Management of top-level windows is done by the *window manager*. The Macintosh and Windows platforms have the window manager built in to the operating system, but in UNIX the window manager is just another application. The window manager controls the position of top-level windows, provides a way to resize windows, open and close them, and implements a border and decorative title for windows. The wm command interacts with the window manager so that the application can control its size, position, and iconified state.

If you need to fine-tune your display, you may need some detailed information about widgets. The winfo command returns all sorts of information about windows, including interior widgets, not just top-level windows.

The wm Command

The wm command has about 20 operations that interact with the window manager. The general form of the command is:

    wm *operation win ?args?*

In all cases the *win* argument must be a toplevel. Otherwise, an error is raised. In many cases, the operation either sets or queries a value. If a new value is not specified, then the current settings are returned. For example, this command returns the current window geometry:

```
wm geometry .
=> 300x200+327+20
```

This command defines a new geometry:

```
wm geometry . 400x200+0+0
```

There are lots of wm operations, and this reflects the complex protocol with UNIX window managers. The summary below lists the subset of operations that I find useful. The operations can be grouped into four main categories:

- *Size, placement and decoration of windows.* Use the geometry and title operations to position windows and set the title bar.
- *Icons.* Use the iconify, deiconify, and withdraw operations to open and close windows. On UNIX, closed windows are represented by an icon.
- *Long-term session state.* Use the protocol operation to get a callback when users destroy windows.
- *Miscellaneous.* Use the transient and overrideredirect operation to get specialized windows. There are platform-specific commands to select different styles of top-level windows.

Toplevel Size, Placement, and Decoration

Each window has a title that appears in the title bar that the window manager places above the window. In a *wish* script, the default title of the main window is the last component of the file name of the script. Use the wm title command to change the title of the window. The title can also appear in the icon for your window, unless you specify another name with wm iconname.

```
wm title . "My Application"
```

Use the wm geometry command to adjust the position or size of your main windows. A geometry specification has the general form *WxH+X+Y*, where *W* is the width, *H* is the height, and *X* and *Y* specify the location of the upper-left corner of the window. The location +0+0 is the upper-left corner of the display. You can specify a negative *X* or *Y* to position the bottom (right) side of the window relative to the bottom (right) side of the display. For example, +0-0 is the lower-left corner, and -100-100 is offset from the lower-right corner by 100 pixels in the X and Y direction. If you do not specify a geometry, then the current geometry is returned.

Example 44–1 Gridded geometry for a canvas.

```
canvas .c -width 300 -height 150
pack .c -fill both -expand true
wm geometry .
=> 300x200+678+477
wm grid . 30 15 10 10
wm geometry .
=> 30x20+678+477
```

Example 44–1 sets up *gridded geometry* for a canvas, which means that the geometry is in terms of some unit other than pixels. With the canvas, use the wm grid command to define the size of the grid. The text and listbox widgets set a grid based on the size of the characters they display. They have a setgrid attribute that turns on gridding, which is described on page 642.

The wm resizable command controls whether a user can resize a window. The following command allows a resize in the X direction, but not in the Y direction:

```
wm resizable . 1 0
```

You can constrain the minimum size, maximum size, and the aspect ratio of a toplevel. The aspect ratio is the width divided by the height. The constraint is applied when the user resizes the window interactively. The minsize, maxsize, and aspect operations apply these constraints.

Some window managers insist on having the user position windows. The sizefrom and positionfrom operations let you pretend that the user specified the size and position in order to work around this restriction.

Table 44–1 summarizes the wm commands that deal with size, decorations, placement:

Table 44–1 Size, placement and decoration window manager operations.

wm aspect *win* ?*a b c d*?	Constrains *win*'s ratio of width to height to be between (*a*/*b* and *c*/*d*).
wm geometry *win* ?*geometry*?	Queries or sets the geometry of *win*.
wm grid *win* ?*w h dx dy*?	Queries or sets the grid size. *w* and *h* are the base size, in grid units. *dx* and *dy* are the size, in pixels, of a grid unit.
wm maxsize *win* ?*width height*?	Constrains the maximum size of *win*.
wm minsize *win* ?*width height*?	Constrains the minimum size of *win*.
wm positionfrom *win* ?*who*?	Queries or sets *who* to be program or user.
wm resizable *win* ?*xok yok*?	Queries or sets ability to resize interactively.
wm sizefrom *win* ?*who*?	Queries or sets *who* to be program or user.
wm stackorder *win*	Returns a list of toplevel windows in stacking order, from lowest to highest. (Tk 8.4)
wm stackorder *win* ?isabove|isbelow *win*?	Returns a boolean result indicating whether or not the first window is currently above or below the second window in the stacking order. (Tk 8.4)
wm title *win* ?*string*?	Queries or sets the window title to *string*.

V. Tk Details

The stackorder operation, introduced in Tk 8.4, returns information about the stacking order of the application's toplevel windows. Given the name of a toplevel, it returns a list of toplevel children windows in stacking order, from lowest to highest. Only those toplevels that are currently mapped to the screen are returned. The following command returns all mapped toplevels in their stacking order:

```
wm stackorder .
```

The stackorder operation can also be used to determine if one toplevel is positioned above or below a second toplevel. When two window arguments separated by either isabove or isbelow are passed, a boolean result indicates whether or not the first window is currently above or below the second window in the stacking order. For example:

```
wm stackorder . isabove .dialog
```

Icons

UNIX window managers let you close a window and replace it with an icon. The window still exists in your application, and users can open the window later. You can open and close a window yourself with the deiconify and iconify operations, respectively. Use the withdraw operation to unmap the window without replacing it with an icon. The state operation returns the current state, which is one of normal, iconified, or withdrawn. If you withdraw a window, you can restore it to the normal state with deiconify.

Windows and Macintosh do not implement icons for program windows. Instead, icons represent files and applications in the desktop environment. When you iconify under Windows, the window gets *minimized* and users can open it by clicking on the taskbar at the bottom of the screen. When you iconify under Macintosh, the window simply gets withdrawn from the screen.

As of Tk 8.3, Windows applications have an additional state, zoomed, which is a full-screen (or "maximized") display mode. Future versions of Tk may support this state for other operating systems

You can set the attributes of UNIX icons with the iconname, iconposition, iconbitmap, and iconmask operations. The icon's mask is used to get irregularly shaped icons. Chapter 41 describes how masks and bitmaps are defined. In the case of an icon, it is most likely that you have the definition in a file, so your command will look like this:

```
wm iconbitmap . @myfilename
```

Starting with Tk 8.3.3, on Windows systems, you can provide the path of a valid Windows icon file (usually .ico or .icr files) when setting the window's icon with the wm iconbitmap command. And if you use the optional -default option, introduced in Tk 8.4, the specified bitmap is used as the default icon for all windows. However, when setting the icon bitmap under windows, remember that the argument you provide must be a filename *without* a leading "@". For example:

```
wm iconbitmap . -default [file join $lib myapp.ico]
```

Table 44–2 summarizes the wm operations that have to do with icons:

Table 44–2 Window manager commands for icons.

wm deiconify *win*	Opens the window *win*.
wm iconbitmap *win* ?*bitmap*?	Queries or defines the bitmap for the icon. UNIX.
wm iconbitmap *win* ?-default? *file*	Sets the icon's bitmap using the specified *file*. The -default option sets the bitmap as the default for all windows of the application. Windows. (Tk 8.3.3)
wm iconify *win*	Closes the window *win*.
wm iconmask *win* ?*mask*?	Queries or defines the mask for the icon. UNIX.
wm iconname *win* ?*name*?	Queries or sets the name on the icon. UNIX.
wm iconposition *win* ?*x y*?	Queries or sets the location of the icon. UNIX.
wm iconwindow *win* ?*window*?	Queries or specifies an alternate window to display when in the iconified state. UNIX.
wm state *win* ?*state*?	Returns normal, iconic, withdrawn or (Windows only) zoomed. If specified, the window is set to the new *state*.
wm withdraw *win*	Unmaps the window. No icon is displayed.

Application Session State

The window manager lets users delete windows with a close operation. When the main Tk window gets deleted, *wish* normally quits. If you have any special processing that must take place when the user deletes a window, you need to intercept the close action. Use the wm protocol operation to register a command that handles the WM_DELETE_WINDOW message from the window manager. This works on all platforms even though "delete" is a UNIX term and "close" is the Windows and Macintosh term:

```
wm protocol . WM_DELETE_WINDOW Quit
```

If you intercept close on the main Tk window (i.e., dot), you must eventually call exit to actually stop your application. However, you can also take the time to prompt the user about unsaved changes, or even let the user change their mind about quitting.

Other window manager messages that you can intercept are WM_SAVE_YOURSELF and WM_TAKE_FOCUS. The first is called periodically by some UNIX session managers, which are described below. The latter is used in the active focus model. Tk (and this book) assumes a passive focus model where the window manager assigns focus to a top-level window.

V. Tk Details

Saving session state.

Some UNIX window managers support the notion of a *session* that lasts between runs of the window system. A session is implemented by saving state about the applications that are running, and using this information to restart the applications when the window system is restarted.

An easy way to participate in the session protocol is to save the command used to start your application. The `wm command` operation does this. The *wish* shell saves this information, so it is just a matter of registering it with the window manager. `argv0` is the command, and `argv` is the command-line arguments:

```
wm command . [linsert $argv 0 $argv0]
```

If your application is typically run on a different host than the one with the display (like in an Xterminal environment), then you also need to record what host to run the application on. Use the `wm client` operation for this. You might need to use *hostname* instead of *uname* on your system:

```
wm client . [exec uname -n]
```

Table 44–3 describes the session-related window manager operations.

Table 44–3 Session-related window manager operations.

`wm client win ?name?`	Records the hostname in the `WM_CLIENT_MACHINE` property. UNIX.
`wm command win ?command?`	Records the start-up command in the `WM_COMMAND` property. UNIX.
`wm protocol win ?name?` `?command?`	Registers a *command* to handle the protocol request *name*, which can be `WM_DELETE_WINDOW`, `WM_SAVE_YOURSELF`, or `WM_TAKE_FOCUS`.

Miscellaneous Window Manager Operations

The UNIX window managers work by reparenting an application's window so that it is a child of the window that forms the border and decorative title bar. The `wm frame` operation returns the window ID of the new parent, or the ID of the window itself if it has not been reparented. The `wm overrideredirect` operation can set a bit that overrides the reparenting. This means that no title or border will be drawn around the window, and you cannot control the window through the window manager.

The `wm group` operation defines groups of windows so that the window manager can open and close them together. One window, typically the main window, is chosen as the leader. The other members of the group are iconified when it is iconified. This is not implemented on Windows and Macintosh, and not all UNIX window managers implement this, either.

The `wm transient` operation informs the window manager that this is a temporary window and there is no need to decorate it with the border and decorative title bar. This is used, for example, on pop-up menus. On Windows, a `transient` window is a toolbar window that does not appear in the task bar. On

Macintosh, the `tk::unsupported::MacWindowStyle` command, which is described on page 489, lets you create different styles of top-level windows.

The `wm attributes` command, added in Tk 8.4, allows you to set or query platform-specific attributes associated with a specific window. The following Windows attributes are supported: `-disabled` gets or sets whether the window is in a disabled state; `-toolwindow` gets or sets the style of the window to toolwindow (as defined in the MSDN); and `-topmost` gets or sets whether this window is displayed above all other windows.

Table 44–4 lists the remaining window manager operations:

Table 44–4 Miscellaneous window manager operations.

`wm attributes win ?...?`	Sets or queries platform-specific window attributes. (Tk 8.4)
`wm colormapwindows win ?windowList?`	Sets or queries the `WM_COLORMAP_WINDOWS` property that orders windows with different colormaps.
`wm focusmodel win ?what?`	Sets or queries the focus model: `active` or `passive`. (Tk assumes the `passive` model.)
`wm frame win`	Returns the ID of the parent of `win` if it has been reparented; otherwise, returns the ID of `win`.
`wm group win ?leader?`	Queries or sets the group leader (a toplevel) for `win`. The window manager may unmap all the group at once.
`wm overrideredirect win ?boolean?`	Sets or queries the override redirect bit that suppresses reparenting by the window manager.
`wm transient win ?leader?`	Queries or marks a window as a transient window working for `leader`, another widget.

The `winfo` Command

The `winfo` command has about 50 operations that return information about a widget or the display. The operations fall into the following categories:

- Sending commands between applications.
- Family relationships.
- Size.
- Location.
- Virtual root coordinates.
- Atoms and IDs.
- Colormaps and visuals.

Sending Commands between Applications

Each Tk application has a name that is used when sending commands between applications using the `send` command, which is described in Chapter 43. The list of Tk applications is returned by the `interps` operation. The `tk appname` command is used to get the name of the application, and that command can also be used to set the application name.

Example 44–2 shows how your application might connect up with several existing applications. It contacts each registered Tk interpreter and sends a short command that contains the application's own name as a parameter. The other application can use that name to communicate back.

Example 44–2 Telling other applications what your name is.

```
foreach app [winfo interps] {
    catch {send $app [list Iam [tk appname]]}
}
```

Table 44–5 summarizes these commands:

Table 44–5 `send` command information.

`tk appname ?`*newname*`?`	Queries or sets the name used with `send`.
`winfo name .`	Also returns the name used for `send`, for backward compatibility with Tk 3.6 and earlier.
`winfo name` *pathname*	Returns the last component of *pathname*.
`winfo ?-displayof` *win*`?` `interps`	Returns the list of registered Tk applications on the same display as *win*.

Widget Family Relationships

The Tk widgets are arranged in a hierarchy, and you can use the `winfo` command to find out about the structure of the hierarchy. The `winfo children` operation returns the children of a window, and the `winfo parent` operation returns the parent. The parent of the main window is null (i.e., an empty string).

A widget is also a member of a class, which is used for bindings and as a key into the resource database. The `winfo class` operation returns this information. You can test for the existence of a window with `winfo exists`, and whether or not a window is mapped onto the screen with `winfo viewable`. Note that `winfo ismapped` is true for a widget that is managed by a geometry manager, but if the widget's top-level window is not mapped, then the widget is not `viewable`.

The `winfo manager` operation tells you what geometry manager is controlling the placement of the window. This returns the name of the geometry manager command. Examples include `pack`, `place`, `grid`, `canvas`, and `text`. The last two indicate the widget is embedded into a canvas or text widget.

Table 44–6 summarizes these `winfo` operations:

Table 44–6 Window hierarchy information.

`winfo children win`	Returns the list of children widgets of *win*.
`winfo class win`	Returns the resource class of *win*.
`winfo exists win`	Returns 1 if *win* exists.
`winfo ismapped win`	Returns 1 if *win* is mapped onto the screen.
`winfo manager win`	Geometry manager: `pack`, `place`, `grid`, `canvas`, or `text`.
`winfo parent win`	Returns the parent widget of *win*.
`winfo viewable win`	Returns 1 if *win* and all its parent windows are mapped.

Widget Size

The `winfo width` and `winfo height` operations return the width and height of a window, respectively. Alternatively, you can ask for the requested width and height of a window. Use `winfo reqwidth` and `winfo reqheight` for this information. The requested size may not be accurate, however, because the geometry manager may allocate more or less space, and the user may resize the window.

Size is not valid until a window is mapped.

A window's size is not set until a geometry manager maps a window onto the display. Initially, a window starts out with a width and height of 1. You can use `tkwait visibility` to wait for a window to be mapped before asking its width or height, or you can use `update` to give Tk a chance to update the display. There are some potential problems with `update` that are discussed on page 608. `Dialog_Wait` in Example 39–1 on page 606 uses `tkwait visibility`.

The `winfo geometry` operation returns the size and position of the window in the standard geometry format: *WxH+X+Y*. In this case the X and Y offsets are relative to the parent widget, or relative to the root window in the case of the main window.

You can find out how big the display is, too. The `winfo screenwidth` and `winfo screenheight` operations return this information in pixels. The `winfo screenmmwidth` and `winfo screenmmheight` return this information in millimeters.

You can convert between pixels and screen distances with the `winfo pixels` and `winfo fpixels` operations. Given a number of screen units such as `10m`, `3c`, or `72p`, these return the corresponding number of pixels. The first form rounds to a whole number, while the second form returns a floating point number. The correspondence between pixels and sizes may not be accurate because users can adjust the pixel size on their monitors, and Tk has no way of knowing about that. Chapter 40 explains screen units on page 612. For example:

```
set pixelsToInch [winfo pixels . 2.54c]
```

Table 44–7 summarizes these operations:

Table 44–7 Window size information.

`winfo fpixels win num`	Converts *num*, in screen units, to pixels. Returns a floating point number.
`winfo geometry win`	Returns the geometry of *win*, in pixels and relative to the parent in the form *WxH+X+Y*
`winfo height win`	Returns the height of *win*, in pixels.
`winfo pixels win num`	Converts *num* to a whole number of pixels.
`winfo reqheight win`	Returns the requested height of *win*, in pixels.
`winfo reqwidth win`	Returns the requested width of *win*, in pixels.
`winfo screenheight win`	Returns the height of the screen, in pixels.
`winfo screenmmheight win`	Returns the height of the screen, in millimeters.
`winfo screenmmwidth win`	Returns the width of the screen, in millimeters.
`winfo screenwidth win`	Returns the width of the screen, in pixels.
`winfo width win`	Returns the width of *win*, in pixels.

Widget Location

Table 44–8 Window location information.

`winfo containing ?-displayof win? win x y`	Returns the pathname of the window at *x* and *y*.
`winfo pointerx win`	Returns the X screen coordinate of the mouse.
`winfo pointery win`	Returns the Y screen coordinate of the mouse.
`winfo pointerxy win`	Returns the X and Y coordinates of the mouse.
`winfo rootx win`	Returns the X screen position of *win*.
`winfo rooty win`	Returns the Y screen position of *win*.
`winfo screen win`	Returns the display identifier of *win*'s screen.
`winfo server win`	Returns the version string of the display server.
`winfo toplevel win`	Returns pathname of toplevel that contains *win*.
`winfo x win`	Returns the X position of *win* in its parent.
`winfo y win`	Returns the Y position of *win* in its parent.

The `winfo x` and `winfo y` operations return the position of the upper-left corner of a window relative to its parent widget. In the case of the main window, this is its location on the screen. The `winfo rootx` and `winfo rooty` return the screen location of the upper-left corner of a widget, even if it is not a toplevel.

The winfo containing operation returns the pathname of the window that contains a point on the screen. This is useful in implementing menus and drag-and-drop applications.

The winfo toplevel operation returns the pathname of the toplevel that contains a widget. If the window is itself a toplevel, then this operation returns its own pathname.

The winfo screen operation returns the display identifier for the screen of the window.

Virtual Root Window

Some window managers use a virtual root window to give the user a larger virtual screen. At any given time, only a portion of the virtual screen is visible, and the user can change the view on the virtual screen to bring different applications into view. In this case, the winfo x and winfo y operations return the coordinates of a main window in the virtual root window (i.e., not the screen).

The winfo vrootheight and winfo vrootwidth operations return the size of the virtual root window. If there is no virtual root window, then these just return the size of the screen.

Correcting virtual root window coordinates.

The winfo vrootx and winfo vrooty are used to map from the coordinates in the virtual root window to screen-relative coordinates. These operations return 0 if there is no virtual root window. Otherwise, they return a negative number. If you add this number to the value returned by winfo x or winfo y, it gives the screen-relative coordinate of the window:

```
set screenx [expr [winfo x $win] + [winfo vrootx $win]]
```

Table 44–9 summarizes these operations:

Table 44–9 Virtual root window information.

winfo vrootheight *win*	Returns the height of the virtual root window for *win*.
winfo vrootwidth *win*	Returns the width of the virtual root window for *win*.
winfo vrootx *win*	Returns the X position of *win* in the virtual root.
winfo vrooty *win*	Returns the Y position of *win* in the virtual root.

Atoms and IDs

An *atom* is an X technical term for an identifier that is registered with the X server. Applications map names into atoms, and the X server assigns each atom a 32-bit identifier that can be passed between applications. One of the few places this is used in Tk is when the selection mechanism is used to interface with different toolkits. In some cases the selection is returned as atoms, which appear as 32-bit integers. The winfo atomname operation converts that number into an atom (i.e., a string), and the winfo atom registers a string with the X server and returns the 32-bit identifier as a hexadecimal string.

Each widget has an ID assigned by the window system. The `winfo id` command returns this identifier. The `winfo pathname` operation returns the Tk pathname of the widget that has a given ID, but only if the window is part of the same application.

Embedding applications.

The `id` operation is useful if you need to embed another application into your window hierarchy. Wish takes a `-use id` command-line argument that causes it to use an existing window for its main window. Other toolkits provide similar functionality. For example, to embed another Tk app in a frame:

```
frame .embed -container true
exec wish -use [winfo id .embed] otherscript.tcl
```

Table 44–10 summarizes these operations:

Table 44–10 Atom and window ID information.

`winfo atom ?-dis-playof win? name`	Returns the 32-bit identifier for the atom *name*.
`winfo atomname ?-dis-playof win? id`	Returns the atom that corresponds to the 32-bit ID.
`winfo id win`	Returns the window ID of *win*.
`winfo pathname ?-dis-playof win? id`	Returns the Tk pathname of the window with *id*, or null.

Colormaps and Visuals

The `winfo depth` returns the number of bits used to represent the color in each pixel. The `winfo cells` command returns the number of colormap entries used by the visual class of a window. These two values are generally related. A window with 8 bits per pixel usually has 256 colormap cells. The `winfo screendepth` and `winfo screencells` return this information for the default visual class.

The `winfo visualsavailable` command returns a list of the visual classes and screen depths that are available. For example, a display with 8 bits per pixel might report the following visual classes are available:

```
winfo visualsavailable .
=> {staticgray 8} {grayscale 8} {staticcolor 8} \
      {pseudocolor 8}
```

The `winfo visual` operation returns the visual class of a window, and the `winfo screenvisual` returns the default visual class of the screen.

The `winfo rgb` operation converts from a color name or value to the red, green, and blue components of that color. Three decimal values are returned. Example 41–2 on page 624 uses this command to compute a slightly darker version of the same color.

Table 44–11 summarizes operations that return information about color-maps and visual classes, which are described in Chapter 41:

Table 44–11 Colormap and visual class information.

winfo cells *win*	Returns the number of colormap cells in *win*'s visual.
winfo colormapfull *win*	Returns 1 if the last color allocation failed.
winfo depth *win*	Returns the number of bits per pixel for *win*.
winfo rgb *win color*	Returns the red, green, and blue values for *color*.
winfo screencells *win*	Returns the number of colormap cells in the default visual.
winfo screendepth *win*	Returns the number of bits per pixel in the screen's default visual.
winfo screenvisual *win*	Returns the default visual of the screen.
winfo visual *win*	Returns the visual class of *win*.
winfo visualsavailable *win*	Returns a list of pairs that specify the visual type and bits per pixel of the available visual classes.

The tk Command

The tk command provides a few miscellaneous entry points into the Tk library.

The appname operation is used to set or query the application name used with the Tk send command. If you define a new name and it is already in use by another application, (perhaps another instance of yourself), then a number is appended to the name (e.g., #2, #3, and so on). This is the syntax of the command:

```
tk appname ?name?
```

Fonts, canvas items, and widget sizes use screen units that are pixels, points, centimeters, millimeters, or inches. There are 72 points per inch. The tk scaling command, which was added in Tk 8.0, is used to set or query the mapping between pixels and points. A scale of 1.0 results in 72 pixels per inch. A scale of 1.25 results in 90 pixels per inch. This gives accurate sizes on a 90 dpi screen or it makes everything 25% larger on a 72 dpi screen. Changing the scale only affects widgets created after the change. This is the syntax of the command:

```
tk scaling ?num?
```

Determining the windowing system.

The tk windowingsystem command, added in Tk 8.4, returns one of x11 (X11-based), win32 (MS Windows), classic (Mac OS Classic), or aqua (Mac OS X Aqua). Traditionally, Tk applications that included platform-dependent code could simply switch on the value of the global tcl_platform(platform) element, which is set to macintosh, unix, or windows. But the introduction of Apple's OS X

V. Tk Details

and the Aqua interface complicated matters. Mac OS X reports `unix` in the `tcl_platform(platform)` element. But its windowing system is not a native X Windows system, so you must use `tk windowingsystem`.

The `caret` operation, introduced in Tk 8.4, sets and queries the caret location for the display of the specified Tk window. The caret is the per-display cursor location used for indicating global focus (for example, to comply with Microsoft Accessibility guidelines), as well as for location of the over-the-spot XIM (X Input Methods) or Windows IME windows.

The `useinputmethods` operation changes the behavior of Tk on X with X Input Methods (XIM). Before Tk 8.3, XIM was recognized and used without question. As of Tk 8.3, they are recognized and initialized, but not used unless XIM is turned on with the `useinputmethods` operation:

```
tk useinputmethods 1
```

Table 44–12 summarizes the `tk` command operations:

Table 44–12   The `tk` command operations.

`tk appname ?name?`	Queries or sets the application name, used by the Tk `send` command.
`tk caret window ?-x x?` `?-y y? ?-height` `height?`	Queries or sets the caret location for the display of the specified Tk *window*. *x* and *y* represent window-relative coordinates. `height` is the height of the current cursor location, or the height of the specified window. Values are returned in option-value pair format. (Tk 8.4)
`tk scaling ?-displayof` `window? ?number?`	Queries or sets the current scaling factor used by Tk to convert between physical units and pixels. *number* is a floating point value that specifies the number of pixels per point on *window*'s display. If *window* is omitted, it defaults to the main window. If *number* is omitted, the current value of the scaling factor is returned.
`tk useinputmethods` `?-displayof window?` `?boolean?`	Queries or sets the state of whether Tk should use XIM (X Input Methods) for filtering events. The resulting state is returned. If XIM support is not available, this will always return 0. If *window* is omitted, it defaults to the main window. If *boolean* is omitted, the current state is returned. (Tk 8.3)
`tk windowingsystem`	Returns the current windowing system: `x11` (X11-based), `win32` (MS Windows), `classic` (Mac OS Classic), or `aqua` (Mac OS X Aqua). (Tk 8.4)

Managing User Preferences

This chapter describes a user preferences package. The resource database stores preference settings. Applications specify Tcl variables that are initialized from the database entries. A user interface lets the user browse and change their settings.

*U*ser customization is an important part of any complex application. There are always design decisions that could go either way. A typical approach is to choose a reasonable default, but then let users change the default setting through a preferences user interface. This chapter describes a preference package that works by tying together a Tcl variable, which the application uses, and a resource specification, which the user sets. In addition, a user interface is provided so that the user need not edit the resource database directly.

App-Defaults Files

We will assume that it is sufficient to have two sources of application defaults: a per-application database and a per-user database. In addition, we will allow for some resources to be specific to color and monochrome displays. The following example initializes the preference package by reading in the per-application and per-user resource specification files. There is also an initialization of the global array `pref` that will be used to hold state information about the preferences package. The `Pref_Init` procedure is called like this:

```
Pref_Init $library/foo-defaults ~/.foo-defaults
```

We assume `$library` is the directory holding support files for the `foo` application, and that per-user defaults will be kept in `~/.foo-defaults`. These are UNIX-oriented file names. When you write cross-platform Tk applications, you

V. Tk Details

will find that some file names are inherently platform-specific. The platform-independent operations described in Chapter 9 are great, but they do not change the fact that user preferences may be stored in `c:/webtk/userpref.txt` on Windows, `Hard Disk:System:Preferences:WebTk Prefs` on Macintosh, and `~/.webtk` on UNIX. I find it useful to have a small amount of platform-specific startup code that defines these pathnames. The preference package uses resource files that work on all platforms:

Example 45–1 Preferences initialization.

```
proc Pref_Init { userDefaults appDefaults } {
    global pref

    set pref(uid) 0;# for a unique identifier for widgets
    set pref(userDefaults) $userDefaults
    set pref(appDefaults) $appDefaults
    PrefReadFile $appDefaults startup
    if [file exists $userDefaults] {
        PrefReadFile $userDefaults user
    }
}
proc PrefReadFile { basename level } {
    if [catch {option readfile $basename $level} err] {
        Status "Error in $basename: $err"
    }
    if {[string match *color* [winfo visual .]]} {
        if [file exists $basename-color] {
            if [catch {option readfile \
                    $basename-color $level} err] {
                Status "Error in $basename-color: $err"
            }
        }
    } else {
        if [file exists $basename-mono] {
            if [catch {option readfile $basename-mono \
                    $level} err] {
                Status "Error in $basename-mono: $err"
            }
        }
    }
}
```

The `PrefReadFile` procedure reads a resource file and then looks for another file with the suffix `-color` or `-mono` depending on the characteristics of the display. With this scheme, a UNIX user puts generic settings in `~/.foo-defaults`. They put color specifications in `~/.foo-defaults-color`. They put specifications for black and white displays in `~/.foo-defaults-mono`. You could extend `PrefReadFile` to allow for per-host files as well.

Throughout this chapter we assume that the `Status` procedure displays messages to the user. It could be as simple as:

```
proc Status { s } { puts stderr $s }
```

Defining Preferences

This section describes the `Pref_Add` procedure that an application uses to define
preference items. A preference item defines a relationship between a Tcl variable
and a resource name. If the Tcl variable is undefined at the time `Pref_Add` is
called, then it is set from the value for the resource. If the resource is not defined,
then the variable is set to the default value.

Hide simple data structures with Tcl procedures.

A default value, a label, and a more extensive help string are associated
with each item, which is represented by a Tcl list of five elements. A few short
routines hide the layout of the item lists and make the rest of the code read better:

Example 45–2 Adding preference items.

```
proc PrefVar { item } { lindex $item 0 }
proc PrefRes { item } { lindex $item 1 }
proc PrefDefault { item } { lindex $item 2 }
proc PrefComment { item } { lindex $item 3 }
proc PrefHelp { item } { lindex $item 4 }

proc Pref_Add { prefs } {
    global pref
    append pref(items) $prefs " "
    foreach item $prefs {
        set varName [PrefVar $item]
        set resName [PrefRes $item]
        set value [PrefValue $varName $resName]
        if {$value == {}} {
            # Set variables that are still not set
            set default [PrefDefault $item]
            switch -regexp -- $default {
                ^CHOICE {
                    PrefValueSet $varName [lindex $default 1]
                }
                ^OFF {
                    PrefValueSet $varName 0
                }
                ^ON {
                    PrefValueSet $varName 1
                }
                default {
                    # This is a string or numeric
                    PrefValueSet $varName $default
                }
            }
        }
    }
}
```

V. Tk Details

The procedures `PrefValue` and `PrefValueSet` are used to query and set the value of the named variable, which can be an array element or a simple variable. The `upvar #0` command sets the variable in the global scope.

Example 45–3 Setting preference variables.

```
# PrefValue returns the value of the variable if it exists,
# otherwise it returns the resource database value
proc PrefValue { varName res } {
    upvar #0 $varName var
    if [info exists var] {
        return $var
    }
    set var [option get . $res {}]
}
# PrefValueSet defines a variable in the global scope.
proc PrefValueSet { varName value } {
    upvar #0 $varName var
    set var $value
}
```

An important side effect of the `Pref_Add` call is that the variables in the preference item are defined at the global scope. It is also worth noting that `PrefValue` will honor any existing value for a variable, so if the variable is already set at the global scope, then neither the resource value nor the default value will be used. It is easy to change `PrefValue` to always set the variable if this is not the behavior you want. Here is a sample call to `Pref_Add`:

Example 45–4 Using the preferences package.

```
Pref_Add {
    {win(scrollside) scrollbarSide {CHOICE left right}
        "Scrollbar placement"
"Scrollbars can be positioned on either the left or
right side of the text and canvas widgets."}
    {win(typeinkills) typeinKills OFF
        "Type-in kills selection"
"This setting determines whether or not the selection
is deleted when new text is typed in."}
    {win(scrollspeed) scrollSpeed 15 "Scrolling speed"
"This parameter affects the scrolling rate when a selection
is dragged off the edge of the window. Smaller numbers
scroll faster, but can consume more CPU."}
}
```

Any number of preference items can be specified in a call to `Pref_Add`. The list-of-lists structure is created by proper placement of the curly braces, and it is preserved when the argument is appended to `pref(items)`, which is the master list of preferences. In this example, `Pref_Add` gets passed a single argument that is a Tcl list with three elements. The Tcl variables are array elements, presumably related to the `Win` module of the application. The resource names are associated with the main application as opposed to any particular widget. They are specified in the database like this:

```
*scrollbarSide: left
*typeinKills: 0
*scrollSpeed: 15
```

The Preferences User Interface

The figure shows the interface for the items added with the `Pref_Add` command given in the previous section. The pop-up window with the extended help text appears after you click on "Scrollbar placement." The user interface to the preference settings is table-driven. As a result of all the `Pref_Add` calls, a single list of all the preference items is built. The interface is constructed by looping through this list and creating a user interface item for each:

Example 45–5 A user interface to the preference items.

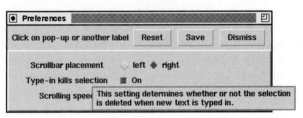

```
proc Pref_Dialog {} {
    global pref
    if [catch {toplevel .pref}] {
        raise .pref
    } else {
        wm title .pref "Preferences"
        set buttons [frame .pref.but -bd 5]
        pack .pref.but -side top -fill x
        button $buttons.quit -text Dismiss \
            -command {PrefDismiss}
        button $buttons.save -text Save \
            -command {PrefSave}
        button $buttons.reset -text Reset \
            -command {PrefReset ; PrefDismiss}
        label $buttons.label \
            -text "Click labels for info on each item"
        pack $buttons.label -side left -fill x
        pack $buttons.quit $buttons.save $buttons.reset \
            -side right -padx 4

        frame .pref.b -borderwidth 2 -relief raised
        pack .pref.b -fill both
        set body [frame .pref.b.b -bd 10]
```

```
        pack .pref.b.b -fill both

        set maxWidth 0
        foreach item $pref(items) {
            set len [string length [PrefComment $item]]
            if {$len > $maxWidth} {
                set maxWidth $len
            }
        }
        set pref(uid) 0
        foreach item $pref(items) {
            PrefDialogItem $body $item $maxWidth
        }
    }
}
```

The interface supports three different types of preference items: boolean, choice, and general value. A boolean is implemented with a checkbutton that is tied to the Tcl variable, which will get a value of either 0 or 1. A boolean is identified by a default value that is either ON or OFF. A choice item is implemented as a set of radiobuttons, one for each choice. A choice item is identified by a default value that is a list with the first element equal to CHOICE. The remaining list items are the choices, with the first one being the default choice. A regexp is used to check for CHOICE instead of using list operations. This is because Tcl 8.0 will complain if the value is not a proper list, which could happen with arbitrary values. If neither of these cases, boolean or choice, are detected, then an entry widget is created to hold the general value of the preference item:

Example 45–6 Interface objects for different preference types.

```
proc PrefDialogItem { frame item width } {
    global pref
    incr pref(uid)
    set f [frame $frame.p$pref(uid) -borderwidth 2]
    pack $f -fill x
    label $f.label -text [PrefComment $item] -width $width
    bind $f.label <1> \
        [list PrefItemHelp %X %Y [PrefHelp $item]]
    pack $f.label -side left
    set default [PrefDefault $item]
    if {[regexp "^CHOICE " $default]} {
        foreach choice [lreplace $default 0 0] {
            incr pref(uid)
            radiobutton $f.c$pref(uid) -text $choice \
                -variable [PrefVar $item] -value $choice
            pack $f.c$pref(uid) -side left
        }
    } else {
        if {$default == "OFF" || $default == "ON"} {
            # This is a boolean
            set varName [PrefVar $item]
            checkbutton $f.check -variable $varName \
```

```
                -command [list PrefFixupBoolean $f.check $varName]
            PrefFixupBoolean $f.check $varName
            pack $f.check -side left
        } else {
            # This is a string or numeric
            entry $f.entry -width 10 -relief sunken
            pack $f.entry -side left -fill x -expand true
            set pref(entry,[PrefVar $item]) $f.entry
            set varName [PrefVar $item]
            $f.entry insert 0 [uplevel #0 [list set $varName]]
            bind $f.entry <Return> "PrefEntrySet %W $varName"
        }
    }
}
proc PrefFixupBoolean {check varname} {
    upvar #0 $varname var
    # Update the checkbutton text each time it changes
    if {$var} {
        $check config -text On
    } else {
        $check config -text Off
    }
}
proc PrefEntrySet { entry varName } {
    PrefValueSet $varName [$entry get]
}
```

In this interface, when the user clicks a radiobutton or a checkbutton, the Tcl variable is set immediately. To obtain a similar effect with the general preference item, the <Return> key is bound to a procedure that sets the associated Tcl variable to the value from the entry widget. PrefEntrySet is a one-line procedure that saves us from using the more awkward binding shown below. Grouping with double quotes allows substitution of $varName, but then we must quote the square brackets to postpone command substitution:

```
    bind $f.entry <Return> "PrefValueSet $varName \[%W get\]"
```

The binding on <Return> is done as opposed to using the -textvariable option because it interacts with traces on the variable a bit better. With trace you can arrange for a Tcl command to be executed when a variable is changed, as in Example 45–10 on page 680. For a general preference item it is better to wait until the complete value is entered before responding to its new value.

The other aspect of the user interface is the display of additional help information for each item. If there are lots of preference items, then there isn't enough room to display this information directly. Instead, clicking on the short description for each item brings up a toplevel with the help text for that item. The toplevel is marked transient so that the window manager does not decorate it:

Example 45–7 Displaying the help text for an item.

```
proc PrefItemHelp { x y text } {
    catch {destroy .prefitemhelp}
    if {$text == {}} {
        return
    }
    set self [toplevel .prefitemhelp -class Itemhelp]
    wm title $self "Item help"
    wm geometry $self +[expr $x+10]+[expr $y+10]
    wm transient $self .pref
    message $self.msg -text $text -aspect 1500
    pack $self.msg
    bind $self.msg <1> {PrefNukeItemHelp .prefitemhelp}
    .pref.but.label configure -text \
        "Click on pop-up or another label"
}
proc PrefNukeItemHelp { t } {
    .pref.but.label configure -text \
        "Click labels for info on each item"
    destroy $t
}
```

Managing the Preferences File

The preference settings are saved in the per-user file. The file is divided into two
parts. The tail is automatically rewritten by the preferences package. Users can
manually add resource specifications to the beginning of the file and they will be
preserved:

Example 45–8 Saving preferences settings to a file.

```
# PrefSave writes the resource specifications to the
# end of the per-user resource file,
proc PrefSave {} {
    global pref
    if [catch {
        set old [open $pref(userDefaults) r]
        set oldValues [split [read $old] \n]
        close $old
    }] {
        set oldValues {}
    }
    if [catch {open $pref(userDefaults).new w} out] {
        .pref.but.label configure -text \
        "Cannot save in $pref(userDefaults).new: $out"
        return
    }
    foreach line $oldValues {
        if {$line == \
                "!!! Lines below here automatically added"} {
```

```
            break
        } else {
            puts $out $line
        }
    }
    puts $out "!!! Lines below here automatically added"
    puts $out "!!! [exec date]"
    puts $out "!!! Do not edit below here"
    foreach item $preferences {
        set varName [PrefVar $item]
        set resName [PrefRes $item]
        if [info exists pref(entry,$varName)] {
            PrefEntrySet $pref(entry,$varName) $varName
        }
        set value [PrefValue $varName $resName]
        puts $out [format "%s\t%s" *${resName}: $value]
    }
    close $out
    set new [glob $pref(userDefaults).new]
    set old [file root $new]
    if [catch {file rename -force $new $old} err] {
        Status "Cannot install $new: $err"
        return
    }
    PrefDismiss
}
```

There is one fine point in `PrefSave`. The value from the entry widget for general-purpose items is obtained explicitly in case the user has not already pressed `<Return>` to update the Tcl variable.

The interface is rounded out with the `PrefReset` and `PrefDismiss` procedures. A reset is achieved by clearing the option database and reloading it, and then temporarily clearing the preference items and their associated variables and then redefining them with `Pref_Add`.

Example 45–9 Read settings from the preferences file.

```
proc PrefReset {} {
    global pref
    # Re-read user defaults
    option clear
    PrefReadFile $pref(appDefaults) startup
    PrefReadFile $pref(userDefaults) user
    # Clear variables
    set items $pref(items)
    set pref(items) {}
    foreach item $items {
        uplevel #0 [list unset [PrefVar $item]]
    }
    # Restore values
    Pref_Add $items
}
```

V. Tk Details

```
proc PrefDismiss {} {
    destroy .pref
    catch {destroy .prefitemhelp}
}
```

Tracing Changes to Preference Variables

Suppose, for example, we want to repack the scrollbars when the user changes their scrollside setting from left to right. This is done by setting a trace on the win(scrollside) variable. When the user changes that via the user interface, the trace routine is called. The trace command and its associated procedure are shown in the next example. The variable must be declared global before setting up the trace, which is not otherwise required if Pref_Add is the only command using the variable.

Example 45–10 Tracing a Tcl variable in a preference item.

```
Pref_Add {
    {win(scrollside) scrollbarSide {CHOICE left right}
        "Scrollbar placement"
"Scrollbars can be positioned on either the left or
right side of the text and canvas widgets."}
}
global win
set win(lastscrollside) $win(scrollside)
trace variable win(scrollside) w ScrollFixup
# Assume win(scrollbar) identifies the scrollbar widget
proc ScrollFixup { name1 name2 op } {
    global win
    if {$win(scrollside) != $win(lastscrollside)} {
        set parent [lindex [pack info $win(scrollbar)] 1]
        pack forget $win(scrollbar)
        set firstchild [lindex [pack slaves $parent] 0]
        pack $win(scrollbar) -in $parent -before $firstchild \
            -side $win(scrollside) -fill y
        set win(lastscrollside) $win(scrollside)
    }
}
```

Improving the Package

One small improvement can be made to Pref_Add. If a user specifies a boolean resource manually, he or she might use "true" instead of one and "false" instead of zero. Pref_Add should check for those cases and set the boolean variable to one or zero to avoid errors when the variables are used in expressions.

The interface lets you dismiss it without saving your preference settings. This is either a feature that lets users try out settings without committing to them, or it is a bug. Fixing this requires introducing a parallel set of variables to shadow the real variables until the user hits `Save`, which is tedious to implement. You can also use a *grab* as described in Chapter 39 to prevent the user from doing anything but setting preferences.

This preference package is a slightly simplified version of one I developed for *exmh*, which has so many preference items that a two-level scheme is necessary. The first level is a menu of preference sections, and each section is created with a single call to `Pref_Add`. This requires additional arguments to `Pref_Add` to provide a title for the section and some overall information about the preference section. The display code changes a small amount. The code for the *exmh* is on the CD-ROM.

V. Tk Details

A User Interface to Bindings

This chapter presents a user interface to view and edit bindings.

A good way to learn about how a widget works is to examine the bindings that are defined for it. This chapter presents a user interface that lets you browse and change bindings for a widget or a class of widgets.

The interface uses a pair of listboxes to display the events and their associated commands. An entry widget is used to enter the name of a widget or a class. There are a few command buttons that let the user add a new binding, edit an existing binding, save the bindings to a file, and dismiss the dialog. Here is what the display looks like:

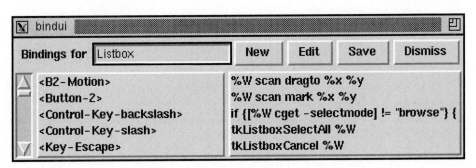

Example 46–1 A user interface to widget bindings.

```
proc Bind_Interface { w } {
    # Our state
    global bind
    set bind(class) $w

    # Set a class used for resource specifications
    set frame [toplevel .bindui -class Bindui]
    # Default relief
    option add *Bindui*Entry.relief sunken startup
    option add *Bindui*Listbox.relief raised startup
    # Default Listbox sizes
    option add *Bindui*key.width 18 startup
    option add *Bindui*cmd.width 25 startup
    option add *Bindui*Listbox.height 5 startup

    # A labeled entry at the top to hold the current
    # widget name or class.
    set t [frame $frame.top -bd 2]
    label $t.l -text "Bindings for" -width 11
    entry $t.e -textvariable bind(class)
    pack $t.l -side left
    pack $t.e -side left -fill x -expand true
    pack $t -side top -fill x
    bind $t.e <Return> [list Bind_Display $frame]

    # Command buttons
    button $t.quit -text Dismiss \
        -command [list destroy $frame]
    button $t.save -text Save \
        -command [list Bind_Save $frame]
    button $t.edit -text Edit \
        -command [list Bind_Edit $frame]
    button $t.new -text New \
        -command [list Bind_New $frame]
    pack $t.quit $t.save $t.edit $t.new -side right

    # A pair of listboxes and a scrollbar
    scrollbar $frame.s -orient vertical \
        -command [list BindYview \
            [list $frame.key $frame.cmd]]
    listbox $frame.key \
        -yscrollcommand [list $frame.s set] \
        -exportselection false
    listbox $frame.cmd \
        -yscrollcommand [list $frame.s set]
    pack $frame.s -side left -fill y
    pack $frame.key $frame.cmd -side left \
        -fill both -expand true

    foreach l [list $frame.key $frame.cmd] {
        bind $l <B2-Motion>\
            [list BindDragto %x %y $frame.key $frame.cmd]
        bind $l <Button-2> \
```

```
            [list BindMark %x %y $frame.key $frame.cmd]
        bind $l <Button-1> \
            [list BindSelect %y $frame.key $frame.cmd]
        bind $l <B1-Motion> \
            [list BindSelect %y $frame.key $frame.cmd]
        bind $l <Shift-B1-Motion> {}
        bind $l <Shift-Button-1> {}
    }
    # Initialize the display
    Bind_Display $frame
}
```

The `Bind_Interface` command takes a widget name or class as a parameter. It creates a toplevel and gives it the `Bindui` class so that resources can be set to control widget attributes. The `option add` command is used to set up the default listbox sizes. The lowest priority, `startup`, is given to these resources so that clients of the package can override the size with their own resource specifications.

At the top of the interface is a labeled entry widget. The entry holds the name of the class or widget for which the bindings are displayed. The `textvariable` option of the entry widget is used so that the entry's contents are available in a variable, `bind(class)`. Pressing `<Return>` in the entry invokes `Bind_Display` that fills in the display.

Example 46–2 `Bind_Display` presents the bindings for a widget or class.

```
proc Bind_Display { frame } {
    global bind
    $frame.key delete 0 end
    $frame.cmd delete 0 end
    foreach seq [bind $bind(class)] {
        $frame.key insert end $seq
        $frame.cmd insert end [bind $bind(class) $seq]
    }
}
```

The `Bind_Display` procedure fills in the display with the binding information. The `bind` command returns the events that have bindings, and what the command associated with each event is. `Bind_Display` loops through this information and fills in the listboxes.

A Pair of Listboxes Working Together

The two listboxes in the interface, `$frame.key` and `$frame.cmd`, are set up to work as a unit. A selection in one causes a parallel selection in the other. Only one listbox exports its selection as the PRIMARY selection. Otherwise, the last listbox to assert the selection steals the selection rights from the other widget. The following example shows the `bind` commands from `Bind_Interface` and the

BindSelect routine that selects an item in both listboxes:

Example 46–3 Related listboxes are configured to select items together.

```
foreach l [list $frame.key $frame.cmd] {
    bind $l <Button-1> \
        [list BindSelect %y $frame.key $frame.cmd]
    bind $l <B1-Motion> \
        [list BindSelect %y $frame.key $frame.cmd]
}
proc BindSelect { y args } {
    foreach w $args {
        $w select clear 0 end
        $w select anchor [$w nearest $y]
        $w select set anchor [$w nearest $y]
    }
}
```

A scrollbar for two listboxes.

A single scrollbar scrolls both listboxes. The next example shows the scrollbar command from Bind_Interface and the BindYview procedure that scrolls the listboxes:

Example 46–4 Controlling a pair of listboxes with one scrollbar.

```
scrollbar $frame.s -orient vertical \
    -command [list BindYview [list $frame.key $frame.cmd]]

proc BindYview { lists args } {
    foreach l $lists {
        eval {$l yview} $args
    }
}
```

The BindYview command is used to change the display of the listboxes associated with the scrollbar. The first argument to BindYview is a list of widgets to scroll, and the remaining arguments are added by the scrollbar to specify how to position the display. The details are essentially private between the scrollbar and the listbox. See page 501 for the details. The args keyword is used to represent these extra arguments, and eval is used to pass them through BindYview. The reasoning for using eval like this is explained in Chapter 10 on page 136.

The Listbox class bindings for <Button-2> and <B2-Motion> cause the listbox to scroll as the user drags the widget with the middle mouse button. These bindings are adjusted so that both listboxes move together. The following example shows the bind commands from the Bind_Interface procedure and the BindMark and BindDrag procedures that scroll the listboxes:

Example 46–5 Drag-scrolling a pair of listboxes together.

```
bind $l <B2-Motion>\
    [list BindDragto %x %y $frame.key $frame.cmd]
bind $l <Button-2> \
    [list BindMark %x %y $frame.key $frame.cmd]

proc BindDragto { x y args } {
    foreach w $args {
        $w scan dragto $x $y
    }
}
proc BindMark { x y args } {
    foreach w $args {
        $w scan mark $x $y
    }
}
```

The BindMark procedure does a scan mark that defines an origin, and Bind-Dragto does a scan dragto that scrolls the widget based on the distance from that origin. All Tk widgets that scroll support yview, scan mark, and scan dragto. Thus the BindYview, BindMark, and BindDragto procedures are general enough to be used with any set of widgets that scroll together.

The Editing Interface

Editing and defining a new binding are done in a pair of entry widgets. These widgets are created and packed into the display dynamically when the user presses the New or Edit button:

Example 46–6 An interface to define bindings.

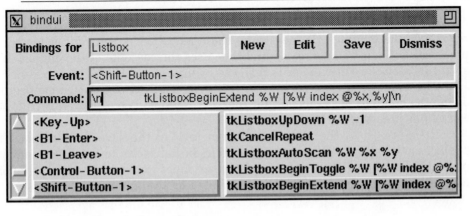

```
proc Bind_New { frame } {
    if [catch {frame $frame.edit} f] {
        # Frame already created
```

```
            set f $frame.edit
        } else {
            foreach x {key cmd} {
                set f2 [frame $f.$x]
                pack $f2 -fill x -padx 2
                label $f2.l -width 11 -anchor e
                pack $f2.l -side left
                entry $f2.e
                pack $f2.e -side left -fill x -expand true
                bind $f2.e <Return> [list BindDefine $f]
            }
            $f.key.l config -text Event:
            $f.cmd.l config -text Command:
        }
        pack $frame.edit -after $frame.top -fill x
    }
    proc Bind_Edit { frame } {
        Bind_New $frame
        set line [$frame.key curselection]
        if {$line == {}} {
            return
        }
        $frame.edit.key.e delete 0 end
        $frame.edit.key.e insert 0 [$frame.key get $line]
        $frame.edit.cmd.e delete 0 end
        $frame.edit.cmd.e insert 0 [$frame.cmd get $line]
    }
```

The -width 11 and -anchor e attributes for the label widgets are specified so that the Event: and Command: labels will line up with the Bindings for label at the top.

Saving and Loading Bindings

All that remains is the actual change or definition of a binding and some way to remember the bindings the next time the application is run. The BindDefine procedure attempts a bind command that uses the contents of the entries. If it succeeds, then the edit window is removed by unpacking it.

The bindings are saved by Bind_Save as a series of Tcl commands that define the bindings. It is crucial that the list command be used to construct the commands properly.

Bind_Read uses the source command to read the saved commands. The application must call Bind_Read as part of its initialization to get the customized bindings for the widget or class. It also must provide a way to invoke Bind_Interface, such as a button, menu entry, or key binding.

Example 46–7 Defining and saving bindings.

```
proc BindDefine { f } {
    if [catch {
        bind [$f.top.e get] [$f.edit.key.e get] \
            [$f.edit.cmd.e get]
    } err] {
        Status $err
    } else {
        # Remove the edit window
        pack forget $f.edit
    }
}
proc Bind_Save { dotfile args } {
    set out [open $dotfile.new w]
    foreach w $args {
        foreach seq [bind $w] {
            # Output a Tcl command
            puts $out [list bind $w $seq [bind $w $seq]]
        }
    }
    close $out
    file rename -force $dotfile.new $dotfile
}
proc Bind_Read { dotfile } {
    if [catch {
        if [file exists $dotfile] {
            # Read the saved Tcl commands
            source $dotfile
        }
    } err] {
        Status "Bind_Read $dotfile failed: $err"
    }
}
```

V. Tk Details

C Programming

Part VI describes C programming and Tcl. The goal of this section is to get you started in the right direction. For serious C programming, you will need to consult the on-line reference material for detailed descriptions of the C APIs.

Chapter 47 provides an introduction to using Tcl at the C programming level. It gets you started with integrating Tcl and Tk into an existing application, and with creating a Tcl extension you can dynamically load into *tclsh* or *wish*. Chapter 48 describes the build environment for Tcl so you can compile Tcl/Tk from the sources, and compile your own extensions. Chapter 49 presents a sample digital clock Tk widget implementation in C. This section ends with Chapter 50, which provides a survey of the facilities in the Tcl and Tk C libraries.

C Programming and Tcl

This chapter explains how to extend a Tcl application with new built-in
commands. Tcl 8.0 replaces the original string-based command interface
with a more efficient dual-ported object interface. This chapter describes
both interfaces.

Tcl is implemented in a C library that
is easy to integrate into an existing application. By adding the Tcl interpreter to
your application, you can configure and control it with Tcl scripts, and with Tk
you can provide a nice graphical interface to it. This was the original model for
Tcl. Applications would be largely application-specific C code and include a small
amount of Tcl for configuration and the graphical interface. However, the basic
Tcl shells proved so useful by themselves that relatively few Tcl programmers
need to worry about programming in C or C++.

Tcl is designed to be easily extensible by writing new command implementations in C. A command implemented in C is more efficient than an equivalent
Tcl procedure. A more pressing reason to write C code is that it may not be possible to provide the same functionality purely in Tcl. Suppose you have a new
device, perhaps a color scanner or a unique input device. The programming
interface to that device is through a set of C procedures that initialize and
manipulate the state of the device. Without some work on your part, that interface is not accessible to your Tcl scripts. You are in the same situation if you
have a C or C++ library that implements some specialized function such as a
database. Fortunately, it is rather straightforward to provide a Tcl interface that
corresponds to the C or C++ interface.

Note: Where this chapter says "C", you can always think "C or C++". There
is also a package called *TclBlend* that lets you extend Tcl by writing Java instead
of C, and to evaluate Tcl scripts from Java. Find out more about *TclBlend* at:

```
http://www.tcl.tk/java/
```

VI. Tcl and C

Basic Concepts

This chapter assumes that you know some C or C++. You do not have to be an expert programmer to use the Tcl APIs. Indeed, one of Tcl's strengths is the ease with which you can extend it by writing C code. This chapter provides a few working examples that explain how to initialize your application and create Tcl commands. It describes how to organize your code into packages. It concludes with notes about compiling Tcl under UNIX, Windows, and Macintosh.

Getting Started

There are two ways to get started writing C code for Tcl applications. The easiest way is to write an *extension* that just adds some new commands to a standard Tcl shell like *tclsh* or *wish*. With this approach the Tcl shell creates a basic framework for you, and your C code just extends this framework with new commands. Tcl supports dynamic loading, so you can compile your extension as a shared library (i.e., DLL) and load it into a running Tcl shell. This is the easiest approach because the Tcl shell handles the details of startup and shutdown, and it provides an interactive console to enter Tcl commands. In the case of *wish*, it also provides the framework for a graphical user interface. Finally, a loadable extension can be shared easily with other Tcl users.

The second way to use the Tcl library is to add it to an existing application. If your application is very simple, it may make sense to turn it into an extension for a standard Tcl shell, which brings you back to the first, simpler approach. However, if your application already has a complex framework (e.g., it is a long-running server process), then you can just add Tcl to it and export the functionality of your application as one or more Tcl commands. Once you do this, you will find that you can extend your application with all the features provided by Tcl.

C Command Procedures and Data Objects

The C or C++ code that implements a Tcl command is called a *command procedure*. The interface to a command procedure is much like the interface to a main program. The inputs are an array of values that correspond exactly to the arguments in the Tcl script command. The result of the command procedure becomes the result of the Tcl command.

There are two kinds of command procedures: string-based and "object-based." I've quoted "object" here because we are really talking about the data representation of the arguments and results. We are not talking about methods and inheritance and other things associated with object oriented programming. However, the Tcl C APIs use a structure called a `Tcl_Obj`, which is called a *dual ported object* in the reference material. I prefer the term "`Tcl_Obj` value".

The string interface is quite simple. A command procedure gets an array of strings as arguments, and it computes a string as the result. Tcl 8.0 generalized strings into the `Tcl_Obj` type, which can have two representations: both a string and another native representation like an integer, floating point number, list, or bytecodes. An object-based command takes an array of `Tcl_Obj` pointers as arguments, and it computes a `Tcl_Obj` as its result. The goal of the `Tcl_Obj` type is to reduce the number of conversions between strings and native representations. Object-based commands will be more efficient than the equivalent string-based commands, but the APIs are a little more complex. For simple tasks, and for learning, you can use just the simpler string-based command interface.

SWIG

David Beasley created a nice tool called SWIG (Simple Wrapper Interface Generator) that generates the C code that implements command procedures that expose a C or C++ API as Tcl commands. This can be a great time saver if you need to export many calls to Tcl. The only drawback is that a C interface may not feel that comfortable to the script writer. Handcrafted Tcl interfaces can be much nicer, but automatically-generated interfaces are just fine for rapid prototyping and for software testing environments. You can learn more about SWIG at its web site:

```
http://www.swig.org/
```

Tcl Initialization

Before you can use your command procedures from Tcl scripts, you need to register them with Tcl. In some cases, you may also need to create the Tcl interpreter, although this is done for you by the standard Tcl shells.

If you are writing an extension, then you must provide an initialization procedure. The job of this procedure is to register Tcl commands with `Tcl_CreateCommand` or `Tcl_CreateObjCommand`. This is shown in Example 47–1 on page 698. The name of this procedure must end with `_Init`, as in `Expect_Init`, `Blt_Init`, or `Foo_Init`, if you plan to create your extension as a shared library. This procedure is called automatically when the Tcl script loads your library with the `load` command, which is described on page 697.

If you are embedding Tcl into an existing application, then you should initialize Tcl with `Tcl_FindExecutable` and `Tcl_CreateInterp`. The first call helps the Tcl runtime initialize itself, and determines the return value for `info nameofexecutable`. `Tcl_CreateInterp` creates an interpreter that includes the standard commands listed in Table 1–4 on page 22. You still have to initialize all your custom commands (e.g., by calling `Foo_Init`) and arrange to run a script using `Tcl_Eval` or `Tcl_EvalFile`. However, there are a lot of details to get right, and Tcl provides a higher level interface in `Tcl_Main` and `Tcl_AppInit`. `Tcl_Main` creates the interpreter for you, processes command line arguments to get an initial script to run, and even provides an interactive command loop. It calls out to `Tcl_AppInit`, which you provide, to complete the initialization of the interpreter. The use of `Tcl_Main` is shown in Example 47–13 on page 720. There are even more details to get right with a Tk application because of the window system and the event loop. These details are hidden behind `Tk_Main`, which makes a similar call out to `Tk_AppInit` that you provide to complete initialization.

Calling Out to Tcl Scripts

An application can call out to the script layer at any point, even inside command procedures. `Tcl_Eval` is the basic API for this, and there are several variations depending on how you pass arguments to the script. When you look up `Tcl_Eval` in the reference material, you will get a description of the whole family of `Tcl_Eval` procedures.

You can also set and query Tcl variables from C using the `Tcl_SetVar` and `Tcl_GetVar` procedures. Again, there are several variations on these procedures that account for different types, like strings or `Tcl_Obj` values, and scalar or array variables. The `Tcl_LinkVar` procedure causes a Tcl variable to mirror a C variable. Modifications to the Tcl variable are reflected in the C variable, and reading the Tcl variable always returns the C variable's value. `Tcl_LinkVar` is built on a more general variable tracing facility, which is exposed to Tcl as the `trace` command, and available as the `Tcl_TraceVar` C API.

A well-behaved extension should provide both a C and Tcl API, but most of the core Tcl and Tk commands do not provide an exported C API. This forces you to eval Tcl scripts to get at their functionality. Example 47–15 on page 725 shows the `Tcl_Invoke` procedure that can help you work around this limitation. `Tcl_Invoke` is used to invoke a Tcl command without the parsing and substitution overhead of `Tcl_Eval`.

Using the Tcl C Library

Over the years the Tcl C Library has grown from a simple language interpreter into a full featured library. An important property of the Tcl API is that it is cross platform: its works equally well on UNIX, Windows, and Macintosh. One can argue that it is easier to write cross-platform applications in Tcl than in Java! Some of the useful features that you might not expect from a language interpreter include:

- A general hash table package that automatically adjusts itself as the hash table grows. It allows various types of keys, including strings and integers.
- A dynamic string (i.e., `DString`) package that provides an efficient way to construct strings.
- An I/O channel package that replaces the old "standard I/O library" found on UNIX with something that is cross-platform, does buffering, allows non-blocking I/O, and does character set translations. You can create new I/O channel types.
- Network sockets for TCP/IP communication.
- Character set translations between Unicode, UTF-8, and other encodings.
- An event loop manager that interfaces with network connections and window system events. You can create new "event sources" that work with the event loop manager.
- Multithreading support in the form of mutexes, condition variables, and thread-local storage.

- A registration system for exit handlers that are called when Tcl is shutting down.

This Chapter focuses just on the Tcl C API related to the Tcl interpreter. Chapter 50 gives a high-level overview of all the procedures in the Tcl and Tk C library, but this book does not provide a complete reference. Refer to the on-line manual pages for the specific details about each procedure; they are an excellent source of information. The manual pages should be part of every Tcl distribution. They are on the book's CD, and they can be found web at:

```
http://www.tcl.tk/man/
```

The Tcl source code is worth reading.

Finally, it is worth emphasizing that the source code of the Tcl C library is a great source of information. The code is well written and well commented. If you want to see how something really works, reading the code is worthwhile.

Creating a Loadable Package

You can organize your C code into a loadable package that can be dynamically linked into *tclsh*, *wish*, or your own Tcl application. The details about compiling the code into the shared library that contains the package are presented in Chapter 48. This section describes a package that implements the `random` Tcl command that returns random numbers.

The `load` Command

The Tcl `load` command is used to dynamically link in a compiled package:

```
load library package ?interp?
```

The `library` is the file name of the shared library file (i.e., the DLL), and `package` is the name of the package implemented by the library. This name corresponds to the `package_Init` procedure called to initialize the package (e.g., `Random_Init`) The optional `interp` argument lets you load the library into a slave interpreter. If the library is in `/usr/local/lib/random.so`, then a Tcl script can `load` the package like this:

```
load /usr/local/lib/random.so Random
```

On most UNIX systems, you can set the `LD_LIBRARY_PATH` environment variable to a colon-separated list of directories that contain shared libraries. If you do that, then you can use relative names for the libraries:

```
load librandom.so Random
```

On Macintosh, the `load` command looks for libraries in the same folder as the Tcl/Tk application (i.e., *Wish*) and in the `System:Extensions:Tool Command Language` folder:

```
load random.shlib Random
```

On Windows, `load` looks in the same directory as the Tcl/Tk application, the current directory, the `C:\Windows\System` directory (or `C:\Windows\System32` on

Windows NT), the `C:\Windows` directory, and then the directories listed in the `PATH` environment variable.

```
load random.dll Random
```

Fortunately, you usually do not have to worry about these details because the Tcl `package` facility can manage your libraries for you. Instead of invoking `load` directly, your scripts can use `package require` instead. The package facility keeps track of where your libraries are and knows how to call `load` for your platform. It is described in Chapter 12.

The Package Initialization Procedure

When a package is loaded, Tcl calls a C procedure named *package*_Init, where *package* is the name of your package. Example 47–1 defines `Random_Init`. It registers a command procedure, `RandomCmd`, that implements a new Tcl command, `random`. When the Tcl script uses the `random` command, the `RandomCmd` procedure will be invoked by the Tcl interpreter. Two styles of command registrations are made for comparison: the original `Tcl_CreateCommand` and the `Tcl_CreateObjCommand` added in Tcl 8.0. The command procedures are described in the next section:

Example 47–1 The initialization procedure for a loadable package.

```
/*
 * random.c
 */
#include <tcl.h>
/*
 * Declarations for application-specific command procedures
 */

int RandomCmd(ClientData clientData,
            Tcl_Interp *interp,
            int argc, CONST char *argv[]);
int RandomObjCmd(ClientData clientData,
            Tcl_Interp *interp,
            int objc, Tcl_Obj *CONST objv[]);

/*
 * Random_Init is called when the package is loaded.
 */

int Random_Init(Tcl_Interp *interp) {
    /*
     * Initialize the stub table interface, which is
     * described in Chapter 48.
     */

    if (Tcl_InitStubs(interp, "8.1", 0) == NULL) {
        return TCL_ERROR;
    }
```

```
        /*
         * Register two variations of random.
         * The orandom command uses the object interface.
         */

        Tcl_CreateCommand(interp, "random", RandomCmd,
                (ClientData)NULL, (Tcl_CmdDeleteProc *)NULL);
        Tcl_CreateObjCommand(interp, "orandom", RandomObjCmd,
                (ClientData)NULL, (Tcl_CmdDeleteProc *)NULL);

        /*
         * Declare that we implement the random package
         * so scripts that do "package require random"
         * can load the library automatically.
         */
        Tcl_PkgProvide(interp, "random", "1.1");
        return TCL_OK;
}
```

Using `Tcl_PkgProvide`

`Random_Init` uses `Tcl_PkgProvide` to declare what package is provided by the C code. This call helps the `pkg_mkIndex` procedure learn what libraries provide which packages. `pkg_mkIndex` saves this information in a package database, which is a file named `pkgIndex.tcl`. The `package require` command looks for the package database files along your `auto_path` and automatically loads your package. The general process is:

- Create your shared library and put it into a directory listed on your `auto_path` variable, or a subdirectory of one of the directories on your `auto_path`.
- Run the `pkg_mkIndex` procedure in that directory, giving it the names of all the script files and shared libraries it should index. Now your shared library is ready for use by other scripts.
- A script uses `package require` to request a package. The correct `load` command for your system will be used the first time a command from your package is used. The `package` command is the same on all platforms:

```
    package require random
    => 1.1
```

This process is explained in more detail on page 175.

A C Command Procedure

Tcl 8.0 introduced a new interface for Tcl commands that is designed to work efficiently with its internal on-the-fly byte code compiler. The original interface to commands was string oriented. This resulted in a lot of conversions between strings and internal formats such as integers, double-precision floating point numbers, and lists. The new interface is based on the `Tcl_Obj` type that can store different types of values. Conversions between strings and other types are done in a lazy fashion, and the saved conversions help your scripts run more efficiently.

This section shows how to build a random number command using both interfaces. The string-based interface is simpler, and we start with that to illustrate the basic concepts. You can use it for your first experiments with command procedures. Once you gain some experience, you can start using the interfaces that use `Tcl_Obj` values instead of simple strings. If you have old command procedures from before Tcl 8.0, you need to update them only if you want extra efficiency. The string and `Tcl_Obj` interfaces are very similar, so you should find updating your command procedures straightforward.

The String Command Interface

The string-based interface to a C command procedure is much like the interface to the `main` program. You register the command procedure like this:

```
Tcl_CreateCommand(interp, "cmd", CmdProc, data, DeleteProc);
```

When the script invokes `cmd`, Tcl calls `CmdProc` like this:

```
CmdProc(data, interp, argc, argv);
```

The `interp` is type `Tcl_Interp *`, and it is a general handle on the state of the interpreter. Most Tcl C APIs take this parameter. The `data` is type `Client-Data`, which is an opaque pointer. You can use this to associate state with your command. You register this state along with your command procedure, and then Tcl passes it back to you when the command is invoked. This is especially useful with Tk widgets, which are explained in more detail in Chapter 49. Our simple `RandomCmd` command procedure does not use this feature, so it passes `NULL` into `Tcl_CreateCommand`. The `DeleteProc` is called when the command is destroyed, which is typically when the whole Tcl interpreter is being deleted. If your state needs to be cleaned up, you can do it then. `RandomCmd` does not use this feature, either.

The arguments from the Tcl command are available as an array of strings defined by an `argv` parameter and counted by an `argc` parameter. This is the same interface that a main program has to its command line arguments. Example 47–2 shows the `RandomCmd` command procedure:

Example 47–2 The `RandomCmd` C command procedure.

```
/*
 * RandomCmd --
 * This implements the random Tcl command. With no arguments
 * the command returns a random integer.
 * With an integer valued argument "range",
 * it returns a random integer between 0 and range.
 */
int
RandomCmd(ClientData clientData, Tcl_Interp *interp,
        int argc, CONST char *argv[])
```

```
{
    int rand, error;
    int range = 0;
    char buffer[20];
    if (argc > 2) {
        interp->result = "Usage: random ?range?";
        return TCL_ERROR;
    }
    if (argc == 2) {
        if (Tcl_GetInt(interp, argv[1], &range) != TCL_OK) {
            return TCL_ERROR;
        }
    }
    rand = random();
    if (range != 0) {
        rand = rand % range;
    }
    sprintf(buf, "%d", rand);
    Tcl_SetResult(interp, buf, TCL_VOLATILE);
    return TCL_OK;
}
```

The return value of a Tcl command is really two things: a result string and a status code. The result is a string that is either the return value of the command as seen by the Tcl script, or an error message that is reported upon error. For example, if extra arguments are passed to the command procedure, it raises a Tcl error by doing this:

```
Tcl_SetResult(interp, "Usage: random ?range?", TCL_STATIC);
return TCL_ERROR;
```

The random implementation accepts an optional argument that is a range over which the random numbers should be returned. The argc parameter is tested to see if this argument has been given in the Tcl command. argc counts the command name as well as the arguments, so in our case argc == 2 indicates that the command has been invoked something like:

```
random 25
```

The procedure Tcl_GetInt converts the string-valued argument to an integer. It does error checking and sets the interpreter's result in the case of error, so we can just return if it fails to return TCL_OK.

```
if (Tcl_GetInt(interp, argv[1], &range) != TCL_OK) {
    return TCL_ERROR;
}
```

Finally, the real work of calling random is done. The result is formatted into a string in a temporary buffer, and the result is set with Tcl_SetResult. A normal return looks like this:

```
sprintf(buffer, "%d", rand);
Tcl_SetResult(interp, buffer, TCL_VOLATILE);
return TCL_OK;
```

VI. Tcl and C

Result Codes from Command Procedures

The command procedure returns a status code that is either `TCL_OK` or `TCL_ERROR` to indicate success or failure. If the command procedure returns `TCL_ERROR`, then a Tcl error is raised, and the result value is used as the error message. The procedure can also return `TCL_BREAK`, `TCL_CONTINUE`, `TCL_RETURN`, which affects control structure commands like `foreach` and `proc`. You can even return an application-specific code (e.g., 5 or higher), which might be useful if you are implementing new kinds of control structures. The status code returned by the command procedure is the value returned by the `Tcl_Eval` family of C APIs, which are described on page 724 and by the `catch` command, which is discussed in more detail on page 83.

Managing the String Result

There is a simple protocol that manages the storage for a command procedure's result string. It involves `interp->result`, which holds the value, and `interp->freeProc`, which determines how the storage is cleaned up. When a command is called, the interpreter initializes `interp->result` to a static buffer of `TCL_RESULT_SIZE`, which is 200 bytes. The default cleanup action is to do nothing.

In earlier versions of Tcl it was safe to access `interp->result` directly. With the addition of the Tcl_Obj interfaces, which are described next, this is no longer always safe. The following procedures should be used to manage the `result` and `freeProc` fields. These procedures automatically manage storage for the result:

```
Tcl_SetResult(interp, string, freeProc)
Tcl_AppendResult(interp, str1, str2, str3, (char *)NULL)
Tcl_AppendElement(interp, string)
```

`Tcl_SetResult` sets the return value to be *string*. The *freeProc* argument describes how the result should be disposed of: `TCL_STATIC` is used in the case where the result is a constant string allocated by the compiler, `TCL_DYNAMIC` is used if the result is allocated with `Tcl_Alloc`, which is a platform- and compiler-independent version of `malloc`, and `TCL_VOLATILE` is used if the result is in a stack variable. In the `TCL_VOLATILE` case, the Tcl interpreter makes a copy of the result before calling any other command procedures. Finally, if you have your own memory allocator, pass in the address of the procedure that should free the result.

`Tcl_AppendResult` copies its arguments into the result buffer, reallocating the buffer if necessary. The arguments are concatenated onto the end of the existing result, if any. `Tcl_AppendResult` can be called several times to build a result. The result buffer is overallocated, so several appends are efficient.

`Tcl_AppendElement` adds the string to the result as a proper Tcl list element. It might add braces or backslashes to get the proper structure.

`Tcl_ResetResult` is called before each command procedure. However, If you have built up a result and want to throw it away (e.g., an error occurs), then you can use `Tcl_ResetResult` to restore the result to its initial state.

The `Tcl_Obj` Command Interface

The `Tcl_Obj` command interface replaces strings with *dual-ported values*. The arguments to a command are an array of pointers to `Tcl_Obj` structures, and the result of a command is also of type `Tcl_Obj`. The replacement of strings by `Tcl_Obj` values extends throughout Tcl. The value of a Tcl variable is kept in a `Tcl_Obj`, and Tcl scripts are stored in a `Tcl_Obj`, too. You can continue to use the old string-based API, which converts strings to `Tcl_Obj` values, but this conversion adds overhead.

The `Tcl_Obj` structure stores both a string representation and a native representation. The native representation depends on the type of the value. Tcl lists are stored as an array of pointers to strings. Integers are stored as 32-bit integers. Floating point values are stored in double-precision. Tcl scripts are stored as sequences of byte codes. Conversion between the native representation and a string are done upon demand. There are APIs for accessing `Tcl_Obj` values, so you do not have to worry about type conversions unless you implement a new type. Example 47–3 shows the `random` command procedure using the `Tcl_Obj` interfaces:

Example 47–3 The `RandomObjCmd` C command procedure.

```
/*
 * RandomObjCmd --
 * This implements the random Tcl command from
 * Example 47-2 using the object interface.
 */
int
RandomObjCmd(ClientData clientData, Tcl_Interp *interp,
        int objc, Tcl_Obj *CONST objv[])
{
    Tcl_Obj *resultPtr;
    int rand, error;
    int range = 0;
    if (objc > 2) {
        Tcl_WrongNumArgs(interp, 1, objv, "?range?");
        return TCL_ERROR;
    }
    if (objc == 2) {
        if (Tcl_GetIntFromObj(interp, objv[1], &range) !=
                TCL_OK) {
            return TCL_ERROR;
        }
    }
    rand = random();
    if (range != 0) {
        rand = rand % range;
    }
    resultPtr = Tcl_GetObjResult(interp);
    Tcl_SetIntObj(resultPtr, rand);
    return TCL_OK;
}
```

Compare Example 47–2 with Example 47–3. You can see that the two versions of the C command procedures are similar. The `Tcl_GetInt` call is replaced with `Tcl_GetIntFromObj` call. This receives an integer value from the command argument. This call can avoid conversion from string to integer if the `Tcl_Obj` value is already an integer.

The result is set by getting a handle on the result object and setting its value. This is done instead of accessing the `interp->result` field directly:

```
resultPtr = Tcl_GetObjResult(interp);

Tcl_SetIntObj(resultPtr, rand);
```

The `Tcl_WrongNumArgs` procedure is a convenience procedure that formats an error message. You pass in `objv`, the number of arguments to use from it, and additional string. The example creates this message:

```
wrong # args: should be "random ?range?"
```

Example 47–3 does not do anything obvious about storage management. Tcl initializes the result object before calling your command procedure and takes care of cleaning it up later. It is sufficient to set a value and return `TCL_OK` or `TCL_ERROR`. In more complex cases, however, you have to worry about reference counts to `Tcl_Obj` values. This is described in more detail later.

If your command procedure returns a string, then you will use `Tcl_SetStringObj`. This command makes a copy of the string you pass it. The new Tcl interfaces that take strings also take length arguments so you can pass binary data in strings. If the length is minus 1, then the string is terminated by a NULL byte. A command that always returned "boring" would do this:

```
resultPtr = Tcl_GetObjResult(interp);

Tcl_SetStringObj(resultPtr, "boring", -1);
```

This is a bit too boring. In practice you may need to build up the result piecemeal. With the string-based API, you use `Tcl_AppendResult`. With the `Tcl_Obj` API you get a pointer to the result and use `Tcl_AppendToObj` or `Tcl_AppendStringsToObj`:

```
resultPtr = Tcl_GetObjResult(interp);

Tcl_AppendStringsToObj(resultPtr, "hello ", username, NULL);
```

Managing `Tcl_Obj` Reference Counts

The string-based interfaces copy strings when passing arguments and returning results, but the `Tcl_Obj` interfaces manipulate reference counts to avoid these copy operations. References come from Tcl variables, from the interpreter's result, and from sharing caused when a value is passed into a Tcl procedure. Constants are also shared. When a C command procedure is called, Tcl does not automatically increment the reference count on the arguments. However, each `Tcl_Obj` referenced by `objv` will have at least one reference, and it is quite common to have two or more references.

The C type definition for `Tcl_Obj` is shown below. There are APIs to access all aspects of an object, so you should refrain from manipulating a `Tcl_Obj` directly unless you are implementing a new type:

Example 47–4 The `Tcl_Obj` structure.

```
typedef struct Tcl_Obj {
    int refCount;        /* Counts number of shared references */
    char *bytes;         /* String representation */
    int length;          /* Number of bytes in the string */
    Tcl_ObjType *typePtr;/* Type implementation */
    union {
        long longValue;  /* Type data */
        double doubleValue;
        VOID *otherValuePtr;
        struct {
            VOID *ptr1;
            VOID *ptr2;
        } twoPtrValue;
    } internalRep;
} Tcl_Obj;
```

Each type implementation provides a few procedures like this:

```
Tcl_GetTypeFromObj(interp, objPtr, valuePtr);

Tcl_SetTypeObj(resultPtr, value);

objPtr = Tcl_NewTypeObj(value);
```

The initial reference count is zero.

The `Tcl_NewTypeObj` allocates storage for a `Tcl_Obj` and sets its reference count to zero. `Tcl_IncrRefCount` and `Tcl_DecrRefCount` increment and decrement the reference count on an object. `Tcl_DecrRefCount` frees the storage for `Tcl_Obj` when it goes to zero. The initial reference count of zero was chosen because functions like `Tcl_SetObjResult` automatically increment the reference count on an object.

The `Tcl_GetTypeFromObj` and `Tcl_SetTypeObj` procedures just get and set the value; the reference count does not change. Type conversions are automatic. You can set a `Tcl_Obj` value to an integer and get back a string or double precision number later. The type implementations automatically take care of the storage for the `Tcl_Obj` value as it changes. Of course, if a `Tcl_Obj` stays the same type, then no string conversions are necessary and accesses are more efficient.

Modifying `Tcl_Obj` Values

It is not safe to modify a shared `Tcl_Obj`. The sharing is only for efficiency: Logically, each reference is a copy, and you must honor this model when creating and modifying `Tcl_Obj` values. `Tcl_IsShared` returns 1 if there is more than one reference to an object. If a command procedure modifies a shared object, it must make a private copy with `Tcl_DuplicateObj`. The new copy starts with a reference count of zero. You either pass this to `Tcl_SetResultObj`, which adds a reference, or you have to explicitly add a reference to the copy with `Tcl_IncrRefCount`.

Example 47–5 implements a `plus1` command that adds one to its argument. If the argument is not shared, then `plus1` can be implemented efficiently

by modifying the native representation of the integer. Otherwise, it has to make
a copy of the object before modifying it:

Example 47–5 The `Plus1ObjCmd` procedure.

```
/*
 * Plus1ObjCmd --
 * This adds one to its input argument.
 */
int
Plus1ObjCmd(ClientData clientData, Tcl_Interp *interp,
        int objc, Tcl_Obj *CONST objv[])
{
    Tcl_Obj *objPtr;
    int i;
    if (objc != 2) {
        Tcl_WrongNumArgs(interp, 1, objv, "value");
        return TCL_ERROR;
    }
    objPtr = objv[1];
    if (Tcl_GetIntFromObj(interp, objPtr, &i) != TCL_OK) {
        return TCL_ERROR;
    }
    if (Tcl_IsShared(objPtr)) {
        objPtr = Tcl_DuplicateObj(objPtr);    /* refCount 0 */
        Tcl_IncrRefCount(objPtr);             /* refCount 1*/
    }
    /*
     * Assert objPtr has a refCount of one here.
     * OK to set the unshared value to something new.
     * Tcl_SetIntObj overwrites the old value.
     */
    Tcl_SetIntObj(objPtr, i+1);
    /*
     * Setting the result object adds a new reference,
     * so we decrement because we no longer care about
     * the integer object we modified.
     */
    Tcl_SetObjResult(interp, objPtr);         /* refCount 2*/
    Tcl_DecrRefCount(objPtr);                 /* refCount 1*/
    /*
     * Now only the interpreter result has a reference to objPtr.
     */
    return TCL_OK;
}
```

Pitfalls of Shared `Tcl_Obj` Values

You have to be careful when using the values from a `Tcl_Obj` structure. The
Tcl C library provides many procedures like `Tcl_GetStringFromObj`,
`Tcl_GetIntFromObj`, `Tcl_GetListFromObj`, and so on. These all operate efficiently by returning a pointer to the native representation of the object. They

will convert the object to the requested type, if necessary. The problem is that shared values can undergo type conversions that may invalidate your reference to a particular type of the value.

Value references are only safe until the next `Tcl_Get*FromObj` *call.*

Consider a command procedure that takes two arguments, an integer and a list. The command procedure has a sequence of code like this:

```
Tcl_ListObjGetElements(interp, objv[1], &objc, &listPtr);
/* Manipulate list */
Tcl_GetIntFromObj(interp, objv[2], &int);
/* list may be invalid here */
```

If, by chance, both arguments have the same value, (e.g., 1 and 1), which is possible for a Tcl list and an integer, then Tcl will automatically arrange to share these values between both arguments. The pointers in `objv[1]` and `objv[2]` will be the same, and the reference count on the `Tcl_Obj` they reference will be at least 2. The first `Tcl_ListObjGetElements` call ensures the value is of type list, and it returns a direct pointer to the native list representation. However, `Tcl_GetIntFromObj` then helpfully converts the `Tcl_Obj` value to an integer. This deallocates the memory for the list representation, and now `listPtr` is a dang-ling pointer! This particular example can be made safe by reversing the calls because `Tcl_GetIntFromObj` copies the integer value:

```
Tcl_GetIntFromObj(interp, objv[2], &int);
Tcl_ListObjGetElements(interp, objv[1], &objc, &listPtr);
/* int is still a good copy of the value */
```

By the way, you should always test your `Tcl_Get*` calls in case the format of the value is incompatible with the requested type. If the object is not a valid list, the following command returns an error:

```
if (Tcl_ListObjGetElements(interp, obj[1], &objc, &listPtr)
        != TCL_OK) {
    return TCL_ERROR;
}
```

The `blob` Command Example

This section illustrates some standard coding practices with a bigger example. The example is still artificial in that it doesn't actually do very much. However, it illustrates a few more common idioms you should know about when creating Tcl commands.

The `blob` command creates and manipulates blobs. Each blob has a name and some associated properties. The `blob` command uses a hash table to keep track of blobs by their name. The hash table is an example of state associated with a command that needs to be cleaned up when the Tcl interpreter is destroyed. The Tcl hash table implementation is nice and general, too, so you may find it helpful in a variety of situations.

You can associate a Tcl script with a blob. When you poke the blob, it invokes the script. This shows how easy it is to associate behaviors with your C extensions. Example 47–6 shows the data structures used to implement blobs.

Example 47–6 The `Blob` and `BlobState` data structures.

```
/*
 * The Blob structure is created for each blob.
 */
typedef struct Blob {
    int N;                 /* Integer-valued property */
    Tcl_Obj *objPtr;       /* General property */
    Tcl_Obj *cmdPtr;       /* Callback script */
} Blob;
/*
 * The BlobState structure is created once for each interp.
 */
typedef struct BlobState {
    Tcl_HashTable hash;        /* List blobs by name */
    int uid;                   /* Used to generate names */
} BlobState;
```

Creating and Destroying Hash Tables

Example 47–7 shows the `Blob_Init` and `BlobCleanup` procedures. `Blob_Init` creates the command and initializes the hash table. It registers a delete procedure, `BlobCleanup`, that will clean up the hash table.

The `Blob_Init` procedure allocates and initializes a hash table as part of the `BlobState` structure. This structure is passed into `Tcl_CreateObjCommand` as the `ClientData`, and gets passed back to `BlobCmd` later. You might be tempted to have a single static hash table structure instead of allocating one. However, it is quite possible that a process has many Tcl interpreters, and each needs its own hash table to record its own blobs.

When the hash table is initialized, you specify what the keys are. In this case, the name of the blob is a key, so `TCL_STRING_KEYS` is used. If you use an integer key, or the address of a data structure, use `TCL_ONE_WORD_KEYS`. You can also have an array of integers (i.e., a chunk of data) for the key. In this case, pass in an integer larger than 1 that represents the size of the integer array used as the key.

The `BlobCleanup` command cleans up the hash table. It iterates through all the elements of the hash table and gets the value associated with each key. This value is cast into a pointer to a `Blob` data structure. This iteration is a special case because each entry is deleted as we go by the `BlobDelete` procedure. If you do not modify the hash table, you continue the search with `Tcl_NextHashEntry` instead of calling `Tcl_FirstHashEntry` repeatedly.

Example 47–7 The `Blob_Init` and `BlobCleanup` procedures.

```
/*
 * Forward references.
 */

int BlobCmd(ClientData data, Tcl_Interp *interp,
        int objc, Tcl_Obj *CONST objv[]);
int BlobCreate(Tcl_Interp *interp, BlobState *statePtr);
void BlobCleanup(ClientData data);

/*
 * Blob_Init --
 *
 *      Initialize the blob module.
 *
 * Side Effects:
 *      This allocates the hash table used to keep track
 *      of blobs. It creates the blob command.
 */
int
Blob_Init(Tcl_Interp *interp)
{
    BlobState *statePtr;
    /*
     * Allocate and initialize the hash table. Associate the
     * BlobState with the command by using the ClientData.
     */
    statePtr = (BlobState *)ckalloc(sizeof(BlobState));
    Tcl_InitHashTable(&statePtr->hash, TCL_STRING_KEYS);
    statePtr->uid = 0;
    Tcl_CreateObjCommand(interp, "blob", BlobCmd,
            (ClientData)statePtr, BlobCleanup);
    return TCL_OK;
}

/*
 * BlobCleanup --
 *      This is called when the blob command is destroyed.
 *
 * Side Effects:
 *      This walks the hash table and deletes the blobs it
 *      contains. Then it deallocates the hash table.
 */

void
BlobCleanup(ClientData data)
{
    BlobState *statePtr = (BlobState *)data;
    Blob *blobPtr;
    Tcl_HashEntry *entryPtr;
    Tcl_HashSearch search;

    entryPtr = Tcl_FirstHashEntry(&statePtr->hash, &search);
```

```
    while (entryPtr != NULL) {
        blobPtr = Tcl_GetHashValue(entryPtr);
        BlobDelete(blobPtr, entryPtr);
        /*
         * Get the first entry again, not the "next" one,
         * because we just modified the hash table.
         */
        entryPtr = Tcl_FirstHashEntry(&statePtr->hash, &search);
    }
    ckfree((char *)statePtr);
}
```

Tcl_Alloc, ckalloc, and malloc

Tcl provides its own memory allocator, `Tcl_Alloc` and `Tcl_Free`, which can be used to replace poor malloc implementations that some systems have. Tcl 8.4 has a new allocator that supports threaded applications well. The memory allocator also supports memory debugging if you compile with `-DTCL_MEM_DEBUG`. A Tcl `memory` command is added that reports on memory use and can help you track down memory problems.

To support optional memory debugging, *tcl.h* defines `ckalloc` and `ckfree` macros that call different allocation routines depending on compile-time options. Because of this, your code should not use `malloc` and `free` directly, nor should it call `Tcl_Alloc` and `Tcl_Free` directly. Use the `ckalloc` and `ckfree` macros everywhere. In general, it is not safe to allocate memory with `Tcl_Alloc` or `ckalloc` and free it with `free`, or allocate memory with `malloc` and free it with `Tcl_Free` or `ckfree`. Also, if you compile some code with `-DTCL_MEM_DEBUG`, and some code without that option, you get an immediate crash.

Parsing Arguments and Tcl_GetIndexFromObj

Example 47–8 shows the `BlobCmd` command procedure. This illustrates a basic framework for parsing command arguments. The `Tcl_GetIndexFromObj` procedure is used to map from the first argument (e.g., "names") to an index (e.g., `NamesIx`). This does error checking and formats an error message if the first argument doesn't match. All of the subcommands except "create" and "names" use the second argument as the name of a blob. This name is looked up in the hash table with `Tcl_FindHashEntry`, and the corresponding `Blob` structure is fetched using `Tcl_GetHashValue`. After the argument checking is complete, `BlobCmd` dispatches to the helper procedures to do the actual work:

Example 47–8 The `BlobCmd` command procedure.

```
/*
 * BlobCmd --
 *
 *      This implements the blob command, which has these
 *      subcommands:
 *          create
 *          command name ?script?
 *          data name ?value?
 *          N name ?value?
 *          names ?pattern?
 *          poke name
 *          delete name
 *
 * Results:
 *      A standard Tcl command result.
 */
int
BlobCmd(ClientData data, Tcl_Interp *interp,
    int objc, Tcl_Obj *CONST objv[])
{
    BlobState *statePtr = (BlobState *)data;
    Blob *blobPtr;
    Tcl_HashEntry *entryPtr;
    Tcl_Obj *valueObjPtr;

    /*
     * The subCmds array defines the allowed values for the
     * first argument. These are mapped to values in the
     * BlobIx enumeration by Tcl_GetIndexFromObj.
     */

    char *subCmds[] = {
        "create", "command", "data", "delete", "N", "names",
        "poke", NULL
    };
    enum BlobIx {
        CreateIx, CommandIx, DataIx, DeleteIx, NIx, NamesIx,
        PokeIx
    };
    int result, index;

    if (objc == 1 || objc > 4) {
        Tcl_WrongNumArgs(interp, 1, objv, "option ?arg ...?");
        return TCL_ERROR;
    }
    if (Tcl_GetIndexFromObj(interp, objv[1], subCmds,
            "option", 0, &index) != TCL_OK) {
        return TCL_ERROR;
    }
    if (((index == NamesIx || index == CreateIx) &&
            (objc > 2)) ||
        ((index == PokeIx || index == DeleteIx) &&
            (objc == 4))) {
```

```
        Tcl_WrongNumArgs(interp, 1, objv, "option ?arg ...?");
        return TCL_ERROR;
    }
    if (index == CreateIx) {
        return BlobCreate(interp, statePtr);
    }
    if (index == NamesIx) {
        return BlobNames(interp, statePtr);
    }
    if (objc < 3) {
        Tcl_WrongNumArgs(interp, 1, objv,
            "option blob ?arg ...?");
        return TCL_ERROR;
    } else if (objc == 3) {
        valueObjPtr = NULL;
    } else {
        valueObjPtr = objv[3];
    }
    /*
     * The rest of the commands take a blob name as the third
     * argument. Hash from the name to the Blob structure.
     */
    entryPtr = Tcl_FindHashEntry(&statePtr->hash,
            Tcl_GetString(objv[2]));
    if (entryPtr == NULL) {
        Tcl_AppendResult(interp, "Unknown blob: ",
                Tcl_GetString(objv[2]), NULL);
        return TCL_ERROR;
    }
    blobPtr = (Blob *)Tcl_GetHashValue(entryPtr);
    switch (index) {
        case CommandIx: {
            return BlobCommand(interp, blobPtr, valueObjPtr);
        }
        case DataIx: {
            return BlobData(interp, blobPtr, valueObjPtr);
        }
        case NIx: {
            return BlobN(interp, blobPtr, valueObjPtr);
        }
        case PokeIx: {
            return BlobPoke(interp, blobPtr);
        }
        case DeleteIx: {
            return BlobDelete(blobPtr, entryPtr);
        }
    }
}
```

Creating and Removing Elements from a Hash Table

The real work of `BlobCmd` is done by several helper procedures. These form the basis of a C API to operate on blobs as well. Example 47–9 shows the `Blob-Create` and `BlobDelete` procedures. These procedures manage the hash table entry, and they allocate and free storage associated with the blob.

Example 47–9 `BlobCreate` and `BlobDelete`.

```
int
BlobCreate(Tcl_Interp *interp, BlobState *statePtr)
{
    Tcl_HashEntry *entryPtr;
    Blob *blobPtr;
    int new;
    char name[20];
    /*
     * Generate a blob name and put it in the hash table
     */
    statePtr->uid++;
    sprintf(name, "blob%d", statePtr->uid);
    entryPtr = Tcl_CreateHashEntry(&statePtr->hash, name, &new);
    /*
     * Assert new == 1
     */
    blobPtr = (Blob *)ckalloc(sizeof(Blob));
    blobPtr->N = 0;
    blobPtr->objPtr = NULL;
    blobPtr->cmdPtr = NULL;
    Tcl_SetHashValue(entryPtr, (ClientData)blobPtr);
    /*
     * Copy the name into the interpreter result.
     */
    Tcl_SetStringObj(Tcl_GetObjResult(interp), name, -1);
    return TCL_OK;
}
int
BlobDelete(Blob *blobPtr, Tcl_HashEntry *entryPtr)
{
    Tcl_DeleteHashEntry(entryPtr);
    if (blobPtr->cmdPtr != NULL) {
        Tcl_DecrRefCount(blobPtr->cmdPtr);
    }
    if (blobPtr->objPtr != NULL) {
        Tcl_DecrRefCount(blobPtr->objPtr);
    }
    /*
     * Use Tcl_EventuallyFree because of the Tcl_Preserve
     * done in BlobPoke. See page 716.
     */
    Tcl_EventuallyFree((char *)blobPtr, Tcl_Free);
    return TCL_OK;
}
```

Building a List

The `BlobNames` procedure iterates through the elements of the hash table using `Tcl_FirstHashEntry` and `Tcl_NextHashEntry`. It builds up a list of the names as it goes along. Note that the object reference counts are managed for us. The `Tcl_NewStringObj` returns a `Tcl_Obj` with reference count of zero. When that object is added to the list, the `Tcl_ListObjAppendElement` procedure increments the reference count. Similarly, the `Tcl_NewListObj` returns a `Tcl_Obj` with reference count zero, and its reference count is incremented by `Tcl_SetObjResult`:

Example 47–10 The `BlobNames` procedure.

```
int
BlobNames(Tcl_Interp *interp, BlobState *statePtr)
{
    Tcl_HashEntry *entryPtr;
    Tcl_HashSearch search;
    Tcl_Obj *listPtr;
    Tcl_Obj *objPtr;
    char *name;
    /*
     * Walk the hash table and build a list of names.
     */
    listPtr = Tcl_NewListObj(0, NULL);
    entryPtr = Tcl_FirstHashEntry(&statePtr->hash, &search);
    while (entryPtr != NULL) {
        name = Tcl_GetHashKey(&statePtr->hash, entryPtr);
        if (Tcl_ListObjAppendElement(interp, listPtr,
                Tcl_NewStringObj(name, -1)) != TCL_OK) {
            return TCL_ERROR;
        }
        entryPtr = Tcl_NextHashEntry(&search);
    }
    Tcl_SetObjResult(interp, listPtr);
    return TCL_OK;
}
```

Keeping References to `Tcl_Obj` Values

A blob has two simple properties: an integer N and a general `Tcl_Obj` value. You can query and set these properties with the `BlobN` and `BlobData` procedures. The `BlobData` procedure keeps a pointer to its `Tcl_Obj` argument, so it must increment the reference count on it:

Example 47–11 The `BlobN` and `BlobData` procedures.

```
int
BlobN(Tcl_Interp *interp, Blob *blobPtr, Tcl_Obj *objPtr)
{
    int N;
    if (objPtr != NULL) {
        if (Tcl_GetIntFromObj(interp, objPtr, &N) != TCL_OK) {
            return TCL_ERROR;
        }
        blobPtr->N = N;
    } else {
        N = blobPtr->N;
    }
    Tcl_SetObjResult(interp, Tcl_NewIntObj(N));
    return TCL_OK;
}
int
BlobData(Tcl_Interp *interp, Blob *blobPtr, Tcl_Obj *objPtr)
{
    if (objPtr != NULL) {
        if (blobPtr->objPtr != NULL) {
            Tcl_DecrRefCount(blobPtr->objPtr);
        }
        Tcl_IncrRefCount(objPtr);
        blobPtr->objPtr = objPtr;
    }
    if (blobPtr->objPtr != NULL) {
        Tcl_SetObjResult(interp, blobPtr->objPtr);
    }
    return TCL_OK;
}
```

Using `Tcl_Preserve` and `Tcl_Release` to Guard Data

The `BlobCommand` and `BlobPoke` operations let you register a Tcl command with a blob and invoke the command later. Whenever you evaluate a Tcl command like this, you must be prepared for the worst. It is quite possible for the command to turn around and delete the blob it is associated with! The `Tcl_Preserve`, `Tcl_Release`, and `Tcl_EventuallyFree` procedures are used to handle this situation. `BlobPoke` calls `Tcl_Preserve` on the blob before calling `Tcl_Eval`. `BlobDelete` calls `Tcl_EventuallyFree` instead of `Tcl_Free`. If the `Tcl_Release` call has not yet been made, then `Tcl_EventuallyFree` just marks the memory for deletion, but does not free it immediately. The memory is freed later by `Tcl_Release`. Otherwise, `Tcl_EventuallyFree` frees the memory directly and `Tcl_Release` does nothing. Example 47–12 shows `BlobCommand` and `BlobPoke`:

Example 47–12 The `BlobCommand` and `BlobPoke` procedures.

```
int
BlobCommand(Tcl_Interp *interp, Blob *blobPtr,
    Tcl_Obj *objPtr)
{
    if (objPtr != NULL) {
        if (blobPtr->cmdPtr != NULL) {
            Tcl_DecrRefCount(blobPtr->cmdPtr);
        }
        Tcl_IncrRefCount(objPtr);
        blobPtr->cmdPtr = objPtr;
    }
    if (blobPtr->cmdPtr != NULL) {
        Tcl_SetObjResult(interp, blobPtr->cmdPtr);
    }
    return TCL_OK;
}
int
BlobPoke(Tcl_Interp *interp, Blob *blobPtr)
{
    int result = TCL_OK;
    if (blobPtr->cmdPtr != NULL) {
        Tcl_Preserve(blobPtr);
        result = Tcl_EvalObj(interp, blobPtr->cmdPtr);
        /*
         * Safe to use blobPtr here
         */
        Tcl_Release(blobPtr);
        /*
         * blobPtr may not be valid here
         */
    }
    return result;
}
```

It turns out that `BlobCmd` does not actually use the `blobPtr` after calling `Tcl_EvalObj`, so it could get away without using `Tcl_Preserve` and `Tcl_Release`. These procedures do add some overhead: They put the pointer onto a list of preserved pointers and have to take it off again. If you are careful, you can omit these calls. However, it is worth noting the potential problems caused by evaluating arbitrary Tcl scripts!

CONST in the Tcl 8.4 APIs

The `const` keyword in C is used to create a read-only variable. Once it is set, it cannot be modified. A common use of CONST is in parameter declarations to imply that the parameter cannot be modified by a procedure. The Tcl API definitions use a CONST macro instead of `const` to allow for older compilers that do not support `const`.

Several of the Tcl APIs were changed in Tcl 8.4 to include CONST where they previously did not. The most significant change is in the signature of string-based command procedures like RandomCmd in this chapter. Changes to tcl.h are generally backward compatible, so this change met with some debate. Most liked the addition of CONST because it allows better error checking, but the changes cause compiler warning messages if you compile old code with the 8.4 tcl.h. In some organizations, even compiler warnings are not allowed in code, so you may be compelled to clean up your code.

There are two reasons you may not be able to change older code. First, you may need to compile the same code against older and newer versions of Tcl. Second, you may not have the time to clean up the code. CONST definitions have a tendency to percolate throughout your code. To support these scenarios, 8.4 adds compile-time defines that change the effect of the CONST additions. Table 47–1 describes these definitions:

Table 47–1 Defines to control the meaning of CONST in the Tcl APIs.

NO_CONST	This defines CONST to nothing so no const keywords are used at all. This define has existed for some time.
USE_NON_CONST	Do not use any of the new CONST keywords added in Tcl 8.4.
USE_COMPAT_CONST	Only use the CONST keywords added for the return values of the Tcl 8.4 APIs. Almost all APIs return CONST values now.

Strings and Internationalization

There are two important topics related to string handling: creating strings dynamically and translating strings between character set encodings. These issues do not show up in the simple examples we have seen so far, but they will arise in more serious applications.

The DString Interface

It is often the case that you have to build up a string from pieces. The Tcl_DString data type and a related API are designed to make this efficient. The DString interface hides the memory management issues, and the Tcl_DString data type starts out with a small static buffer, so you can often avoid allocating memory if you put a Tcl_String type on the stack (i.e., as a local variable). The standard code sequence goes something like this:

```
Tcl_DString ds;
Tcl_DStringInit(&ds);
Tcl_DStringAppend(&ds, "some value", -1);
Tcl_DStringAppend(&ds, "something else", -1);
Tcl_DStringResult(interp, &ds);
```

The Tcl_DStringInit call initializes a string pointer inside the structure to point to a static buffer that is also inside the structure. The Tcl_DStringAppend call grows the string. If it would exceed the static buffer, then a new buffer is allocated dynamically and the string is copied into it. The last argument to `Tcl_DStringAppend` is a length, which can be minus 1 if you want to copy until the trailing NULL byte in your string. You can use the string value as the result of your Tcl command with `Tcl_DStringResult`. This passes ownership of the string to the interpreter and automatically cleans up the `Tcl_DString` structure.

If you do not use the string as the interpreter result, then you must call `Tcl_DStringFree` to ensure that any dynamically allocated memory is released:

```
Tcl_DStringFree(&ds);
```

You can get a direct pointer to the string you have created with `Tcl_DStringValue`:

```
name = Tcl_DStringValue(&ds);
```

There are a handful of additional procedures in the `DString` API that you can read about in the reference material. There are some that create lists, but this is better done with the `Tcl_Obj` interface (e.g., `Tcl_NewListObj` and friends).

To some degree, a `Tcl_Obj` can replace the use of a `Tcl_DString`. For example, the `Tcl_NewStringObj` and `Tcl_AppendToObj` allocate a `Tcl_Obj` and append strings to it. However, there are a number of Tcl API procedures that take `Tcl_DString` types as arguments instead of the `Tcl_Obj` type. Also, for small strings, the `DString` interface is still more efficient because it can do less dynamic memory allocation.

Character Set Conversions

As described in Chapter 15, Tcl uses UTF-8 strings internally. UTF-8 is a representation of Unicode that does not contain NULL bytes. It also represents 7-bit ASCII characters in one byte, so if you have old C code that only manipulates ASCII strings, it can coexist with Tcl without modification.

However, in more general cases, you may need to convert between UTF-8 strings you get from `Tcl_Obj` values to strings of a particular encoding. For example, when you pass strings to the operating system, it expects them in its native encoding, which might be 16-bit Unicode, ISO-Latin-1 (i.e., iso-8859-1), or something else.

Tcl provides an encoding API that does translations for you. The simplest calls use a `Tcl_DString` to store the results because it is not possible to predict the size of the result in advance. For example, to convert from a UTF-8 `string` to a `Tcl_DString` in the system encoding, you use this call:

```
Tcl_UtfToExternalDString(NULL, string, -1, &ds);
```

You can then pass `Tcl_DStringValue(&ds)` to your system call that expects a native string. Afterwards you need to call `Tcl_DStringFree(&ds)` to free up any memory allocated by `Tcl_UtfToExternalDString`.

To translate strings the other way, use `Tcl_ExternalToUtfDString`:

```
Tcl_ExternalToUtfDString(NULL, string, -1, &ds);
```

The third argument to these procedures is the length of `string` in bytes (not characters), and minus 1 means that Tcl should calculate it by looking for a

NULL byte. Tcl stores its UTF-8 strings with a NULL byte at the end so it can do this.

The first argument to `these procedures` is the encoding to translate to or from. NULL means the system encoding. If you have data in nonstandard encodings, or need to translate into something other than the system encoding, you need to get a handle on the encoding with `Tcl_GetEncoding`, and free that handle later with `Tcl_FreeEncoding`:

```
encoding = Tcl_GetEncoding(interp, name);
Tcl_FreeEncoding(encoding);
```

The names of the encodings are returned by the `encoding names` Tcl command, and you can query them with a C API, too.

Windows has a quirky string data type called TCHAR, which is an 8-bit byte on Windows 95/98, and a 16-bit Unicode character on Windows NT and Windows CE. If you use a C API that takes an array of TCHAR, then you have to know what kind of system you are running on to use it properly. Tcl provides two procedures that deal with this automatically. `Tcl_WinTCharToUf` works like `Tcl_ExternalToUtfDString`, and `Tcl_WinUtfToTChar` works like `Tcl_UtfToExternalDString`:

```
Tcl_WinUtfToTChar(string, -1, &ds);
Tcl_WinTCharToUtf(string, -1, &ds);
```

Finally, Tcl has several procedures to work with Unicode characters, which are type `Tcl_UniChar`, and UTF-8 encoded characters. Examples include `Tcl_UniCharToUtf`, `Tcl_NumUtfChars`, and `Tcl_UtfToUniCharDString`. Consult the reference materials for details about these procedures.

Tcl_Main and Tcl_AppInit

This section describes how to make a custom main program that includes Tcl. However, the need for custom main programs has been reduced by the use of loadable modules. If you create your commands as a loadable package, you can just `load` them into *tclsh* or *wish*. Even if you do not need a custom main, this section will explain how all the pieces fit together.

The Tcl library supports the basic application structure through the `Tcl_Main` procedure that is designed to be called from your `main` program. `Tcl_Main` does three things:

- It calls `Tcl_CreateInterp` to create an interpreter that includes all the standard Tcl commands like `set` and `proc`. It also defines a few Tcl variables like `argc` and `argv`. These have the command-line arguments that were passed to your application.
- It calls `Tcl_AppInit`, which is not part of the Tcl library. Instead, your application provides this procedure. In `Tcl_AppInit` you can register additional application-specific Tcl commands.
- It reads a script or goes into an interactive loop.

You call `Tcl_Main` from your main program and provide an implementation
of the `Tcl_AppInit` procedure:

Example 47–13 A canonical Tcl main program and `Tcl_AppInit`.

```
/* main.c */
#include <tcl.h>
int Tcl_AppInit(Tcl_Interp *interp);
/*
 * Declarations for application-specific command procedures
 */
int Plus1ObjCmd(ClientData clientData,
             Tcl_Interp *interp,
             int objc, Tcl_Obj *CONST objv[]);

main(int argc, char *argv[]) {
    /*
     * Initialize your application,
     * then initialize and run Tcl.
     */
    Tcl_Main(argc, argv, Tcl_AppInit);
    exit(0);
}
/*
 * Tcl_AppInit is called from Tcl_Main after the Tcl
 * interpreter has been created, and before the script file
 * or interactive command loop is entered.
 */
int
Tcl_AppInit(Tcl_Interp *interp) {
    /*
     * Tcl_Init reads init.tcl from the Tcl script library.
     */
    if (Tcl_Init(interp) == TCL_ERROR) {
       return TCL_ERROR;
    }
    /*
     * Register application-specific commands.
     */
    Tcl_CreateObjCommand(interp, "plus1", Plus1ObjCmd,
          (ClientData)NULL, (Tcl_CmdDeleteProc *)NULL);
    Random_Init(interp);
    Blob_Init(interp);
    /*
     * This file is read if no script is supplied.
     */
    Tcl_SetVar(interp, "tcl_rcFileName", "~/.mytcl",
       TCL_GLOBAL_ONLY);
    /*
     * Test of Tcl_Invoke, which is defined on page 725.
     */
    Tcl_Invoke(interp, "set", "foo", "$xyz [foo] {", NULL);
    return TCL_OK;
}
```

The `main` program calls `Tcl_Main` with the `argc` and `argv` parameters passed into the program. These are the strings passed to the program on the command line, and `Tcl_Main` will store these values into Tcl variables by the same name. `Tcl_Main` is also given the address of the initialization procedure, which is `Tcl_AppInit` in our example. `Tcl_AppInit` is called by `Tcl_Main` with one argument, a handle on a newly created interpreter. There are three parts to the `Tcl_AppInit` procedure:

- The first part initializes the various packages the application uses. The example calls `Tcl_Init` to set up the script library facility described in Chapter 12. The core Tcl commands have already been defined by `Tcl_CreateInterp`, which is called by `Tcl_Main` before the call to `Tcl_AppInit`.
- The second part of `Tcl_AppInit` does application-specific initialization. The example registers the command procedures defined earlier in this Chapter.
- The third part defines a Tcl variable, `tcl_RcFileName`, which names an application startup script that executes if the program is used interactively.

You can use your custom program just like *tclsh*, except that it includes the additional commands you define in your `Tcl_AppInit` procedure. The sample makefile on the CD creates a program named *mytcl*. You can compile and run that program and test `random` and the other commands.

Tk_Main

The structure of Tk applications is similar. The `Tk_Main` procedure creates a Tcl interpreter and the main Tk window. It calls out to a procedure you provide to complete initialization. After your `Tk_AppInit` returns, `Tk_Main` goes into an event loop until all the windows in your application have been destroyed.

Example 47–14 shows a `Tk_AppInit` used with `Tk_Main`. The main program processes its own command-line arguments using `Tk_ParseArgv`, which requires a Tcl interpreter for error reporting. The `Tk_AppInit` procedure initializes the clock widget example that is the topic of Chapter 49:

Example 47–14 A canonical Tk `main` program and `Tk_AppInit`.

```
/* main.c */
#include <tk.h>

int Tk_AppInit(Tcl_Interp *interp);

/*
 * A table for command line arguments.
 */
char *myoption1 = NULL;
int myint2 = 0;
```

VI. Tcl and C

```
static Tk_ArgvInfo argTable[] = {
    {"-myoption1", TK_ARGV_STRING, (char *) NULL,
        (char *) &myoption1, "Explain myoption1"},
    {"-myint2", TK_ARGV_CONSTANT, (char *) 1, (char *) &myint2,
        "Explain myint2"},
    {"", TK_ARGV_END, },
};

main(int argc, char *argv[]) {
    Tcl_Interp *interp;
    /*
     * Call this before creating any interpreters.
     */
    Tcl_FindExecutable();
    /*
     * Create an interpreter for the error message from
     * Tk_ParseArgv. Another one is created by Tk_Main.
     * Parse our arguments and leave the rest to Tk_Main.
     */
    interp = Tcl_CreateInterp();
    if (Tk_ParseArgv(interp, (Tk_Window) NULL, &argc, argv,
            argTable, 0) != TCL_OK) {
        fprintf(stderr, "%s\n", interp->result);
        exit(1);
    }
    Tcl_DeleteInterp(interp);

    Tk_Main(argc, argv, Tk_AppInit);
    exit(0);
}
int ClockCmd(ClientData clientData,
            Tcl_Interp *interp,
            int argc, CONST char *argv[]);
int ClockObjCmd(ClientData clientData,
            Tcl_Interp *interp,
            int objc, Tcl_Obj *CONST objv[]);
void ClockObjDestroy(ClientData clientData);

int
Tk_AppInit(Tcl_Interp *interp) {
    /*
     * Initialize packages
     */
    if (Tcl_Init(interp) == TCL_ERROR) {
        return TCL_ERROR;
    }
    if (Tk_Init(interp) == TCL_ERROR) {
        return TCL_ERROR;
    }
    /*
     * Define application-specific commands here.
     */
    Tcl_CreateCommand(interp, "wclock", ClockCmd,
        (ClientData)Tk_MainWindow(interp),
        (Tcl_CmdDeleteProc *)NULL);
```

```
    Tcl_CreateObjCommand(interp, "oclock", ClockObjCmd,
        (ClientData)NULL, ClockObjDestroy);
    /*
     * Define start-up filename. This file is read in
     * case the program is run interactively.
     */
    Tcl_SetVar(interp, "tcl_rcFileName", "~/.mytcl",
        TCL_GLOBAL_ONLY);
    return TCL_OK;
}
```

The Event Loop

An event loop is used to process window system events and other events like timers and network sockets. The different event types are described later. All Tk applications must have an event loop so that they function properly in the window system environment. Tk provides a standard event loop with the `Tk_MainLoop` procedure, which is called at the end of `Tk_Main`. The *wish* shell provides an event loop automatically. The *tclsh* shell does not, although you can add an event loop using pure Tcl as shown in Example 16–2 on page 230.

Some applications already have their own event loop. You have two choices if you want to add Tk to such an application. The first is to modify the existing event loop to call `Tcl_DoOneEvent` to process any outstanding Tcl events. The `unix` directory of the source distribution has a file called `XtTest.c` that adds Tcl to an Xt (i.e., Motif) application. The other way to customize the event loop is to make your existing events look like Tcl *event sources*, and register them with the event loop. Then you can just use `Tk_Main`. There are four event classes, and they are handled in the following order by `Tcl_DoOneEvent`:

- Window events. Use the `Tk_CreateEventHandler` procedure to register a handler for these events. Use the `TCL_WINDOW_EVENTS` flag to process these in `Tcl_DoOneEvent`.
- File events. Use these events to wait on slow devices and network connections. On UNIX you can register a handler for all files, sockets, and devices with `Tcl_CreateFileHandler`. On Windows and Macintosh, there are different APIs for registration because there are different system handles for files, sockets, and devices. On all platforms you use the `TCL_FILE_EVENTS` flag to process these handlers in `Tcl_DoOneEvent`.
- Timer events. You can set up events to occur after a specified time period. Use the `Tcl_CreateTimerHandler` procedure to register a handler for the event. Use the `TCL_TIMER_EVENTS` flag to process these in `Tcl_DoOneEvent`.
- Idle events. These events are processed when there is nothing else to do. Virtually all the Tk widgets use idle events to display themselves. Use the `Tcl_DoWhenIdle` procedure to register a procedure to call once at the next idle time. Use the `TCL_IDLE_EVENTS` flag to process these in `Tcl_DoOneEvent`.

VI. Tcl and C

Invoking Scripts from C

The main program is not the only place you can evaluate a Tcl script. You can use the `Tcl_Eval` procedure essentially at any time to evaluate a Tcl command:

```
Tcl_Eval(Tcl_Interp *interp, char *script);
```

The return value of `Tcl_Eval` is a return code like `TCL_OK`, `TCL_ERROR`, `TCL_BREAK`, `TCL_CONTINUE`, or `TCL_RETURN`. The result of the command is obtained with `Tcl_GetStringResult` or `Tcl_GetObjResult`. Those APIs return whatever was set with the `Tcl_SetResult`, `Tcl_SetObjResult`, or the other APIs used to set the result of a command procedure.

The `script` is evaluated in the current Tcl procedure scope, which may be the global scope. Similarly, calls like `Tcl_GetVar` and `Tcl_SetVar` access variables in the current scope. If for some reason you want a new procedure scope, the easiest thing to do is to call your C code from a Tcl procedure used for this purpose. It is not easy to create a new procedure scope with the exported C API.

`Tcl_Eval` modifies its argument.

You should be aware that `Tcl_Eval` may modify the string that is passed into it as a side effect of the way substitutions are performed. If you pass a constant string to `Tcl_Eval`, make sure your compiler has not put the string constant into read-only memory. If you use the *gcc* compiler, you may need to use the `-fwritable-strings` option. Chapter 48 shows how to get the right compilation settings for your system.

Variations on Tcl_Eval

There are several variations on `Tcl_Eval`. The possibilities include strings or `Tcl_Obj` values, evaluation at the current or global scope, a single string (or `Tcl_Obj` value) or a variable number of arguments, and optional byte-code compilation. The most general string-based eval is `Tcl_EvalEx`, which takes a counted string and some flags:

```
Tcl_EvalEx(interp, string, count, flags);
```

The flags are `TCL_GLOBAL_EVAL` and `TCL_EVAL_DIRECT`, which bypasses the byte-code compiler. For code that is executed only one time, `TCL_EVAL_DIRECT` may be more efficient. `Tcl_GlobalEval` is equivalent to passing in the `TCL_GLOBAL_EVAL` flag. The `Tcl_VarEval` procedure takes a variable number of strings arguments and concatenates them before evaluation:

```
Tcl_VarEval(Tcl_Interp *interp, char *str, ..., NULL);
```

`Tcl_EvalObj` takes an object as an argument instead of a simple string. The string is compiled into byte codes the first time it is used. If you are going to execute the script many times, then the `Tcl_Obj` value caches the byte codes for you. The general `Tcl_Obj` value interface to `Tcl_Eval` is `Tcl_EvalObjEx`, which takes the same flags as `Tcl_EvalEx`:

```
Tcl_EvalObjEx(interp, objPtr, flags);
```

For variable numbers of arguments, use `Tcl_EvalObjv`, which takes an array of `Tcl_Obj` pointers. This routine concatenates the string values of the various `Tcl_Obj` values before parsing the resulting Tcl command:

```
Tcl_EvalObjv(interp, objc, objv);
```

Bypassing `Tcl_Eval`

In a performance-critical situation, you may want to avoid some of the overhead associated with `Tcl_Eval`. David Nichols showed me how to call the implementation of a C command procedure directly. The trick is facilitated by the `Tcl_GetCommandInfo` procedure that returns the address of the C command procedure for a Tcl command, plus its client data pointer. The `Tcl_Invoke` procedure is shown in Example 47–15. It is used much like `Tcl_VarEval`, except that each of its arguments becomes an argument to the Tcl command without any substitutions being performed.

For example, you might want to insert a large chunk of text into a text widget without worrying about the parsing done by `Tcl_Eval`. You could use `Tcl_Invoke` like this:

```
Tcl_Invoke(interp, ".t", "insert", "insert", buf, NULL);
```

Or:

```
Tcl_Invoke(interp, "set", "foo", "$xyz [blah] {", NULL);
```

No substitutions are performed on any of the arguments because `Tcl_Eval` is out of the picture. The variable `foo` gets the following literal value:

```
$xyz [blah] {
```

Example 47–15 shows `Tcl_Invoke`. The procedure is complicated for two reasons. First, it must handle a Tcl command that has either the object interface or the old string interface. Second, it has to build up an argument vector and may need to grow its storage in the middle of building it. It is a bit messy to deal with both at the same time, but it lets us compare the object and string interfaces. The string interfaces are simpler, but the object interfaces run more efficiently because they reduce copying and type conversions.

Example 47–15 Calling C command procedure directly with `Tcl_Invoke`.

```
#include <tcl.h>

/*
 * Tcl_Invoke --
 *      Directly invoke a Tcl command or procedure
 *
 *      Call Tcl_Invoke somewhat like Tcl_VarEval
 *      Each arg becomes one argument to the command,
 *      with no further substitutions or parsing.
 */
    /* VARARGS2 */ /* ARGSUSED */
```

```
int
Tcl_Invoke TCL_VARARGS_DEF(Tcl_Interp *, arg1)
{
    va_list argList;
    Tcl_Interp *interp;
    char *cmd;              /* Command name */
    char *arg;              /* Command argument */
    char **argv;            /* String vector for arguments */
    int argc, i, max;       /* Number of arguments */
    Tcl_CmdInfo info;       /* Info about command procedures */
    int result;             /* TCL_OK or TCL_ERROR */

    interp = TCL_VARARGS_START(Tcl_Interp *, arg1, argList);
    Tcl_ResetResult(interp);

    /*
     * Map from the command name to a C procedure
     */
    cmd = va_arg(argList, char *);
    if (! Tcl_GetCommandInfo(interp, cmd, &info)) {
        Tcl_AppendResult(interp, "unknown command \"",
            cmd, "\"", NULL);
        va_end(argList);
        return TCL_ERROR;
    }

    max = 20;               /* Initial size of argument vector */

#if TCL_MAJOR_VERSION > 7
    /*
     * Check whether the object interface is preferred for
     * this command
     */

    if (info.isNativeObjectProc) {
        Tcl_Obj **objv;     /* Object vector for arguments */
        Tcl_Obj *resultPtr; /* The result object */
        int objc;

        objv = (Tcl_Obj **) ckalloc(max * sizeof(Tcl_Obj *));
        objv[0] = Tcl_NewStringObj(cmd, strlen(cmd));
        Tcl_IncrRefCount(objv[0]); /* ref count == 1*/
        objc = 1;

        /*
         * Build a vector out of the rest of the arguments
         */

        while (1) {
            arg = va_arg(argList, char *);
            if (arg == (char *)NULL) {
                objv[objc] = (Tcl_Obj *)NULL;
                break;
            }
            objv[objc] = Tcl_NewStringObj(arg, strlen(arg));
```

```
            Tcl_IncrRefCount(objv[objc]); /* ref count == 1*/
            objc++;
            if (objc >= max) {
                /* allocate a bigger vector and copy old one */
                Tcl_Obj **oldv = objv;
                max *= 2;
                objv = (Tcl_Obj **) ckalloc(max *
                        sizeof(Tcl_Obj *));
                for (i = 0 ; i < objc ; i++) {
                    objv[i] = oldv[i];
                }
                Tcl_Free((char *)oldv);
            }
        }
        va_end(argList);

        /*
         * Invoke the C procedure
         */
        result = (*info.objProc)(info.objClientData, interp,
                objc, objv);

        /*
         * Make sure the string value of the result is valid
         * and release our references to the arguments
         */
        (void) Tcl_GetStringResult(interp);
        for (i = 0 ; i < objc ; i++) {
            Tcl_DecrRefCount(objv[i]);
        }
        Tcl_Free((char *)objv);

        return result;
    }
#endif
    argv = (char **) ckalloc(max * sizeof(char *));
    argv[0] = cmd;
    argc = 1;

    /*
     * Build a vector out of the rest of the arguments
     */
    while (1) {
        arg = va_arg(argList, char *);
        argv[argc] = arg;
        if (arg == (char *)NULL) {
            break;
        }
        argc++;
        if (argc >= max) {
            /* allocate a bigger vector and copy old one */
            char **oldv = argv;
            max *= 2;
            argv = (char **) ckalloc(max * sizeof(char *));
            for (i = 0 ; i < argc ; i++) {
```

```
                argv[i] = oldv[i];
            }
            Tcl_Free((char *) oldv);
        }
    }
    va_end(argList);

    /*
     * Invoke the C procedure
     */
    result = (*info.proc)(info.clientData, interp, argc, argv);

    /*
     * Release the arguments
     */
    Tcl_Free((char *) argv);
    return result;

}
```

This version of `Tcl_Invoke` was contributed by Jean Brouwers. He uses `TCL_VARARGS_DEF` and `TCL_VARARGS_START` macros to define procedures that take a variable number of arguments. These standard Tcl macros hide the differences in the way you do this on different operating systems and different compilers. It turns out that there are numerous minor differences between compilers that can cause portability problems in a variety of situations. Happily, there is a nice scheme used to discover these differences and write code in a portable way. This is the topic of the next chapter.

Compiling Tcl and Extensions

This chapter explains how to build Tcl from the source distribution, and how to create C extensions that are built according to the standard Tcl Extension Architecture (TEA).

Compiling Tcl from the source distribution is easy. One of the strengths of Tcl is that it is quite portable, so it has been built on all kinds of systems including Unix, Windows, Macintosh, AS/400, IBM mainframes, and embedded systems. However, it can be a challenge to create a Tcl extension that has the same portability. The Tcl Extension Architecture (TEA) provides guidelines and samples to help extension authors create portable Tcl extensions. TEA is a result of collaboration within the Tcl user community, and the version described here is the 2nd generation known as TEA2.

This chapter starts with a walk through of how Tcl itself is built. This serves as a model for building extensions. There are also some by-products of the Tcl build process that are designed to make it easier to build your extensions. So if you are an extension author, you will almost always want to get started by compiling Tcl itself.

You can find the Tcl and Tk sources on the CD-ROM, and on the Web:

```
http://www.tcl.tk/software/tcltk/
```

Source distributions can be found at the Tcl FTP site:

```
ftp://ftp.tcl.tk/pub/tcl/
```

The on-line CVS repository for Tcl software is explained here:

```
http://www.tcl.tk/software/tcltk/netcvs.html
http://www.sourceforge.net/projects/tcl
```

If you have trouble with these URLs, please check this book's Web site for current information about the Tcl sources:

```
http://www.beedub.com/book/
```

VI. Tcl and C

Standard Directory Structure

The Source Distribution

Table 48–1 describes the directory structure of the Tcl source distribution. The Tk distribution is similar, and you should model your own source distribution after this. It is also standard to place the Tcl, Tk, and other source packages under a common source directory (e.g., /usr/local/src or /home/welch/cvs). In fact, this may be necessary if the packages depend on each other.

Table 48–1   The Tcl source directory structure.

tcl8.4	The root of the Tcl sources. This contains a README and license_terms file, and several subdirectories.
tcl8.4/compat	This contains .c files that implement procedures that are otherwise broken in the standard C library on some platforms. They are only used if necessary.
tcl8.4/doc	This contains the reference documentation. Currently this is in *nroff* format suitable for use with the UNIX *man* program. The goal is to convert this to XML.
tcl8.4/generic	This contains the generic .c and .h source files that are shared among Unix, Windows, and Macintosh.
tcl8.4/mac	This contains the .c and .h source files that are specific to Macintosh. It also contains *Code Warrior* project files.
tcl8.4/library	This contains init.tcl and other Tcl files in the standard Tcl script library.
tcl8.4/library/encoding	This contains the Unicode conversion tables.
tcl8.4/library/*package*	There are several subdirectories (e.g., http2.3) that contain Tcl script packages.
tcl8.4/test	This contains the Tcl test suite. These are Tcl scripts that exercise the Tcl implementation.
tcl8.4/tools	This is a collection of scripts used to help build the Tcl distribution.
tcl8.4/unix	This contains the .c and .h source files that are specific to UNIX. This also contains the *configure* script and the Makefile.in template.
tcl8.4/unix/dltest	This contains test files for dynamic loading.
tcl8.4/unix/*platform*	These can be used to build Tcl for several different platforms. You create the *package* directories yourself.
tcl8.4/win	This contains the .c and .h source files that are specific to Windows. This also contains the *configure* script and the Makefile.in template. This may contain a makefile.vc that is compatible with *nmake*.

The Installation Directory Structure

When you install Tcl, the files end up in a different arrangement than the one in the source distribution does. The standard installation directory is organized so that it can be shared by computers with different machine types (e.g., Windows, Linux, and Solaris). The Tcl scripts, include files, and documentation are all in shared directories. The applications and programming libraries (i.e., DLLs) are in platform-specific directories. You can choose where these two groups of files are installed with the `--prefix` and `--exec-prefix` options to *configure*, which is explained in detail in the next section. Table 48–2 shows the standard installation directory structure:

Table 48–2 The installation directory structure.

`arch/bin`	This contains platform-specific applications. On Windows, this also contains binary libraries (i.e., DLLs). Typical `arch` names are `solaris-sparc`, `linux-ix86`, and `win-ix86`.
`arch/lib`	This contains platform-specific binary libraries on UNIX systems (e.g., `libtcl8.4.so`)
`bin`	This contains platform-independent applications (e.g., Tcl script applications).
`doc`	This contains documentation.
`include`	This contains public `.h` files.
`lib`	This contains subdirectories for platform-independent script packages. Packages stored here are found automatically by the Tcl auto loading mechanism described in Chapter 12.
`lib/tcl8.2`	This contains the contents of the `tcl8.4/library` source directory, including subdirectories.
`lib/package`	This contains Tcl scripts for *package*. Example *package* directories include `tk8.4` and `itcl3.2`.
`man`	This contains reference documentation in UNIX *man* format.

If you are an expert in *configure*, you may be aware of other options that give you even finer control over where the different parts of the installation go. However, because of the way Tcl automatically searches for scripts and binary libraries, you should avoid deviating from the recommended structure.

Building Tcl from Source

Compiling Tcl from the source distribution is a two-step process: configuration, which uses a `configure` script; then compiling, which is controlled by the *make* program. The `configure` script examines the current system and makes various settings that are used during compilation. When you run `configure`, you make some basic choices about how you will compile Tcl, such as whether you will compile with debugging systems, or whether you will turn on threading support. You also define the Tcl installation directory with `configure`. You use *make* to compile the source code, install the compiled application, run the test suite, and clean up after yourself.

The *make* facility is familiar to any Unix programmer. By using the freely available Cygwin tools, you can use `configure` and *make* on Windows, too. You have two compiler choices on Windows, the free *mingw* compiler and the Microsoft VC++ compiler. However, *gcc* is not supported for Tcl builds on Windows.

Windows and Macintosh programmers may not have experience with *make*. The source distributions may also include project files for the Microsoft *Visual C++* compiler and the Macintosh development environments. It may be easier for you to use these project files, especially on the Macintosh. Look in the `win` and `mac` subdirectories of the source distribution for these project files. However, the focus of this chapter is on using `configure` and *make* to build your Tcl applications and extensions.

Configure and Autoconf

Autoconf is a clever and, unfortunately, complex system for creating portable build environments. By using *autoconf*, a developer on Windows or Linux can generate a `configure` script and a Makefile template that is usable by other developers on Solaris, HP-UX, FreeBSD, AIX, or any system that is vaguely UNIX-like. The `configure` script examines the current system and turns the Makefile template into a platform specific Makefile. The three steps: setup, configuration and make, are illustrated by the build process for Tcl and Tk:

- **Setup**. The developer of a source code package creates a `configure.in` template that expresses the system dependencies of the source code. They use the *autoconf* program to process this template into a `configure` script. The developer also creates a `Makefile.in` template. Creating these templates is described later. The Tcl and Tk source distributions already contain the `configure` script, which can be found in the `unix` and `win` subdirectories.
- **Configure**. A user of a source code package runs `configure` on the computer system they will use to compile the sources. This step converts `Makefile.in` to a `Makefile` suitable for the platform and configuration settings. If you have only one platform, simply run `configure` in the `unix` (or `win`) directory:

```
% cd /usr/local/src/tcl8.4/unix
% ./configure flags
```

The `configure` flags are described in Table 48–3. I use `./configure` because I do not have . on my `PATH`. Furthermore, I want to ensure that I run the configure script from the current directory! If you build for multiple platforms, create subdirectories of `unix` and run `configure` from there. For example, here we use `../configure`:

```
% cd /usr/local/src/tcl8.2/unix
% mkdir linux
% cd linux
% ../configure flags
```

- **Make**. The `configure` script uses the `Makefile.in` template to generate the `Makefile`. Once `configure` is complete, you build your program with *make*:

  ```
  % make
  ```

  You can do other things with *make*. To run the test suite, do:

  ```
  % make test
  ```

  To install the compiled program or extension, do:

  ```
  % make install
  ```

The Tcl Extension Architecture defines a standard set of actions, or make targets, for building Tcl sources. Table 48–4 on page 740 shows the standard *make* targets.

Make sure you have a working compiler.

As the `configure` script executes, it prints out messages about the properties of the current platform. You can tell if you are in trouble if the output contains either of these messages:

```
checking for cross compiler ... yes
```

or

```
checking if compiler works ... no
```

Either of these means that `configure` has failed to find a working compiler. In the first case, it assumes that you are configuring on the target system but will cross-compile from a different system. In the second case, an attempt to compile a tiny sample program failed. In either case, the resulting `Makefile` is useless. While cross-compiling is common on embedded processors, it is rarely necessary on UNIX and Windows. I see these messages only when my UNIX environment isn't set up right to find the compiler.

Many UNIX venders no longer bundle a working compiler. Fortunately, the freely available *gcc* compiler has been ported to nearly every UNIX system. You should be able to search the Internet and find a ready-to-use *gcc* package for your platform.

On Windows, Tcl is built with either the free *mingw* compiler the Microsoft *Visual C++* compiler. It ships with a batch file, `vcvars32.bat`, that sets up the environment so that you can run the Microsoft compiler from the command line. You should read that file and configure your environment so that you do not have to remember to run the batch file all the time.

Standard Configure Flags

Table 48–3 shows the standard options for Tcl configure scripts. These are implemented by a configure library file (`aclocal.m4` and `tcl.m4`) that you can use in your own configure scripts. The facilities provided by `tcl.m4` are described in more detail later.

VI. Tcl and C

Table 48–3 Standard configure flags.

`--prefix=`*dir*	Defines the root of the installation directory hierarchy. The default is `/usr/local`.
`--exec-prefix=`*dir*	This defines the root of the installation area for platform-specific files. This defaults to the `--prefix` value. An example setting is `/usr/local/solaris-sparc`.
`--enable-gcc`	Uses the *gcc* compiler instead of the default system compiler.
`--disable-shared`	Disables generation of shared libraries and Tcl shells that dynamically link against them. Statically linked shells and static archives are built instead.
`--enable-symbols`	Compiles with debugging symbols.
`--enable-threads`	Compiles with thread support turned on.
`--with-tcl=`*dir*	Specifies the location of the build directory for Tcl.
`--with-tk=`*dir*	Specifies the location of the build directory for Tk.
`--with-tclinclude=`*dir*	Specifies the directory that contains `tcl.h`.
`--with-tcllib=dir`	Specifies the directory that contains the Tcl binary library (e.g., `libtclstubs.a`).
`--with-x11include=dir`	Specifies the directory that contains `X11.h`.
`--with-x11lib=dir`	Specifies the directory that contains the X11 binary library (e.g., `libX11.6.0.so`).

Any flag with `disable` or `enable` in its name can be inverted. Table 48–3 lists the nondefault setting, however, so you can just leave the flag out to turn it off. For example, when building Tcl on Solaris with the *gcc* compiler, shared libraries, debugging symbols, and threading support turned on, use this command:

```
configure --prefix=/home/welch/install \
     --exec-prefix=/home/welch/install/solaris \
     --enable-gcc --enable-threads --enable-symbols
```

Keep all your sources next to the Tcl sources.

Your builds will go the most smoothly if you organize all your sources under a common directory. In this case, you can specify the same configure flags for Tcl and all the other extensions you will compile. In particular, you must use the same `--prefix` and `--exec-prefix` so that everything gets installed together.

If your source tree is not adjacent to the Tcl source tree, then you must use `--with-tclinclude` or `--with-tcllib` so that the header files and runtime library can be found during compilation. Typically, this can happen if you build an extension under your home directory, but you are using a copy of Tcl that has been installed by your system administrator. The `--with-x11include` and `--with-x11lib` flags are similar options necessary when building Tk if your X11 installation is in a nonstandard location.

Installation

The `--prefix` flag specifies the main directory (e.g., `/home/welch/install`). The directories listed in Table 48–2 are created under this directory. If you do not specify `--exec-prefix`, then the platform-specific binary files are mixed into the main `bin` and `lib` directories. For example, the *tclsh8.4* program and `libtcl8.4.so` shared library will be installed in:

```
/home/welch/install/bin/tclsh8.4
/home/welch/install/lib/libtclsh8.4.so
```

The script libraries and manual pages will be installed in:

```
/home/welch/install/lib/tcl8.4
/home/welch/install/man
```

If you want to have installations for several different platforms, then specify an `--exec-prefix` that is different for each platform. For example, if you use `--exec-prefix=/home/welch/install/freebsd`, then the *tclsh8.4* program and `libtcl8.4.so` shared library will be installed in:

```
/home/welch/install/freebsd/bin/tclsh8.4
/home/welch/install/freebsd/lib/libtclsh8.4.so
```

The script libraries and manual pages will remain where they are, so they are shared by all platforms. Note that Windows has a slightly different installation location for binary libraries. They go into the `arch/bin` directory along with the main executable programs.

Using Stub Libraries

One problem with extensions is that they get compiled for a particular version of Tcl. As new Tcl releases occur, you find yourself having to recompile extensions. This was necessary for two reasons. First, the Tcl C library tended to change its APIs from release to release. Changes in its symbol table tie a compiled extension to a specific version of the Tcl library. Another problem occurred if you compiled *tclsh* statically and then tried to dynamically load a library. Some systems do not support back linking in this situation, so *tclsh* would crash. Paul Duffin created a *stub library* mechanism for Tcl that helps solve these problems.

The main idea is that Tcl creates two binary libraries: the main library (e.g., `libtcl8.4.so`) and a stub library (e.g., `libtclstub.a`). All the code is in the main library. The stub library is just a big jump table that contains addresses of functions in the main library. An extension calls Tcl through the jump table. The level of indirection makes the extension immune to changes in the Tcl library. It also handles the back linking problem. If this sounds expensive, it turns out to be equivalent to what the operating system does when you use shared libraries (i.e., dynamic link libraries). Tcl has just implemented dynamic linking in a portable, robust way.

To make your extension use stubs, you have to compile with the correct flags, and you must add a new call to your extensions `Init` procedure (e.g.,

VI. Tcl and C

Sample_Init). The TCL_USE_STUBS compile-time flag turns the Tcl C API calls into macros that use the stub table. The Tcl_InitStubs call ensures that the jump table is initialized, so you must call Tcl_InitStubs as the very first thing in your Init procedure. A typical call looks like this:

```
if (Tcl_InitStubs(interp, "8.1", 0) == NULL) {
    return TCL_ERROR;
}
```

Tcl_InitStubs is similar in spirit to Tcl_PkgRequire in that you request a minimum Tcl version number. Stubs have been supported since Tcl 8.1, and the API will evolve in a backward-compatible way. Unless your extension uses new C APIs introduced in later versions, you should specify the lowest version possible so that it is compatible with more Tcl applications.

Using autoconf

Autoconf uses the *m4* macro processor to translate the configure.in template into the configure script. The configure script is run by /bin/sh (i.e., the Bourne Shell). Creating the configure.in template is simplified by a standard *m4* macro library that is distributed with *autoconf*. In addition, a Tcl distribution contains a tcl.m4 file that has additional *autoconf* macros. Among other things, these macros support the standard configure flags described in Table 48–3.

Configure macros are hard.

Creating configure templates can be complex and confusing. There are several layers of macro processing: *m4* macros in configure.in, shell variables in configure, *autoconf* substitutions in Makefile.in, and Makefile variables. The days I have spent trying to change the Tcl configuration files really made me appreciate the simplicity of Tcl! Fortunately, there is now a standard set of Tcl-specific *autoconf* macros and a sample Tcl extension that uses them. By editing the configure.in and Makefile.in sample templates, you can ignore the details of what is happening under the covers.

The tcl.m4 File

The Tcl source distribution includes tcl.m4 and aclocal.m4 files. The *autoconf* program looks for the aclocal.m4 file in the same directory as the configure.in template. In our case, the aclocal.m4 file just includes the tcl.m4 file. In the TEA sample extension described later, the tcl.m4 file is kept in a tclconfig subdirectory.

The tcl.m4 file defines macros whose names begin with TEA (for Tcl Extension Architecture). The standard *autoconf* macro names begin with AC. This book does not provide an exhaustive explanation of all these *autoconf* macros. Instead, the important ones are explained in the context of the sample extension.

The tcl.m4 file replaces the tclConfig.sh found in previous versions of Tcl. (Actually, tclConfig.sh is still produced by the Tcl 8.4 *configure* script, but its use is deprecated.) The idea of `tclConfig.sh` was to capture some important results of Tcl's *configure* so that they could be included in the *configure* scripts used by an extension. However, it is better to recompute these settings when configuring an extension because, for example, different compilers could be used to build Tcl and the extension. So, instead of including `tclConfig.sh` into an extension's *configure* script, the extension's `configure.in` should use the TEA macros defined in the *tcl.m4* file.

Makefile Templates

Autoconf implements yet another macro mechanism for the `Makefile.in` templates. The basic idea is that the *configure* script sets shell variables as it learns things about your system. Finally, it substitutes these variables into `Makefile.in` to create the working `Makefile`. The syntax for the substitutions in `Makefile.in` is:

> `@configure_variable_name@`

For example, the `--prefix` command line value is put into the `prefix` shell variable, and then substituted into the `Makefile.in` template wherever `@prefix@` occurs. Often, the *make* variable and the shell variable have the same name. For example, the following statement in `Makefile.in` passes the `TCL_LIBRARY` value determined by `configure` through to the `Makefile`:

> `TCL_LIBRARY = @TCL_LIBRARY@`

The `AC_SUBST` macro specifies what shell variables should be substituted in the `Makefile.in` template. For example:

> `AC_SUBST(TCL_LIBRARY)`

The Sample Extension

This section describes the sample extension that is distributed as part of the Tcl Extension Architecture (TEA) standard. The goal of TEA is to create a standard for Tcl extensions that makes it easier to build, install, and share Tcl extensions. The sample Tcl extension is on the CD, and it can be found on the Web at:

> `ftp://ftp.tcl.tk/pub/tcl/examples/tea/`

There is also documentation on the Web at:

> `http://www.tcl.tk/software/tcltk/tea/`

The extension described here is stored in the network CVS repository under the module name `samplextension`. If you want direct access to the latest versions of Tcl source code, you can learn about the CVS repository at this web page:

> `http://www.tcl.tk/software/tcltk/netcvs.html`

The sample extension implements the Secure Hash Algorithm (SHA1). Steve Reid wrote the original SHA1 C code, and Dave Dykstra wrote the original Tcl interface to it. Michael Thomas created the standard configure and Makefile templates, and Jeff Hobbs updated the sample for TEA2.

Instead of using the original name, `sha1`, the example uses a more generic name, `sample`, in its files, libraries, and package names. When editing the sample templates for your own extension, you can simply replace occurrences of "sample" with the appropriate name for your extension. The sample files are well commented, so it is easy to see where you need to make the changes.

`configure.in`

The `configure.in` file is the template for the `configure` script. This file is very well commented. The places you need to change are marked with `__CHANGE__`. The first macro to change is:

```
AC_INIT(generic/sample.h)
```

The `AC_INIT` macro lists a file that is part of the distribution. The name is relative to the `configure.in` file. Other possibilities include `../generic/tcl.h` or `src/mylib.h`, depending on where the configure.in file is relative to your sources. The `AC_INIT` macro is necessary to support building the package in different directories (e.g., either `tcl8.4/unix` or `tcl8.4/unix/solaris`). The next thing in `configure.in` is a set of variable assignments that define the package's name and version number:

```
PACKAGE = sample
MAJOR_VERSION = 0
MINOR_VERSION = 4
PATCH_LEVEL =
```

The package name determines the file names used for the directory and the binary library file created by the Makefile. This name is also used in several configure and Makefile variables. You will need to change all references to "sample" to match the name you choose for your package.

The version and patch level support a three-level scheme, but you can leave the patch level empty for two-level versions like `0.4`. If you do specify a patch-level, you need to include a leading "." or "p" in it. These values are combined to create the version number like this:

```
VERSION = ${MAJOR_VERSION}.${MINOR_VERSION}${PATCH_LEVEL}
```

The `configure.in` file has a bunch of magic to determine the name of the shared library file (e.g., `sample04.dll`, `libsample.0.4.so`, `sample.0.2.shlib`, etc.). You need to change the macro to match your package name. Define `samplestub_LIB_FILE` if you want to generate a stub library:

```
AC_SUBST(sample_LIB_FILE)
AC_SUBST(samplestub_LIB_FILE)
```

There are several standard TEA macros in `configure.in` that expand to a set of rules to determine the compiler and other settings. Most of these you can leave alone. Although in some cases you need to change the sample if you are creating a Tk extension, or if you need to use internal Tcl or Tk header files. For example, you may need to add TEA_PATH_TKCONFIG and TEA_LOAD_TKCONFIG, and to choose between TEA_PUBLIC_TCL_HEADERS, TEA_PRIVATE_TCL_HEADERS and between `TEA_PUBLIC_TK_HEADERS` and `TEA_PRIVATE_TK_HEADERS`. Using private headers (i.e., `tclInt.h`) is strongly discouraged.

There is also a platform-specific section where you may which to adjust the `CLEANFILES` and `EXTRA_SOURCES` macros to match your needs. This section also defines the `BUILD_sample` macro on Windows. Windows compilers create a special case for shared libraries (i.e., DLLs). When you compile the library itself, you need to declare its functions one way. When you compile code that uses the library, you need to declare its functions another way. This complicates `sample.h`. Happily, the complexity is hidden inside the `BUILD_sample` macro. We will show later how this is used in `sample.h` to control the definition of the `Sample_Init` procedure.

The last macro in `configure.in` determines which templates are processed by the configure script. The sample generates the `Makefile` from the `Makefile.in` template with this directive:

```
AC_OUTPUT([Makefile])
```

Makefile.in

The `Makefile.in` template is converted by the `configure` script into the `Makefile`. The sample `Makefile.in` is well commented so that it is easy to see where to make changes. There are a few variables with `sample` in their name. In particular, `sample_LIB_FILE` corresponds to a variable name in the configure script. You need to change both files consistently:

```
sample_LIB_FILE = @sample_LIB_FILE@
```

The `@varname@` syntax is used to substitute the configure variable with its platform-specific name (e.g., `libsample.dll` or `libsample.so`). You must define the set of source files and the corresponding object files that are part of the library. In the sample, `sample.c` implements the core of the Secure Hash Algorithm, and the `tclsample.c` file implements the Tcl command interface:

```
sample_SOURCES  = sample.c tclsample.c @EXTRA_SOURCES@
```

The object file definitions use the `OBJEXT` variable that is `.o` for UNIX and `.obj` for Windows:

```
sample_OBJECTS  = $(sample_SOURCES:.c=.@OBJEXT@)
```

The header files that you want to have installed are assigned to the `GENERIC_HDRS` variable. The `srcdir` Make variable is defined during *configure* to be the name of the directory containing the file named in the `AC_INIT` macro:

```
GENERIC_HDRS    = $(srcdir)/generic/sample.h
```

The sample Makefile includes several standard targets. Even if you decide not to use the sample `Makefile.in` template, you should still define the targets listed in Table 48–4 to ensure your extension is TEA compliant. Plans for automatic build environments depend on every extension implementing the standard make targets. The targets can be empty, but you should define them so that *make* will not complain if they are used.

VI. Tcl and C

Table 48–4 TEA standard Makefile targets.

`all`	Makes these targets in order: `binaries`, `libraries`, `doc`.
`binaries`	Makes executable programs and binary libraries (e.g., DLLs).
`libraries`	Makes platform-independent libraries.
`doc`	Generates documentation files.
`install`	Makes these targets in order: `install-binaries`, `install-libraries`, `install-doc`.
`install-binaries`	Installs programs and binary libraries.
`install-libraries`	Installs script libraries.
`install-doc`	Installs documentation files.
`test`	Runs the test suite for the package.
`depend`	Generates makefile dependency rules.
`clean`	Removes files built during the make process.
`distclean`	Removes files built during the configure process.

Standard Header Files

This section explains a technique you should use to get symbols defined properly in your binary library. The issue is raised by Windows compilers, which have a notion of explicitly importing and exporting symbols. When you build a library you export symbols. When you link against a library, you import symbols. The `BUILD_sample` variable is defined on Windows when you are building the library. This variable should be undefined on UNIX, which does not have this issue. Your header file uses this variable like this:

```
#ifdef BUILD_sample
#undef TCL_STORAGE_CLASS
#define TCL_STORAGE_CLASS DLLEXPORT
#endif /* BUILD_sample */
```

The `TCL_STORAGE_CLASS` variable is used in the definition of the `EXTERN` macro. You must use `EXTERN` before the prototype for any function you want to export from your library:

```
EXTERN int Sample_Init _ANSI_ARGS_((Tcl_Interp *Interp));
```

The `_ANSI_ARGS_` macro is used to guard against old C compilers that do not tolerate function prototypes.

Using the Sample Extension

You should be able to configure, compile, and install the sample extension without modification. On my Solaris machine, the binary library is named `sample0.4.so`, while on my Windows NT machine the library is named `sample04.dll`. The package name is `Tclsha1`, and it implements the `sha1` Tcl command. Ordinarily these names would be more consistent with the file names and package names in the template files. However, the names in the sample are designed to be easy to edit in the template. Assuming that you use `make install` to copy the binary library into the standard location for your site, you can use the package from Tcl like this:

```
package require Tclsha1
sha1 -string "some string"
```

The `sha1` command returns a 128 bit encoded hash function of the input string. There are a number of options to `sha1` you can learn about by reading the manual page that is included with the extension.

Writing a Tk Widget in C

This chapter describes the implementation of a simple clock widget. Two implementations are shown: the original string-based command interface and the Tcl_Obj command interface.

A custom widget implemented in C has the advantage of being efficient and flexible. However, it requires more work, too. This chapter illustrates the effort by explaining the implementation of a clock widget. It is a digital clock that displays the current time according to a format string. This is something you could implement in several lines of Tcl using a label widget, the `clock` command, and `after` for periodic updates. However, the point of the example is to show the basic structure for a Tk widget implemented in C, not how much easier Tcl programming is :-). The implementation of a widget includes:

- A data structure to describe one instance of the widget.
- A class procedure to create a new instance of the widget.
- An instance procedure to operate on an instance of the widget.
- A set of configuration options for the widget.
- A configuration procedure used when creating and reconfiguring the widget.
- An event handling procedure.
- A display procedure.
- Other widget-specific procedures.

Two implementations are compared: string-based and `Tcl_Obj` based. The version that uses `Tcl_Obj` values can interpret command line options more efficiently. A new option parsing package hides most of the details. The string-based version of each procedure is shown first, and then the `Tcl_Obj` version is shown for comparison. The display portion of the code is the same in the two versions.

VI. Tcl and C

Initializing the Extension

The widget is packaged as an extension that you can dynamically load into *wish*. Example 49–1 shows the `Clock_Init` procedure. It registers two commands, clock and oclock, which use the string-based and `Tcl_Obj` interfaces, respectively. It also initializes the stub table, which is described in Chapter 48, and declares a package so that scripts can load the widget with `package require`.

Example 49–1 The `Clock_Init` procedure.

```
int ClockCmd(ClientData clientData,
          Tcl_Interp *interp,
          int argc, CONST char *argv[]);
int ClockObjCmd(ClientData clientData,
          Tcl_Interp *interp,
          int objc, Tcl_Obj *CONST objv[]);
void ClockObjDelete(ClientData clientData);

/*
 * Clock_Init is called when the package is loaded.
 */

int Clock_Init(Tcl_Interp *interp) {
    if (Tcl_InitStubs(interp, "8.1", 0) == NULL) {
        return TCL_ERROR;
    }
    Tcl_CreateCommand(interp, "wclock", ClockCmd,
            (ClientData)NULL, (Tcl_CmdDeleteProc *)NULL);
    Tcl_CreateObjCommand(interp, "oclock", ClockObjCmd,
            (ClientData)NULL, ClockObjDelete);
    Tcl_PkgProvide(interp, "Tkclock", "1.0");
    return TCL_OK;
}
```

The Widget Data Structure

Each widget is associated with a data structure that describes it. Any widget structure will need a pointer to the Tcl interpreter, the Tk window, and the display. The interpreter is used in most of the Tcl and Tk library calls, and it provides a way to call out to the script or query and set Tcl variables. The Tk window is needed for various Tk operations, and the display is used when doing low-level graphic operations. The rest of the information in the data structure depends on the widget. The different types will be explained as they are used in the rest of the code. The structure for the clock widget follows:

Example 49–2 The Clock widget data structure.

```c
#include "tk.h"
#include <sys/time.h>

typedef struct {
    Tk_Window tkwin;          /* The window for the widget */
    Display *display;         /* Tk's handle on the display */
    Tcl_Interp *interp;       /* Interpreter of the widget */
    Tcl_Command widgetCmd;    /* clock instance command. */
    Tk_OptionTable optionTable; /* Used to parse options */
    /*
     * Clock-specific attributes.
     */
    int borderWidth;          /* Size of 3-D border */
    Tcl_Obj *borderWidthPtr;  /* Original string value */
    int relief;               /* Style of 3-D border */
    Tk_3DBorder background;    /* Color for border & background */
    XColor *foreground;       /* Color for the text */
    XColor *highlight;        /* Color for active highlight */
    XColor *highlightBg;      /* Color for neutral highlight */
    int highlightWidth;       /* Thickness of highlight rim */
    Tcl_Obj *highlightWidthPtr; /* Original string value */
    Tk_Font tkfont;           /* Font info for the text */
    char *format;             /* Format for time string */
    /*
     * Graphic contexts and other support.
     */
    GC textGC;                /* Text graphics context */
    Tk_TimerToken token;      /* Periodic callback handle*/
    char *clock;              /* Pointer to the clock string */
    int numChars;             /* length of the text */
    int textWidth;            /* in pixels */
    Tcl_Obj *widthPtr;        /* The original width string value*/
    int textHeight;           /* in pixels */
    Tcl_Obj *heightPtr;       /* The original height string value*/
    int padX;                 /* Horizontal padding */
    Tcl_Obj *padXPtr;         /* The original padX string value*/
    int padY;                 /* Vertical padding */
    Tcl_Obj *padYPtr;         /* The original padY string value */
    int flags;                /* Flags defined below */
} Clock;
/*
 * Flag bit definitions.
 */
#define REDRAW_PENDING  0x1
#define GOT_FOCUS       0x2
#define TICKING         0x4
```

The Widget Class Command

The Tcl command that creates an instance of a widget is known as the *class command*. In our example, the clock command creates a clock widget. The command procedure for `clock` follows. The procedure allocates the `Clock` data structure. It registers an event handler that gets called when the widget is exposed, resized, or gets the focus. It creates a new Tcl command that operates on the widget. Finally, it calls `ClockConfigure` to set up the widget according to the attributes specified on the command line and the default configuration specifications.

Example 49–3 The `ClockCmd` command procedure.

```
int
ClockCmd(clientData, interp, argc, argv)
    ClientData clientData;/* Main window of the app */
    Tcl_Interp *interp; /* Current interpreter. */
    int argc;             /* Number of arguments. */
    CONST char **argv;   /* Argument strings. */
{
    Tk_Window main = (Tk_Window) clientData;
    Clock *clockPtr;
    Tk_Window tkwin;

    if (argc < 2) {
        Tcl_AppendResult(interp, "wrong # args: should be \"",
            argv[0], " pathName ?options?\"", (char *) NULL);
        return TCL_ERROR;
    }
    tkwin = Tk_CreateWindowFromPath(interp, main,
            argv[1], (char *) NULL);
    if (tkwin == NULL) {
        return TCL_ERROR;
    }
    /*
     * Set resource class.
     */
    Tk_SetClass(tkwin, "Clock");
    /*
     * Allocate and initialize the widget record.
     */
    clockPtr = (Clock *) Tcl_Alloc(sizeof(Clock));
    clockPtr->tkwin = tkwin;
    clockPtr->display = Tk_Display(tkwin);
    clockPtr->interp = interp;
    clockPtr->borderWidth = 0;
    clockPtr->highlightWidth = 0;
    clockPtr->relief = TK_RELIEF_FLAT;
    clockPtr->background = NULL;
    clockPtr->foreground = NULL;
    clockPtr->highlight = NULL;
    clockPtr->highlightBg = NULL;
    clockPtr->tkfont = NULL;
    clockPtr->textGC = None;
    clockPtr->token = NULL;
    clockPtr->clock = NULL;
    clockPtr->format = NULL;
    clockPtr->numChars = 0;
```

```
    clockPtr->textWidth = 0;
    clockPtr->textHeight = 0;
    clockPtr->padX = 0;
    clockPtr->padY = 0;
    clockPtr->flags = 0;
    /*
     * Register a handler for when the window is
     * exposed or resized.
     */
    Tk_CreateEventHandler(clockPtr->tkwin,
        ExposureMask|StructureNotifyMask|FocusChangeMask,
        ClockEventProc, (ClientData) clockPtr);
    /*
     * Create a Tcl command that operates on the widget.
     */
    clockPtr->widgetCmd = Tcl_CreateCommand(interp,
        Tk_PathName(clockPtr->tkwin),
        ClockInstanceCmd,
        (ClientData) clockPtr, (void (*)()) NULL);
    /*
     * Parse the command line arguments.
     */
    if (ClockConfigure(interp, clockPtr,
            argc-2, argv+2, 0) != TCL_OK) {
        Tk_DestroyWindow(clockPtr->tkwin);
        return TCL_ERROR;
    }
    Tcl_SetResult(interp, Tk_PathName(clockPtr->tkwin),
            TCL_VOLATILE);
    return TCL_OK;
}
```

The Tcl_Obj version, ClockObjCmd, does some additional work to set up an option table that is used to efficiently parse the command line options to the clock command. The option table is created the first time the clock command is used. The clientData for ClockObjCmd is initially NULL; it is used to store the option table once it is initialized. While ClockCmd uses the clientData to store a reference to the main Tk window, ClockObjCmd uses the Tk_MainWindow procedure to get a reference to the main Tk window.

Example 49–4 The ClockObjCmd command procedure.

```
int
ClockObjCmd(clientData, interp, objc, objv)
    ClientData clientData;/* Main window of the app */
    Tcl_Interp *interp; /* Current interpreter. */
    int objc;           /* Number of arguments. */
    Tcl_Obj **objv;     /* Argument values. */
{
    Tk_OptionTable optionTable;
    Clock *clockPtr;
    Tk_Window tkwin;
```

VI. Tcl and C

```
if (objc < 2) {
    Tcl_WrongNumArgs(interp, 1, objv, "pathName ?options?");
    return TCL_ERROR;
}
optionTable = (Tk_OptionTable) clientData;
if (optionTable == NULL) {
    Tcl_CmdInfo info;
    char *name;

    /*
     * Initialize the option table for this widget the
     * first time a clock widget is created. The option
     * table is saved as our client data.
     */

    optionTable = Tk_CreateOptionTable(interp, optionSpecs);
    name = Tcl_GetString(objv[0]);
    Tcl_GetCommandInfo(interp, name, &info);
    info.objClientData = (ClientData) optionTable;
    Tcl_SetCommandInfo(interp, name, &info);
}
tkwin = Tk_CreateWindowFromPath(interp,
        Tk_MainWindow(interp),
        Tcl_GetString(objv[1]), (char *) NULL);
if (tkwin == NULL) {
    return TCL_ERROR;
}
/*
 * Set resource class.
 */
Tk_SetClass(tkwin, "Clock");
/*
 * Allocate and initialize the widget record.
 */
clockPtr = (Clock *) ckalloc(sizeof(Clock));
clockPtr->tkwin = tkwin;
clockPtr->display = Tk_Display(tkwin);
clockPtr->interp = interp;
clockPtr->optionTable = optionTable;
clockPtr->borderWidth = 0;
clockPtr->borderWidthPtr = NULL;
clockPtr->highlightWidth = 0;
clockPtr->highlightWidthPtr = NULL;
clockPtr->relief = TK_RELIEF_FLAT;
clockPtr->background = NULL;
clockPtr->foreground = NULL;
clockPtr->highlight = NULL;
clockPtr->highlightBg = NULL;
clockPtr->tkfont = NULL;
clockPtr->textGC = None;
clockPtr->token = NULL;
clockPtr->clock = NULL;
clockPtr->format = NULL;
clockPtr->numChars = 0;
clockPtr->textWidth = 0;
```

```
        clockPtr->widthPtr = NULL;
        clockPtr->textHeight = 0;
        clockPtr->heightPtr = NULL;
        clockPtr->padX = 0;
        clockPtr->padXPtr = NULL;
        clockPtr->padY = 0;
        clockPtr->padYPtr = NULL;
        clockPtr->flags = 0;
        /*
         * Register a handler for when the window is
         * exposed or resized.
         */
        Tk_CreateEventHandler(clockPtr->tkwin,
            ExposureMask|StructureNotifyMask|FocusChangeMask,
            ClockEventProc, (ClientData) clockPtr);
        /*
         * Create a Tcl command that operates on the widget.
         */
        clockPtr->widgetCmd = Tcl_CreateObjCommand(interp,
            Tk_PathName(clockPtr->tkwin),
            ClockInstanceObjCmd,
            (ClientData) clockPtr, (void (*)()) NULL);
        /*
         * Parse the command line arguments.
         */
        if ((Tk_InitOptions(interp, (char *)clockPtr,
                optionTable, tkwin) != TCL_OK) ||
            (ClockObjConfigure(interp, clockPtr,
                objc-2, objv+2, 0) != TCL_OK)) {
            Tk_DestroyWindow(clockPtr->tkwin);
            return TCL_ERROR;
        }
        Tcl_SetStringObj(Tcl_GetObjResult(interp),
            Tk_PathName(clockPtr->tkwin), -1);
        return TCL_OK;
}
```

The Widget Instance Command

For each instance of a widget, a new command is created that operates on that widget. This is called the *widget instance command*. Its name is the same as the Tk pathname of the widget. In the clock example, all that is done on instances is to query and change their attributes. Most of the work is done by `Tk_ConfigureWidget` and `ClockConfigure`, which are shown in the next section. The `ClockInstanceCmd` command procedure is shown in the next example:

Example 49–5 The `ClockInstanceCmd` command procedure.

```
static int
ClockInstanceCmd(clientData, interp, argc, argv)
    ClientData clientData;/* A pointer to a Clock struct */
```

VI. Tcl and C

```
        Tcl_Interp *interp; /* The interpreter */
        int argc;            /* The number of arguments */
        CONST char *argv[]; /* The command line arguments */
{
        Clock *clockPtr = (Clock *)clientData;
        int result = TCL_OK;
        char c;
        int len;
        if (argc < 2) {
            Tcl_AppendResult(interp, "wrong # args: should be \"",
                argv[0], " option ?arg arg ...?\"", (char *) NULL);
            return TCL_ERROR;
        }
        c = argv[1][0];
        len = strlen(argv[1]);
        if ((c == 'c') && (strncmp(argv[1], "cget", len) == 0)
                && (len >= 2)) {
            if (argc != 3) {
                Tcl_AppendResult(interp,
                    "wrong # args: should be \"",
                    argv[0], " cget option\"",
                    (char *) NULL);
                return TCL_ERROR;
            }
            result = Tk_ConfigureValue(interp, clockPtr->tkwin,
                configSpecs, (char *) clockPtr, argv[2], 0);
        } else if ((c == 'c') && (strncmp(argv[1], "configure", len)
                == 0) && (len >= 2)) {
            if (argc == 2) {
                /*
                 * Return all configuration information.
                 */
                result = Tk_ConfigureInfo(interp, clockPtr->tkwin,
                    configSpecs, (char *) clockPtr,
                    (char *) NULL,0);
            } else if (argc == 3) {
                /*
                 * Return info about one attribute, like cget.
                 */
                result = Tk_ConfigureInfo(interp, clockPtr->tkwin,
                    configSpecs, (char *) clockPtr, argv[2], 0);
            } else {
                /*
                 * Change one or more attributes.
                 */
                result = ClockConfigure(interp, clockPtr, argc-2,
                    argv+2,TK_CONFIG_ARGV_ONLY);
            }
        } else {
            Tcl_AppendResult(interp, "bad option \"", argv[1],
                "\": must be cget, configure, position, or size",
                (char *) NULL);
            return TCL_ERROR;
        }
        return result;
}
```

Example 49–6 shows the `ClockInstanceObjCmd` procedure. It uses the `Tk_GetIndexFromObj` routine to map the first argument to an index, which is then used in a switch statement. It uses the `Tk_GetOptionValue` and `Tk_GetOptionInfo` procedures to parse the widget configuration options.

Example 49–6 The `ClockInstanceObjCmd` command procedure.

```
static int
ClockInstanceObjCmd(clientData, interp, objc, objv)
    ClientData clientData;/* A pointer to a Clock struct */
    Tcl_Interp *interp;  /* The interpreter */
    int objc;            /* The number of arguments */
    Tcl_Obj *objv[];     /* The command line arguments */
{
    Clock *clockPtr = (Clock *)clientData;
    CONST char *commands[] = {"cget", "configure", NULL};
    enum command {CLOCK_CGET, CLOCK_CONFIGURE};
    int result;
    Tcl_Obj *objPtr;
    int index;

    if (objc < 2) {
        Tcl_WrongNumArgs(interp, 1, objv,
            "option ?arg arg ...?");
        return TCL_ERROR;
    }
    result = Tcl_GetIndexFromObj(interp, objv[1], commands,
        "option", 0, &index);
    if (result != TCL_OK) {
        return result;
    }
    switch (index) {
        case CLOCK_CGET: {
            if (objc != 3) {
                Tcl_WrongNumArgs(interp, 1, objv,
                    "cget option");
                return TCL_ERROR;
            }
            objPtr = Tk_GetOptionValue(interp,
                    (char *)clockPtr,
                    clockPtr->optionTable,
                    (objc == 3) ? objv[2] : NULL,
                    clockPtr->tkwin);
            if (objPtr == NULL) {
                return TCL_ERROR;
            } else {
                Tcl_SetObjResult(interp, objPtr);
            }
            break;
        }
        case CLOCK_CONFIGURE: {
            if (objc <= 3) {
                /*
                 * Return one item if the option is given,
```

```
           * or return all configuration information.
           */
          objPtr = Tk_GetOptionInfo(interp,
                  (char *) clockPtr,
                  clockPtr->optionTable,
                  (objc == 3) ? objv[2] : NULL,
                  clockPtr->tkwin);
          if (objPtr == NULL) {
              return TCL_ERROR;
          } else {
              Tcl_SetObjResult(interp, objPtr);
          }
      } else {
          /*
           * Change one or more attributes.
           */
          result = ClockObjConfigure(interp, clockPtr,
              objc-2, objv+2);
      }
  }
}
return TCL_OK;
}
```

Configuring and Reconfiguring Attributes

When the widget is created or reconfigured, then the implementation needs to allocate the resources implied by the attribute settings. Each clock widget uses some colors and a font. These are described by graphics contexts that parameterize operations. Instead of specifying every possible attribute in graphics calls, a graphics context is initialized with a subset of the parameters, and this is passed into the graphic commands. The context can specify the foreground and background colors, clip masks, line styles, and so on. The clock widget allocates a graphics context once and reuses it each time the widget is displayed.

There are two kinds of color resources used by the widget. The focus highlight and the text foreground are simple colors. The background is a Tk_3DBorder, which is a set of colors used to render 3D borders. The background color is specified in the attribute, and the other colors are computed based on that color. The code uses Tk_3DBorderColor to map back to the original color for use in the background of the widget.

After the resources are set up, a call to redisplay the widget is scheduled for the next idle period. This is a standard idiom for Tk widgets. It means that you can create and reconfigure a widget in the middle of a script, and all the changes result in only one redisplay. The REDRAW_PENDING flag is used to ensure that only one redisplay is queued up at any time. The ClockConfigure procedure is shown in the next example:

Example 49–7 `ClockConfigure` allocates resources for the widget.

```
static int
ClockConfigure(interp, clockPtr, argc, argv, flags)
    Tcl_Interp *interp;/* For return values and errors */
    Clock *clockPtr; /* The per-instance data structure */
    int argc;        /* Number of valid entries in argv */
    char *argv[];    /* The command line arguments */
    int flags;       /* Tk_ConfigureWidget flags */
{
    XGCValues gcValues;
    GC newGC;

    /*
     * Tk_ConfigureWidget parses the command line arguments
     * and looks for defaults in the resource database.
     */
    if (Tk_ConfigureWidget(interp, clockPtr->tkwin,
            configSpecs, argc, argv, (char *) clockPtr, flags)
              != TCL_OK) {
      return TCL_ERROR;
    }
    /*
     * Give the widget a default background so it doesn't get
     * a random background between the time it is initially
     * displayed by the X server and we paint it
     */
    Tk_SetWindowBackground(clockPtr->tkwin,
        Tk_3DBorderColor(clockPtr->background)->pixel);
    /*
     * Set up the graphics contexts to display the widget.
     * The context is used to draw off-screen pixmaps,
     * so turn off exposure notifications.
     */
    gcValues.background =
        Tk_3DBorderColor(clockPtr->background)->pixel;
    gcValues.foreground = clockPtr->foreground->pixel;
    gcValues.font = Tk_FontId(clockPtr->tkfont);
    gcValues.graphics_exposures = False;
    newGC = Tk_GetGC(clockPtr->tkwin,
        GCBackground|GCForeground|GCFont|GCGraphicsExposures,
        &gcValues);
    if (clockPtr->textGC != None) {
        Tk_FreeGC(clockPtr->display, clockPtr->textGC);
    }
    clockPtr->textGC = newGC;
    /*
     * Determine how big the widget wants to be.
     */
    ComputeGeometry(clockPtr);
    /*
     * Set up a call to display ourself.
     */
    if ((clockPtr->tkwin != NULL) &&
            Tk_IsMapped(clockPtr->tkwin)
```

```
        && !(clockPtr->flags & REDRAW_PENDING)) {
      Tk_DoWhenIdle(ClockDisplay, (ClientData) clockPtr);
      clockPtr->flags |= REDRAW_PENDING;
    }
    return TCL_OK;
}
```

Example 49–8 shows the `ClockObjConfigure` procedure. The `Tk_SetOptions` interface, which is used to set fields in the `Clock` data structure, has one potential problem. It is possible that some configuration options are correct, while others cause errors. In this case, `ClockObjConfigure` backs out the changes, so the whole configuration has no effect. This requires a two-pass approach, with the second pass used to restore the original values. `Tk_SetOptions` has a feature that lets you classify changes to the widget. The `GEOMETRY_MASK` and `GRAPHICS_MASK` are bits defined by the clock widget to divide its attributes into two classes. It changes its graphics context or recomputes its geometry only if an attribute from the appropriate class is changed.

Example 49–8 `ClockObjConfigure` allocates resources for the widget.

```
static int
ClockObjConfigure(interp, clockPtr, objc, objv)
    Tcl_Interp *interp;/* For return values and errors */
    Clock *clockPtr; /* The per-instance data structure */
    int objc;        /* Number of valid entries in argv */
    Tcl_Obj *objv[]; /* The command line arguments */
{
    XGCValues gcValues;
    GC newGC;
    Tk_SavedOptions savedOptions;
    int mask, error;
    Tcl_Obj *errorResult;

    /*
     * The first time through this loop we set the
     * configuration from the command line inputs. The second
     * pass is used to restore the configuration in case of
     * errors
     */
    for (error = 0 ; error <= 1 ; error++) {
        if (!error) {
            /*
             * Tk_SetOptions parses the command arguments
             * and looks for defaults in the resource
             * database.
             */
            if (Tk_SetOptions(interp, (char *) clockPtr,
                  clockPtr->optionTable, objc, objv,
                  clockPtr->tkwin, &savedOptions,
                  &mask) != TCL_OK) {
                continue;
            }
```

```
    } else {
        /*
         * Restore options from saved values
         */
        errorResult = Tcl_GetObjResult(interp);
        Tcl_IncrRefCount(errorResult);
        Tk_RestoreSavedOptions(&savedOptions);
    }
    if (mask & GRAPHICS_MASK) {
        /*
         * Give the widget a default background so it doesn't
         * get a random background between the time it is
         * initially displayed by the system and we paint it
         */
        Tk_SetBackgroundFromBorder(clockPtr->tkwin,
                clockPtr->background);
        /*
         * Set up the graphics contexts to display the widget.
         * The context is used to draw off-screen pixmaps,
         * so turn off exposure notifications.
         */
        gcValues.background =
            Tk_3DBorderColor(clockPtr->background)->pixel;
        gcValues.foreground = clockPtr->foreground->pixel;
        gcValues.font = Tk_FontId(clockPtr->tkfont);
        gcValues.graphics_exposures = False;
        newGC = Tk_GetGC(clockPtr->tkwin,
        GCBackground|GCForeground|GCFont|GCGraphicsExposures,
            &gcValues);
        if (clockPtr->textGC != None) {
            Tk_FreeGC(clockPtr->display, clockPtr->textGC);
        }
        clockPtr->textGC = newGC;
    }
    /*
     * Determine how big the widget wants to be.
     */
    if (mask & GEOMETRY_MASK) {
        ComputeGeometry(clockPtr);
    }
    /*
     * Set up a call to display ourself.
     */
    if ((clockPtr->tkwin != NULL) &&
            Tk_IsMapped(clockPtr->tkwin)
            && !(clockPtr->flags & REDRAW_PENDING)) {
        Tk_DoWhenIdle(ClockDisplay,
            (ClientData) clockPtr);
        clockPtr->flags |= REDRAW_PENDING;
    }
    /*
     * All OK, break out and avoid error rollback.
     */
    break;
}
```

```
    if (!error) {
        Tk_FreeSavedOptions(&savedOptions);
        return TCL_OK;
    } else {
        Tcl_SetObjResult(interp, errorResult);
        Tcl_DecrRefCount(errorResult);
        return TCL_ERROR;
    }
}
```

Specifying Widget Attributes

Several of the fields in the `Clock` structure are attributes that can be set when the widget is created or reconfigured with the `configure` operation. The `Tk_ConfigureWidget` procedure is designed to help you manage the default values, their resource names, and their class names. It works by associating a widget option with an offset into the widget data structure. When you use a command line argument to change an option, `Tk_ConfigureWidget` reaches into your widget structure and changes the value for you. Several types are supported, such as colors and fonts, and `Tk_ConfigureWidget` handles all the memory allocation used to store the values. Example 49–9 shows the `Tk_ConfigSpec` type used to represent information about each attribute:

Example 49–9 The `Tk_ConfigSpec` typedef.

```
typedef struct Tk_ConfigSpec {
    int type;
    char *name;
    char *dbName;
    char *dbClass;
    char *defValue;
    int offset;
    int specflags;
    Tk_CustomOption *customPtr;
} Tk_ConfigSpec;
```

The initial field is a type, such as `TK_CONFIG_BORDER`. Colors and borders will be explained shortly. The next field is the command-line flag for the attribute, (e.g., `-background`). Then comes the resource name and the class name. The default value is next, (e.g., `light blue`). The offset of a structure member is next, and the `Tk_Offset` macro is used to compute this offset. The `specflags` field is a bitmask of flags. The two used in this example are `TK_CONFIG_COLOR_ONLY` and `TK_CONFIG_MONO_ONLY`, which restrict the application of the configuration setting to color and monochrome displays, respectively. You can define additional flags and pass them into `Tk_ConfigureWidget` if you have a family of widgets that share most, but not all, of their attributes. The `tkButton.c` file in the Tk sources has an example of this. The `customPtr` is used if you have a `TK_CONFIG_CUSTOM` type, which is explained in detail in the manual page for `Tk_ConfigureWidget`. Example 49–10 shows the `Tk_ConfigSpec` specification of widget attributes for the clock widget.

Example 49–10 Configuration specs for the clock widget.

```
static Tk_ConfigSpec configSpecs[] = {
    {TK_CONFIG_BORDER, "-background", "background",
        "Background", "light blue",
        Tk_Offset(Clock, background), TK_CONFIG_COLOR_ONLY},
    {TK_CONFIG_BORDER, "-background", "background",
        "Background", "white", Tk_Offset(Clock, background),
        TK_CONFIG_MONO_ONLY},
    {TK_CONFIG_SYNONYM, "-bg", "background", (char *) NULL,
        (char *) NULL, 0, 0},
    {TK_CONFIG_SYNONYM, "-bd", "borderWidth", (char *) NULL,
        (char *) NULL, 0, 0},
    {TK_CONFIG_PIXELS, "-borderwidth", "borderWidth",
        "BorderWidth","2", Tk_Offset(Clock, borderWidth), 0},
    {TK_CONFIG_RELIEF, "-relief", "relief", "Relief",
        "ridge", Tk_Offset(Clock, relief), 0},
    {TK_CONFIG_COLOR, "-foreground", "foreground",
        "Foreground", "black", Tk_Offset(Clock, foreground),0},
    {TK_CONFIG_SYNONYM, "-fg", "foreground", (char *) NULL,
        (char *) NULL, 0, 0},
    {TK_CONFIG_COLOR, "-highlightcolor", "highlightColor",
        "HighlightColor", "red", Tk_Offset(Clock, highlight),
        TK_CONFIG_COLOR_ONLY},
    {TK_CONFIG_COLOR, "-highlightcolor", "highlightColor",
        "HighlightColor", "black",
        Tk_Offset(Clock, highlight),TK_CONFIG_MONO_ONLY},
    {TK_CONFIG_COLOR, "-highlightbackground",
        "highlightBackground", "HighlightBackground",
        "light blue", Tk_Offset(Clock, highlightBg),
        TK_CONFIG_COLOR_ONLY},
    {TK_CONFIG_COLOR, "-highlightbackground",
        "highlightBackground", "HighlightBackground",
        "black", Tk_Offset(Clock, highlightBg),
        TK_CONFIG_MONO_ONLY},
    {TK_CONFIG_PIXELS, "-highlightthickness",
        "highlightThickness","HighlightThickness",
        "2", Tk_Offset(Clock, highlightWidth), 0},
    {TK_CONFIG_PIXELS, "-padx", "padX", "Pad",
        "2", Tk_Offset(Clock, padX), 0},
    {TK_CONFIG_PIXELS, "-pady", "padY", "Pad",
        "2", Tk_Offset(Clock, padY), 0},
    {TK_CONFIG_STRING, "-format", "format", "Format",
        "%H:%M:%S", Tk_Offset(Clock, format), 0},
    {TK_CONFIG_FONT, "-font", "font", "Font",
        "Courier 18",
        Tk_Offset(Clock, tkfont), 0},
    {TK_CONFIG_END, (char *) NULL, (char *) NULL,
        (char *) NULL, (char *) NULL, 0, 0}
};
```

There is an alternative to the `Tk_ConfigureWidget` interface that understands `Tcl_Obj` values in the widget data structure. It uses a a similar type, `Tk_OptionSpec`, and `Tk_ConfigureWidget` is replaced by the `Tk_SetOptions`, `Tk_GetOptionValue`, and `Tk_GetOptionInfo` procedures. Example 49–11 shows the `Tk_OptionSpec` type.

Example 49–11 The `Tk_OptionSpec` typedef.

```
typedef struct Tk_OptionSpec {
    Tk_OptionType type;
    char *optionName;
    char *dbName;
    char *dbClass;
    char *defValue;
    int objOffset;
    int internalOffset;
    int flags;
    ClientData clientData;
    int typeMask;
} Tk_OptionSpec;
```

The `Tk_OptionSpec` has two offsets, one for normal values and one for `Tcl_Obj` values. You can use the second offset to set `Tcl_Obj` values directly from the command line configuration. The `TK_CONFIG_PIXELS` type uses both offsets. The pixel value is stored in an integer, and a `Tcl_Obj` is used to remember the exact string (e.g., `0.2cm`) used to specify the screen distance. Most of the functionality of the `specflags` field of `Tk_ConfigSpec` (e.g., `TK_CONFIG_MONO_ONLY`) has been changed. The flags field accepts only `TK_CONFIG_NULL_OK`, and the rest of the features use the `clientData` field instead. For example, the color types uses `clientData` for their default on monochrome displays. The `typeMask` supports a general notion of grouping option values into sets. For example, the clock widget marks attributes that affect geometry and color into different sets. This lets the widget optimize its configuration procedure. Example 49–12 shows the `Tk_OptionSpec` specification of the clock widget attributes.

Example 49–12 The `Tk_OptionSpec` structure for the clock widget.

```
#define GEOMETRY_MASK 0X1
#define GRAPHICS_MASK 0X2

static Tk_OptionSpec optionSpecs[] = {
    {TK_OPTION_BORDER, "-background", "background",
        "Background", "light blue", -1,
        Tk_Offset(Clock, background), 0,
        (ClientData) "white", GRAPHICS_MASK},
    {TK_OPTION_SYNONYM, "-bg", "background", (char *) NULL,
        (char *) NULL, -1, 0, 0, 0, 0},
    {TK_OPTION_PIXELS, "-borderwidth", "borderWidth",
        "BorderWidth", "2", Tk_Offset(Clock, borderWidthPtr),
```

```
        Tk_Offset(Clock, borderWidth),
        0, 0, GEOMETRY_MASK},
    {TK_OPTION_SYNONYM, "-bd", "borderWidth", (char *) NULL,
        (char *) NULL, -1, 0, 0, 0, 0},
    {TK_OPTION_RELIEF, "-relief", "relief", "Relief",
        "ridge", -1, Tk_Offset(Clock, relief), 0, 0, 0},
    {TK_OPTION_COLOR, "-foreground", "foreground",
        "Foreground", "black",-1, Tk_Offset(Clock, foreground),
        0, (ClientData) "black", GRAPHICS_MASK},
    {TK_OPTION_SYNONYM, "-fg", "foreground", (char *) NULL,
        (char *) NULL, -1, 0, 0, 0, 0},
    {TK_OPTION_COLOR, "-highlightcolor", "highlightColor",
        "HighlightColor", "red",-1, Tk_Offset(Clock, highlight),
        0, (ClientData) "black", GRAPHICS_MASK},
    {TK_OPTION_COLOR, "-highlightbackground",
        "highlightBackground", "HighlightBackground",
        "light blue",-1, Tk_Offset(Clock, highlightBg),
        0, (ClientData) "white", GRAPHICS_MASK},
    {TK_OPTION_PIXELS, "-highlightthickness",
        "highlightThickness","HighlightThickness",
        "2", Tk_Offset(Clock, highlightWidthPtr),
        Tk_Offset(Clock, highlightWidth), 0, 0,
        GEOMETRY_MASK},
    {TK_OPTION_PIXELS, "-padx", "padX", "Pad",
        "2", Tk_Offset(Clock, padXPtr),
        Tk_Offset(Clock, padX), 0, 0, GEOMETRY_MASK},
    {TK_OPTION_PIXELS, "-pady", "padY", "Pad",
        "2", Tk_Offset(Clock, padYPtr),
        Tk_Offset(Clock, padY), 0, 0, GEOMETRY_MASK},
    {TK_OPTION_STRING, "-format", "format", "Format",
        "%H:%M:%S",-1, Tk_Offset(Clock, format), 0, 0,
        GEOMETRY_MASK},
    {TK_OPTION_FONT, "-font", "font", "Font",
        "Courier 18",
        -1, Tk_Offset(Clock, tkfont), 0, 0,
        (GRAPHICS_MASK|GEOMETRY_MASK)},
    {TK_OPTION_END, (char *) NULL, (char *) NULL,
        (char *) NULL, (char *) NULL, -1, 0, 0, 0, 0}
};
```

Table 49–1 lists the correspondence between the configuration type of the option and the type of the associated field in the widget data structure. The same types are supported by the Tk_ConfigSpec and Tk_OptionSpec types, with a few exceptions. The TK_CONFIG_ACTIVE_CURSOR configuration type corresponds to the TK_OPTION_CURSOR; both of these set the widgets cursor. The TK_CONFIG_MM and TK_CONFIG_CURSOR types are simply not supported by Tk_OptionSpec because they were not very useful. The TK_OPTION_STRING_TABLE replaces TK_CONFIG_CAP_STYLE and TK_CONFIG_JOIN_STYLE with a more general type that works with Tcl_GetIndexFromObj. In this case, the clientData is an array of strings that are passed to Tcl_GetIndexFromObj. The index value corresponds to the integer value returned from procedures like Tk_GetCapStyle.

Table 49–1 Configuration flags and corresponding C types.

TK_CONFIG_ACTIVE_CURSOR TK_OPTION_CURSOR	Cursor
TK_CONFIG_ANCHOR TK_OPTION_ANCHOR	Tk_Anchor
TK_CONFIG_BITMAP TK_OPTION_BITMAP	Pixmap
TK_CONFIG_BOOLEAN TK_OPTION_BOOLEAN	int (0 or 1)
TK_CONFIG_BORDER TK_OPTION_BORDER	Tk_3DBorder *
TK_CONFIG_CAP_STYLE	int (see Tk_GetCapStyle)
TK_CONFIG_COLOR TK_OPTION_COLOR	XColor * clientData **is monochrome default.**
TK_CONFIG_CURSOR	Cursor
TK_CONFIG_CUSTOM	
TK_CONFIG_DOUBLE TK_OPTION_DOUBLE	double
TK_CONFIG_END TK_OPTION_END	(signals end of options)
TK_CONFIG_FONT TK_OPTION_FONT	Tk_Font
TK_CONFIG_INT TK_OPTION_INT	int
TK_CONFIG_JOIN_STYLE	int (see Tk_GetJoinStyle)
TK_CONFIG_JUSTIFY TK_OPTION_JUSTIFY	Tk_Justify
TK_CONFIG_MM	double
TK_CONFIG_PIXELS TK_OPTION_PIXELS	int objOffset **used for original value.**
TK_CONFIG_RELIEF TK_OPTION_RELIEF	int (see Tk_GetRelief)
TK_CONFIG_STRING TK_OPTION_STRING	char *
TK_OPTION_STRING_TABLE	The clientData **is an array of strings used** **with** Tcl_GetIndexFromObj
TK_CONFIG_SYNONYM TK_OPTION_SYNONYM	(alias for other option) clientData **is the name of another option.**
TK_CONFIG_UID	Tk_Uid
TK_CONFIG_WINDOW TK_OPTION_WINDOW	Tk_Window

Displaying the Clock

There are two parts to a widget's display. First, the size must be determined. This is done at configuration time, and then that space is requested from the geometry manager. When the widget is later displayed, it should use the `Tk_Width` and `Tk_Height` calls to find out how much space was actually allocated to it by the geometry manager. Example 49–13 shows `ComputeGeometry`. This procedure is identical in both versions of the widget.

Example 49–13 `ComputeGeometry` computes the widget's size.

```
static void
ComputeGeometry(Clock *clockPtr)
{
    int width, height;
    Tk_FontMetrics fm;      /* Font size information */
    struct tm *tmPtr;       /* Time info split into fields */
    struct timeval tv;      /* BSD-style time value */
    int bd;                 /* Padding from borders */
    char clock[1000];       /* Displayed time */

    /*
     * Get the time and format it to see how big it will be.
     */
    gettimeofday(&tv, NULL);
    tmPtr = localtime(&tv.tv_sec);
    strftime(clock, 1000, clockPtr->format, tmPtr);
    if (clockPtr->clock != NULL) {
        ckfree(clockPtr->clock);
    }
    clockPtr->clock = ckalloc(1+strlen(clock));
    clockPtr->numChars = strlen(clock);

    bd = clockPtr->highlightWidth + clockPtr->borderWidth;
    Tk_GetFontMetrics(clockPtr->tkfont, &fm);
    height = fm.linespace + 2*(bd + clockPtr->padY);
    Tk_MeasureChars(clockPtr->tkfont, clock,
        clockPtr->numChars, 0, 0, &clockPtr->textWidth);
    width = clockPtr->textWidth + 2*(bd + clockPtr->padX);

    Tk_GeometryRequest(clockPtr->tkwin, width, height);
    Tk_SetInternalBorder(clockPtr->tkwin, bd);
}
```

Finally, we get to the actual display of the widget! The routine is careful to check that the widget still exists and is mapped. This is important because the redisplay is scheduled asynchronously. The current time is converted to a string. This uses the POSIX library procedures `gettimeofday`, `localtime`, and `strftime`. There might be different routines on your system. The string is painted into a pixmap, which is a drawable region of memory that is off-screen. After the whole display has been painted, the pixmap is copied into on-screen memory to avoid flickering as the image is cleared and repainted. The text is painted first, then the borders. This ensures that the borders overwrite the text if the widget has not been allocated enough room by the geometry manager.

This example allocates and frees the off-screen pixmap for each redisplay. This is the standard idiom for Tk widgets. They temporarily allocate the off-screen pixmap each time they redisplay. In the case of a clock that updates every second, it might be reasonable to permanently allocate the pixmap and store its pointer in the `Clock` data structure. Make sure to reallocate the pixmap if the size changes.

After the display is finished, another call to the display routine is scheduled to happen in one second. If you were to embellish this widget, you might want to make the uptime period a parameter. The `TICKING` flag is used to note that the timer callback is scheduled. It is checked when the widget is destroyed so that the callback can be canceled. Example 49–14 shows `ClockDisplay`. This procedure is identical in both versions of the widget.

Example 49–14 The `ClockDisplay` procedure.

```
static void
ClockDisplay(ClientData clientData)
{
    Clock *clockPtr = (Clock *)clientData;
    Tk_Window tkwin = clockPtr->tkwin;
    GC gc;                      /* Graphics Context for highlight
*/
    Tk_TextLayout layout;    /* Text measurement state */
    Pixmap pixmap;           /* Temporary drawing area */
    int offset, x, y;        /* Coordinates */
    int width, height;       /* Size */
    struct tm *tmPtr;        /* Time info split into fields */
    struct timeval tv;       /* BSD-style time value */

    /*
     * Make sure the clock still exists
     * and is mapped onto the display before painting.
     */
    clockPtr->flags &= ~(REDRAW_PENDING|TICKING);
    if ((clockPtr->tkwin == NULL) || !Tk_IsMapped(tkwin)) {
        return;
    }
    /*
     * Format the time into a string.
     * localtime chops up the time into fields.
     * strftime formats the fields into a string.
     */
    gettimeofday(&tv, NULL);
    tmPtr = localtime(&tv.tv_sec);
    strftime(clockPtr->clock, clockPtr->numChars+1,
        clockPtr->format, tmPtr);
    /*
     * To avoid flicker when the display is updated, the new
```

```
 * image is painted in an offscreen pixmap and then
 * copied onto the display in one operation. Allocate the
 * pixmap and paint its background.
 */
pixmap = Tk_GetPixmap(clockPtr->display,
    Tk_WindowId(tkwin), Tk_Width(tkwin),
    Tk_Height(tkwin), Tk_Depth(tkwin));
Tk_Fill3DRectangle(tkwin, pixmap,
    clockPtr->background, 0, 0, Tk_Width(tkwin),
    Tk_Height(tkwin), 0, TK_RELIEF_FLAT);

/*
 * Paint the text first.
 */
layout = Tk_ComputeTextLayout(clockPtr->tkfont,
    clockPtr->clock, clockPtr->numChars, 0,
    TK_JUSTIFY_CENTER, 0, &width, &height);
x = (Tk_Width(tkwin) - width)/2;
y = (Tk_Height(tkwin) - height)/2;
Tk_DrawTextLayout(clockPtr->display, pixmap,
    clockPtr->textGC, layout, x, y, 0, -1);

/*
 * Display the borders, so they overwrite any of the
 * text that extends to the edge of the display.
 */
if (clockPtr->relief != TK_RELIEF_FLAT) {
    Tk_Draw3DRectangle(tkwin, pixmap,
        clockPtr->background,
        clockPtr->highlightWidth,
        clockPtr->highlightWidth,
        Tk_Width(tkwin) - 2*clockPtr->highlightWidth,
        Tk_Height(tkwin) - 2*clockPtr->highlightWidth,
        clockPtr->borderWidth, clockPtr->relief);
}
if (clockPtr->highlightWidth != 0) {
    GC gc;

    /*
     * This GC is associated with the color, and Tk caches
     * the GC until the color is freed. Hence no freeGC.
     */

    if (clockPtr->flags & GOT_FOCUS) {
        gc = Tk_GCForColor(clockPtr->highlight, pixmap);
    } else {
        gc = Tk_GCForColor(clockPtr->highlightBg, pixmap);
    }
    Tk_DrawFocusHighlight(tkwin, gc,
        clockPtr->highlightWidth, pixmap);
}
/*
 * Copy the information from the off-screen pixmap onto
 * the screen, then delete the pixmap.
 */
```

VI. Tcl and C

```
    XCopyArea(clockPtr->display, pixmap, Tk_WindowId(tkwin),
        clockPtr->textGC, 0, 0, Tk_Width(tkwin),
        Tk_Height(tkwin), 0, 0);
    Tk_FreePixmap(clockPtr->display, pixmap);

    /*
     * Queue another call to ourselves. The rate at which
     * this is done could be optimized.
     */
    clockPtr->token = Tk_CreateTimerHandler(1000,
        ClockDisplay, (ClientData)clockPtr);
    clockPtr->flags |= TICKING;
}
```

The Window Event Procedure

Each widget registers an event handler for expose and resize events. If it implements a focus highlight, it also needs to be notified of focus events. If you have used other toolkits, you may expect to register callbacks for mouse and keystroke events too. You should not need to do that. Instead, use the regular Tk bind facility and define your bindings in Tcl. That way they can be customized by applications. This procedure is identical in both versions of the widget.

Example 49–15 The `ClockEventProc` handles window events.

```
static void
ClockEventProc(ClientData clientData, XEvent *eventPtr)
{
    Clock *clockPtr = (Clock *) clientData;
    if ((eventPtr->type == Expose) &&
        (eventPtr->xexpose.count == 0)) {
            goto redraw;
    } else if (eventPtr->type == DestroyNotify) {
        Tcl_DeleteCommandFromToken(clockPtr->interp,
                clockPtr->widgetCmd);
        /*
         * Zapping the tkwin lets the other procedures
         * know we are being destroyed.
         */
        clockPtr->tkwin = NULL;

        if (clockPtr->flags & REDRAW_PENDING) {
            Tk_CancelIdleCall(ClockDisplay,
                (ClientData) clockPtr);
            clockPtr->flags &= ~REDRAW_PENDING;
        }
        if (clockPtr->flags & TICKING) {
            Tk_DeleteTimerHandler(clockPtr->token);
            clockPtr->flags &= ~TICKING;
        }
```

```
        /*
         * This results in a call to ClockDestroy.
         */
        Tk_EventuallyFree((ClientData) clockPtr,
            ClockDestroy);
    } else if (eventPtr->type == FocusIn) {
        if (eventPtr->xfocus.detail != NotifyPointer) {
            clockPtr->flags |= GOT_FOCUS;
            if (clockPtr->highlightWidth > 0) {
                goto redraw;
            }
        }
    } else if (eventPtr->type == FocusOut) {
        if (eventPtr->xfocus.detail != NotifyPointer) {
            clockPtr->flags &= ~GOT_FOCUS;
            if (clockPtr->highlightWidth > 0) {
                goto redraw;
            }
        }
    }
    return;
redraw:
    if ((clockPtr->tkwin != NULL) &&
            !(clockPtr->flags & REDRAW_PENDING)) {
        Tk_DoWhenIdle(ClockDisplay, (ClientData) clockPtr);
        clockPtr->flags |= REDRAW_PENDING;
    }
}
```

Final Cleanup

When a widget is destroyed, you need to free up any resources it has allocated. The resources associated with attributes are cleaned up by `Tk_FreeOptions`. The others you must take care of yourself. The `ClockDestroy` procedure is called as a result of the `Tk_EventuallyFree` call in the `ClockEventProc`. The `Tk_EventuallyFree` procedure is part of a protocol that is needed for widgets that might get deleted when in the middle of processing. Typically the `Tk_Preserve` and `Tk_Release` procedures are called at the beginning and end of the widget instance command to mark the widget as being in use. `Tk_EventuallyFree` will wait until `Tk_Release` is called before calling the cleanup procedure. The next example shows `ClockDestroy`:

Example 49–16 The `ClockDestroy` cleanup procedure.

```
static void
ClockDestroy(clientData)
    ClientData clientData;/* Info about entry widget. */
{
    register Clock *clockPtr = (Clock *) clientData;
```

```
/*
 * Free up all the stuff that requires special handling,
 * then let Tk_FreeOptions handle resources associated
 * with the widget attributes.
 */
if (clockPtr->textGC != None) {
    Tk_FreeGC(clockPtr->display, clockPtr->textGC);
}
if (clockPtr->clock != NULL) {
    Tcl_Free(clockPtr->clock);
}
if (clockPtr->flags & TICKING) {
    Tk_DeleteTimerHandler(clockPtr->token);
}
if (clockPtr->flags & REDRAW_PENDING) {
    Tk_CancelIdleCall(ClockDisplay,
        (ClientData) clockPtr);
}
/*
 * This frees up colors and fonts and any allocated
 * storage associated with the widget attributes.
 */
Tk_FreeOptions(configSpecs, (char *) clockPtr,
    clockPtr->display, 0);
Tcl_Free((char *) clockPtr);
}
```

The version of `ClockDestroy` that uses the `Tcl_Obj` interfaces calls `Tk_FreeConfigOptions` instead of `Tk_FreeOptions`. The `ClockObjDelete` command is called when the `oclock` command is removed from the interpreter. This has to clean up the option table used to parse options, if it has been initialized. There is no corresponding delete procedure for the string-based version of the widget. Example 49–17 shows `ClockObjDelete`.

Example 49–17 The `ClockObjDelete` command.

```
void
ClockObjDelete(ClientData clientData)
{
    Tk_OptionTable optionTable = (Tk_OptionTable) clientData;
    if (optionTable != NULL) {
        Tk_DeleteOptionTable(optionTable);
    }
}
```

C Library Overview

This chapter provides a bird's eye view of the facilities in the Tcl and Tk C libraries. For details of the APIs, you will need to consult the on-line reference material.

C libraries provide comprehensive access to the Tcl and Tk implementation. You have complete control over the Tcl script environment, plus you can extend Tcl and Tk by writing new features in C. You can implement new commands, I/O channels, event sources, widgets, canvas items, image types, and geometry managers. The platform-independent I/O subsystem and the event loop are available for use from C. This chapter provides an overview of the Tcl and Tk C libraries.

For serious C programming, you need to consult the on-line reference material. The manual pages describe groups of related C procedures. For example, on UNIX, you can run *man* on individual procedures and see the documentation for the whole group of related procedures:

```
man Tcl_CreateCommand
```

The Windows Help and HTML versions are indexed by procedure. You can find the HTML on the CD-ROM and the Web:

```
http://www.tcl.tk/man/
```

The Tcl and Tk sources are also excellent reference material. The code is well written with a consistent style that encourages lots of comments. Virtually all the exported APIs are used by Tcl and Tk themselves, so you can read the source code to see how the APIs are used. The Tcl and Tk sources are on the CD-ROM in `tcl8.4` and `tk8.4` directories. Chapter 48 describes the source directory structure and how to build Tcl from the source code.

VI. Tcl and C

An Overview of the Tcl C Library

Application Initialization

The `Tcl_Main` and `Tcl_AppInit` procedures are illustrated by Example 47–13 on page 720. They provide a standard framework for creating main programs that embed a Tcl interpreter. `Tcl_Init` is used to source the `init.tcl` script. `Tcl_SourceRCFile` sources the per-user startup file (e.g., `.tclshrc`). `Tcl_SetMainLoop` is used to set up an event loop (e.g., by Tk).

The `Tcl_InitStubs` procedure must be called during initialization by an extension that has been linked against the Tcl stub library, which is described on page 735. `Tcl_InitStubs` is illustrated in Example 47–1 on page 698.

The `Tcl_FindExecutable` searches the system to determine the absolute file name of the program being run. This should be called early, before `Tcl_Main` or `Tcl_CreateInterp`. Once `Tcl_FindExecutable` has been called, `Tcl_GetNameOfExecutable` can be used to get the value of the program name.

Creating and Deleting Interpreters

A Tcl interpreter is created and deleted with the `Tcl_CreateInterp` and `Tcl_DeleteInterp` procedures. You can find out whether an interpreter is in the process of being deleted with the `Tcl_InterpDeleted` call. You can register a callback to occur when the interpreter is deleted with `Tcl_CallWhenDeleted`. Unregister the callback with `Tcl_DontCallWhenDeleted`.

Slave interpreters are created and manipulated with `Tcl_CreateSlave`, `Tcl_GetSlave`, `Tcl_GetSlaves`, `Tcl_GetMaster`, `Tcl_CreateAlias`, `Tcl_CreateAliasObj`, `Tcl_GetAlias`, `Tcl_GetAliasObj`, `Tcl_GetAliases`, `Tcl_GetInterpPath`, `Tcl_IsSafe`, `Tcl_MakeSafe`, `Tcl_ExposeCommand`, and `Tcl_HideCommand`.

Creating and Deleting Commands

Register a new Tcl command with `Tcl_CreateCommand`, and delete a command with `Tcl_DeleteCommand`. The `Tcl_GetCommandInfo` and `Tcl_SetCommandInfo` procedures query and modify the procedure that implements a Tcl command and the `ClientData` that is associated with the command. When a command is created, a token is returned. The following procedures manipulate the command using the token: `Tcl_GetCommandInfoFromToken`, `Tcl_SetCommandInfoFromToken`, and `Tcl_DeleteCommandFromToken`. A command that uses the `Tcl_Obj` interface is created with `Tcl_CreateObjCommand`. Command procedures are illustrated in Chapter 47.

Dynamic Loading and Packages

`Tcl_PkgRequire` checks a dependency on another package. `Tcl_PkgProvide` declares that a package is provided by a library. These procedures are equivalent to the `package require` and `package provide` Tcl commands. The `Tcl_PkgPresent` procedure returns the version number of the package, if it is loaded. `Tcl_PkgProvideEx`, `Tcl_PkgRequireEx`, and `Tcl_PkgPresentEx` let you set and query the clientData associated with the package. The `Tcl_StaticPackage` call is used by statically linked packages so that scripts can `load` them into slave interpreters.

Managing the Result String

The result string is managed through the `Tcl_SetResult`, `Tcl_AppendResult`, `Tcl_AppendElement`, `Tcl_GetStringResult`, and `Tcl_ResetResult` procedures. The object interface is provided by `Tcl_SetObjResult` and `Tcl_GetObjResult`.

Error information is managed with the `Tcl_AddErrorInfo`, `Tcl_AddObjErrorInfo`, `Tcl_SetErrorCode`, `Tcl_SetObjErrorCode`, `Tcl_SetErrorCodeVA`, `Tcl_LogCommandInfo`, and `Tcl_PosixError` procedures. The `Tcl_WrongNumArgs` generates a standard error message. `Tcl_SetErrno`, `Tcl_GetErrno`, `Tcl_ErrnoId`, and `Tcl_ErrnoMsg` provide platform-independent access to the `errno` global variable that stores POSIX error codes.

Memory Allocation

The `Tcl_Alloc`, `Tcl_Realloc`, and `Tcl_Free` procedures provide platform- and compiler-independent functions to allocation and free heap storage. Use these instead of `alloc`, `realloc`, and `free`. Note that Tcl_Alloc and Tcl_Realloc will panic if no memory is available. The following procedures will return a NULL pointer instead of panicking: `Tcl_AttemptAlloc`, `Tcl_AttemptRealloc`. The `Tcl_Preserve` and `Tcl_Release` procedures work in concert with `Tcl_EventuallyFree` to guard data structures against premature deallocation. These are described on page 715.

The following macros are layers over the memory APIs that provide extra debugging support if the `TCL_MEM_DEBUG` compile-time option is used: `ckalloc`, `ckfree`, `ckrealloc`, `attemptckalloc`, `attemptckrealloc`. To view the debugging information, use `Tcl_DumpActiveMemory` or `Tcl_ValidateAllMemory`. Use `Tcl_InitMemory` to create the `memory` Tcl command that provides script-level access to these APIs.

Lists

You can chop a list up into its elements with `Tcl_SplitList`, which returns an array of strings. You can create a list out of an array of strings with `Tcl_Merge`. This behaves like the `list` command in that it will add syntax to the strings so that the list structure has one element for each of the strings. The `Tcl_ScanElement`, `Tcl_ScanCountedElement`, `Tcl_ConvertCountedElement`, and `Tcl_ConvertElement` procedures are used by `Tcl_Merge`. The object interface to lists is provided by `Tcl_NewListObj`, `Tcl_SetListObj`, `Tcl_ListObjIndex`,

VI. Tcl and C

`Tcl_ListObjLength,    Tcl_ListObjAppendList,    Tcl_ListObjAppendElement,`
`Tcl_ListObjGetElements,` and `Tcl_ListObjReplace`.

Command Parsing

If you are reading commands, you can test for a complete command with
`Tcl_CommandComplete`. You can do backslash substitutions with `Tcl_Backslash`.
A more formal Tcl parser is provided by these procedures: `Tcl_ParseCommand`,
`Tcl_ParseExpr`, `Tcl_ParseBraces`, `Tcl_ParseQuotedString`, `Tcl_ParseVarName`,
`Tcl_ParseVar` and `Tcl_FreeParse`. The result of the parse is a sequence of
tokens,   which   you   can   evaluate   with   `Tcl_EvalTokens`   and
`Tcl_EvalTokensStandard`.

Command Pipelines

The `Tcl_OpenCommandChannel` procedure does all the work of setting up a
pipeline between processes. It handles file redirection and implements all the
syntax supported by the `exec` and `open` commands. Use `Tcl_WaitPid` to wait for
the process to complete.

If the command pipeline is run in the background, then a list of process
identifiers is returned. You can detach these processes with `Tcl_DetachPids`,
and you can clean up after them with `Tcl_ReapDetachedProcs`.

Tracing the Actions of the Tcl Interpreter

There are several procedures that let you trace the execution of the Tcl
interpreter and provide control over its behavior. `Tcl_CreateTrace` and
`Tcl_CreateObjTrace` register a procedure that is called before the execution of
each Tcl command. Remove the registration with `Tcl_DeleteTrace`. Traces on
individual   commands   are   controlled   with   `Tcl_TraceCommand`,
`Tcl_UntraceCommand,` and `Tcl_CommandTraceInfo`.

You can trace modifications and accesses to Tcl variables with
`Tcl_TraceVar` and `Tcl_TraceVar2`. The second form is used with array elements.
Remove the traces with `Tcl_UntraceVar` and `Tcl_UntraceVar2`. You can query
the traces on variables with `Tcl_VarTraceInfo` and `Tcl_VarTraceInfo2`.

Evaluating Tcl Commands

There is a large family of procedures that evaluate Tcl commands.
`Tcl_Eval` evaluates a string as a Tcl command. `Tcl_VarEval` and `Tcl_VarEvalVA`
take a variable number of string arguments and concatenates them before evaluation. The `Tcl_EvalFile` command reads commands from a file. `Tcl_GlobalEval`
evaluates a string at the global scope. The `Tcl_EvalEx` procedure takes flags.
The `TCL_GLOBAL_EVAL` flag causes evaluation at the global scope. The
`TCL_EVAL_DIRECT` flags does evaluation without first compiling the script to byte
codes.

`Tcl_EvalObj` and `Tcl_GlobalEvalObj` provide an object interface. Their argument is a script object that gets compiled into byte codes and cached. Use these procedures if you plan to execute the same script several times. The `Tcl_EvalObjEx` procedure takes the evaluation flags described above. The `Tcl_EvalObjv` procedure takes an array of `Tcl_Obj` that represent the command and its arguments. Unlike the other procedures, `Tcl_EvalObjv` does not do substitutions on the arguments to the command.

If you are implementing an interactive command interpreter and want to use the history facility, then call `Tcl_RecordAndEval` or `Tcl_RecordAndEvalObj`. This records the command on the history list and then behaves like `Tcl_GlobalEval`.

You can set the recursion limit of the interpreter with `Tcl_SetRecursionLimit`. If you are implementing a new control structure, you may need to use the `Tcl_AllowExceptions` procedure. This makes it acceptable for `Tcl_Eval` and friends to return something other than `TCL_OK` and `TCL_ERROR`.

If you want to evaluate a Tcl command without modifying the current interpreter result and error information, use `Tcl_SaveResult`, `Tcl_RestoreResult`, and `Tcl_DiscardResult`.

The `Tcl_SubstObj` procedure implements the mechanics of the `subst` Tcl command.

Reporting Script Errors

If your widget makes a callback into the script level, what do you do when the callback returns an error? Use the `Tcl_BackgroundError` procedure that invokes the standard `bgerror` procedure to report the error to the user.

Manipulating Tcl Variables

You can set a Tcl variable with `Tcl_SetVar` and `Tcl_SetVar2`. These two procedures assign a string value, and the second form is used for array elements. The `Tcl_SetVar2Ex` procedure assigns a `Tcl_Obj` value to the variable, and it can be used with array elements. You can retrieve the value of a Tcl variable with `Tcl_GetVar` and `Tcl_GetVar2`. The `Tcl_GetVar2Ex` procedure returns a `Tcl_Obj` value instead of a string. In the rare case that you have the name of the variable in a `Tcl_Obj` instead of a simple string, you must use `Tcl_ObjSetVar2` procedure and `Tcl_ObjGetVar2`. You can delete variables with `Tcl_UnsetVar` and `Tcl_UnsetVar2`.

You can link a Tcl variable and a C variable together with `Tcl_LinkVar` and break the relationship with `Tcl_UnlinkVar`. Setting the Tcl variable modifies the C variable, and reading the Tcl variable returns the value of the C variable. If you need to modify the Tcl variable directly, use `Tcl_UpdateLinkedVar`.

Use the `Tcl_UpVar` and `Tcl_UpVar2` procedures to link Tcl variables from different scopes together. You may need to do this if your command takes the name of a variable as an argument as opposed to a value. These procedures are used in the implementation of the `upvar` Tcl command.

Evaluating Expressions

The Tcl expression evaluator is available through the `Tcl_ExprLong`, `Tcl_ExprDouble`, `Tcl_ExprBoolean`, and `Tcl_ExprString` procedures. These all use the same evaluator, but they differ in how they return their result. The object interface to expressions is implemented with `Tcl_ExprLongObj`, `Tcl_ExprDoubleObj`, `Tcl_ExprBooleanObj`, and `Tcl_ExprObj`. You can register the implementation of new math functions by using `Tcl_CreateMathFunc`, and you can query them with `Tcl_GetMathFuncInfo` and `Tcl_ListMathFuncs`.

Converting Numbers

You can convert strings into numbers with the `Tcl_GetInt`, `Tcl_GetDouble`, and `Tcl_GetBoolean` procedures. The `Tcl_PrintDouble` procedure converts a floating point number to a string. Tcl uses it any time it must do this conversion.

Tcl Objects

Tcl 8.0 uses dual-ported objects instead of strings to improve execution efficiency. The basic interface to objects is provided by `Tcl_NewObj`, `Tl_DuplicateObj`, `Tcl_IncrRefCount`, `Tcl_DecrRefCount`, `Tcl_InvalidateStringRep`, and `Tcl_IsShared`. Example 47–5 on page 706 and Example 47–15 on page 725 illustrate some of these procedures. You can define new object types. The interface consists of `Tcl_RegisterObjType`, `Tcl_GetObjType`, `Tcl_AppendAllObjTypes`, and `Tcl_ConvertToType`.

Primitive Object Types

The basic Tcl object types are boolean, integer, double-precision real, and string. The types provide procedures for creating objects, setting values, and getting values: `Tcl_NewBooleanObj`, `Tcl_SetBooleanObj`, `Tcl_GetBooleanFromObj`, `Tcl_NewDoubleObj`, `Tcl_SetDoubleObj`, `Tcl_GetDoubleFromObj`, `Tcl_NewIntObj`, `Tcl_GetIntFromObj`, `Tcl_SetIntObj`, `Tcl_NewLongObj`, `Tcl_GetLongFromObj`, and `Tcl_SetLongObj`. 64-bit integers are supported with `Tcl_NewWideInt`, `Tcl_SetWideInt`, and `Tcl_GetWideIntFromObj`.

String Object Types

The `Tcl_Obj` values are used to store strings in different encodings. The natural string value in a `Tcl_Obj` is UTF-8 encoded. There can also be Unicode (i.e., 16-bit characters) or ByteArray (i.e., 8-bit characters) format strings stored in a `Tcl_Obj`. Conversions among these string types are done automatically. However, certain operations work best with a particular string encoding, and the `Tcl_Obj` value is useful for caching an efficient representation.

These procedures operate on string objects with the UTF-8 encoding: `Tcl_NewStringObj`, `Tcl_SetStringObj`, `Tcl_GetString`, `Tcl_GetStringFromObj`,

`Tcl_AppendToObj`, `Tcl_AppendStringsToObj`, and `Tcl_AppendObjToObj`. These procedures operate on Unicode strings: `Tcl_NewUnicodeObj`, `Tcl_SetUnicodeObj`, `Tcl_AppendUnicodeToObj`, `Tcl_GetUnicode`, `Tcl_GetUnicodeFromObj`, `Tcl_GetRange`, `Tcl_GetUniChar`. The `Tcl_AppendObjToObj` preserves the existing representation (e.g., Unicode or UTF-8) of the string being appended to.

The `Tcl_GetCharLength` returns the length in characters of the string. `Tcl_SetObjLength` procedure sets the storage size of the string in bytes, which is generally different from the character length. This can be used to overallocate a string in preparation for creating a large one. Use `Tcl_AttemptSetObjLength` to avoid a panic if you cannot grow the object to the requested size.

The `Tcl_Concat` and `Tcl_ConcatObj` procedures operate like the concat Tcl command. Its input is an array of strings (for `Tcl_Concat`) or `Tcl_Obj` values (for `Tcl_ConcatObj`). They trim leading and trailing white space from each one, and concatenate them together into one string with a single space character between each value.

ByteArrays for Binary Data

The ByteArray `Tcl_Obj` type is used to store arbitrary binary data. It is simply an array of 8-bit bytes. These are its procedures: `Tcl_NewByteArrayObj`, `Tcl_SetByteArrayObj`, `Tcl_GetByteArrayFromObj`, and `Tcl_SetByteArray-Length`.

Dynamic Strings

The Tcl dynamic string package is designed for strings that get built up incrementally. You will need to use dynamic strings if you use the `Tcl_TranslateFileName` procedure. The procedures in the package are `Tcl_DStringInit`, `Tcl_DStringAppend`, `Tcl_DStringAppendElement`, `Tcl_DStringStartSublist`, `Tcl_DStringEndSublist`, `Tcl_DStringLength`, `Tcl_DStringValue`, `Tcl_DStringSetLength`, `Tcl_DStringFree`, `Tcl_DString-Result`, and `Tcl_DStringGetResult`. Dynamic strings are explained in more detail on page 717.

Character Set Encodings

The procedures that convert strings between character set encodings use an abstract handle on a particular encoding. The `Tcl_GetEncoding` and `Tcl_FreeEncoding` procedures allocate and release these handles. `Tcl_SetSystemEncoding` is called by Tcl to set the encoding for the current system. `Tcl_CreateEncoding` creates a new encoding. The `Tcl_GetEncodingName` and `Tcl_GetEncodingNames` procedures query the available encodings. The encodings are stored in files in default location, which you query and set with `Tcl_GetDefaultEncodingDir` and `Tcl_SetDefaultEncodingDir`.

There are three sets of procedures that translate strings between encodings. The easiest to use are `Tcl_ExternalToUtfDString` and `Tcl_UtfToExternalDString`, which put the result into a `Tcl_DString`. These are built on top of `Tcl_ExternalToUtf` and `Tcl_UtfToExternal`, which are harder to use because they have to deal with partial conversions at the end of the buffer. The `Tcl_WinTCharToUtf` and `Tcl_WinUtfToTChar` procedures are for use with Windows `TChar` type, which is an 8-bit character on Windows 98 and a 16-bit Unicode character on Windows NT.

There are many utility procedures for operating on Unicode and UTF-8 strings: `Tcl_UniChar`, `Tcl_UniCharToUtf`, `Tcl_UtfToUniChar`, `Tcl_UniCharToUtfDString`, `Tcl_UtfToUniCharDString`, `Tcl_UniCharLen`, `Tcl_UniCharNcmp`, `Tcl_UtfCharComplete`, `Tcl_NumUtfChars`, `Tcl_UtfFindFirst`, `Tcl_UtfFindLast`, `Tcl_UtfNext`, `Tcl_UtfPrev`, `Tcl_UniCharAtIndex`, `Tcl_UtfAtIndex`, and `Tcl_UtfBackslash`.

These procedures convert Unicode characters to different cases: `Tcl_UniCharToUpper`, `Tcl_UniCharToLower`, and `Tcl_UniCharToTitle`. These procedures convert strings: `Tcl_UtfToUpper`, `Tcl_UtfToLower`, `Tcl_UtfToTitle`. The procedures compare Unicode strings: `Tcl_UniCharCaseMatch` and `Tcl_UniCharNcasecmp`.

These procedures test classification of Unicode characters: `Tcl_UniCharIsAlnum`, `Tcl_UniCharIsAlpha`, `Tcl_UniCharIsControl`, `Tcl_UniCharIsDigit`, `Tcl_UniCharIsGraph`, `Tcl_UniCharIsLower`, `Tcl_UniCharIsPrint`, `Tcl_UniCharIsPunct`, `Tcl_UniCharIsSpace`, `Tcl_UniCharIsUpper`, and `Tcl_UniCharIsWordChar`.

AssocData for per Interpreter Data Structures

If your extension needs to store information that is not associated with any particular command, you can associate it with an interpreter with *AssocData*. The `Tcl_SetAssocData` registers a string-valued key for a data structure. The `Tcl_GetAssocData` gets the data for a key, and `Tcl_DeleteAssocData` removes the key and pointer. The registration also includes a callback that is made when the interpreter is deleted. This is a layer on top of the hash table package described next.

Hash Tables

Tcl has a nice hash table package that automatically grows the hash table data structures as more elements are added to the table. Because everything is a string, you may need to set up a hash table that maps from a string-valued key to an internal data structure. The procedures in the package are `Tcl_InitHashTable`, `Tcl_InitObjHashTable`, `Tcl_InitCustomHashTable`, `Tcl_DeleteHashTable`, `Tcl_CreateHashEntry`, `Tcl_Delete-HashEntry`, `Tcl_FindHashEntry`, `Tcl_GetHashValue`, `Tcl_SetHashValue`, `Tcl_GetHashKey`, `Tcl_FirstHashEntry`, `Tcl_NextHashEntry`, and `Tcl_HashStats`. Hash tables are used in the `blob` command example presented in Chapter 47.

Option Processing

`Tcl_GetIndexFromObj` and `Tcl_GetIndexFromObjStruct` provide a way to look up keywords in a table. They are designed to work with options on a Tcl command. `Tcl_GetIndexFromObj` is illustrated in Example 47–8 on page 711.

Regular Expressions and String Matching

The regular expression library used by Tcl is exported through the `Tcl_RegExpMatch`, `Tcl_RegExpCompile`, `Tcl_RegExpExec`, and `Tcl_RegExpRange` procedures. The `Tcl_Obj` version of this interface uses the `Tcl_RegExpMatchObj`, `Tcl_GetRegExpFromObj`, `Tcl_RegExpExecObj` and `Tcl_GetRegExpInfo` procedures. The `string match` function is available through the `Tcl_StringMatch` and `Tcl_StringCaseMatch` procedures.

Event Loop Implementation

The event loop is implemented by the *notifier* that manages a set of *event sources* and a queue of pending events. The *tclsh* and *wish* applications already manage the event loop for you. The simplest interface is provided by `Tcl_DoOneEvent`. In some cases, you may need to implement new event sources. Use `Tcl_CreateEventSource` and `Tcl_DeleteEventSource` to create and destroy an event source. An event source manipulates the events queue with `Tcl_QueueEvent`, `Tcl_DeleteEvents`, and `Tcl_SetMaxBlockTime`.

Each thread runs a notifier. You can enqueue events for another thread's notifier with `Tcl_ThreadQueueEvent`. After you do this, you must signal the other thread with `Tcl_ThreadAlert`. The ID of the current thread is returned from `Tcl_GetCurrentThread`.

The notifier is implemented with a public API so that you can replace the API with a new implementation for custom situations. This API consists of `Tcl_InitNotifier`, `Tcl_FinalizeNotifier`, `Tcl_WaitForEvent`, `Tcl_AlertNotifier`, `Tcl_Sleep`, `Tcl_CreateFileHandler`, and `Tcl_DeleteFileHandler`.

If you want to integrate Tcl's event loop with an external one, such as the Xt event loop used by Motif, then you can use the following procedures: `Tcl_WaitForEvent`, `Tcl_SetTimer`, `Tcl_ServiceAll`, `Tcl_ServiceEvent`, `Tcl_GetServiceMode`, and `Tcl_SetServiceMode`. There is an example application of this in the `unix/xtTest.c` file.

File Handlers

Use `Tcl_CreateFileHandler` to register handlers for I/O streams. You set up the handlers to be called when the I/O stream is ready for reading or writing, or both. File handlers are called after window event handlers. Use `Tcl_DeleteFileHandler` to remove the handler.

`Tcl_CreateFileHandler` is UNIX-specific because UNIX has a unified handle for files, sockets, pipes, and devices. On Windows and the Macintosh, there are different system APIs to wait for events from these different classes of I/O objects. These differences are hidden by the channel drivers for sockets and pipes. For nonstandard devices, the best thing is to create a channel driver and event source for them.

Timer Events

Register a callback to occur at some time in the future with `Tcl_CreateTimerHandler`. The handler is called only once. If you need to delete the handler before it gets called, use `Tcl_DeleteTimerHandler`.

Idle Callbacks

If there are no outstanding events, the Tk makes idle callbacks before waiting for new events to arrive. In general, Tk widgets queue their display routines to be called at idle time. Use `Tcl_DoWhenIdle` to queue an idle callback, and use `Tcl_CancelIdleCall` to remove the callback from the queue. The `Tcl_Sleep` procedure delays execution for a specified number of milliseconds.

Input/Output

The Tcl I/O subsystem provides buffering and works with the event loop to provide event-driven I/O. The interface consists of `Tcl_OpenFileChannel`, `Tcl_OpenCommandChannel`, `Tcl_MakeFileChannel`, `Tcl_GetChannel`, `Tcl_GetChannelNames`, `Tcl_GetChannelNamesEx`, `Tcl_GetOpenFile`, `Tcl_RegisterChannel`, `Tcl_UnregisterChannel`, `Tcl_DetachChannel`, `Tcl_IsStandardChannel`, `Tcl_Close`, `Tcl_Read`, `Tcl_ReadChars`, `Tcl_Gets`, `Tcl_Write`, `Tcl_WriteObj`, `Tcl_WriteChars`, `Tcl_Flush`, `Tcl_Seek`, `Tcl_Tell`, `Tcl_Eof`, `Tcl_GetsObj`, `Tcl_InputBlocked`, `Tcl_InputBuffered`, `Tcl_OutputBuffered`, `Tcl_Ungets`, `Tcl_ReadRaw`, `Tcl_WriteRaw`, `Tcl_GetChannelOption`, and `Tcl_SetChannelOption`.

I/O Channel Drivers

Tcl provides an extensible I/O subsystem. You can implement a new channel (i.e., for a UDP network socket) by providing a Tcl command to create the channel and registering a set of callbacks that are used by the standard Tcl I/O commands like `puts`, `gets`, and `close`. The interface to channels consists of these procedures: `Tcl_CreateChannel`, `Tcl_GetChannel`, `Tcl_GetChannelType`, `Tcl_GetChannelInstanceData`, `Tcl_GetChannelName`, `Tcl_GetChannelHandle`, `Tcl_GetChannelMode`, `Tcl_BadChannelOption`, `Tcl_GetChannelBufferSize`, `Tcl_SetDefaultTranslation`, `Tcl_SetChannelBufferSize`, and `Tcl_NotifyChannel`.

The `Tcl_CreateChannelHandler` and `Tcl_DeleteChannelHandler` are used in the interface to the main event loop. The `Tcl_CreateCloseHandler` and `Tcl_DeleteCloseHandler` set and delete a callback that occurs when a channel is closed. The `Tcl_GetStdChannel` and `Tcl_SetStdChannel` are used to manipulate the standard input and standard output channels of your application.

Network sockets are created with `Tcl_OpenTcpClient` and `Tcl_OpenTcpServer`. The `Tcl_MakeTcpClientChannel` provides a platform-independent way to create a Tcl channel structure for a socket connection.

The `Tcl_StackChannel`, `Tcl_UnstackChannel`, `Tcl_GetTopChannel`, and `Tcl_GetStackedChannel` procedures support layering of I/O channels. This can be used to push compression- or encryption-processing modules onto I/O channels.

The driver for a channel type implements a set of procedures that are registered in a `Tcl_ChannelType` structure. This structure has changed format in a backward compatible way so that older stub-enabled extensions can interoperate with newer versions of Tcl. The version of the channel type structure is returned with `Tcl_ChannelVersion`. The following accessor functions should be used instead of accessing the structure directly: `Tcl_ChannelBlockModeProc`, `Tcl_ChannelBlockModeProc`, `Tcl_ChannelCloseProc`, `Tcl_ChannelClose2Proc`, `Tcl_ChannelInputProc`, `Tcl_ChannelOutputProc`, `Tcl_ChannelSeekProc`, `Tcl_ChannelWideSeekProc`, `Tcl_ChannelSetOptionProc`, `Tcl_ChannelGet-OptionProc`, `Tcl_ChannelWatchProc`, `Tcl_ChannelGetHandleProc`, `Tcl_ChannelFlushProc`, and `Tcl_ChannelHandlerProc`.

Each I/O channel is registered with one or more interpreters, and each of these is recorded in a reference count. `Tcl_SpliceChannel` and `Tcl_CutChannel` are used to add or remove a channel from the per-interpreter channel list. The reference count and registration are queried with `Tcl_IsChannelShared`, `Tcl_IsChannelExisting`, and `Tcl_IsChannelRegistered`. `Tcl_ChannelBuffered` queries the amount of data buffered in the channel. In addition, each interpreter is bound to a particular thread, so `Tcl_GetChannelThread` is used to find the right thread to notify about I/O events. `Tcl_ClearChannelHandlers` will remove all handlers in order to deactivate a channel.

Manipulating File Names

The `Tcl_SplitPath`, `Tcl_JoinPath`, and `Tcl_GetPathType` procedures provide the implementation for the `file split`, `file join`, and `file pathtype` Tcl commands that are used to manipulate file names in a platform-independent manner. The `Tcl_TranslateFileName` procedure converts a file name to native syntax. It also expands tilde (~) in file names into user home directories.

Examining the File System

Tcl 8.4 provides a broad set of `Tcl_FS` procedures to access the file system. These procedures provide portability across UNIX, Windows, and Macintosh. They also support the Virtual File System interface; that all C extensions that use these APIs will automatically access any embedded file systems.

These procedures are for basic file system operations: `Tcl_FSCopyFile`, `Tcl_FSCopyDirectory`, `Tcl_FSCreateDirectory`, `Tcl_FSDeleteFile`,

VI. Tcl and C

`Tcl_FSRemoveDirectory`, `Tcl_FSRenameFile`, `Tcl_FSListVolumes`, `Tcl_FSLink`, `Tcl_FSLstat`, `Tcl_FSUtime`, `Tcl_FSFileAttrsGet`, `Tcl_FSFileAttrsSet`, `Tcl_FSFileAttrStrings`, `Tcl_FSStat`, `Tcl_FSAccess`, `Tcl_FSOpenFileChannel`, `Tcl_FSGetCwd`, `Tcl_FSChdir`, `Tcl_FSMatchInDirectory`, `Tcl_FSFileSystemInfo`, and `Tcl_AllocStatBuf`.

These procedures are used for `source` and `load`: `Tcl_FSEvalFile`, `Tcl_FSLoadFile`.

These procedures are used for platform-independent file name manipulation: `Tcl_FSGetPathType`, `Tcl_FSPathSeparator`, `Tcl_FSJoinPath`, `Tcl_FSSplitPath`, `Tcl_FSEqualPaths`, `Tcl_FSGetNormalizedPath`, `Tcl_FSJoinToPath`, `Tcl_FSConvertToPathType`, `Tcl_FSGetInternalRep`, `Tcl_FSGetTranslatedPath`, `Tcl_FSNewNativePath`, `Tcl_FSGetNativePath`, and `Tcl_FSGetTranslatedStringPath`.

The following APIs are now deprecated in favor of the corresponding `Tcl_FS` procedures: `Tcl_Stat`, `Tcl_Access`, `Tcl_Chdir` and `Tcl_GetCwd`.

Virtual File System Implementations

A Virtual File System (VFS) is implemented by registering a set of procedures that handle various aspects of file system access. The procedures include `Tcl_FSRegister`, `Tcl_FSUnregister`, `Tcl_FSData`, `Tcl_FSMountsChanged`, and `Tcl_FSGetFileSystemForPath`.

Thread Support

The Tcl library is thread safe. The procedures listed here provide a convenient, cross-platform API for programming with threads. The following procedures serialize access to data structures: `Tcl_MutexLock`, `Tcl_MutexUnlock`, `Tcl_ConditionWait`, and `Tcl_ConditionNotify`. Thread local storage is provided by `Tcl_GetThreadData`. All of these procedures are self-initializing, so there are no explicit initialization calls. There are, however, `Tcl_ConditionFinalize` and `Tcl_MutexFinalize`.

The following procedures manage thread life cycle: `Tcl_CreateThread`, `Tcl_ExitThread`, `Tcl_JoinThread`, and `Tcl_FinalizeThread`.

The `Tcl_CreateThreadExitHandler` procedure registers a procedure that is called when a thread is terminated. In particular, it can clean up thread local storage. Use `Tcl_DeleteThreadExitHandler` to remove a registration.

Working with Signals

Tcl provides a simple package for safely dealing with signals and other asynchronous events. You register a handler for an event with `Tcl_AsyncCreate`. When the event occurs, you mark the handler as ready with `Tcl_AsyncMark`. When the Tcl interpreter is at a safe point, it uses `Tcl_AsyncReady` to determine which handlers are ready, and then it uses `Tcl_AsyncInvoke` to call them. Your application can call `Tcl_AsyncInvoke`, too. Use `Tcl_AsyncDelete` to unregister a handler.

Exit Handlers

The `Tcl_Exit` procedure terminates the application. The `Tcl_Finalize` procedure cleans up Tcl's memory usage and calls exit handlers, but it does not exit. This is necessary when unloading the Tcl DLL. The `Tcl_CreateExitHandler` and `Tcl_DeleteExitHandler` set up callbacks that occur when `Tcl_Exit` is called.

Macintosh

The Macintosh platform has a number of APIs used to manipulate Mac-specific resources and to register handlers for Mac-specific events: `Tcl_MacSetEventProc`, `Tcl_MacConvertTextResource`, `Tcl_MacEvalResource`, `Tcl_MacFindResource`, `Tcl_GetOSTypeFromObj`, `Tcl_SetOSTypeObj`, and `Tcl_NewOSTypeObj`.

Panic

`Tcl_Panic` is used to abort the application if some serious internal error occurs. `Tcl_PanicVA` takes a variable number of arguments. You can alter the default behavior of `Tcl_Panic` by setting a handler with `Tcl_SetPanicProc`. The panic macro calls `Tcl_Panic`.

Miscellaneous

`Tcl_GetHostName` returns the name of the current machine. This is the same as the `info hostname` value. `Tcl_GetTime` returns the current time in seconds and microseconds. `Tcl_GetVersion` returns the version and patch level of the Tcl interpreter. `Tcl_PutEnv` sets a value in the environment, and should be used instead of `putenv`.

`Tcl_SignalId` and `Tcl_SignalMsg` convert between signal numbers (e.g., 9) and signal names (e.g., `"SIGKILL"`).

An Overview of the Tk C Library

Main Programs and Command-Line Arguments

The `Tk_Main` procedure does the standard setup for your application's main window and event loop. The `Tk_ParseArgv` procedure parses command-line arguments. This procedure is designed for use by main programs. It uses a table of `Tk_ArgvInfo` records to describe your program's arguments. These procedures are illustrated by Example 47–14 on page 721.

If your extension uses the Tk library, you should link against the Tk stub library. In this case, you must call `Tk_InitStubs` in your extension's initialization routine.

Creating Windows

The `Tk_Init procedure` creates the main window for your application. The `Tk_CreateWindow` and `Tk_CreateWindowFromPath` are used to create windows for widgets. The actual creation of the window is delayed until an idle point. You can force the window to be created with `Tk_MakeWindowExist` or destroy a window with `Tk_DestroyWindow`.

The `Tk_MainWindow` procedure returns the handle on the application's main window. The `Tk_MapWindow` and `Tk_UnmapWindow` are used to display and withdraw a window, respectively. The `Tk_MoveToplevelWindow` call is used to position a top-level window. `Tk_GetNumMainWindows` returns the number of main windows opened by the current process.

Translate between window names and the `Tk_Window` type with `Tk_Name`, `Tk_PathName`, and `Tk_NameToWindow`. You can convert from an operating system window ID to the corresponding `Tk_Window` with `Tk_IdToWindow` procedure.

`Tk_SetClassProcs` registers widget-specific handlers to react to system wide font and color changes, to create platform-specific windows, and to handle modal input loops.

Application Name for Send

The name of the application is defined or changed with `Tk_SetAppName`. This name is used when other applications send it Tcl commands using the `send` command.

Configuring Windows

The configuration of a window includes its width, height, cursor, and so on. Tk provides a set of routines that configure a window and also cache the results. This makes it efficient to query these settings because the system does not need to be contacted. The window configuration routines are `Tk_ConfigureWindow`, `Tk_ResizeWindow`, `Tk_MoveWindow`, `Tk_MoveResizeWindow`, `Tk_SetWindowBorderWidth`, `Tk_DefineCursor`, `Tk_ChangeWindowAttributes`, `Tk_SetWindowBackground`, `Tk_SetWindowColormap`, `Tk_UndefineCursor`, `Tk_SetWindowBackgroundPixmap`, `Tk_SetWindowBorderPixmap`, `Tk_MoveWindow`, and `Tk_SetWindowBorder`.

Command Options

The `Tk_CreateOptionTable`, `Tk_SetOptions`, `Tk_GetOptionValue`, `Tk_GetOptionInfo`, `Tk_RestoreSavedOptions`, `Tk_FreeSavedOptions`, `Tk_InitOptions`, `Tk_FreeConfigOptions`, and `Tk_DeleteOptionTable` procedures are used to parse command line options with procedures that use `Tcl_Obj` values. Canvas item types are supported by `Tk_CanvasTagsOption`.

`Tk_AddOption` is used to add a value to the option database. This creates defaults for command line options that are not explicitly passed to widget commands.

Window Coordinates

The coordinates of a widget relative to the root window (the main screen) are returned by `Tk_GetRootCoords`. The `Tk_GetVRootGeometry` procedure returns the size and position of a window relative to the virtual root window. The `Tk_CoordsToWindow` procedure locates the window under a given coordinate.

Window Stacking Order

Control the stacking order of windows in the window hierarchy with `Tk_RestackWindow`. Windows higher in the stacking order obscure lower windows.

Window Information

Tk keeps lots of information associated with each window, or widget. The following calls are fast macros that return the information without calling the X server: `Tk_WindowId`, `Tk_Parent`, `Tk_StrictMotif`, `Tk_Display`, `Tk_DisplayName`, `Tk_ScreenNumber`, `Tk_Screen`, `Tk_X`, `Tk_Y`, `Tk_Width`, `Tk_Height`, `Tk_Changes`, `Tk_Attributes`, `Tk_IsMapped`, `Tk_IsTopLevel`, `Tk_IsContainer`, `Tk_IsEmbedded`, `Tk_ReqWidth`, `Tk_ReqHeight`, `Tk_InternalBorderWidth`, `Tk_MinReqWidth`, `Tk_MinReqHeight`, `Tk_InternalBorderLeft`, `Tk_InternalBorderRight`, `Tk_InternalBorderTop`, `Tk_InternalBorderBottom`, `Tk_Visual`, `Tk_Depth`, and `Tk_Colormap`.

Configuring Widget Attributes

The `Tk_ConfigureWidget` procedure parses command-line specification of attributes and allocates resources like colors and fonts. Related procedures include `Tk_Offset`, `Tk_ConfigureInfo`, `Tk_ConfigureValue`, and `Tk_FreeOptions`. `Tk_GetScrollInfo` and `Tk_GetScrollInfoObj` parse arguments to scrolling commands like the `xview` and `yview` widget operations.

The Selection and Clipboard

Retrieve the current selection with `Tk_GetSelection`. Clear the selection with `Tk_ClearSelection`. Register a handler for selection requests with `Tk_CreateSelHandler`. Unregister the handler with `Tk_DeleteSelHandler`. Claim ownership of the selection with `Tk_OwnSelection`. Manipulate the clipboard with `Tk_ClipboardClear` and `Tk_ClipboardAppend`.

Event Loop Interface

The standard event loop is implemented by `Tk_MainLoop`. If you write your own event loop, you need to call `Tcl_DoOneEvent` so that Tcl can handle its events. Call `Tcl_DoOneEvent` with `TCL_DONT_WAIT` until it returns 0 to indicate no more events need to be processed. If you read window events directly, (e.g., through `Tk_CreateGenericHandler`), you can dispatch to the correct handler for the event with `Tk_HandleEvent`. Note that most of the event loop is implemented in the Tcl library, except for `Tk_MainLoop` and the window event handler interface that are part of the Tk library. You can create handlers for file, timer, and idle events after this call. Restrict or delay events with the `Tk_RestrictEvent` procedure.

Handling Window Events

Use `Tk_CreateEventHandler` to set up a handler for specific window events. Widget implementations need a handler for expose and resize events, for example. Remove the registration with `Tk_DeleteEventHandler`. You can set up a handler for all window events with `Tk_CreateGenericHandler`. This is useful in some modal interactions where you have to poll for a certain event. If you get an event you do not want to handle yourself, you can push it onto the event queue with `Tk_QueueWindowEvent`. `Tk_CollapseMotionEvents` will eliminate extra motion events from the queue. `Tk_RestrictEvents` will filter and selectively delay events. Delete the event handler with `Tk_DeleteGenericHandler`. `Tk_CreateClientMessageHandler` is used for WM_PROTOCOL events. Delete the handler with `Tk_DeleteClientMessageHandler`.

Event Bindings

The routines that manage bindings are exported by the Tk library, so you can manage bindings yourself. For example, the canvas widget uses the API to implement bindings on canvas items. The procedures are `Tk_CreateBindingTable`, `Tk_DeleteBindingTable`, `Tk_CreateBinding`, `Tk_DeleteBinding`, `Tk_BindEvent`, `Tk_GetBinding`, `Tk_GetAllBindings`, and `Tk_DeleteAllBindings`.

Keyboard Grab

`Tk_Grab` and `Tk_Ungrab` change the state of any keyboard grab, which is used to restrict input to a particular window.

Handling Graphic Protocol Errors

You can handle graphic protocol errors by registering a handler with `Tk_CreateErrorHandler`. Unregister it with `Tk_DeleteErrorHandler`. UNIX has an asynchronous interface, so the error will be reported sometime after the offending call was made. You can call the Xlib XSynchronize routine to turn off the asynchronous behavior in order to help you debug.

Using the Resource Database

The `Tk_GetOption` procedure looks up items in the resource database. The resource class of a window is set with `Tk_SetClass`, and the current class setting is retrieved with `Tk_Class`.

Managing Bitmaps

Tk maintains a registry of bitmaps by name, (e.g., `gray50` and `questhead`). You can define new bitmaps with `Tk_DefineBitmap`, and you can get a handle on the bitmap from its name with `Tk_GetBitmap`. Related procedures include `Tk_NameOfBitmap`, `Tk_SizeOfBitmap`, `Tk_GetBitmapFromData`, `Tk_FreeBitmap`, `Tk_AllocBitmapFromObj`, `Tk_GetBitmapFromObj`, and `Tk_FreeBitmapFromObj`.

Creating New Image Types

`Tk_CreateImageType` and `Tk_InitImageArgs` are used to register the implementation of a new image type. The registration includes `image` command options and several procedures that call back into the implementation to support creation, display, and deletion of images. When an image changes, the widgets that display it are notified by calling `Tk_ImageChanged`. The `Tk_NameOfImage` procedure returns the Tcl name of an image. The `Tk_GetImageMasterData` returns the client data associated with an image type.

Using an Image in a Widget

The following routines support widgets that display images. `Tk_GetImage` maps from the name to a `Tk_Image` data structure. `Tk_RedrawImage` causes the image to update its display. `Tk_SizeOfImage` tells you how big it is. When the image is no longer in use, call `Tk_FreeImage`. The `Tk_DeleteImage` deletes an image.

Photo Image Types

One of the image types is `photo`, which has its own C interface for defining new formats. The job of a format handler is to read and write different image formats such as `GIF` or `JPEG` so that the `photo` image can display them. The `Tk_CreatePhotoImageFormat` procedure sets up the interface. There are several support routines for photo format handlers. The `Tk_FindPhoto` procedure maps from a photo name to its associated `Tk_PhotoHandle` data structure. The image is updated with `Tk_PhotoBlank`, `Tk_PhotoPutBlock`, and `Tk_PhotoPutZoomedBlock`. The image values can be obtained with `Tk_PhotoGetImage`. The size of the image can be manipulated with `Tk_PhotoExpand`, `Tk_PhotoGetSize`, and `Tk_PhotoSetSize`.

VI. Tcl and C

Canvas Object Support

The C interface for defining new canvas items is exported via the `Tk_CreateItemType` procedure. The description for a canvas item includes a set of procedures that the canvas widget uses to call the implementation of the canvas item type. The `Tk_GetItemTypes` returns information about all types of canvas objects. The support routines for the managers of new item types are `Tk_CanvasGetCoord`, `Tk_CanvasDrawableCoords`, `Tk_CanvasSetStippleOrigin`, `Tk_CanvasTkwin`, `Tk_CanvasWindowCoords`, and `Tk_CanvasEventuallyRedraw`. The following procedures help with the generation of postscript: `Tk_CanvasPsY`, `Tk_CanvasPsBitmap`, `Tk_CanvasPsColor`, `Tk_CanvasPsFont`, `Tk_CanvasPsPath`, and `Tk_CanvasPsStipple`. If you are manipulating text items directly, then you can use the `Tk_CanvasGetTextInfo` procedure to get a description of the selection state and other details about the text item.

Geometry Management

A widget requests a certain size with the `Tk_GeometryRequest` procedure. If it draws a border inside that area, it calls `Tk_SetInternalBorder`. The geometry manager responds to these requests, although the widget may get a different size. The `Tk_ManageGeometry` procedure sets up the relationship between the geometry manager and a widget. The `Tk_MaintainGeometry` procedure arranges for one window to stay at a fixed position relative to another widget. This is used by the place geometry manager. The relationship is broken with the `Tk_UnmaintainGeometry` call. The `Tk_SetGrid` call enables gridded geometry management. The grid is turned off with `Tk_UnsetGrid`.

String Identifiers (UIDS)

Tk maintains a database of string values such that a string appears in it only once. The `Tk_Uid` type refers to such a string. You can test for equality by using the value of `Tk_Uid`, which is the string's address, as an identifier. A `Tk_Uid` is used as a name in the various `GetByName` calls introduced below. The `Tk_GetUid` procedure installs a string into the registry.

Note: The table of `Tk_Uid` values is a memory leak. The leak is not serious under normal operation. However, if you continually register new strings as `Tk_Uid` values, then the hash table that records them continues to grow. This table is not cleaned up when Tk is finalized. The mapping from a string to a constant is better served by the `Tcl_GetIndexFromObj` call.

Colors, Colormaps, and Visuals

Use `Tk_GetColor`, `Tk_GetColorByValue`, `Tk_AllocColorFromObj`, and `Tk_GetColorFromObj` to allocate a color. You can retrieve the string name of a color with `Tk_NameOfColor`. When you are done using a color, you need to call `Tk_FreeColor` or `Tk_FreeColorFromObj`. You can get a graphics context for drawing a particular color with `Tk_GCForColor`. Colors are shared among widgets, so it is important to free them when you are done using them. Use `Tk_GetColormap` and `Tk_FreeColormap` to allocate and free a colormap. Colormaps are shared, if possible, so you should use these routines instead of the platform-specific routines to allocate colormaps. The window's visual type is set with `Tk_SetWindowVisual`. You can get a visual context with `Tk_GetVisual`.

3D Borders

The three-dimensional relief used for widget borders is supported by `Tk_Get3DBorder`, `Tk_3DBorderGC`, `Tk_Draw3DRectangle`, `Tk_Fill3DRectangle`, `Tk_Draw3DPolygon`, `Tk_Free3DBorder`, `Tk_Fill3DPolygon`, `Tk_3DVerticalBevel`, `Tk_3DHorizontalBevel`, `Tk_SetBackgroundFromBorder`, `Tk_NameOf3DBorder`, `Tk_3DBorderColor`, `Tk_Alloc3DBorderFromObj`, `Tk_Get3DBorderFromObj`, and `Tk_Free3DBorderFromObj`. Widgets use `Tk_DrawFocusHighlight` to draw their focus highlight.

Mouse Cursors

Allocate a cursor with `Tk_GetCursor`, `Tk_GetCursorFromData`, `Tk_GetCursorFromObj`, and `Tk_AllocCursorFromObj`. Map back to the name of the cursor with `Tk_NameOfCursor`. Release the cursor resource with `Tk_FreeCursor` or `Tk_FreeCursorFromObj`. `Tk_SetCaretPos` sets the per-window caret position, which is used for over-the-spot X Input Methods and Windows IME windows.

Fonts and Text Display

Allocate a font with `Tk_GetFont`, `Tk_GetFontFromObj`, or `Tk_AllocFontFromObj`. Get the name of a font with `Tk_NameOfFont`. Release the font with `Tk_FreeFont` or `Tk_FreeFontFromObj`. Once you have a font, you can get information about it with `Tk_FontId`, `Tk_FontMetrics`, and `Tk_PostscriptFontName`. `Tk_MeasureChars`, `Tk_TextWidth`, `Tk_DrawChars`, and `Tk_UnderlineChars` measure and display simple strings. `Tk_ComputeTextLayout`, `Tk_FreeTextLayout`, `Tk_DrawTextLayout`, `Tk_UnderlineTextLayout`, `Tk_CharBbox`, `Tk_DistanceToTextLayout`, `Tk_PointToChar`, `Tk_IntersectTextLayout`, and `Tk_TextLayoutToPostscript` measure and display multiline, justified text.

Graphics Contexts

A graphics context records information about colors, fonts, line drawing styles, and so on. Instead of specifying this information on every graphics operation, a graphics context is created first. Individual graphics operations specify a particular graphic context. Allocate a graphics context with `Tk_GetGC` and free it with `Tk_FreeGC`.

VI. Tcl and C

Allocate a Pixmap

A pixmap is a simple color image. Allocate and free pixmaps with `Tk_GetPixmap` and `Tk_FreePixmap`.

Screen Measurements

Translate between strings like `4c` or `72p` and screen distances with `Tk_GetPixels`, `Tk_GetPixelsFromObj`, `Tk_GetMMFromObj`, and `Tk_GetScreenMM`. The first call returns pixels (integers); the second returns millimeters as a floating point number.

Relief Style

Window frames are drawn with a particular 3D relief such as raised, sunken, or grooved. Translate between relief styles and names with `Tk_GetRelief`, `Tk_GetReliefFromObj`, and `Tk_NameOfRelief`.

Text Anchor Positions

Anchor positions specify the position of a window within its geometry parcel. Translate between strings and anchor positions with `Tk_GetAnchor`, `Tk_GetAnchorFromObj`, and `Tk_NameOfAnchor`.

Line Cap Styles

The line cap defines how the end point of a line is drawn. Translate between line cap styles and names with `Tk_GetCapStyle` and `Tk_NameOfCapStyle`.

Line Join Styles

The line join style defines how the junction between two line segments is drawn. Translate between line join styles and names with `Tk_GetJoinStyle` and `Tk_NameOfJoinStyle`.

Dashed Lines

`Tk_GetDash` converts from a string to a dash pattern.

Text Justification Styles

Translate between line justification styles and names with `Tk_GetJustify`, `Tk_GetJustifyFromObj`, and `Tk_NameOfJustify`.

Atoms

An atom is an integer that references a string that has been registered with the system. Tk maintains a cache of the atom registry to avoid contacting the system when atoms are used. Use `Tk_InternAtom` to install an atom in the registry, and `Tk_GetAtomName` to return the name given an atom.

X Resource ID Management

Each window system resource like a color or pixmap has a resource ID associated with it. The `Tk_FreeXId` call releases an ID so it can be reused. This is used, for example, by routines like `Tk_FreeColor` and `Tk_FreePixmap`.

Windows Application Handles

`Tk_GetHINSTANCE` returns the global application handle for Windows. `Tk_GetHWND` returns the Windows `HWND` identifier for the Tk window. `Tk_HWNDToWindow` maps from the Windows handle to the corresponding Tk window.

VI. Tcl and C

P A R T

VII

Changes

Part VII describes the changes between versions of Tcl and Tk. These chapters are useful to quickly determine what features were added in each release.

Chapter 51 describes changes in Tcl 7.4 and Tk 4.0.

Chapter 52 describes changes in Tcl 7.5 and Tk 4.1.

Chapter 53 describes changes in Tcl 7.6 and Tk 4.2.

The Tcl and Tk version numbers were unified in the next release, Tcl/Tk 8.0, which is described in Chapter 54.

Chapter 55 describes changes in Tcl/Tk 8.1.

Chapter 56 describes changes in Tcl/Tk 8.2.

Chapter 57 describes changes in Tcl/Tk 8.3.

Chapter 58 describes changes in Tcl/Tk 8.4.

VII

Changes

C H A P T E R **51**

Tcl 7.4/Tk 4.0

This chapter has notes about upgrading your application to Tcl 7.4 and Tk 4.0
from earlier versions of Tk such as Tk 3.6. This includes notable new
features that you may want to take advantage of as well as things that
need to be fixed because of incompatible changes.

*P*orting your scripts from any of the Tk
version 3 releases is easy. Not that many things have changed. The sections in
this chapter summarize what has changed in Tk 4.0 and what some of the new
commands are.

wish

The *wish* shell no longer requires a `-file` (or `-f`) argument, so you can drop this
from your script header lines. This flag is still valid but no longer necessary.

The class name of the application is set from the name of the script file
instead of always being `Tk`. If the script is `/usr/local/bin/foobar`, then the
class is set to `Foobar`, for example.

Obsolete Features

Several features that were replaced in previous versions are now completely
unsupported.

The variable that contains the version number is `tk_version`. The ancient
(version 1) `tkVersion` is no longer supported.

Button widgets no longer have `activate` and `deactivate` operations.
Instead, configure their `state` attribute.

Menus no longer have `enable` and `disable` operations. Instead, configure their `state` attribute.

The `cget` Operation

All widgets support a `cget` operation that returns the current value of the specified configuration option. The following two commands are equivalent:

```
lindex [$w config option] 4
$w cget option
```

Nothing breaks with this change, but you should enjoy this feature.

Input Focus Highlight

Each widget can have an input focus highlight, which is a border that is drawn in color when the widget has the input focus. This border is outside the border used to draw the 3D relief for widgets. It has the pleasant visual effect of providing a little bit of space around widgets, even when they do not have the input focus. The addition of the input focus highlight does not break anything, but it changes the appearance of your interfaces a little. In particular, the highlight on a canvas obscures objects that are at its edge. See page 616 for a description of the generic widget attributes related to the input focus highlight.

Bindings

The hierarchy of bindings has been fixed so that it is actually useful to define bindings at each of the global (i.e., `all`), class, and instance levels. The new `bindtags` command defines the order among these sources of binding information. You can also introduce new binding classes (e.g., `InsertMode`), and bind things to that class. Use the `bindtags` command to insert this class into the binding hierarchy. The order of binding classes in the `bindtags` command determines the order in which bindings are triggered. Use `break` in a binding command to stop the progression, or use `continue` to go on to the next level.

```
bindtags $w [list all Text InsertMode $w]
```

The various `Request` events have disappeared: `CirculateRequest`, `ConfigureRequest`, `MapRequest`, and `ResizeRequest`. The `Keymap` event is gone, too.

Extra modifier keys are ignored when matching events. Although you can still use the `Any` wild card modifier, it is no longer necessary. The `Alt` and `Meta` modifiers are set up in a general way so that they are associated with the `Alt_L`, `Alt_R`, `Meta_L`, and `Meta_R` keysyms.

Chapter 29 describes bindings starting at page 435.

Scrollbar Interface

The interface between scrollbars and the scrollable widgets has changed. Happily, the change is transparent to most scripts. If you hook your scrollbars to widgets in the straightforward way, the new interface is compatible. If you use the `xview` and `yview` widget commands directly, however, you might need to modify your code. The old interface still works, but there are new features of these operations that give you even better control. You can also query the view state, so you do not need to watch the scroll `set` commands to keep track of what is going on. Finally, scrollable widgets are constrained so that the end of their data remains stuck at the bottom (right) of their display. In most cases, nothing is broken by this change. Chapter 33 describes the scrollbar protocol starting at page 501.

pack info

Version 3 of Tk introduced a new syntax for the `pack` command, but the old syntax was still supported. This continues to be true in nearly all cases except the `pack info` command. If you are still using the old packer format, you should probably take this opportunity to convert to the new packer syntax.

The problem with `pack info` is that its semantics changed. The new operation used to be known as `pack newinfo`. In the old packer, `pack info` returned a list of all the slaves of a window and their packing configuration. Now `pack info` returns the packing configuration for a particular slave. You must first use the `pack slaves` command to get the list of all the slaves and then use the (new) `pack info` to get their configuration information. Chapter 25 describes the pack geometry manager starting at page 396.

Focus

The focus mechanism has been cleaned up to support different focus windows on different screens. The `focus` command takes a `-displayof` argument. Tk remembers which widget inside each toplevel has the focus. When the focus is given to a toplevel by the window manager, Tk automatically assigns focus to the right widget. The `-lastfor` argument queries which widget in a toplevel will get the focus by this means. Chapter 39 describes focus starting at page 603.

The `focus default` and `focus none` commands are no longer supported. There is no real need for `focus default` anymore, and `focus none` can be achieved by passing an empty string to the regular `focus` command.

The `tk_focusFollowsMouse` procedure changes from the default explicit focus model where a widget must claim the focus to one in which moving the mouse into a widget automatically gives it the focus.

The `tk_focusNext` and `tk_focusPrev` procedures implement keyboard traversal of the focus among widgets. Most widgets have bindings for `<Tab>` and `<Shift-Tab>` that cycle the focus among widgets.

The send Command

The `send` command has been changed so that it does not time out after five seconds but instead waits indefinitely for a response. Specify the `-async` option if you do not want to wait for a result. You can also specify an alternate display with the `-displayof` option. Chapter 43 describes `send` starting on page 648.

The name of an application can be set and queried with the new `tk appname` command. Use this instead of `winfo name "."`.

Because of the changes in the `send` implementation, it is not possible to use `send` between Tk 4.0 applications and earlier versions.

Internal Button Padding

Buttons and labels have new defaults for the amount of padding around their text. There is more padding now, so your buttons get bigger if you use the default `padX` and `padY` attributes. The old defaults were one pixel for both attributes. The new defaults are `3m` for `padX` and `1m` for `padY`, which map into three pixels and ten pixels on my display.

There is a difference between buttons and the other button-like widgets. An extra two pixels of padding is added, in spite of all `padX` and `padY` settings in the case of simple buttons. If you want your checkbuttons, radiobuttons, menubuttons, and buttons with all the same dimensions, you'll need two extra pixels of padding for everything but simple buttons.

Radiobutton Value

The default value for a radiobutton is no longer the name of the widget. Instead, it is an empty string. Make sure that you specify a `-value` option when setting up your radiobuttons.

Entry Widget

The `scrollCommand` attribute changed to `xScrollCommand` to be consistent with other widgets that scroll horizontally. The `view` operation changed to the `xview` operation for the same reason. Chapter 34 describes the entry widget starting on page 507.

The `delete` operation has changed the meaning of the second index so that the second index refers to the character immediately following the affected text. The selection operations have changed in a similar fashion. The `sel.last` index refers to the character immediately following the end of the selection, so deleting from `sel.first` to `sel.last` still works. The default bindings have been updated, of course, but if you have custom bindings, you must fix them.

Menus

The menu associated with a menubutton must be a child widget of the menubutton. Similarly, the menu for a cascade menu entry must be a child of the menu.

The `@y` index for a menu always returns a valid index, even if the mouse cursor is outside any entry. In this case, it simply returns the index of the closest entry, instead of `none`.

The `selector` attribute is now `selectColor`.

The `postcascade` operation posts the menu of a `cascade` entry:

```
$menu postcascade index
```

The insert operation adds a menu entry before a specified entry:

```
$menu insert index type options...
```

Chapter 30 describes menus starting at page 462.

Listboxes

Listboxes changed quite a bit in Tk 4.0. See Chapter 35 for all the details. There are now four Motif-like selection styles, and two of these support disjoint selections. The `tk_listboxSingleSelect` procedure no longer exists. Instead, configure the `selectMode` attribute of the listbox. A listbox has an active element, which is drawn with an underline. It is referenced with the `active` index keyword.

The selection commands for listboxes have changed. Change:

```
$listbox select from index1
$listbox select to index2
```

to:

```
$listbox select anchor index1
$listbox select set anchor index2
```

The `set` operation takes two indices, and `anchor` is a valid index, which typically corresponds to the start of a selection.

You can selectively clear the selection and query whether there is a selection in the listbox. The command to clear the selection has changed. It requires one or two indices. Change:

```
$listbox select clear
```

to:

```
$listbox select clear 0 end
```

No geometry Attribute

The frame, toplevel, and listbox widgets no longer have a `geometry` attribute. Use the `width` and `height` attributes instead. The `geometry` attribute was confused with geometry specifications for top-level windows. The use of `width` and `height` is more consistent. Note that for listboxes the `width` and `height` are in terms of lines and characters, while for frames and toplevels, they are in screen units.

Text Widget

The tags and marks of the text widgets have been cleaned up a bit, justification and spacing are supported, variable tab stops can be defined, and you can embed widgets in the text display.

A mark now has a gravity — either left or right — that determines what happens when characters are inserted at the mark. With right gravity you get the old behavior: The mark gets pushed along by the inserted text by sticking to the right-hand character. With left gravity it remains stuck. The default is right gravity. The `mark gravity` operation changes it.

When text is inserted, it picks up only tags that are present on both sides of the insert point. Previously it would inherit the tags from the character to the left of the insert mark. You can also override this default behavior by supplying tags to the insert operation.

The widget scan operation supports horizontal scrolling. Instead of using marks like `@y`, you need a mark like `@x,y`.

For a description of the new features, see Chapter 36.

Color Attributes

Table 51–1 lists the names of the color attributes that changed. These attributes are described in more detail in Chapter 41 starting at page 620.

Table 51–1 Changes in color attribute names.

Tk 3.6	Tk4.0
`selector`	`selectColor`
`Scrollbar.activeForeground`	`Scrollbar.activeBackground`
`Scrollbar.background`	`troughColor`
`Scrollbar.foreground`	`Scrollbar.background`
`Scale.activeForeground`	`Scale.activeBackground`
`Scale.background`	`troughColor`
`Scale.sliderForeground`	`Scale.background`
`(did not exist)`	`highlightBackground`
`(did not exist)`	`highlightColor`

Color Allocation and `tk colormodel`

In Tk 3.6, color allocations could fail if the colormap was full. In this case, Tk would revert its colormodel to monochrome and use only black and white. The `tk colormodel` command was used to query or set the colormodel. In Tk 4.0, color allocations do not fail. Instead, the closest possible color is allocated. Because of this, the `tk colormodel` operation is no longer supported. Use the `winfo visual` command, which is described on page 624, to find out the characteristics of your display.

Canvas `scrollincrement`

The canvas widget changed the `scrollIncrement` attribute to a pair of attributes: `xScrollIncrement` and `yScrollIncrement`. The default for these is now one-tenth the width (height) of the canvas instead of one pixel. Scrolling by one page scrolls by nine-tenths of the canvas display.

The Selection

The selection support has been generalized in Tk 4.0 to allow use of other selections such as the CLIPBOARD and SECONDARY selections. The changes do not break anything, but you should check out the new `clipboard` command. Some other toolkits, notably OpenLook, can paste data only from the clipboard. Chapter 38 describes the selection starting at page 591.

The `bell` Command

The `bell` command rings the bell associated with the terminal. You need to use the *xset* program to modify the parameters of the bell such as volume and duration. This command is described on page 497.

Tcl 7.5/Tk 4.1

Tk 4.1 is notable for its cross-platform support. Your Tk scripts can run on
Windows, Macintosh, and UNIX. The associated Tcl release, 7.5, saw
significant changes in event-driven I/O, network sockets, and multiple
interpreters.

Cross-platform support, network sockets,
multiple Tcl interpreters, and an enhanced `foreach` command are the highlights
of Tcl 7.5 and Tk 4.1.

Cross-Platform Scripts

Cross-platform support lets a Tcl/Tk script run unchanged on UNIX, Windows,
and Macintosh. However, you can still have platform dependencies in your program. The most obvious dependency is if your script executes other programs or
uses C-level extensions. These need to be ported for your script to continue to
work.

File Name Manipulation

File naming conventions vary across platforms. New file operations were
added to help you manipulate file names in a platform-independent manner.
These are the `file join`, `file split`, and `file pathtype` operations, which are
described on page 110. Additional commands to copy, delete, and rename files
were added in Tcl 7.6

Newline Translations

Windows and Macintosh have different conventions for representing the end of line in files. These differences are handled automatically by the new I/O subsystem. However, you can use the new `fconfigure` command described on page 231 to control the translations.

The `tcl_platform` Variable

In practice you may need a small amount of platform-specific code. The `tcl_platform` array holds information about the computer and operating system that your script is running on. This array is described on page 193. You can use a script file with the name of the platform to isolate all your platform-specific code. The following command sources either `unix.tcl`, `windows.tcl`, or `macintosh.tcl` from your script library:

```
source [file join $lib $tcl_platform(platform).tcl]
```

The `console` Command

The Windows and Macintosh versions of *wish* have a built-in console. The commands you enter in the console are evaluated in the main Tcl interpreter, but the console is really implemented in another Tcl interpreter to avoid conflicts. You can show and hide the console with the `console` command, which is described on page 29.

The `clock` Command

The `clock` command eliminates the need to `exec date` to get the time of day in Tcl. The equivalent is:

```
clock format [clock seconds]
```

The `format` operation takes an optional format string that lets you control the date and time string. There is also `clock scan` to parse clock values, and `clock clicks` to get high resolution clock values. The `clock` command is described on page 183.

The `load` Command

The `load` command supports shared libraries (i.e., DLLs) that implement new Tcl commands in compiled code. With this feature, the preferred way to package extensions is as a shared library. This eliminates the need to compile custom versions of *wish* if you use extensions. The details about creating shared libraries are described on page 697. For example, you could load the `Tix` library with:

```
load libtix.so Tix
```

The `info` command added two related operations, `sharedlibextention` and `nameofexecutable`, which are described on page 192.

The package Command

The package command provides an alternate way to organize script libraries. It also supports extensions that are added with the load command. The package command supports a provide/require model where packages are provided by scripts in a library, and your application specifies what it needs with package require commands. The package facility supports multiple versions of a package, if necessary. Packages are described on page 173.

Multiple foreach loop variables

This is one of my favorite features. The foreach command supports multiple loop variables and multiple value lists. This means that you can assign values to multiple variables during each loop iteration. The values can come from the same list or from lists that are processed in parallel. Multiple foreach loop variables are described on page 81. For example, you can iterate through the contents of an array with:

```
foreach {name value} [array get arrName] {
    # arrName($name) is $value
}
```

Event Loop Moves from Tk to Tcl

To support network sockets, the event loop was moved from Tk to Tcl. This means that the after and update commands are now part of Tcl. The fileevent command was added to support nonblocking I/O. The vwait command was added to Tcl and is equivalent to the tkwait variable command. Event-driven I/O is described in Chapter 16 starting on page 227.

The tkerror command has been replaced by bgerror. This is the procedure that is called when an error occurs while processing an event. Backwards compatibility is provided if you already define tkerror. These procedures are described on page 202.

Network Sockets

The socket command provides access to TCP/IP sockets. There are C APIs to define new *channels*, and there are extensions that provide UDP and other protocols. Chapter 17 describes sockets starting on page 239. Example 43–4 on page 653 uses sockets as a replacement for the Tk send command.

`info hostname`

The `info hostname` command was added to find out your host identifier.

The `fconfigure` Command

The best way to use sockets is with event-driven I/O. The `fileevent` command provides part of the solution. You also need to be able to control the blocking behavior and buffering modes of sockets. The `fconfigure` command lets you do this and more. You can also control the newline translation modes and query socket-specific settings. The `fconfigure` command is described on page 231.

Multiple Interpreters and Safe-Tcl

Chapter 19 describes the new `interp` command and the Safe-Tcl security mechanism. You can create multiple Tcl interpreters in your application and control them with the `interp` command. You create command aliases so that the interpreters can exchange Tcl commands. If an interpreter is created in a safe mode, then its set of Tcl commands is restricted so that its scripts cannot harm your computer or application. However, with aliases you can give the untrusted scripts limited access to resources.

The `grid` Geometry Manager

Chapter 26 describes the new `grid` geometry manager that provides a table-like metaphor for arranging widgets. Like `pack`, `grid` is constraint-based, so the grid automatically adjusts if widgets change size or if widgets are added and deleted. The `grid` command was influenced by the `blt_table` geometry manager, but it is a whole new implementation.

The Text Widget

Several new operations were added to the text widget. The `dump` operation provides a way to get all the information out of the widget, including information about tags, marks, and embedded windows. The `mark next` and `mark previous` operations let you search for marks. The `tag prevrange` is the complement of the existing `tag nextrange` operation.

The Entry Widget

The `bbox` operation was added to the entry widget. This is used to refine the bindings that do character selection and set the input cursor.

Tcl 7.6/Tk 4.2

Tk 4.2 saw improvements in its cross-platform support., including virtual events, additions to the `file` command, improvements to the `exec` command on Windows, and the addition of common dialogs for choosing colors and selecting files. The `grid` geometry manager was rebuilt to improve its layout algorithm.

Grid saw a major rewrite for Tk 4.2 to improve its layout algorithm. Cross-platform scripts were enhanced by the addition of standard dialogs and virtual events. Tcl 7.6 saw improvements in `exec` and pipelines on Windows. The Macintosh version got a significant performance boost from a new memory allocator.

More `file` Operations

The `file` command was rounded out with `copy`, `rename`, `delete`, and `mkdir` operations. These operations are described on page 112.

Virtual Events

The new `event` command defines virtual events like `<<Cut>>` `<<Copy>>` and `<<Paste>>`. These virtual events map to different physical events on different platforms. For example, `<<Copy>>` is `<Control-c>` on Windows and `<Command-c>` on Macintosh. You can write your scripts in terms of virtual events, and you can define new virtual events for your application. You can also use the `event` command to generate events for testing purposes. Virtual events and the `event` command are described starting at page 446.

Standard Dialogs

Several standard dialogs were added to Tk. These let you display alerts, prompt the user, choose colors, and select files using dialogs that are implemented in native look for each platform. For example, to ask the user a yes/no question:

```
tk_messageBox -type yesno \
    -message "Ok to proceed?" \
    -icon question
=> yes
```

To open an existing file:

```
set file [tk_getOpenFile]
```

The standard dialogs are described in Chapter 39 starting at page 599.

New grid Geometry Manager

The grid geometry manager was overhauled to improve its layout algorithm, and there were several user-visible changes. The weights on rows and columns that affect resize behavior were changed from floating point values to integers. A -pad row and column attribute was added to provide padding for a whole row or column. The columnconfigure and rowconfigure operations now return the current settings if given no arguments. There are two new grid operations. The update operation forces an update of the grid layout. The remove operation removes a widget from the grid but remembers all its grid settings, so it is easy to put it back into the grid later.

Macintosh unsupported1 Command

The unsupported1 command provides access to different window styles on the Macintosh. If supported, it might be a style operation in the wm command, but it is Macintosh-specific, so it is not fully supported. However, you can use it to get several different styles of Macintosh windows. This command is described on page 489.

Tcl/Tk 8.0

Tcl 8.0 includes an on-the-fly byte code compiler that improves performance of scripts from two to 20 times depending on what commands they use. The Tk version number was set to match Tcl. Tk 8.0 uses native buttons, menus, menubars, and scrollbars. Font objects allow flexible font handling in a platform-independent way.

Tcl 8.0 added a byte-code compiler that improves performance dramatically. The compiler is transparent to Tcl scripts, so you do not have to do anything special to take advantage of it. The other main addition to Tcl is support of binary data. It is now safe to read binary data into Tcl variables, and new commands convert between strings and binary representations.

Tk 8.0 has native look and feel on UNIX, Windows, and Macintosh. This is due to native buttons, native menus, native scrollbars, and a new cross-platform menu bar facility. A new cross-platform font facility improves the font support. Tk also has support for application embedding, which is used in the Web browser plug-in described in Chapter 20.

The Tcl Compiler

The Tcl Compiler is an *on-the-fly* compiler that is virtually transparent to Tcl scripts. The compiler translates a script to byte codes the first time it evaluates it. If the script is evaluated again, such as in a loop or in a procedure body, then the byte codes are executed and the translation step is saved. If a procedure is redefined, then the compiler discards any translated byte codes for it.

The compiler uses a dual-ported object model instead of the simple string-based model used in earlier versions of Tcl. The dual-ported objects hold a string value and a native representation of that string such as an integer, double-precision floating point value, or compiler byte codes. This makes it possible to save translations between strings and the native representations. The object model is described in Chapter 47 starting at page 703.

The performance improvement for your application will depend on what features you use. Math expressions and list accesses are much faster. Overall you should expect a factor of 2 speedup, and I have heard reports of 10 and 20 times improvement in parts of some applications.

Compile-Time Errors

The compiler catches some sorts of errors earlier than the pure interpreted version. The first time a compiler runs a procedure, it translates the whole thing to byte codes first. If there are syntax errors at the end of the procedure, it prevents any code in the procedure from running.

A similar problem occurs with list data. If a string is not a perfect list, then the list commands will fail when parsing it, even if they do not use the damaged part of the list. For example, `lindex` used to process only enough of a list to find the requested element. In Tcl 8.0 the whole list is converted into a native representation. Errors at the end of a list will prevent you from getting elements at the beginning. This is mainly an issue when you use list operations on arbitrary input data.

Binary String Support

Tcl now supports binary data. This means that an embedded NULL byte no longer terminates a value. Instead, Tcl keeps a byte count for its string objects. This is facilitated by the switch from simple strings to dual-ported objects.

The `binary format` and `binary scan` commands support conversions between binary data and strings. These are described on page 59. The `unsupported0` command was improved and became the `fcopy` command, which is described on page 250.

Namespaces

Chapter 14 describes the Tcl namespace facility that partitions the global scope for variables and procedures. Namespaces are optional. Simple scripts can avoid them, but larger applications can use them for structuring. Library packages should also use namespaces to facility code sharing without conflict.

Safe-Tcl

Hidden commands were added to the Safe-Tcl security model. Instead of removing unsafe commands from an interpreter, the commands are hidden. The master can invoke hidden commands inside a slave. This is necessary so that the command sees the correct context. This adds new operations to the `interp` command: `invokehidden`, `hide`, `expose`, and `hidden`. Hidden commands are described on page 297.

Initialization of a safe interpreter with a *safe base* that supports auto loading and a standard `exit` alias has been abstracted into a Tcl interface. The `safe::interpCreate` and `safe::interpInit` procedures create or initialize a slave with the safe base. The `safe::interpDelete` procedure cleans up. The safe base is described on page 300.

To support the `Trusted` security policy, the `interp marktrusted` command was added. This promotes an unsafe interpreter back into a trusted one. Of course, only the master can do this.

New lsort

The `lsort` command was reimplemented. The new implementation is reentrant, which means that you can use `lsort` inside a sorting function called by `lsort`. New options have lessened the need for custom sorting procedures, too. The `-dictionary` option sorts cases together, and it handles numbers better. The `-index` option sorts lists on a key field. These are described on page 70.

tcl_precision Variable

The `tcl_precision` variable was removed in the 8.0p2 release and added back in the 8.0.3 release. Its default value was increased from 6 to 12, which should be enough for most applications.

Year 2000 Convention

The `clock` command now implements the following standard convention for two-digit year names:

70–99 map to 1970–1999.

00–69 map to 2000–2069.

Actually, the ability to parse a date value after 2037 and before 1903 may be limited on your system by the size of an integer (e.g., 32-bits) and the clock *epoch*, which is January 1, 1970 on Windows and most UNIX systems.

Http Package

A Tcl implementation of the HTTP/1.0 protocol was added to the Tcl script library. The `http::geturl` command is described on page 251.

Serial Line I/O

Support for serial line devices was added to `fconfigure`. The `-mode` argument specifies the baud rate, parity setting, and the number of data and stop bits. The `-mode` option to `fconfigure` is described on page 234.

Windows has some special device names that always connect you to the serial line devices when you use `open`. They are `com1` and `com2`. UNIX has names for serial devices in `/dev`. Interactive applications can open the current terminal with `/dev/tty`.

As of this writing, there is no way to open serial devices on the Macintosh. I expect a new `serial` command for this purpose, or possibly a flag to `open`.

Platform-Independent Fonts

A platform-independent font-naming system was added in Tk 8.0. Names like `times 10 bold` are interpreted on all platforms. The `font` command lets you create font objects that can be associated with widgets. The `font metrics` command returns detailed size information. The `font` command is described on page 640.

The `tk scaling` Command

The `tk scaling` command queries or sets the mapping from pixels to points. Points are used with fonts, and points and other screen measures are used in the canvas. The `tk scaling` command is described on page 669.

Application Embedding

Tk supports application embedding. Frames and toplevels have a `-container` attribute that indicates that they embed another application. This is necessary for geometry management and focus protocols. Frames and toplevels have a `-use` parameter that embeds them into an existing window. *Wish* also takes a `-use` command-line argument. Embedding is described on pages 489 and 312.

Native Menus and Menubars

Tk 8.0 has a native menubar mechanism. You define a menu and associate it with a toplevel. On the Macintosh, this menu appears along the top of the screen when the window is activated. On Windows and UNIX, the menubar appears along the top of the window. This facility is described on page 464.

Tear-off menus now track any changes to the menu they were created from. As part of this, the `-transient` attribute was replaced with a `-type` attribute.

You can create multicolumn menus with the `-columnbreak` attribute.

CDE Border Width

On UNIX, the default border width changed from two to one to match the CDE look and feel.

Native Buttons and Scrollbars

Buttons, menus, and scrollbars are native widgets on Windows and Macintosh. This goes a long way to providing your applications with a native look. The bindings on the text and entry widgets were also tuned to match platform standard bindings. See page 392 for an example of the same Tk program on all platforms.

Buttons on all platforms support a `-default` attribute, which has three values: `active`, `normal`, and `disabled`. The `active` state displays like a default button. The `normal` state displays like a regular button, but leaves room for the highlight used in the `active` state. The `disabled` state, which is the default, may be smaller. You still need to program a key binding that invokes the button.

Images in Text Widgets

The text widget supports embedded images. They work much like the embedded windows but provide a more efficient way to embed images. These are described on page 544.

No Errors from `destroy`

The `destroy` command used to raise an error if the window did not exist. Now it does not.

grid rowconfigure

The `grid columnconfigure` and `rowconfigure` commands take an argument that specifies a row or column. This value can be a list:

```
grid columnconfigure {0 3} -weight 1
```

The Patch Releases

There was a hiatus in the development of the 8.0 release as John Ousterhout left Sun Microsystems to form Scriptics Corporation. The 8.0p2 release was made in the fall of 1997, about the same time the first alpha release of 8.1 was made. Almost a year later, there were a series of patch releases: 8.0.3, 8.0.4, and 8.0.5, which were made in conjunction with releases of the *TclPro* development tools. The main changes in these patch releases were in C APIs, which were added to support *TclPro Wrapper* and *TclPro Compiler*. These tools are introduced on

page 200. There were only a few changes after 8.0p2 that were visible to Tcl
script writers, and these are documented here.

fconfigure -error

The fconfigure -error option was added so that you can find out whether
or not an asynchronous socket connection attempt has failed. It returns an
empty string if the connection completed successfully. Otherwise, it returns the
error message.

tcl_platform(debug)

A new element was added to the tcl_platform variable to indicate that Tcl
was compiled with debugging symbols. The motivation for this is the fact that a
Windows application compiled with debugging symbols cannot safely load a DLL
that has been compiled without debugging symbols. Similarly, an application
compiled without debugging symbols cannot safely load a DLL that does have
debugging symbols. The problem is an artifact of the Microsoft C runtime
library.

When you build Tcl DLLs with debugging symbols their name has a trailing
"d", such as tcl80d.dll instead of tcl80.dll. By testing tcl_platform(debug),
a savvy application can attempt to load a matching DLL.

tcl_findLibrary

The tcl_findLibrary procedure was added to help extensions find their
script library directory. This is used by Tk and other extensions. The big picture
is that Tcl has a complex search path that it uses to find its own script library. It
searches relative to the location of *tclsh* or *wish* and assumes a standard installation or a standard build environment. The search supports sites that have several Tcl installations and helps extensions find their correct script library. The
usage of tcl_findLibrary is:

        tcl_findLibrary *base version patch script enVar varName*

The *base* is the prefix of the script library directory name. The *version* is
the main version number (e.g., "8.0"). The *patch* is the full patch level (e.g.,
"8.0.3"). The *script* is the initialization script to source from the directory. The
enVar names an environment variable that can be used to override the default
search path. The *varName* is an output parameter that is set to the name of the
directory found by tcl_findLibrary. A side effect of tcl_findLibrary is to
source the script from the directory. An example call is:

        tcl_findLibrary tk 8.0 8.0.3 tk.tcl TK_LIBRARY tk_library
    tcl_findLibrary is described on page 180.

`auto_mkindex_old`

The `auto_mkindex` procedure was reimplemented by Michael McLennan to support [incr Tcl] classes and methods. This changed the semantics somewhat so that all procedures are always indexed. Previously, only procedures defined with the word "`proc`" starting at the beginning of a line were indexed. The new implementation sources code into a safe interpreter and watches for `proc` commands however they are executed, not how they are typed into the source file. The old version of `auto_mkindex` was saved as `auto_mkindex_old` for those applications that used the trick of indenting procedure definitions to hide them from the indexing process.

Windows Keysyms for Start and Menu Keys

The Microsoft keyboards have special keys that bring up the Start menu and trigger menu traversal. New keysyms `App`, `Menu_L`, and `Menu_R` were added for these keys.

The `MouseWheel` Event

The `MouseWheel` event was added to support the scrolling wheel built into Microsoft mice. There is a `%D` event parameter that gets replaced with a positive or negative number to indicate relative scrolling motion.

Transparent Fill on Canvas Text

Canvas text items now honor the convention that an empty `fill` attribute turns them transparent. This convention was previously implemented for all other canvas item types. This feature makes it easy to hide items with:

```
$canvas itemconfigure item -fill ""
```

`safe::loadTk`

This procedure was extended to take a `-display` *displayname* argument so that you can control where the main window of the safe interpreter is created. Its `-use` argument was extended to take either window IDs or Tk window pathnames.

Tcl/Tk 8.1

Tcl/Tk 8.1 features Unicode support for internationalization, thread safety, and
a new regular expression package.

Tcl 8.1 should probably have been
called Tcl 9.0. The internal changes required to support Unicode caused a major
overhaul that touched nearly the entire implementation. At the same time, the
code base was cleaned up so that it could be used in multithreaded environments, and it added a platform-independent dynamic loading facility (i.e., stub
libraries). Finally, thanks to Henry Spencer, an all new regular expression package was added that brings Advanced Regular Expressions to Tcl. However, in
spite of all these changes, scripts written for earlier versions of Tcl are very compatible with Tcl 8.1.

Unicode and Internationalization

The effect of Unicode on Tcl scripts is actually very limited. There is a new backslash sequence, \u*XXXX*, that specifies a 16-bit Unicode character. There are also
facilities to work with character set encodings and message catalogs.

fconfigure -encoding

The Tcl I/O system supports character set translations. It automatically
converts files to Unicode when it reads them in, and it converts them to the
native system encoding during output. The `fconfigure -encoding` option can be
used to specify alternate encodings for files. This option is described on page 219.

The encoding Command

The encoding command provides access to the basic encoding mechanism used in Tcl. The encoding convertfrom and convertto operations convert strings between different encodings. The encoding system operation queries and sets the encoding used by the operating system. The encoding command is described on page 222.

The msgcat Package

Message catalogs are implemented by the msgcat package, which is described on page 226. A message catalog stores translations of user messages into other languages. Tcl makes message catalogs easy to use.

UTF-8 and Unicode C API

The effects of Unicode on the Tcl C API is more fundamental. Tcl uses UTF-8 to represent Unicode internally. This encoding is compatible with ASCII, so Tcl extensions that pass only ASCII strings to Tcl continue to work normally. However, to take advantage of Unicode, Tcl extensions need to translate strings into UTF-8 or Unicode before calling the Tcl C library. There is a C API for this. An example of its use is shown on page 718.

Thread Safety

The Tcl C library is thread-safe. This means that you can use Tcl in an application that uses threads. The threading model for Tcl is a thread can have one or more Tcl interpreters, but a Tcl interpreter cannot be used by different threads. For communication between threads, Tcl provides the ability to send Tcl scripts to an interpreter in another thread.

The Tcl C library provides mutex variables, condition variables, and thread local storage. These primitives are used by Tcl internally, and they are meant to be used by Tcl extensions to serialize access to their own data structures. The Tcl library allows different implementations of the threading primitives. This is done to support Unix, Windows, and Macintosh. Tcl uses native threads on Windows, and Posix pthreads on Unix. MacOS does not have true threads, so it is easy to provide the required thread API.

The testthread Command

Tcl 8.1 does not export threads to the script level, except through the testthread testing command. (Chapter 21 describes the Thread extension built for Tcl 8.3 and Tcl 8.4 that extends the testthread package described here.) You can try out testthread by compiling the *tcltest* program instead of the regular *tclsh* shell. Table 55–1 describes the testthread operations, which are implemented in the `generic/tclThreadTest.c` file. These operations are likely to be similar to those of the API provided by the more general threading extension, but you should check the documentation associated with that extension for more details.

Table 55-1 The `testthread` command.

`testthread create ?script?`	Creates a new thread and a Tcl interpreter. Runs *script* after creating the Tcl interpreter. If no *script* is specified, the new thread waits with `testthread wait`.
`testthread id`	Returns the thread ID of the current thread.
`testthread errorproc proc`	Registers *proc* as a handler for errors from other threads. If they terminate with a Tcl error, this procedure is called with the error message and `errorInfo` values as arguments. Otherwise, a message is printed to `stderr`.
`testthread exit`	Terminates the current thread.
`testthread names`	Returns a list of thread IDs.
`testthread send id ?-async? script`	Sends a script to another thread for evaluation. If `-async` is specified, the command does not wait for the result.
`testthread wait`	Enters the event loop. This is used by worker threads to wait for scripts to arrive for evaluation. Threads can also use `vwait` for this purpose.

Advanced Regular Expressions

An all new regular expression implementation supports Unicode and *Advanced Regular Expressions*, which are described in detail in Chapter 11. The new regular expression syntax has been added in a way that is compatible with earlier versions of regular expressions. There are also new `regexp` and `regsub` command options to control the new regular expression engine.

New String Commands

The string command was enhanced with several new operations that include string classification operations (`string is`), character string mappings (`string map`), title case conversion (`string totitle`), an easier-to-use equality test (`string equal`), and new string manipulation commands (`string repeat` and `string replace`). The `-nocase` and `-length` options have been added to commands like `string compare` and `string tolower`. These additions are listed in Table 4-1 on page 50 and explained in more detail in Chapter 4. Note: These only appeared in the Tcl 8.1.1 patch release.

The DDE Extension

Dynamic Data Exchange (DDE) is a communication protocol used among Windows applications. The protocol exchanges data with a server identified by name. Each service implements a number of operations known as *topics*. The data exchange can be synchronous or asynchronous. The `dde` command is implemented as an extension that is distributed with Tcl. You must use `package require dde` to load the extension. Table 55–2 summarizes the `dde` command.

Table 55–2 The dde command options.

`dde servername ?topic?`	Registers the current process as a DDE service with name `TclEval` and the given `topic`. If `topic` is not specified, this command returns the currently registered topic.
`dde ?-async? execute service topic data`	Sends *data* to the `service` with the given `topic`.
`dde ?-async? eval topic cmd ?arg ...?`	Sends *cmd* and its arguments to the `TclEval` service with the given `topic`. This is an alternative to the Tk send command.
`dde ?-async? poke service topic data`	Similar to the `execute` operation, but some services export operations under `poke` instead of `execute`.
`dde ?-async? request service topic item`	Fetches the named *item* from the `service` with the given `topic`.
`dde services server topic`	Returns `server` and `topic` if that server currently exists; otherwise, it returns the empty string.
`dde services server {}`	Returns all the topics implemented by `server`.
`dde services {} topic`	Returns all servers that implement `topic`.
`dde services {} {}`	Returns all server, topic registrations.

Miscellaneous

Serial Line I/O

The Windows serial line drivers were converted to use threads, so you can wait for I/O with `fileevent` when using serial devices. There is no API change here, but this was a limitation on Windows that was annoying in previous Tcl releases.

tcl_platform(user)

The `tcl_platform(user)` array element records the currently logged in user. This masks differences in environment variables and system calls used to get this information on different platforms.

CHAPTER **56**

Tcl/Tk 8.2

Tcl 8.2 is primarily a bug fix and stabilization release. This release is
recommended instead of Tcl 8.1.

Tcl 8.2 adds almost no new features at
the Tcl script level. Instead, it adds a few new C APIs that enable some interesting extensions to be added without having to modify the core Tcl distribution. At
the same time, Scriptics focused on the outstanding bug reports in order to make
the 8.2 release as stable as possible.

The Trf Patch

Andreas Kupries contributed a mechanism that allows I/O channel processing
modules to be stacked onto open I/O channels. This adds a new
`Tcl_StackChannel` C API, but there are no changes visible at the Tcl script level.
However, it enables several interesting extensions such as compression and
encryption (e.g., SSL) to be added to Tcl. Andreas has an extension that exports
the channel filter mechanism to the Tcl script level. This is used primarily for
testing, but you can also use it for script-level data filters.

Faster String Operations

The UTF-8 encoding has the drawback that characters are not all the same size:
They are either one, two, or three bytes in length. The variable-sized characters
make operations like `string length`, `string index`, and `string range` quite slow

in comparison to a system that uses fixed-sized characters. A new Unicode string type, which uses 16-bit characters, was added to support faster string operations. This change does not cause any changes that are visible to Tcl scripts, except for improved performance in comparison to Tcl 8.1.

Empty Array Names

Perhaps the only change in Tcl 8.2 visible to Tcl scripts is support for empty array names. This is a quirk you can get by using name spaces or `upvar`, but it was previously difficult to use directly. For example, the syntax `$::foo::(item)` references an array. That worked in any version of Tcl that supported namespaces. However, in Tcl 8.2 you can also use `$(item)` directly, which implies that the array name is the empty string. This trick is exploited by Jean-Luc Fontain's *STOOOP* object-oriented extension.

Browser Plugin Compatibility

The Web Browser plugin requires changes to the event loop mechanism because Tcl is embedded in an application with its own event loop. While the C APIs have supported alternate event loops since Tcl 8.0.3, it has been difficult to do this sort of embedding without recompiling Tcl. The `Tcl_SetNotifier` API was added to support embedding a "stock" Tcl interpreter.

Finer Control of Windows Serial Port Monitoring

On Windows systems, Tcl polls the serial ports for fileevents at the default rate of approximately every 10 milliseconds. Tcl 8.2 introduced the `fconfigure -pollinterval` option to give the ability to specify a shorter polling interval.

Regular Expression Expanded Syntax Option

Although Tcl 8.1 introduced support for expanded regular expression syntax (where whitespace and comments are ignored), it required you the signal the expanded syntax by including the `(?x)` option embedded in the regular expression string. Tcl 8.2 introduced the `regexp -expanded` option as an alternate way of enabling expanded regular expression syntax.

Tcl/Tk 8.3

Tcl/Tk 8.3 enhanced the capabilities of the canvas widget through the incorporation of the popular "dash" patch, as well as providing incremental improvements to other Tcl/Tk features.

Tcl 8.3 incorporated several key contributed patches, particularly for Tk. Jan Nijtmans's dash and image patches provided many handy features such as dashed lines on the canvas, improved image support, and more. Bringing these patches into the Tcl core not only provided new features usable in general Tcl scripts, but it allowed people to use several popular extensions and tools without the need for manually applying these patches and recompiling Tcl.

New File Manipulation Commands and Options

The new `file channels` command returns a list of open I/O channels, which can be sockets, regular files, or channels created by extensions. It accepts an optional glob pattern argument (e.g., `sock*`) to constrain the list.

The `file atime` and `file mtime` commands now accept an optional argument to set the access time or modification time of the specified file. This gives you the ability to perform the equivalent of the Unix `touch` command in pure Tcl code.

In addition to the previous ability to set file permissions using the same octal code format as the Unix `chmod` command, the `-permissions` option of the `file attributes` command now allows you to set file permissions symbolically. You can use the same symbolic attributes as the Unix `chmod` command (for example, `u+s`, `go-rw` to add sticky bit for user and remove read and write permissions for group and other). A simplified `ls`-style string, of the form `rwxrwxrwx` (the string must be 9 characters) is also supported (for example, `rwxr-xr-t` is equivalent to 01755).

New `glob` Options

New `-directory`, `-join`, `-path`, and `-types` options for `glob` command make it easier to manipulate directories in a platform-independent manner. "Matching File Names with `glob`" on page 122 describes these new options.

Regular Expression Command Enhancements

Both `regexp` and `regsub` gained a `-start` option, which indicates a starting offset into the string being matched. The new `regexp -inline` option can return the matching characters, rather than storing them in a variable. The `regexp -all` option finds all occurrences of the match pattern; in conjunction with the `-inline` option it returns all the matches as a list, whereas without the `-inline` option it returns the number of matches.

Direct Return of `scan` Matches

If you don't provide any variables to store the results of a `scan` command, it now returns its matches directly as a list.

Removing Duplicate List Elements with `lsort`

The new `lsort -unique` option removes duplicate elements from a list as it is sorted.

Deleting Elements from an Array

The new `array unset` command deletes all elements from an array whose key matches be given glob-style pattern. If no pattern is provided, the command deletes the array variable and all of its elements.

Enhanced `clock` Features

The `clock scan` command was extended to support common ISO 8601 date and time formats. An "easter egg" was included in both `clock scan` and `clock format` so that they understand the Stardate format (try `%Q` with `clock format`).

The `clock clicks -milliseconds` option was added to guarantee a millisecond granularity to the returned values.

Support for Delayed Package Loading in `pkg_mkIndex`

The new `pkg_mkIndex -lazy` option generates a package index file that delays actual loading of a package until an application attempts to use one of the commands provided by the package. Without this option, the generate package immediately loads its command when an application executes it `package require` command.

The Img Patch

The `Img` patch adds an alpha channel, better transparency support, and improved GIF support, including the ability to save GIF images. See the "Bitmaps and Images" section starting on page 625 for more information about these features. This patch also supports other image types (e.g., JPEG) that can be loaded as extensions; script-level support for other image types is typically provided through the Img extension, which can be used now without patching the Tcl core.

The Dash Patch

The "dash patch" added a variety of new Tk features — primarily to the canvas widget, but in other areas as well.

Canvas Improvements

The dash patch provided several significant improvements to the canvas widget:

- Canvas coordinates may be specified as a single list argument instead of individual arguments, which makes it easier to construct commands.
- Many items now support the notion of a dash pattern for outlines, implemented through a variety of new item options containing the word `dash`. Windows 95 supports only single-pixel wide dashed lines, whereas other platforms support thick dashed lines.
- The canvas now includes a `state` attribute, which modifies the default state of the canvas. Individual canvas objects all have their own `-state` attributes, which may override the default canvas state. Items also have new attributes to control their appearance based upon their state. The attributes that start with `-active` control the appearance when the mouse pointer is over the item, while the attributes starting with `-disabled` con-

trol the appearance when the state is disabled. Additionally, disabled canvas items don't react to canvas bindings.

- Advanced tag searching is available for all canvas operations that accept a tag or item ID as an argument. This adds the ability to search for canvas items based on boolean expressions of tag values.

- The canvas can generate Postscript for embedded images on all platforms. Additionally, on Unix platforms, it can generate Postscript for embedded widgets currently displayed on the screen (that is, displayed within the canvas's viewport and not obscured by other windows).

- The internal implementation of the canvas now uses `Tcl_Obj` values, which improved its performance.

Hidden Text

Tags in text widgets now include an `-elide` attribute, to hide text with that tag. This feature is used by the popular *TkMan* manual page browser, which can be used now without patching the Tcl core.

Pointer Warping

Tk applications now have the ability to move the mouse under program control. Use the `event generate -warp` option when generating KeyPress, KeyRelease, ButtonPress, ButtonRelease, or Motion events. For example:

```
event generate .c <Motion> -warp 1 -x 10 -y 20
```

Entry Widget Validation

New options were added to the entry widget for input validation. The options specify command callbacks that are made at various times, such as when the entry widget takes input focus, loses input focus, or has its value change. The commands are subject to `%` keyword substitution similar to the substitutions in event bindings. The keywords are used to get the name of the entry widget (e.g., `%W`), the character that is being added, and so forth. (See "Entry Widget Validation" on page 822.)

Other New Tk Features

Listbox Enhancements

Listboxes have a new `listVariable` attribute to link the contents of the listbox to a variable that contains a list value (in much the same way that the `textVariable` option is used in several other widgets). Listboxes also have new `itemconfigure` and `itemcget` operations to set and query the color of individual items.

New Directory Chooser Dialog

A new `tk_chooseDirectory` command allows users to browse a directory hierarchy and select a directory, in much the same way as the `tk_getOpenFile` command works for regular files.

Window Manager Interactions with Toplevel Windows

The `wm state` command now accepts an optional argument allowing you to set the state of a toplevel. On Windows systems, `wm state` also supports a new `zoomed` state for maximized windows.

Support Added for Windows System Cursors

On Windows systems, you can now use Windows system cursors in `.ani` and `.cur` files by using the format `-cursor @`*`filename`* when setting a widget's cursor.

Mousewheel Support for Listbox and Text Widgets on Unix

Default binding were added to listbox and text widgets so that on Unix system that report mousewheel events as `<ButtonPress-4>` and `<ButtonPress-5>` events, the listbox and text widgets respond to the mousewheel.

New Quadruple Event Modifier

You can use `Quadruple` as a modifier (e.g., `<Quadruple-ButtonPress-1>`.)

X Input Methods (XIM)

A new `tk useinputmethods` command changes the behavior of Tk on X where X Input Methods (XIM) were recognized and used without question. With 8.3, they are recognized and initialized, but not used unless XIM is turned on (`tk useinputmethods 1`). This should only affect users with special input methods, and the new default behavior should be more beneficial to the average user.

The Patch Releases

A series of 8.3 patch releases mainly provided incremental improvements and bug fixes, but did add a few new features. The 8.3.5 patch release was a final stabilization release for the 8.3 series, and was released concurrently with version 8.4.1. The only significant new feature of 8.3.5 versus the previous patch release was the ability of the canvas to generate Postscript for embedded widgets on Windows platforms, which was concurrently added with the 8.4.1 patch release.

Detection of Entry Validation Type

The `%v` substitution for entry widget validation reports the type of validation that triggered the callback (`key`, `focusin`, `focusout`, `forced`). (8.3.1)

Macintosh File Selection Dialog Enhancement

On the Macintosh — when Navigation Services are installed — the `tk_getOpenFile` and `tk_getSaveFile` commands accept a `-message` option to specify a message to include in the client area of the dialog. (8.3.1)

State Attributes for Label Widgets

The label widget now supports a `state` attribute, with `normal`, `active`, and `disabled` states. (8.3.1) Additionally, it has new `activeBackground` and `active-Foreground` attributes to control its appearance in the `active` state (8.3.2), and a `disabledForeground` attribute to control its appearance in the `disabled` state (8.3.1).

Support for Windows Icons

On Windows systems, you can provide the path of a valid Windows icon file (usually `.ico` or `.icr` files) when setting the window's icon with the `wm iconbit-map` command. (8.3.3)

New Reference Pages

The online documentation includes new `colors`, `cursors`, and `keysyms` reference pages, documenting the supported color names, cursor names, and keysyms. (8.3.2)

Tcl/Tk 8.4

Tcl 8.4 provided significant performance improvements, many new commands and options, and three new Tk widgets.

Speed was a primary objective of Tcl/Tk 8.4. Version 8.0 provided major performance improvements to Tcl with the introduction of the bytecode compiler. But new features added in version 8.1 (in particular, multi-threaded support and internationalization support with Unicode strings) slowed down Tcl significantly. The goal for 8.4 was for scripts to run as fast as — or faster than — they did under 8.0, and the goal was achieved in almost all areas of the language.

Tcl/Tk 8.4 is perhaps the most significant release since 8.1 in terms of new features. Virtually all aspects of the language gained new functionality, and new widgets were added to the core for the first time since version 8.0.

Version 8.4 also marked the transition from Tcl being under the sole control of John Ousterhout to its management by the Tcl Core Team (TCT), which is composed of a group people who have been instrumental to Tcl's development over the years. The TCT is responsible for determining changes and new features for upcoming versions of Tcl. They also work with maintainers, who have responsibility over specific aspects of Tcl/Tk, and other community volunteers to actually implement the changes. Anyone can suggest a new feature or change to Tcl by submitting a Tcl Improvement Proposal (TIP). A description of the TIP process and a list of all submitted TIPs are available at *http://www.purl.org/tcl/tip*. Development of the 8.4 release was already in progress before the TIP process was in place, so not all new 8.4 features were controlled by TIPs; however, in this chapter, any new feature that was proposed by a TIP has that TIP number indicated.

64-Bit Support

Changes to several commands provide better support for 64-bit values, even on 32-bit platforms. (TIP #72) The changes implemented were designed to maximize backward compatibility.

64-Bit Arithmetic

The `expr` command now supports 64-bit (wide integer) arithmetic. Integer constants unable to fit in a signed 32-bit value are treated as wide integers, unless they exceed the capacity of 64 bits, in which case they are treated as double-precision floating point values. The result of an arithmetic operation is a double if at least one of the operands is a double, a wide integer if at least one of the operands is a wide integer, and a normal integer otherwise.

The `int()` function always returns a non-wide integer (converting by dropping the high bits), and the new `wide()` function always returns a wide integer (converting by sign-extending).

The `incr` command can increment variables containing 64-bit values correctly, but can accept only 32-bit values as amounts to increment by.

64-Bit Value Conversions

The `format` and `scan` commands now support the `l` modifier for use with integer-handling conversion specifiers (`d`, `u`, `i`, `o`, and `x`), which tells them to work with 64-bit values. The `binary` command gained new `w` and `W` specifiers for its `format` and `scan` subcommands, which operate on 64-bit wide values in a fashion analogous to the existing `i` and `I` specifiers (that is, smallest byte to largest, and largest byte to smallest, respectively).

64-Bit Filesystem Support

All Tcl commands interacting with the filesystem (`file`, `glob`, `seek`, and `tell`) work correctly for files larger than 2 GB.

Native Word Size Detection

The `tcl_platform` array contains a new `tcl_platform(wordSize)` element, which gives the native size of machine words on the host platform.

Additional Filesystem Features and Commands

Virtual Filesystems

Tcl is now "virtual filesystem (VFS) aware," which allows filesystem interaction and input/output to take place on something other than the system's native filesystem. (TIP #17) This means that, given appropriate extensions, any ordinary Tcl code can use the standard file commands: cd, pwd, glob, file, open, etc. and operate on "virtual files" without realizing it. Such virtual files can be remote files (on FTP sites or over an HTTP connection) or inside archives (for example, Zip or tar files).

The basic Tcl distribution doesn't expose the capability of manipulating virtual filesystems at the Tcl script level. However, the new C APIs enables several interesting extensions and applications. TclVFS is the extension that allows standard Tcl scripts to "mount" and use virtual filesystems. TclVFS includes support for virtual filesystem types including: FTP, HTTP, WebDAV, Zip archives, tar archives, MetaKit databases, and Tcl namespaces. TclKit, which provides a method of distributing single-file, standalone executables written in Tcl/Tk, is also based on Tcl's VFS capabilities. TclKit is described in Chapter 22.

New `file` Subcommands and `glob` Options

The file command gained several new subcommands, primarily to support the new virtual filesystem capabilities described above (TIP #17): file normalize, file separator, and file system. TIP #17 added the glob -tail option. TIP #99 added the file link command for creating hard and symbolic links. See "The file Command" on page 108 for more information on the file subcommands, and "Matching File Names with glob" on page 122 for more information on glob.

New and Enhanced List Commands

Tcl 8.4 added several new commands and options that increase performance when manipulating lists:

- The new lset command allows you to directly change the value of an individual list element. This is much faster than using lreplace to replace the element with a new value. See "The lset Command" on page 66.
- The lindex command now accepts multiple indices to allow retrieval of values in nested lists. See "Getting List Elements: llength, lindex, and lrange" on 68.
- Many new options were added to lsearch for faster and more flexible list searching. You can use the -sorted, -ascii, -decreasing, -dictionary, -increasing, -integer, and -real options indicate that the list is already sorted in various ways, which allows lsearch to use a more efficient searching algorithm. TIP #80 added the -all, -inline, -not, and -start options, giving you the ability to do things such as retrieve multiple elements with a search. See "Searching Lists: lsearch" on page 69.

Array Searching and Statistics

New `-exact`, `-glob`, and `-regexp` options to the `array names` command allow you to specify the type of pattern matching to use when searching for array element names. The new `array statistics` command returns statistics about the array internals, used primarily for debugging and profiling purposes.

Enhanced Support for Serial Communications

The `fconfigure -handshake`, `-queue`, `-sysbuffer`, `-timeout`, `-ttycontrol`, `-ttystatus`, and `-xchar` options provide much finer control over serial port communications than was available under previous versions of Tcl. See "The `fconfigure` Command" on page 231 for a description of these options.

New String Comparison Operators

Two new string comparison operators, `eq` and `ne`, can be used to force a string equality or inequality comparison everywhere that you can evaluate an expression (for example, `expr`, `for`, `if`, and `while`).

Command Tracing

Tcl now has the ability to trace commands as well as variables. (TIP #62) Options include triggering actions: before or after executing any specified command; before or after entering any command within a specified procedure; when a command is renamed; or when a command is deleted. A new command syntax for creating and using variable traces was also added, to match the features of command tracing. The old syntax for variable traces will be retained for now for backwards compatibility, but its use is deprecated. For more information on using traces, see "Tracing Variables and Commands" on page 193.

Additional Introspection Commands

Several new commands support more introspection and control of the Tcl interpreter:

- `info functions` returns a list of all the math functions currently defined. (TIP #15)
- `info script` now accepts an optional pathname argument. If provided, it becomes the return value for all future invocation of `info script` for the duration of the session. This can be useful in virtual file system applications.

- `interp recursionlimit` sets and returns the maximum depth for nested Tcl procedure calls and other operations that create Tcl stack frames. (TIP #87)
- `namespace exists` reports whether or not a specified namespace exists.

Other Tcl Changes

Unsetting Nonexistent Variables

With the `-nocomplain` option, `unset` suppresses any possible errors. A new `--` option also allows you to delete variables that might have the same name as any `unset` options.

Direct Return of Substituted String with **regsub**

The final `regsub` argument (the name of the variable in which to store the substituted string) is now optional. If omitted, `regsub` simply returns the substituted string (or the original string, of no substitutions were made). (TIP #76)

Increased Time Resolution on Windows

Previously, the `time` command, the `clock clicks` command, and all related functions were limited to a resolution of (typically) 10 milliseconds on Windows systems. Tcl 8.4 on Windows now features microsecond precision with accuracy in the tens of microseconds. (TIP #7)

Bug Fixed in **fcopy** to Respect Channel Encodings

The `fcopy` command in prior versions of Tcl improperly ignored the encodings of the channels. Now `fcopy` respects the channel encodings, and performs proper translations on the data if the channels have different encodings.

New Tk Widgets

Tk 8.4 features three new widgets:

- A `spinbox` is an extended entry widget that allows the user to move, or "spin," through a fixed set of values, such as times or dates, in addition to editing the value as in an entry.
- A `labelframe` is very similar to the standard frame, but also has the ability to display a label. (TIP #18)
- A `panedwindow` contains any number of panes, arranged horizontally or vertically. Each pane contains one widget, and each pair of panes is separated by a moveable sash, which causes the widgets on either side of the sash to be resized. (TIP #41)

Text Widget Undo Mechanism and Other Enhancements

The text widget gained several new features in Tk 8.4:

- A mechanism for unlimited undoing and redoing of changes was added. (TIP #26) When the new `-undo` option is set to a Boolean true value, the widget records every insert and delete action on a stack. Default key bindings allow the user to undo and redo changes, and a programmatic interface gives the application full control over the undo and redo stacks. (See "The Undo Mechanism" on page 548.)
- The text widget generates a `<<Modified>>` virtual event whenever the contents of the widget changes. (TIP #26)
- The text widget generates a `<<Selection>>` virtual event whenever the text selection of the widget changes. (TIP #26)
- The text widget's `delete` and `get` operations now accept multiple ranges, instead of only a single character or range of characters. (TIP #93)

New pack and grid Features

Asymmetric Padding

Both the `pack` and `grid` commands now support asymmetric padding. If you provide a single screen distance value to either `-padx` or `-pady`, then that value is used for both the left and right (or top and bottom) padding around the widget, just as it has been in previous versions of Tk. But now if you provide a 2-element list of screen distance values, then the first value determines the padding on the left (top), and the second value determines the padding on the right (bottom).

Uniform Rows and Columns in grid

The new `-uniform` option for `grid columnconfigure` and `grid rowconfigure` makes it easier to create layouts with equal-sized cells. (TIP #37)

Displaying Both Text and an Image in a Widget

In previous versions of Tk, labels, menu entries, and the various button widgets could not display text and a bitmap or image at the same time. Tk 8.4 introduced the `compound` attribute, which specifies whether the widgets should display both an image (or bitmap) and text, and if so, where the image should be placed relative to the text. (TIP #11)

New Button Relief Attributes

Buttons, checkbuttons, and radiobuttons all gained an `-overrelief` option, which specifies a relief style to use when the mouse cursor is over the widget. Checkbutton and radiobutton widgets also gained an `-offrelief` option, which specifies the relief style to use for the widget when the widget is in an "off" state and the indicator is not drawn. These new relief options make it much easier to create "toolbars" from a collection of button widgets. (TIP #82)

Controlling the State of Entries and Listboxes

The entry and listbox widgets gained new options for controlling their state:

- The entry widget `state` attribute now supports a `readonly` value. When an entry is in the `readonly` state, the value displayed cannot be changed by either the application or the user, and the insertion cursor is never displayed. However, the user can still select the contents of the widget. The entry widget also supports new `disabledForeground`, `disabledBackground`, and `readonlyBackground` attributes to control its appearance in the different states.
- The listbox widget now supports a `state` attribute, with `normal` and `disabled` states, and a `disabledForeground` attribute to control its appearance in the disabled state. Additionally, a new `activeStyle` attribute controls the style in which the active element is drawn. (TIP #94)

More Window Manager Interaction

Several `wm` subcommands were added to provide additional interaction with the window manager and control over toplevel windows:

- `wm attributes` returns or sets platform-specific attributes associated with a window. (TIP #95)
- `wm stackorder` returns information about the stacking order of an application's toplevel windows. (TIP #74)
- `wm iconbitmap` accepts a new `-default` option on Windows platforms for designating a default icon bitmap for all of an application's toplevel windows. (TIP #8)
- `tk windowingsystem` returns the current Tk windowing system, one of `x11` (X11-based), `win32` (MS Windows), `classic` (Mac OS Classic), or `aqua` (Mac OS X Aqua). (TIP #108)

Other Tk Changes

Mouse Button Repeat Control

You can now configure how buttons, scales, scrollbars, and spinboxes respond when the user holds down a mouse button or key for that widget. The `repeatDelay` attribute specifies the number of milliseconds a button or key must be held down before it begins to auto-repeat, and the `repeatInterval` attribute determines the number of milliseconds between auto-repeats.

Better Support for Image Transparency

Tk 8.4 provides greater access to transparency information for photo images. Photo image object commands now support a `transparency` subcommand with `get` and `set` operations, which respectively get and set the transparency setting of individual pixels in the image. (TIP #14) Additionally, a new `-compositingrule` option to the `copy` subcommand allows you to specify how transparent pixels in the source image are combined with the destination image. (TIP #98)

Selecting Multiple Files with `tk_getOpenFile`

The `tk_getOpenFile -multiple` option allows a user to select multiple files to open, returning the files selected as a list.

Fixed-Width Button Support on Windows Systems

On Windows systems, the `button width` attribute now accepts a negative value to specify a minimum width, enabling better compliance with native Windows look-and-feel.

Easier Access to Clipboard Contents

A new `clipboard get` subcommand returns the contents of the clipboard — equivalent to `selection get -selection CLIPBOARD`.

Determining if an Image is Used

The `image inuse` command returns whether or not a specified image is in use by any widget.

New Events and Substitutions for Window Managers

To enable writing Tk-based window managers, Tk 8.4 added support for five new event types: `<CirculateRequest>`, `<Create>`, `<MapRequest>`, `<Resize-Request>`, and `<ConfigureRequest>`. The `%i` and `%P` event substitutions were also added. (TIP #47)

Caret Management for Improved XIM/IME Support

A new `tk caret` command sets and queries the caret location for the display of the specified Tk window. The caret is the per-display cursor location used for indicating global focus (for example, to comply with Microsoft Accessibility guidelines), as well as for location of the over-the-spot XIM (X Input Methods) or Windows IME windows. (TIP #96)

New `bell` Option to Prevent Resetting Screen Savers

The `bell` command has the side effect of resetting the screen saver for the screen, which usually makes the screen visible again. The new `-nice` option prevents the `bell` command from resetting the screen saver.

Generating Postscript for Embedded Widgets

The Tk 8.4.1 patch release added the ability on Windows for the canvas to generate Postscript for embedded widgets currently displayed on the screen (that is, displayed within the canvas's viewport and not obscured by other windows). This capability was added concurrently with the 8.3.5 patch release.

About The CD-ROM

This chapter describes what is available on the CD-ROM.

The CD-ROM contains Tcl/Tk software distributions, the examples from the book, and a collection of Tcl-related software found on the Internet. The CD is one volume in a hybrid format that is readable on UNIX (ISO 9660 format with Rock Ridge extensions), Windows (Joliet format with long file names), and Macintosh (HFS). Kudos to the ISO standard for supporting multiple formats simultaneously, and to the Linux *mkisofs* application used to create the disk image.

The Tcl/Tk distributions are in the `tcl_84` and `tcl_83` folders. The `.tar.gz` files there are source distributions that can be unpacked on a UNIX system with a command like this:

```
gunzip < tcl8.4.2.tar.gz | tar xvf -
```

You can compile the source code like this (there are more detailed instructions in Chapter 48):

```
cd tcl8.4.2/unix
./configure
make
```

There are also source distributions in `.zip` files that contain the same files as the `.tar.gz` packages. There are Windows installers in `.exe` files that install ready-to-run Tcl/Tk interpreters and script libraries.

The `tcl8_4` folder contains Macintosh distributions in `.bin` files for MacOS 9. The `.dmg` files are the Tcl/Tk Aqua distribution for MacOS X. You should be able to double-click those files to install Tcl/Tk on those platforms.

The `ActiveTcl` folder contains the *ActiveTcl*[*] binary distributions and demo copies of *TclDevKit*, which is described in more detail on page 200. *TclDevKit* provides a set of development tools including a debugger and syntax checker. You can get a demo license for the tools at:

```
http://www.activestate.com/products/Tcl_Dev_Kit
```

The `exsource` folder contains the examples from the book. These are automatically extracted from the book files. The `browser.tcl` script lets you view and try out the examples.

The `tclhttpd3.4.3` directory contains an unpacked version of the TclHttpd distribution. You should be able to start the server by loading the `bin/httpd.tcl` script into `wish` or `tclsh`. The script starts a Web server on port 8015.

The `tclkit8.4.2` and `tclkit8.4.1` directories contain versions of *Tclkit* for a variety of platforms, plus the source so you can build this extended Tcl/Tk interpreter yourself. Copy the appropriate build to a convenient location and rename it to *tclkit*. Use *tclkit* to run the Starkits found under the `sdarchive` directory.

The `wiki` directory contains a copy of `http://wiki.tcl.tk` in the form of a Starkit. You can browse this copy by running this command. The `-readonly` is necessary if you run directly off of the CD-ROM:

```
tclkit wiki/wikit.kit wiki/wikit.tkd -readonly
```

The `handheld` directory contains distributions of Tcl/Tk created for small hand-held devices, including PalmOS, DOS, and Windows CE. Support for Windows CE will be included in future "core" Tcl/Tk distributions.

The `extensions` and `applications` folders contain software downloaded from the Internet. Most of these were downloaded from projects on SourceForge:

```
http://www.sourceforge.net
```

The `mingw` directory contains a copy of the free *mingw* C compiler for Windows. To build Tcl/Tk on Windows with *mingw*, you will also need a *Cygwin* installation, which you can find at:

```
http://www.cygwin.com
```

The `CD_UTILS` folder contains software you may find helpful, such as Winzip and a version of Tar for Macintosh. I have also included scripts I used to create the CD.

Technical Support

Prentice Hall does not offer technical support for this software. If there is a problem with the media, however, you may obtain a replacement CD by emailing a description of the problem. Send your email to:

```
disc_exchange@prenhall.com
```

---

[*] ActiveTcl is a trademark of ActiveState Corporation.

Index

Symbols

#, pad with spaces in format 58
$ in regular expressions 155
$, dollar sign 18
% in clock format 184
% in event bindings 449
( ) for arrays 95
( ) in regular expressions 155
(?!re) in regular expressions 155
(?:re) in regular expressions 155
(?=re) in regular expressions 155
(?abc) in regular expressions 155
* in regular expressions 154
*, matching character 53
*? in regular expressions 155
+ in regular expressions 154
+, format character 58
+? in regular expressions 155
-, left justify string in format 58
., (dot) in regular expressions 154
/bin/sh to run a Tcl script 27
/debug, Application Direct URL 282
/mail, Application Direct URL 283
/status, Application Direct URL 281
? in regular expressions 155
?, string match character 53
?? in regular expressions 155
@ in binary format 60
[ ] in regular expressions 155
[ ] in string match 53
[ ], command substitution 18
[. .] in regular expressions 155
[: :] in regular expressions 155
[= =] 155
[incr Tcl] From The Ground Up, book lviii
[incr Tcl] object system 214
\\, backslash 20
\0 in regular expressions 157
\A in regular expressions 156
\a in regular expressions 156
\a, bell 20
\B in regular expressions 156
\b in regular expressions 156
\b, backspace 20
\c in regular expressions 155
\cX in regular expressions 156
\D in regular expressions 156
\d in regular expressions 156
\e in regular expressions 156
\f in regular expressions 156

\f, form feed 20
\M in regular expressions 156
\m in regular expressions 156
\n in regular expressions 156
\n, newline 20
\r in regular expressions 156
\r, carriage return 20
\S in regular expressions 156
\s in regular expressions 156
\t in regular expressions 156
\t, tab 20
\uXXXX in regular expressions 157
\v in regular expressions 157
\v, vertical tab 20
\W in regular expressions 157
\x in regular expressions 157
\xhh in regular expressions 157
\xy in regular expressions 157
\xyz in regular expressions 157
\Y in regular expressions 157
\y in regular expressions 157
\Z in regular expressions 157
^ in regular expressions 155
{ } for argument grouping 4
{m,n} in regular expressions 155
{m,n}? in regular expressions 155
| in regular expressions 155
~ in file names 124

Numerics

0, o, in binary format 58
3D Border 785
3D relief sampler 614
3dDarkShadow, system color 622
3dLight, system color 622
64-Bit
    Arithmetic 826
    Filesystem Support 826
    Value Conversions 826

A

A, a, in binary format 60
abbreviation of commands 179
-about, regexp option 158
-above, event option 449
abs(x), absolute value 21
AC_INIT 738
AC_OUTPUT 739
AC_SUBST 738
accepting socket connections 240

access time, file 108
acos(x), arccosine 21
activate canvas objects 566
activate, button operation 467
Activate, window event 439, 442
activeBackground, widget attribute 620
ActiveBorder, system color 622
activeBorderWidth, widget attribute 615
ActiveCaption, system color 622
activeForeground, widget attribute 620
activeRelief, widget attribute 615
addinput. See fileevent.
addtag, canvas operation 581
Advanced Regular Expressions 815
advanced regular expressions 149
after, safe alias 308
after, Tcl command 228
aliases defined by the browser package 317
aliases, command 296
aliases, introspection on 296
-all, lsearch option 70
Allocate a Pixmap 786
Allocation, Memory 769
alnum, in regular expressions 156
alnum, string class 54
alpha, in regular expressions 156
alpha, string class 54
Alt, key modifier 444
alternation in regular expressions 147
anchor position, pack 404
Anchor Positions, Text 786
anchor the selection, entry widget 514
anchor, widget attribute 616
anchoring a regular expression 147
Anchoring text in a label or button 617
animation with images 627
animation with update 405, 609
ANSI_ARGS 740
Any, key modifier 445
app-defaults file 477, 671
append mode, open 117
append to clipboard 594
append to list 66
APPEND, open mode 117
append, Tcl command 56
AppleScript on Macintosh 107
applets 311
application activation 442
application and user resources 483
application class 476
application class warning 476
application deactivation 442
Application Direct URL 262
  /debug 282
  /mail 283

/status 281
  e-mail form results. 283
  form handlers 272
  specifying content type 265
application embedding 489, 808
Application Initialization 768
application name 669, 780
appname, tk command operation 664
AppWorkspace, system color 622
Aqua window system, Mac OS X 670, 831
arc canvas item 567
arccosine function 21
Architecture, Tcl Extension 729
-archive, file property 115
arcsine function 21
arctangent function 21
argc, Tcl variable 31
args, example 424, 614
args, parameter keyword 88, 134
Arguments and Tcl_GetIndexFromObj, Parsing 710
Arguments, Main Programs and Command-Line 779
argv, saving for window session 662
argv, Tcl variable 29, 80
argv0, and Starkit VFS access 355
arithmetic on text indices 533
arithmetic operators 20
array 96
  ArrayInvert 99
  collecting variables 99
  complex indices 100
  convert to list 98
  created with variable trace 196
  empty variable name 818
  for a Database 41
  for simple database 100
  global 182
  list of 103
  names of indices 98
  searching and statistics 828
  set from list 98
  syntax 95
  Tcl command 97
arrow keys 441
arrow on canvas 570
-ascii, lsearch option 70
ascii, string class 54
asin(x), arcsine 21
aspect ratio, message widget 493, 613
aspect ratio, of window 659
AssocData for per Interpreter Data Structures 774
Associating State with Data 92
asymmetric padding 402, 413
Asymmetric padding in geometry managers 830
-async, send option 648
asynchronous I/O 232

asynchronous message sending, threads
   329–330
atan(x), arctangent 21
atan2(y,x), arctangent 21
atime, file access time 114
Atom and window ID information 668
atom, in C 787
attemptckalloc 769
attemptckrealloc 769
attribute 371
   activeBackground 620
   activeBorderWidth 615
   activeForeground 620
   activeRelief 615
   anchor 616
   aspect 613
   background 620
   bitmap 627
   borderWidth 615
   button widgets 459
   Canvas Widget 586
   colormap 624
   colors, all 620
   configuring in C 781
   cursor 631
   disabledBackground 620
   disabledForeground 620
   elementBorderWidth 615
   entry widget 515
   exportSelection 642
   file 109
   foreground 620
   Frames and Toplevels 486
   geometry, old 795
   height 613
   highlightBackground 616
   highlightColor 616, 620
   highlightThickness 616
   image 625
   insertBackground 620, 631
   insertBorderWidth 631
   insertOffTime 631
   insertOnTime 631
   insertWidth 631
   justify 641
   Label Widget 491
   length 613
   listbox widget 528
   menu entries 469
   Message Widget 494
   of Fonts 636
   options and resources 372
   orient 613
   padX 616
   padY 616
   platform-specific window 663
   readonlyBackground 620
   relief 615
   Scale Widget 496
   scrollbar widget 504
   selectBackground 620, 642
   selectBorderWidth 642
   selectColor 620
   selectForeground 620, 642
   setgrid 642
   size 612
   spinbox widget 515
   text tags 536
   text widget 554
   troughColor 620
   types, in C 756
   visual 624
   width 613
   wrapLength 641
AUTH_TYPE, CGI environment variable 280
auto extracting applications 354
auto loading and auto_import 215
auto loading, description 178
auto, end of line translation 234
auto_import, procedure hook 215
auto_index, Tcl variable 31
auto_mkindex_old 811
auto_noexec, Tcl variable 107, 179
auto_noload, disable library 178
auto_path, Tcl variable 172, 177, 180
autoconf, configure and 732
autoconf, tcl.m4 file 736
autoconf, using 736
automatic decompression 354
automatic program execution 107, 179
automatic quoting 65
auto-repeat, timing control 832

B

B, b, in binary format 60
b, regular expression option 157
back references 151
background error handler 202
background errors 771
background for area covered by insert cursor
   515
background I/O reader 229
background processes, in C 770
background, execute in 106
Background, system color 622
background, widget attribute 620
backslash character, \\ 20
backslash escapes in regular expressions 156
backslash quoting 147
backslash sequences 7, 18, 20
backslash-newline, in quoted string 493
backspace character, \b 20
BackSpace key 441
Ball, Steve lviii
balloon help 678
basic authentication using http::geturl 256
baud rate, I/O channel 234
bd. Synonym for borderwidth.
Beasley, David 695
beep. See bell.
bell character, \a 20
bell, prevent resetting screen savers 833

bell, Tk command 497

bg. Synonym for background.

bgerror 771

bgerror, background error handler 202

binaries, make target 740

binary
  conversion types 60
  data and file I/O 62
  data, ByteArrays 773
  data, pack 59
  data, unpack 59
  encoding 221
  end of line translation 234
  registry value type 126
  string support 806
  Tcl command 59

bind, canvas command 582

bind, Tk command 435

Bind_Display 685

Bind_Edit 688

Bind_Interface 684

Bind_New 687

Bind_Read 689

Bind_Save 689

BindDefine 689

BindDragto 687

binding 435
  adding to 436
  arrow keys 441
  break and continue 438
  button modifiers 443
  canvas object 560, 563
  canvas selection 595
  canvas text objects 576
  class 437
  command to event 435
  continue 438
  destroy window 442
  different binding tags 438
  double click 444
  entry widget 513
  event syntax 439
  event types 439
  execute in the global scope 436
  global 437
  in C code 782
  keyboard events 440
  listbox
    browse selection 525
    extended selection 526
    multiple selection 527
    single selection 525
  Meta and Escape 446
  mouse events 441
  order of execution 437
  scale widget 495
  scrollbar widget 503
  sequence of events 445
  tab key 604
  tag, defining 439
  text tags 540
  text widget 549
  Tk 4.0 changes 792
  top-level windows 443

user interface for 683
window changes size 442
window dragging 425
X, Y coordinates 449

BindMark 687

BindSelect 686

bindtags, Tk command 437

BindYview 686

bit blit 629

bitmap
  built-in 627
  canvas item 568
  definition in C code 783
  for icon 661
  image type 626
  in label 491
  on canvas 568
  widget attribute 627

blank, in regular expressions 156

blinking cursor 515, 631

Blob and BlobState 708

blob Command Example 707

Blob_Init and BlobCleanup procedures 709

BlobCommand and BlobPoke 716

BlobCreate and BlobDelete 713

BlobData and BlobN 715

BlobNames procedure 714

BlobState data structures 708

-blocking, fconfigure option 231

-blocksize, http::geturl option 252

BLT lviii

body, http::geturl result 253

bold 638

bold text 537, 639

Bonet, Achim 483

book Web site 729

book, font weight 638

boolean expressions 75

boolean preference item 676

boolean, string class 54

borders
  3D 785
  and padding 617
  and relief attributes 615
  are drawn in the canvas 558
  vs. padding, example 618

-borderwidth, event option 450

borderWidth, widget attribute 615

Borenstein, Nathaniel 291

bound quantifiers 151

bounding box, canvas 582

bounding box, of text 551

box on canvas 574

break, Tcl command 83
  bindings 438

Brouwers, Jean 728

browse selection mode, listbox 525

browser for the code examples 384

browser package aliases 317
Browser Plugin Compatiblity 818
browser Tcl plugin 314
browser::displayForm 317
browser::displayURL 317
browser::getForm 317
browser::getURL 317
browser::getURL callbacks 317
browser::status 317
-buffering, fconfigure option 231
buffering, I/O channel 233
-buffersize, fconfigure option 231
Building a List 714
Building Tcl from Source 731
built-in bitmaps 627
built-in commands, finding 190
bulleted list 544
button 453
    as event modifier 444
    associated with a Tcl procedure 456
    associated with variables 458
    attributes 459
    command 380
    container for 380, 397
    emulate in text widget 541
    event option 449
    fixed width 832
    fixing a troublesome situation 455
    image and text together 626
    minimum width 832
    mouse as event modifiers 443
    number, mouse 449
    operations 461
    padding 794
    padding vs. packer padding 402
    problems with command 454
    procedures for commands 455
    relief attributes 831
    row of 380, 397
    scope of command 454
    Tk widget 453
    user-defined 479
Button, window event 439
ButtonFace, system color 622, 623
ButtonFrame, system color 623
ButtonHighlight, system color 622
ButtonPress, window event 439
ButtonRelease, window event 439
ButtonShadow, system color 622
ButtonText, system color 622, 623
byte code compiler 200, 805
ByteArrays for Binary Data 773

C

C command procedure. See command proce-
    dure
C compiler for Windows, mingw 836
C Library, Using the Tcl 696
C Programming and Tcl 693

C programming with Critcl 201
C shell history, comparison 198
C variables linked to Tcl variables 696
C, creating commands in 768
C, evaluate Tcl command from 770
c, in binary format 60
c, in string format 57
C, Invoking Scripts from 724
c, regular expression option 157
C, Tcl_Eval runs Tcl commands from 724
calculating clicks per second 185
call by name 91
call stack, viewing 190, 200
callbacks 132, 191
    code wrapper 212
    idle 776
    into a namespace 211
    scope for 211
    socket accept 240
Calling C command with Tcl_Invoke 725
Calling Out to Tcl Scripts 696
canvas 557
    "Hello, World!" 559
    active objects 566
    adding tags 581
    arc object 567
    arrow 570
    attributes 586
    bindings on objects 563
    bindings, text object 576
    bitmap object 568
    borders obscure items 558
    bounding box 563, 582
    C interface 784
    circle 572
    convert mouse to canvas x, y 582
    coordinate space 557
    coordinates vs. screen coordinates 587
    coordinates, large 587
    copy and paste 595
    dashed lines 566, 821
    disabled objects 566
    display list 581
    drag object 558
    embedded window 579
    events coordinates 587
    find overlapping vs. find closest 576
    gridded geometry 658
    hidden objects 566
    hints 587
    hit detection 576, 588
    image object 569
    large scroll area 558
    line object 570
    min max scale 561
    moving objects 560
    object bindings 560
    object support in C 784
    objects with many points 588
    oval object 572
    polygon object 573
    postscript 583
    proposed improvements 821
    rectangle object 574

resources for objects 588
rotation 588
scaling objects 563, 588
scroll increment 580
scroll region 558, 587
selection handler example 595
set or query item coordinates 582
spline 570
state 566
stroke drawing example 571
summary of operations 581
tag on object 559, 561
tag persistence 561
tags are not persistent 561
tags vs. object IDs 561
tags, logical combination 560
text object attributes 578
text object bindings 576
text operations 575
transparent text 811
Cap Styles, Line 786
Caps Lock key 444
CaptionText, system color 622
capturing program output 378
capturing subpatterns 148
caret 670
Caret Management for XIM/IME Support 833
carriage return character, \r 20
carriage-return line-feed translation 231
cascaded menus 388
case. See switch.
catalog files
    managing message 223
    sample message 224
catalogs, message 222
    namespaces and 225
catch
    catching more than errors 84
    errors from open 118
    example 83, 84
    possible return values 84
    Tcl command 83
cavity model, pack 398
cd, Tcl command 122
cd, Tcl command, multi-threaded scripts and
    332
CDE Border Width 809
ceil(x), next highest integer 21
cells in colormap 669
center, anchor position 616
centering a window 421
centimeters 557
cget, widget operation 467, 612
CGI 35
    Application, Guestbook 33
    argument parsing 165
    definition of 35
    Directories 289
    environment variables 280
    example script 36
    html package 276
    ncgi.tcl package 44

script library for 37
Cgi_Header 38
Cgi_Parse and Cgi_Value 165
Chained conditional with elseif 77
change directory 122
changing a list variable 66
Changing Command Names with rename 89
changing the system encoding 218
changing widgets 371, 612
channel
    drivers, I/O 776
    flush I/O 116
    see input/output
    stacking 817
    threads and 333–337
-channel, http::geturl option 252
character
    class names 54
    classes in regular expressions 156
    code 20, 152
    from strings 72
character set 145, 218
    conversions 718
    encoding 231, 235, 773
    of URL 253
checkbutton, Tk widget 458
child windows 665
children, of namespace 213
choice preference item 676
choosing items from a listbox 520
choosing the parent for packing 407
Chopping File Pathnames 111
circle, canvas object 572
Circulate, window event 439
CirculateRequest, window event 439
ckalloc 709, 769
ckfree 769
ckrealloc 769
class
    application 476
    application, warning 476
    event binding 437
    of application 791
    resource 476, 665
    widget 369
clean, make target 740
clear clipboard 594
clear photo image 629
clear the selection 518
clicks per second 185
clicks, clock operation 184
client machine, window session 662
client of HTTP 243
client of the echo service 242
client side of remote evaluation 654
client sockets 239
ClientData 768
Clipboard access 832
CLIPBOARD selection 594, 781

clipboard, Tk command 594
clock formatting keywords 184
clock seconds 184
clock widget 743
Clock widget data structure 745
clock, Tcl command 800
Clock_Init procedure 744
ClockCmd command procedure 746
ClockConfigure allocates resources for the
    widget 753
ClockDestroy cleanup procedure 765
ClockDisplay procedure 762
ClockEventProc handles window events 764
ClockInstanceCmd command procedure 749
ClockInstanceObjCmd command procedure
    751
ClockObjCmd command procedure 747
ClockObjConfigure, Tcl_Obj version 754
ClockObjDelete command 766
clone, menu operation 467
close a window 442
close errors from pipes 382
close window callback 661
close, Tcl command 121
Closing I/O channels 121
cntrl, in regular expressions 156
code checker 200
code generation 46
code, procedure for callbacks 212
code, read the Tcl source 697, 705
Codes from Command Procedures 702
coding style 181
collating elements 153
color 619
    allocating in C 752
    attributes 620
    bisque 621
    computing darker shades 624
    convert to number 669
    dialog to choose 602
    exhaustion 669
    greyscale 624
    name 623
    of text 537
    palettes 621
    resource class 621
    resource names 478, 620
    reverse video 621
    RGB specification 622
    static colormap 624
    Tk 4.0 new attributes 796
    values 621
    values, in C 784
    Windows system 622
colormap 668
    allocation 669
    cells 669
    command-line argument 30
    event 439
    for frame 487

    in C 785
    size of default 669
    widget attribute 624
columnbreak menu attribute 469
columns of widgets 411
columns, uniform size 830
com port 828
combobox
    See spinbox.
comm communication package, tcllib 647
command
    abbreviations 179
    aliases for safe interpreters 296
    aliases, saving as Tcl commands 297
    body 11
    build with list 130
    built-in, finding 190
    buttons 380
    C interface, String 700
    C interface, Tcl_Obj 703
    call with Tcl_Invoke 725
    callbacks 191
    complete Tcl command 191
    creating and deleting 768
    defined by a namespace, listing 212
    evaluate from C 770
    evaluation 190
    example, blob 707
    for entry widget 508
    from C using Tcl_Eval 724
    hidden from safe interpreters 295
    history 179, 197
    http::geturl option 252
    implement in C 700, 768
    list-related 64
    lookup 208
    on radiobutton or checkbutton 459
    parsing in C 770
    passing variable names 93
    prefix callbacks 132
    reading commands 191
    substitution 5
    syntax 4
    that concatenates its arguments 131
    that uses regular expressions 170
Command key, Macintosh 443
command procedure 699
    and Data Objects 694
    BlobCmd 711
    call with Tcl_Invoke 725
    RandomCmd 700
    RandomObjCmd 703
    Result Codes from 702
Command tracing 828
command-line
    argument
        colormap 30
        display 30
        geometry 30
        name 30
        sync 30
        to Wish 30
        use 30
        visual 30
    arguments 29, 80, 652, 662
    arguments, in C 779

arguments, main programs and 779
    parsing 80
comments 16
    in line 17
    in regular expressions 154
    in resource file 478
    in switch 78
Communicating Processes 651
compare, string command 50
Comparing file modify times 114
Comparing strings 52, 53
comparing text indices 533, 551
comparison function, sorting a list 71
compatibility, regular expression patterns
    149
compiler, byte code 805
compiler, make sure you have a working 733
compiler, Microsoft Visual C++ 732
compiler, Tcl Dev Kit 200
Compile-Time Errors 806
Compiling Tcl and Extensions 729
compiling Tcl and extensions
    multi-threaded support 323
complex indices for arrays 96
compound attribute to display text and image
    830
compound, widget attribute 626
ComputeGeometry computes the widget's size
    761
Computing a darker color 624
concat and eval 134
concat and lists 131
concat, list, double quotes comparison 67
concat, Tcl command 67
concatenate strings and lists 67
condition variables 340–342
    standard use 341
conditional, if then else. 76
-config filename, TclHttpd 286
config/plugin.cfg file 318
configure
    and autoconf 732
    flags, Standard 733
    macros are hard 736
    widget operation 467, 612
    window event 440
Configure, window event 442
configure.in 732, 738
ConfigureRequest, window event 440
configuring
    attributes, in C 752, 781
    read-write channels 235
    Security Policies 318
    widget attributes 371, 611
    window, in C 780
    windows 780
conflict between namespace and global vari-
    ables 207
Connect client to an eval server 651

connect, socket 239
connection state, TclHttpd 261
console, Tcl command 29, 800
CONST in the Tcl 8.4 APIs 716
constructing code with the list command 130
Constructing Lists 65
constructing procedures dynamically 133
containers. See frame.
containing window 666
content type for Application Direct URL 265
CONTENT_LENGTH, CGI environment vari-
    able 280
CONTENT_TYPE, CGI environment variable
    280
Content-Encoding for URL 253
Content-Type of URL 253
Contexts, Graphics 785
continue in bindings 438
continue, Tcl command 83
    bindings 438
Control key event 444
Control Structure Commands 75
control, string class 54
controlling terminal 117
conversion types, binary 60
conversions between encodings 221
Conversions, Character Set 718
conversions, string format 57
convertfrom, encoding 222
Converting Between Arrays and Lists 98
converting existing packages to namespaces
    213
Converting Numbers 772
convertto, encoding 222
cookie, HTTP, setting in TclHttpd 279
coordinate space, canvas 557
coordinates of mouse event 436
coordinates, general 666
Coordinates, Window 781
copy and paste 591
copy image area 629
Copy options for photo images 630
Copy, virtual event 447
Copying Files 112
corner grips 422
correct quoting with eval 136
cos(x), cosine 21
cosh(x), hyperbolic cosine 21
-count, event option 449
counting with regsub 163
covering a window with place 422
Cox, Christopher 598
cr, end of line translation 234
CREAT, open mode 117
create

commands in C 768
directories 112
elements in a hash table 713
file pathnames 110
file, open 117
hash tables in C 708
hierarchy of interpreters 293
image types in C 783
interpreter in C 768
interpreter in scripts 292
interpreters 293
interpreters in C 768
loadable package 697
Starpack 354
threads 324–327
window event 440
windows in C 780
-creator, file attribute 116
Critcl, tool for mixing C and Tcl 201
crlf, end of line translation 234
cross-platform 193
cancel event 383
clipboard 592
file naming 110
scripts 799
virtual events 383
ctime, file change time 114
curly braces 4
group arguments to eval with 137
positioning is important 76
stripped off 4
vs. double quotes 8
current directory 122
multi-threaded scripts and 332
current, namespace 213
cursor
blinking 515, 631
entry widget 515
hide mouse 632
in C 785
mouse 633
text insert 631
widget attribute 631
widget option in C 760
Custom Dialogs 602
cut and paste 591
Cut, virtual event 447
CVS repository for Tcl software 729
Cygwin UNIX environment for Windows 732,
836

D

d, in binary format 60
d, in string format 57
Darley, Vince 349
dashed lines, canvas 566
data encapsulation 673
data in a Metakit view 360
Data Objects, C Command Procedures and
694
Data Structures with Arrays 99

Data Structures, AssocData for per Interpreter 774
data transformation 163
-data, for image 627
Data, Using Tcl_Preserve and Tcl_Release to
Guard 715
database
Metakit 360
ODBC lviii
simple in-memory 41, 103
using the resource 783
data-driven user interface 676
date formatting 184
date parsing 184
date, getting current 184
day, %d 184
DDE Extension 816
Deactivate, window event 440, 442
debug URL for TclHttpd 282
Debug, procedure 199
debug, text widget 551
debugger and TclHttpd 282
debugger, Tcl Dev Kit 200
debugging 199
debugging Tk applications with tkinspect 201
declaring variables 5, 208
decoding HTML entities 166
decoration, window 659
-decreasing, lsearch option 70
default button 402
default parameter values 88
-default, tk_messageBox option 600
-defaultextension, tk_getOpenFile option 600
defining new binding tags 439
delete
characters in entry 514
commands in C 768
files 113
interpreter 292
interpreters in C 768
list element by value 69
menu items 467
namespace 213
text in text widget 532, 551
the section 514
-delta, event option 450
demibold, font 638
depend, make target 740
depth, screen 669
destroy
hash tables 708
no errors 809
Tk command 605
widget 605
window 605
window event 440, 442
detached window 486
-detail, event option 449
Determining if an image is used 832

dev, file attribute 114
dialog
    buiding with procedure 606
    custom 602
    data-driven approach 676
    message for 493
    simple example 607
    to make choice 599
    window for 486
dictionary search rules 70
-dictionary, lsearch option 70
dictionary. See array.
digit, in regular expressions 156
digit, string class 55
direct color visual class 624
-direct, pkg_mkIndex option 174
directory
    create 109
    current 122
    file test 108
    for packages 731
    structure, installation 731
    structure, Tcl source 730
    Tcl script from C 731
directory selection dialog 600
disabled canvas objects 566
disabled entry 516
disabledForeground, widget attribute 620
DisabledText, system color 622
--disable-shared 734
disabling the library facility 178
display list graphics 581
display space, with pack 401
display, command-line argument 30
Display, Fonts and Text 785
Displaying Both Text and an Image in a Wid-
    get 830
-displayof, send option 648
distclean, make target 740
distribution, Tcl source code 730
dither image 629
dlineinfo, text operation 551
DLL, loading into Tcl 174, 697
DLLEXPORT 740
DNS client 238
doc, installation directory 740
doc, make target 731
Doc_AddRoot 278
Doc_CheckTemplates 278
Doc_Coookie 279
Doc_Dynamic 279
Doc_Error sock 279
Doc_ErrorPage 278
Doc_IndexFile 278
Doc_IsLinkToSelf 279
Doc_NotFound 279
Doc_NotFoundPage 278
Doc_PublicHtml 278

Doc_Redirect 279
Doc_Root 278
Doc_SetCookie 279
Doc_Subst 279
Doc_TemplateInterp 279
Doc_TemplateLibrary 278
Doc_Webmaster 279
-docRoot directory 286
document root, TclHttpd 286, 287
document type handler, TclHttpd 265
DOCUMENT_ROOT, CGI environment vari-
    able 280
dollar sign syntax 18
DOS to UNIX 121
DOS, Tcl/Tk distributions for 836
double click 444
double quotes
    and eval 137
    compared to concat and list 67
    vs. curly braces 8
double(x), convert to floating point 21
Double, event 445
double, string class 55
Double-click, warning about 444
downloading files with http::geturl 254
dp_send, Tcl command 132
drag object on canvas 558
drag out a box 574
drag out a selection 513
drag windows, bindings 425
drag-and-drop 667
drawing application, ImPress 598
Drivers, I/O Channel 776
DString interface 717, 773
Duffin, Paul 735
dump, text operation 552
dword, registry value type 126
dword_big_endian 126
Dykstra, Dave 737
Dynamic HTML, CGI 35
dynamic linking 174, 697
Dynamic Loading and Packages 768
Dynamic Strings, DString 773

E

e or E, in string format 57
e, anchor position 616
e, regular expression option 157
echo server, multi-threaded example 335
echo service, example 241
EchoArgs 29
edit bindings for canvas text 576
editable text 531
Effective Tcl/Tk Programming, book lviii
elementBorderWidth, widget attribute 615

else. See if.
elseif. See if.
Emacs-like binding for Meta and Escape 446
e-mail application, exmh 171
e-mail, sending from TclHttpd 283
embed_args and plugin, variables 314
embed_args, Tcl variable 31
embedded
    application in window 30
    applications 668
    images for a bulleted list 544
    images in text 544
    options, the (?x) syntax 157
    Tk windows 312
    widgets in text 542
    window in frame 489
    window on canvas 579
Employee DB example 100
Empty Array Names 818
--enable-gcc 734
--enable-symbols 734
--enable-threads 734
encoding
    binary 221
    changing the system 218
    character set, in C 773
    character sets 218
    conversions between 221
    fconfigure option for character sets 219, 231
    for X font 638
    I/O channels 219
    scripts in different 220
    system 218
    Tcl command 222, 814
end-of-file
    character 234
    condition 120
    makes a channel readable 229
end-of-line
    character 20, 231
    translations 234
engineering manual, Tcl 182
Enter, window event 440
entry 507
    adjust selection 514
    attributes 515
    binding to commands 508
    bindings 513
    blinking cursor 515
    changes in Tk 4.1 802
    get the contents 517
    hidden value for password 516
    indices 517
    insert string 517
    long strings in 510
    move cursor 514
    operations 517
    read only state 831
    read-only 510
    scrolling 518
    state 831
    tips for use 510
    Tk 4.0 changes 794
    Tk widget 507

    validating contents 508
    variable for value 507
    with label 508
entrycget, menu operation 467
entryconfigure, menu operation 467
env, Tcl variable to hold environment 31
Environment Variables 124
environment variables
    CGI 280
    multi-threaded scripts and 332
eof channel 116
eof, Tcl command 120
-eofchar, fconfigure option 231
eq, string comparison 828
equal sized widgets, grid 418
equal, string command 50
Equal-sized labels 614
equivalence classes 153
errno 769
error
    background, in Tcl 771
    catching 83
    errorCode, variable 85
    errorInfo, variable 83, 85
    fconfigure option 231
    from return 86
    handler for Tk 202
    http::geturl result 253
    information in C 769
    reporting script 771
    Tcl command 85
    thread error handling 328, 331–332
    X protocol 782
Escape key 441
eval
    and double quotes 137
    example 482, 534
    in aliases 302
    in namespace 213
    server 652
    server for remote evaluation of code 652
    Tcl command 130
    user input 191
    wrapper procedure example 134
Evaluating Expressions from C 772
Evaluating Tcl Commands from C 770
event
    % keywords summary 449
    bindings 435
    bindings, in C 782
    for Tk-Based Window Managers 833
    generating 447, 448
    handler, in C 782
    handler, resize in C 764
    keywords 448
    modifier 443
    sequences 445
    syntax, bindings 439
    text is selected 830
    text widget is modified 830
    Tk command 448
    types, binding 439
    virtual 446

event loop 227
    event sources 723
    I/O handler 229
    implementation 775
    in C, Timer 776
    in C, Window 782
    in tclsh 230
    interface 781
    moves from Tk to Tcl 801
    threads and 325
event-driven programming 227
-exact, lsearch option 70
Examining a Metakit database 360
Examining the File System 777
example browser 384
Example Plugins 314
Example, The blob Command 707
exception. See catch.
exceptions 702
EXCL, open mode 117
exclusive open 117
exec
    ExecLog procedure 377
    limitations on Windows 107
    syntax for I/O redirection 106
    Tcl command for running programs 106
--exec-prefix=dir 734
executable, is file 108
execute programs automatically 179
executing programs 382
execution environment 192
exists, array command 98
exists, interp operation 292
exit
    command alias 296
    handlers 779
    hidden command 301
    multi-threaded scripts and 332
    Tcl command 124
exmh, e-mail application 171
exp(x), exponential 21
expand vs. fill, with pack 400
expand, more than one widget 404
expand_sz, registry value type 126
expanded regular expressions allow com-
    ments 154
-expanded, regular expression option 158
Expanding Tilde in File Names 124
expanding variables in resources 484
Expect lviii
Expect, Tcl extension 119
Exploring Expect, book lvii
exponential function 21
export from namespace 213
exporting and importing procedures 210
exportSelection, widget attribute 642
expose, interp operation 292
Expose, window event 440

expr, Tcl command 6
expressions
    and string matching, regular 775
    evaluating 772
    from C code 772
extend a selection 518
extended selection mode, listbox 526
extension
    architecture, Tcl 729
    compiling 729
    many bundled in kitten Starkit 357
    multi-threaded scripts, using in 323
    of file name 108
    the programming sample 737
EXTERN 740

F

f, in binary format 60
f, in string format 57
false, string class 55
family, font 638
fblocked, Tcl command 233
fconfigure
    changes in Tcl 8.0 810
    changes in Tcl 8.1 813
    changes in Tk 4.1 802
    file encodings and 219
    Tcl command 231
fcopy
    and channel encodings 829
    HttpCopyDone example 249
    Tcl command 250
feedback, to user 609
fg. Synonym for foreground.
fifo, special file 114
file
    64-bit support 826
    atime, access time 108
    attributes 109, 114
    base name 109
    change modify time 819
    change name 109
    channel names 819
    compare modify times 114
    copy 108
    current script 191
    delete 108
    dialogs 600
    directory create 109
    encodings and fconfigure 219
    end of line character 121
    end-of-file 120
    equality test 115
    exists test 108
    extension 108
    fifo 109
    find by name 123
    finding with info script 38
    for image 627
    for preferences 679
    handlers, in C 775
    hidden command 301
    I/O and Binary Data 62

in a simple Starkit 353
is executable 108
is plain 108
join pathnames 108
limited access with safe interp 304
lstat 109
mkdir 109
mtime, modify time 109
multiple threads accessing 333
name change 109
name manipulation 799
name manipulation in C 777
name patterns 122
native name 109
of widget attributes 478
open dialog 600
open for I/O 116
operations added in Tcl 7.6 803
ownership 109
partial re-write 678
pathname type 109
read line by line 120
read symlink value 109
readable test 109
rename 109
rootname 109
size 109
split pathnames 109
stat 109
stat, array elements 114
symbolic and hard link 113
symbolic and hard links 827
symbolic link 109
tail 109
Tcl command 108
tilde in names 124
type 109
writable test 109
file selection dialog 600
file system interface, VFS 351
File System, Examining the 777
File_Process 140
fileevent and end of file 229
fileevent, Tcl command 229, 382
-filetypes, tk_getOpenFile option 600
fill vs. expand, with pack 400
-fill, pack option 400
find file by name 123
find related files 191
find text in widget 542
finding files with info script 38
first, string command 50
Fixed-Width Button Support on Windows
     Systems 832
flat, relief 615
floor(x), next lowest integer 21
flush, Tcl command 118
Flynt, Clif lvii
fmod(x,y), floating point modulo 21
focus 599
     and dialogs 603
     changes from keyboard traversal 516
     event generation and 448

event option 449
events 438
grab 604
grab, tkwait sequence 605
grabbing the focus 604
highlight 616, 792
highlight color 515
introduction 368
model of window 663
tab binding 604
Tk 4.0 changes 793
Tk command 603
tk_focusNext 604
focus, input 603
FocusIn, window event 440
FocusOut, window event 440
font
     actual 641
     and text attributes 635
     attributes of 636
     command summary 641
     creating named 641
     failure to find 639
     fall back to fixed 640
     family or typeface 636
     in C code 785
     measure 641
     metrics 640
     missing 480
     names 641
     platform-independent 808
     resource 477
     scaling size 669
     selection dialog 643
     selection example 643
     selection program, Unix 639
     system 637
     Tk command 640
Fontain, Jean-Luc 818
FontWidget handles missing fonts 639
for loop, example 82
for, Tcl command 82
foreach, multiple loop variables 801
foreach, Tcl command 79
foreground, widget attribute 620
forget namespace import 213
forget, package operation 176
form
     and processing form data, HTML 42
     data, TclHttpd 261
     feed character, \f 20
     handlers 272
     HTML with browser::getForm 317
     newguest.html 43
     self-checking HTML 276
     with entry widgets 508
format date and time 184
Format flags 58
Format Templates 59
format text with message widget 493
-format, image 630
format, Tcl command 56
Formatting strings 57

foundry, font 638
frame 485
    as container 368, 380
    attributes 486
    colormap 487
    nested for packing 399
    packing example 396
    positioned on canvas 579
    reparented 663
    size 396
    Tk widget 485
free 769
FTP access, via VFS 352
FTP client 238
FTP server 238
full screen 660
function definition. See procedure

G

g or G, in string format 57
gamma value 628
generating events 447, 448
geometry
    command-line argument 30
    gridding 642
    gridding, canvas 658, 659
    gridding, listbox 529
    management in C 784
    manager 367
        canvas 579
        pack 396, 409
        panedwindow 430
        place 421
        text 543
    manager, name 665
    of widget 666
    of window 659
    old attribute 795
    propagation, turning off 397
GET, HTTP protocol 244
gets, Tcl command 120
gid, file attribute 114
GIF 783
GIF image format 628
glob options added in Tcl 8.3 820
-glob, lsearch option 70
glob, string matching 53
glob, Tcl command 122
global arrays 99, 182
global binding 437
global command goes inside a procedure 90
global scope and the variable command 215
global, Tcl command 90
goto 83
Grab Can Fail 607
grab, Tk command 604
Grabbing the Focus 604
graph, in regular expressions 156
graph, string class 55

Graphic Protocol Errors, Handling 782
Graphical Applications with Tcl & Tk, book
    lviii
graphics context 752, 785
gravity of text marks 534, 552
Gravity, window event 440
GrayText, system color 622
greyscale visual class 624
grid
    added in Tk 4.1 802
    asymmetric padding 413
    basic example 411
    changes in Tk 4.2 804
    changes in Tk 8.0 809
    command summary 419
    external padding 413
    internal padding 414
    -ipadx and -ipady 414
    minimum size 417
    multiple widgets in a cell 414
    options 419
    pack, combining with 395, 411
    -padx and -pady 413
    panedwindow and 430
    resize behavior 417
    row and column constraints 416
    row and column padding 416
    row and column span 415, 416
    row and column specifications 413
    sticky settings 412, 414
    text widget and scrollbar 417
    Tk command 411, 419
    uniform rows and columns 830
    weights 418
    window under mouse, query 419
gridded geometry 642
gridded geometry for a canvas 658
gridded geometry, in C 784
gridded, resizable listbox 642
griddied geometry for a listbox 529
grips on corners 422
groove, relief 615
group file ownership 114
group leader, window 663
group your patterns with curly braces 144
-group, file attribute 115
grouping rules 17
guard data with, Tcl_Preserve and
    Tcl_Release 715
Guestbook CGI Application 33
guestbook.cgi 36, 40, 41

H

H, h, in binary format 60
-handler, http::geturl option 252
handlers
    exit 779
    file 775
    graphic protocol errors 782
    window events 782

hard and symbolic links 827
hard link, file 113
Harrison, Mark lviii, 214
hash table 95
    creating and destroying 708
    creating and removing elements 713
    package, in C 774
hbox, window layout 397
HEAD, HTTP 245
Header Files, Standard 740
-headers, http::geturl option 252
height
    event option 449
    of image 628
    of widget 666
    virtual root window 667
    widget attribute 613
Hello, World! Tk program 369
Hello, World!, canvas example 558
Help menu 464
help pop-up 678
hexadecimal string 55
hidden
    canvas objects 566
    commands 297
    commands, exposing 292
    field 516
    file attribute 116
    text 822
hide the mouse cursor 632
hide, interp operation 292
high resolution timer 185
Highlight, system color 622, 623
highlightBackground, widget attribute 616
highlightColor, widget attribute 616, 620
HighlightText, system color 623
highlightThickness, widget attribute 616
HINSTANCE, Windows application handle
    787
history syntax, Tcl 197
history, command 179
history, Tcl command 197
hit counts, TclHttpd 281
hit detection, in canvas 576
Hobbs, Jeff 201, 737
horizontal and vertical layout, nested 398
horizontal fill in a menu bar 400
horizontal window layout 397
hostname 193
Hot Tip
    abbreviate history commands 197
    always use thread::wait to enter a thread's
        event loop 331
    append is efficient 56
    args and eval 135
    array elements on demand 195
    array for module data 182
    attribute resource names 372
    Big lists can be slow 64

bind callback is in global scope 436
borders, padding, and highlight 618
braces get stripped off 4
bugs in transferring sockets between threads
    334
button command procedures 455
canvas borders obscure features 558
canvas hints 587
canvas stroke example 572
canvas tags are not persistent 561
careful file open 118
color, convert to RGB 623
combining pack and grid 395, 411
comments at the end of line 17
comments in switch 78
configure tags early 537
create managed widgets as children of a paned-
    window 431
curly brace placement 76
detecting windowing system 669
do not declare Tcl variables 5
double-click warning 441
embedding applications 668
end-of-file makes a channel readable 229
entry, displaying end of string 510
errors on close 121
eval and double quotes 137
exit kills all threads 332
expr is unreliable for string comparison 52
find file by name 123
find overlapping vs. find closest 576
font, fall back to fixed 640
global inside procedures 90
grab can fail 607
grid weights when shrinking 418
group command bodies with braces for safety
    12
group expressions with braces 111
group expressions with braces for performance
    16
grouping before substitution 10
I/O operations and fileevent 229
labels that change size 490
list handling in C code 769
list with foreach 80
list, after, and send 131
main thread must be the last one to terminate
    324
menu accelerator, consistent 473
menu index pattern 467
message text layout 493
mouse cursors, all shown 633
mutexes rely on threads being "good citizens"
    339
name of the current interpreter 296, 318
namespace import takes a snapshot 211
only exported names appear in package index-
    es. 210
open a process pipeline 118
pack the scrollbar first 407
packing widgets to a side 398
parentheses do not group 96
partially qualified names can refer to two differ-
    ent objects. 209
pipelines and error output 382
procedures to hide list structure 673
quotes lose list structure 131
resources, general patterns first 477

result string, managing in C 702
Scotty extension supports many network protocols 238
script name, don't use widget names 476
scrollbar for two listboxes 686
scrolling widgets on a canvas 579
send requires X authority 648
send, constructing commands 651
single round of interpretation 7
size not set until mapped 665
standard I/O channels in multi-threaded scripts 333
Starkit VFS access 355
string conversions by expr 52
synchronous messages can deadlock multi-threaded scripts 329
Tcl_Eval may modify its string 724
Tcl_Obj initial reference count is zero 705
text mark gravity 534
The list command does automatic quoting 65
thread::join blocks 327
threads might not start immediately after creation 325
Tk isn't truly thread-safe 323
tkwait on global variable 605
traces on entry values 677
trapping errors from pipelines 382
update, using safely 609
Upvar aliases do not work 93
Use arrays to collect related variables 99
use canvas tags instead of IDs 561
variable for widget name 370
virtual root window coordinates 667
Watch out for long pathnames 26
widget data, safety in C 765
window session protocol 662
window size, getting correct 580
hour, %H 184
how auto loading works 178
HTML
A Quick Introduction 34
comments, removing 170
Dynamic Pages 35
entity decoder 166
form data mapped to procedure arguments 189
form, self-checking 276
Page, Beginning 38
simple parser 168
tags, partial list 34
Tcl template file 266, 269
templates, for site structure 268
templates, form handlers 274
html package, tcllib 261, 276
Html_DecodeEntity 167
Html_Parse 168
http 807
HTTP download 254
http package 253
HTTP, network protocol 243
http::cleanup 253, 255
http::code 253
http::config 251
http::data 253
http::error 253
http::formatQuery 254
http::geturl 251, 252
http::geturl options 252
http::geturl state array 253
http::register 255
http::reset 255
http::size 253
http::status 253
http::unregister 255
http::wait 253
HTTP_ACCEPT, CGI environment variable 280
HTTP_AUTHORIZATION, CGI environment variable 280
HTTP_COOKIE, CGI environment variable 280
HTTP_FROM, CGI environment variable 280
Http_Get fetches the contents of a URL 247
Http_Head validates a URL 245
HTTP_REFERER, CGI environment variable 280
HTTP_USER_AGENT, CGI environment variable 280
HttpCopyDone is used with fcopy 249
Httpd_Error 277
Httpd_Redirect 277
Httpd_ReturnData 277
Httpd_ReturnFile 277
Httpd_SelfUrl 277
HttpGetText reads text URLs 249
HTTPS URL access 255
HWND, Windows identifier 787
hyperbolic cosine function 21
hyperbolic sine function 21
hyperbolic tangent function 21
hypot(x,y), hypoteneus 21

I

I, i, in binary format 60
i, in string format 57
i, regular expression option 157
I/O Channel Drivers 776
I/O events, in C 723, 775
icon
bitmap 661
name 661
position 661
window for 661
icon bitmap for toplevels 831
ID Management, X Resource 787
Identifiers (UIDS), String 784
idle events, in C 228, 723, 776
if, Tcl command 76
image
and namespaces 215

and text in a widget 830
and text on a button 626
C interface 783
C interface, photo 783
clear 629
command summary 626
copy 629
create options, in text 545
determine if used 832
dither 629
Img extension for more formats 628
in text widget 552, 809
load from file 629
masks 627
on canvas 569
save to file 629
supported formats 628
Tk command 626
transparency 629, 832
widget attribute 625
IME 833
IME windows 785
Img Tk extension for image formats 628
Img Tk extention for image formats 821
Implementing join in Tcl 73
import from namespace 213
import takes a snapshot, namespace 211
importing and exporting procedures 210
ImPress, drawing application 598
InactiveBorder, system color 623
InactiveCaption, system color 623
InactiveCaptionText, system color 623
inch, screen measurement 557
include, directory 731
incr procedure, improved 92
incr Tcl, object system 214
incr, Tcl command 13, 92
-increasing, lsearch option 70
increment a variable 13
index
    a character, entry widget 517
    canvas text object 575
    entry widget 517
    modifiers for text widgets 533
    of loadable packages 699
    of menu item 467
    string operation 50
    text widget 531, 552
indices, listbox widget 522
-indices, regular expression option 158
infinite loop 13
info hostname 802
info script, finding files relative to 38
info, Tcl command 186
InfoBackground, system color 623
InfoText, system color 623
init.tcl, location during startup 180
initialization
    application 768
    extension 744
    of Tcl 695

procedure, for a package 698
-inline, lsearch option 70
ino, file attribute (inode) 114
input data into Tcl lists 72
input focus 368, 381, 603
input focus highlight 792
input/output
    binary data 62
    channel properties 231, 232
    channels, stacking 817
    command summary 116, 123
    configuration 232
    events, in C 228
    from C 776
    from safe interpreters 299
    redirection 106
inscope, namespace operation 213
insert
    items into menu 467
    position, setting entry 513
    string into entry widget 517
    text in text widget 532, 552
insertBackground, widget attribute 620, 631
insertBorderWidth, widget attribute 631
insertOffTime, widget attribute 631
insertOnTime, widget attribute 631
insertWidth, widget attribute 631
Inspector, Tcl Dev Kit 201
install, make target 740
Installation Directory Structure 731
Installation, Tcl 735
install-binaries, make target 740
install-doc, make target 740
install-libraries, make target 740
int(x), truncate to integer 21
-integer, lsearch option 70
integer, string class 55
integrating TclHttpd with your application 258
interactive command entry 29
interactive command history 196
interactive resize 659
interactive, detecting 31
Interface, DString 717
Interface, String Command 700
Interface, Tcl_Obj Command 703
internal padding, -ipady 401
Internationalization 717, 813
internationalization 217
Internet Explorer 311
interp, for TclHttpd 279
interp, Tcl Command 292
interpreter
    creating 293
    creating in C 768
    data structures, AssocData 774
    exists test 292
    hierarchy of 293
    internal state 186

name as a command 294
namespaces and 215
registry of names 664
thread-enabled 323
tracing commands in C 770
interprocess communication. See send.
intranet applications, Tcl plug-in 311
Introduction to HTML 34
introspection 212
introspection, with pack 406
invoke menu item from program 467
invokehidden, interp operation 292
Invoking Scripts from C 724
IP address, TclHttpd 286
-ipadx and -ipady pack options 401
IRC client 238
is, string command 50
iso8859, fonts 638
issafe, interp operation 292
italic text 537, 639
itcl, object-oriented Tcl 214
iterator in Tcl, creating new 102, 140

J

Jacl, Tcl interpreter in Java lii
Java li
Java Tcl Interpreter, Jacl lii
Javascript lii
Javascript, access from Tcl plug-in 316
Johnson, Eric lviii
join in Tcl, Implementing 73
Join Styles, Line 786
join, file names 108
join, Tcl command 72
joinable threads 326–327
JPEG image format 628, 783
justify
    in text widget 536, 538
    string 58
    text in C 786
    widget attribute 641

K

Keeping References to Tcl_Obj Values 714
Kenny, Kevin 27
keyboard
    bindings and focus 380
    event, generate 448
    events 440
    focus traversal 604
    grab 604, 782
    Key events 438
    map 445
    selection, menu 465
    shortcuts and focus 608
-keycode, event option 449
KeyPress, window event
    Key, window event 440

KeyRelease, window event 440
keysym
    keyboard symbol 450
    what is generated by your keyboard 441
-keysym, event option 450
kitten extension bundle, Starkit 357
Kupries, Andreas 817

L

label
    and an entry 380
    arranging 494
    attributes 491
    displaying different strings 490
    image and text together 626
    lining up 676, 688
    multiline 491
    size 490
    state 831
    Tk widget 490
    width and wrap length 491
labelframe
    attributes 486
    Tk widget 486
Landers, Steve 351
lappend, Tcl command 66
lassign, list assignment with foreach. 139
last, string command 50
Layout attributes for text 641
Layout attributes for widgets 616
ldelete, Tcl procedure 69
Leave,window event 440
length, string command 50
length, widget attribute 613
Lewis, Brian 315
lf, end of line translation 234
lib, directory 731
Libes, Don lvii, 44, 383
libraries make target 740
library
    and imported commands, loading 215
    based on the tclIndex File 176
    directory, Tcl 192
    how it works 178
    index 177
    introduction 171
    of procedures 171
    regular expression C 775
    search path 177
    shared 697
    Tcl C 696, 768
    Tk C 779
    using stubs 735
light font 638
limit recursion depth 829
Limitations of exec on Windows 107
limited socket access 302
limited temporary files 304
lindex, Tcl command 68, 71
Line Cap Styles 786

Line Join Styles 786
line on canvas 570
line segment performance 588
line spacing in text widget 538
-line, regular expression option 158
-lineanchor, regular expression option 158
-linestop, regular expression option 158
link, registry value type 126
linked listboxes 520
linking, dynamic 697
links, symbolic and hard 827
linsert, Tcl command 68
list
    accessing nested 827
    and concat 131
    append elements 66
    assignment into 139
    automatic quoting 65
    command summary 64
    comparison with double quotes and concat 67
    constructing commands 130, 131, 456,
        482, 651, 688
    convert to array 98
    delete by value 69
    efficient modification 66
    eliminating duplicate values 71
    extract element 68
    find matching element 69
    generating Tcl commands 46
    implement a stack 101
    insert elements 68
    join into string 72
    length of 68
    manipulation in C code 714, 769
    modifying 68
    nested lists and lset 66
    of arrays 103
    performance of 64
    quote arguments to send 650
    replace elements 68
    searching 64
    sorting 64
    splice together 67
    split string into 71
    sublist 68
    summary of operations 64
    syntax 63
    Tcl command 65
    with foreach 81
    with interp eval 294
listbox 519
    attributes 528
    bindings 524
    browse selection 525
    disabled state 831
    extended selection 526
    geometry gridding 529
    indices 522
    linked 520
    multiple selection 527
    operations 522
    pair of 520
    pair working together 685
    scroll bindings 527
    selecting items 520
    selectMode attribute 524
    single selection 525
    state 831
    Tk 4.0 changes 795
    Tk widget 519
    virtual events 528
    with optional scrollbars 502
listen, sockets 240
listing commands defined by a namespace
    212
llength, Tcl command 68
load
    automatic package 173
    changes in Tk 4.1 800
    hidden command 301
    into slave interpreters 312
    pkg_mkIndex option 174
    shared libraries 178
    Tcl Command 178
    Tcl command 312, 697
    tclIndex file 178
loadable package, creating 697
loadable package, initialization 698
loading option database files 477
loading package
    programming API 768
locale, specifying a 223
locate your script files, trick to 191
locating packages, auto_path variable 172
locating the Tcl script library 180
location of icon 661
location of window 666
Lock, caps lock 444
log files, TclHttpd 289
Log Procedure 382
log(x), logarithm 21
log10(x) 21
logging
    multi-threaded example 333
logging the output of a program 378
-longname, file property 115
look-ahead in regular expressions 152
looking at all widget attributes 371
looking at marks 546
looking at tags 546
lookup, command 208
loop
    break & continue 83
    event 227
    for 82
    foreach 79
    reading input 120
    while 79
LoVerso, John 479
lower case conversion 50
lower, in regular expressions 156
lower, string class 55
lower, Tk command 409
lrange, Tcl command 68
lreplace, example 639

lreplace, Tcl command 68
lsearch, Tcl command 64
lset, Tcl command 66
lsort, changes in Tcl 8.0 807
lsort, Tcl command 70

M

m, regular expression option 157
Mac OS X Aqua, window system 831
Macintosh
  Apple menu 464
  auto_path 172
  Classic and Aqua windowing systems 669
  command key 443
  file types 601
  look and feel 393
  mouse cursors 632
  serial devices 235
  shared libraries 174
  shared library location 697
  source Tcl from resource 28
  system colors 623
  system font size 637
  unsupported1 Command 804
  window styles. 489
  zoom, full 660
Mackerras, Paul 628
MacWindowStyle 663
mail, sending from TclHttpd 283
main program
  Command-Line Arguments 779
  Tcl_AppInit, Tcl 720
  Tk_AppInit, Tk 721
main thread, terminating 324
Makefile targets, TEA standard 740
Makefile Templates 737
Makefile.in 733, 739
man, installation directory 731
managing
  bitmaps 783
  geometry 784
  global state 387
  message catalog files 223
  Tcl_Obj reference counts 704
  the result string 702, 769
  user preferences 671
  X resource id 787
manipulating
  file names 777
  files and directories 112
  menus and menu entries 466
  Tcl variables 771
manual, on-line 372
map, string command 50
Map, window event 440, 442
Mapping Strings 55
mapping windows for display 369
MapRequest, window event 440
mark gravity, text 534
mark position in text 382, 534
marktrusted, interp operation 292

-maskdata, for image 627
-maskfile, for image 627
match, string command 50
matching
  characters 145
  file names with glob 122
  precedence 148
  regular expressions and string 775
math
  64-bit 826
  expressions 6
  functions, built-in 21
  functions, querying 828
maximum size, window 659
McLennan, Michael lviii, 214
Measurements, Screen 786
medium, font weight 638
Memory Allocation 769
memory, Tcl Command 769
memory, Tcl command 710
menu 462
  accelerator 469, 473
  accelerator linked to bindings 473
  add items 467
  apple 464
  attributes for entries 469
  attributes for widget 468
  button for 462
  by name package 470
  cascade 388
  cascaded menu helper procedure 472
  clone for tearoff 467
  define with resource database 482
  delete items 467
  entries via resources 481
  entry index keywords 467
  example of different types 463
  example, screen shot 463
  help 464
  invoke action from script 467
  keyboard selection 465
  menubar 464
  menubuttons 462
  multicolumn 469
  multicolumn palette 465
  operations on entries 466
  packing a menubar 403
  pop-up 465
  post on screen 468
  system 464
  system color 623
  tear off 468
  Tk widget 462
  unpost from display 468
  user defined 481
  virtual events 466
Menu, system color 623
MenuActive, system color 623
MenuActiveText, system color 623
menubutton, Tk widget 462
MenuDisabled, system color 623
MenuGet maps from name to menu 471
MenuText, system color 623

message
 arranging text 494
 attributes 494
 formats long lines of text 493
 text layout 493
 Tk widget 493
Message Box 600
message catalogs 222
 example 224
 managing 223
 namespaces and 225
Meta key 444, 446
Metakit
 adding data to a view 362
 an embedded database 349
 creating a view or table 361
 data model 359
 examining data 360
 selecting rows 361
 tables and views 360
microsecond precision for time 829
Microsoft VC++ compiler 732
Microsoft Word special characters 55
millimeters 557
MIME type 265
min max scale, example 561
mingw, free Windows C compiler 836
minimize, window operation 660
minimum button width 832
minimum size, pane in panedwindow 430
minimum size, window 659
minimum widget size, with grid 417
minute, %M 184
missing font 480
mkdir, make directory 109
Mod, general event modifier bit 444
-mode, event option 449
-mode, fconfigure option for serial devices 232
mode, file attribute 114
Modified, virtual event 830
modifiers, event 443
modify time, file attribute 109
modifying a list 66, 68
Modifying Tcl_Obj Values 705
module data 182
module prefix for procedure names 181
module support 181
month, %B 184
Motion, window event 440
Mounting VFS 352
mouse 632
 button repeat control 832
 coordinates 666
 cursor on Windows 632
 cursors 785
 cursors, all possible 633
 event coordinates 436
 event, generate 448
 events 441
 hide cursor 632
 moving 448
 warping 448
MouseWheel event 811
MouseWheel, window event 440, 442
move cursor, entry widget 514
moving the mouse 448
msgcat package 226, 814
msgcat::mc 226
msgcat::mcload 226
msgcat::mclocale 226
msgcat::mcpreferences 226
msgcat::mcset locale 226
msgcat::mcunknown 225, 226
mtime, file attribute 114
multi_sz, registry value type 126
multicolumn palette menus 465
multiline labels 491
multiple
 foreach loop variables 801
 interpreters 392
 interpreters and Safe-Tcl 291, 802
 loop variables with foreach 81
 return values 139
 selection mode, listbox 527
 value lists with foreach 82
multi-threaded Tcl scripts. See threads.
multiway branch, switch 77
mutexes 339
mv. See file rename

N

n, anchor position 616
n, regular expression option 157
name
 command-line argument 30
 giving out yours 664
 manipulating file 777
 namespace syntax 213
 of all interpreters 664
 of atom 668
 of color 623
 of current interpreter 296, 318
 of encoding 222
 of fonts 641
 of geometry manager for window 665
 of I/O channels 819
 of images 626
 of interpreter, in C 780
 of interpreter, send 648, 664, 669
 of packages 176
 of procedure 11
 of text marks 552
 of variable 5
 of widgets 370
 on icon 661
 qualified namespace 208
 quirks in namespaces 216
 window server 666
Named Fonts 637

namespace 205
    added in Tcl 8.0 806
    and upvar 93
    callbacks and 211
    check if one exists 829
    converting packages to use 213
    efficient variable references 208
    import takes a snapshot 211
    listing commands 212
    message catalogs 225
    name manipulation 213
    nested 209
    original 213
    Tcl command 213
    uplevel, and 216
    using 205
    variables 207
    widgets, images, and interpreters 215
Native Buttons and Scrollbars 809
native file name 109
native look and feel 392
Native Menus and Menubars 808
ncgi package 44, 261
ne, anchor position 616
ne, string comparison 828
nested frames 399
nested lists 827
nested namespaces 209
Netscape Navigator 311
network programming 237
network server 242
Network Sockets 801
networking extensions, tcllib 238
New Image Types, Creating 783
newguest.cgi script 45, 47
newguest.html Form 43
newline character 20
newline sensitive matching 153
Newline Translations 799
Newman, Matt 349
Nichols, David 725
Nijtmans, Jan liii, 819
nlink, file attribute 114
NNTP client 238
NO_CONST 717
-nocase, regexp option 158
NOCTTY, open mode 117
NONBLOCK, open mode 117
nonblocking I/O 117, 232
none, registry value type 126
nongreedy quantifiers 151
normal, font 638
-not, lsearch option 70
Numbers, Converting 772
numeric value, widget for 495
nw, anchor position 616

O

o, in string format 57
Object Support, Canvas 784
Object Types, Primitive 772
Object Types, String 772
object-oriented, [incr Tcl] 214
objects with many points 588
Objects, C Command Procedures and Data
    694
Objects, Tcl 772
ODBC lviii
offRelief, widget attribute 615
on-line manual 372
open
    a window 660
    a window, binding 442
    catching errors from 118
    client socket with a timeout 240
    connection to an HTTP server 243
    file dialog 600
    file for an unsafe interpreter 300
    file for writing 117
    files for I/O 116
    Process Pipeline 118
    server socket 240
    Tcl command 116
operators, arithmetic 20
option database. See resource.
option menus 465
Option Processing 775
option, Tk command 477
optional scrollbars 502
Options to the standard file dialogs 600
options vs. attributes vs. resources 372
Oracle lviii
OraTcl lviii
Order, Window Stacking 781
Organizing source into packages 357
orient, widget attribute 613
original namespace 213
Ousterhout, John xlix, lvii, 809
oval, canvas object 572
overRelief, widget attribute 615
override redirect 663
-override, event option 449
-overstrike, font attribute 636
-owner, file attribute 115
ownership, file 109

P

p, regular expression option 157
pack 395
    asymmetric padding 402
    binary data 59
    command options 409
    display space 401
    expand vs. fill 400

grid, combining with 395, 411
into other relatives 407
nested frames 399
order of children 406
packing order 406
packing space and display space 399
padding 402
padding vs. button padding 402
panedwindow and 430
resizing windows 403
scrollbars first 407
space for 399
Tk 4.0 changes 793
Tk command 409
unexpected results 399
package 171
convert to namespaces 213
creating a loadable 697
directory 731
dynamic loading 768
html 261
implemented in C code 174
index 699
index file 173
initialization in C 698
ncgi 44, 261
Tcl command 176, 801
version numbers 173
versions, comparing 176
packaging sources in starkits 357
padding
and anchors 616
around widgets 402
asymmetric 402, 413, 830
button vs. packer 402
in buttons 794
provided by labels and buttons 617
widget 617
-padx and -pady, pack options 402
padX, widget attribute 616
padY, widget attribute 616
page array, TclHttpd 279
page layout application 598
palette menus 465
PalmOS, Tcl/Tk distributions for 836
pane manager 423
Pane_Create sets up vertical or horizontal
    panes 423
PaneDrag adjusts the percentage 426
panedwindow 429–434
adding panes 430
creating managed widgets 431
minimum pane size 430
orientation of panes 429
pane order 430
positioning pane contents 430
removing panes 431
PaneGeometry updates the layout 426
parameters, variable number of 88
parent
directory 108
for pack 407
namespace 213
window 600, 601, 602, 665

Parentheses are not a grouping mechanism
    96
parity, serial interface 234
parsing
arguments 424
arguments and Tcl_GetIndexFromObj 710
command-line arguments 80
Tcl commands in C 770
URLs 238
pass by reference 91
Passing Arrays by Name 99
password entry, hidden value 516
password, prompting for 605
paste 591
canvas example 592
PRIMARY or CLIPBOARD selection 592
selection at the insert cursor 513
virtual event 447
PATH_INFO, CGI environment variable 280
PATH_TRANSLATED, CGI environment vari-
    able 280
pathname from window ID 668
pattern match
glob, file name match 122
glob, string match 53
menu entries 467
resource database 476
switch command 77
URL regular expression 159
-peername, fconfigure socket option 231
-peerport, fconfigure option 231
performance
appending strings 56
canvas items 588
declaring variables 208
faster string operations 817
improving expression 16
tuning 202
performance improvements 825
Perl 1
-permissions, file attribute 115
PGM image format 628
Photo image attributes 628
Photo image operations 629
photo, C interface 783
pid, Tcl command 124
pie slice, canvas 567
pipes 122
and errors 382
closing 383
fileevent 229
setting up in C 770
Pitfalls of Shared Tcl_Obj Values 706
pixel depth 669
pixels 638
pixels per inch 669
pixmap
configuration type 760
image format 628
in C 786

off screen 762
pkg_mkIndex options 174
pkg_mkIndex, Tcl command 173, 699
pkgIndex.tcl in a Starkit 354
place
    basics 421
    event option 449
    geometry manager 421
    panedwindow and 430
    Tk command 427
placement options 427
plain file 108
Platform-Independent Fonts 808
Platform-Specific End of Line Characters 120
Platform-specific file attributes 115
plugin
    examples, web browser 314
    Tcl 8.2 support 818
    Tcl in a Web page 314
plus, in bindings 436
Plus1ObjCmd procedure 706
Pointer Warping 822
pointer warping 448
points 638
points per pixel 639
polygon, canvas item 573
POP3 client 238
POP3 server 238
pop-up menus 465
port, TclHttpd 286
position
    a window above a sibling 422
    in text widget 534
    in virtual root window 667
    relative to widget 421
    text anchor 786
POSIX
    errorCode 85
    file access 117
    flags for open 117
post menu on screen 468
POST, form data 247
POST, HTTP protocol 247
postcascade , menu operation 468
Postscript for Widgets Embedded on a Canvas
    Under Windows 833
postscript from canvas 583
pow(x,y), power 21
PPM image format 628
precision, of expressions 15
Predefined Variables 31
Pref_Add 673
Pref_Dialog 675
Pref_Init 672
PrefDialogItem 676
PrefDismiss 680
PrefEntrySet 677
preferences 671

data definition 673
help 678
initialization 672
items, adding 673
read from file 679
saving to file 678
user interface 675
variables 674
PrefFixupBoolean 677
PrefItemHelp 678
--prefix=dir 734
PrefReadFile 672
PrefReset 679
PrefSave 678
PrefValue 674
PrefValueSet 674
present working directory. See current directory.
Preserving errorInfo when calling error 85
preserving threads 330–331
PRIMARY selection 593
Primitive Object Types 772
print
    a procedure definition 188
    environment variable values 124
    in regular expressions 156
    See puts.
    string class 55
    variable by name 92
PrintByName, Tcl procedure 459
printer points 557
printf. See format command
private procedure 182
proc, Tcl command 11, 87
procedure
    arguments from HTML forms 189
    array parameters 99
    as parameter 191
    characters allowed in names 11
    construct dynamically 133
    definition 11, 87
    for button commands 455
    importing and exporting 210
    introspection 188
    library 171
    multiple return values 139
    naming conventions 181
    printing definition 188
    query definition 188
    small is good 673
    to build dialogs 606
    variable scope 87
process ID 124
Processing HTML Form Data 42
profiling Tcl code 203
program and Tcl_AppInit, Tcl main 720
program and Tk_AppInit, Tk main 721
program arguments, TclHttpd 286
program output, saving 378
programming
    and Tcl, C 693

entry widgets 517
listboxes 520
scales 497
scrollbars 505
-progress, http::geturl option 252
prompt for a password 605
Prompter Dialog 607
Prompting for input 119
property of widget. See attribute.
Property, window event 440
Protocol Errors, Handling Graphic 782
protocol handler, window manager 662
provide, package operation 176
provide/require package model 171
proxy, web server 244
pseudo color visual class 624
punct, in regular expressions 156
punct, string class 55
Puoplo, Gerald lviii
putenv 779
puts, limited with safe interp 306
puts, Tcl command 119
pwd, Tcl command 122

Q

q, regular expression option 157
qualified names 208
qualified names, performance 208
qualifiers, namespace operation 213
Quantifiers in regular expressions 146
-query, http::geturl option 252
QUERY_STRING, CGI environment variable
    280
querying aliases 296
questhead 783
quirks, namespaces 216
quit application, protocol to 661
quit button 378
quotes compared to concat and list 67
quoting
    and eval 129, 136
    and regular expressions 144
    automatic 65
    tips, funny values 7
    tips, grouping 10

R

radiobutton, Tk widget 458
Raines, Paul lviii
raise an error 85
raise, Tk command 409
raised, relief 615
Raising an error with return 86
rand(), random number 21
Random Access I/O 121
random number

example 91
example using namespaces 206, 209
function 21
in C 701
RandomCmd C command procedure 700
RandomObjCmd C command procedure 703
RDONLY, open mode 117
RDWR, open mode 117
read
    and evaluate 191
    commands from a socket 653
    file line by line 120
    I/O in background 233
    option database file 477
    options for photo images 630
    Tcl command 120
    Tcl commands from a file 26, 191
    Tcl source code 697, 705
readable, file 109
readline. See gets.
readlink, file operation 109
readlink, with file link command 113
readonly
    entry 516
    entry widget 510
    open 117
    state 511
    text widget 389
    variables 195
readonly, file attribute 116
-real, lsearch option 70
realloc 769
records, with arrays 99
rectangle on canvas 574
recursion limit 829
redefining procedures 89
redirect URL request 279
redisplay. See update.
redo. See history.
reference count, zero initial value 705
Reference Counts, Managing Tcl_Obj 704
References to Tcl_Obj Values, Keeping 714
Referencing an array indirectly 97
reflection and debugging 183
regexp
    command options 70, 158
    in text search 542
    lsearch option 70
    Tcl command 158
register image format, in C 783
registry, font 638
registry, Tcl command 126
regsub
    counting with 163
    direct return of substituted string 829
    Tcl command 162
regular expression 143, 158
    C library 775
    new for Tcl 8.1 815
    syntax 145, 154
Reid, Steve 737

relative and absolute window sizes 422
relative position of windows 421
releasing threads 330–331
Relief Style 786
relief, button 831
relief, widget attribute 615
Remote eval using sockets 653
REMOTE_ADDR, CGI environment variable 280
REMOTE_USER, CGI environment variable 280
Removing Elements from a Hash Table 713
rename, Tcl command 89
Renaming Files and Directories 113
Reparent, window event 440
reparented frame 663
repeating a string 50
replacing substring 50
Reporting Script Errors 771
REQUEST_METHOD, CGI environment variable 280
REQUEST_URI, CGI environment variable 280
requested hight of widget 666
require, package operation 176
ResEdit, Macintosh 28, 29
ResizeRequest, window event 440
resizing
    and -expand 403
    grids 418
    text and scrollbar 381
    windows 387, 403
    windows, effect of expand 404
resource 475
    associated with Tcl variable 673
    attribute names 372
    attribute vs. options vs. 372
    class 476
    color 478
    database access 479
    database description 475
    example 684
    file example 478
    font 477
    for all button widgets 460
    for canvas objects 588
    ID Management, X 787
    introduction 475
    loading from files 477, 672
    lookup in C code 783
    Macintosh 28
    name patterns 476
    non-standard names 482
    order of patterns 477
    specifications 372
    user vs. application 483
    with variable references 484
resource class, color 621
Resource_ButtonFrame, defines buttons 480
Resource_GetFamily merges resources 483

resource_list, registry value type 126
RESOURCE_MANAGER property 476
Result Codes from Command Procedures 702
result string, managing in C 702, 769
return codes, Tcl_Eval 702
Return key 441
return multiple values 139
return, Tcl command 11, 86
reverse video 621
RGB color values 622, 623
ridge, relief 615
ring the bell 497
Rooms. See Virtual Root.
root window ID 450
-root, event option 450
root, file name 109
-rootx, event option 450
-rooty, event option 450
Rose, Marshall 291
Roseman, Mark 359
rotation not supported, canvas 588
round(x), round to integer 21
row insert, Metakit view 362
row of buttons 397
rows of widgets 411
rows, uniform size 830
RS 232, serial devices 235
rubber banding 574
Run procedure 381
Running Programs with exec 105
runs Tcl commands from C, Tcl_Eval 724

S

s, anchor position 616
s, in string format 57
s, regular expression option 157
S, s, in binary format 60
safe after command 307
safe base 300
safe interpreter, creating 301
safe interpreters 295
safe::interpAddToAccessPath 301
safe::interpConfigure 301
safe::interpCreate 301
safe::interpDelete 301
safe::interpFindInAccess 301
safe::interpInit 301
safe::loadTk 811
safe::setLogCmd 301
Safesock security policy 302
Safe-Tcl 291, 802, 806
Safe-Tk and the Browser Plugin 311
Safe-Tk Restrictions 313
same width widgets with grid 418

Sample Extension 737
sample message catalog files 224
sample regular expressions 161
saving preferences 678
Saving session state 662
saving state as Tcl commands 688
scale of screen units 669
scale widget 495
    attributes 496
    bindings 495
    canvas implementation 561
    operations 497
    Tk widget 495
    variable 495
scaling canvas objects 563
scan, Tcl command 58
scanf. See scan command
scope
    for callbacks 211
    global variables 90
    local variables 89
screen
    coordinates vs. canvas coordinates 587
    depth 669
    for toplevel 487
    height 666
    identifier 666
    measurement units 557, 613
        converting 666
        in C 786
        scaling 669
    multiple 486
    position of window 666
    relative coordinates 667
    width 666
screen savers and bell 833
Script Errors, Reporting 771
script library 171
    initialization 178
    setting with TCL_LIBRARY 180
    using 37
script, current 191
script, namespace callbacks 213
SCRIPT_NAME, CGI environment variable
    280
Scriptics Corporation 809
scripts and the library 191
Scripts from C, Invoking 696, 724
scripts in different encodings 220
scroll entry widget 518
Scroll_Set manages optional scrollbars 501
scrollbar 499
    attributes 504
    automatic hiding 502
    bindings 503
    entry widget 516
    example 500, 502
    for canvas 558
    for listbox 527
    for two widgets 686
    horizontal or vertical 613
    operations 505

protocol with widgets 501
    set size 501
    system color 623
    Tk widget 499
    widgets on a canvas 579
    with text 381
ScrollFixup 680
sdarchive, starkit archive 351
sdx, starkit development tool 352
se, anchor position 616
search operation, in text 542
search path, library 172, 177
searching
    arrays 97
    lists 69, 827
    text widget 542, 552
    through files 387
second, %S 184
secure hash algorithm, sha1 740
Secure sockets 817
secure web access 255
security policies 301
    and Browser Plugin 315
    configuration 318, 319
    configured for each client 318
    creating 320
    feature sets 319
    Safesock 302
    Tempfile 304
seek, Tcl command 121
select loop, Tcl interface 228
select text in entry widget 513
select. See fileevent.
selectBackground, widget attribute 620, 642
selectBorderWidth, widget attribute 642
selectColor, widget attribute 620
selectForeground, widget attribute 620, 642
Selecting data with mk::select 361
Selecting Multiple Files with tk_getOpenFile
    832
selection
    adjust, entry widget 513
    and clipboard in C 781
    attributes 642
    canvas example 588, 595
    clear 518
    CLIPBOARD 594
    deleting 514
    exporting to X 642
    handler example 595
    model 591
    ownership 595
    PRIMARY 593
    text widget 540
    Tk command 594
    virtual event 830
selectMode, for listbox 524
self-checking form 276
self-contained Tcl distribution 350
self-updating applications 364
send 648

application name in C 780
command information 664
command options 648
command to another application 649
constructing command reliably 651
name of interpreter 648, 664
timeout changed in Tk 4.0 794
Tk command 648
X authority required 648
sender application 650
-sendevent, event option 450
sending messages to threads 328–330
serial ports 235, 808, 816, 828
-serial, event option 449
server socket options 241
server sockets 240
server, multi-threaded example 335
SERVER_NAME, CGI environment variable
280
SERVER_PORT, CGI environment variable
280
SERVER_PROTOCOL, CGI environment variable 280
SERVER_SOFTWARE, CGI environment variable 280
services, on Windows 201
session, window system 662
client 662
command 662
saving 662
Set Conversions, Character 718
set, Tcl command 5, 13
setgrid, widget attribute 642
sha1, secure hash algorithm 740
share, I/O channels with interp 292
shared libraries 171, 174, 697
shared resources, threads 332
Shared Tcl_Obj Values, Pitfalls of 706
shared variables, threads 337–338
sharing code as Starkits 357
Shen, Sam 201
Shift key 444
-shortname, file property 115
-shrink, image operation 630
shrinking frames and pack propagate 396
signal handling, in C 778
Signals, Working with 778
significant digits 15
Simple Records 99
sin(x), sine 21
single selection mode, listbox 525
sinh(x), hyperbolic sine 21
SiteFooter 270
SiteMenu 270
SitePage 269
size
attributes 613

font attribute 636
not valid until window is mapped 665
of file 109
of integer word 826
of label 490
placement and decoration 659
relative to widget 421
-slant, font attribute 636
slaves, interp operation 292
sleep, Tcl_Sleep 776
sleep. See after.
Smith, Chad lviii
SMTP client 238
SMTP server 238
socket 237
accepting connections 240
added in Tcl 7.5 801
client side 239
client timeout 240
connect to HTTP server 243
limited with safe interp 302
listen 240
peer address 231
read Tcl commands from 653
server example 242
special file 114
Tcl Command 239
socket I/O, non-blocking 228
solid, relief 615
sort 70
-sorted, lsearch option 70
sorting lists 70
source
example 688
hidden command 301
in safe interpreters 301
loading code into TclHttpd 267, 282
Tcl command 26, 28
source code
best location 734
compiling Tcl from 731
distribution, Tcl 730
is worth reading,Tcl 697, 705
source files relative to current script 38
SourceForge 836
space
around widgets 402
in array indices 96
in regular expressions 156
in string format 58
string class 55
spacing, widgets 617
special characters in character sets 145
specifying a locale 223
Spencer, Henry 143, 813
spinbox 511
attributes 515
splice lists together 67
spline curve on canvas 570
split data into Tcl lists 72
split file names 109
split, Tcl command 71

sqrt(x), square root 21
square brackets 18
srand(x), random number seed 21
SSL and TLS 255
SSL channel plugin 817
stack depth limit 829
stack trace 83, 190
stack, data structure 101
stack, example 101
stacking I/O channels 817
stacking order, window 407, 409, 431, 660, 663, 781
standalone Tcl script 26
Standard Configure Flags 733
Standard Dialogs 599, 804
Standard Directory Structure 730
Standard Header Files 740
Standard Makefile targets, TEA 740
standard options 372
Standard Tcl Library 38
    networking extensions 238
    Starkit main.tcl file 358
    tcllib 261, 276
starkit
    accessing its VFS 355
    archive 351
    create a simple one 352
    creating tclhttpd.kit 356
    examine the virtual file system 355
    files in 353
    kitten extension bundle 357
    main program 353
    packaging Tcl applications 350
    sdx development tool 352
    sharing among applications 357
    starkit::autoextend and auto_path 356
    starkit::startup return values 358
    starpacks 351
    storing application data 362
    thin clients 364
    Wiki 363
starpack 358
    how to create 354
    Tclkit and Starkits 351
-start, lsearch option 70
stat, file attributes 109
stat, symlink attributes 109
state
    canvas and canvas items 566
State of Entries, Listboxes, and Labels 831
state of window 661
-state, event option 449
static code checker 200
static color visual class 624
status, http::geturl result 253
Status, Tcl procedure 672
status, TclHttpd 281
stderr, standard error output 4
stdin, standard input 4

stdout, standard output 4
sticky geometry settings 425
-sticky, grid option 412
stop bits, serial interface 234
Stop procedure 383
store widget names in variables 370
Storing application data in a Starkit 362
strftime 761
strftime, see clock format
string 49
    characters from 72
    class names 54
    classification 50, 54
    command interface in C 700
    command, changes in Tcl 8.1 815
    comparison 52, 53
    comparison operators 828
    comparison, using expr 52
    concatenate 67
    display. See label.
    dynamic (DString) in C 773
    effect of backslash-newline 493
    encoding conversions 222
    expressions 52
    extract a character 50
    find last substring 50
    identifiers (UIDS) in C 784
    indices 51
    internationalization in C 717
    length in characters 50
    mapping to new strings 55
    match simple pattern 50
    matching 53
    matching, regular expressions in C 775
    object types in C 772
    processing with subst 141
    repeating 50
    replacing substring 50
    result, managing in C 702, 769
    storage size 50
    Tcl command 49, 50
stroke, canvas example 572
structures, with arrays 99
Stub Libraries, Using 735
style
    guide, Tcl 182
    Line Cap 786
    Line Join 786
    Relief 786
    Text Justification 786
subpatterns to parse strings 160
subst
    document templates 279
    Tcl command 140
    template example 269
substitution
    and hidden commands 298
    before grouping 10
    no eval 140
    rules 17
-subwindow, event option 450
summary of package loading 175
summary of the Tk Commands 373

Sun Microsystems l, 809
sunken, relief 615
sw, anchor position 616
SWIG 695
switch
    example 482
    on exact strings 78
    substitutions in patterns 78
    Tcl command 77
    with "fall through" cases 78
Sybase lviii
SybTcl lviii
symbolic and hard links 827
symbolic link 109
symbolic link, file 113
sync, command-line argument 30
synchronous message sending, threads 328–
    329
syntax 17
    advanced regular expressions 155
    arrays 95
    character code 20
    command 4
    curly braces 4
    dollar sign 18
    I/O pipelines 106
    list 63
    regular expressions 154
    square brackets 18
    Tcl Dev Kit Checker 200
system colors, Windows 622
system encoding 218
system font 637
system menus 464
-system, file attribute 115

T

t, regular expression option 157
tab character, \t 20
Tab key 441
tab stops 540
tab to change focus 604
tab, default binding 604
Table, Hash 708, 713
table-like layouts, grid 411
Tables or views in a Metakit database 360
tag
    canvas vs. text 561
    canvas widget 559, 561
    canvas, logical combination 560
    text widget 535, 537
        attributes 535
        bindings 540
        initialization 537
tail, file name 109
tan(x), tangent 21
tanh(x), hyperbolic tangent 21
target, interp operation 292
TChar 774

Tcl 719
Tcl 7.4 791
Tcl 7.5 lii, 799
Tcl 7.6 lii, 803
Tcl 8.0 Patch Releases 809
Tcl and Extensions, Compiling 729
Tcl and the Tk Toolkit, book lvii
Tcl and Tk sources, on the web 729
Tcl books
    [incr Tcl] From The Ground Up lviii
    Building Network Management Tools with Tcl/
        Tk lviii
    Effective Tcl/Tk Programming lviii
    Exploring Expect lvii
    Graphical Applications with Tcl & Tk lviii
    Tcl and the Tk Toolkit lvii
    Tcl/Tk for Programmers lviii
    Tcl/Tk in a Nutshell lviii
    Tcl/Tk Tools lviii
    Tcl/Tk: A Developer's Guide lvii
    Web Tcl Complete lviii
Tcl C Library 696, 768
Tcl Command
    memory 769
Tcl command
    after, timer events 228
    append, strings 56
    array, data type 97
    bgerror, error handler 202, 771
    binary, convert between string and binary 59
    break, exit loop 83
    catch, error handler 83
    cd, change directory 122
    close, I/O channel 121
    concat, concatenate strings and lists 67
    console, Windows and Macintosh 29, 800
    continue, loop 83
    dde, dynamic data exchange 816
    encoding, character sets 222
    eof, test end of file 120
    error, raise error 85
    eval, evaluate a string 130
    exec, run programs 106
    exit, terminate 124
    expr, math expressions 6
    fblocked, I/O channel 233
    fconfigure, I/O channel properties 231
    fcopy, I/O channel copy 250
    file, operate on files 108
    fileevent, select I/O channel 229, 382
    flush, I/O channel 118
    for, loop 82
    foreach, loop 79
    format, strings 56
    from C, Tcl_Eval 724, 770
    generating with list 46
    gets, read line 120
    glob, match file names 122
    global, variables 90
    history, of commands 197
    if, conditional 76
    incr, improved version 92
    incr, increment variable 13
    info, introspection 186
    interp, create interpreter 292

join, merge lists 72
lappend, append to list 66
lindex, element from list 68, 71
linsert, modify list 68
list for code generation 46
list, create lists 65
list-related commands 64
llength, list length 68
load, compiled extensions 178, 697
lrange, list sublist 68
lreplace, modify list 68
lset 66
lsort, sort list 70
memory, for debugging malloc/free 710
namespace, variables and procedures 207, 213
number executed 190
open, I/O channel 116
package, manage libraries 176
pid, get process ID 124
pkg_mkIndex, generate package index 173
proc, define procedures 11, 87
puts, print line 119
pwd, get working directory 122
read, I/O channel 120
regexp, match regular expression 158
registry, Windows 126
regsub, regular expression substitution 162
rename, commands and procedures 89
return, from procedure 11, 86
scan, parsing strings 58
See also Tk command
seek, move I/O channel offset 121
set, getting variable value 13
set, variable assignment 5
socket, network 239
source, read Tcl script file 26
split, data into list 71
string, collection of operations 50
subst, substitute Tcl in data 140
switch, multiway branch 77
table of 22
tell, read I/O channel offset 121
testthread 815
time, measure command speed 202
trace, variables 193
unknown, command fallback 178
unset, delete variable 15
uplevel, evaluate in different scope 138
upvar, variable references 91
vwait, wait for event 230
while, loop 79
writing commands to files 688
Tcl Core Team, TCT 825
Tcl Dev Kit development tools 200
Tcl distribution, self-contained 350
Tcl Engineering Manual 182
Tcl Extension Architecture 729
Tcl Extention Architecture (TEA) 736
Tcl Improvement Proposal, TIP 825
Tcl Initialization 695
Tcl library 192
Tcl main program and Tcl_AppInit 720
Tcl Objects 772
Tcl Scripts, Calling Out to 696

Tcl Service Manager 201
Tcl shell library environment 179
Tcl shell, sample program 389, 652
Tcl source code is worth reading 697, 705
Tcl source directory structure 730
Tcl Style Guide 182
Tcl variable
    argc 31
    argv 29, 80, 662, 800
    auto_index 31
    auto_noexec 107, 179
    auto_noload 178
    auto_path 172, 177, 180
    embed_args 31
    env 31, 124
    errorCode 85
    errorInfo 83, 85
    from C 771
    tcl_interactive 31
    tcl_library 180, 192
    tcl_patchLevel 31
    tcl_pkgPath 180
    tcl_platform 31
    tcl_precision 15
    tcl_prompt1 31
    tcl_version 31
Tcl version 192
Tcl, C Programming and 693
Tcl, compiling from source 729, 731
Tcl, CVS repository 729
tcl.m4 autoconf macros 736
Tcl/Tk
    8.4 825
Tcl/Tk 8.0 lii, 805
Tcl/Tk 8.1 liii, 813
Tcl/Tk 8.2 liii, 817
Tcl/Tk 8.3 819
Tcl/Tk for Programmers, book lviii
Tcl/Tk for Real Programmers, book lvii
Tcl/Tk in a Nutshell, book lviii
Tcl/Tk Tools, book lviii
Tcl_Access 778
Tcl_AddErrorInfo 769
Tcl_AddObjErrorInfo 769
Tcl_Alert-Notifier 775
Tcl_Alloc 769
Tcl_Alloc and Tcl_Free 710
Tcl_AllocStatBuf 778
Tcl_AllowExceptions 771
Tcl_AppendAllObjTypes 772
Tcl_AppendElement 702, 769
Tcl_AppendObjToObj 773
Tcl_AppendResult 702, 712, 750, 751, 769
Tcl_AppendStringsToObj 704, 773
Tcl_AppendToObj 773
Tcl_AppendUnicodeToObj 773
Tcl_AppInit 695, 719, 720, 768
Tcl_AsyncCreate 778
Tcl_AsyncDelete 778

Tcl_AsyncInvoke 778
Tcl_AsyncMark 778
Tcl_AsyncReady 778
Tcl_AttemptAlloc 769
Tcl_AttemptRealloc 769
Tcl_AttemptSetObjLength 773
Tcl_BackgroundError 771
Tcl_Backslash 770
Tcl_BadChannelOption 776
TCL_BREAK 724
Tcl_CallWhenDeleted 768
Tcl_CancelIdleCall 776
Tcl_ChannelBlockModeProc 777
Tcl_ChannelBuffered 777
Tcl_ChannelClose2Proc 777
Tcl_ChannelCloseProc 777
Tcl_ChannelFlushProc 777
Tcl_ChannelGetHandleProc 777
Tcl_ChannelGetOptionProc 777
Tcl_ChannelHandlerProc 777
Tcl_ChannelInputProc 777
Tcl_ChannelOutputProc 777
Tcl_ChannelSeekProc 777
Tcl_ChannelSetOptionProc 777
Tcl_ChannelType 777
Tcl_ChannelVersion 777
Tcl_ChannelWatchProc 777
Tcl_ChannelWideSeekProc 777
Tcl_Chdir 778
Tcl_ClearChannelHandlers 777
Tcl_Close 776
Tcl_CommandComplete 770
Tcl_CommandTraceInfo 770
Tcl_Concat 773
Tcl_ConcatObj 773
Tcl_ConditionFinalize 778
Tcl_ConditionNotify 778
Tcl_ConditionWait 778
TCL_CONTINUE 724
Tcl_ConvertCountedElement 769
Tcl_ConvertElement 769
Tcl_ConvertToType 772
Tcl_CreateAlias 768
Tcl_CreateAliasObj 768
Tcl_CreateChannel 351, 776
Tcl_CreateChannelHandler 776
Tcl_CreateCloseHandler 776
Tcl_CreateCommand 695, 699, 744, 747,
    749, 768
Tcl_CreateEncoding 773
Tcl_CreateEventSource 775
Tcl_CreateExitHandler 779
Tcl_CreateFileHandler 775
Tcl_CreateHashEntry 713, 774
Tcl_CreateInterp 695, 722, 768

Tcl_CreateMathFunc 772
Tcl_CreateObjCommand 695, 709, 720, 768
Tcl_CreateObjTrace 770
Tcl_CreateSlave 768
Tcl_CreateThread 778
Tcl_CreateThreadExitHandler 778
Tcl_CreateTimerHandler 776
Tcl_CreateTrace 770
Tcl_CutChannel 777
Tcl_DecrRefCount 706, 713, 727, 756, 772
Tcl_DeleteAssocData 774
Tcl_DeleteChannelHandler 776
Tcl_DeleteCloseHandler 776
Tcl_DeleteCommand 764, 768
Tcl_DeleteCommandFromToken 768
Tcl_DeleteEvents 775
Tcl_DeleteEventSource 775
Tcl_DeleteExitHandler 779
Tcl_DeleteFileHandler 775
Tcl_Delete-HashEntry 774
Tcl_DeleteHashTable 774
Tcl_DeleteInterp 722, 768
Tcl_DeleteThreadExitHandler 778
Tcl_DeleteTimerHandler 776
Tcl_DeleteTrace 770
Tcl_DelteHashEntry 713
Tcl_DetachChannel 776
Tcl_DetachPids 770
Tcl_DiscardResult 771
Tcl_DontCallWhenDeleted 768
Tcl_DoOneEvent 775, 781
Tcl_DoWhenIdle 776
Tcl_DString 774
Tcl_DStringAppend 717, 773
Tcl_DStringAppendElement 773
Tcl_DStringEndSublist 773
Tcl_DStringFree 773
Tcl_DStringGetResult 773
Tcl_DStringInit 717, 773
Tcl_DStringLength 773
Tcl_DString-Result 773
Tcl_DStringSetLength 773
Tcl_DStringStartSublist 773
Tcl_DStringValue 718, 773
Tcl_DumpActiveMemory 769
Tcl_DuplicateObj 705, 772
Tcl_Eof 776
Tcl_ErrnoId 769
Tcl_ErrnoMsg 769
TCL_ERROR 724, 771
Tcl_Eval 695, 696, 724, 770, 771
Tcl_Eval modifies its argument. 724
Tcl_Eval, Bypassing 725
Tcl_Eval, return codes 702
TCL_EVAL_DIRECT 770

Tcl_EvalEx 724, 770
Tcl_EvalFile 695, 770
Tcl_EvalObj 716, 771
Tcl_EvalObjEx 724, 771
Tcl_EvalObjv 725, 771
Tcl_EvalTokens 770
Tcl_EvalTokensStandard 770
Tcl_EventuallyFree 713, 769
Tcl_Exit 779
Tcl_ExitThread 778
Tcl_ExposeCommand 768
Tcl_ExprBoolean 772
Tcl_ExprBooleanObj 772
Tcl_ExprDouble 772
Tcl_ExprDoubleObj 772
Tcl_ExprLong 772
Tcl_ExprLongObj 772
Tcl_ExprObj 772
Tcl_ExprString 772
Tcl_ExternalToUtf 774
Tcl_ExternalToUtfDString 718, 774
Tcl_Finalize 779
Tcl_FinalizeNotifier 775
Tcl_FinalizeThread 778
Tcl_FindExectuable 695
Tcl_FindExecuatable 768
Tcl_FindHashEntry 774
tcl_findLibrary 180, 810
Tcl_FirstHashEntry 709, 714, 774
Tcl_Flush 776
Tcl_Free 727, 769
Tcl_Free, Tcl_Alloc and 710
Tcl_FreeEncoding 719, 773
Tcl_FreeParse 770
Tcl_FSAccess 778
Tcl_FSChdir 778
Tcl_FSConvertToPathType 778
Tcl_FSCopyDirectory 777
Tcl_FSCopyFile 777
Tcl_FSCreateDirectory 777
Tcl_FSData 778
Tcl_FSDeleteFile 351, 777
Tcl_FSEqualPaths 778
Tcl_FSEvalFile 778
Tcl_FSFileAttrsGet 778
Tcl_FSFileAttrsSet 778
Tcl_FSFileAttrStrings 778
Tcl_FSFileSystemInfo 778
Tcl_FSGetCwd 778
Tcl_FSGetFileSystemForPath 778
Tcl_FSGetInternalRep 778
Tcl_FSGetNativePath 778
Tcl_FSGetNormalizedPath 778
Tcl_FSGetPathType 778
Tcl_FSGetTranslatedPath 778

Tcl_FSGetTranslatedStringPath 778
Tcl_FSJoinPath 778
Tcl_FSJoinToPath 778
Tcl_FSLink 778
Tcl_FSListVolumes 778
Tcl_FSLoadFile 778
Tcl_FSLstat 778
Tcl_FSMatchInDirectory 778
Tcl_FSMountsChanged 778
Tcl_FSNewNativePath 778
Tcl_FSOpenFileChannel 778
Tcl_FSPathSeparator 778
Tcl_FSRegister 778
Tcl_FSRemoveDirectory 778
Tcl_FSRenameFile 778
Tcl_FSSplitPath 778
Tcl_FSStat 778
Tcl_FSUnregister 778
Tcl_FSUtime 778
Tcl_Get*FromObj warning 707
Tcl_GetAlias 768
Tcl_GetAliases 768
Tcl_GetAliasObj 768
Tcl_GetAssocData 774
Tcl_GetBoolean 772
Tcl_GetBooleanFromObj 772
Tcl_GetByteArrayFromObj 773
Tcl_GetChannel 776
Tcl_GetChannelBufferSize 776
Tcl_GetChannelHandle 776
Tcl_GetChannelInstanceData 776
Tcl_GetChannelMode 776
Tcl_GetChannelName 776
Tcl_GetChannelNames 776
Tcl_GetChannelNamesEx 776
Tcl_GetChannelOption 776
Tcl_GetChannelThread 777
Tcl_GetChannelType 776
Tcl_GetCharLength 773
Tcl_GetCommandInfo 726, 748, 768
Tcl_GetCommandInfoFromToken 768
Tcl_GetCurrentThread 775
Tcl_GetCwd 778
Tcl_GetDefaultEncodingDir 773
Tcl_GetDouble 772
Tcl_GetDoubleFromObj 772
Tcl_GetEncoding 719, 773
Tcl_GetEncodingName 773
Tcl_GetEncodingNames 773
Tcl_GetErrno 769
Tcl_GetHashKey 774
Tcl_GetHashValue 710, 774
Tcl_GetHostName 779
Tcl_GetIndexFromObj 710, 711, 751, 775, 784

Tcl_GetIndexFromObjStruct 775
Tcl_GetInt 701, 703, 772
Tcl_GetInterpPath 768
Tcl_GetIntFromObj 707, 772
Tcl_GetListFromObj 707
Tcl_GetLongFromObj 772
Tcl_GetMaster 768
Tcl_GetMathFuncInfo 772
Tcl_GetNameOfExecutable 768
Tcl_GetObjResult 703, 724, 755, 769
Tcl_GetObjType 772
Tcl_GetOpenFile 776
Tcl_GetOSTypeFromObj 779
Tcl_GetPathType 777
Tcl_GetRange 773
Tcl_GetRegExpFromObj 775
Tcl_GetRegExpInfo 775
Tcl_Gets 776
Tcl_GetServiceMode 775
Tcl_GetSlave 768
Tcl_GetSlaves 768
Tcl_GetsObj 776
Tcl_GetStackedChannel 777
Tcl_GetStdChannel 777
Tcl_GetString 772
Tcl_GetStringFromObj 772
Tcl_GetStringResult 724, 769
Tcl_GetThreadData 778
Tcl_GetTime 779
Tcl_GetTopChannel 777
Tcl_GetUniChar 773
Tcl_GetUnicode 773
Tcl_GetUnicodeFromObj 773
Tcl_GetVar 696, 771
Tcl_GetVar2 771
Tcl_GetVar2Ex 771
Tcl_GetVersion 779
Tcl_GetWideIntFromObj 772
TCL_GLOBAL_EVAL 770
Tcl_GlobalEval 770, 771
Tcl_GlobalEvalObj 771
Tcl_HashStats 774
Tcl_HashTable 708
Tcl_HideCommand 768
Tcl_IncrRefCount 705, 726, 755, 772
Tcl_Init 720, 768
Tcl_InitCustomHashTable 774
Tcl_InitHashTable 709, 774
Tcl_InitMemory 769
Tcl_InitNotifier 775
Tcl_InitObjHashTable 774
Tcl_InitStubs 698, 736, 744, 768
Tcl_InputBlocked 776
Tcl_InputBuffered 776
tcl_interactive, Tcl variable 31

Tcl_InterpDeleted 768
Tcl_InvalidateStringRep 772
Tcl_Invoke 720
Tcl_Invoke bypasses Tcl_Eval 725
Tcl_IsChannelExisting 777
Tcl_IsChannelRegistered 777
Tcl_IsChannelShared 777
Tcl_IsSafe 768
Tcl_IsShared 706, 772
Tcl_IsStandardChannel 776
Tcl_JoinPath 777
Tcl_JoinThread 778
TCL_LIBRARY, environment variable 180
tcl_library, Tcl variable 180, 192
Tcl_LinkVar 696, 771
Tcl_ListMathFuncs 772
Tcl_ListObjAppendElement 714, 770
Tcl_ListObjAppendList 770
Tcl_ListObjGetElements 770
Tcl_ListObjIndex 769
Tcl_ListObjLength 770
Tcl_ListObjReplace 770
Tcl_LogCommandInfo 769
Tcl_MacConvertTextResource 779
Tcl_MacEvalResource 779
Tcl_MacFindResource 779
Tcl_MacSetEventProc 779
Tcl_Main 695, 768
Tcl_Main and Tcl_AppInit 719
Tcl_MakeFileChannel 776
Tcl_MakeSafe 768
Tcl_MakeTcpClientChannel 777
TCL_MEM_DEBUG 769
Tcl_Merge 769
Tcl_MutexFinalize 778
Tcl_MutexLock 778
Tcl_MutexUnlock 778
Tcl_NewBooleanObj 772
Tcl_NewByteArrayObj 773
Tcl_NewDoubleObj 772
Tcl_NewIntObj 772
Tcl_NewListObj 714, 769
Tcl_NewLongObj 772
Tcl_NewObj 772
Tcl_NewStringObj 726, 772
Tcl_NewUnicodeObj 773
Tcl_NewWideInt 772
Tcl_NextHashEntry 774
Tcl_NotifyChannel 776
Tcl_NumUtfChars 774
Tcl_Obj 705
Tcl_Obj Command Interface, The 703
Tcl_Obj reference count 705
Tcl_Obj Reference Counts, Managing 704
Tcl_Obj structure., The 705

Tcl_Obj Values, Keeping References to 714
Tcl_Obj Values, Modifying 705
Tcl_Obj Values, Pitfalls of Shared 706
Tcl_Obj version of Tk widget 743
Tcl_ObjGetVar2 771
Tcl_ObjSetVar2 771
TCL_OK 724, 771
Tcl_OpenCommandChannel 770, 776
Tcl_OpenFileChannel 776
Tcl_OpenTcpClient 777
Tcl_OpenTcpServer 777
Tcl_OutputBuffered 776
Tcl_Panic 779
Tcl_PanicVA 779
Tcl_ParseBraces 770
Tcl_ParseCommand 770
Tcl_ParseExpr 770
Tcl_ParseQuotedString 770
Tcl_ParseVar 770
Tcl_ParseVarName 770
tcl_patchLevel, Tcl variable 31
tcl_pkgPath, Tcl variable 180
Tcl_PkgPresent 769
Tcl_PkgPresentEx 769
Tcl_PkgProvide 699, 744, 768
Tcl_PkgProvide, Using 699
Tcl_PkgProvideEx 769
Tcl_PkgRequire 768
Tcl_PkgRequireEx 769
tcl_platform 800
        threaded element 323
tcl_platform, debug element 810
tcl_platform, Tcl variable 31
tcl_platform, user element 816
Tcl_PosixError 769
tcl_precision variable 15
tcl_precision, changes in Tcl 8.0 807
Tcl_Preserve 716, 769
Tcl_PrintDouble 772
tcl_prompt1, Tcl variable 31
Tcl_PutEnv 779
Tcl_QueueEvent 775
Tcl_Read 776
Tcl_ReadChars 776
Tcl_ReadRaw 776
Tcl_Realloc 769
Tcl_ReapDetachedProcs 770
Tcl_RecordAndEval 771
Tcl_RecordAndEvalObj 771
Tcl_RegExpCompile 775
Tcl_RegExpExec 775
Tcl_RegExpExecObj 775
Tcl_RegExpMatch 775
Tcl_RegExpMatchObj 775
Tcl_RegExpRange 775

Tcl_RegisterChannel 776
Tcl_RegisterObjType 772
Tcl_Release 716, 769
Tcl_ResetResult 702, 726, 769
Tcl_RestoreResult 771
TCL_RETURN 724
tcl_safeCreateInterp 301
tcl_safeDeleteInterp 301
tcl_safeInitInterp 301
Tcl_SaveResult 771
Tcl_ScanCountedElement 769
Tcl_ScanElement 769
Tcl_Seek 776
Tcl_ServiceAll 775
Tcl_ServiceEvent 775
Tcl_SetAssocData 774
Tcl_SetBooleanObj 772
Tcl_SetByteArray-Length 773
Tcl_SetByteArrayObj 773
Tcl_SetChannelBufferSize 776
Tcl_SetChannelOption 776
Tcl_SetCommandInfo 748, 768
Tcl_SetCommandInfoFromToken 768
Tcl_SetDefaultEncodingDir. 773
Tcl_SetDefaultTranslation 776
Tcl_SetDoubleObj 772
Tcl_SetErrno 769
Tcl_SetErrorCode 769
Tcl_SetErrorCodeVA 769
Tcl_SetHashValue 713, 774
Tcl_SetIntObj 703, 706, 772
Tcl_SetListObj 769
Tcl_SetLongObj. 772
Tcl_SetMainLoop 768
Tcl_SetMaxBlockTime 775
Tcl_SetNotifier 818
Tcl_SetObjErrorCode 769
Tcl_SetObjLength 773
Tcl_SetObjResult 706, 751, 756, 769
Tcl_SetOSTypeObj 779
Tcl_SetRecursionLimit 771
Tcl_SetResult 702, 769
Tcl_SetServiceMode 775
Tcl_SetStdChannel 777
Tcl_SetStringObj 704, 713, 749, 772
Tcl_SetSystemEncoding 773
Tcl_SetTimer 775
Tcl_SetUnicodeObj 773
Tcl_SetVar 696, 720, 771
Tcl_SetVar2 771
Tcl_SetVar2Ex 771
Tcl_SetWideInt 772
Tcl_SignalId 779
Tcl_SignalMsg 779
Tcl_Sleep 775, 776

Tcl_SourceRCFile 768
Tcl_SpliceChannel 777
Tcl_SplitList 769
Tcl_SplitPath 777
Tcl_StackChannel 777
Tcl_Stat 778
TCL_STATIC 702
Tcl_StaticPackage 769
TCL_STORAGE_CLASS 740
Tcl_StringCaseMatch 775
Tcl_StringMatch 775
Tcl_SubstObj 771
Tcl_Tell 776
Tcl_ThreadAlert 775
Tcl_ThreadQueueEvent 775
Tcl_TraceCommand 770
Tcl_TraceVar 696, 770
Tcl_TraceVar2 770
Tcl_TranslateFileName 773, 777
Tcl_Ungets 776
Tcl_UniChar 774
Tcl_UniCharAtIndex 774
Tcl_UniCharCaseMatch 774
Tcl_UniCharIsAlnum 774
Tcl_UniCharIsAlpha 774
Tcl_UniCharIsControl 774
Tcl_UniCharIsDigit 774
Tcl_UniCharIsGraph 774
Tcl_UniCharIsLower 774
Tcl_UniCharIsPrint 774
Tcl_UniCharIsPunct 774
Tcl_UniCharIsSpace 774
Tcl_UniCharIsUpper 774
Tcl_UniCharIsWordChar 774
Tcl_UniCharLen 774
Tcl_UniCharNcasecmp 774
Tcl_UniCharNcmp 774
Tcl_UniCharToLower 774
Tcl_UniCharToTitle 774
Tcl_UniCharToUpper 774
Tcl_UniCharToUtf 774
Tcl_UniCharToUtfDString 774
Tcl_UnlinkVar 771
Tcl_UnregisterChannel 776
Tcl_UnsetVar 771
Tcl_UnsetVar2 771
Tcl_UnstackChannel 777
Tcl_UntraceCommand 770
Tcl_UntraceVar 770
Tcl_UntraceVar2 770
Tcl_UpdateLinkedVar 771
Tcl_UpVar 771
Tcl_UpVar2 771
Tcl_UtfAtIndex 774
Tcl_UtfBackslash 774

Tcl_UtfCharComplete 774
Tcl_UtfFindFirst 774
Tcl_UtfFindLast 774
Tcl_UtfNext 774
Tcl_UtfPrev 774
Tcl_UtfToExternal 774
Tcl_UtfToExternalDString 718, 774
Tcl_UtfToLower 774
Tcl_UtfToTitle 774
Tcl_UtfToUniChar 774
Tcl_UtfToUniCharDString 774
Tcl_UtfToUpper 774
Tcl_ValidateAllMemory 769
TCL_VARARGS_START 726
Tcl_VarEval 724, 770
Tcl_VarEvalVA 770
Tcl_VarTraceInfo 770
Tcl_VarTraceInfo2 770
tcl_version, Tcl variable 31
TCL_VOLATILE 702
Tcl_WaitForEvent 775
Tcl_WaitPid 770
Tcl_WinTCharToUtf 719, 774
Tcl_WinUtfToTChar 719, 774
Tcl_Write 776
Tcl_WriteChars 776
Tcl_WriteObj 776
Tcl_WriteRaw 776
Tcl_WrongNumArgs 703, 769
TclBlend, Java integration lii
tclConfig.sh 736
Tcler's Wiki 363, 836
Tclets, network applications 311
TclHttpd
    adding source code 267
    architecture 258
    configuration parameters 286
    debug URL 282
    displaying values 282
    document root 286, 287
    document type handler 265
    domain handler 260
    e-mail, sending 283
    error page 278
    group ID 286
    hit counters 281
    HTML template 269
    integrating with application 258
    IP address 286
    log files 289
    not found page 278
    page array 279
    port 286
    quick start configuration 284
    script library 286
    self-checking form 276
    source code distribution 284
    sourcing Tcl scripts 282
    starkit main program 356, 357, 359
    starkit, creating 356

TclPro Debugger, using 282
templates 288
URL domain handler 261
user ID 286
vfs directory 357
webmaster e-mail 279, 286
tclIndex file 177
Tclkit
    and Starkits 349
    Tcl/Tk interpreter 349
    thin clients 363
    zlib compression 354
tcllib
    html package 276
    Standard Tcl Library 276
TclODBC lviii
tclPkgUnknown 175
TclPro Debugger and TclHttpd 282
TclPro is now Tcl Dev Kit 200
tclsh, application 172
TclVFS extension 827
TclX lviii
TCP/IP 239
TCT, Tcl Core Team 825
TEA 729
TEA standard Makefile targets 740
TEA, Tcl Extention Archtecture 736
TEA_LOAD_TKCONFIG 738
TEA_PATH_TCLCONFIG 738
TEA_PATH_TKCONFIG 738
TEA_PRIVATE_TCL_HEADERS 738
TEA_PRIVATE_TK_HEADERS 739
TEA_PUBLIC_TCL_HEADERS 738
TEA_PUBLIC_TK_HEADERS 739
tell, I/O channel 116
tell, Tcl command 121
Tempfile security policy 304
template
    binary format 59
    configure.in 732
    for procedure body 133
    HTML 288
    Makefile.in 733
    SiteMenu and SiteFooter 270
terminal, controlling 117
terminate
    thread 330–331
terminate process 124
test, make target 740
testthread, Tcl command 815
text 531
    anchor positions, in C 786
    and image in a widget 830
    and image on a button 626
    attributes 554
    attributes for tags 535
    attributes from multiple tags 537
    bindings 392, 549
    bold 537
    bounding box 551
    bulleted list 544
    changes in Tk 4.1 802
    clearing marks 552
    color 537
    compare indices 551
    configure tags early 537
    debug setting 551
    deleting 532, 551
    display and fonts, in C 785
    dumping widget contents 552
    embedded window 543, 553
    entry widget 507
    find range of tag 546
    finding marks 552
    get string from widget 552
    hidden 822
    images 552
    in a message widget 493
    index 531, 552
    index arithmetic 533
    insert cursor 631
    insert string 552
    inserting 532, 552
    italic 537
    justification 536, 538
    justification, in C 786
    line spacing 538
    mark 392, 534
        gravity 534, 552
        introspection 546
        names 552
    modification, event 830
    on canvas 575
    operations 551
    read-only 389
    scan for fast scrolling 552
    scrolling operations 553
    search widget 552
    searching 542
    selection 540
    selection event 830
    tabs 540
    tag 392, 535
        bindings 540
        initialization 537
        introspection 546
        operations 553
    Tk 4.0 changes 796
    Tk widget 531
    two scrollbars 500
    underlined 537
    undo mechanism 548, 830
    view line 553
    virtual events 551
    widget introspection 545
    with scrollbar 381
text variable, entry widget 507
textvariables and upvar 93
then. See if.
thin clients and starkits 363, 364
Thomas, Michael 737
Thread extension 322
    commands 343
    loading 324
    See also threads.
thread namespace 343
    See also tpool namespace, tsv namespace

thread::attach 334, 344
thread::cond 340—342, 344
thread::configure 331, 344
thread::create 324—327, 344
thread::detach 334, 344
thread::errorproc 331, 344
thread::eval 344
thread::exists 344
thread::id 344
thread::join 326, 345
thread::mutex 339, 345
thread::names 345
thread::preserve 330, 345
thread::release 330, 345
thread::send 328—330, 345
thread::transfer 334, 345
thread::unwind 345
thread::wait 325, 345
thread pools 342—343
    configuration options 348
Thread Support 778, 814, 815
threads 321—348
    asynchronous messages 329—330
    channels 333—337
    compiling for support 323
    condition variables 340—342
    configuration options 345
    creating 324—327
    creation vs execution 325
    current directory 332
    deadlock with synchronous messages 329
    definition 321
    echo server example 335
    environment variables 332
    error handling 328, 331—332
    event loop 325
    extensions 323
    file access from multiple 333
    ID, thread 324
    joinable 326—327
    killing 330—331
    logging example 333
    main thread termination 324
    messages 328—330
    mutexes 339
    preserving 330—331
    releasing 330—331
    sending messages 328—330
    server example 335
    shared resources 332
    shared variables 337—338
    synchronous messages 328—329
    Tcl interpreters and 323
    tcl_platform(threaded) 323
    thread namespace 343
    thread pools 342—343
    thread safety 323
    thread support, testing for 323
    threading model in Tcl 322
    tpool namespace 347
    transferring I/O channels 334—337
    transferring sockets 334
    tsv namespace 346
tilde in file names 124
tilde key, asciicircum 441
time
    event option 449

formatting 184
getting current 184
in microseconds 829
parsing 184
resolution on Windows 829
stamps in a log 202
Tcl command 202
timeout on client socket 240
-timeout, http::geturl option 252
Timer Events 776
timer events, in C 228, 723
timer, high resolution 185
timer. See after.
TIP, Tcl Improvement Proposal 825
title case conversion 51
-title, of standard dialog 602
title, of window 658
title, supressing 663
Tix lviii
Tk 4.0, porting issues 791
Tk 4.1, porting issues 799
Tk 4.2, porting issues 803
Tk 8.0, porting issues 805
Tk 8.1, porting issues 813
Tk 8.2, porting issues 817
Tk 8.3, porting issues 819, 835
Tk by example 377
Tk C Library 779
tk colormodel, removed in Tk 4.0 797
Tk command
    bell 497
    bind, events 435
    bindtags, binding groups 437
    clipboard, cut and paste 594
    destroy, window 605
    event, generation 448
    focus, on window 603
    font, control 640
    grab, focus 604
    grid, geometry manager 411, 419
    image, manipulation 626
    lower, window 409
    option, resource database 477
    pack, geometry manager 409
    place, geometry manager 427
    raise, window 409
    See also widgets.
    selection, cut and paste 594
    send, command to application 648
    tk, miscellaneous 669
    tkerror 202
    tkwait, for event 605
    unsupported1, window styles 489
    update, events 609
    winfo, window info 663
    wm, window control 657
Tk command summary 373
Tk fundamentals 367
Tk in Child Interpreters 312
Tk main program and Tk_AppInit 721
Tk manual pages 372

tk scaling 808
Tk thread safety 323
Tk widget attributes and the resource data-
    base 372
Tk widget-creation commands 373
Tk widget-manipulation commands 374
tk, Tk command 669
Tk_3DBorder 760
Tk_3DBorderColor 785
Tk_3DBorderGC 785
Tk_3DHorizontalBevel 785
Tk_3DVerticalBevel 785
Tk_Alloc3DBorderFromObj 785
Tk_AllocBitmapFromObj 783
Tk_AllocColorFromObj 784
Tk_AllocCursorFromObj 785
Tk_AllocFontFromObj 785
Tk_Anchor 760
Tk_AppInit, Tk main program and 721
Tk_Attributes 781
Tk_BindEvent 782
tk_bisque, for Tk 3.6 color scheme 621
Tk_CancelIdleCall 764, 766
Tk_CanvasDrawableCoords 784
Tk_CanvasEventuallyRedraw 784
Tk_CanvasGetCoord 784
Tk_CanvasGetTextInfo 784
Tk_CanvasPsBitmap 784
Tk_CanvasPsColor 784
Tk_CanvasPsFont 784
Tk_CanvasPsPath 784
Tk_CanvasPsStipple 784
Tk_CanvasPsY 784
Tk_CanvasSetStippleOrigin 784
Tk_CanvasTagsOption 780
Tk_CanvasTkwin 784
Tk_CanvasWindowCoords 784
Tk_Changes 781
Tk_ChangeWindowAttributes 780
Tk_CharBbox 785
tk_chooseColor 602
tk_chooseDirectory 600
Tk_Class 783
Tk_ClearSelection 781
Tk_ClipboardAppend 781
Tk_ClipboardClear 781
Tk_CollapseMotionEvents 782
Tk_Colormap 781
Tk_ComputeTextLayout 763, 785
TK_CONFIG_ACTIVE_CURSOR 760
TK_CONFIG_ANCHOR 760
TK_CONFIG_BITMAP 760
TK_CONFIG_BOOLEAN 760
TK_CONFIG_BORDER 760
TK_CONFIG_CAP_STYLE 760

TK_CONFIG_COLOR 760
TK_CONFIG_CURSOR 760
TK_CONFIG_CUSTOM 760
TK_CONFIG_DOUBLE 760
TK_CONFIG_END 760
TK_CONFIG_FONT 760
TK_CONFIG_INT 760
TK_CONFIG_JOIN_STYLE 760
TK_CONFIG_JUSTIFY 760
TK_CONFIG_MM 760
TK_CONFIG_PIXELS 760
TK_CONFIG_RELIEF 760
TK_CONFIG_STRING 760
TK_CONFIG_SYNONYM 760
TK_CONFIG_UID 760
TK_CONFIG_WINDOW 760
Tk_ConfigSpec 756, 758
Tk_ConfigSpec typedef 756
Tk_ConfigureInfo 750, 781
Tk_ConfigureValue 750, 751, 781
Tk_ConfigureWidget 753, 781
Tk_ConfigureWidget flags and corresponding
    C types 760
Tk_ConfigureWindow 780
Tk_CoordsToWindow 781
Tk_CreateBinding 782
Tk_CreateBindingTable 782
Tk_CreateClientMessageHandler 782
Tk_CreateErrorHandler 782
Tk_CreateEventHandler 747, 749, 782
Tk_CreateGenericHandler 782
Tk_CreateImageType 783
Tk_CreateItemType 784
Tk_CreateOptionTable 748, 780
Tk_CreatePhotoImageFormat 783
Tk_CreateSelHandler 781
Tk_CreateTimerHandler 764
Tk_CreateWindow 780
Tk_CreateWindowFromPath 746, 748, 780
Tk_DefineBitmap 783
Tk_DefineCursor 780
Tk_DeleteAllBindings 782
Tk_DeleteBinding 782
Tk_DeleteBindingTable 782
Tk_DeleteClientMessageHandler 782
Tk_DeleteErrorHandler 782
Tk_DeleteEventHandler 782
Tk_DeleteGenericHandler 782
Tk_DeleteImage 783
Tk_DeleteOptionTable 766, 780
Tk_DeleteSelHandler 781
Tk_DeleteTimerHandler 764, 766
Tk_Depth 781
Tk_DestroyWindow 749, 780
tk_dialog, built-in dialog 599

Tk_Display 746, 781
Tk_DisplayName 781
Tk_DistanceToTextLayout 785
Tk_DoWhenIdle 754, 755, 765
Tk_Draw3DPolygon 785
Tk_Draw3DRectangle 763, 785
Tk_DrawChars 785
Tk_DrawFocusHighlight 763, 785
Tk_DrawTextLayout 763, 785
Tk_EventuallyFree 765
Tk_Fill3DPolygon 785
Tk_Fill3DRectangle 763, 785
Tk_FindPhoto 783
tk_focusFollowsMouse 603
tk_focusNext 604
Tk_Font 760
Tk_FontId 785
Tk_FontMetrics 785
Tk_Free3DBorder 785
Tk_Free3DBorderFromObj 785
Tk_FreeBitmap 783
Tk_FreeBitmapFromObj 783
Tk_FreeColor 784, 787
Tk_FreeColorFromObj 784
Tk_FreeColormap 785
Tk_FreeConfigOptions 780
Tk_FreeCursor 785
Tk_FreeCursorFromObj 785
Tk_FreeFont 785
Tk_FreeFontFromObj 785
Tk_FreeGC 766, 785
Tk_FreeImage 783
Tk_FreeOptions 766, 781
Tk_FreePixmap 764, 786, 787
Tk_FreeSavedOptions 756, 780
Tk_FreeTextLayout 785
Tk_FreeXId 787
Tk_GCForColor 785
Tk_GeometryRequest 761, 784
Tk_Get3DBorder 785
Tk_Get3DBorderFromObj 785
Tk_GetAllBindings 782
Tk_GetAnchor 786
Tk_GetAnchorFromObj 786
Tk_GetAtomName 787
Tk_GetBinding 782
Tk_GetBitmap 783
Tk_GetBitmapFromData 783
Tk_GetBitmapFromObj 783
Tk_GetCapStyle 786
Tk_GetColor 784
Tk_GetColorByValue 784
Tk_GetColorFromObj 784
Tk_GetColormap 785
Tk_GetCursor 785

Tk_GetCursorFromData 785
Tk_GetCursorFromObj 785
Tk_GetDash 786
Tk_GetFont 785
Tk_GetFontFromObj 785
Tk_GetFontMetrics 761
Tk_GetGC 753, 785
Tk_GetHINSTANCE 787
Tk_GetHWND 787
Tk_GetImage 783
Tk_GetImageMasterData 783
Tk_GetItemTypes 784
Tk_GetJoinStyle 786
Tk_GetJustify 786
Tk_GetJustifyFromObj 786
Tk_GetMMFromObj 786
Tk_GetNumMainWindows 780
tk_getOpenFile 600
tk_getOpenFile, selecting multiple files 832
Tk_GetOption 783
Tk_GetOptionInfo 752, 780
Tk_GetOptionValue 780
Tk_GetPixels 786
Tk_GetPixelsFromObj 786
Tk_GetPixmap 763, 786
Tk_GetRelief 786
Tk_GetReliefFromObj 786
Tk_GetRootCoords 781
tk_getSaveFile 600
Tk_GetScreenMM 786
Tk_GetScrollInfo 781
Tk_GetScrollInfoObj 781
Tk_GetSelection 781
Tk_GetString 748
Tk_GetUid 784
Tk_GetVisual 785
Tk_GetVRootGeometry 781
Tk_Grab 782
Tk_HandleEvent 782
Tk_Height 781
Tk_HWNDToWindow 787
Tk_IdToWindow 780
Tk_Image 783
Tk_ImageChanged 783
Tk_Init 722, 780
Tk_Init procedure 780
Tk_InitImageArgs 783
Tk_InitOptions 749, 780
Tk_InitStubs 779
Tk_InternalBorderBottom 781
Tk_InternalBorderLeft 781
Tk_InternalBorderRight 781
Tk_InternalBorderTop 781
Tk_InternalBorderWidth 781
Tk_InternAtom 787

Tk_IntersectTextLayout 785
Tk_IsContainer 781
Tk_IsEmbedded 781
Tk_IsMapped 753, 781
Tk_IsTopLevel 781
Tk_Justify 760
tk_listboxSingleSelect 795
Tk_Main 721, 779
Tk_MainLoop 781, 782
Tk_MaintainGeometry 784
Tk_MainWindow 780
Tk_MakeWindowExist 780
Tk_ManageGeometry 784
Tk_MapWindow 780
Tk_MeasureChars 761, 785
tk_messageBox 600
Tk_MinReqHeight 781
Tk_MinReqWidth 781
Tk_MoveResizeWindow 780
Tk_MoveToplevelWindow 780
Tk_MoveWindow 780
Tk_Name 780
Tk_NameOf3DBorder 785
Tk_NameOfAnchor 786
Tk_NameOfBitmap 783
Tk_NameOfCapStyle 786
Tk_NameOfColor 784
Tk_NameOfCursor 785
Tk_NameOfFont 785
Tk_NameOfImage 783
Tk_NameOfJoinStyle 786
Tk_NameOfJustify 786
Tk_NameOfRelief 786
Tk_NameToWindow 780
Tk_Offset 781
TK_OPTION_ANCHOR 760
TK_OPTION_BITMAP 760
TK_OPTION_BOOLEAN 760
TK_OPTION_BORDER 760
TK_OPTION_COLOR 760
TK_OPTION_CURSOR 760
TK_OPTION_DOUBLE 760
TK_OPTION_END 760
TK_OPTION_FONT 760
TK_OPTION_INT 760
TK_OPTION_JUSTIFY 760
TK_OPTION_PIXELS 760
TK_OPTION_RELIEF 760
TK_OPTION_STRING 760
TK_OPTION_STRING_TABLE 760
TK_OPTION_SYNONYM 760
TK_OPTION_WINDOW 760
Tk_OptionSpec 758
Tk_OptionSpec typedef 758
Tk_OptionTable 747

Tk_OwnSelection 781
Tk_Parent 781
Tk_ParseArgv 722, 779
Tk_PathName 747, 780
Tk_PhotoBlank 783
Tk_PhotoExpand 783
Tk_PhotoGetImage 783
Tk_PhotoGetSize 783
Tk_PhotoHandle 783
Tk_PhotoPutBlock 783
Tk_PhotoPutZoomedBlock 783
Tk_PhotoSetSize 783
Tk_PointToChar 785
Tk_PostscriptFontName 785
Tk_QueueWindowEvent 782
Tk_RedrawImage 783
Tk_ReqHeight 781
Tk_ReqWidth 781
Tk_ResizeWindow 780
Tk_RestackWindow 781
Tk_RestoreSavedOptions 755, 780
Tk_RestrictEvent 782
Tk_RestrictEvents 782
Tk_Screen 781
Tk_ScreenNumber 781
Tk_SetAppName 780
Tk_SetBackgroundFromBorder 755, 785
Tk_SetCaretPos 785
Tk_SetClass 746, 748, 783
Tk_SetClassProcs 780
Tk_SetGrid 784
Tk_SetInternalBorder 761, 784
Tk_SetOptions 754, 780
tk_setPalette 621
Tk_SetWindowBackground 753, 780
Tk_SetWindowBackgroundPixmap 780
Tk_SetWindowBorder 780
Tk_SetWindowBorderPixmap 780
Tk_SetWindowBorderWidth 780
Tk_SetWindowColormap 780
Tk_SetWindowVisual 785
Tk_SizeOfBitmap 783
Tk_SizeOfImage 783
Tk_StrictMotif 781
Tk_TextLayoutToPostscript 785
Tk_TextWidth 785
Tk_Uid 760
Tk_UndefineCursor 780
Tk_UnderlineChars 785
Tk_UnderlineTextLayout 785
Tk_Ungrab 782
Tk_UnmaintainGeometry 784
Tk_UnmapWindow 780
Tk_UnsetGrid 784
Tk_Visual 781

Tk_Width 781
Tk_Window 760, 780
Tk_WindowId 781
Tk_X 781
Tk_Y 781
tkerror, Tcl procedure 202
tkinspect 201
tkman, UNIX program 372
tkwait with global variables 605
tkwait, Tk command 605
TLS secure socket extension 255
tolower, string command 50
toolbars 615
toolwindow, Windows 663
toplevel
    attributes 486
    icon bitmap 831
    of widget 666
    Tk widget 486
    window styles 489
totitle, string command 51
toupper, string command 51
tpool namespace 347
    See also thread namespace, tsv namespace
    tpool::create 347
    tpool::get 347
    tpool::names 348
    tpool::post 347
    tpool::preserve 348
    tpool::release 348
    tpool::wait 347
trace 193
    command execution 828
    example for preferences 680
    execution, in C 770
    Tcl command 193
    variables, in C 770
tranparent images 629
transfer, I/O channel to interp 292
transferring I/O channel
    threads 334–337
transforming data to program with regsub
    163
transient window 663
-translation, fconfigure option 231
Transparent Fill on Canvas Text 811
transparent images 832
transpose characters 514
Tranter, Jeff lviii
trapping errors from pipelines 382
Trf Patch 817
trig functions 21
trim, string command 51
trimleft, string command 51
trimright, string command 51
triple click 444
troublesome button command 454
troughColor, widget attribute 620
true color visual class 624

true, string class 55
TRUNC, open mode 117
truncate file, open 117
tsv namespace 346
    See also thread namespace, tpool namespace
    tsv::append 346
    tsv::exists 346
    tsv::get 338, 346
    tsv::incr 346
    tsv::lappend 346
    tsv::lindex 346
    tsv::linsert 346
    tsv::llength 346
    tsv::lock 346
    tsv::lpop 346
    tsv::lpush 346
    tsv::lrange 346
    tsv::lreplace 346
    tsv::lsearch 346
    tsv::move 347
    tsv::names 347
    tsv::object 347
    tsv::pop 347
    tsv::set 338, 347
    tsv::unset 347
turn data into list 72
Turning off geometry propagation 397
two screens 486
type
    conversions are automatic 705
    of file 116, 122
    of images 626
    of menu item 468
    Tcl_Obj in C 772
typeface. See font.
type-in widget. See entry.

U

u, in string format 57
Uhler, Stephen 163, 168
uid, user ID 114
-underline, font attribute 636
underlined text 537
undo mechanism, text widgets 548
undo, in text widget 830
Unicode and Internationalization 813
Unicode and UTF-8 220
Unicode Fonts 637
Uniform Rows and Columns in grid 830
uniform widget size, grid 418
UNIX look and feel 394
UNIX Tcl Scripts 26
UNIX to DOS 121
unknown backslash sequences are an error
    147
unknown, in safe interpreters 301
unknown, Tcl command 178
unmap window 408, 661
Unmap, window event 440, 442
unpack binary data 59

unpost, menu operation 468
unset, Tcl command 15
Unsetting Nonexistent Variables 829
unsupported1, Tk command 489, 804
untrusted scripts 291
update idletasks is safer 609
update, automatic application 364
update, Tk command 609
uplevel, namespaces and 216
uplevel, Tcl command 138
upper case conversion 51
upper, in regular expressions 156
upper, string class 55
upvar
    aliases do not work with Tk widget text vari-
        ables 93
    example 459, 674
    namespaces 93
    Tcl command 91
    textvariables 93
    variable traces 93
URI manipulation 238
URL
    access from Tcl 243
    character set 253
    Content-Encoding 253
    copy to file 254
    CVS repository 729
    Decoding 164
    domain handler, TclHttpd 261
    fetch with HTTP 243
    get with browser::displayURL 317
    implementing by a program 260
    redirection 279
    Tcl source location 729
    this book's home page 729
Url_Decode 164
Url_DecodeQuery 278
Url_Encode 278
Url_PrefxInstall 278
use, command-line argument 30
USE_COMPAT_CONST 717
USE_NON_CONST 717
User and Group ID 287
user customization 671
user feedback 609
user interface to preferences 675
user-defined buttons 479
user-defined menus 481
UTF-8 and Unicode 220, 814

V

-validate, http::geturl option 252
validation, entry contents 508
value, delete list element by 69
Values, Keeping References to Tcl_Obj 714
Values, Modifying Tcl_Obj 705
Values, Pitfalls of Shared Tcl_Obj 706

variable 187
    aliases with upvar 92
    args 88
    argv 29, 80, 662
    argv0 662
    array 96
    assignment 5
    auto_noexec 107, 179
    auto_noload 178
    auto_path 172, 177, 180
    call by name 91
    characters allowed in names 5
    command at global scope 215
    command line arguments 29
    currently defined 187
    declaring 5, 208
    deleting 15
    efficient names 208
    embed_args 314
    environment 124
    errorCode 85
    errorInfo 83, 85
    for button 458
    for entry text 507, 516
    for label text 490
    for listbox 529
    for scale widget 495
    from preferences 674
    increment 13
    manipulate from C code 771
    names 5
    namespace 207
    namespace vs. global conflict 207
    pass by reference 91
    plugin 314
    predefined, list of 31
    print by name 92
    PrintByName 459
    read-only 195
    scope and procedures 90
    Tcl command 207
    tcl_library 180, 192
    tcl_pkgPath 180
    tcl_platform 800
    tcl_precision 15
    test if defined 15
    thread-shared 337—338
    trace access 193
    trace, array example 196
    wait for modification 605
Variable number of arguments 88
variable, linked to C variable 696
variables
    unsetting nonexistent 829
Vasiljevic, Zoran 322
vbox, vertical layout 397
vcompare, package operation 176
-verbose, pkg_mkIndex option 174
version number, Tcl 192
version numbers 192
version, patch level 31
versions, of packages 171, 173
vertical layout 397
vertical tab character, \v 20
VFS 826

view text contents 553
viewable window 665
Virtual Events 803
virtual events
    <<ListboxSelect>> 528
    <<MenuSelect>> 466
    <<Modified>> 551
    <<Selection>> 551
virtual events for cut, copy, and paste 446
Virtual File Systems 351
Virtual File Systems (VFS) and Starkits 355
Virtual Filesystems 826
virtual root coordinates, correcting 667
virtual root window 667
Visibility, window event 440
visual
    available 669
    class, widget attribute 624, 669
    command-line argument 30
    default 669
    of window 669
volume, of bell 498
vwait, Tcl command 230

W

w, anchor position 616
w, in binary format 60
w, in regular expressions 157
w, regular expression option 157
wait for Tk event 605
warping, mouse (pointer) 448
Web browser status line 317
Web browser Tcl plugin 314
Web server, TclHttpd 257
Web Tcl Complete, book lviii
webmaster e-mail, TclHttpd 279, 286
weekday, %a 184
-weight, font attribute 636
when to use regular expressions 144
while loop to read input 79
while, Tcl command 79
white space 4
wide integer 826
widget
    attributes 371
    attributes, in C 781
    C data structure 744
    class command, in C 745
    class definition 369
    cleanup in C 765
    container. See frame.
    containing 666
    data structure, in C 744
    definition 367
    destroy 605
    destroy, in C 765
    display in C 761
    embed in text 543
    frame for container 368

geometry 666
height 666
hide by unmapping 408
image, from C 783
implemented in C 743
instance command, in C 749
introduction 367
names in variables 370
naming 370
reconfigure 371
screen of 666
screen position 666
spacing between 617
Tcl_Obj version 743
toplevel of 666
unmapping 408
width 666
X, Y coordinate 666
widgets
    button 453
    canvas 557
    checkbutton 458
    entry 507
    frame 485
    label 490
    labelframe 486
    listbox 519
    menu 462
    menubutton 462
    message 493
    namespaces and 215
    panedwindow 429–434
    radiobutton 458
    scale 495
    scrollbar 499
    spinbox 511
    text 531
    toplevel 486
width
    equal with grid 418
    event option 449
    of widget 666
    virtual root window 667
    widget attribute 613
Wikit, a wiki wiki 836
Wikit, a Wiki-Wiki 363
window
    Activate event 442
    aspect ratio 659
    binding on close 442
    binding on open 442
    changes size 442
    children 665
    class, resource 665
    close 661
    close or delete callback 661
    colormap 668
    configuration in C 780
    Configure event 442
    coordinates, in C 781
    create options, in text 544
    creating in C 780
    current state 661
    decoration 659
    deiconify 661
    deleting 605
    depth of screen pixels 669

Destroy event 442
detached 486
embedded in canvas 579
embedding 489
events, in C 228, 723
exists 665
family relationships 664
focus model 663
general information in C 781
geometry 659
geometry manager 665
gridding 659
group 663
grouping when closed 663
hierarchy 367
hierarchy information 665
icon bitmap 660
iconify 661
icons for 661
ID of 668
layout in <Configure> binding 425
location information. 666
manager 379, 657
manager, miscellaneous 663
Map event 442
mapped onto display 665
maximized 660
maxsize 659
minimize 660
minsize 659
mouse location 666
MouseWheel event 442
name of 664
open 661
open, is 665
override redirect 663
parent 665
pathname 668
placement 659
platform-specific attributes 663
position from 659
protocol handler 662
protocol, miscellaneous 662
resize, interactive 387
rooms 667
screen information 666
server name 666
session state 662
size from 659
stacking order 409, 431, 660, 663
stacking order, in C 781
startup command 662
state 661
styles 489
system color 623
system, detecting 669
title 379, 658
toplevel of 666
transient 663
unmap 661
Unmap event 442
virtual root 667
visibile 665
visual 668, 669
visual of 669
wait for destroy 605
wait for visibility 605
withdraw 661

Window C compiler, mingw 836
window manager interaction 831
window manager, Tk-based 833
WindowBody, system color 623
WindowFrame, system color 623
Windows 632
    and exec problems 107
    auto_path 172
    com ports 235
    DLL location 697
    look and feel 393
    mouse cursors 632
    platform-specific window attributes 663
    services, Tcl applications as 201
    shared libraries 174
    Start and Menu Keys 811
    Start Menu 27
    system colors. 622
    system font size 637
    system menu 464
    text mode files 234
    toolwindow 663
Windows Application Handles 787
Windows CE, Tcl/Tk for 836
Windows IME 670
WindowText, system color 623
winfo, Tk command 663
Wippler, Jean-Claude 349
Wish command line options 30
wish, application 172
withdraw window 661
--with-tcl=dir 734
--with-tclinclude=dir 734
--with-tcllib=dir 734
--with-tk=dir 734
--with-x11include=dir 734
--with-x11lib=dir 734
wm, Tk command 657
WM_DELETE_WINDOW 661
WM_PROTOCOL 782
Word size detection, integer 826
Word, Microsoft, special characters 55
wordchar, string class 55
wordend, string command 51
wordstart, string command 51
Working 778
Working with Signals 778
World Wide Web 243
wrapLength, widget attribute 641
wrapping Tcl applications 350, 353
writable, file 109
write only, open 117
Write options for photo images 631
Writing a Tk Widget in C 743
WRONLY, open mode 117

X

X authority, send 648

X Font Names 638
X ID for resource, in C 787
X Input Methods 670, 785
X protocol errors 782
X resource database. See resource.
X Resource ID Management 787
X selection, export string to 515
-x, event option, event option 449
x, regular expression option 157
X, x, in binary format 60
X, x, in string format 57
X, Y coordinate of widget 666
X, Y coordinates, in event 449
X, Y mouse coordinates 666
XColor 760
XCopyArea 764
Xdefaults. See resource.
xdigit, in regular expressions 156
xdigit, string class 55
Xerox PARC 1
xfontsel, UNIX program 639
xhost list and send 649
XIM, X Input Method 833
xlsfonts, UNIX program 639
xmodmap, program 445
xrdb. See resource.
xset program 498
XSynchronize 782
xview scrollbar operation 502

Y

-y, event option 449
year 184
Year 2000 Compliance 807
year 2000 compliance 186
ypostion, menu operation 468
yview scrollbar operation 502

Z

Zeltserman, Dave lviii
Zimmer, Adrian lviii
zip file via VFS 352
zlib compression 354
zlib to automatically compress Tclkit 354
zoom box style 489
zoomed, window 660

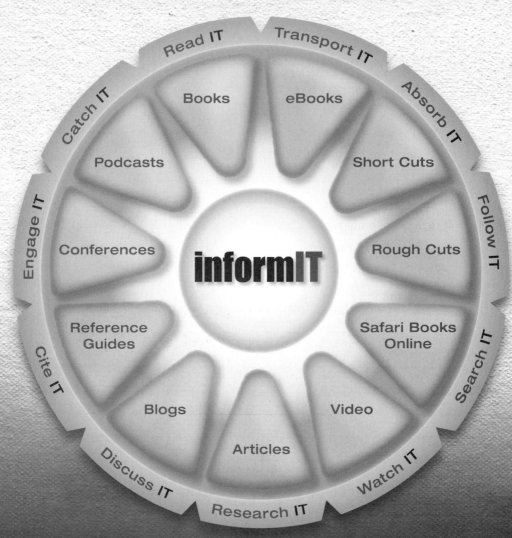